Dictionary
of Ulster Biography

COMPILED BY KATE NEWMAN
FOR THE ULSTER HISTORY

from research funded by the Cultural
and the International Fund for

*With many thanks
for the staff of
Ballycastle Library*

Kate Newmann
20/12/93

THE INSTITUTE OF IRISH STUDIES
THE QUEEN'S UNIVERSITY OF BELFAST

Published 1993
The Institute of Irish Studies
The Queen's University of Belfast

Grateful acknowledgement for financial assistance is made to the International Fund for Ireland and the Cultural Traditions programme of the Community Relations Council which aims to encourage acceptance and understanding of cultural diversity.

© Author

British Library Cataloguing-in-Publication Data. A catalogue record for this book is available from the British Library.

ISBN: 0 85389 478 7 PB
ISBN: 0 85389 479 5 HB

Printed by W & G Baird Ltd, Antrim
Cover design by Rodney Miller Associates
'Mother and Child'; Colin Middleton, by kind permission of Ms Laura Stinson

For my supervisor, Mr John Magee.

Kate Newmann was born in Holywood, County Down, in 1965. Her family moved to Hillsborough, County Down, and then to Dromore, County Down. She was educated at Friends' School Lisburn, County Antrim. Before reading English at King's College, Cambridge, she worked for a year at the Museum of Cretan Ethnology, and learnt Modern Greek. After graduating she taught English as a Foreign Language in Rhodes, Greece, and later completed a Master of Arts degree at the University of Ulster, Coleraine. Following a period of unemployment and free-lancing, she became first Cultural Traditions junior fellow at the Institute of Irish Studies. She is currently assistant editor at the Institute of Irish Studies, Queen's University, Belfast. She lives in Ballycastle, County Antrim.

INTRODUCTION

This dictionary includes people from the nine counties of Ulster who have distinguished themselves. They have either been born here, or have been educated here, or have worked here, or have represented here, or have died here, or have been buried here. What unites them all is that they are no longer alive. My apologies for any errors which I have unwittingly propagated and my regrets for those deserving people who have been inadvertently omitted. It is a celebration of extraordinary lives; a book not only for the reference shelves; a book to be read and enjoyed.

ACKNOWLEDGEMENTS

I am grateful to those who assisted me: the members of the Ulster History Circle; Ms RoseAnne Donnelly; Mr Michael Smallwood and Mr Seamus Scanlon and the library of Queen's University; Ms Mary Hughes, Mr John Killen, Mr Gerry Healy and Mr John Gray and the staff of the Linen Hall Library; Dr Alan Gailey and Mr John Moore and the Ulster Folk and Transport Museum, Cultra; Ms Belinda Jupp, Mr Terence Reeves-Smith and Mr Tom McErlean of the Department of Historic Monuments; Ms Michelle Neill and the Public Record Office; Belfast Central Library; Ms Margaret Iliff, Ms Marian Maloney, Ms Joan Coyles and Ballycastle Library; the *Irish News*; the *News-Letter*; Mr Brian Dempster and the BBC; Mr Samuel Hamill, Mr Peter King and Mr Walter McAuley and the *Belfast Telegraph*; Dr S. B. Kennedy, Ms Eileen Black, Dr William Maguire and the Ulster Museum; Mr Bernard Loughlin and Ms Mary Loughlin and the Tyrone Guthrie Centre; Ms Angelique Day, Dr Patrick McWilliams and Ms Noreen Dobson of the Ordnance Survey Memoirs of Ireland Project; the members of the Place-names Project, Celtic Department, Queen's University, Belfast; Mr Czernicevsky and the Polish Cultural Institute in London; the Korean Tourist Board in London; Dr Liam Ronaine and Donegal County Council; Ms Anne Peoples, Ms Moira Craig and Mr Dick Sinclair and the Central Library in Derry; Mr Sam Burnside, Mr Jim Craig and Ms Liz Weir of the Verbal Arts Centre, Derry; Dr William Crawford and the Federation for Ulster Local Studies, and its Historical Society Members; Dr Damian Smyth and Dr Pól Ó Muirí of *Fortnight*; Ms Ruth Taillon and Ms Elsie Best and the Mary Ann McCracken Historical Society; Glynis Barr and Larne Council; the Killybegs Writers; the Derry Women's Writing Group; Word of Mouth; Ms Joan Maguire, Dr Brian Walker, Ms Brenda Graham, Mr Michael Quinn, Ms Daphne Smyth, Ms Joan Sloane, Dr Sophie Hillan-King, Dr Valerie Hall and the Institute of Irish Studies, Queen's University; Ms. Nellis; Mr Hugh Boyd; Dr Peter Collins; Mr Tony Canavan; Dr Hiram Morgan; Ms Anne Craig; Ms Anne Casement; Dr Rosemary Cullen Owen; Dr Mary Cullen; Mr Denis Cassidy; Dr Cahal Dallat; Ms Ruth Hooley; Ms Martina O'Hare; Professor Alun Evans; Mr Francis Gallagher; Ms Cathy Gage; the Right Honorable Patrick MacNaghten; Ms Purdy and Ms Elizabeth Hutchinson; Ms Montgomery; Dr Holmes; Ms Christine Heslip; Father Patrick Hickey; Mr Ted Hickey; Ms Margaret Martin; Professor Ronnie Buchanan; Mr Keith Haines; Mr John Kennedy; Ms Kate Middleton; Mr John Kelly; Mr Canray Fontenot; Dr Maria Luddy; Ms Elizabeth Lynas; Mr Kevin McClenaghan; Mr Michael Longley; Ms Linde Lunney; Mr John Fairleigh; Mr Aodán Mac Póilin and the Ultach Trust; Mr Damian Gorman; Ms Ann McKay; Dr Virginia Crossman; Mr James Simmons; Mr John McGuckian; Ms Medbh McGuckian; Ms Bridget Anne Ryan; Mr Feargus McGarvey; Mr Michael Campbell; the McConaghie family of Stranocum; Ms Kathleen McPeake; Mr Francis Byrne; Ms Sabina Wichert; Ms Mairead Byrne; Mr Aidan Walsh; Mr John Molden; Ms Paula Meehan; Mr Theo Dorgan; Mr John P. McBride; Mr Mícheál Ó Mainnín; Father Brian Mac Cuarta; Dr Michael Newmann; Mr John Metcalf; Dr Theresa Moriarty; Ms Mary Campbell; Mr Gabriel Murphy; Mr Robert McKelvey; Mr Graham Mawhinney; Mr John Robb; Mr Robert McKinstry; Dr Mary O'Dowd; Dr Margaret Mullett; Mr Malcolm Scott; Ms Rosanna Trainor; Ms Helen Wogan; Mr Roger Weatherup; Mr Richard Bennett; Mr Jonathon Bardon; Dr Diarmaid Ó Doibhlin, Dr Bruce Stewart and Professor Robert Welch, University of Ulster, Coleraine; Mr Adrian Rice; Ms Etta Bell; Mr C. Beck; Mr Robert Foy; Mr Alan Davison and Dr Brian Trainor and the Ulster Historical Foundation.

ΟΙΝΟΣ ΠΑΝΤΑΣ ΕΥΕΛΠΙΔΑΣ ΠΟΙΕΙ
ΑΡΙΣΤΟΤΕΛΗΣ

For most of history, 'Anonymous'
was a woman.

Virginia Wolff

The ideal author of this work would have a considerable knowledge of each part of the subject, be impartial in respect of all of
them, and be able to see and to present the vast system as an
integrated whole. No such person exists.

Christmas Humphries
Preface to *Buddhism*

A

ABERCORN, MARQUIS OF see HAMILTON, JAMES

ABERNETHY, JOHN 1680–1740
John Abernethy was born in Brigh, near Stewartstown, County Tyrone, and lived for some time in Ballymena, County Antrim, and Coleraine, County Londonderry. He studied at the University of Glasgow and at Edinburgh. Before he was twenty-one he preached in Dublin and was appointed minister of a congregation in Antrim, where he was ordained in 1703. When he was recalled to Dublin in 1717, he defied the synod and opted to stay in Antrim. When the division among Presbyterians occurred, Abernethy led the Unitarians or Non-subscribers. He was prominent in The Belfast Society and the 'New Light' Movement. In 1730 he went to minister in Dublin. He was frequently at variance with the Presbyterian Church especially on the issue of exclusion from army service. He was opposed to the Test Act. Despite being a strict believer in temperance, he died from what was described as 'gout in the head'. He published tracts and books, including *Sermons on the Being and Perfections of God* which was reprinted many times and was favourably criticised by Samuel Johnson.

ABERNETHY, WILLIAM d. *c*.1930
William Abernethy probably came from near Comber, County Down. He learned his trade with a Belfast photographer and set up a business in High Street, Belfast, in 1886. For many years he was successful as a portrait photographer and opened branches in Bangor and Newry, County Down. He visited the Holy Land. With the advent of polyfoto in Belfast his business declined.

ABRAHAM, JAMES JOHNSTON 1876–1963
James Abraham was born in Coleraine, County Londonderry, and was educated there and at Trinity College, Dublin, where he studied medicine. He practised in County Clare and was appointed Resident Medical Officer to London Dock Hospital and Rescue Home in 1908. In 1914 he travelled to Serbia, where he administered to the Serbian army and played a major part in bolstering morale. He coped with inadequate supplies, outbreaks of typhoid, scarlet fever, recurrent fever, smallpox and a typhus epidemic. He was the first doctor on location to diagnose typhus, and he and the Serbian Army Medical Corps managed to contain it. He was then called to the Middle East and latterly became a Harley Street specialist. He was created a Knight of St John Consulting Surgeon at the Princess Beatrice Hospital in London. He was a Fellow of the Royal Society of Medicine, President of the Irish Medical Graduates' Association and in 1949 won the Arnott Medal. He was author of *The Night Nurse* (1913); *Surgeon's Journal; Balkan Log* and *The Surgeon's Log*, which ran to thirty-one editions. He was awarded an honorary doctorate in 1946.

ACHESON, ANNE CRAWFORD 1882–1962
Anne Acheson was born in Portadown, County Armagh, and was educated at Victoria College, Belfast, Belfast School of Art and the Royal College of Art, London. She studied sculpture under Lanteri and exhibited at the Royal Academy and internationally. She was awarded the CBE in 1919. She lived in London and Glenavy, County Antrim.

ACHESON, ARCHIBALD 1776–1849
Archibald Acheson was born in County Armagh and was educated at Oxford University. He was elected member of parliament for County Armagh, and served from 1798 to 1807. He was 2nd Earl of Gosford and became Governor General of

Canada. He advocated the unpopular policy of conciliation both in Ireland and in Canada, and because of opposition he resigned.

ADAIR, ROBERT ALEXANDER SHAFTO
c.1811–1886

Robert Adair was born in Ballymena, County Antrim, and was member of parliament for Cambridge from 1847 to 1852, and from 1854 to 1857. In 1869 he unsuccessfully contested East Suffolk and County Antrim. In 1872 he was created a peer. He was Lord Lieutenant of County Antrim, and a Fellow of the Royal Society. Among his works are *Antrim in 1847* and *Ireland and her Servile War*.

ADAMNÁN,(EUNAN) ST c.624–704

Adamnán was born in County Donegal and was Abbot of Raphoe, which he may have founded. He became ninth abbot of the monastic community of Iona, in 679. He visited Aldfrith, King of Northumbria, who had studied on Iona and who persuaded Adamnán to agree to the Roman view in the controversy over the date of Easter, though Adamnán's monks were not won over. He was prominent at the Synod of Tara in 697 and won acceptance for his 'law of the innocents' which protected non-combatants in war. *Cáin Adamnáin* contains a draft of this law. He also ensured that a law exempting women from military service was passed. His greatest work was *Vita Sancti Columbae*, the life of St Columba, and he also wrote *De Locis Sanctis*, an account of Bishop Arculf's pilgrimage to the Holy Land. *Fís Adamnáin*, which appears in a twelfth-century manuscript, is now regarded as a much later work and wrongly attributed to him. His feast-day is on the 23rd of September.

ADAMS, FRANCES M. J. 1882–1987

Frances Adams was born in Omagh, County Tyrone, and was educated at Queen's College, Belfast, where she studied zoology, physiology and botany. At London University she studied plant pathology and carried out research on wild white clover for the Department of Agriculture at Aberystwyth University. When she returned to Belfast, she was appointed lecturer in botany at the College of Technology. She was a member of the Belfast Naturalists' Field Club and served as its President. After she retired she took up motoring and water-colour painting and exhibited with the Ulster Society of Women Artists. She, with her sister, Dr Elizabeth Hunt and her brother, Dr John Adams, appears in the *Guinness Book of Records* for the extraordinary fact that they all lived to over the age of a hundred. She died in Rostrevor, County Down.

ADRAIN, ROBERT 1775–1843

Robert Adrain was born in Carrickfergus, County Antrim, and fought in the rebellion of 1798. He escaped to America and became Professor of Mathematics in Columbia College, New York, and Vice-Provost of the University of Pennsylvania. He was the author and editor of many mathematical works, including *Exponential Law of Error*, and published in many journals such as the *Analyst* and the *Mathematical Diary*. In 1818 Volume I of the *Transactions of The American Philosophical Society* published those of his papers which dealt with his calculations on the measurements of the earth. He died in New Brunswick.

AE see RUSSELL, GEORGE WILLIAM.

ÁEDÁN, ST (or MOGUE or MÁEDÓC, ST) 560–632

Áedán was born in Brackley Lough, County Cavan, and was educated in Wales. When he returned to Ireland, he established monasteries in Wexford. He was the first Bishop of Ferns, where he died, and was patron saint of Uí Cheinnsealaigh or Wexford. His feast-day is on the 31st of January.

ÁEDH MAC AINMERECH 566–593

Áedh was king of the Northern Uí Néill. He called a convention at Dromkett, near Limavady, County Londonderry which had a three-fold aim: to attempt to curtail the activity of the bards, to impose a heavier tribute on Scottish Dalriada, and to depose the King of Ossory. St Columcille came from Iona to the convention. King Áedh fell at the Battle of Dunbolg.

AGNEW, JAMES WILLSON 1815–1901
James Willson Agnew was born in Ballyclare, County Antrim, and studied medicine at Glasgow. After practising medicine in Sydney, he went to Hobart and helped found the Royal Society of Tasmania. He became Premier of Tasmania in 1886 and was knighted. He died in Hobart.

AIKEN, FRANK 1898–1983
Frank Aiken was born in Camlough, County Armagh, and attended the Christian Brothers' School at Newry. He became commandant of the 4th Northern Division of the Irish Republican Army in 1921, and Chief of Staff in 1923. Subsequent to 1932 he was appointed by de Valera as Minister for Defence and from 1945 to 1948 he was Minister of Finance. In 1951 he became Minister of External Affairs and served as Tánaiste from 1959 to 1969. He retired from ministerial office in 1969 and from the Dáil in 1973. He was awarded honorary doctorates from the National University of Ireland and Trinity College, Dublin.

ALEXANDER, CECIL FRANCES (née HUMPHREYS) 1818–1895
Cecil Frances Alexander was born in Dublin but her girlhood was spent at Redcross, County Wicklow. Throughout her life she was a keen supporter of the Oxford Movement. Her *Hymns for Little Children* (1848) included such universal favourites as 'Once in Royal David's City', 'All Things Bright and Beautiful' and 'There is a Green Hill Far Away', and it was reprinted sixty-nine times. She spent her adult life mainly in Derry and Strabane as the wife of Bishop Alexander. There she wrote tracts, poetry and hymns, a collection of which was published a year after her death. She was an active philanthropist and protector of animals. Gounod is said to have remarked that some of her lyrics 'seemed to set themselves to music'.

ALEXANDER, ELEANOR d. 1934
Eleanor Alexander was born in Strabane, County Tyrone, the daughter of Cecil Frances and William Alexander. She was educated at home and wrote poetry which was published in the *Spectator* and other periodicals. Her novels include *Lady Anne's Walk*; *The Rambling Rector* (1904) and *The Lady of the Well*. She was awarded an MBE and created Lady of Grace, St John of Jerusalem.

ALEXANDER, HAROLD RUPERT LEOFRIC GEORGE 1891–1969
Harold Alexander was born in Caledon, County Tyrone. He was educated at Harrow and Sandhurst and served with the Irish Guards in the First World War in France, and later in India. He was awarded the Military Cross, the Legion of Honour and the Russian Order of St Anne. During the Second World War he served in Burma, the Middle East, North Africa and Italy, eventually becoming Allied commander in the Mediterranean with the rank of field-marshal. After the war he was appointed first Governor-General of Canada, and from 1952 to 1954, served as Minister of Defence in the government of Winston Churchill. He received the Order of Merit in 1959 and was raised to the peerage as the Earl Alexander of Tunis and Errigal.

ALEXANDER, ROBERT 1910–1943
Bob Alexander was born in Belfast. He won eleven international rugby caps for Ireland between 1936 and 1939. He played fourteen times, including all three Test matches, for the 1938 British and Irish Lions in South Africa. He also played cricket for Ireland. He was killed in action in Burma while serving as a captain in the Royal Inniskilling Fusiliers.

ALEXANDER, WILLIAM 1824–1911
William Alexander was born in Derry and after an Oxford education became Bishop of Derry in 1867. He was appointed Archbishop of Armagh in 1893 and later became Primate of All Ireland. He was married to Cecil Frances Alexander the famous hymn-writer. He published prolifically both sermons and poetry. His titles include *Logics of Life and Light*, (1878) and his lectures 'Evidences of Christianity' appear in a book, *Primary Convictions*. He died in Torquay.

ALISON, FRANCIS 1705–1779
Francis Alison was born in County Donegal, was educated in Glasgow, and became a Presbyterian minister. He emigrated to

America in 1735 and for many years was Vice-Provost of the College of Philadelphia and pastor of the First Presbyterian Church. He died in Philadelphia, leaving instructions that all his slaves were to be freed.

ALLAWAY, ALBERT JOHN 1904–1983
Albert John Allaway was born in Yorkshire and worked as an engineer from the age of fourteen to twenty-four. He returned to education through the Workers' Education Association and in 1931 graduated from Sheffield University with first-class honours. For the next seven years he was employed by the Extra-Mural Department of the University of Manchester. During his time as Director of Extra-Mural Studies at Queen's University, Belfast, 1938 to 1946, it was his policy to make classes accessible in all areas of Northern Ireland. He was also responsible for the education of the armed forces throughout the war. In 1946 he took over the adult education services in Leicester. He was a justice of the peace, President of the Educational Centres Association, and of the National Federation of Community Associations. The Queen's Jubilee Medal was bestowed on him for his contribution to the work of the National Council of Social Service, and he was elected President of the Transactional Analysis Group.

ALLEY, JEROME 1760–1826
Jerome Alley was educated at Trinity College, Dublin and became Rector of Drumcar in the diocese of Armagh. He was a poet and author, and among his works is a study of world religions.

ALLINGHAM, WILLIAM 1824–1889
William Allingham was born in Ballyshannon, County Donegal, and was educated there. As a young man he was employed in banking and customs and excise, moving to Coleraine, County Londonderry, as Controller of Customs in 1860. His much-anthologised poem 'The Fairies' was written on a tour of duty in Killybegs. He published one play and many volumes of poetry, his first in 1850. He had a close connection with the Pre-Raphaelites: Millais and Rossetti illustrated his collection *Day and Night Songs*, and he was a friend of Tennyson, Thomas Carlyle and Leigh Hunt. He edited *Fraser's Magazine* and published in 1864 *Laurence Bloomfield in Ireland.*

ALLMAN, GEORGE JAMES 1812–1898
George Allman was born in Cork and was educated at Belfast Academical Institution and Trinity College, Dublin. He was a Fellow of the Royal College of Surgeons in Ireland and in 1844 became Professor of Botany at Trinity College, Dublin. Ten years later he became a Fellow of the Royal Society and from 1855 to 1870 held the Chair of Natural History at Edinburgh University. While at Edinburgh he gained the degree of Doctor of Laws. The Royal Society bestowed on him the Royal Medal in 1873, and in 1878 the Royal Irish Academy presented him with the Cunningham Medal. From 1874 to 1883 he was President of the Linnean Society, and in 1896 was presented with its Gold Medal. In 1879 he was President of the British Association and became a Royal Commissioner on Fisheries. He published many monographs on natural history.

ALMENT, MARY MARTHA 1834–1908
Mary Martha Alment was born in Derry and studied art in Dublin. Her tutor, Henry McManus, was headmaster of what became the School of Design in 1849, and it was during that period that women were first admitted as students. From 1858 until her death, Mary Martha Alment frequently exhibited at the Royal Hibernian Academy, at the Dublin Sketching Club, and at the Watercolour Society of Ireland. She was chiefly a landscape painter.

ALMERIA see HAMILTON, ELIZABETH

ANDERSON, JAMES 1881–1915
James Anderson was born in Derry and graduated from the Royal University of Ireland in 1905. In 1907 he was called to the Bar and in 1910 became Professor of Political Economy and Jurisprudence at University College, Cork. In 1914 he was appointed Reid Professor of Criminal and Constitutional Law at Trinity College, Dublin.

ANDERSON, JOHN 1815–1905
John Anderson was born in County Londonderry and was a prominent geologist

and bibliographer. He was Treasurer of the Belfast Natural History and Philosophical Society, President of the Belfast Naturalists' Field Club and a Fellow of the Geological Society. His works include a *History of the Linen Hall Library*, and a five-part *Catalogue of Early Belfast Printed Books, 1694–1830*. He died in Holywood, County Down.

ANDERSON, LILY 1922–1982

Lily Anderson became a member of the Communist Party from 1942, and served on its sub-committees for education, social services and women. She was an active supporter of the Nursery Mother's Action Campaign, established in Belfast in 1964–66 to demand the provision of nursery schools, many of which had functioned during the war, but in times of peace, were felt to be 'for lazy mothers'. She was successful in obtaining two new nursery schools in Belfast. She died in an accident in Bulgaria.

ANDERSON, MARGARET 1881–1956

Margaret Anderson was born in Ballinran, Kilkeel, County Down. She left school when she was eleven years old and at the age of thirteen went to Waringstown, County Down, to work as a medical receptionist. She subsequently went to England to train as a nurse in Leeds Union Infirmary. She qualified as a State Registered Nurse and obtained her state certificate of midwifery. In 1916 she joined the Queen Alexandra's Imperial Military Nursing Reserve and was awarded the Royal Red Cross, the highest award that could be conferred on a woman for war service. It was presented to her by King George V in 1919. In 1921 she went to Iraq as a nurse and on her return to England in 1924, was appointed assistant matron at the Royal Infirmary, Truro, Cornwall. In 1926 she returned to Ireland as matron of the temporary hospital in the Silent Valley. In 1932 she again went to England, as matron of a hospital near Oxford, and remained there until 1939. During the Second World War, despite being fifty-eight years old, she rejoined the nursing reserve and took part in several sorties across the Channel during the evacuation of Dunkirk.

ANDREWS, JOHN MILLER 1871–1956

John Andrews was born in Comber, County Down and was educated at the Royal Belfast Academical Institution. He became director of the family linen bleaching firm, and of the Belfast Ropeworks. He was one of the honorary secretaries of the Ulster Unionist Council, and a founder-member of the Ulster Unionist Labour Association. He became Unionist member of parliament for County Down and was unopposed in every election from 1921. He served from 1921 to 1937 as Minister of Labour, from 1937 to 1940 as Minister of Finance and was the second Prime Minister of Northern Ireland from 1940 to 1943, when he resigned. He was County Grand Master of the Orange Institution in County Down and served on the Institution's All Ireland Council and Imperial Grand Council of the World.

ANDREWS, MARY 1852–1914

Mary Andrews was born in Belfast. She was Honorary Secretary of the geological section of the Belfast Naturalists' Field Club and she contributed geological photographs to the British Association. Among her published works are *The Early History of Magnetism*; *Dykes in Antrim and Down*; *Notes on Moel Tryfaen* and *Notes on Some Igneous Rocks in Antrim and Down*.

ANDREWS, MICHAEL 1874–1934

Michael Andrews was educated in England and Brussels and became fluent in several European languages. He was directly descended from Thomas Andrews of Ardoyne who in 1819 had established a damask-weaving factory. Michael rose from the position of manager to director of the Royal Damask-Weaving Factory at Ardoyne and chairman of the Power Loom Manufacturers' Association. Alongside this he became an expert on cartography, especially the development of maps and nautical charts from the fourteenth century to the seventeenth century. His library, including his unique collection of photographs and maps, was bequeathed to the Royal Geographical Society.

ANDREWS, THOMAS 1813–1885

Thomas Andrews was born in Belfast and

was educated in Belfast, Dublin, Glasgow and Edinburgh, where he qualified as a doctor of medicine. He worked in Paris under Dumas, the distinguished chemist, became a Fellow of the Royal Society, a member of the Royal Irish Academy and a member of the Belfast Natural History and Philosophical Society. He established a medical practice in Belfast, and during the cholera epidemic of 1832 he published valuable research on the blood of sufferers. Having taught in the Royal Belfast Academical Institution for eleven years, he was subsequently appointed Vice-President and Professor of Chemistry of Queen's College, Belfast, where he established the School of Medicine. He published *The Church in Ireland*, advocating its disestablishment, and was involved in social issues, writing a paper *Suggestions for Checking the Hurtful Use of Alcoholic Beverages by the Working Classes*. It was, however, as a chemist that he achieved international recognition, his research on ozone and gases being of particular significance. He became Honorary Fellow of the Royal Society of Edinburgh and President of the British Association for the Advancement of Science in 1876. When he died, his students at Queen's presented his portrait to the university and funded the Andrews Studentship in Chemistry.

ANDREWS, THOMAS 1873–1912
Thomas Andrews was born in Comber, County Down, and began work in Harland & Wolff's shipyard in Belfast at the age of sixteen. He studied design after work and eventually became managing director in 1907. He was chief designer of the *Titanic*, and when it sank on its maiden voyage he drowned with the ship. Comber remembers him in the naming of its Memorial Hall.

ANNESLEY, HUGH 1831–1908
Hugh Annesley was born in Dublin and was educated at Eton and Trinity College, Dublin. In 1851 he entered the army where he attained the rank of lieutenant-colonel in 1860, having been severely wounded in the Kaffir War. He returned to Ireland in 1871 and in 1875 became 5th Earl of Castlewellan. From 1857 to 1874 he was Conservative member of parliament for

Cavan. He was a horticulturalist, and established the arboretum at Castlewellan. From the late 1850s to the early 1900s he was also a keen amateur photographer, and published a botanical book which he illustrated with his own photographs. His collection is in the Public Record Office, Belfast. He died in Castlewellan.

ANNESLEY, MABEL 1881–1959
Lady Mabel Annesley was born in Castlewellan, County Down. In 1895 she attended the Frank Calderon School of Animal Painting. From 1920 to 1921, she studied wood engraving at the Central School of Art and Design, and illustrated a limited edition of *Songs from Robert Burns*. She was a member of the Belfast Art Society and of the Society of Wood Engravers. She exhibited in her studio in Lombard Street, Belfast and in London, Dublin and Manchester. Her work can be seen in the Ulster Museum, Belfast and in the British Museum.

ANTRIM (COUNTESS OF), ANGELA (née SYKES) 1911–1984
Lady Angela Antrim was educated privately and eventually went to Belgium to train under the sculptor D'Havlosse. She also attended the British School in Rome. She sculpted in a studio in London, often in stone and on a very large scale. She married the 8th Earl of Antrim and at the outbreak of the Second World War, moved to Glenarm Castle in County Antrim, where she lived until her death. She carried out a number of public commissions in stone, such as those at St Joseph's Church, Ballygally, County Antrim, and at the parliament buildings, Newfoundland. She exhibited with the Royal Hibernian Academy and the Irish Exhibition of Living Art. Her later work consists largely of models cast in bronze, because in 1962 she suffered an injury to her hand which prevented her from sculpting.

ARBUCKLE, JAMES 1700–1734
James Arbuckle is thought to have been born in County Down. Having qualified as a doctor of medicine in Glasgow, he became a teacher, poet and essayist, and ran the *Dublin*

Weekly Journal. He published two collections of poetry, *Snuff* (1717) and *Glotta* (1721), and an essay on Swift, *Momus Mistaken.*

ARCHDALL, MERVYN 1723–1791
Mervyn Archdall, whose ancestors had settled in County Fermanagh, was a minister, antiquarian and genealogist. He collected coins, medals and seals and published a major reference work, *Monasticon Hibernicum,* in 1786. He was a member of the Royal Irish Academy. In 1789 Archdall brought out an edition of *Lodge's Peerage of Ireland.*

ARCHER, FRANCIS 1803–1875
Francis Archer was born in Belfast and practised medicine in Liverpool. He was a founder member of the Belfast Natural History and Philosophical Society and President of the Liverpool Natural History Society. He had a collection of conch shells which was donated to Birmingham University after his death.

ARCHER, WILLIAM 1830–1897
William Archer was born in Magherahamlet, County Down. He was a naturalist and in 1875 was elected Fellow of the Royal Society and Librarian of the Royal Dublin Society. In 1877 he was appointed director of the National Library of Ireland, where he established a dictionary catalogue. In 1879 he was awarded the Cunningham Gold Medal of the Royal Irish Academy for his scientific achievements.

ARMOUR, JAMES BROWN 1841–1928
James Armour was born in Lisboy, Ballymoney, County Antrim, and was educated at the Royal Belfast Academical Institution and Queen's Colleges, Belfast and Cork, where he studied classics. He became a Presbyterian minister at Ballymoney in 1869 and founded the Intermediate School there. He lectured at Magee College, Derry. He was politically outspoken in support of Home Rule, the Tenant Right movement and the controversial proposal for a Catholic university. He felt that politics ought not to divide the Presbyterian Church, but he firmly believed that partition would be disastrous for Ulster. He served on the Senate of Queen's University, Belfast, where he favoured the teaching of the Irish language and scholastic philosophy. He was made honorary chaplain to the Lord Lieutenant during the First World War and retired from the ministry in 1925. [Biography by his son, 1934]

ARMSTRONG, ALEXANDER 1818–1899
Alexander Armstrong was born in Crahan, County Fermanagh, and was educated at Trinity College, Dublin, and in Edinburgh. As a doctor he joined the navy and spent four years in this capacity, searching the polar regions for Sir John Franklin's expedition. He served in the Crimean War, in North America and in Malta and became Director-General of the medical department of the navy. He was knighted and elected Fellow of the Royal Society. His journal *Personal Narrative of the Discovery of the North-West Passage,* for which he won the Gilbert Blane Gold Medal, was published in 1857, and *Observations on Naval Hygiene* in 1858.

ARMSTRONG, GEORGE 1792–1857
George Armstrong was born in Drogheda, County Louth and educated at Trinity College, Dublin. He was ordained in the Established Church in 1815, became a clergyman in Bangor, County Down, and firmly supported Catholic Emancipation. He contributed prolifically to periodicals. He moved to Bristol where he joined the Unitarian church as a minister and died there.

ARMSTRONG, GEORGE FRANCIS SAVAGE *c.* 1845–1906
George Savage Armstrong was born in County Down, and was educated at Trinity College, Dublin. He produced two volumes on the history of his mother's family, the Savages of the Ards peninsula. He was Professor of History and Literature in Queen's College, Cork. He wrote a satire, *Mephistopheles in Broadcloth* (1888), much poetry, a biography of his brother Edmund, and *Stories of Wicklow* (1886).

ARMSTRONG, JAMES 1780–1839
James Armstrong was born in Ballynahinch, County Down, and was educated at Trinity

7

College, Dublin and at Edinburgh. He was ordained a Unitarian minister in 1806, was one of the founders of the Irish Unitarian Society in 1830, and was involved in the establishment of the Association of Irish Non-Subscribing Presbyterians in 1835. He received a Doctorate of Divinity from the University of Geneva and among his published works are *The Sin Against the Holy Ghost* (1836); *A Sermon Vindicating the Principles of Unitarian Christianity* (1838) and *An Ordination Sermon*, an important source for the history of Irish Presbyterianism. He was a member of the Belfast Literary Society, and of the Royal Irish Academy.

ARMSTRONG, RICHARD 1815–1880
Richard Armstrong was born in County Armagh, and graduated in law at Trinity College, Dublin. He was called to the Bar in 1839 and in 1854 became Queen's Counsel. He served as member of parliament for Sligo from 1865 to 1868.

ASH, THOMAS b. 1660
Thomas Ash was born in Eglinton, County Londonderry, and went to school in Derry in 1671. In 1684 he was manager of his father's estates in County Antrim and at the age of twenty-five was appointed coroner for County Londonderry. In 1689 he moved from Ashbrook into Derry city to live. At the beginning of the siege in this year, he was lieutenant and then a captain in one of the city regiments. During this period, he kept a journal which recorded the incidents and events which happened during the hundred-and-five-day blockade. It was not published until 1792.

ASHE, ANDREW 1758–1838
Andrew Ashe was born in Lisburn, County Antrim, and because of his musical ability on the flute was sent to England for special tuition at the expense of his benefactor, Count Bentinck. He became the most renowned player in Brussels, Dublin and London, 'being one of the first to use the additional keys'. He played for the Italian opera and later returned to Dublin.

ASHE, ST GEORGE c.1658–1718
St George Ashe was born in Roscommon and was educated at Trinity College, Dublin, where he was later appointed Provost. He became Bishop of Cloyne, Clogher and Derry, and as a friend of Jonathan Swift, is reputed to have officiated at the alleged marriage of Swift and Stella in 1716.

ASTON, WILLIAM GEORGE 1841–1911
William George Aston was born in County Londonderry and attended Queen's College, Belfast. He became a Doctor of Literature at the Royal University of Ireland. He was Consul-General of Korea from 1884 to 1886. He was fluent in Japanese, translating widely into English and compiling, in 1869 and 1872, two Japanese grammars, for both the spoken and written language. He is said to have sent the first Japanese child for education to Belfast. His was the first European translation of *Nihongi: The Ancient Chronicles of Japan* and this was followed by *Japanese Literature* and *Shinto*. He was a prolific contributor to the Royal Asiatic Society of London and to the Transactions of the Asiatic Society of Japan.

ATHILL, LOMBE 1827–1910
Lombe Athill was born in Asder, County Fermanagh, and graduated in medicine at Trinity College, Dublin. He was Master of the Rotunda Hospital in Dublin and specialised in gynaecology, performing the first successful ovariotomy in Ireland. He wrote *Recollections*, which was published one year after his death.

ATKINS, JAMES 1799–1833
James Atkins was born in Belfast. He trained with his father, who was a coach, house and sign painter in Belfast, and then at the Drawing School of the Belfast Academical Institution from 1817 to 1819. He was sent to Italy, sponsored by a group of patrons, and remained in Rome and Florence for the next thirteen years, during which time he became an accomplished portrait painter. In 1832 he went from Rome to Constantinople to paint the Sultan. He later moved to Malta, where he died. The contents of his studio were bought by Narcissus Batt, one of his patrons. His work was shown posthumously at the Belfast Association of Artists' exhibitions of 1836, 1837 and 1838.

ATKINSON, JOHN 1844–1932

John Atkinson was born in Drogheda, County Louth, and was educated at Queen's College, Galway. He was called to the Bar in 1865 and served as Solicitor-General from 1889 to 1892. For a brief period in 1892 he served as Attorney-General, a post which he reoccupied from 1895 to 1905. He was also Unionist member of parliament for North Londonderry.

ATKINSON, WILLIAM CHRISTOPHER 1902–1992

William Atkinson was born in Belfast and was educated at Queen's University, Belfast. From 1926 until 1932 he was a lecturer in Spanish at Durham University. In that year he was appointed Stevenson Professor of Spanish at Glasgow University. He introduced the study of Portuguese language and literature and by the late 1950s his department offered an honours course in Latin American history and literature, the first of its kind in the United Kingdom. From 1944 unitl 1947 he was Dean of the Faculty of Arts. He served in the Foreign Office during the Second World War and translated newspapers and documents. From 1966 to 1972 he was Director of the Institute of Latin American Studies of Glasgow. He lectured extensively in Latin America and was nominated Honorary Professor of the National University of Colombia. He received a Rockefeller Award for research in Latin America. He was a member of the Hispanic Society of America and was appointed Carnegie Research Fellow to the United States in 1955. He was made a Commander of the Order of Prince Henry the Navigator in 1972 in recognition of his services to Portugal. Among his many publications are *The History of Spain and Portugal; The Remarkable Life of Don Diego* and *The Conquest of New Granada*. He also wrote articles for the *Encyclopaedia Britannica* and for a time edited the *Bulletin of Hispanic Studies*.

AUCHINLECK, CLAUDE 1884–1981

Claude Auchinleck was born in County Tyrone but as a small child went to India, where his father was a colonel in the Indian Army. In 1903 he joined the Indian Army as a second lieutenant. During the First World War he fought the Turkish Army at the Suez Canal and in Mesopotamia. In 1917 he was promoted to brigade-major. In 1936 he became major-general and Deputy Chief of the General Staff and had gained a reputation as a commander on the North-West Frontier. During the Second World War he came back to England to organise and command the new 4th Corps. Later he was appointed commander of the military forces in northern Norway and was eventually given command of the 5th Corps, before becoming General Officer Commanding-in-Chief. In 1940 he was appointed Commander-in-Chief in India with the title of general, but in 1941 became a commander in the Middle East. He created the 8th Army which fought against Rommel. In 1943 he returned to India and later formed the 14th Army which defeated the Japanese in Burma. In 1946 he was promoted to the rank of field-marshal and in 1947 became Supreme Commander of all armed forces in India and Pakistan. He was known by the Indians as Lord of War. When India gained independence in 1947, Claude Auchinleck left. He became a colonel of the Inniskilling Fusiliers.

AVERELL, ADAM 1754–1847

Adam Averell was born in Mullan, County Tyrone, and was educated at Trinity College, Dublin. Having been ordained, he was appointed curate of Aghaboe and became acquainted with John Wesley, under whose influence he became a Methodist. He relinquished his wife, property and parish 'to unreservedly devote himself to preaching in different parts of the country'. He kept a journal and having left the mainstream Methodists, served as President of the Primitive Wesleyan Conference for nearly thirty years. [Biography by Stewart and Revington, 1849]

AYTON, ALEXANDER fl.1865–1901

Alexander Ayton had a photographic studio in Shipquay Place, Derry from 1865 to 1901. He took many photographs in Donegal and one of these, 'Open Air Mass 1867' has been much reproduced.

B

BABINGTON, WILLIAM 1756–1833
William Babington was born in Port-glenone, County Antrim, and received his medical education at Guy's Hospital, London, where he practised as a physician after serving as a naval surgeon. He was a Fellow of the Royal Society, and he founded the Geological Society. Among his works is *New System of Mineralogy*. His monument is in St Paul's Cathedral, London.

BAGENAL, HENRY c.1556–1598
Henry Bagenal was an Elizabethan soldier who succeeded his father as Marshal of the army in Ireland in 1590. In 1591 his sister Mabel became the third wife of Hugh O'Neill, Earl of Tyrone; Henry Bagenal was opposed to the marriage. In 1595 the armies of both men clashed at the Yellow Ford, two miles from Armagh. Henry Bagenal was killed by a musket ball when he lifted the visor of his helmet, and his army was defeated.

BAGENAL, MABEL 16th century
Mabel Bagenal was the sister of Henry Bagenal, who refused to allow Hugh O'Neill to marry her. Hugh defied him and married Mabel, who was half his age, secretly. Henry Bagenal tried to prove that Hugh was not properly divorced from his first wife, and two years after the marriage, he still witheld the dowry which had been left to Mabel by her father. She has often been cited by historians as the cause of hostilities between O'Neill and Bagenal, the 'Helen of the Elizabethan Wars', though this simplistic assessment has been discredited. In 1594, Hugh and Mabel were described as papists, who supported seminary priests.

BAIRD, ROBERT HUGH HANLEY 1855–1934
Robert Baird was born in Belfast and was educated at the Royal Belfast Academical Instution. In 1869 he was an apprentice compositor and a year later worked for the *Belfast Telegraph*, which had been founded by his father. He had sole control of this newspaper from 1886 and established many other papers. He was a justice of the peace and Deputy Lieutenant and was knighted in 1921.

BALLANCE, JOHN 1839–1893
John Ballance was born in Glenavy, County Antrim and was educated at Glenavy National School and Wilson's Academy, Belfast. When he was fourteen, he was apprenticed to an ironmonger. In 1866 he emigrated to New Zealand. There he became involved in journalism and founded and edited the *Wanganui Herald*. He served in the Maori war of 1867, and entered parliament in 1875. After a career in politics he became Premier of New Zealand in 1891, bringing its first Liberal government to power. During this period his policies were seen as radical and forward-looking in regard to land reform and votes for women, and he introduced the world's first welfare state. This association with prosperity gained him the title of 'Rainmaker'.

BAMBRICK, JAMES (JOE, or 'HEAD, HEEL OR TOE') 1905–1983
Joe Bambrick was born in Belfast. During the course of his career he played soccer for Rockville, Ulster Rangers, Bridgemount, Glentoran, Linfield, Chelsea and Walsall. He was the first British player to score a double hat-trick in a full international match against Wales at Celtic Park in 1930. He won eleven international caps between 1929 and 1938. In the 1929-30 season with Linfield he scored ninety-four goals. He scored thirty-three goals for Chelsea in only fifty-nine games. Between the years 1925 to 1940 it is said that he scored approximately a thousand goals.

10

BARBER, SAMUEL c.1738–1811
Samuel Barber was born in Killead, County Antrim, and became a Presbyterian minister. He was colonel of the Volunteers from 1782 and was imprisoned for his part in the 1798 rebellion. He died in Rathfriland, County Down.

BARCLAY, JOSEPH 1831–1881
Joseph Barclay was born in County Tyrone and was educated at Trinity College, Dublin. He was involved in missionary work among the Jews and became the Bishop of Jerusalem in 1861. He translated portions of the Talmud into English.

BARNARD, ANDREW FRANCIS 1773–1855
Andrew Barnard was born in Fahan, County Donegal. In 1794 he joined the army and fought in Canada, the West Indies, the Peninsular War and was wounded at Waterloo. He became a general, and susequently Governor of Chelsea Hospital, and was knighted.

BARNETT, GEORGE 1876–1965
George Barnett lived most of his life in Owenreagh, Sixtowns, County Londonderry. He was a geologist and archaeologist and discovered Beaghmore Bronze Age site in County Tyrone. He suggested that it was a lunar observatory. He experimented by making his own stone tools modelled on those of the Stone Age. He had an intimate knowledge of the north-east Tyrone landscape and frequently contributed artifacts to Draperstown Museum.

BARRE, WILLIAM J. 1830–1867
William Barre was born in Newry, County Down and as an architect practised in Newry and Belfast. He designed many major public buildings in Belfast, including the Ulster Hall and the Albert Memorial.

BARRINGTON, MARGARET 1896–1982
Margaret Barrington was born in Malin, County Donegal, and was educated in, among other places, Dungannon and at Trinity College, Dublin. In 1926 she married Liam O'Flaherty, her second husband. She wrote many short stories, and in 1939 published a novel, *My Cousin Justin. David's Daughter, Tamar,* a selection of her short stories, was published in 1982, five months after her death. During the 1930s she wrote a woman's page for the *Tribune* and lived in England. She helped refugees from Nazi Germany and was an active supporter of the Republicans in the Spanish Civil War. In the 1940s she returned to Ireland and lived in West Cork in almost total obscurity.

BARRY, REDMOND 1866–1913
Redmond Barry was born in Cork and was educated at the Royal University of Ireland. He was called to the Bar and later became a Liberal member of parliament for North Tyrone, from 1907 to 1911. He was appointed Solicitor-General and in 1909, Attorney-General. He became Lord Chancellor in 1911.

BARTON, DUNBAR PLUNKETT 1853–1937
Dunbar Barton was educated in England and was called to the Bar in 1880. From 1885 to 1891 he was professor and lecturer at King's Inns and served as Unionist member of parliament for Mid-Armagh from 1893 to 1900. He was Solicitor-General from 1898 and in 1900 was appointed a judge of the High Court. He was a member of the Royal Irish Academy and the Royal Society of Antiquaries of Ireland and he served on the Senate of the National University of Ireland. Among his publications are *Bernadotte, Prince and King; Links between Ireland and Shakespeare; Timothy Healy* and *Links between Shakespeare and the Law.*

BATTY, WILLIAM HENRY WEST see BETTY

BAX, ARNOLD EDWARD TREVOR 1883–1953
Arnold Bax was an English composer who made many visits to County Donegal, lived in Glencolumbkille for a number of years during the 1920s and was heavily influenced by Irish literature and folklore. He was knighted in 1937 and in 1941 became Master of the King's (later Queen's) Musick. He wrote seven symphonies and several symphonic poems, including 'The

Garden of Fand' and 'Tintagel' as well as a violin concerto, a cello concerto, piano solos and music for choral and chamber groups. He wrote several novels under the pseudonym Dermot O'Byrne. In his autobiography, *Farewell My Youth*, he writes of his dying wish as being 'to gaze from his window at Glen Head in late evening'.

BEATTY, FRANCIS S. fl. 1839–1860
Francis Beatty is listed in the 1839 Belfast Directory as 'engraver and linen ornament manufacturer'. Only weeks after Daguerre had published his method of photography by mercury vapour development of silver iodide exposed on a copper plate, Francis Beatty produced a Daguerrotype of the Long Bridge in Belfast. In 1841 Richard Beard, who had bought the Daguerrotype concession for England and Wales, engaged Beatty, when he opened the first photographic studio in London. The following year, Beatty opened his own studio in Castle Street, Belfast, but soon his business collapsed. He contributed regularly to photographic journals and in 1860 took out a patent for early experiments in photo-lithography.

BECKETT, SAMUEL 1906–1989
Samuel Beckett was born in Foxrock, Dublin, and was educated at Portora Royal School, Enniskillen, and Trinity College, Dublin. He lectured in English in Paris, where he became a close friend of James Joyce, and in French at Trinity College, Dublin. Returning to Paris in 1932, he wrote several novels, *Murphy; Watt; Molloy; Malone Dies* and *The Unnamable*. It was with his plays that he made his international reputation, beginning with *Waiting for Godot* in 1952, followed by *Endgame; Krapp's Last Tape* and *Happy Days* as well as many shorter works. His *Collected Poems* (1930–1978) was published in 1984, and he wrote several volumes of short stories, including *More Pricks than Kicks* and *No's Knife*. He was awarded the Nobel Prize for Literature in 1969. He died in Paris renowned as one of the great writers of the twentieth century.

BEGGS, THOMAS 1789–1847
Thomas Beggs was born in Glenwhirry, County Antrim. When he was six years of age, the family moved to Whiteabbey on the shore of Belfast Lough, and Thomas went to sea in a coasting vessel. He was shipwrecked off Rathlin Island, and returned home. He moved to Ballyclare, County Antrim, and became employed in a local bleachworks. He contributed poems to the *Belfast Penny Journal*, the *News-Letter* and the *Banner of Ulster*. His first book, *Miscellaneous Pieces in Verse*, was published in 1819. He intended to go to France to work in a linen firm, but when this didn't materialise, and he found himself unemployed, he set out on a north Antrim walking tour. The following year, *Rathlin* was published, and a year later, *The Rhyming Pedagogue*. He moved to Belfast in 1825 to work in the bleachworks, and in 1828 published *The Momento, a Choice Variety of Original Poems*. In 1830 he published a prose work, *Nights in a Garrett*. Despite again becoming unemployed, and having to rely on his brother for food and shelter for himself and his family, he continued to publish. Eventually he was re-employed and given a cottage. He is buried in Ballylinny, near Ballyclare, County Antrim, in an unmarked grave.

BELFAST, EARL OF see CHICHESTER, FREDERICK RICHARD

BELL, ARTIE *c.*1915–1972
Artie Bell was born in Belfast. He was a motorcycle sprinter, a grasstrack rider, a hill-climber and a car rallyer, having competed in the Circuit of Ireland Rally. He is best known as a road racer and was a member of the Norton factory team. He won the Isle of Man Senior T.T. race in 1948 and the 1950 Isle of Man Junior T.T. on Norton motorcycles. He also won the 1947 and 1948 Dutch T.T. and the 1948 Swiss Grand Prix. In 1949 he finished fifth in the 500cc World Championship, and in 1950, fourth in the 350cc World Championship. During 1950 he had a serious accident in the Belgian Grand Prix, leaving him unable to race.

BELL, CHARLES DENT 1819–1898
Charles Dent Bell was born in Ballymaguigan, County Londonderry, and was educated at Trinity College, Dublin. He

was ordained in the Church of England and appointed Canon of Carlisle. He was a prolific writer of prose and religious verse.

BELL, GEORGE 1794–1877
George Bell was born in Fermanagh and fought at Badajoz in 1812 and Sebastopol in 1855. He rose to the rank of general and was knighted.

BELL, HENRY NUGENT 1792–1822
Henry Bell was born in Bellvue, County Fermanagh. He was educated at the Inner Temple, and became a specialist in genealogy and ancient laws and titles. He was the brother of Sir George Bell.

BELL, JAMES 1824–1908
James Bell was born in Armagh and was educated at University College, London. He was appointed consulting chemist to the government of India after running the Somerset House laboratory. He was Companion of the Bath and a Fellow of the Royal Society.

BELL, JOHN 1793–1861
John Bell was born in Camelon, near Falkirk, Stirlingshire, Scotland, but at the age of twenty he was known in Newry, County Down, as a landscape painter. In the course of the next seven years he had a number of letters and articles published in the local press, and he lived in Armagh, Newry, Dundalk and Dublin. He was an antiquarian, collecting, it is said 'anything from flint arrowheads to traditional Irish harps'. In 1839 he was employed as drawing master at the Royal School, Dungannon. In 1844 he was elected a Fellow of the Society of Antiquaries of Scotland and five years later a member of the Royal Irish Academy. During this period he was collecting both antiquities and folklore in County Tyrone and investigating a number of archaeological sites throughout Ulster. His drawings frequently illustrated his own archaeological research. When the Irish Antiquities Exhibition took place in Belfast in 1852, John Bell's collection was by far the largest. It was bequeathed to the Society of Antiquaries in Edinburgh and went to their museum.

BELL, ROBERT 1864–1934
Robert Bell served his apprenticeship at the Harland & Wolff shipyard and spent the next forty years of his life working as a hot rivetter. He was interested in geology and became a member of Belfast Naturalists' Field Club. He collected zeolite minerals for which he gained an international reputation.

BELL, SAM HANNA 1909–1990
Sam Hanna Bell was born in Glasgow, but came to live in County Down when he was nine years old. After a variety of jobs he began to work for BBC Northern Ireland as a features producer in 1946, retiring in 1969. During this period, he and Michael J. Murphy collected folklore, and with Seán O'Boyle, he collected traditional music. This material was used in the many radio programmes he wrote and produced, and is in the B.B.C. Archive in the Ulster Folk and Transport Museum, Cultra, County Down. He also wrote a great deal about the theatre and the arts, and several novels, among which are *The Hollow Ball* and *A Man Flourishing*. His novel *December Bride* was published in 1951, reprinted in 1982, and filmed in 1991. He was editor of *The Arts in Ulster*.

BELMORE, 4th EARL OF, see LOWRY-CORRY, SOMERSET

BENEN, ST (or BENIGNUS) d.468
Benen is said to have been baptised by St Patrick in 433 and to have travelled on St Patrick's behalf to all parts of Ireland. He is believed to have succeeded in 465 to the see of Armagh, where he died in 468. His feast-day is on the 9th of November.

BENN, EDWARD 1798–1874
Edward Benn was born in Tandragee, County Armagh, and began working in the brewing trade with his brother George in Downpatrick, County Down. They then moved to Glenravel estate where they distilled potatoes. In 1837 he was a member of the Belfast Natural History and Philosophical Society, and he bequeathed his collection of antiquities to it. He wrote many papers, including 'Objects in Glass'.

He, along with his brother George, established the Belfast Hospital for Diseases of the Skin in Glenravel Street in 1875; the Benn Ulster Eye, Ear and Throat Hospital; and the Samaritan Hospital. His donation allowed Royal Belfast Academical Institution to open a school of mathematics, and another donation enabled the Poorhouse in Clifton Street to build two new wings.

BENN, GEORGE 1801–1882
George Benn was born in Tandragee, County Armagh. During his time as a pupil at Belfast Academy and Belfast Academical Institution he wrote a *History of Belfast*, published in 1823. This topic continued to preoccupy him, and in 1877 and 1880 he published two volumes of a new edition, which utilised William Pinkerton's research. He contributed articles to several journals. For a time he was a distiller in Downpatrick, County Down, and later a farmer and distiller on the family estate at Glenravel, Ballymena. He moved to Liverpool, but when iron ore was dicovered on the Glenravel estate, he returned home. He and his brother Edward were responsible for the establishment of three hospitals in Belfast: the Samaritan Hospital, the Hospital for Diseases of the Skin and the Benn Ulster Eye, Ear and Throat Hospital. His collection of antiquities was presented to the Ulster Museum.

BENNETT, ALEC 1897–1973
Alec Bennett was born in Craigantlet, County Down. He was a motor-cycle racer and rode dirt track in Canada, and then as a road tester for Sunbeam. In the 1920s he won eleven of the twenty-nine top events in which he rode, seven of which were European Grand Prix events. In 1923 in the International Six Days Trial he won a Gold Medal. He had a motorcycle business in Hampshire until his death.

BERESFORD, JOHN CLAUDIUS 1738–1805
John Beresford was born in Dublin and was educated at Kilkenny College and Trinity College, Dublin. In 1760 he was called to the Bar but never practised. From 1760 until 1805 he was member of parliament for

Waterford. In 1768 he became a Privy Counsellor, in 1770 a Comissioner of Revenue and in 1780 First Comissioner of Revenue. He was instrumental in the building of the new Custom House in Dublin and the extension of the quays. He was a close colleague of Pitt's, and a strong supporter of the Act of Union. His seat was at Walworth in County Londonderry, where he died.

BERESFORD, JOHN GEORGE 1773–1862
John George Beresford was born in Dublin and was educated at Eton and Oxford. He entered the Church and came to Armagh in 1822 as Archbishop and Primate of All Ireland, having been Bishop of Cork and Ross, Raphoe, and Clogher and Archbishop of Dublin. He was Vice-Chancellor of Dublin University and later Chancellor. He restored the Cathedral of Armagh as well as installing a campanile in the library-square of Trinity College, Dublin. As the son of the first Marquis of Waterford he became Lord George Beresford. He published sermons, and is buried in Armagh Cathedral.

BERESFORD, JOHN POO c.1768–1844
John Beresford joined the navy and attained the rank of admiral. He was a member of parliament for Chatham, Berwick and Coleraine and in 1814 was created a baronet.

BERESFORD, WILLIAM 1742–1819
William Beresford was educated at Trinity College, Dublin, and became Doctor of Divinity in 1780. In that year he was appointed Bishop of Dromore, and two years later Bishop of Ossory. In 1794 he was given the Archbishopric of Tuam and in 1812 was created Baron Decies.

BERKELEY, GEORGE 1685–1753
George Berkeley was born at Dysart Castle, County Kilkenny, and was educated at Trinity College, Dublin, where he became a fellow. He travelled in Europe and when he returned to Ireland, wrote: 'Essay Towards Preventing the Ruin of Great Britain'. He entered the Church and was made Dean of Derry in 1724. During this period he sought financial support for a proposed

college in the Bermudas which never came to fruition. Three years were spent in Rhode Island where he wrote *Alciphron*. He became Bishop of Cloyne in 1734. His interest in Irish social and economic issues was reflected in *The Querist*, a work in three volumes. He retired to Oxford where he subsequently died, and he is buried in Christ Church Cathedral. He published many influential works.

BERWICK, EDWARD 1750–1820
Edward Berwick was born in County Down. He was educated at Trinity College, Dublin, where he antagonised the provost, Major Hely Hutchinson, by refusing to vote for parliamentary candidates of the provost's nomination. In 1775 Edward Berwick was deprived of his scholarship, ostensibly because he had not been in residence for the required period, but after putting his case before the archbishops of Armagh and Dublin, he was re-instated. He was ordained in the Church of Ireland and became rector of Tullylish, County Down, from where he moved to Leixlip, County Dublin and then Clongish, County Longford, as domestic chaplain to the Earl of Moira. He published theological and classical works, including *A Treatise on the Government of the Church*, 1811. Subsequently, he became chaplain to the Marquis of Hastings, under whose patronage he edited the *Rawdon Papers*.

BEST, RICHARD IRVINE 1872–1959
Richard Best was born in Ulster and studied in Paris. He became a renowned Celtic scholar and was Senior Professor of Celtic Studies at the Dublin Institute of Advanced Studies. He published such works as *The Irish Mythological Cycle and Celtic Mythology*, *The Martyrology of Tallaght*, and *The Book of Leinster, formerly Lebar Na Nuachongbála*. He was Director of the National Library and President of the Royal Irish Academy. His major publication is judged to be *Bibliography of Irish Philology and Manuscript Literature, Publications 1913–1941*. He was elected an Honorary Fellow of the Bibliographical Society of Ireland, had two honorary doctorates conferred upon him, and was awarded the highly regarded Leibniz Medal of the Royal Prussian Academy.

BETTY (or BATTY), WILLIAM HENRY WEST 1791–1874
William Henry West Betty came from Dromore, County Down, and was a well-known boy actor, under the name of 'Young Roscius'. He played on the London stage, and it has been claimed that Pitt the Younger adjourned parliament so that he could see Betty playing in *Hamlet*. Betty is said to have retired at the age of twenty-one with a large fortune.

BIGGAR, JOSEPH GILLIS 1828–1890
Joseph Biggar was born in Belfast. He was a provisions merchant and became active in nationalist politics, sitting as member of parliament for Cavan from 1874 to 1890. He was the originator of the policy of 'obstruction' in the House of Commons. A Presbyterian who converted to Catholicism, he was a member of the Fenians from 1875 to 1877, and treasurer of the Land League.

BIGGER, FRANCIS JOSEPH 1863–1926
Francis Joseph Bigger was born in Belfast and was educated at the Royal Belfast Academical Institution, of which his grandfather was a founder, and in Liverpool. Though he began to practise as a solicitor in 1888, he was devoted to the study of Irish archaeology and Ulster history. He revived the *Ulster Journal of Archaeology* and restored many ruined castles and churches. A member of the Royal Irish Academy, he believed in the worth of Irish culture, especially folk music and song, and he advocated learning the Irish language. He was elected Fellow of the Royal Society of Antiquaries of Ireland and produced a series of pamphlets: *Irish Penal Crosses*; *The Ulster Land War of 1770*; and *The Northern Leaders of '98*. In 1924 he edited *Ulster Dialect Words and Phrases*. His private library of three thousand volumes was given to the Belfast Public Library. A selection of his work, *Articles and Sketches*, was published a year after his death.

BING, GEOFFREY HENRY CECIL 1909–1977
Geoffrey Bing was born in County Down and was educated at Tonbridge, Oxford

University and Princeton University. He was a lawyer, and served in Gibraltar, Ghana and Nigeria. During the war he was a signals officer, and afterwards he became a Labour member of parliament for Hornchurch. From 1957 to 1961 he was Attorney-General in Ghana under President Nkrumah. He was author of the best-selling *John Bull's Other Island* and of *Reap the Whirlwind.* He became a Companion of the Order of St Michael and St George in 1960.

BINGHAM, JOHN 1908–1988
John Bingham became 7th Baron Clanmorris of Bangor Castle in 1960. He was a prolific author of crime and spy novels. His obituary in *The Times* acknowledged his ability to bring authentic police and intelligence procedures to his writing. He had worked for MI5.

BINGHAM, MADELEINE 1912–1988
Madeleine Bingham married John Bingham, 7th Baron Clanmorris of Bangor Castle. Among other works she published *The Man from the Ministry* in 1946 and *Peers and Plebs* in 1976.

BIRCH, THOMAS LEDLIE d.1808
Thomas Ledlie Birch was born in County Down and was ordained in the Presbyterian Church in 1752. A United Irishman, he was court-martialled at Lisburn in 1798, and had to flee to America. He published many sermons.

BIRKETT, GEORGE fl. 1614
George Birkett was a brick-layer and builder from London. He was sent over to Ulster by the Drapers' Company of the City of London, to build the castle at Moneymore, the Drapers' Plantation in County Londonderry. By 1620, six stone and six timber houses had been erected. He was appointed Surveyor by the parishioners of Donoghenry, near Stewartstown, County Tyrone, to repair their ruined parish church.

BIRMINGHAM, GEORGE A. see HANNAY, JAMES OWEN

BLACK, JAMES early 19th century
Little is known of James Black, except for his large oil painting, the 'City of Armagh', which was presented to Armagh town commissioners in 1870. He painted shop signs and some local portraits. According to the *Belfast News-Letter* of the 10th of February, 1829, James Black was returning home one evening, past a butcher's, when he interfered in a row between the butcher and his wife. He was struck on the head with a cleaver, and died a few days later.

BLACK, JOSEPH 1728–1799
Joseph Black was an eminent chemist and physician, born in Bordeaux of Belfast parents. He was educated, initially at home by his mother, then in Belfast and at the Universities of Glasgow and Edinburgh. In 1754 he took the degree of Doctor of Medicine, and his inaugural thesis was regarded highly by the pneumatic school of medicine. He made valuable observations about 'fixed air' (carbon dioxide), was appointed Professor of Chemistry at Glasgow in 1756 and began research into the nature and properties of heat. Lavoisier, who developed Black's theories, recommended him as an Associate of the Académie Royale des Sciences in Paris. In 1766 he became Professor of Chemistry at Edinburgh University. He was artisitic and musical and belonged to many learned societies both in England and Europe. He died suddenly 'and was discovered sitting before his usual frugal meal of bread, prunes and milk – his death had been so calm that the mug of milk set down upon his knee remained unspilled'. James Watt's first steam engine used Black's research and he is acknowledged for having laid the foundation of modern chemistry. His *Lectures on Chemistry* were published in many editions.

BLACK, ROBERT 1752–1817
Robert Black was born in County Armagh and was educated in Glasgow. In 1777 he was ordained in the Presbyterian Church at Dromore, County Down and was bitterly opposed to the United Irishmen. He did, however, support Catholic Emancipation and the reform of the electoral system. He had considerable contact with Lord Castlereagh, to whom he gave advice. He was appointed synod agent for the 'regium

donum', a post which he occupied from 1788 until his death. In 1801 he received an honorary doctorate from America. His theology was regarded as controversial, as was his support for the Arian, William Porter. Among other works he published *A Catechism*. He committed suicide by throwing himself into the River Foyle.

BLACK, SAMUEL 1762–1832

Samuel Black was probably born in County Down. He was educated at Edinburgh University and studied anatomy, surgery, materia medica, midwifery, the theory and practice of medicine, natural philosophy and botany. He graduated in 1786 as a doctor of medicine. His thesis, which dealt with the properties of water, is in the library of Queen's University, Belfast. He set up a medical practice in Newry, County Down, in the late 1780s and though he spent some time in Dublin, resided there until his death. His major contribution was his diagnosis of angina and his dissection of four cases of angina pectoris. In his book, *Clinical and Pathological Reports* (1818), he listed people who were liable to develop heart disease: men, people psychologically stressed, those with an accumulation of fat around the heart, those who ate well and did not exercise. He also listed those who were not: women, foot soldiers, the poor and the French. In 1795 his first paper on angina pectoris was published, where he noted that through dissection he had observed 'ossification of the arteries of the heart'. In 1812 he is mentioned in the first edition of the *Boston Medical and Surgical Journal*. In 1817, he treated victims of the typhus epidemic in Newry, and in 1821 published 'Account of the Fever Lately Epidemic in Ireland'. He also made a significant contribution to the study of neurology, diabetes and public health.

BLACKER, VALENTINE 1778–1826

Valentine Blacker was born in Armagh and made his career in the army. He was a Companion of the Bath. He was promoted to the rank of colonel and was appointed Surveyor-General of India where he wrote *The History of the Mahratta War*.

BLACKER, WILLIAM 1777–1855

William Blacker was born in Armagh and was educated at Trinity College, Dublin. He was present at the 'Battle of the Diamond' and subsequently became a prominent Orangeman. He was appointed to the rank of colonel in the army and wrote many songs, publishing *Ardmagh* in 1848.

BLACKHAM, DOROTHY ISABEL 1896–1975

Dorothy Blackham was born in Dublin and trained as an artist in the Royal Hibernian Academy, The Metropolitan School of Art, and Goldsmith's College, London, from 1921 to 1922. She taught art for a period and was awarded medals at the Tailteann Festivals of 1928 and 1932. She worked in Gibraltar among refugees from 1939 until 1945. She married and moved to Donaghadee, County Down, where she continued to paint under her maiden name. She designed posters, Christmas cards, and worked in oils, water-colours and tempera as well as producing drawings for the *Bell* and other magazines. She exhibited widely at the Royal Academy, the Ulster Women Artists' Group, the Royal Hibernian Academy, the Royal Society of British Artists, the Ulster Academy, the Watercolour Society of Ireland, and the Arts and Crafts Society of Ireland. Examples of her work are in the Hugh Lane Municipal Gallery, Dublin.

BLACKWOOD, FREDERICK WILLIAM HAMILTON TEMPLE 1826–1902

Frederick Blackwood, 1st Marquis of Dufferin and Ava, was born in Florence and was educated at Eton and Oxford. In 1847 he went to Skibbereen to help famine victims. He returned to his estates at Clandeboye and managed them for ten years. After various senior ministerial appointments, he became Governor-General of Canada from 1872 to 1878, Ambassador to Russia, to Turkey, to Egypt, to Italy and to France and Governor-General of India from 1884 to 1888. One of the most distinguished diplomats of Victorian Britain, he wrote many books, including *Letters from High Latitudes*. He died at Clandeboye, County Down.

BLACKWOOD, HARIOT (née ROWAN HAMILTON) fl. 1872–1891

Hariot Blackwood, Marchioness of Dufferin and Ava, was the wife of Frederick Blackwood, 1st Marquis of Dufferin and Ava. They lived at Clandeboye, County Down. From 1872 to 1879 she accompanied him when he was made Governor-General of Canada, from 1879 to 1881 when he was British Ambassador to Russia and from 1881 to 1883 when he was British Ambassador to Turkey. She subsequently published *My Russian and Turkish Journals* in 1916. When Frederick Blackwood was appointed Viceroy of India from 1884 to 1888, Hariot again accompanied him. She was interested in photography and the Public Record Office of Northern Ireland has her album, entitled 'My First Efforts in Photography, India 1886'. While she was in India she founded the Countess of Dufferin's Fund in Support of the National Association for Supplying Female Medical Aid to the Women of India. The fund eventually provided Zenana wards and hospitals, such as the Dufferin Maternity Hospital, Agra, and the Dufferin Hospital for Women, Agpur. Money was set aside for the training of Indian nurses and female doctors. Rudyard Kipling dedicated to her a poem, 'The Song of the Women'. Her journal, *Our Viceregal Life in India*, was published in 1891.

BLACKWOOD, HELEN SELENA (née SHERIDAN) 1807–1867

Helen Blackwood grew up in South Africa, and returned to England to live at Hampton Court Palace with her family after her father died. She married Captain Blackwood, who succeeded to the barony of Dufferin in 1839. They lived in Italy, England and Clandeboye, County Down. In 1863 she went to Egypt and after a trip on the Nile with her son, wrote *Lispings from Low Latitudes, or Extracts from the Journal of the Honorable Impulsia Gushington.* Her play, *Finesse, or a Busy Day in Messina* was produced at the Haymarket Theatre, London, later the same year. In 1862 she re-married, Lord Gifford, fourteen years her junior, when he received terminal injuries and was brought to her house to be nursed. Her son, Frederick Blackwood, wrote of her 'I doubt whether there have been any who combined, with so high spirit, such strong unerring good sense, tact, and discretion'. She was the author of many famous Irish ballads, for example 'The Bay of Dublin', 'Terence's Farewell' and 'The Irish Emigrant'. In 1894 a collection of her work was published privately.

BLACKWOOD, HENRY 1770–1832

Henry Blackwood was born in Ballyleidy, County Down. He served as a captain in the navy. In 1792 he went to France to learn French and was suspected of spying, as a result of which he had to flee. On the morning of Trafalgar, he witnessed the will of his friend Admiral Horatio Nelson who gave him command of all the frigates. He became a baronet in 1814, was appointed Commander-in-Chief in the East Indies, and was knighted in 1819. He became a vice-admiral in 1821. He died in Ballyleidy.

BLACKWOOD, HENRY JOSEPH JAMES 1920–1992

Harry Blackwood was born in Armagh and was educated there and at Queen's University, Belfast, where he took a degree in dental surgery in 1941. In 1945 he graduated in medicine and he held various junior posts in surgery in the Harrogate and District General Hospital. He was Resident Surgical Officer at the Baguley EMS Hospital, Altrincham and in 1948 was appointed Registrar at the Royal Dental Hospital in London. He was a prominent dental scientist and was awarded a Nuffield Foundation Fellowship at the London Hospital. In 1959 he attained a Doctorate of Medicine at Queen's University, Belfast. He contributed to the Bone and Tooth Society and edited the proceedings of their conferences. His own research centred on the anatomy and diseases of the teeth and oral tissues. He was Honorary Consultant in Oral Pathology at the Royal Dental Hospital and a Fellow of the Royal College of Pathologists. In 1983 he became President of the Odontological Section of the Royal Society of Medicine.

BLAKELEY, FLETCHER 1783–1862

Fletcher Blakeley was born in Ballyroney,

County Down, and was educated at Glasgow. He was ordained in Moneyrea, County Down. A Unitarian minister, he resigned in 1857, but continued to preach until the installation of his successor. He was in favour of education, supported the rights of tenants and wrote many controversial books. He was joint editor of the *Bible Christian* (1830–33).

BLAND, HUMPHREY *c.*1686–1763
Humphrey Bland was born in Lisburn, County Antrim. He joined the army and fought at Culloden before being appointed Governor of Gibraltar and later Commander-in-Chief in Scotland.

BLAND, LILLIAN 1878–1971
Lillian Bland was born in Kent, and at the age of twenty-eight came to live at Tobercoran House, the family home in Carnmoney, near Belfast. By this stage she had earned a reputation as a press photographer and sports writer. Her aspirations were fired by the achievements of the Wright brothers in the USA and she began to construct a bi-plane glider, and was the first woman in the British Isles, possibly in the world, to design, build and fly her own plane. She named the plane 'Mayfly' with deliberate irony. The 'Mayfly' did fly, and she fitted an engine by A. V. Roe & Company. This modified craft flew successfully in 1910. It is said that her father's offer of a car diverted her attention to running a motor agency, and she then married and left for Vancouver. At the age of ninety-three the *Belfast Telegraph* quoted her as saying that the only excitement left to her was gambling.

BLAYNEY, ANDREW THOMAS 1770–1834
Andrew Blayney, 11th Baron Blayney, was born in Castleblayney, County Monaghan. He joined the army in 1789 and fought in Flanders, Egypt, the Cape and the Peninsular War, where he was taken prisoner in 1810. He was held for four years and wrote an account of his imprisonment. In 1819 he attained the rank of lieutenant-general.

BLYTHE, ERNEST (DE BLAGHD, EARNÁN) 1889–1975
Ernest Blythe was born in Magheragall, near Lisburn, County Antrim, where he was educated. At the age of fifteen he went to work in Dublin. During his stay he learned Irish, and Seán O'Casey reputedly encouraged him to join the Irish Republican Brotherhood. He returned to the North as a journalist for the *North Down Herald.* He became involved in the Irish Volunteer movement and was many times imprisoned as a consequence. He was elected to the Dáil in 1918, and later served under W. T. Cosgrave as Minister of Finance. He held other ministerial posts and was Vice-President of the Executive Council. He retired from politics in 1936. From this point he devoted time and energy to the Irish language revival in the form of an Irish language theatre and the establishment of an official Irish press, An Gúm. He was managing director of the Abbey Theatre from 1939 to 1967 and in 1957 published the autobiographical work *Trasna na Bóinne,* followed in 1969 with *Slán le hUltaibh.* His other publications include a volume of poetry in 1938 and *Briseadh na Teorann* in 1955.

BODLEY, JOSIAS *c.* 1550–1617
Josias Bodley was born in Exeter and was educated at Merton College, Oxford. After a military career in Ireland and Europe he came to Ireland as Director-General of the Fortifications and Buildings in Ireland. In 1614 he was appointed by the Lord Deputy to inquire into the progress of the London Companies' plantations in County Londonderry. His report was presented to James I.

BOND, OLIVER 1762–1798
Oliver Bond was born in County Londonderry. He had a woollen business in Dublin and was active in Irish politics, joining the United Irishmen on their formation in 1791. Despite a term of imprisonment in Newgate, by 1797 he was enthusiastically engaged in administering the United Irishmen's oath, and enrolling and arming men. Meetings of the Leinster Directory of United Irishmen took place at his house which was the setting for the resolution

'We will pay no attention to any measure which the Parliament of this kingdom may adopt, to divert the public mind from the grand object we have in view; as nothing short of the entire and complete regeneration of our country can satisfy us.' He was tried and convicted for high treason on the 24th of July, 1798, and after six weeks in prison died suddenly. He is buried in St Michan's graveyard, Dublin.

BORU, BRIAN 941–1014
Brian Boru was born in Thomond and became King of Munster in 978. It is said that he united the kingdoms under his rule, reformed the Church and defeated the Scandanavian settlers of Dublin at the Battle of Clontarf where he died, having gained sovereignty over all of Ireland. His body was brought to Armagh and buried in the Cathedral.

BOULTER, HUGH 1671–1742
Hugh Boulter was born in London and was educated at Oxford. He held, among other eminent positions, the chaplaincy to George I, the bishopric of Bristol and in 1724 became Archbishop of Armagh. During the nineteen years of his primacy in Armagh he was deeply politically involved on behalf of the English government. On his death he left his estate for the purchase of glebes for the Irish clergy. His inability to make converts to Protestantism was a source of great concern to him: 'I can assure you the Papists are here so numerous that it highly concerns us in point of interest . . . to bring them and theirs over to the knowledge of the true religion; and one of the most likely methods we can think of is...instructing and converting the young generation . . . The ignorance and obstinacy of the adult Papists is such that there is not much hope of converting them.' He published *Letters, containing an Account of the Most Interesting Transactions which Passed in Ireland from 1724 to 1738.*

BOURKE, RICHARD SOUTHWELL 1822–1872
Richard Bourke, Lord Naas, subsequently 6th Earl of Mayo, was born in Dublin and was member of parliament for Kildare from 1847 to 1852 and for Coleraine from 1852 to 1857. He was Chief Secretary for Ireland during the Fenian rising in 1867. He succeeded as Earl of Mayo, was knighted and appointed Governor-General of India. He was shot while visiting penal settlements in the Andaman Islands.

BOWDEN, JOHN 1916–1988
Jack Bowden played hockey for Lisnagarvey and won Irish Senior Cup medals in 1945, 1946, 1951 and 1952. Between 1938 and 1950, he won nineteen hockey international caps for Ireland. He was a member of the Irish hockey side which won four Triple Crowns, in 1938, 1939, 1947 and 1949. Between 1946 and 1955 he also played cricket for Ireland on eighteen occasions.

BOWEN, GRETTA 1880–1981
Gretta Bowen was born in Dublin, but lived most of her life in Belfast. As a widow, she reared three sons, two of whom, George and Arthur Campbell, were artists. She was seventy years old when she discovered her own artistic talent. An article was written about her in *The Times* and she exhibited at the Irish Exhibition of Living Art, the Royal Hibernian Academy, and the Oireachtas. She had one-woman exhibitions in the Bell Gallery in 1965 and the Tom Caldwell Gallery in 1970 and 1976. The Arts Council of Northern Ireland commissioned her son George to paint her portrait in 1975. She attracted international attention and her work is represented in the Ulster Museum.

BOYCE, JOHN (pseud. PEPPERGRASS, PAUL) 1810–1864
John Boyce was born in County Donegal and educated at Maynooth. He emigrated to the United States in 1845, eight years after being ordained. He published lectures, and a number of novels, including *Shandy Maguire* (1848); *The Spaewife* and *Mary Lee*, under his pseudonym Paul Peppergrass. He also published lectures on the influence of Catholicity on the Arts and Sciences.

BOYD, HENRY *c.*1750–1832
Henry Boyd was born near Dromore, County Down. He was educated at Trinity College,

Dublin, and became a vicar in Rathfriland and chaplain to the Earl of Charleville. He wrote poems and translated into English Dante's *Inferno* and *Divine Comedy*.

BOYD, HUGH MACAULEY 1746–1794

Hugh Macauley Boyd was born in Ballycastle, County Antrim and was educated at Trinity College, Dublin. He edited the political paper, the *Freeholder* in Dublin, before going to London, where he joined the club attended by Johnson, Goldsmith and Burke. He accompanied Lord Macartney to India as his secretary and was captured and imprisoned by the French. He became Master-Attendant in Madras where he edited the *Madras Courier* and other Anglo-Indian journals. His miscellaneous works were published between 1798 and 1800, and there were many who believed him (rather than Sir Philip Francis) to be the author of the 'Junius Letters', which had appeared in the *Public Advertiser*, London, from 1769 to 1772, attacking George III and his ministers.

BOYD, JOHN McNEILL 1812–1861

John McNeill Boyd was born in Derry and became a captain in the Royal Navy. He served in the Baltic and is remembered chiefly for his bravery in attempting to rescue a crew in a hurricane near Kingstown, an action which cost him his life.

BOYD, JOHN ST CLAIR 1858–1918

John St Clair Boyd was born in Holywood, County Down, and was educated at Queen's College, Belfast. He graduated as a medical doctor. He moved to the Birmingham and Midland Hospital for Women, where he worked as a surgical assistant. In 1888 he returned to Belfast and worked at the Hospital for Sick Children, Queen Street, as assistant surgeon. In 1889 he became gynaecologist at the Ulster Hospital for Children and Women. He was then appointed Senior Surgeon to the Samaritan Hospital. He was the first President of the Belfast Gaelic League, which had grown out of the Belfast Naturalists' Field Club, in 1895. He was also President of the Dublin Pipers' Club and adjudicated at musical festivals.

BOYD, WILLIAM d.1772

William Boyd was a Presbyterian minister in Macosquin, County Londonderry. He was one of the leaders in the Bann Valley exodus. When in 1718 over 200 men of Aghadowey and Macosquin districts petitioned the king to be allowed to found a colony in New Hampshire, America. Those who emigrated settled at Nutfield, which they renamed Londonderry. They founded the linen industry in the land of their adoption. William Boyd returned to Ireland to minister in County Donegal, where he died.

BOYLE, MICHAEL *c.*1609–1702

Michael Boyle, the eldest son of Richard Boyle, Archbishop of Tuam, was educated at Trinity College, Dublin, and in 1640 he became Dean of Cloyne. In 1641 he was Chaplain-General to the English army in Munster, and later became Bishop of Cork, Cloyne and Ross. In 1661 he became Archbishop of Dublin, and in 1665 he was appointed Lord Chancellor. During this period he founded a town, Blessington, in County Wicklow. In 1679 he became Archbishop of Armagh.

BOYLE, PATRICK 1905–1982

Patrick Boyle was born in Ballymoney, County Antrim, and was educated at Coleraine, County Londonderry. After a long career in the Ulster Bank, he published his first novel, *Like Any Other Man.* He afterwards published three collections of short stories: *At Night All Cats Are Grey; All Looks Yellow to the Jaundiced Eye* and *A View from Calvary. The Port Wine Stain* was a selected volume published in Dublin in 1983. He was a member of the Irish Academy of Letters.

BRABAZON, WILLIAM d.1552

William Brabazon was the Vice-Treasurer and Receiver-General in Ireland for eighteen years. In 1543 he was responsible for receiving the surrender of the Abbeys closed by Henry VIII. In 1543, 1546 and 1549 he was Lord Justice. In 1547 he became an Irish privy councillor. He built the fort at Philipstown and suggested the repair of Athlone Castle. In 1552 he died in Carrickfergus and was buried in Dublin.

BRADFORD, ROBERT 1941–1981
Robert Bradford was born in Limavady, County Londonderry, where his family were evacuated in the Second World War. They returned to the Donegall Road area of Belfast when he was three years old. He left school at the age of fifteen to train as a professional footballer. He was, for a short period, on the list of Sheffield Wednesday, but returned to Belfast and played full-back for Glenavon and Distillery, and later for Queen's University, Belfast. He resumed his education at the age of seventeen and attended Edgehill College which was attached to Queen's University. He was ordained a Methodist minister in 1963. He joined the Unionist party and the Orange Order and was elected to Westminster as the Official United Unionist candidate for South Belfast in 1974. He was re-elected eight months later with a large majority and was again re-elected in 1979. He was in favour of the death penalty. He devoted much time to the social needs of his constituents. He was shot dead at a community hall.

BRADY, THOMAS c.1752–1827
Thomas Brady was born in Cootehill, County Cavan, and was educated in Vienna where he was training for the priesthood. It is said that he attracted the attention of Empress Maria Theresa of Austria. He joined her army, gaining promotion quickly and fought against Napoleon in defence of Austria. He became a privy councillor and a baron and Governor of Dalmatia. He married into the imperial family and died in Vienna.

BRAITHWAITE, CHARLES 1876–1941
Charles Braithwaite was born in Lisburn, County Antrim and attended the School of Art in Belfast until the turn of the century. He went to London where he studied art, craft-work and design at the Royal College of Art. He exhibited with both the Irish Arts and Crafts Society and the English Arts and Crafts Society, and specialised in lettering and illuminated work. His illumi-nations were used for the poems of, among others, Moira O'Neill, Dante Gabriel Rossetti and Elizabeth Browning and an illuminated memorial board was placed in All Souls' Non-Subscribing Presbyterian Church, Elmwood Avenue, Belfast. He, with others, established the Ulster School of Arts and Crafts in Chichester Street, Belfast. In 1911 he joined the staff of the School of Art and taught writing, illumi-nating and lettering. He was an Associate of the Royal Hibernian Academy, and ex-hibited there and at the Arts and Crafts Society. He was a member of the Guild of Irish Art-Workers and Honorary Secretary to the Ulster Committee of the Arts and Crafts Society of Ireland from 1909 to 1925. From 1909 until his death he taught art in Methodist College, Belfast.

BRAMHALL, JOHN 1593–1663
After a distinguished career in the English Church, John Bramhall became Bishop of Derry in 1634 and then Archbishop of Armagh. He was in close contact with the English monarchy and was complimented by Charles I for his service in Ireland, though he had to flee the country after the king's troops were defeated at the Battle of Marston Moor. After the Restoration he was empow-ered as Primate to consecrate archbishops and bishops, one of whom was Jeremy Taylor, the Bishop of Down and Dromore. As a member of the House of Lords he used his considerable influence to increase the Church's capital. The most prominent of his many writings is an attack on Hobbes entitled *The Catching of the Leviathan*.

BRAND, THOMAS NORMAN 1899–1938
Thomas Brand played rugby and was se-lected for the 1924 Lions tour of South Africa. He was capped for the Lions before going on to be capped for Ireland. He accidently drowned in Poole, Dorset.

BRANDT, MURIEL 1909–1981
Muriel Brandt was born in Belfast, attended the Royal College of Art in London, and later married and settled in Dublin. She was commissioned to paint the portraits of many Dublin notables, among them Sir Alfred Chester Beatty. She also painted the

panels in the Franciscan church of Adam and Eve, on Merchant's Quay, Dublin.

BRESLIN, CORMAC 1901–1978
Cormac Breslin was born in County Donegal and was educated at St Eunan's College, Letterkenny. From 1937 to 1977 he was a Dáil deputy. He was Leas Ceann Comhairle from 1951 to 1967 and Ceann Comhairle from 1967 to 1973.

BRIDLE, KATHLEEN 1897–1989
Kathleen Bridle studied at the Metropolitan School of Art, Dublin and at the Royal College of Art, London. She settled in County Fermanagh in 1926 and taught art there for many years. One of her pupils was T. P. Flanagan. She was an academician of the Royal Ulster Academy.

BRISTOL, EARL OF see HERVEY, FREDERICK AUGUSTUS

BROGAN, HARRY 1905–1977
Harry Brogan was born in Holywood, County Down, though soon after his birth his parents moved to Dublin. He was active in Irish theatre, on stage, on radio and later on television and film. He was a permanent member of the Abbey Theatre company.

BRONTË, PATRICK 1777–1861
Patrick Brontë was born in Ballynaskeagh, County Down, and his original family name was O'Prunty or Brunty. He was a local schoolmaster, but then attended St John's College, Cambridge, and became vicar of Haworth in Yorkshire. Though he wrote and published prolifically himself, it is the work of his three daughters, Charlotte, Emily and Anne (all of whom he survived) which has impressed the world. His own publications include *Cottage Poems; The Rural Minstrel* and *The Maid of Killarney*.

BROOKE, BASIL 1888–1973
Basil Brooke was born in Colebrook, County Fermanagh, and was educated at Winchester and Sandhurst. He won two military honours in the First World War: the Military Cross and the Croix de Guerre. Having returned to manage his estate in Colebrook, in 1922 he was appointed Commandant of the Ulster Special Constabulary. He became a Unionist member of the Stormont parliament and held various ministerial posts, including Minister of Agriculture in 1933 and Minister of Commerce and Minister of Production in 1941, culminating in his appointment as Prime Minister of Northern Ireland in 1943, a position which he retained for twenty years. In 1952, he was created Viscount Brookborough. He was a prominent member of the Orange Order.

BROOKE, CHARLOTTE 1740–1793
Charlotte Brooke was born in Rantavan, County Cavan, and was educated at home, where she studied Irish language and literature. She collected, translated and in 1789 published *Reliques of Irish Poetry*. She also published *The School for Christians in Dialogues, for the Use of Children* in 1791, and edited her father, Henry Brooke's works. Many of her translations from Gaelic poetry were published in *Bolg an tSolair* in 1795. Her tragedy, *Belisarius,* was never printed. She was a friend of Maria Edgeworth.

BROOKE, HENRY *c.*1703–1783
Henry Brooke was born in Rantavan, County Cavan, and was educated in Rantavan, at Dr Sheridan's School in Capel Street, Dublin and at Trinity College, Dublin. He went to London to study law and befriended Swift and Pope. He wrote political pamphlets on the need for the abolition of the penal laws and for equal rights, though he opposed the Jacobite rebellion and in 1745 published *The Farmer's Letters to the Protestants of Ireland,* warning them to prepare against such an occurence. An oratorio, an opera and several novels including, in five volumes, *The Fool of Quality* (1766–7) were also published by him. Among his plays are *Gustavus Vasa; The Earl of Westmoreland* and *The Earl of Essex.* He was the father of twenty-two children, one of whom was Charlotte. He died in Dublin.

BROOKE, STOPFORD AUGUSTUS 1832–1916
Stopford Brooke was born in Glendoen,

County Donegal, and was educated at Trinity College, Dublin. After he had taken holy orders, he was chaplain to Queen Victoria and her daughter, the Empress of Germany, though he later became a Unitarian. For many years he was president of the Irish Literary Society in London and editor of a *Treasury of Irish Poetry*. Among his publications are sermons, poems, essays and criticism. [Biography by L. P. Jacks]

BROWN, ANDREW 1744–1797

Andrew Brown was born in Ulster and was educated at Trinity College, Dublin. He went to America in the service of the British army, settled there, and later fought on the side of the Americans in the War of Independence, rising to the rank of major. His subsequent career was varied, ranging from founding a women's college to the editing of a newspaper, the *Federal Gazette*. He died while attempting to save his wife and three children from a fire in their home.

BROWN, JOHN 1850–1911

John Brown was born in Waringstown, County Down, and was educated at the Royal Belfast Academical Institution, and in Bonn. He worked in his father's damask and linen manufacturing factories, though at the age of thirty-five he resigned in order to devote his time to scientific pursuits. He was a member of the British Association and an Associate of the Institute of Electrical Engineers, a Fellow of the Physical Society and a Fellow of the Royal Society. He wrote many scientific papers on voltaic action and electrolysis. His last paper was entitled 'Removal of the Voltaic Potential Difference by Heating in Oil'. At the age of thirty he arrived at the best possible method of construction of the Rumkorf Coil. Ten years later his paper on the subject of 'Education and Schools' was read before the Belfast Natural History and Philosophical Society, asserting that 'In a good school the pupils should learn how to learn'. He was a member of many clubs. In 1895 he bought a steam car, and in 1905 he exhibited the first motor-car in Belfast. His motoring led to an awareness of road surfaces; he invented the 'Viagraph' to record the condition of the surface, and he was President of the Irish Roads Improvement Association.

BROWN, STEPHEN JAMES MEREDITH 1881–1962

Stephen Brown was born in Holywood, County Down, and was educated at Clongowes Wood College. He was ordained as a Jesuit in 1914. He published three scholarly works : *A Reader's Guide to Irish Fiction*; *A Guide to Books on Ireland* and *Ireland in Fiction*. He also edited *Catalogue of Tales and Novels by Irish Writers*. He was a campaigner for libraries, founding the Central Catholic Library. He was Director of the Academy of Christian Art.

BROWN, THOMAS WATERS 1879–1944

Thomas Brown was born in Newtownards, County Down, and was educated at Campbell College, Belfast, and Queen's College, Belfast. In 1907 he was called to the Bar and from 1918 to 1922 served as Unionist member of parliament for North Down. In 1921 he was appointed Attorney-General and later became a judge in the Northern Ireland High Court.

BROWN, WILLIAM 1784–1864

William Brown was born in Ballymena, County Antrim, which he left to enter the linen trade in Baltimore. He was highly successful and opened a branch in Liverpool at the age of twenty-five. He sat as member of parliament for Lancashire and became chairman of the Atlantic Telegraph Company. He was created a baronet and established a free library and museum in Liverpool.

BROWNE, FRANCES 1816–1879

Frances Browne was born in Stranorlar, County Donegal, and because of smallpox in infancy, was blind. She educated herself by memorising passages from dictionaries and grammar books. Her poems were first published in the *Irish Penny Journal* from 1840 to 1844. In 1847 she went to Edinburgh with her sister, determined to live by writing. She was a prolific author, and one of her books, *Granny's Wonderful Chair and the Stories It Told*, published in 1857, became internationally famous. She settled in London and was granted a small pension by Sir Robert Peel to whom she had dedicated her second volume of poems, *The Star of Ateghei* (1844). Other works include *Lyrics and Miscellaneous Poems* and *Pictures and Songs of Home.*

BROWNE, HAMILTON d.1916
Hamilton Browne was born in Comber, County Down, and is remembered for his exploits in the wars in the Antipodes, which gained him the nickname of 'Maori Browne'. He became a colonel and died in Jamaica.

BROWNE, THOMAS GEORGE 1888–1963
Thomas Browne was born in Moneymore, County Londonderry, and was educated at Cookstown Academy and the Veterinary College of Ireland. In 1913 he became a member of the Royal College of Veterinary Surgeons in England, and from 1915 to 1953 was Professsor of Anatomy at the Veterinary College of Ireland, where he was Principal from 1941 to 1953. He was responsible for negotiations which led to the affiliation of the Veterinary College with the National University of Ireland and Trinity College, Dublin.

BROWNE, WILLIAM FRAZER 1903–1931
William Browne was a rugby captain for Campbell College, Belfast. Between 1925 and 1928 he was capped twelve times for Ireland.

BROWNING, MICIAIH d.1689
Miciaih Browning was born in Derry. He is remembered for driving his vessel, the *Mountjoy*, through a boom placed across the River Foyle during the siege of Derry thus bringing supplies to the beleaguered city. He was shot dead before the boat reached Derry quay. It is said that Robert Browning, the poet, was interested in a possible genealogical link with Miciaih's family and that this link is now established.

BROWNLOW, ARTHUR (or CHAMBERLAIN, ARTHUR) 1645–1710
Arthur Chamberlain was born in Ardee, County Louth, and was educated at Trinity College, Dublin. When he reached twenty-one he inherited the Brownlow estates in Armagh from his maternal grandfather and changed his surname to Brownlow. In 1697 he was appointed High Sheriff of Armagh, and from 1692 unitl 1710 he served as a member of parliament. He brought the linen industry to Lurgan, where it thrived. He came into possession of the Book of Armagh and twelve Irish manuscripts. In the last quarter of the seventeenth century he was patron of the Irish scribe, Eoghan Mac Oghannáin, who was based in southeast Ulster. He himself translated Irish poems into English.

BRUCE, EDWARD d.1318
Edward Bruce took part in the Ayreshire Campaign in 1307, and in 1308 subdued Galloway. In 1313 he attacked Dundee and besieged Sterling Castle. In 1314 he commanded the right wing at Bannockburn. In 1315 he took Carrickfergus and was crowned King of Ireland. He marched towards Limerick but retreated to Carrickfergus in 1317. He was killed in battle in Dundalk.

BRUCE, JAMES 1660–1730
James Bruce was born in County Down and ordained as a Presbyterian minister. He established a 'philosophical school' in Killyleagh, County Down.

BRUCE, JAMES ANDREW THOMAS b.1846
James Bruce was born at Downhill Castle, County Londonderry, and later became Admiral of the Fleet. His son, Henry Bruce, who was born in Ballyscullion, was also Admiral of the Fleet.

BRUCE, MICHAEL 1686–1735
Michael Bruce was born in Killyleagh, County Down, where his father, James Bruce had founded a college. He was ordained as a Presbyterian minister, but on adopting Arianism he lost popularity. He lectured in Belfast and is thought to have written *Narratives of the Seven Synods.*

BRUCE, WILLIAM 1757–1841
William Bruce was born in Dublin and was

educated there at Trinity College. After studying theology in Glasgow and Warrington, he was ordained in the Presbyterian Church in 1779 and became Principal of Belfast Academy. An active volunteer, he took part in the national convention at the Rotunda, Dublin 1783. With Henry Joy, he compiled *Belfast Politics: a collection of the debates, resolutions and other proceedings of that town in the years 1792 and 1793*. He was opposed to the United Irishmen and in 1798 he served in the yeomanry. An historian and theologian, he was an early member of the Belfast Literary Society of which he became President, and a founder member of the Unitarian Society. He was also President of the Linen Hall Library from 1798 to 1817.

BRUCE-JOY, ALBERT 1842–1924

Albert Bruce-Joy was born in Dublin and was educated at Becker's School, Offenbach, in Paris and at King's College, London. At the Royal Academy School of Art in London, he studied to become a sculptor. He twice visited America and many of his statues are there. In 1878 he was awarded one of three medals given to British sculptors. In 1893 he was appointed a member of the Royal Hibernian Academy. He was responsible for the figure of Lord Kelvin in the Botanic Gardens, Belfast, modelled a bust of King Edward VII, and made his death mask. Examples of his work are in the National Portrait Gallery, the British Museum and the Ulster Museum.

BRUEN, JAMES 1920–1972

Jimmy Bruen was born in Belfast but played for Cork as an amateur international golfer. At the age of sixteen he was British boys champion. In 1937 and 1938 he won the Barton Shield followed by the Senior Cup in 1939. He won the Irish Close Championship in 1937 and 1938 and the Irish Amateur Open in 1938. At the age of eighteen he played in the Walker Cup at St Andrew's, the youngest player to do so until the record was broken in 1981. He won two further Walker Cup places in 1949 and 1951. At the age of nineteen, he led the qualifiers for the British Open. In 1946 he won the British Amateur Championship.

He was leading amateur in 1937, 1938 and 1939 in the Irish Open and he played twenty-four Home International matches. He was also an international selector from 1959 to 1962 and was captain and president of Cork Golf Club.

BRYCE, JAMES 1767–1857

James Bryce was of Scottish origin and was installed as minister of Killaig, Macosquin parish, County Londonderry in 1805. He was the founder of the Associate Presbytery of Ireland.

BRYCE, JAMES 1806–1877

James Bryce was born at Killaig, Coleraine, County Londonderry, and educated by his parents, both of whom were classical scholars, and by his elder brother Reuben. In 1826 he was appointed Master of the Mathematical and Commercial Department of Belfast Academy. He introduced the teaching of natural history and printed a catalogue entitled *Tables of Simple Minerals, Rocks and Shells, with Local Catalogues of Species for use by the Students of Natural History in Belfast Academy*. He was elected a Fellow of the Geological Societies of London and Dublin in recognition of his work on the fossils of Antrim. In the *Geological Magazine* he described the true origin of the Giant's Causeway, originally proffered by Nicholas Desmarest and William Hamilton but then erroneously discredited, and he produced a paper on the mineral resources of the north of Ireland. As secretary of the Natural History Society he gave a lecture on 'The Method of Supplying Large Towns with Water by Artesian Wells and on the Question of its Applicability to Belfast'. In 1846 he published a *Cyclopaedia of Geography*, and in 1877 he died in a fall from a cliff in the Highlands of Scotland. A memorial stone marks the spot at Foyers.

BRYCE, JAMES 1838–1922

James Bryce was born in Belfast and became Viscount Bryce of Dechmount. He was educated in Glasgow and at Trinity College, Oxford, and was elected to a fellowship in Oriel College. He began publishing in 1864 with his book *The Holy Roman Empire* and was called to the Bar at

Lincoln's Inn. He was appointed Regius Professor of Civil Law at Oxford and British Ambassador to the USA and published many travel books: *Transcaucasia and Ararat; South Africa; South America* as well as *Modern Democracies; Studies in History and Jurisprudence* and *Studies in Contemporary Biography*. He resigned his professorship and entered parliament as a Liberal. When he died in 1922 he had been President of the Board of Trade, Under-Secretary for Foreign Affairs, Chief Secretary for Ireland, had received honorary degrees from thirty-three universities and belonged to thirty-five learned societies. His travels were worldwide, and the British Museum Catalogue contains ninety-two entries under his name. He was awarded the Order of Merit. The latter years of his life were spent in helping to establish the League of Nations.

BRYSON, SAMUEL 1778–1853
Samuel Bryson was born in Belfast and became a surgeon in the army. He returned to Belfast and worked on the staff of the Old Royal Hospital in Frederick Street. He wrote and collected several manuscripts in the Irish language and in 1805 published *Remains of the Irish Bards*. He promoted the study of the Irish language and literature, and Belfast Public Library is the repository for his work.

BULLOCK, JOHN WILLIAM see BULLOCK, SHAN F.

BULLOCK, SHAN F. (BULLOCK, JOHN WILLIAM) 1865–1935
Shan Bullock was born as John William Bullock in Crom, County Fermanagh, and his early childhood was spent around Crom Castle, where his father was steward. He was educated at Farra, County Westmeath. Having worked on his father's farm, he went to London and became a civil servant. He published two volumes of short stories: *The Awkward Squad* (1893) and *Ring o' Rushes* (1896) and many novels, including *By Thrasna River* (1895), *The Squireen* (1903), *Dan the Dollar*, and *Robert Thorne*. He published an autobiography and a final book of fiction, *The Loughsiders*, as well as two volumes of poetry: *Mores et Vita* and

Gleanings. His play *Snow-Drop Jane* was produced in Belfast in 1915. He was a member of the Irish Academy of Letters and was awarded the OBE.

BUNTING, EDWARD 1773–1843
Edward Bunting was born in Armagh and at the early age of eleven became sub-organist in St Anne's Church, Belfast. The McCracken family befriended him, and he taught music for a livelihood. Following the Festival of Irish Harpers in Belfast in 1792, he became interested in collecting traditional Irish folksongs and tunes. He published *A General Collection of the Ancient Irish Music* in 1796, and further collections were published in 1809 and 1840. Bunting has been criticised for modifying and mutilating what he heard, though his publishers must accept more than part of the blame, since many of his original manuscripts have been much amended by them. He went to live in Dublin, where he was organist at St Stephen's Church. The material which he collected is unique and has been utilised by many, such as Thomas Moore.

BURDEN, HENRY 1835–1893
Henry Burden was born in Belfast and was educated at the Royal Belfast Academical Institution and Queen's College, Belfast, where he studied medicine and won several awards. In 1860 he was appointed demonstrator of anatomy in Queen's College and in the same year was elected a member of the Clinical and Pathological Society. In 1861 he became a member of the Royal College of Surgeons. For a short time he worked in the Maternity Hospital under his father, Professor William Burden. From 1888 to 1889 he was President of the Ulster Medical Society and was pathologist to the Belfast Royal Hospital until his death. Throughout his life he was active as a member of the Belfast Literary Society, the Belfast Natural History and Philosophical Society, the Belfast Naturalists' Field Club and the Royal Irish Academy.

BURDEN, WILLIAM 1798–1879
William Burden was born in India, but his parents died when he was twelve and he

27

was sent home to Belfast to live with his aunts and to attend the Belfast Academy. He abandoned a business career in order to study medicine. He went to Glasgow, where he obtained his degree, and on returning to Belfast was elected a member of the Belfast Medical Society. For three years he was a medical practitioner in Newry. From 1838 to 1870 he was physician to the Belfast Maternity Hospital, and from 1840 to 1849 he lectured on midwifery to the Royal Belfast Academical Institution, where in 1848 he was promoted to President of the Faculty of Medicine. He was the first professor elected to the Chair of Midwifery in Queen's College, in 1849. His portrait hangs in Queen's University.

BURGESS, JAMES HOWARD c.1817–1890
James Burgess worked for many years in the Carrickfergus, County Antrim, area. He contributed twenty-five illustrations to Halls' *Ireland, its Scenery, Character,* published in 1841. He also published *Illustrations of the North of Ireland,* which had a guide to the Giant's Causeway. Most of his work is of Irish coastal scenes, but he also painted in England and Scotland. He had a drawing academy in Belfast. Examples of his work are held by the Linen Hall Library, the Ulster Museum, Belfast Harbour Office, and the National Library of Ireland, Dublin.

BURKE, WILLIAM 1792–1829
William Burke was born in Urney, County Tyrone. In 1818 he moved to Scotland to work on a canal as a navvy. By 1827 he was living in a lodging house in Edinburgh kept by William Hare from Derry. Burke and Hare sold for dissection the body of an elderly person who had died in the house. They received £10 from Dr Robert Knox of Edinburgh University. In the next few years they disposed of at least fifteen people by intoxicating and then suffocating them and selling them to Dr Knox. In 1828 neighbours became suspicious when Marjorie Campbell disappeared and her corpse turned up in Dr Knox's house. On the 28th of January 1829, on the evidence of Hare, Burke was found guilty of murder and hanged in Edinburgh. His body was given to anatomists.

BURKITT, DENIS PARSONS 1911–1993
Denis Burkitt was born in Enniskillen, County Fermanagh. After qualifying in medicine from Trinity College, Dublin, he served as a surgeon in the Royal Army Medical Corps from 1941 to 1946. From 1946 until 1964 he was government surgeon in Uganda. During this period, he discovered a cancer which was caused by a virus, now known universally as 'Burkitt's Lymphona'. He served from 1964 until 1976 on the Medical Research Council External Scientific Staff. He received the highest scientific honours, became a Fellow of the Royal Society in 1972, a member of the Academie de Sciences in 1990, and he won the United States Bower Prize in 1993. He was the recipient of honorary degrees from many countries. Because of him, the sciences of nutrition, gastroenterology and epidemiology were revolutionised when he advocated a high fibre diet, the benefits of which he had observed in Africa. From 1976 to 1984 he was Honorary Senior Research Fellow at St Thomas's Hospital Medical School.

BURROWS, J. W. fl. 1901–1913
J. W. Burrows had a photographic business in Strabane, County Tyrone, from 1901 to 1913. He also owned and ran the Pallidrome, and the local dance hall. His business was bought by Herbert Cooper, and Burrows's work was presented to the Public Record Office of Northern Ireland as part of the Cooper Collection, which is the largest single collection of photographs in Ireland. About 20,000 of the 200,000 plate glass negatives are concerned with events in Counties Tyrone and Donegal.

BURY, JOHN BAGNELL 1861–1927
John Bagnell Bury was born in Monaghan and was educated at Foyle College, Derry and Trinity College, Dublin. He became Professor of Modern History at Trinity College, Dublin, in 1893, and at Cambridge in 1902. In 1898 he was also briefly Professor of Greek at Trinity College, Dublin and he edited Pindar and Gibbon. He was a Fellow of Bristol Academy and a Harvard Lecturer. Among his best known works are *History of Rome, History of Greece, Life of St.*

Patrick; *The Ancient Greek Historians*; *History of the Later Roman Empire* and *A History of Freedom of Thought*. He edited the *Cambridge Ancient History*. Honours were bestowed on him by numerous universities and international learned societies.

BUTLER, PIERCE 1652–1740
Pierce Butler was 3rd Viscount of Galmoy. He took part in the siege of Derry as a colonel of horse. He fought in the Battle of the Boyne and the Battle of Aughrim. He was one of the signatories of the Treaty of Limerick and was finally outlawed. In France, James II created him Earl of Newcastle and he remained there to serve as a colonel of an Irish cavalry regiment. In 1697 his estates in Ireland were confiscated.

BUTLER, WILLIAM ARCHER 1814–1848
William Butler was born in Clonmel, County Tipperary, and was educated at Trinity College, Dublin, where he became Professor of Moral Philosophy. He was appointed rector of Raymochey, County Donegal, and devoted much energy to alleviating the suffering of the famine victims. Among his works are sermons and lectures which were published posthumously. He was a friend of William Wordsworth. He died in County Donegal.

BUTT, ISAAC 1813–1879
Isaac Butt was born in Glenfin, County Donegal, and was educated at Raphoe and Trinity College, Dublin. In 1833 the *Dublin University Magazine* was co-founded by him, and he served as its editor from 1834 to 1838. From 1836 to 1841 he held the Chair of Political Economy. He was called to the Bar in 1838 and became Queen's Counsel in 1844. He established the *Protestant Guardian*, a Dublin weekly newspaper, but having been a supporter of the Union, in opposition to O'Connell, by 1848 he had shifted his political stance and defended William Smith O'Brien. In 1869 he was appointed President of the Amnesty Association and in 1870 was one of those who founded the Home Government Association, later to become the Home Rule League. He served as a member of parliament for Harwich, Youghal and later for Limerick, but was displaced as party leader by Parnell. He was the author of many political and historical works, including *The Handbook of the Land*; *Land Tenure in Ireland* and *The Problem with Irish Education*. Among his works of fiction are *The Gap of Barnesmore*, *Chapters of College Romance* and *Irish Life in Court and Castle*. He died in Dublin and is buried in Stranorlar, County Donegal.

BUTTERS, MARY early 19th century
Mary Butters lived in Carrickfergus, County Antrim, and had the reputation for being a sorceress. A case arising from the death of three people was recorded in the *Ordnance Survey Memoirs of Ireland* in 1839. The jury returned the verdict that they found Mary Butters guilty of 'making use of some noxious ingredients, in the manner of a charm, to recover or relieve from witchcraft a cow, the property of Alexander Montgomery'.

BYERS, JOHN WILLIAM 1853–1920
John William Byers was born in Shanghai, the son of Margaret Byers. He came to Belfast to study at the Academical Institution and Queen's College, where he became Professor of Midwifery. An authority on diseases relating specifically to women and children, he published numerous medical papers, and was knighted in 1906. He also cultivated his interest in the myths and dialects of Ulster.

BYERS, MARGARET 1832–1912
Margaret Byers was born in Rathfriland, County Down, and was educated in Nottingham where she became a teacher. Her headmistress, whose maxim was, 'Women can do anything under God', is said to have had a profound influence on her. She married in 1852, and she and her husband left for China as missionaries. She showed great courage and fortitude when, on their return journey, when she was barely twenty years old, she had to look after a new-born infant and her ailing husband, who died eight days before their ship reached New York. When she returned to Ireland, she taught in the Ladies' Collegiate School in Cookstown, County Tyrone, before establishing her own school, Victoria College, in Belfast. This institution

occupied many sites but eventually moved from Lower Crescent to University Road. Margaret Byers was a teacher, a businesswoman, a pioneer of higher education for girls, a philanthropist and a suffragist. She said: 'My aim was to provide for girls an education...as thorough as that which is afforded to boys in the schools of the highest order.' In 1905 she was given an honorary degree by Trinity College, Dublin and in 1908 Queen's University, Belfast, appointed her to its Senate.

BYRNE, CHARLES 1761–1783
Charles Byrne was born in Littlebridge, near Derry. He had a tumour on his pituitary gland which stimulated unnatural growth and affected his intelligence. By the time he was twenty-one years old he was over seven feet tall. He travelled to London, where he formed a partnership with Count Joseph Borulwaski, who was only three feet tall, and together they gave exhibitions throughout the country. It was said that John Hunter, the surgeon, offered Byrne a sum of money for his body, which he wished to place in his museum, but Byrne refused. A very heavy drinker, Byrne died at the age of twenty-two, of tuberculosis, and Hunter procured his body and mounted it in a glass case. It is now in the College of Surgeons in London.

BYRNE, DONN see O'BEIRNE, BRIAN

BYRNE, FRANCIS (DEARG) 1903–1987
Francis Byrne was born in Kilcar, County Donegal and was educated locally. As a boy he was hired to work the land. He and his brother Mickey Byrne (1899–1980) were masters of the self-taught fiddle music of Donegal. They played to raise money for Father McDyer's co-operative scheme in Glencolumbkille. They composed music and oral poetry and told stories on any given occasion. Francis was the lead fiddler and Mickey played octave fiddle. They were revered by musicians all over the world, such as Sean Maguire and Boys of the Lough, many of whom came to visit Kilcar. Frequent recordings were made, especially by Ciarán Mac Mathúna from Radio Éireann. They won numerous prizes at Fleadhs and the Francie Dearg Memorial Fleadh is held on the 23rd of July in Kilcar. They are listed in RTÉ archives.

BYRNE, JOSEPH ALOYSIUS 1874–1942
Joseph Byrne was born in Derry and was educated in England and Belgium. In 1893 he joined the British army and was appointed Inspector-General of the Royal Irish Constabulary in 1916. He was knighted. In 1920 he was suspended with full pay because of his political views.

BYRNE, PATRICK d.1863
Patrick Byrne was born in Farney, County Monaghan. He was blind, but learned to play the harp at the school for harpers in Belfast. He was known as 'Young Byrne'. In 1845 he represented Ireland in Edinburgh, and later he played before Queen Victoria at Balmoral. A photograph of him survives.

BYRON, WILLIAM d.1961
Billy Byron was an International Rugby forward and won many Senior Cup medals for North of Ireland Football Club. Between 1896 and 1899 he was capped eleven times for Ireland and was one of the five players to play in all matches in Ireland's Second Triple Crown success in 1899.

C

CAINNECH, ST (CANICE or KENNETH)
6th century
Cainnech was born in Drumrammer, near Limavady, County Londonderry, and was the patron saint of Kilkenny. He studied at Clonard around 543, and is said to have visited Columba at Iona. He belonged to the Corca-dalan of Ulster and founded churches at Aghaboe and Kilkenny and a school at Drumachose. He was the son of the famous poet Lydach, and his feast-day is on the 11th of October.

CAIRNES, DAVID 1645–1722
David Cairnes was born in Derry and became a lawyer. He played a prominent part in the defence of Derry in the early stages of the siege. In 1689 he was appointed lieutenant-colonel of a regiment. For thirty years after the war he served Derry as a member of parliament, and was appointed Recorder of the city. He is buried in the cathedral churchyard.

CAIRNÍN, ST d.653
Cairnín was Abbot of Iniscaltra, Lough Derg, County Donegal. He became an anchorite, and large numbers of people went to Lough Derg to seek him out. The Franciscan convent in Donegal preserved his manuscript, which contained a commentary on the 119th Psalm. It was then housed in Rome, but in 1871 was returned to the Dublin Franciscans. His feast-day is on the 24th March.

CAIRNS, HUGH McCALMONT 1819–1885
Hugh Cairns was born in Belfast and was educated at Trinity College, Dublin. He became a lawyer in 1844 and a member of parliament for Belfast from 1852 to 1866. By 1867 he had been raised to the peerage and the following year became Lord Chancellor of England.

CALDWELL, ROBERT 1814–1891
Robert Caldwell was born in Clady, County Tyrone, and was educated in Glasgow. In 1837 he went to Madras as a missionary and during this period translated the Bible and the Book of Common Prayer into the Tamil language. He wrote a great deal on Indian history and Indian languages and was consecrated Bishop of Tinnevelly in 1877. He died at Kodaikanal in 1891. His work, *Reminiscences; Madras,* was published in 1894.

CALLAN, BERNARD (BRIAN UA CATHALÁIN) 1750–1804
Bernard Callan was born in Farney, County Monaghan, and was educated in Antwerp. In 1780 he was appointed parish priest of the parishes of Inniskeen and Donaghmoyne, County Monaghan. He instigated the building of Drumcatton and Taplagh Churches. He was an Irish scholar and he commissioned an Irish prayer book in 1800. It was reprinted in 1819, 1825 and 1835, and was known as *The Spiritual Rose.* He composed both prose and poetry in Irish, English and Latin, and many of his manuscripts are in the Franciscan archives in Killiney.

CAMPBELL, AGNES 16th century
Agnes Campbell, Lady of Kintyre, was reared at the Court of the Stuarts. She married James MacDonald, to whom she bore Angus, Donald Gorm and Finula. In 1569 she again married, Turlough Luineach O'Neill, who hoped, through her influence in Scotland, to obtain a constant supply of mercenary soldiers. Although, with her daughter Finula, she was responsible for recruiting most of the Scots mercenaries who served in Ireland at that time, she did not always comply with Turlough's wishes. She strove to establish her sons Angus and Donald Gorm MacDonald in the Glens of Antrim as rivals

tò Sorley Boy, whom Turlough had hoped to keep as an ally. She helped Turlough establish Strabane as a small town.

CAMPBELL, ALEXANDER c.1786–1866
Alexander Campbell was born in Ballymena, County Antrim. Having studied theology at Glasgow University, he became a Presbyterian minister. He emigrated to Bethany in Western Virginia and left the Presbyterian Church. He and his father established several congregations which disapproved of all sects and became known as the Disciples of Christ, or Campbellites. In 1840 they founded a college. By 1867 approximately half a million people in the United States were followers. Alexander Campbell published various theological works including *The Christian Baptist*. He believed that the possession of slaves ought not to disqualify one from church membership. He died in West Virginia. [Life by Richardson, 1868]

CAMPBELL, ARTHUR 1863–1954
Arthur Campbell was born near Derry. He worked all his life on methods of establishing fundamental electrical standards. He made a major contribution under Sir Richard Glazebrook to the National Physical Laboratory, the reputation of which became world-wide. He was awarded the Duddell Medal of the Physical Society.

CAMPBELL, FREDERICK GEORGE 1917–1979
George Campbell was born in Arklow, County Wicklow, but spent his formative years in Belfast and was educated in Dublin, London and Paris. He began to paint and after the Second World War was involved in founding the Living Art Exhibition. He was a member of the Royal Hibernian Academy and won, among other awards, the Douglas Hyde Gold Medal in 1966 and the Oireachtas Prize for Landscape in 1969. The Spanish government conferred on him the honour of Knight Commander of Spain, and indeed Spain, where he lived for twenty-five years, is the subject of many of his paintings, as is Belfast and the west of Ireland. As well as exhibiting his paintings in Canada, Gibral-

tar, Holland, Spain and America, he exhibited with his brother Arthur, and with his mother, Gretta Bowen. He made stained glass windows for Galway Cathedral and played the flamenco guitar. He was a close friend of Gerard Dillon. In 1970 he illustrated the *Guide to the National Monuments in the Republic of Ireland.*

CAMPBELL, J. early 20th century
J. Campbell was a soccer international midfielder and played for Cliftonville and Distillery. He won Irish Cup medals in 1896, 1897, 1900, 1901 and 1907. He was capped fifteen times for Ireland between 1896 and 1904 and scored one international goal.

CAMPBELL, JAMES 1758–1818
James Campbell was born in Cairncastle, County Antrim, and was taught locally. He learnt to weave, and moved to Ballynure, County Antrim, where he worked as a journeyman, and then to Ballybracken, County Antrim. He was a United Irishman, and was arrested in 1798. His papers, which contained all his poems written up to that point, were seized by the authorities, and not returned. His work was later edited by Alexander McDowell and the *Posthumous Works of James Campbell of Ballynure*, was published in 1820, two years after his death.

CAMPBELL, JAMES JOSEPH 1910–1979
J. J. Campbell was born in Belfast and was educated at St Malachy's College, Belfast, and Queen's University. He taught for a year at Methodist College, Belfast, and in 1931 was appointed classics master in St Malachy's College. He was strongly nationalist in his youth, and published *Orange Terror*, though he subsequently modified his views. He became lecturer in education at St Mary's Training College in 1950, and later head of the Education Department at St Joseph's College of Education. In 1969 he was Director of the Institute of Education at Queen's University, Chairman of Convocation at Queen's and a member of the Senate. He was editor of the *Irish Bookman* and published widely in journals and newspapers. He was a member of the BBC Advisory Council, and a noted broadcaster. He served on many committees,

notably the Cameron Commission on the disturbances in Northern Ireland in 1969. He died in Belfast and bequeathed his collection of books to the Linen Hall Library.

CAMPBELL, JOHN 1663–1730

John Campbell was educated at Trinity College, Dublin, and ordained in 1687. In the same year he went to Seagoe parish, in Portadown, County Armagh, and remained there for the rest of his life. He was also rector of Killead and was chaplain to Viscount Massereene. He took an active part in the siege of Derry in 1689. He was one of eighteen Anglican clergymen who both fought, and held daily services in the beleaguered city. After the siege he accompanied his friend, the Reverend George Walker, to the Battle of the Boyne, where Walker was killed. John Campbell returned to Seagoe and is buried there.

CAMPBELL, JOHN 1862–1929

John Campbell was born in Templepatrick, County Antrim, and was educated at Queen's College, Belfast. In 1887 he graduated as a Doctor of Medicine and in 1909 as Doctor of Laws. He was a Fellow of the Royal College of Surgeons. He served during the First World War and held many hospital appointments. From 1921 to 1925 he was member of parliament for Queen's University and was Chairman of Convocation. In 1925 he was knighted. He published *A History of Unitarianism* and works on obstetrics and gynaecology.

CAMPBELL, JOHN PATRICK 1883–1962

John Patrick Campbell was born in Belfast and trained as an artist in the Belfast School of Art. Some of his earliest illustrations appeared in Irish text publications of the Gaelic League under the name Seaghan Mac Cathmhaoil. He was involved in the Ulster Literary Theatre and was an actor as well as designing costumes. He reproduced a portrait of Sir Samuel Ferguson for the centenary of the poet's birth, and he illustrated Mary A. Hutton's *The Tain*. In 1911 he emigrated to the United States and during his stay there, illustrated many books. However, his greatest achievement in the memories of those who knew him there,

was an Irish pageant produced in the Armory, Thirty-first, New York.

CAMPBELL, JOHN P. 1923–1968

Johnny Campbell was born in Belfast. He played soccer for Belfast Celtic and Fulham. He was an outside-left and was capped twice for Northern Ireland in 1951. He was an Ulster 100 and 200 yards sprint champion.

CAMPBELL, JOSEPH (MAC CATHMHAOIL, SEOSAMH) 1879–1944

Joseph Campbell was born in Belfast. He was educated locally and contributed to the journal *Uladh* and to the Ulster Literary Theatre, where his play *The Little Cowherd of Sláinge* was performed in 1905. He collected many traditional songs, such as 'My Lagan Love'. He became secretary of the Irish National Literary Society in London, and published several books of poetry and song: *The Garden of the Bees; The Rush Light; The Man Child; Earth of Cualann* and *The Gilly of Christ*. He wrote a play, *Judgement*, which was performed at the Abbey in 1912. When the Civil War broke out he was arrested and interned for two years. In 1923 he emigrated to New York and remained at Fordham University until 1935, when he returned to Ireland. His collected poems were published in Dublin in 1963. [Biography: *Joseph Campbell: Poet and Nationalist 1879–1944* by N. Saunders and A. A. Kelly, 1988]

CAMPBELL, SAMUEL BURNSIDE BOYD 1889–1971

Samuel Campbell was a rugby international forward. He played for Edinburgh University and Derry. Between 1911 and 1913 he won twelve international caps. He won a Military Cross in the First World War.

CAMPBELL, THOMAS 1733–1795

Thomas Campbell was born in Glack, County Tyrone, and was educated at Trinity College, Dublin. He became a clergyman and visited London, where he met Dr Johnson and is mentioned by Boswell. He wrote many controversial works, including *A Philosophical Survey of the South of Ireland*, which adopts an Englishman for its narrator. He became Chancellor of St

McCartan's, and his diary was published posthumously in 1854.

CAMPBELL, THOMAS JOSEPH d.1946
Thomas Campbell was born in Belfast and educated at the Christian Brothers' School and St Malachy's College. He was editor of the *Irish News* from 1895 to 1906. In 1900 he was called to the Bar and was the first treasurer of the Northern Ireland Bar and the first secretary of the Northern Ireland Circuit. He became King's Counsel in 1918, represented the Nationalist party after 1929, in both houses of the Northern Ireland parliament, and ended his career as a county court judge. He was author of *Fifty Years of Ulster.*

CAMPBELL, WILLIAM HOWARD 1859–1910
William Campbell was born and educated in Derry and graduated from Edinburgh University in 1880. He was ordained and went to India, as a missionary where he became an authority on the Telugu language. He wrote a grammar and three other works in this language. He was also an entomologist and discovered approximately sixty new species of moth.

CANNING, ALBERT b.1832
Albert Canning was the son of 1st Lord Garvagh. He lived in Rostrevor, County Down and was Deputy-Lieutenant for Counties Down and Londonderry. He achieved a reputation in the field of literary history and published about thirty works, which included a study of Shakepeare.

CANNING, GEORGE 1730–1771
George Canning was born in Garvagh, County Londonderry, and was educated at Trinity College, Dublin. He was banished to London on an allowance of £150 a year and failed in attempts both to become a lawyer and to establish himself in the wine trade. When George Canning married Mary Ann Costello, his father in his anger stopped the allowance; he therefore turned to writing for a living. Although he published articles, *Poems,* a translation of *Anti-Lucretius,* and (in desperation) his own personal love-letters, he died 'in a wretched garret in Holborn, in a state of the most abject poverty', leaving a child, George, one year of age, who was to become Prime Minister in 1827.

CARBERY, ETHNA see MacMANUS, ANNA.

CAREY, JOHN 1800–1891
John Carey was born at Duneane, County Antrim, was educated at the Belfast Academical Institution, and became a Presbyterian minister in Ballymena. He claimed he was a descendant of the sister of Anne Boleyn. In 1839 he was minister of Albany, County Tyrone. He later moved to Brookvale Presbyterian church in County Down. He was involved in a shooting incident, and though he was arrested, lack of evidence led to his release. It is unclear how he spent the next seven years. In 1850 he went to live in Rarity Cottage, Toome. He earned a reputation during the Famine for lending money at extortionate rates of interest, but, at the same time he was said to have been a benefactor to the destitute. He erected a fine pump in Toome and built a small schoolhouse, but it is his 'Temple of Liberty, Learning and Select Amusement' for which he is remembered. This extraordinary building had seating for one thousand five hundred people and had a fine organ and a fifty-candle chandelier. Its library contained five thousand books. It survived until 1910, when it was burnt to the ground.

CAREY, JOSEPH W. 1859–1937
Joseph Carey received his early art training in the firm of Marcus Ward & Company, Belfast, and eventually formed a business partnership with Richard Thomson. His water-colour sketches, produced in a presentation album in 1915 are in the Armagh County Museum. He was an active member of the Belfast Art Society and a member of the Ulster Academy of Arts. His picture, 'Sailing Ships off Blackhead, County Antrim', painted in 1912, is in the Belfast Harbour Office, and 'British Fleet Anchored in Bangor Bay, 1914–18 War' is in the Town Hall, Bangor. Other examples of his work are in the Ulster Museum, the

Linen Hall Library, and the Ulster Folk and Transport Museum, Cultra, County Down.

CARLETON, GUY 1724–1808

Guy Carleton was born in Strabane, County Tyrone, and entered the Guards where he became a lieutenant-colonel of the 72nd Foot. He served in America and became colonel in 1762. From 1775 to 1777 he was Governor of Quebec. He drove the Americans from Quebec and consolidated the victory in a naval battle on Lake Champlain in October, 1776. In the same year he was knighted. In 1778 he became a lieutenant-general and subsequently was promoted to the post of commander-in-chief in America. On his return to Great Britain he was created Baron Dorchester and for ten years he was Governor of British North America. He died in England.

CARLETON, WILLIAM 1794–1869

William Carleton was born in Prillisk near Clogher, County Tyrone, into a family which spoke both Irish and English. The youngest of fourteen children, he attended a hedge school and a school in Donagh, County Monaghan. It is said that he was drawn to the priesthood, but converted to Protestantism when he married. After a motley series of occupations which varied from tutoring to taxidermy and an attempt to join the army, he was befriended by the Reverend Caesar Otway, who encouraged him to write. The *Christian Examiner* printed his story 'The Lough Derg Pilgrimage', and this confirmed him in his choice of career. This was followed by *Traits and Stories of the Irish Peasantry* in five volumes; *Fardarougha the Miser* (1839); *The Black Prophet*, a story of the Famine; and *The Tithe Proctor*. He was a prolific writer and 'farmed his talents as he might have farmed his fields if he had had any, putting in the crop that suited the market'. Towards the end of his life he received a Civil List pension of £200 a year. He returned once to the Clogher Valley during the Famine in 1847. He died in Dublin and is buried in Mount Jerome Cemetery. [Biographies by O'Donoghue; and by Benedict Kiely: *Poor Scholar*, 1947]

CARLILE, ANN JANE (née HAMILL) 1775–1864

Ann Jane Carlile was born in Ruskey, County Monaghan. She had a drapery business. After her husband, the Reverend Francis Carlile died, she lived in Derry for fifteen years from 1911. When three of her seven children died, she went to Dublin, where she was a member of the Female Gaol Committee and was engaged in the visiting of prisons and the founding of temperance associations. During this period she met Elizabeth Fry. She made frequent visits to Belfast, England and Scotland, to advocate the formation of temperance associations there and invented the title 'Band of Hope' to describe such organisations.

CARMICHAEL, AMY BEATRICE 1867–1938

Amy Carmichael was born in Millisle, County Down and was educated at Harrogate, Yorkshire, and in Belfast. She went to Japan as a missionary in 1893 and to India in 1895, where she remained until her death. She was the author of thirty-five publications, including: *Gold by Moonlight*; *Ploughed Under*, *From Sunrise Land* and *Gold Cord*. None of her books carried her photograph, and she is reputed to have said: 'I think nothing can be less beautiful than I am, and there are enough "not" beautiful things in the world without my adding to the number'.

CARNDUFF, THOMAS 1886–1956

Thomas Carnduff was born in the Sandy Row district of Belfast and spent his early childhood in Dublin, where he was educated at the Royal Hibernian School and the Royal Military College. He worked as a butcher's boy, in a thread and needle factory, in a printing house, as a drover in a linen factory and in the Belfast shipyards. He joined the Young Citizens' Volunteers and fought in the First World War in the Royal Engineers. He was involved in the Labour and trade union movements and active in the Independent Orange Order. He was a friend of Peadar O'Donnell and supported the Connolly Association. All his life he had written poetry, and in 1936 he formed the Young Ulster Literary

Society and was a member of the Irish PEN Club. He wrote for several newspapers and magazines, including the *Bell* and published books of poems, one of which was *Songs from the Shipyard and Other Poems*. He wrote many plays: *Workers*; *Traitors*; *Castlereagh*; *Industry*; *The Stars Foretell* and *Murder at Stranmillis*. Some of these were performed in the Abbey Theatre, Dublin and the Empire Theatre, Belfast; *The Birth of a Giant* was a play written for radio. His later years were spent working as a caretaker in the Linen Hall Library, where his portrait now hangs.

CARNEY, WINIFRED 1887–1943
Winifred Carney was born in Bangor, County Down, was educated at the Christian Brothers' School in Donegall Street, Belfast and was for a time a junior teacher there. She qualified as a secretary and shorthand typist from Hughes' Commercial Academy, one of the first women to do so. She worked as a clerk and became involved in the Gaelic League, in the Suffragist movement and in socialist activities. In 1912 she met James Connolly and became secretary of the Textile Workers' Union, which was in practice the women's section of the Belfast branch of the Irish Transport and General Workers' Union, though officially part of the Irish Women Workers' Union. She typed Connolly's articles for publication and became a friend and confidant. In Cumann na mBan, she taught first aid and was very proficient in rifle practice. She was summoned to Dublin by Connolly on the 4th April 1916, and as adjutant she joined the insurgents in the General Post Office, where they were garrisoned. She stayed with Connolly after he had been wounded. In 1917 she was the Belfast delegate to the Cumann na mBan convention and a year later stood as Sinn Féin candidate with the view to establishing a Workers' Republic. She lost the election, but continued to work for the Irish Transport and General Workers' Union until 1928. In 1924 she had joined the Labour Party. In 1928 she married George McBride in Wales, and they moved back to Belfast. She alienated people who could not understand why she would wish to spend her life with 'an Orangeman'. In the 1930s she joined the Belfast Socialist Party. Her grave in Milltown Cemetery remains unmarked.

CARSON, ALEXANDER b.1776
Alexander Carson was born in Stewartstown, County Tyrone, and was educated in Glasgow. He became a Presbyterian minister at Tobermore, County Londonderry, but had leanings towards Baptist theology and resigned in 1804. He wrote prolifically on theological subjects, and his work is published in six volumes. He received an honorary degree from two American universities. [Biography by Moore and Douglas]

CARSON, EDWARD HENRY 1854–1935
Edward Carson was born in Dublin, and was educated at Portarlington and Trinity College, Dublin, and was called to the Irish Bar in 1877. He joined the Leinster Circuit and in 1887 became junior Counsel to the Attorney-General. He was appointed Queen's Counsel in 1889 and Solicitor-General for Ireland in 1892. From 1892 to 1918 he was member of parliament for Dublin University. In 1893 he was called to the English Bar and became Queen's Counsel in 1894, receiving a knighthood in 1900. He is remembered for his cross-examination of Oscar Wilde. When the Conservative party went out of office in 1905, he was already a leading member and in 1910 he accepted the leadership of the Irish Unionists in the Westminster parliament. He was prominent in forming the Ulster Volunteers, who were trained, illegally armed, and prepared to oppose Home Rule. When the Liberal government gave way to a coalition in the spring of 1915, he was appointed Attorney General, but resigned this post after a few months because of his dissatisfaction with how the war was being conducted. In 1916 he accepted the office of First Lord of the Admiralty and in 1917 entered the war Cabinet, resigning again in 1918. In the same year he abandoned his seat for Dublin University and became member of parliament for the Duncairn division of Belfast. He refused the invitation to be Prime Minister of Northern

Ireland, regarding partition as a defeat. He resigned from politics and was given a life peerage as Baron Carson of Duncairn. He was buried in St Anne's Cathedral after a state funeral in Belfast. [Biographies by E. Marjoribanks and Paul Bew].

CARY, ARTHUR JOYCE LUNEL 1888–1957
Joyce Cary was born in Derry and was educated at Tunbridge Wells and Clifton College. After an attempt to become an artist he graduated in law from Trinity College, Oxford. In 1912–13 he served in the Balkan War with the Red Cross, and having joined the Nigerian political service, fought in the Cameroons in the First World War, where he was wounded. Ill health forced him to return to Oxford in 1920, and his first novel, *Aissa Saved,* was published. He published many novels and short stories, including his autobiographical novel, *A House of Children.* His best known trilogy is *The Horse's Mouth; Herself Surprised* and *To Be a Pilgrim.*

CASEMENT, ANNE BEATRICE (née HODGES) 1887–1975
Anne Beatrice Casement came to live in Magherintemple, Ballycastle, County Antrim, on her marriage to Captain John Casement. She opened her home in 1941 as the first nursery unit for young evacuees from Belfast. She was a member of the North Antrim Hospital Management Committee and of the Dalriada Hospital Management Committee, and she was active in the Ulster Unionist party. In 1956 she was awarded the OBE. She died in Ballycastle, County Antrim.

CASEMENT, FRANCES MABEL (née HARRISON) 1886–1972
Frances Casement was born in Dublin. During the First World War she worked for the Soldiers', Sailors' and Airmens' Families Association in Dublin, and in London in the Second World War. She served on the War Pensions Committee. She was Irish Ladies Golf Champion in 1910, 1911 and 1912, and was runner-up in 1913. She died in Ballymoney, County Antrim.

CASEMENT, FRANCIS 1881–1967
Francis Casement was born in Dublin and spent his childhood in Ballycastle, County Antrim, where he later lived from 1946 to 1967. He was educated in Coleraine Academical Institution and Trinity College, Dublin. He was an Irish International Rugby Player, being capped three times in 1906 for the side which won the Triple Crown. A year later he joined the Royal Army Medical Corps. He served in the First World War as brevet lieutenant colonel in Gallipoli and on the Western Front. He was mentioned three times in despatches. In 1915 he was awarded the Legion d'Honneur, the Distinguished Service Order in 1917, its Bar in 1918 and the Order of St John. In 1922 he was principal medical officer in Mauritius. He was Assistant Director General of Army Medical Services in 1935, and Deputy Director two years later. In 1938 he was Deputy Director of General Medical Services, Southern Command, and from 1940 until 1941, was Honorary Surgeon to King George VI. During 1941 he was also Principal Medical Officer for the Ministry of Health. After his retirement in 1946, he served on the Northern Ireland Grand Jury, and was High Sheriff for County Antrim in 1951. He was the husband of Frances Mabel Harrison. He died in Ballycastle, County Antrim.

CASEMENT, ROGER 1864–1916
Roger Casement was born in Sandycove, Dublin, and was educated at Ballymena Academy, County Antrim. He was employed in the British Consular Service from 1895 to 1913, from which position he exposed cruelties in the Congo and on the rubber plantations of Brazil, where he was Consul-General. He received a knighthood in 1911 and retired from the colonial services in 1912. He joined the Irish Volunteer movement in 1913 and the Sinn Féin movement in 1914 and went to Germany to appeal for armed aid. On his return in a German submarine, he was arrested in County Kerry, tried in London for high treason, and was found guilty and hanged in 1916. His collected writings were published in 1958, and *The Black Diaries of Roger Casement,* which had been used to prejudice public opinion

against him, were published in Europe and America in 1959. He is buried in Glasnevin Cemetery, his body having been returned to Ireland in 1965. In the words of Bulmer Hobson, he 'literally gave away everything he had to help the national movement. He raised money to defend prisoners, to feed school children in the Gaeltacht, to finance Gaelic colleges and to keep our small and insolvent newspapers in existence'. [Biography by Brian Inglis, 1993]

CASSELLS (or CASSEL), RICHARD 1690–1751
Richard Cassells was German and he came to Ireland early in the eighteenth century. He was an architect and built a house, no longer surviving, for Sir Gustavus Hume in Enniskillen. He designed the Rotunda Lying-In Hospital; the printing house at Trinity College, Dublin; Powerscourt, County Wicklow, and the Newry canal, which was the first inland navigation in the British Isles. What is now the Agricultural College in County Cavan is a house designed by him.

CASSIDY, JAMES 1892–1970
James Cassidy was born in the Sandy Row area of Belfast and, when he was old enough, started work in Linfield Mill, originally as a part-timer, and at the age of fourteen as a full-time apprentice hacklemaker. During the First World War he joined the Royal Army Medical Corps and was stationed in Salonica. He returned home in 1919, having been awarded various medals. Until 1927 he worked at Linfield Mill and then became a full-time missionary on behalf of Belfast City Missions in the Donegall Road area. He worked for forty years in the service of the working-class people of Belfast.

CASTLEREAGH, VISCOUNT see STEWART, ROBERT.

CAULFIELD, JAMES 1728–1799
James Caulfield was 1st Earl of Charlemont. He was born in Dublin, but the family estates were in County Tyrone and County Armagh. He planned the village of Moy, said to be modelled on Marengo in Lom-

bardy. He was Commander-in-Chief of the Irish Volunteers and served against the French in Carrickfergus in 1760. He was the first President of the Royal Irish Academy. He is buried in Armagh. [*The Volunteer Earl*, Maurice Craig, 1948]

CELLACH, ST (CELESTINE or CELSUS) c.1079–1129
Cellach was born in Armagh and at the age of twenty-seven, was consecrated archbishop of that diocese. In 1121 he became Bishop of Dublin. He was active in the Church, both intellectually and practically, repairing Armagh Cathedral in 1125. He acted in a conciliatory role on many occasions, the most notable being the truce between the King of Connaught and the King of Munster in 1128. His pupil, St Malachy, he recommended to succeed him. He died in Ardpatrick, County Limerick, and was remembered for his outstanding contribution to the organisation of the Church. His feast-day is on the 6th of April.

CENTLIVRE, SUSANNA (née FREEMAN) 1667–1722
Susanna Centlivre was born in County Tyrone, where her father had been granted land in the plantation of Ulster. At the age of fifteen she ran away to Liverpool and from there walked to London. She was befriended by Arthur Hammond, who persuaded her to go with him as his valet to Cambridge University, dressed in boy's clothes. After some years she left for London, where she married a man who was soon to be killed in a duel. Her second husband was also killed in a duel within a year of their marriage. She began to write for the stage, and her first play was *The Purjured Husband*, which, though not a success, was watched by Queen Anne's chef, Joseph Centlivre, who was struck by the beauty of Susanna, playing the tragic heroine, and married her. Their house near Charing Cross often hosted the literati of the day. Susanna, who spoke several languages, wrote a number of successful comedies. *The Wonder! A Woman Keeps a Secret*, 1714, starred Garrick, and another of her plays, *A Bold Stroke for a Wife*, was very

popular. She is buried in the Church of St Martin-in-the-Fields.

CHARLEMONT, JAMES 1880–1949
James Charlemont was a viscount and was educated at Winchester and commissioned in the Coldstream Guards in 1914. He had previously taken part in the Ulster Volunteer movement against Home Rule. In 1938, he was co-founder of the Irish Association, of which he remained the first president for eight years.

CHARLES, JOHN JAMES 1845–1912
John Charles was born in Cookstown, County Tyrone, and was educated at Queen's College, Belfast, and abroad. In 1865 he graduated as Doctor of Medicine and for the next ten years was a lecturer in Anatomy in Queen's College, Belfast. He moved to Queen's College, Cork, where until 1907 he was Professor of Anatomy and Physiology.

CHARLES, RICHARD HAVELOCK 1858–1934
Richard Charles was born in Cookstown, County Tyrone, and was educated at Queen's College, Cork, in Dublin and in Europe. He became a medical doctor, won a gold medal for scholarship and was a Fellow of the Royal College of Surgeons in Ireland. He joined the Indian Medical Service in 1882 and rose to the rank of major-general. He was appointed physician to the Prince of Wales and Serjeant-Surgeon to King George V. He was President of the Medical Board and Professor of Surgery at Calcutta and Lahore. He was knighted and awarded the Grand Cross of the Star of India.

CHARLES, ROBERT HENRY 1855–1931
Robert Charles was born in Cookstown, County Tyrone, the brother of Richard Charles. He was educated at Queen's College, Belfast, Trinity College, Dublin, and was ordained in 1883 to a curacy in Whitechapel, London, and two years later, to Kensington. From 1898 to 1899 he lectured at Oxford University and again from 1905 to 1914. He was Professor of Biblical Greek at Trinity College, Dublin, from 1898

to 1906. In 1913 he became a canon and six years later Archdeacon of Westminster. He translated manuscripts from the Greek, Hebrew, Armenian, Ethiopic, Syriac, Slavonic and Aramaic and published lectures and sermons.

CHARLEY, WILLIAM THOMAS 1833–1904
William Charley was born in Finaghy, County Antrim, and was educated in Oxford. After a career in law he became member of parliament for Salford from 1868 to 1880. He was made Queen's Counsel and knighted. In 1878 he was appointed Common Serjeant of the City of London, an appointment which he filled for the next fourteen years. He published many works on legal subjects.

CHERMSIDE, ROBERT ALEXANDER 1787–1860
Robert Chermside was born in Portaferry, County Down, and joined the army as an assistant surgeon. He served in the Peninsular War and at the Battle of Waterloo. He became a physician to the British Embassy in Paris, and, after a long and distinguished medical career, was knighted in 1835. He died at Oxford.

CHESNEY, CHARLES CORNWALLIS 1826–1876
Charles Chesney was born in Packolet near Kilkeel, County Down. Having been educated at the Royal Military Academy, Woolwich, he entered the Royal Engineers in 1845 and rose to the rank of colonel by 1873. He wrote many books, including *Campaigns in Virginia and Maryland; Waterloo Lectures* and *Essays on Modern Military Biography*, many of which became textbooks. He was Professor of Military History at Sandhurst, where he lectured on the American Civil War while it was still in progress. He died on military duty.

CHESNEY, FRANCIS RAWDON 1789–1872
Francis Chesney was born in Packolet near Kilkeel, County Down. At the age of nine he is said to have held a commission in the yeomanry and later attended the Military

Academy at Woolwich. He made a personal tour of Napoleon's battlefields after the Penninsular War in order to study battle strategy. In 1814 when he returned to County Down he rescued the crew of a French ship which had grounded, and was presented with the Medal of the Société des Naufrages. In 1829, as lieutenant of artillery he went to Egypt to explore the possibilities of Egyptian and Syrian routes to India. During this trip, which lasted for three years, he visited Damascus, Tiberius, and Djerash, until he reached El Werdi and the Euphrates, which he sailed on a raft. He was able to report the feasibility of a Suez Canal, hence his epithet 'Father of the Suez Canal'. Because of the success of this venture, a second exploration was instigated in 1835 under Chesney's command. The party landed in Syria and transported across the desert two small steamboats which they assembled on the banks of the Euphrates. Despite one of the boats sinking with the loss of twenty people, Chesney managed, with the remaining boat, to explore the Euphrates, the Tigris and the Karum, and to chart these waters. This venture took him to India, and he did not return to London until 1837. By 1843 he had risen in rank and was appointed Commandant of Hong Kong, and returned in 1851 to Packolet. He was sent on two missions to Constantinople in order to assess the possibilities of a railway system. During this period he rose from the rank of colonel, through major general, to general in 1868. He published many works, including those on the exploration of the Rivers Tigris and Euphrates, a book on firearms and artillery, and another on the Russo-Turkish campaigns. He was a Fellow of the Royal Society, a Fellow of the Royal Geographic Society and had conferred on him a Doctorate of Civil Law by Oxford University. [Life by his wife and his daughter, Mary Damant, 1893]

CHESNEY, GEORGE TOMKYNS 1830–1895

George Chesney was probably born at Packolet, Kilkeel, County Down. He joined the Bengal Engineers in 1848 and served through the Indian Mutiny. He rose to be a general and became President of Cooper's Hill Engineering College from 1871 to 1880. He was knighted in 1890 and served as a member of parliament for Oxford until 1895. He wrote novels and a famous skit *The Battle of Dorking*.

CHICHESTER, ARTHUR 1563–1625

Arthur Chichester was born in England but fled to Ireland having been accused of committing robbery. He was Captain of one of Drake's ships which sailed to the West Indies, and in France he was knighted by Henry IV. In 1595 he was knighted once again for service in wars in Ireland, where Lodge regarded him as active in the attempt 'to plough and break up that barbarous nation by conquest, and then sow it with seeds of civility'. He was commander at Carrickfergus in 1599 and was involved in warring with O'Neill. In 1604 he was appointed Lord Deputy and was instrumental in encouraging the Ulster plantation after the Flight of the Earls in 1607. In 1612 he was created Baron Chichester of Belfast and given Inishowen. He summoned the first meeting of parliament in Ireland for twenty-seven years and established a Protestant majority. During his office as Lord Deputy the harp was added to the English arms on the coinage. In 1622 he was sent on a mission to Europe, and returned to die in London, though he is buried in the Church of St Nicholas at Carrickfergus, where a monument has been erected to his memory.

CHICHESTER, ARTHUR 1606–1675

Arthur Chichster was the son of Viscount Chichester. In 1639 he was member of parliament for County Antrim, and at the outbreak of the rebellion in 1641, he raised troops in Carrickfergus. In 1643 he was made Governor of Carrickfergus, but on his refusal to take the covenant prescribed by the parliament in 1644, he withdrew from Ulster. In 1647 he was created Earl of Donegal, and took his seat in the House of Lords in 1661. He died in Belfast and was buried in Carrickfergus.

CHICHESTER, FREDERICK RICHARD 1827–1853

Frederick Chichester was born in Belfast

and was educated at Eton. He gave the proceeds from his earliest musical compositions to the relief of the Famine in 1846. He was president of the Classical Harmonists' Society established in Belfast in 1852. He lectured in working men's clubs in Belfast on poets and poetry, and wrote several novels, among which is *Two Generations*. He also published a book on Naples, where he died. He was Earl of Belfast, which was a courtesy title.

CHICHESTER, WILLIAM 1813–1883

William Chichester was born at Kilmore, County Londonderry, and was educated at Foyle College, Derry, the High School, Shrewsbury and Trinity College, Dublin. He was ordained in 1837 and later inherited the O'Neill estates. An extinct peerage was restored to Chichester under the title of Baron O'Neill of Shane's Castle in 1868.

CHURCHILL-LUCK MRS (née SPOTTISWOODE-ASHE) (pseud. HAMILTON. M.) b.1860

Mrs Churchill-Luck was born in County Londonderry and was a prolific novelist. Her works include *Across an Ulster Bog* (1896); *Beyond the Boundary* (1902) and *On an Ulster Farm* (1904).

CIARÁN, ST 6th century

Ciarán was educated at Clonard and Scattery Island and was founder of Clonmacnoise in 549. It is said by some that he was the author of the *Táin Bó Cúailnge* and that he was of an ancient Ulster family. His feast-day is on the 9th of September.

CILLIAN, ST 7th century

Cillian was born near Virginia, County Cavan, and was an apostle of Franconia. On the 8th of July 689, which is his feast-day, he was martyred in Würtzburg.

CINNAMOND, ROBERT 1884–1968

Robert Cinnamond was born in Ballinderry, County Antrim. He was a folk singer who collected over two hundred songs. He was still recording songs when he was over seventy years old.

CLANNY, WILLIAM REID 1776–1850

William Clanny was born in Bangor, County Down, and studied medicine at Edinburgh. After serving in the navy he invented a safety lamp for miners, an invention which preceeded Davy's and for which he received a gold medal from the Society of Arts.

CLARK, MILES 1960–1993

Miles Clark was born in Magherafelt, County Londonderry. At the age of thirteen, he wrote to Brigadier Smeeton, for advice on how to plan a single-handed transatlantic passage. At the age of seventeen he joined Operation Drake in the Panamanian rain-forest. When he was a geography student at Downing College, Cambridge, he organised an expedition to climb volcanoes, and undertake scientific research in Atka, in the Aleutian Archipelago. He joined the army and in 1984 was one of the oarsmen who rowed Tim Severin's replica Greek Galley through the Black Sea to Georgia. In the mid 1980s he became a full-time writer and photographer. He worked as features editor for *Yachting Monthly*, contributed to many magazines, and wrote a short book on sky-diving. In 1991 he published *High Endeavours*, his biography of Miles and Beryl Smeeton. In 1992 he sailed his family's sixty-year-old wooden yacht, *Wild Goose* to the Arctic Circle, into the White Sea, through canals and rivers to the Black Sea and the Mediterranean. At the time of his death he was writing a book about his travels.

CLARKE, ADAM c.1760–1832

Adam Clarke was born in County Londonderry, and was apprenticed to the linen business. Though a Quaker, he became a pupil of a Methodist school near Bristol, where he prepared himself for the ministry. He studied Hebrew and Oriental languages. In 1782 he was ordained by Wesley, and over the next twenty years, his preaching attracted large crowds. In 1802 he published a bibliographical dictionary in six volumes. As a consequence of this he became a member of the Royal Society of Antiquaries and of the Royal Irish Academy. The University of St Andrew's conferred upon him the degrees of Master of Arts and Doctor of Laws. As well as many other works, he published *The Holy Bible with a Commentary and Notes* in eight volumes and devoted much of his life to this work. He established several schools in Ulster and a small museum, and collected a valuable library. He died of cholera during a visit to England. His last words were 'Am I blue?' [Biographies by his daughter (1833) and Everett and Etheridge]

CLARKE, HARRY 1889–1931
Harry Clarke studied at the Metropolitan School of Art under A. E. Childe. As well as being an accomplished decorative painter and illustrator, he became a stained glass artist. He created the series of stained glass Stations of the Cross in Lough Derg basilica and the windows in the cathedral in Letterkenny, County Donegal. His work is on display in the Municipal Gallery of Modern Art, Dublin.

CLARKE, JOSEPH 1758–1834
Joseph Clarke was born in Desertlin, County Londonderry, and was educated in Glasgow and Edinburgh. He became a prosperous and distinguished physician, practising in Dublin, and it is said that of nearly four thousand cases of parturition he attended in his private practice during forty-four years, there were only twenty-two fatalities. He was Master of the Rotunda Hospital for seven years, during which time he kept an invaluable record. [Biography by Collins 1849]

CLARKE, MARGARET (née CRILLEY) 1888–1961
Margaret Clarke was born in Newry, County Down and she trained at Newry Technical School and the Dublin Metropolitan School of Art under Orpen in 1905. She won medals for oil painting, and first exhibited in the Royal Hibernian Academy in 1913. She visited Aran in order to paint and in 1914 married Harry Clarke. She used her children and her family as subjects for her pictures, and received many commissions from the 1920s onwards. She painted portraits of among others, Lennox Robinson, President de Valera, and Archbishop McQuaid. She taught in the Dublin School

of Art and the Royal Hibernian Academy, and won many prizes for her work. After her husband died in 1931 she directed the Harry Clarke Stained Glass Studios, with her daughter. She was a member of the Royal Hibernian Academy. She was buried in Redford cemetery, Greystones, County Wicklow and her work is in the National Gallery of Ireland, the Ulster Museum and in Cork and Limerick.

CLARKE, MAUD VIOLET 1892–1935
Maud Clarke was born in Belfast and was educated in Belfast, Dublin and Oxford. She returned to Belfast as deputy Professor of History at Queen's University. In 1919 she was appointed tutor at Somerville College, Oxford, and in 1922 became a fellow. She was involved in the fourth volume of the *Oxford History of England* and a book on medieval representation. She died in Carnmoney, County Antrim.

CLARKE, THOMAS J. 1858–1916
Thomas Clarke was born on the Isle of Wight, of Irish parents. He spent his early years in Dungannon, County Tyrone, and emigrated to America in 1881. He joined Clan na Gael and was arrested in London for attempting to dynamite public buildings. He returned to America after he was released from his life sentence, and finally settled in Dublin in 1907. His was the first signature to the republican proclamation in Easter Week 1916. He was subsequently court-martialled, condemned to death and executed.

CLIVE, CATHERINE (née RAFTER) 1711–1785
Kitty Clive is believed to have been born in the north of Ireland. While still very young she separated from her husband, Richard Clive, who was a barrister, and became an actress. She was admired by Handel, and Dr Johnson said of her, 'Clive, Sir, is a good thing to sit by; she always understands what you say'. She was continually mentioned by contemporaries such as Garrick, who played opposite her in her last performance. In her retirement to Strawberry Hill, where she became a close friend and neighbour of Horace Walpole, she

remained a focus for public attention. She wrote several pieces for the theatre, of which *The Rehearsal* was the only one printed. [Biography by Percy Fitzgerald (1888)]

CLOTWORTHY, JOHN d.1665
John Clotworthy was born near Antrim and became a noted soldier. He was later knighted and created First Lord Massareene. He upheld the claims of the Presbyterian leaders before Ormond, the Lord Lieutenant, in 1661.

COBURN, JOSEPH 1835–1890
Joe Coburn was born in Middletown, County Armagh and moved to America. He was a prize-fighting boxer and fought a draw against Ned Price in Boston in 1856 and won against Mike McCoole in 1863. He fought twice for the world title against Jem Mace in 1864.

COIGLY, JAMES 1762–1798
James Coigly was born in County Armagh, and was educated in Paris for the priesthood. He returned to Armagh and became involved with the United Irishmen. He attempted to return to France, but was arrested at Margate and sentenced to death for possessing treasonable documents.

COLE, FLORENCE c.1778–1862
Florence Cole was the third daughter of the 1st Earl of Enniskillen. She lived at Florencecourt, near Enniskillen, County Fermanagh, and sketched prolifically. She is noted for her cut-out work with paper. Her sketch books have been presented to the National Trust for Northern Ireland and are displayed at Florencecourt.

COLE, GALBRAITH LOWRY 1772–1842
Galbraith Cole was born in Dublin and entered the army, serving in the West Indies and in Egypt. He was member of parliament for Enniskillen and Fermanagh for twenty years. He rose to the rank of general and served in the Penninsular War. He was knighted, and from 1823 to 1833 he served as Governor of Mauritius and the Cape. A monument to him stands on Fort Hill in Enniskillen.

COLE, WILLIAM d.1653
William Cole was born in England but settled in County Fermanagh in 1607. He had the title of 'captain of the long boats and barges' bestowed upon him and he carried out his duties at Ballyshannon and Lough Erne. He was first Provost of Enniskillen. He was knighted in 1617 and was the first to give warning to the Lord Deputy, of the impending uprising of 1641. At this time he raised a regiment and protected Enniskillen for King Charles I. He is buried in St Michan's Church, Dublin.

COLE, WILLIAM WILLOUGHBY 1807–1887
William Cole, 3rd Earl of Enniskillen, collected over 10,000 specimens of fossil fish which were housed in a specially built museum at Florence Court, his family home. The Science Museum in London now possesses his invaluable collection.

COLGAN, JOHN (Ó COLGÁIN, SEÁN) c.1590–1657
John Colgan was born in Donegal and educated at Louvain where he entered the Franciscan order in 1618. He was asked to write a history of Irish saints, along with Aodh Mac an Bhaird, and *Acta Sanctorum Veteris et Majoris Scotiae seu Hiberniae* contains the biographies of saints with feast-days from January to March. He also wrote *Trias Thaumaturga* on the lives of Saints Patrick, Brigid and Columba, as well as a *Life of Johannes Duns Scotus*. He retired from the post of Professor of Theology at Louvain in 1645. He was the first to describe the work of Michael O'Clery and his colleagues as *The Annals of the Four Masters*. [Biography by O'Hanlon]

COLLIE, (or CORRIE) GEORGE 1904–1975
George Collie was born in Carrickmacross, County Monaghan, and was educated at St Kevin's Metropolitan School, Blackpitts, Dublin, the Royal Hibernian Academy and the Metropolitan School of Art. In 1927 he won the Taylor Art Scholarship, which allowed him to travel. He studied art in Paris at both the Académie Colorossie and the Grande Chaumerie, and in London at the Royal College of Art. When he returned to Dublin, where he opened his own

studio and school in Schoolhouse Lane, he taught in the National College of Art. He gained a reputation as a portrait painter, and President de Valera and Cardinal D'Alton were among his subjects. In the parish church, Bailieborough, County Cavan, he painted the Stations of the Cross.

COLMÁN, ST 553–610
Colmán was born in Glenelly, County Tyrone. He visited St Columba, who was his uncle, at Iona, and subsequently founded an abbey at Muckamore, County Antrim, and a monastery at Land Elo Lynally, County Offaly. He requested to be buried in Clonard and his feast-day is on the 26th of September.

COLMCILLE, ST (COLUMCILLE or COLUMBA) 521–597
Colmcille was born in Gartan, County Donegal; his baptismal name was Crimthann. He was educated at Moville and possibly Strangford and under St Finian at Clonard, where he was ordained. He founded monasteries in Swords, Durrow, Kells and Derry. He is said to have inscribed the Gospels and instructed others in the art of illuminating texts. One of these Gospel books, the Book of Durrow, is now in the library of Trinity College, Dublin. He sailed with twelve companions to Scotland from Derry in 563 and founded the Abbey of Iona. He returned briefly to Ireland in 575 to attend the Council of Dromkett. He wrote poetry in Irish and Latin, notably the Latin hymn *Altus Prosator*, and a Latin manuscript of the Psalms is said to be in his handwriting. His biography was written by St Adamnán. His feast-day is on the 9th of June.

COLTON JOHN d.1404
John Colton was born in Norfolk. In 1373 he was appointed Lord Treasurer of Ireland and in 1374 became the Dean of St Patrick's, Dublin. He became Lord Chancellor in 1380 and Lord Justice in 1382. In 1381 he was raised to the primacy by Pope Urban VI. He wrote *Visitation of the Diocese of Derry* in 1397 and it was published in 1850 with a preface by William Reeves. He is buried in the Church of St Peter at Drogheda, County Louth.

COLUM, PÁDRAIC 1881–1972
Pádraic Colum was born in County Longford and reared on his grandfather's farm in County Cavan. He worked as a clerk in the railway clearing-house in Dublin and began to write in 1903. His plays *Broken Soil* (later renamed *The Fiddler's House*); *The Land* and *Thomas Muskerry* were produced for the theatre. He was the author of lyrics such as 'She Moved Through the Fair'. In 1907 his first collection of poems *The Wild Earth* was published. Before moving to America, where he taught comparative literature at Columbia University, he co-founded the *Irish Review*. During his stay in America he published folk tales in the *New York Tribune* and was invited by the government of Hawaii to investigate their myths and legends and to write them as children's stories. His collected poems appeared in 1953. He was given doctorates from both University College, Dublin, and Columbia University, and he was awarded the Gregory Medal of the Irish Academy of Letters. He published a biography of Arthur Griffith and in collaboration with his wife Mary, *Our Friend James Joyce*. He was given a grant by the American-Irish Foundation and he was President of the United Arts Club. He died in Connecticut and is buried in Sutton, County Dublin.

COLUMBA, ST, see COLMCILLE

COLUMBÁN, ST, see COLUMBANUS

COLUMBANUS, ST (COLUMBÁN) 543–615
Columbanus was born in Leinster and studied under Comgall in the monastery at Bangor, County Down. He went to Britain and then to France as a missionary and founded monasteries at Annegray, Luxeuil and Fontaine. He drew up a Rule for his monks which was approved by the Council of Macon in 627 but it was superseded by the Benedictine Rule. He was expelled from Gaul by Theodoric II of Burgundy because Columbanus had criticised the immorality of his court. He travelled through Switzerland and founded a monastery at Bobbio in Italy, where he died. His writings including his Rule, letters, poems and sermons,

are in Latin. His feast-day is celebrated on the 21st of November.

COLUMCILLE, ST, see COLMCILLE

COLVILL, ALEXANDER 1700–1777
Alexander Colvill was born in Newtownards, County Down, and was educated at Edinburgh. He was installed at Dromore, County Down in 1725 as a Presbyterian clergyman. During this period he published many controversial works and in 1745 commanded a volunteer corps.

COMGALL, ST (or CONGAL) 516–601
Comgall was born in Magheramorne, County Antrim, to a distinguished Dalriada family. In his youth he relinquished the life of a soldier and travelled to St Fintan at Clonenagh, though he disliked the rigours of monastic life. He was ordained a priest at Clonmacnoise and retreated to an island in Lough Erne. Before retiring to Bangor, County Down, where he founded a monastery and established a Rule, he had already founded several ecclesiastical houses, including that of Camus, near Coleraine. Pilgrims were attracted to the monastery, and it is said that Cormac, King of Uí Cheinnsealaigh, retired there. With St Brendan, Comgall visited St Colmcille in the western isles of Scotland. He died in Bangor, and his feast-day is on the 10th of May.

CONALL CERNACH 1st century
Conall Cernach was a Red Branch Knight. He is continually mentioned in legend as one of those who avenged the death of Cú Chulainn and is said to have received his military training from Fergus mac Róigh at Emain Macha.

CONCANNON, HELENA (née WALSH) 1878–1952
Helena Concannon was born in Maghera, County Londonderry, and was educated at Maghera, Loretto College, Coleraine, County Londonderry, and at Dublin, Berlin, Rome and Paris. She was fluent in Irish. She was a member of Dáil Éireann for the National University of Ireland from 1933 to 1937, and became a senator in 1938.

She wrote many books, among which are *Daughters of Banba*, *Irish Nuns in Penal Days*, *The Blessed Oliver Plunkett* and *Women of Ninety-Eight*.

CONGAL CLÁEN 7th century
Congal Cláen was a King of Ulster who raised an army of mercenaries to fight against the High King, Domnall mac Áedo. He was killed at the Battle of Moira, County Down, in 637 and his army was destroyed.

CONN, WILLIAM H. 1895–1973
Billy Conn was educated at the Ulster Provincial School, which is now Friends' School, Lisburn, County Antrim. In 1921 he was employed as a commercial artist by W. & G. Baird Ltd. He was appointed staff artist to the *Belfast Telegraph* in 1946 and contributed cartoons to *Ireland's Saturday Night*, among which was his regular cartoon, 'The Doings of Larry O'Hooligan'. He exhibited at the Royal Hibernian Academy and contributed black and white drawings to the *Dublin Opinion* and other magazines. He was a member of the Ulster Arts Club and the Royal Ulster Academy.

CONNOLLY, JAMES 1868–1916
James Connolly was born in Edinburgh of County Monaghan parents and was self-educated. When he was twenty-seven he moved to Ireland, where he became a leading member of the Irish trade union movement. He was resident in Belfast from 1910 to 1914 as organiser for the Irish Transport Workers' Union. Although much of his writing was historical and political such as *Erin's Hope*, *The End and the Means* and *Labour in Irish History*, he wrote a play *Under Which Flag?* and a number of poems. He also established trade union journals: *The Harp*, *The Irish Worker* and *The Worker's Republic* and was renowned as both a journalist and a public speaker. In 1896 he founded the Irish Socialist Republican Party and during a seven-year stay in America he was an organiser for the Industrial Workers of the World. In 1912 and 1913 he was involved, with James Larkin, in establishing an Irish Labour Party: the Congress Party. During the lock-out of 1913 to 1914, he joined Larkin in Dublin and in 1914

organised the Citizen Army. He was appointed military commander of the republican forces in Dublin, took a leading role in the 1916 Easter Rising, and was subsequently executed. [Biography by Samuel Levenson].

CONNOLLY, JOSEPH b.1885
Joseph Connolly was born in Belfast and educated at St Malachy's College, Belfast. From 1921 to 1922 he represented the Irish Free State as Consul-General in America, from 1928 to 1936 he was Fianna Fáil member of the Irish Senate, and in 1932 he deputised for de Valera at the Council of the League of Nations. He became Chairman of the Board of Public Works in 1936.

CONOLLY, WILLIAM d.1729
William Conolly was born in Ballyshannon, County Donegal. He became a barrister and Speaker of the Irish House of Commons from 1715 to 1729. He was a Commisioner of Revenue and a Lord Justice, and served both Donegal, from 1692 to 1699 and County Londonderry from 1703 to 1729 as a member of parliament. Linen scarves were first worn at his funeral to encourage the linen trade.

CONOR MAC NESSA (CONCHOBAR mac NESSA) 1st century
Conor Mac Nessa was the son of Nessa, who married Fergus mac Róigh, King of Ulster, on condition that Conor should reign for one year. He proved himself to be a wise and just king and was requested to continue to occupy the throne of Ulster. In a myth we are told that a magic ball of lime and human brains wounded him and became embedded in his forehead and that his physicians declared that if the ball were removed, his death would ensue. This happened when he was made aware by magical means, of the crucifixion, and he is thus reputed to have died in A.D.33. He established the Red Branch Knights and extended the boundaries of Ulster. His name is prominent as a hero in this period of Irish history.

CONOR, WILLIAM 1881–1968
William Conor was born in Belfast and attended Cliftonpark Central National School and the Government School of Design, Belfast. After an apprenticeship as a poster designer at a printer's, and by painting in his spare time, he was able to fund himself for further study in Dublin and Paris. His first exhibition was in Belfast in 1914 and he was officially commissioned during the war to record soldiers and munition workers. He was elected to the Royal Hibernian Academy in 1947, and was awarded the OBE in 1952. He was a member of the National Society of Painters and Sculptors, London, and of the Royal Ulster Academy of Arts, of which he was President in 1957. In the same year he received an honorary Master of Arts degree from Queen's University. He exhibited in London, Paris and New York, and his works have been sold to various public galleries throughout the world.

CONWAY, WILLIAM 1913–1977
William Conway was born in Belfast, and was educated at Barrack Street Christian Brothers' School and Queen's University, Belfast. He entered Maynooth, was ordained in 1937, and became a Doctor of Divinity in 1938. He attended the Gregorian University of Rome from 1938 to 1941. During the next two years he was a teacher of English and Latin at St Malachy's College, Belfast. He held the Chairs of Moral Theology and of Canon Law at Maynooth until 1958, and became Vice-President of the College in 1957. He edited the *Irish Theological Quarterly* and published a book, *Problems of Canon Law*, in 1950. After a term as administrator of St Mary's parish, Dundalk, and of acting as auxiliary to Cardinal D'Alton, William Conway was appointed Archbishop of Armagh and Primate of All Ireland in 1963. In 1965 he was created cardinal. He chaired the first synod of bishops in Rome in 1967 and was a member of four Vatican congregations. He was instrumental in establishing Trócaire. He was a member of the Pontifical Commission for the Revision of Canon Law. He died in Armagh.

COOKE, HENRY 1788–1868
Henry Cooke was born at Grillagh, near Maghera, County Londonderry. He

was educated locally and at the University of Glasgow. In 1808 he was ordained in the Presbyterian ministry and was given a parish in Duneane near Randalstown, later moving to Donegore, near Templepatrick, County Antrim. In 1815 he resumed his studies at Glasgow and in 1817 he entered Trinity College and attended medical classes, preaching to various Presbyterian congregations on Sundays. By 1818 he was pastor of Killyleagh, County Down. He was bitterly opposed to the Unitarian elements within the Irish Presbyterian Church, and ultimately brought about their separation. His followers built him a church in May Street, Belfast, where he preached until his death. He was Moderator of the Synod of Ulster in 1824, and twice Moderator of the General Assembly in 1841 and 1862. He abhorred the restricted use of the Scriptures in the new system of Irish National Education and by 1839 had urged the Synod of Ulster to establish a system of education of its own. He campaigned repeatedly against O'Connell's Irish policy, for example during the Protestant demonstration in Hillsborough in 1834 and at the anti-Repeal meeting in Belfast in 1841. Jefferson College in the United States conferred a doctorate upon him, and in 1837 Trinity College, Dublin did likewise. In 1839 he was given the freedom of Dublin by the corporation. He was instrumental in establishing the Free Church of Scotland. He devoted much time to an *Analytical Concordance of Scripture*, the manuscript of which was destroyed by fire in a London hotel. He edited a new version of *Brown's Family Bible*. He was appointed President of Belfast Theological College, and in 1849 he became Dean of Residence for Presbyterian students in Belfast. As late as 1867, within a year of his death, he gave a public speech in Hillsborough opposing the disestablishment of the Church of Ireland. [Biography by J.L. Porter 1871]

COOLEY, THOMAS 1740–1784
Thomas Cooley was born in England and came to Ireland as an architect. He designed the Royal Exchange as well as many other buildings in Dublin. In Armagh he designed the public library and the addition of a tower to Armagh Cathedral.

COON, ALAN DANIEL 1867–1938
Alan Daniel Coon was born in Buffalo, New York and was Attorney-at-Law in the United States. In 1902 he came to Ireland and opened a photographic studio in Derry where he produced posters and many picture postcards. He opened photographic businesses in Letterkenny, County Donegal and Moira, County Down. He owned cinemas in Letterkenny, Buncrana and Killybegs, County Donegal and one in Belfast. He travelled around in a caravan which contained a photographic studio and a dark room. He also gave cinematographic shows. He died in Moira and is buried there.

COOPER, HERBERT FREDERICK THOMAS 1874–1960
Herbert Cooper was born in Hammersmith, London, and came to Strabane, County Tyrone, where he bought the photographic business of J. W. Burrows in 1913. The Cooper Collection, which was given to the Public Record Office of Northern Ireland by his son, Mr H. D. H. Cooper, is the largest single collection of photographs in Ireland. Among the 200,000 plate glass negatives, some of J. W. Burrows's work is included.

COPLEY, CLARA d.1949
Clara Copley came from a circus family and lived in a Romany caravan, which was sold after her death to a farmer who lived in it in preference to his own house. She had a boxing booth, and later a wooden hall on Chapel Fields in Belfast where boxing tournaments took place. Ma Copley (as she was popularly known) began her career in the 1930s when there was no work and young men were willing to fight for the chance of winning money. One of these was Rinty Monaghan, who became fly-weight champion of the world when he knocked out Jackie Patterson at the King's Hall in 1948. Others were Bunty Doran, who became Irish champion; Tommy Armour, who knocked out the British champion Eric Boon; and Jimmy Warnock, who beat the world fly-weight champion,

Benny Lynch. It was said of Clara Copley, 'she was a woman in a man's world – the world of prize fighting'.

COPPIN, WILLIAM 1805–1895
William Coppin was born in Kinsale, County Cork. As a boy he saved six customs men from drowning when their boat overturned on the river Shannon. He went to St John, New Brunswick and in 1825, designed a boat which could run on the frozen rivers. In 1829 he produced his first ship. While in the West Indies studying navigation he met merchants from Londonderry who ordered a boat, the 'Edward Reid', which arrived in Derry in 1831 after only a nineteen day voyage. William Coppin came to live in Derry and built many boats and captained the 'Robert Napier' which he had built and which ran between Derry and Liverpool. In 1839 he launched his first ship 'City of Derry'. Londonderry Corporation presented Captain Coppin with an inscribed silver service. In 1841 his ship 'Great Northern' was driven by an Archimedean screw propeller and in 1843 it was berthed at the East India Inner Dock and an article and drawings appeared in the Illustrated London News. William Coppin next turned to salvage work and was elected a town councillor. In the 1880s he designed and built a triple-hulled iron ship, the 'Tripod Express' which sailed the Atlantic. He also invented the artificial light fish-catching apparatus in 1886. In the mid-nineteenth century he employed five hundred men.

CORBREUS, ST (COIRPRE) d.570
Corbreus was the first Bishop of Coleraine, where he presided over a priory of Canons Regular, which continued to flourish until 930, when its abbot was killed by the Danes. It is said that Corbreus was kidnapped from Ireland as a boy and educated in Galloway.

CORDNER, JOSEPH 1875–c.1960
Joe Cordner was born in Lurgan, County Armagh, and opened a cycle shop in Derry in 1900. He built his own aeroplane and flew at Buncrana in 1910. He invented and patented the slotted wing.

CORMACÁN ÉIGEAS MAC MÁELBRIGDE d.946
Cormacán 'the Learned' was chief poet to Muirchertach, King of Ulster. He wrote a poem celebrating the king's tour of Ireland in 941/42.

CORRY, ISAAC 1755–1813
Isaac Corry was born in Newry, County Down, and educated at Trinity College, Dublin. He was member of parliament for Newry from 1776 to 1800, and served as Chancellor of the Irish Exchequer in 1798 and Surveyor of Crown Lands in 1799. He fought a duel with Grattan in 1800. From 1802 to 1806 he sat in the Westminster parliament for Newry, but was defeated in elections in 1806 and 1807.

COULTER, JOHN 1888–1976
John Coulter was born in Belfast and emigrated to Canada in 1936, where he became an important playwright and producer, with plays such as Rich; Family Portrait; Holy Manhattan; God's Ulsterman and The Drums are Out. He also wrote a biography of Sir Winston Churchill; a novel, Turf Smoke, and a volume of poetry, The Blossoming Thorn.

COUSINS, JAMES HENRY SPROULL 1873–1956
James Cousins was born in Belfast, where he was educated. He was private secretary to the Lord Mayor of Belfast until he moved to Dublin. The first play produced by the Irish Dramatic Company in 1902 was his The Sleep of the King, and in the same year The Racing Lug was first performed. He taught English in the High School, Harcourt Street, Dublin and in 1908 joined the Theosophical Society. After a short period in Liverpool he went to Madras as literary sub-editor of New India, published by the leading Theosophist, Annie Besant. For the next twenty-two years he was involved with the Theosophical College at Madanapalle, where he served as Principal. From 1938 he worked for the Indian government in various capacities, advising on the arts. He published several volumes of poetry in Ireland: Ben Madigan and other poems; The Voice of One; The Quest and Etain

the Beloved and Other Poems, but the bulk of his work, over a hundred books, was published in India. These included *Sea-Change*; *Collected Poems 1894–1940*; *Heathen Essays* and an autobiography, *We Two Together*, written with Margaret Cousins. In Mysore and Travancore he established the first public Art Galleries in India.

COUSINS, MARGARET (née GILLESPIE) 1878–1954

Margaret Cousins was born in Boyle, County Roscommon, and was educated at the local National and Intermediate Schools, the Victoria High School for Girls, Derry and the Royal Irish Academy of Music. At the Royal University of Ireland she took a degree in music. She became a teacher of music and later taught in a kindergarten. In 1908, along with Hanna Sheehy Skeffington, she founded the radical and militant Irish Women's Franchise League, of which she became the treasurer. She organised Sylvia Pankhurst's visit to Derry in 1910 and in the same year represented Ireland at the Parliament of Women in London, where she was arrested and sentenced to six months' imprisonment. In 1915 she went to India with James Cousins, her husband, and by 1916 had become the first non-Indian member of the Indian Women's University at Poona. In 1917 she was one of the founder members of the Indian Women's Association and from 1919 to 1920 was headmistress of the National Girls' School in Bangalore. She was the first woman magistrate in India. She was a Theosophist and was awarded the Founder's Silver Medal of the Theosophical Society in 1928. She was imprisoned for a year in 1932 because she addressed a public meeting in Madras to object to alterations to the penal code. Among her publications were books and pamphlets on art, philosophy and education. The joint autobiography, written with her husband, *We Two Together* was published in 1950. She was presented several times with generous amounts of money from the Indian government and the Prime Minister, Nehru, in appreciation of her services to the country. From 1943 she was paralysed, and she died at Adyar.

COWAN, EDWARD PORTER c.1840–1890

Edward Cowan was a whiskey distiller. In the early 1880s he was appointed Mayor of Belfast, and in 1881 he was knighted. He was Lord Lieutenant of Antrim and Custos Rotulorum for the county, responsible for the appointment of magistrates. He was Chairman of the Board of the Ulster Bank, Director of the Great Northern Railway and Director of the Belfast Steamship Company. He was actively opposed to Home Rule. He died of typhoid fever.

COWAN, SAMUEL KENNEDY 1850–1918

Samuel Cowan was born in Lisburn, County Antrim, and was educated at Trinity College, Dublin. He was a prolific writer of verses for Christmas cards. Many of his poems were set to music by composers including Sir Arthur Sullivan. He published *Sung by Six: Collected Poems of Six Poets*; *Poems*; *Victoria the Good*; and *From Ulster's Hills*. He served as a major in the militia.

COYLE, KATHLEEN 1883–1952

Kathleen Coyle was born in Derry. She suffered an accident at the age of three, when her foot caught in the spokes of a pram. A delay in treatment resulted in her having to wear a built-up shoe. She had a tutor and did not attend school. She wrote her first short story when she was nine, and when it was lost swore she would never write again. In her youth the family house burnt down. She and her mother and a brother went to live in Liverpool, where she worked in a library. She later worked in an editor's office in London and then moved to Dublin, where she became involved in both the Labour movement and the Suffragettes. She began to write as a means of supporting her two small children. Her first book was published when she was living in London before she travelled abroad to Belgium and Paris, where she knew Nora and James Joyce. She wrote nineteen books, thirteen of which are novels; one, *The French Husband*, was written under economic pressure in eleven days. She published two autobiographies, *A Flock of Birds* and *The Magical Realm*, which deals with her childhood in Derry: 'It is absurd to think that life begins for us at birth. The pattern is set far back, we merely step into the process.'

COYNE, JOSEPH STERLING 1803–1868
Joseph Coyne was born in Birr, County Offaly and was educated in Dungannon, County Tyrone, and Dublin. He contributed to the *Comet* and wrote several farces, some of which were staged at the Theatre Royal, Dublin. In 1837 he went to London and during his stay there wrote over sixty dramatic pieces, some of which were translated into French and German. He was a co-founder of *Punch*.

CRAIG, JAMES b.1861
James Craig was born in Castlecatt, near Bushmills, County Antrim. He was educated at Coleraine Academical Institution and Trinity College, Dublin. He became President of the Royal College of Physicians in Ireland, and was physician to the Lord Lieutenant of Ireland.

CRAIG, JAMES 1871–1940
James Craig was born in Belfast and was educated in Edinburgh. Before serving with the Royal Irish Rifles in the South African War, he was a stockbroker in Belfast. In 1906 he was elected member of parliament for East Down and continued to represent the constituency until 1918, when he transferred to Mid Down. He supported Carson in the anti-Home Rule lobby and was Ulster representative at the Buckingham Palace Conference on the Third Home Rule Bill in 1914. He organised the Ulster Volunteer Force and during the First World War he was Quartermaster-General in France, of the 36th (Ulster) Division, which consisted largely of Ulster Volunteers. Before being knighted in 1918 he held office as a parliamentary secretary in the British government, led by Lloyd George. In 1920 he was appointed First Lord of the Admiralty. He participated in the drafting of the Government of Ireland Act which led to the establishment of the parliament of Northern Ireland. He was elected member of parliament for North Down and in 1921 he became the first Prime Minister of Northern Ireland, a position he held until his death. He was insrumental in abolish-

ing the proportional representation voting system. He was created Viscount Craigavon of Stormont in 1927, and was buried at Stormont.

CRAIG, JAMES HUMBERT 1878–1944
James Craig was born in Belfast and spent his childhood in Ballyholme, County Down. He was educated at a private school, and for a short period at the Belfast School of Art. He lived in Tornamona Cottage, Cushendun, County Antrim, and devoted himself to painting, although he had no formal training. He visited the continent on several occasions, and painted in Swtzerland, the south of France and northern Spain. In 1928 he was elected to the Royal Hibernian Academy and exhibited there. He was also a member of the Royal Ulster Academy. In 1928 he exhibited along with Paul Henry at the Fine Arts Society in London and he illustrated Richard Hayward's *In Praise of Ulster* in 1938. Among his principal works is 'The Road To Maam Cross, Connemara'. His work is in many collections, including the National Gallery of Ireland and the Ulster Museum. His widow Annie bequeathed a dozen paintings to Bangor Borough Council.

CRAIG, JOSEPH c.1900–1958
Joe Craig was born in Ballymena, County Antrim. He was a successful motor cyclist and raced for the firm of Norton in the 1920s. From c.1937 to 1958 he became Engineering Director of Norton. He was killed in a car crash.

CRAWFORD, ADAIR 1748–1795
Adair Crawford was born in Crumlin, County Antrim, and studied medicine at Glasgow and Edinburgh Universities. He was Professor of Chemistry at the Royal Military Academy at Woolwich, and distinguished himself with his research in chemical physiology. His publication, *Experiments and Observations on Animal Heat, and the Inflammation of Combustible Bodies, Being an Attempt to Resolve these Phenomena into a General Law of Nature*, was of great importance. He was a Fellow of the Royal Society and physician to St Thomas's Hospital.

CRAWFORD, EBENEZER 1830–1874

Ebenezer Crawford was born in Belfast and studied art at the Belfast School of Design, and later in London. From 1859 to 1873 he exhibited about a dozen pictures at the Royal Academy, which included 'The Smithy, Redbay Cave, County Antrim', painted in 1861. The Ulster Museum has a sketch drawn by him.

CRAWFORD, JULIA 1799–1860

Julia Crawford was born in County Cavan. She wrote several novels, but is remembered for her song, 'Kathleen Mavourneen', which was published in the *Metropolitan Magazine*, London 1830. She also published *Irish Songs, set to music by F. M. Crouch* in 1840.

CRAWFORD, THOMAS 1824–1895

Thomas Crawford was born in County Down, and was educated in Edinburgh after which he entered the army medical service. He served in Burma and the Crimea with the 18th Royal Irish, and in India during the Mutiny. He was promoted to surgeon-general in 1876, and became Director-General of the Medical Department of the Army. He was knighted for his services.

CRAWFORD, WILLIAM ERNEST b. 1891

Ernie Crawford was born in Belfast and was a rugby international full-back. He played for Malone, Lansdowne Cardiff and the Barbarians. In 1920 he won the first of his thirty caps and he was captain of the side on fifteen occasions. He was an Irish rugby selector and from 1957–1958 was President of the Irish Rugby Football Union. He was also a soccer player and played for Bohemians and Cliftonville.

CRAWFORD, WILLIAM SHARMAN 1781–1861

William Sharman Crawford was born in County Down and became High Sheriff of that county in 1811. He was an advocate of emancipation and is known as the 'Father of Tenant Right'. In 1835 he became member of parliament for Dundalk. He had a chequered career in politics and was not in favour of Repeal, preferring a federal parliamentary system. He was elected member of parliament for Rochdale in 1841 and in 1846 formed the Ulster Tenant Right Association. He stood for election in County Down in 1852, but was defeated. He died in Crawfordsburn, County Down.

CRAWFORD, WILLIAM THOMAS c.1740–1800

William Crawford was born in Crumlin, County Antrim, and was educated in Glasgow. He was ordained Presbyterian minister of Strabane and established an academy there. He published *Volunteer Sermons*; *Translations from Turretin* and a *History of Ireland* (1783) which adopts an epistolary form and is a valuable contemporary account of the 'Whiteboys' and the 'Oakboys'. He eventually moved to Holywood, County Down, where he died.

CREAGH, RICHARD c.1525–1585

Richard Creagh was born in Limerick and was educated in theology at Louvain, after his ordination returning to Limerick. In 1560 the papal nuncio invited him to Rome where he was consecrated Archbishop of Armagh by Pope Pius IV in 1564. While conducting a service he was arrested, sent to London and confined in the Tower. He escaped to Belgium and via Spain returned to Armagh in 1566. In Armagh Cathedral he preached to both O'Neill and O'Donnell. Once again he was imprisoned in the Tower, where he died after an internment of eighteen years. He wrote two works in Latin, *The Origin of the Irish Language* and *Controversies of Faith*, as well as a catechism in Irish.

CREAGH, WILLIAM 1828–1901

William Creagh was born in Newry, County Down, and joined the Bombay Infantry in 1845. He served through the Indian Mutiny and the Second Afghan War. He became a major-general in 1879 and was renowned for his part in building two hundred miles of military roads in India.

CREMER, PATRICK THOMAS 1875–1953

Patrick Cremer was born at Greaghnafarna, County Cavan. He trained as a teacher at Marlborough Street College, Dublin. He taught in Plymouth and then returned to

Ireland to teach in Rockwell College, Cashel. There he met and became a close friend of de Valera. He invented a system of teaching handwriting, the 'Cremer unit system'. By the 1930s the system, in conjunction with 'Cremer Right-Line copy-books', was in use in schools all over Ireland.

CRICHTON, F.E. (MRS) b.1877
Mrs Crichton was born in Belfast and educated at a private school in Richmond. She travelled in Italy, Switzerland and Germany and published short stories, childrens books and novels, among which are *The Soundless Tide* (1911); *Tinker's Hollow* (1912) and *The Blind Side of the Heart.*

CROFTS, FREEMAN WILLS 1879–1957
Freeman Crofts was born in Dublin and was educated at the Methodist and Campbell Colleges, Belfast. He was a civil engineer by profession, but was also a successful detective story writer. His books have been translated into both Danish and Dutch, and published in America.

CROKER, JOHN WILSON 1780–1857
John Wilson Croker was born in Galway, though some sources say Waterford, and was educated at Trinity College, Dublin. In 1807 he became a Tory member of parliament for Downpatrick, County Down, and was active in the literary and political circles of London, founding the *Atheneum* and co-founding and contributing to the *Quarterly Review* along with Scott, Canning and Southey. It is said that Disraeli, in his novel *Coningsby*, portrayed Croker as the character Rigby. He served as First Secretary to the Admiralty from 1809 to 1830. He published *Stories for Children from English History; Boswell's Johnson; Military Events of the French Revolution* and *A Sketch of the State of Ireland, Past and Present*, though he is perhaps best known for his savage review of John Keats's 'Endymion'. He also wrote a history of the guillotine and supposedly first applied the label 'Conservative' to the Tory party. He was responsible for erecting Nelson's column in Dublin.

CROLLY, GEORGE 1813–1878
George Crolly was born in Downpatrick, County Down, and was educated at Maynooth. He became a parish priest in Belfast in 1837 and Professor of Theology at Maynooth in 1843. He assisted Gavan Duffy to establish the *Vindicator* newspaper, and he published three volumes on *Moral Theology* and a biography of Archbishop Crolly, who was his uncle.

CROLLY, WILLIAM 1780–1849
William Crolly was born at Ballykilbeg, County Down. He was educated at Maynooth and was ordained in 1806, and taught in the college for the next six years. In 1812 he was appointed to the parish of Belfast, in 1825 he was consecrated Bishop of Down and Conor, and in 1835 he became Archbishop of Armagh. He advocated integrated education, particularly in the form of the Queen's Colleges, one of which he thought should be established in Armagh. He is buried in the Catholic cathedral of Armagh. [Biography by George Crolly (1852)]

CROMER, GEORGE d.1542
George Cromer was appointed Archbishop of Armagh in 1522 and Lord Chancellor in 1532. He was active in denouncing Henry VIII's decrees against the Church and was subsequently removed from the chancellorship. He and his followers were fervent in their allegiance to the pope, but in 1539 he was suspended by the Holy See and once more was favoured by the king.

CROMMELIN, MARIA HENRIETTA (MAY) DE LA CHEROIS 1850–1930
May Crommelin was born in Carrowdore Castle, County Down and educated at home. She was a descendant of Louis Crommelin. She spent her early life in Ireland, later lived in London, and travelled a great deal. She became a Fellow of the Royal Geographic Society. Later in life she nursed and helped Belfast refugees during the First World War. She wrote more than thirty novels, travel books and many short stories. Her publications include *Orange Lily and other stories; Black Abbey* (1880); *Over the Andes from Chile to Peru* (1896) and *The Golden Bow* (1912).

CROMMELIN, LOUIS 1652–1727

Louis Crommelin was born in Picardy, France. In 1685 the family moved to Amsterdam to escape religious persecution. On the invitation of William III he came to Lisburn, County Antrim, bringing with him a colony of Huguenots, having investigated the linen industry throughout Ireland in 1697. He established a factory at the foot of Bridge Street, on the River Lagan, in Lisburn, and in 1699, he was appointed 'Overseer of the Royal Linen Manufacture of Ireland'. In 1705 he opened a factory in Kilkenny and in the same year published *Essay on the Improving of the Hempen and Flaxen Manufactures in the Kingdom of Ireland*. He imported new skills and methods from Europe and revitalised the Irish linen industry.

CRONE, ANNE 1915–1972

Anne Crone was born in Dublin. She was a teacher in County Fermanagh, and a novelist. She wrote *Bridie Steen* which was published in New York, and twice reprinted; *This Pleasant Lea* and *My Heart and I*. She died in Belfast.

CRONE, JOHN SMYTH 1858–1945

John Crone was born and educated in Belfast and practised medicine in London. He founded and edited the *Irish Book Lover* and wrote *A Concise Dictionary of Irish Biography*. He was elected to the Royal Irish Academy and was President of the Irish Literary Society in London from 1918 to 1925. He wrote *Henry Bradshaw: His Life and Works*, and collaborated with F. J. Bigger in editing Bigger's biography, *In Remembrance*.

CROSKERY, THOMAS 1830–1886

Thomas Croskery was born in Carrowdore, County Down, and was educated at the Royal Belfast Academical Institution. He became a reporter and edited *Banner of Ulster*. He was ordained in 1860 and appointed Professor of Logic at Magee College, Derry, in 1875, and Professor of Theology in 1879. He wrote many articles and became Doctor of Divinity in 1883. He died in Derry.

CROSS, ERIC 1905–1980

Eric Cross was born in Newry, County Down, though reared and educated in England. His career as a chemical engineer spanned the invention of synthetic marble and the making of knitting needles from bicycle spokes. He is known for a book of short stories, *The Taylor and Ansty*, which was published in 1942 and was banned by the Irish Censorship Board for twenty years after its publication. Another collection, *Silence is Golden*, was published in 1978. He wrote for RTE and the BBC.

CROSSAGH, SHANE 18th century

Shane Crossagh was a notorious highwayman in the districts of Moyola and the Roe and Faughan valleys. One of his most secure hiding-places was at the Ness waterfall, where the Burntollet joins the Faughan. His exploits have become legendary.

CROSSLEY, FRANCIS WILLIAM 1839–1879

Francis Crossley was born in Glenburn, County Antrim, and was educated at the Royal School, Dungannon. He served with the Tyrone militia. He became apprenticed in Sir William Armstrong's works, where he developed a gas engine. He established a large firm at Openshaw and subsequently manufactured Crossley motors and engines. He was renowned for his work as a philanthropist. [Biography by Rendel Harris (1899)]

CROSSLEY, WILLIAM JOHN 1844–1911

William Crossley was born in Glenburn, County Antrim, and was educated at the Royal School, Dungannon. He joined his brother Francis in the manufacture of Crossley motors and engines. In 1906 he became a member of parliament for Altrincham and was made a baronet in 1909. He was appointed the first Director of the Manchester Canal Company.

CROWLEY, NICHOLAS J. 1819–1857

Nicholas Crowley was born in Dublin and educated at Dublin Society's School. In 1832 he became a student at the Royal Hibernian Academy, and had a portrait in the annual exhibition. The next year, when he was fourteen, he contributed six portraits. He lived in Belfast from 1835 to 1836, and painted portraits. During this period he showed forty-seven pictures at the Royal Academy. In 1836 he was one of the founder members of the Belfast Association of Artists and in 1837 became a member of the Royal Hibernian Academy. In this year he left for London, though he made frequent visits to Belfast. Many of his pictures were owned by Sir Tyrone Guthrie, his great grandson, and the Ulster Museum has a self-portrait.

CROZIER, FRANCIS RAWDON MOIRA
1796–1848

Francis Crozier was born in Banbridge, County Down. He entered the navy in Cork as a volunteer at the age of fourteen and rose through the ranks, passing his exams in 1817. He sailed with Captain Parry on three of his Arctic voyages, in 1821, 1824 and 1827, when he served as lieutenant. After a mission to find missing whalers, he was appointed commander in 1837. He commanded the *Terror*, under Captain Ross on a voyage to the Antarctic Ocean, and again in 1845 under Franklin, on an expedition to find the North-West Passage. This expedition did not return, and it was not until 1850 that the missing ships were discovered. In 1854, Dr Rae learned from the Innuit that the whole party had died of cold and starvation on Montreal Island. In 1857 Captain McClintock spent two years trying to locate traces, and discovered a document which verified that the ships had been deserted, along with other evidence. The extreme west point of King William's Island was named 'Cape Crozier', and it is generally acknowledged that Sir John Franklin, Captain Crozier and the crews were the first discoverers of the North-West Passage. As well as carrying out botanical research, he compiled books of data on tides and navigation and set up observatories. He was a Fellow of the Royal Society and received a medal for Arctic discoveries. The forensic scientist, Dr Beatty recently examined the remains of some of those who had perished during the expedition, and these revealed a vitamin C deficiency and evidence of cannibalism. In comparison to Innuit bones, those of crew members also had huge doses of lead, which he suspects was contained in the pottery glaze and the table-ware on board, as well as in primitive canned foods. The symptoms of lead poisoning and scurvy are very similar: anorexia, weakness, anaemia, abdominal pains, poor decision-making and neurosis. Tests on hair showed acute lead poisoning from the first eight months of the voyage and decreased considerably as the crew ate less. Death rates among officers was higher because they always ate off pewter. Banbridge has erected a monument to Captain Crozier's memory.

CROZIER, JOHN BAPTIST 1853–1920
John Crozier was born in Ballyhaise, County Cavan, and was educated at Trinity College, Dublin. He was ordained in 1876, and became Vicar of Holywood. In 1896 he was appointed Canon of St Patrick's Cathedral, then Bishop of Ossory and later of Down and Connor. He was appointed Archbishop of Armagh in 1911, and died there.

CÚ CHULAINN 1st century
Cú Chulainn was a Red Branch Knight. He was a mythological figure, associated with South East Ulster, and was a cousin of Conall Cernach, and of the three sons of Uisliu. He was initiated into the military order at seven years of age and was educated in arms in Britain by Scáthach, a female warrior. He died when he was twenty-seven years of age and there are contradictory accounts of how and where this happened. He is a major figure in Irish literature. It is said his head and right hand were buried at Tara. His home fort was Dún Dealgan, present day Dundalk.

CULLEN, PAUL 1803–1878
Paul Cullen was born in Prospect, County Kildare, and was educated in Rome and ordained as a priest in 1829. He later became the Vice-Rector and then Rector of the Irish College in Rome. He was appointed Archbishop of Armagh in 1849 and a year later presided over the Synod of Thurles which recommended the establishment of a Catholic university. Two years later he was translated to Dublin. He became the first Irish cardinal in 1866. Four years later at the

Vatican Council, he formulated the definition of papal infallibility. He was also Apostolic Delegate. He opposed the Young Irelanders and the Fenians. He founded the Catholic University, Clonliffe seminary and the Mater Misericordiae Hospital in Dublin, as well as churches, convents and schools.

CUMMING, WILLIAM 1769–1852
William Cumming was probably born in Ulster and earned renown as an artist, particularly for his female portraits. He was one of the founder members of the Royal Hibernian Academy and was President of this institution from 1829 to 1832.

CUMMINGS, JAMES SLEATOR 1819–1852
James Sleator Cummings was born in County Monaghan. He joined the army and was killed in action in the Khyber Pass, Afghanistan. His *Six Years' Diary* reflects his experience as a subaltern in India during that period. It was published posthumously, and a memorial tablet was erected to him in St Patrick's Cathedral, Dublin.

CUNNINGHAM, ROBERT OLIVER 1841–1918
Robert Cunningham was born in Scotland and was educated at Edinburgh University. He went on a scientific expedition and published his chief work, *The Natural History of the Straits of Magellan*, in 1871. He contributed papers to the Zoological Society and the Linnean Society, the latter based on his voyage to Patagonia. In 1871 he was appointed Professor of Natural History at Queen's College, Belfast, a position which he occupied for thirty-one years, during which time he had various degrees and a fellowship conferred upon him. He died in Devonshire.

CURLD, JOHN fl.1709
John Curld is known only for his architectural plans for Castle Coole, County Fermanagh, a country house which he designed for James Corry in 1709. His plans were skilled, which would lead to the conclusion that he was an experienced architect. Curld's house was later replaced by the current Castle Coole.

CURRAN, JOHN OLIVER 1819–1847
John Curran was born at Trooperfield, near Lisburn, County Antrim. It is said that at the age of four he chose to become a vegetarian. He studied in Glasgow and Dublin and became a medical doctor in 1843. By 1846, after a study of Paris hospitals, he returned to Ireland to work at the King and Queen's College of Physicians. He was a gifted doctor, a member of the Royal Irish Academy, and contributed to medical literature. He died of typhus during the Famine when he was twenty-eight years old.

CURTIS, PATRICK 1740–1832
Patrick Curtis was educated at Salamanca and was head of the Irish College there for forty years. Because of his knowledge of Spain, he was able to assist Wellington during the Peninsular War and was arrested as a spy by the French. He returned to Ireland in 1813 and was given a warm recommendation by Wellington. In 1819 he was appointed Archbishop of Armagh.

CUSACK, MARGARET ANNE 1832–1899
Margaret Cusack was born in Dublin and joined the Anglican sisterhood in London. In 1858 she became a Catholic, taking the religious name Sister Mary Frances Clare. In 1860 she came to Newry to the Irish Poor Clares, who worked with young women. She went to Kenmare, County Kerry, to open a foundation, and from 1879 to 1880 she collected funds for the relief of the poor. In 1881 she left the order. She gained the approval of Pope Leo XIII in 1884 to found the Sisters of Peace. She went to America to guide and train immigrant Irish girls though she had to abandon the project when it received an indifferent reception. She published biographies of Saints Patrick, Columba and Brigid and of O'Connell and Father Mathew as well as pamphlets on women and works of fiction, for example *Ned Rusheen* (1871) and *Tim O'Halloran's Choice* (1877). She reverted to Anglicanism and bitterly attacked Catholicism. In 1889 she published her autobiography *The Nun of Kenmare*, and in the following year died in Warwickshire.

CUSACK SMITH, WILLIAM 1766–1836
William Cusack Smith was born in Dublin and was educated at Eton and Oxford. In 1788 he was called to the Bar and seven years later was appointed King's Counsel. He was a member of parliament for Donegal Borough. He was founder of *The Flapper* in 1796. In 1800 he was appointed Solicitor-General and within a year became Baron of the Exchequer. In 1834 his conduct as a judge was debated in parliament. Among his publications were poems and pamphlets.

CUSH, WILBUR W. 1928–1981
Wilbur Cush was born in Lurgan, County Armagh. He was a soccer international halfback, inside-forward and wing-half. He played for Shankill YMCA, Glenavon, Leeds United and Portadown. He was capped twenty-six times for Northern Ireland. He scored five international goals, and was a member of the World Cup Squad in 1958.

He played in all five matches and scored the winning goal against Czechoslovakia. He also played for the Irish League.

CUSHEN, LORD see McNEILL, RONALD

CUST, WILLIAM d.1908
William Cust was born in Magilligan, County Londonderry. He emigrated to Canada, where he engaged in ranching and mining. He was a pioneer, and 'Cust's House' was, at the turn of the century, the last outpost of civilisation.

CUTHBERT, WILLIAM MITCHEL 1859–1917
William Cuthbert was born in Dungiven, County Londonderry, and emigrated to South Africa in October 1881. His father had been a tanner in Coleraine, and William built up a hugely successful leather business. He befriended and employed many young immigrants from Ulster.

D

DALEY, VICTOR JAMES 1858–1905
Victor James Daley was born in Navan, County Armagh, and after a term as a clerk at Plymouth he emigrated to Australia. He was considered the leading poet in Australia and had two volumes of verse published. He died in Sydney after a life-long connection with the Australian press. [Biography by A. G. Stephens 1905]

DALLÁN, ST d. *c.*600
Dallán was born in what is now County Cavan. He was also known as Dallán Forgaill and he was a scholar. At a convention of bards at Dromkett in 575 he recited his poem on St Colmcille, who was present. His feast-day is on the 29th of January.

D'ALTON, JOHN F. 1883–1963
John D'Alton was born in Claremorris, County Mayo, and was educated at Blackrock, Clongowes Wood College and the Irish College, Rome. In 1908 he was ordained and undertook postgraduate studies in Oxford and Cambridge. In 1912 he was appointed to the Chair of Ancient Classics in Maynooth, becoming President of the college in 1936. In 1942 he became Bishop of Meath and four years later was translated to Armagh as Archbishop and Primate of All Ireland. In 1953 he became a Cardinal. When the second Vatican Council met, Cardinal D'Alton was appointed as a member of the Central Preparatory Commission. He returned to Ireland in 1962. Among his publications are *Horace and His Age: A Study in Historical Background; Roman Literary Theory and Criticism: A Study in Tendencies* and *Selections from St John Chrysostom.*

DALY, FRED 1911–1990
Fred Daly was born in Portrush, County Antrim and was a professional golfer. In 1944 he was appointed pro at Balmoral where he remained until 1990. He won the Irish Open in 1946 and in 1947 won the British Open Golf Championship. He won the British Professional Matchplay title in 1947, 1948 and 1952. He attained Ryder Cup honours three times, in 1947, 1949 and 1953. He won the Ulster professional title eleven times and the Irish Professional Championship three times. He won many cups and was awarded the MBE in 1983. In 1984 he became the third golfer to join the Texaco Hall of Fame.

D'ARCY, CHARLES FREDERICK 1859–1938
Charles Frederick D'Arcy was born in Dublin and was educated at Trinity College, Dublin. He was ordained in 1884 and in 1903 became Bishop of Clogher, four years later of Ossory, Ferns and Leighlin, and in 1911 of Down, Connor and Dromore. He was opposed to Home Rule and signed the Ulster Covenant in 1912. In 1919 he was elected Archbishop of Dublin, and a year later was translated to Armagh. Among his publications are *A Short Study of Ethics; Idealism and Theology; Science and Creation; God Is Science* and *The Adventures of a Bishop.*

DARGAN, WILLIAM 1799–1867
William Dargan was born in County Carlow and worked on engineering projects in England under Telford. He was contracted to build many railways in Ireland, including the Dublin railway and the Ulster canal. He financially guaranteed the great Dublin Exhibition of 1853 and entertained Queen Victoria on her visit to the country. He later declined a baronetcy. He fell from a horse in 1866 and sustained a serious injury which terminated his career.

DARLEY, JOHN fl. 1664
John Darley was a mason and carpenter. He is first mentioned as having worked on a wall and one tower of Lisburn Castle, County Antrim. He built a house for William Benson in Lisburn and was much

sought after as a craftsman. He was said to be 'a little of a Quaker'. When the town of Lisburn was destroyed by fire Darley's work was probably also destroyed.

DARLEY, JOHN RICHARD 1799–1884
John Darley was born in Fairfield, County Monaghan, and was educated at Trinity College, Dublin. He was appointed headmaster of Dundalk Grammar School in 1826, and of the Royal School, Dungannon in 1831. In 1874 he was consecrated Bishop of Kilmore. Among his publications are *The Grecian Drama* and *Homer*.

DARRAGH, WILLIAM 1813–1892
William Darragh was born in Hillsborough, County Down, was educated in Belfast and was for forty-seven years curator of the Belfast Museum.

DAVIDSON, SAMUEL 1806–1899
Samuel Davidson was born in Kellswater, County Antrim, and was educated at Belfast Academical Institution. He became a Presbyterian minister in 1833 and was later appointed Professor of Biblical Criticism in Belfast. Lancashire Independent College, Manchester, employed him in the same capacity, but because of his heterodox views he resigned in 1856. He published many theological works, including *The Text of the Old Testament Considered*. He was one of the pioneers of English biblical criticism, and his autobiography was published in 1890.

DAVIDSON, SAMUEL 1846–1921
Samuel Davidson was born in Belfast and went to India to help his cousins run a tea plantation. In 1877 he designed a tea-drier and later set up his own firm in Belfast to construct driers. This led to the design of the Sirocco forward-bladed centri-fugal fan.

DAVIES, JOHN 1569–1626
John Davies came to Ireland in 1603 as Solicitor-General. Three years later he became Attorney-General and then made a full report of the Flight of the Earls. In 1608 he went to Ulster to indict Hugh O'Neill, Earl of Tyrone, and Rory O'Donnell, Earl of Tyrconnell. As a consequence of the jury's having convicted O'Neill, John Davies acquired four thousand acres of land in County Tyrone He flouted the stipulation that houses should be built and freeholders planted. He returned to England in 1619. He published *A Discovery of the True Causes Why Ireland Was Never Entirely Subdued nor Brought under Obedience to the Crown of England until the Beginning of His Majesty's Happy Reign* (1612).

DAVIES, JOHN HENRY 1838–1909
John Davies was born in England; he came to Ireland as a boy and was educated at a private school run by the Society of Friends. He was involved in the linen business as manager of a bleach works near Lisburn and later near Banbridge and was a recognised authority on the linen trade. He became interested in botany, had a wide knowledge of Irish flora and was a member of the Belfast Naturalists' Field Club. He studied mosses and discovered several new varieties. He published papers in the *Phytologist* and the *Irish Naturalist*.

DAVIS, FRANCIS 1810–1885
Francis Davis, originally from Cork, was a muslin weaver and later an assistant librarian at Queen's College, Belfast. He was editor of the *Belfastman's Journal* and contributed poetry to several newspapers, including the *Nation*. His collected poems were published in 1878 and he was known as 'The Belfastman'.

DAWSON, ARTHUR 1695–1775
Arthur Dawson was born in Castledawson, County Londonderry, and was a lawyer, a poet and a baron. He was author of the song 'Bumper, Squire Jones', which was written to a composition of his contemporary, Carolan, in honour of Squire Jones of Moneyglass, near Toome.

DAWSON, JOSHUA 1660–1725
Joshua Dawson's family came from Dawson's Bridge, County Londonderry. He served as member of parliament for County Wicklow from 1713 to 1714. He is remembered for having built the Mansion House in Dawson Street, Dublin, in 1710.

DAY, JOHN GODFREY FITZMAURICE 1874–1938

Godfrey Day was born into the family of the Bishop of Clogher, was educated in England, and was ordained a rector of the Church of Ireland. From 1914 until 1920 he was Canon of Christ Church Cathedral, Dublin. From 1920 until 1938 he was Bishop of Ossory, Ferns and Leighlin, and was then appointed Archbishop of Armagh.

DEASE, WILLIAM c.1750–1798

William Dease was born in Lisney, County Cavan, and was educated in Dublin and Paris, where he became a surgeon. He helped to found the Royal College of Surgeons in Dublin and served as its first professor, then later as its first President. In 1798 he died in mysterious circumstances. His publications include *Observations on Wounds in the Head; Different Methods of Treating the Venereal Diseases; Radical Cure of Hydrocele* and *Observations on Midwifery*. A statue and a bust have been erected to his memory in the hall of the College of Surgeons.

DE BLÁCAM, AODH 1890–1951

Aodh de Blácam was born in London, the son of an Ulster family. He learned Irish in London from Robert Lynd, and in 1915 went to Ireland as a journalist. He was interned by the Black and Tans for his nationalist writings. He published *The Story of Colmcille* in 1929; *Gaelic Literature Surveyed* in the same year, and *The Life of Wolfe Tone* in 1935. Other books were *Towards the Republic* and *The Black North*; as well as the lives of Irish saints. He was also a playwright, having written *King Dan* and *Two Kingdoms*. He worked on the staff of the *Irish Times*, was editor of the *Standard* and wrote for the *Irish Press* under the pseudonym 'Roddy the Rover'. Until 1947 he was a member of the Fianna Fáil executive, but resigned to join Clann na Poblachta. He was defeated in the election for County Louth in 1948, but became a member of the Emigration Commission and later Director of Publicity of the Department of Health.

DE BLAGHD, EARNÁN see BLYTHE, ERNEST

DE BURGH, ELIZABETH b.1332

Elizabeth de Burgh was the daughter of William de Burgh, the 'Brown Earl', who was murdered at the instigation of his cousins. Elizabeth was sole heir to the Earldom of Ulster, and was taken to England by her mother while still a child. She later married Lionel, Duke of Clarence, the son of Edward III, who became 5th Earl of Ulster on their marriage in 1352. Although he was unable to enforce his rights, through him the English royal family had a claim to the large de Burgh estates in Ireland, which right they revived in Tudor times.

DE BURGH, RICHARD d.1326

Richard de Burgh was the son of Walter de Burgh and Maud de Lacy and was educated at the court of Henry III. He was known as the 'Red Earl', 2nd Earl of Ulster, and was successful in his campaigns against the Scots, whereby he was made general of the Irish forces. He founded many monasteries. He feasted the Anglo-Norman knights and then confined himself to a monastery, where he died the same year.

DE BURGH, WALTER d.1271

Walter de Burgh was the son of Richard de Burgh, Lord of Connaught. He married Maud de Lacy, daughter of Hugh de Lacy, Earl of Ulster. When Maud's father died in 1243 Walter de Burgh became Earl of Ulster.

DE BURGH, WILLIAM 1312–1332

William de Burgh was the grandson of Richard de Burgh. When his grandfather died, William succeeded to the earldom of Ulster at the age of fourteen; he was known as the 'Brown Earl'. He captured his cousin, Sir Walter and starved him to death in Greencastle, County Galway in 1332. He was murdered by Robert FitzRichard de Mandeville on his way to Carrickfergus, County Antrim. Three hundred of Mandeville's followers, it is said, were killed for this murder.

DECIES, BARON see BERESFORD, WILLIAM 1742–1819

DE COURCY, JOHN *c.*1150–1219
John de Courcy served under Henry II and came to Ireland after Strongbow's death. He moved northwards and seized Downpatrick, and despite attempts to remove him by troops raised under MacDunlevy, de Courcy stood his ground. He allotted portions of Down and Antrim to his followers. Gerald of Wales describes him as being 'of fair complexion' with large, strong limbs. De Courcy married Affreca, daughter of the King of Man and the Isles. She founded many religious establishments, among them the Cistercian Grey Abbey, County Down. King John would have taken de Courcy prisoner, but he managed to defeat the king's forces at Down in 1204. Eventually he was committed to the Tower of London, and it is said that he was sent from there to champion King John in single combat. This he did successfully, and the king restored him to his estates. Apparently he tried to land in Ireland, but was prevented fifteen times by storms, so he retired to France, where he died.

DE LACY, HUGH d. 1243
Hugh de Lacy was created Earl of Ulster in 1205, and obtained John de Courcy's Ulster estates after his death. In 1210 he fled to France, returning to England in 1221. He subsequntly returned to his estates in Ulster.

DELANEY, THOMAS 1947–1979
Thomas Delaney was born in Dublin, and was educated at Blackrock College and University College, Dublin. His excavation work at Carrickfergus has earned him a place as one of the country's leading archaeologists. He was the only Irish member of the British Archaeological Society. At the time of his death he was head of the Department of Medieval Archaeology at the Queen's University, Belfast.

DELANY, MARY [PENDARVES] (née GRANVILLE) 1700–1788
Mary Delany was born in Wiltshire. When she was widowed after her marriage to Alexander Pendarves in 1724, she left Cornwall to live in London. In 1743 she married the Reverend Patrick Delany, later Dean of Down, who was a close friend of Jonathan Swift, and came to live at Delville, near Dublin. They frequently visited Ulster. Her career as an artist developed when she came to Ireland. She drew and described landscapes wherever they visited. She also designed and embroidered fabrics and was a competent musician. Her major work, *Hortus Siccus,* 900 cut paper depictions of plants, which she began in 1772, is in the British Museum. Her letters and biography were published by her great great niece in 1861–2 in 6 volumes. A selection of these were published in 1991 under the title *Letters from Georgian Ireland,* edited by Angélique Day.

DELANY, PATRICK *c.*1684–1768
Patrick Delany, was educated at Trinity College, Dublin, of which he was made a fellow in 1709. He was appointed Dean of Down in 1744 and was a close friend of Swift, to whom he was executor and who described him as 'the most eminent preacher we have'. The work for which he is remembered is *Observations upon Lord Orrery's Remarks upon the Life and Writings of Dr Jonathan Swift.* In the three-volume *Revelations Examined with Candour* he deals with such issues as the defence of polygamy and Old Testament dietary laws. He published *An Historical Account of the Life and Reign of King David* in three volumes. In 1757 he founded the *Humanist,* a journal which denounced, for example, the docking of horses' tails. His bust is in the library of Trinity College.

DELARGY, JAMES HAMILTON (Ó DUILEARGA, SÉAMUS) 1899–1980
James Delargy was born in Cushendall, County Antrim. When he was two years old his father died, and a few years later his family moved to Glenariff, County Antrim. In 1907 James was sent to a convent school in Kilcool, County Wicklow, after which he was educated at Castleknock College and University College, Dublin. At the age of sixteen he made his first trip to the Gaeltacht on Rathlin Island. He visited the Aran Islands, Donegal and the Hebrides and recorded his first tale in Antrim Irish at Waterfoot. His degree in Celtic Studies led him to become a lecturer at University College, Dublin, and in 1945 he gave the Sir John Rhys Memorial

Lecture to the British Academy. He became Professor of Folklore in 1946. He was fluent in various Celtic languages, French, German, Swedish and Icelandic. He was instrumental in establishing the Folklore of Ireland Society, and edited its journal *Béaloideas*, for forty-six years. The Irish Folklore Commission, under Delargy's directorship collected, recorded and transcribed stories and folklore of a dying oral tradition. His publications include *The Gaelic Storyteller, Leabhar Sheáin Í Chonaill* and *Seanchas ón Oileán Tiar.* He received honorary doctorates from Scandinavia, Nova Scotia, Wales and three Irish universities and was decorated by the governments of Sweden and Iceland.

DEMPSEY, ALEXANDER 1852–1920
Alexander Dempsey was born in Ballymoney, County Antrim. He was educated at St Malachy's College, Belfast, the Catholic University Medical School, Dublin, and Queen's College, Galway. He took the degree of Doctor of Medicine of the Royal University and the Diploma of the Royal College of Surgeons, Ireland in 1874. In the same year, he set up a medical practice in Donegall Street, Belfast, and he was one of the founder members of the North of Ireland Branch of the British Medical Association, of which he was Honorary Secretary and later President. He was a member of the Ulster Medical Association, and was its President from 1880 to 1891. He contributed numerous papers on medicine to both these societies, and to leading medical journals. In 1880 he was appointed a magistrate of the city of Belfast. He was closely associated with both the initiation and extension of the Mater Infirmorum Hospital. In 1911, he had a knighthood conferred upon him. He became a justice of the peace and was a Fellow of the Royal Society of Medicine, London, and the Royal Academy of Medicine, Ireland.

DENVIR, JOHN 1834–1916
John Denvir was born in Bushmills, County Antrim, and moved to Liverpool, where he managed and edited the *Catholic Times*, the *United Irishman* and the *Nationalist*. In 1870 he published 'Denvir's Penny Library', a series of books on Irish poetry, history and biography, and these were immensely popular. He published a pamphlet, *The Catalpa*, in 1877; *The Irish in Britain* in 1892, and in 1910 his autobiography *Life Story of an Old Rebel.*

DE PALATIO, OCTAVIAN d.1513
Octavian de Palatio lived in Florence and was sent to Armagh to be Archbishop by Pope Sixtus IV in 1480. He died having ruled his diocese for thirty-three years.

DESMOND, BRIDGET (née BYRNE) 1865–1911
Bridget Desmond was born in County Donegal. She married John Desmond, and settled in Claudy, County Londonderry. She began her business by having shirts made up by out-workers, on behalf of Tillie & Henderson, one of the largest shirt manufacturers in Londonderry. She journeyed once a week in her pony and trap to collect the cut garments, and to distribute them to the houses of the out-workers. She purchased sewing machines from the Singer Company for hire by her workers, and these were paid for on a weekly basis. Later she decided to centralise the work by bringing the girls into the family home. Soon all the rooms were taken up and the first Desmond factory came into being. Her husband John joined her in building up the business which is now a major clothing supplier.

DESPARD, CHARLOTTE (née FRENCH) 1844–1939
Charlotte Despard was born in England of Anglo-Irish parents. In 1890 she became a Catholic and until the 1920s was an active suffragist. She came to Ireland during 1916, shared a house with Maud Gonne, and was an active supporter of Sinn Féin. She visited the Soviet Union in 1930 and returned to Ireland with the anomalous identity of a Catholic Communist. She came to Belfast, where she eventually died. She is buried at Glasnevin Cemetery.

DE VALERA, RUAIDHRÍ 1916–1978
Ruaidhrí De Valera was born in Dublin and educated at University College, Dublin. From 1946 to 1957 he was the Place-names

and Archaeological Officer with the Ordnance Survey. From 1957 to 1978 he was Professor of Celtic Archaeology at University College, Dublin. With Sean Ó Nualláin he published *Survey of the Megalithtic Tombs of Ireland* in four volumes and he revised Seán Ó Ríordáin's *Antiquities of the Irish Countryside.* He died in Enniskillen, County Fermanagh.

DEVEREUX, ROBERT 1567–1601
Robert Devereux was born in Herefordshire and educated at Trinity College, Cambridge. He succeeded his father, Walter Devereux, as 2nd Earl of Essex. In 1585 he fought in the Low Countries and became a favourite of Queen Elizabeth I. In 1596 he took Cadiz and destroyed the Spanish fleet, but after a quarrel with the queen he was sent to Ireland as Lord Lieutenant and Governor-General to fight against Hugh O'Neill. He garrisoned Newry, Dundalk, Drogheda, Wicklow and Naas, but defied his order to march against O'Neill in Ulster. Various expeditions in Ireland were unsucessful and cost him half his army, though after a defeat, he was said to decimate his own soldiers. In 1599 he met Hugh O'Neill and they concluded a peace, regarded in England as a dishonourable and dangerous treaty. Queen Elizabeth sent him an aggrieved letter and he returned, without her permission, to London where he was detained, a prisoner in his own home. He was tried at Westminster Hall, where his protégé and former friend, Francis Bacon, spoke for the prosecution. He was eventually executed. During his lifetime he wrote numerous sonnets.

DEVEREUX, WALTER c.1540–1576
Walter Devereux was born in Carmarthenshire, Wales and in 1558 succeeded to his grandfather's titles, 3rd Baron Ferrers and Viscount Hereford. He became a Knight of the Garter and was created Earl of Essex in 1572 by Queen Elizabeth I. He came to Ulster in order to colonise it and was granted the district of Clandeboye, County Down. The English had failed to settle Ulster, which was under the domination of the O'Neills, led by Sir Brian MacPhelim and Turlough Luineach. They

were supported by the Scots under Sorley Boy MacDonnell. In 1573, Essex was appointed Captain-General, and Governor of Ulster the following year. He was involved in two acts of treachery, the first when his soldiers slaughtered the retainers of Brian MacPhelim O'Neill, at a banquet held by Essex, supposedly in their honour. The O'Neills were removed to Dublin where they were executed. In 1575 the entire population of Rathlin was slaughtered: six hundred men, women and children, probably at his instigation. After that, his plan for colonisation was abandonded by order of the Queen. In 1576 he was appointed Earl Marshal of Ireland and granted the Barony of Farney, County Monaghan. The following year he died in Dublin of dysentery. He is buried at Carmarthen.

DEVLIN, JOSEPH 1871–1934
Joseph Devlin was born in Hamill Street, Belfast, and was educated at Divis Street Christian Brothers' School. Before becoming a journalist on the *Irish News*, he worked as a barman. He was returned as member of parliament for North Kilkenny in 1902 and won the West Belfast seat in 1906. He served in the Northern Ireland parliament for Antrim. Until his death he was President of the Ancient Order of Hibernians, which he had revived in 1905. He defeated Eamon de Valera in the Falls division of Belfast in 1918 and retained the seat until 1922. He also represented Fermanagh and Tyrone at Westminster from 1929 to 1934, founded a holiday home for working women and funded outings for Belfast children.

DICKEY, EDWARD O'RORKE 1894–1977
Edward O'Rorke Dickey was born in Belfast and was educated at Wellington College and Trinity College, Cambridge. He studied art at Westminster School of Art in London, and exhibited with the New English Art Club and the Royal Academy. After the First World War he lived in Antrim. He was an original member of the Society of Wood Engravers, and his woodcuts illustrated Richard Rowley's book of poems, *Workers.* He also published *A Picture Book of British Art* in 1931. During the 1920s he had been an art master at Oundle School, and

later became Professor of Fine Art and Director of King Edward VII School of Art, King's College, University of Durham from 1926 to 1931. For the next twenty-six years he was inspector of art for the Ministry of Education. His work is in the Ulster Museum, and the Cork and Limerick Municipal Art Galleries as well as the British Museum. He was awarded the CBE.

DICKIE, GEORGE 1812–1882

George Dickie was born in Aberdeen and studied arts, then medicine at the Universities of Aberdeen and Edinburgh. After lecturing on botany in King's College, Aberdeen, he became University Librarian there. He was appointed first Professor of Natural History at Queen's College, Belfast, in 1849. In 1860 he returned to Aberdeen University, where he became Professor of Botany. He was made a Fellow of the Linnean Society in 1863, an Honorary Fellow of the Edinburgh Botanical Society in 1877, and a Fellow of the Royal Society of London in 1881. He published papers on botanical subjects and was the foremost authority on marine algae. Among his works are the *Flora of Aberdeen; A Botanist's Guide to the Counties of Aberdeen, Banff and Kincardine* and *A Flora of Ulster.*

DICKSON, CHARLES 1886–1978

Charles Dickson was born in County Down and was educated in Belfast, where he became a medical practitioner. He was a civil servant and in France and Belgium served in the Royal Army Medical Corps in the First World War. From 1962 to 1970 he edited the *Irish Journal of Medical Science.* He published *The Life of Michael Dwyer; The Wexford Rising in 1798* and *Revolt in the North* and was an authority on late 18th-century Ireland.

DICKSON, WILLIAM STEEL 1744–1824

William Dixon was born in Carnmoney, County Antrim, and was educated in Glasgow, where he gratuated as Doctor of Divinity in 1783. He was Presbyterian minister of Ballyhalbert and Portaferry, County Down. He was a supporter of the Volunteer movement and joining the United Irishmen, was Adjutant-General for County Down in 1798. On the eve of the rising he was imprisoned in Fort George, Scotland, until 1802. He was called to a small congregation at Keady, County Armagh, and ministered there for thirteen years. In 1812 he published *Sermons* and *Narrative of Exile.* He died in poverty in Belfast.

DILL, EDWARD MARCUS 1810–1862

Edward Marcus Dill was born in Knowehead, County Londonderry, and was educated in Glasgow. He was ordained in Cookstown, County Tyrone, in 1835 as a Presbyterian minister. He was responsible for erecting churches in Cork and Clonakilty and was instrumental in raising funds in America to aid the sufferers of the Famine in 1848. He published *Ireland's Miseries; The Grand Cause and Cure* and *The Gathering Storm* .

DILL, JOHN 1881–1944

John Dill was born in Lurgan, County Armagh, and was educated at Cheltenham College and Sandhurst Military College. He served in South Africa and in the First World War and was promoted to Commandant of the British Army Staff College. On reaching the rank of lieutenant-general he became Director of Military Operations at the War Office. In 1937 he went to France as corps commander and was appointed Chief of Staff in 1940. In 1942 he led the British Military Mission in Washington, where he died in 1944.

DILL, SAMUEL 1844–1925

Samuel Dill was born in Hillsborough, County Down, and was educated at the Royal Belfast Academical Institution and Queen's College, Belfast. He gained further degrees from Oxford and became governor of Owens College and Victoria University, Manchester, from 1880 to 1889. In 1890 he was appointed Professor of Greek and Pro-Chancellor of Queen's College, Belfast. He published several works on the Roman Empire and was knighted in 1909.

DILLON, GERARD 1916–1971

Gerard Dillon was born off the Falls Road, Belfast and educated at Raglan Street School, and the Christian Brothers' School. In 1930 he was apprenticed to a house painter and attended the Belfast College of

Art for a short period. From 1934 to 1939 he lived in London, where he began to paint. In 1942, when he returned to Dublin, he had his first one-man show. He spent some time painting in Connemara with George Campbell. He exhibited at the Irish Exhibition of Living Art in Dublin, in 1943. From 1945 until 1968 he spent much of his time in London. He held several one-man shows, both in Belfast and in Dublin. As well as painting, he was commissioned by the Dublin Tourist Board to create a wall hanging, and he designed sets, costumes and posters for the Abbey Theatre. He exhibited in America and Rome. From 1969 to 1971 he lectured in Dublin, and his painting 'Black Lake' was reproduced on a postage stamp issued from Dublin. His work appears in practically all the principal Irish collections and includes landscapes, murals and etchings. He settled in Dublin in 1968.

DIXON, EDITH (née CLARK) d. 1964
Edith, Lady Dixon, was a benefactor. Both she and her husband, Sir Thomas Dixon, Lieutenant of Belfast, (d.1950) were deeply involved with charitable work. They founded the Sir Thomas and Lady Dixon Convalescent Hospital. This was Cairndhu House, their former home, which they presented, with 100 acres, to the Hospitals Authority. They gave 4 acres of land to Larne, and this is now known as Dixon Park, and money was donated for a new church hall at Drains Bay. Another gift was the Dixon Nurses' Home of the Benn Hospital in Belfast. Sir Thomas left a legacy to found a scholarship in Larne Grammar School, and Lady Dixon presented money to Queen's University for bursaries. In 1953 she presented Wilmont House Estate at Drumbeg to Belfast Corporation, and it was converted into a residential home for the elderly. She was awarded an OBE after the First World War and she held high office in many national organisations. She was first Mayoress of Larne.

DIXON, JOSEPH 1806–1866
Joseph Dixon was born in Coalisland, County Tyrone, and was educated at Maynooth where he was ordained in 1829. He became Dean and Professor of Hebrew,

and succeeded Cardinal Cullen as Archbishop of Armagh. He wrote a *General Introduction to Scriptures* in 1852 and *The Blessed Cornelius* in 1855. [Biography by M. F. Cusack].

DOBBS, ARTHUR 1689–1765
Arthur Dobbs was born in Scotland, though his family came from Castle Dobbs, County Antrim. In 1720 he was appointed High Sheriff of County Antrim and Mayor of Carrickfergus, a position which he attained three times. He was a member of parliament for Carrickfergus for many years and in 1728, he became Deputy Governor of the town. He was appointed Surveyor-General of Ireland in 1733 and ordered much new building. He was a co-founder of the Royal Dublin Society. At his instigation, two vessels were sent in 1740 to find a North-West Passage to India. A point of land on Hudson's Bay is known as Cape Dobbs. He was appointed Governor of North Carolina in 1753. He published two important works :*An Essay on the Trade and Improvement of Ireland* and *An Account of the Countries adjoining to the Hudson's Bay*. He was a keen bee-keeper and botanist and made perceptive observations about pollination. His letter 'Concerning Bees and Their Methods of Gathering Wax and Honey' was sent to the Royal Society. He joined with merchants to form the Ohio Company of Virginia, and at the age of seventy-three, he married Justina Davis who was fifteen years old. Later the same year he suffered a stroke. He died in North Carolina.

DOBBS, FRANCIS 1750–1811
Francis Dobbs was born in County Antrim. He was called to the Bar and came to public notice as the northern Volunteer corps representative to the Dungannon Convention in 1782. He was engrossed by the prophetical scriptures and frequently predicted the end of the world; consequently he was known as 'Millenium Dobbs'. He served as member of parliament for Charlemont. He published a *Letter to Lord North* and a *Universal History* in several volumes. He felt that, through reference to various scriptures, he had proved that the union between Great Britain and Ireland was forbidden, and he

made a public speech to this effect, which was printed and sold widely: *Memoirs of F. Dobbs Esq. – Also Genuine Reports of his Speech in Parliament on the Subject of an Union and Prediction of the Second Coming of the Messiah, with Extracts from his Poem on the Millenium.* He published *The Patriot King* in 1774, and *Poems* in 1788.

DOBBS, MARGARET EMMELINE 1873–1961

Margaret Dobbs was born in Dublin but spent much of her life in Cushendun, County Antrim. Along with Roger Casement and Francis Bigger she was one of the organisers of the Feis in Glenariff in 1904, and was active on the Feis Committee until the end of her life. She was an Irish scholar and felt that 'Ireland without Irish is quite meaningless'. She wrote plays, among which is *She's Going to America.* She was closely involved with the Irish language schools in Rathlin, and at Gortahork, County Donegal. In 1916 she put forward £600 towards the defence of Roger Casement, a close friend. When she died, despite the fact that her family requested a private funeral, hundreds of people from the Glens attended.

DOCWRA (or DOWCRA), HENRY 1560–1631

Henry Docwra came to Ireland as a young man. He was given command of an army with which to subdue the north on the outbreak of the rebellion of Hugh O'Neill. Having sailed up Lough Foyle, he left a garrison at Culmore and took Derry. He is reputed to have been the founder of the modern city, since many streets and houses were built at his instigation. He published *A Narration of the Services Done by the Army Employed to Lough Foyle under the Leading of Me, Sir Henry Dowcra, Knight.*

DODD, WILLIAM HUSTON 1844–1930

William Dodd was born in Rathfriland, County Down, and was educated at the Royal Belfast Academical Institution and Queen's College, Belfast. In 1873 he was called to the Bar, and in 1896 he was appointed President of the Statistical and Social Enquiry Society. He served as a High Court judge from 1907 to 1924.

DODDINGTON (DODINGTON), EDWARD fl. 1602

Edward Doddington was first noted in Ireland as a Captain of Foot, active in Munster during the Tyrone War. He afterwards became Constable of Dungiven Castle, County Londonderry and Killybegs Castle, County Donegal. In 1612 he is mentioned as one of the Burgesses of the newly incorporated town of Limavady, County Londonderry. He has been credited with the design of the town walls of Derry, and he also built a house at Crossalt, with a bawn and two turrets. He was the first to build in Coleraine, County Londonderry, in the English style. He was knighted.

DODDS, ERIC ROBERTSON 1893–1979

Eric Dodds was educated at Campbell College, Belfast, in Scotland, Dublin, and at Balliol College, Oxford. He taught classics in Reading and Birmingham Universities, and from 1936 to 1960 held the Chair of Greek at Oxford. He was also President of the Society for Psychical Research from 1961 to 1963, and during the 1960s was a lecturer on Swan's Hellenic Cruises. He was a friend of Auden and of Stephen McKenna, whose *Journals and Letters* he edited. He was Louis MacNeice's literary executor and friend and edited *The Strings are False* and the *Collected Poems.* His own books include *Select Passages Illustrating Neoplatonism*, 1923; *The Greeks and the Irrational*, 1951 and *The Ancient Concept of Progress and Other Essays on Greek Literature and Belief*, 1973. His autobiography, *Missing Persons*, won the Duff Cooper Award in 1979.

DOHERTY, JOHN 1895–1980

John Doherty was a member of a family of travelling tinsmiths who circulated in the South-west Donegal area. They made fiddles from tin and because they were cheap they became extremely popular. He was a fiddler and his style was distinguished by the use of strict tempo – one bow stroke per note – and by the staccato sound, mimicked from the highland pipes chanter. The music was performed for dancing in the kitchen. As John Doherty said, 'The old musicians . . . would take music from the sound of the sea, or they would go alongside the river at the time of the flood and they would take music from that. They would take music from the chase of the hound and the hare.'

DOHERTY, PETER DERMONT ('PETER THE GREAT') 1913–1990
Peter Doherty was born in Magherafelt, County Londonderry. He was an international scoccer player and played for Glentoran, then Blackpool and later Manchester City and Derby County. From 1946 to 1949 he was player manager at Huddlesfield Town and later played for Doncaster Rovers and Bristol City. He played sixteen matches for Northern Ireland between 1936 and 1951 and scored the equalizer against England in 1947. He was the second soccer player to be elevated to the Texaco Hall of Fame. From 1951 to 1962 he was Northern Ireland's first international team manager and led his team to qualify for the World Cup finals in 1958 where they won through to the quarter finals.

DOLLING, ROBERT WILLIAM RADCLYFFE 1851–1901
Robert Dolling was born in Magheralin, County Down, and was educated at Harrow and Cambridge. He worked as a land agent at Kilrea, County Londonderry, and from 1870 to 1878 was involved in social work in Dublin. Before being ordained in 1885 he worked in the London slums and was known as 'Brother Bob'. The next ten years of his life are documented in his publication *Ten Years in a Portsmouth Slum*. He moved from Portsmouth, and as 'Father Dolling', went as vicar to St Xavier's, Poplar in 1898 where he continued his philanthropic endeavours. It is said that he died from overwork. [Biographies by Osborne and Clayton]

DONAGHY, JOHN LYLE 1902–1947
John Lyle Donaghy was educated at Larne Grammar School and Trinity College, Dublin. He was a schoolmaster by profession and published poetry: *At Dawn Above Aherlow* in 1926 and *Into the Light* in 1934.

DONAHOE, PATRICK 1811–1901
Patrick Donahoe was born in Munnery, County Cavan. When he was ten years old he went to Boston, where he became apprenticed to a printer. He initiated the *Boston Pilot*, an Irish literary journal. He became a publisher and a bookseller, but in 1872 his printing house was destroyed and in 1878 he was forced to sell the *Boston Pilot*. Later he began to print *Donahoe's Magazine*, which was a success and enabled him to buy back the *Boston Pilot* in 1881.

DONLEVY, ANDREW 1694–1765
Andrew Donlevy was educated in Sligo and Paris. He was a prefect of the Irish College in Paris and later Dean of Raphoe. He published *The Catechism or Christian Doctrine* and *The Elements of the Irish Language* which was printed in both Irish and English.

DONNAN, FREDERICK GEORGE 1870–1956
Frederick Donnan was born in Holywood, County Down, and was educated at Queen's College, Belfast, and in Berlin, Leipzig and London. He was an honorary graduate of the National University of Ireland and of other universities. He was a Fellow of the Royal University of Ireland from 1898 to 1901 and later an examiner there. In 1902 he was assistant professor at University College, London and from 1903 to 1904 was a lecturer in Chemistry at the Royal College of Science, Dublin.

DONN BYRNE see O'BEIRNE, BRIAN

DONNELLY, CHARLES 1910–1937
Charles Donnelly was born near Dungannon, County Tyrone, and was educated at University College, Dublin, where he belonged to the group which included Cyril Cusack and Flann O'Brien. He contributed poetry to *Comhthrom Féinne*. He went to London, where he worked for the Republican Congress. He submitted a thesis on military strategy in 19th-century Spain and volunteered to fight in Spain with the International Brigade. He joined the Abraham Lincoln Battalion and was killed on the Jarama front.

DONNELLY, JAMES 1822–1893
James Donnelly was born in Annahagh, County Monaghan, and was educated at Maynooth. In 1848 he was appointed to a

professorship at St MacCartan's Seminary, and he spent four years from 1852 in America raising funds for the Catholic University. He became a professor in the Irish College in Paris, and in 1864 was consecrated Bishop of Clogher. He saw the completion of Monaghan Cathedral and the building of St MacCartan's Seminary and St Louis Convent.

DONNOLLY, ROBERT 19th century
Robert Donnolly came from Portadown, County Armagh, and it is thought that he was a weaver. He published many poems, most in broadsheet form which he illustrated himself. His two volumes of poetry were *Poems on Various Subjects*, 1867 and *The Poetical Works of Robert Donnolly*, 1882.

DONOVAN, JOHN THOMAS 1878–1922
John Donovan was born in Belfast and studied law. In 1914 he became Nationalist member of parliament for West Wicklow and served as Honorary Secretary of the National Volunteers. He visited Australia and New Zealand on two occasions as envoy of the Nationlist Party.

DORAN, JOSEPH M. late 19th century
Joseph Doran trained at the School of Art in Belfast and specialised in the design of wall-papers, printed and woven textiles, metal-work and enamel-work. As a student he exhibited at the Belfast Art and Industrial Exhibition and in 1895 at the Arts and Crafts Society of Ireland. Two years later he won a national bronze medal and one of only nine Queen's Prizes for Advanced Design. In 1899 he won a scholarship to South Kensington to study for three years and produced textile designs for a number of manufacturers. In 1906 and in 1911 he exhibited at the English Arts and Crafts Society his printed linens and cottons as well as jewellery, enamelling, carved ivory and embriodered panels for clothes. In 1909 he was included in the *Studio Year Book*, a survey of the leading European designers and craftsmen. Though he had an international reputation, and lived in Chelsea, he joined the Guild of Irish Art-Workers and was an honorary member of the Ulster Arts Club.

DORAN, JOSEPH 1907–1989
Joseph Doran was born in Kilkeel, County Down and was educated at Kilkeel and Strawberry Hill Training College in London. He returned to Keady, County Armagh, as a teacher and became principal of Brackney School and Moneydarragh School, County Down. He was appointed the first principal of St Columban's Secondary School at Kilkeel. He wrote many articles for the *Mourne Observer* and the *Rathfriland Outlook* as well as scripts for radio and television. He was a keen walker and among his publications are *Hill Walks in the Mournes*, *My Mourne*, with a preface by Estyn Evans; *Wayfarer in the Mournes* and *Turn up the Lamp*, the latter consisting of childhood recollections.

DORRIAN, PATRICK 1814–1885
Patrick Dorrian was born in Downpatrick, County Down, and was educated in Maynooth, where he was ordained in 1833. He served as a curate in Belfast for ten years and was parish priest in Loughinisland, County Down, from 1847 to 1860, at which time he became Coadjutor Bishop of Down and Connor. He was consecrated in St Malachy's Church, Belfast and eventually succeeded as Bishop in 1865. He died in Dublin.

DOUGHERTY, JAMES BROWN 1844–1934
James Dougherty was born in Garvagh, County Londonderry, and was educated at Queen's College, Belfast. He was ordained a Presbyterian minister and settled in Nottingham. In 1879 he was appointed Professor of Logic and English at Magee College, Derry, a post which he occupied for the next sixteen years. In 1908 he became Under-Secretary to the Lord Lieutenant and Clerk of the Privy Council. He was knighted and served as member of parliament for Derry City from 1914 to 1918.

DOUGLAS, ARTHUR COATES 1902–1937
Arthur Douglas was a sportsmaster and a rugby and cricket international. He was capped for Ireland five times and won five Ulster Senior Cup medals. He scored two international tries, one on his debut against France. He played cricket for Ireland in

thirteen internationals between 1925 and 1933.

DOUGLAS, JAMES 1867–1940

James Douglas was born in Belfast. He moved to London, and became assistant editor and literary critic of the *London Star*. Subsequently he became editor of the *Sunday Express* in 1920 and held this position until 1931. Among his published work is *The Unpardonable Sin* (1907); an edition of the *Poems and Songs of Robert Burns* and *The Man in the Pulpit*.

DOUGLAS, JOHN C. 1778–1850

John Douglas was born in Lurgan, County Armagh, and graduated as a medical doctor in 1803. He began a practice in Dublin and was instrumental in establishing a school of midwifery which had a very high reputation. He was a Fellow and President of the College of Physicians, Dublin.

DOWCRA, see DOCWRA, HENRY

DOWDALL, GEORGE 1487–1558

George Dowdall was appointed to the primacy of Armagh in 1543. Pope Paul III declined to sanction his appointment. He refused to adopt English ritual and during the reign of Edward VI, went into exile in France. He was restored to the primacy by Queen Mary in 1554.

DOWSE, RICHARD 1824–1890

Richard Dowse was born in Dungannon, County Tyrone, and was educated at Trinity College, Dublin. In 1852 he was called to the Bar and became Queen's Counsel in 1863. From 1864 to 1872 he served as member of parliament for Derry, after which he was appointed Baron of the Exchequer.

DOYLE, LYNN C. see MONTGOMERY, LESLIE ALEXANDER

DOYLE-JONES, FRANCIS W. d.1938

Francis Doyle-Jones was the sculptor responsible for the statue of St Patrick erected near Downpatrick in 1932. He was a member of the Royal Hibernian Academy and the Royal Academy, London. He also sculpted the bust of T. M. Kettle in St Stephen's Green, Dublin.

DRENLINCOURT, PETER 1644–1722

Peter Drenlincourt was a French Huguenot who came to Ireland to act as chaplain to the Duke of Ormond. He was appointed Precentor of Christ Church, Dublin, in 1681 and resigned a further preferment as Archdeacon of Leighlin when he became Dean of Armagh in 1690. His only published work is *A Speech to the Duke of Ormond and the Privy Council, to Return the Humble Thanks of the French Protestants Arrived in this Kingdom and Graciously Received*. He is buried in Armagh Cathedral, where a monument has been raised to his memory. The Drenlincourt Charity School was founded in Armagh in 1732.

DRENNAN, WILLIAM 1754–1820

William Drennan was born in Belfast, was educated at Glasgow University, studied medicine at Edinburgh and practised as a gynaecologist in Belfast and Newry. He went to Dublin to work, was one of the founding members of the United Irishmen, and wrote many political and religious pamphlets. He was tried for sedition in 1794 but was acquitted. Following this, he withdrew from active involvement in the United Irishmen though he remained committed to radical politics and was a tireless advocate of Catholic Emancipation. He returned to Belfast after 1800 and relinquished his medical practice. He collaborated with John Templeton and John Hancock to establish the Belfast Academical Institution, an interdenominational school, and to publish the *Belfast Magazine*. In 1815 *Fugitive Pieces* was published and he translated the *Electra* of Sophocles. He coined the phrase 'Emerald Isle' in 'When Erin First Rose', 1795. He requested that his coffin should pass by the Academical Institution 'and let six poor Protestants and six poor Catholics get a guinea piece for carriage of me, and a priest and a dissenting clergyman with any other friends that chuse'. *Glendalough and Other Poems* was published posthumously in 1859.

DREW, THOMAS 1838–1910

Thomas Drew was born in Belfast and was a pupil of Charles Lanyon. He was the architect responsible for the restoration work on the two Protestant cathedrals in

Dublin, Christ Church and St Patrick's. He was President of the Royal Society of Antiquaries of Ireland as well as being President of the Royal Hibernian Academy. He was knighted in 1900 and in 1910 was offered the Professorship of Architecture at the National University of Ireland, but died a few weeks later. Among his architectural designs are the Graduates' Memorial Building, Trinity College, Dublin, the Masonic Boys' School, Clonskeagh and Belfast Cathedral.

DRUMM, JAMES 1896–1974

James Drumm was born in Derrygooney, County Monaghan, and was educated at St Macartan's College, and University College, Dublin where he became Professor of Science. He was primarily a chemist and industrial technologist. He developed and manufactured batteries which were capable of being charged at very high rates. In 1930 the 'Drumm battery' was mounted in a demonstration rail coach and the result was that two 'Drumm trains' were built, which could travel with passengers at a speed of forty-seven miles per hour for eighty miles on one single charge. These trains served the lines from Connolly Station and Harcourt Street Station, to Bray in the years between 1930 and 1950. In 1940, government aid was withdrawn and the project was never fully developed. James Drumm was a member of the Senate of the National University of Ireland and in 1935 was appointed Vice-President of the Federation of Irish Industries. He was the first to import stainless steel into Ireland and was a member of the Board of the Emergency Scientific Research Bureau. He died in Dublin.

DRUMMOND, JAMES LAWSON 1783–1853

James Lawson Drummond was born in Larne, County Antrim, and was educated at the Belfast Academy. He became an apprentice surgeon in the Royal Navy and then studied medicine in Edinburgh. In 1814 he was Physician to Belfast Dispensary and four years later was appointed Professor of Anatomy and Physiology in the Belfast Academical Institution. From 1835 to 1836

he was Professor of Botany, and he was instrumental in founding the Faculty of Medicine of which he became the first President. He was the first President of the Belfast Natural History Society. He was a founder of the Belfast Museum.

DRUMMOND, WILLIAM HAMILTON 1778–1865

William Hamilton Drummond was born in Larne, County Antrim, and was educated in Belfast and Glasgow. He was ordained in Belfast in 1800 and became minister of Holywood, County Down. He opened a boarding school at Mount Collier, outside Belfast, but left for a parish in Dublin in 1815. He wrote a great deal of poetry as well as history, and his books include *Ancient Irish Minstrelsy*, 1852; *The Battle of Trafalgar, The Giant's Causeway, Clontarf* and *Bruce's Invasion of Ireland*, and he paraphrased many poems from Old Irish sources. He died in Dublin. [Memoir by Reverend J. Scott Porter, 1867]

DRUMMOND, WILLIAM HENRY 1854–1907

William Drummond was born in Mohill, County Leitrim, and grew up in County Donegal. When he was about eleven years old his family emigrated to Canada and on his father's death his education was interrupted. He worked in Quebec as a telegrapher and completed his education at Montreal High School, McGill College and Bishop's Medical College, where he graduated in medicine. Before setting up a practice in Stornaway near Lake Megantic, he worked at the Western Hospital. After practising for a time in Knowlton, he returned to Montreal. He was a renowned athlete, excelling in weight-throwing, snowshoeing and fast walking. Although he was a successful practitioner and Professor of Medical Jurisprudence, it is for his poetry that he became known. He published *The Habitant and other French-Canadian poems; Johnny Courteau and other poems* and *The Voyageur and other poems*. The poems are remarkable in so far as they are written in the patois. Drummond's *Poetical Works* includes many poems about Ireland, but in Canada it is his dialect verse that won him fame. On his headstone are engraved lines by Moira O'Neill, the poet from the Glens of Antrim.

DRURY, SUSANNA fl.1733–1770
Susanna Drury was the sister of Dublin miniature painter, Franklin Drury who died in 1771. It is not known where she trained as an artist, though it is likely to have been London, because of the subjects she chose to paint. From 1690 onwards the Giant's Causeway attracted a great deal of attention and in about 1740 was depicted by Susanna Drury in two fine paintings which won the £25 premium prize. These served as the basis for a pair of magnificent engravings by Francois Vivares, which received wide European circulation. It was the second half of the 18th century before any progress was made in an explanation of the Causeway. In 1765 and 1771 the French geologist Nicholas Desmarest suggested that basalt such as that of the causeway was really consolidated lava which had been poured from volcanic eruptions. Desmarest had never visited the Causeway, but he had studied Susanna Drury's illustrations carefully, and for some years thereafter areas of columnar basalt in France, Germany or wheresoever they might occur, were known as 'Giant's Causeways'.

DRYER, JOHN 19th century
John Dryer, who was Danish, came to work at Armagh Observatory in 1882. His special interest was nebulae and star clusters, and he had already published on the subject. He was author of a second Armagh catalogue of stars and was requested by the Royal Astronomical Council to publish a comprehensive book which would include his own and Herschel's information. The seminal text *New General Catalogue of Nebulae and Star Clusters* is still used by astronomers throughout the world.

DUB DÁ LÉITHE MAC MÁEL MUIRE d.1064
Dub dá Léithe was Reader of Divinity at Armagh and in 1049 became abbot. He was the author of the chronicle of Ireland mentioned in the *Annals of Ulster* and *Annals of the Four Masters*.

DUCHAL, JAMES 1697–1761
James Duchal was born in Antrim and was educated at the University of Glasgow. He subsequently became a minister of a small congregation in Cambridge. Later he came to Antrim as a Presbyterian clergyman and then to Dublin to minister to the dissenting congregation in Wood Street. He published many theological works and wrote hundreds of sermons. A selection of these was published in three volumes after his death.

DUFFERIN, MARQUIS OF see BLACKWOOD, FREDERICK WILLIAM TEMPLE

DUFFERIN, LADY see BLACKWOOD, HARIOT

DUFFERIN, HELEN SELENA see BLACKWOOD

DUFFIN, EMMA 20th century
Emma Duffin was born in Belfast. She enlisted as a Voluntary Auxiliary Detachment nurse in the First World War and worked in front-line hospitals in Northern France and in Egypt. Initially, she was an untrained auxiliary nurse tending to the wounded as they were brought in, and changing and maintaining dressings. She kept a diary during this period. In 1941, during the Second World War, her experience of nursing in war-time was called upon. On the night of the 15th to the 16th of April, 1941, during the raid on Belfast by some two hundred Luftwaffe bombers, over nine hundred people were killed. Emma reported to Belfast market which was being used as a morgue. The experience left a profound impression, which she recorded in her diaries of the Second World War. These diaries are now in the Public Record Office of Northern Ireland.

DUFFY, BERNARD 1882–1952
Bernard Duffy was born in Carrickmacross, County Monaghan. In 1907 he was called to the Bar. He was a prolific writer and his novels include *Oriel* (1918) and *The Rocky Road* (1929). Among his plays are *Cupboard Love, The Coiner, The Plot* and *The Countercharm.*

DUFFY, CHARLES GAVAN 1816–1903

Gavan Duffy was born in Monaghan and was educated at local hedge schools. He worked in Dublin and Belfast as a journalist, and though called to the Bar in 1845, he did not practise. He joined the Young Ireland movement, was founder of the *Belfast Vindicator* in 1839 and co-founder of the *Nation*, a weekly journal, in 1842, but it was suppressed in 1848 and Duffy was arrested. In 1849 he was released and he revived the *Nation*, and in 1852 was elected member of parliament for New Ross. His attempts at land reform were thwarted by the House of Lords, and in 1855 he emigrated to Australia. In 1871 he became Prime Minister of Victoria and was knighted in 1873. He returned to Europe and in 1892 was elected President of the Irish Literary Society in London. He established the New Irish Library, and among his publications are a history of the Young Ireland movement; his autobiography, *My Life in Two Hemispheres; Four Years of Irish History* and *Life of Thomas Davis*. He died in Nice and is buried in Glasnevin Cemetery, Dublin.

DUFFY, JAMES 1809–1871

James Duffy was born in Monaghan and was educated at a hedge school. Before starting his own bookselling business in 1830, he worked as a bookseller's assistant in Dublin. He sold the popular twopenny edition of *Boney's Oraculum* or *Napoleon's Book of Fate* and then launched his Popular Sixpenny Library. He published the work of such writers as Mangan and Carleton and the writings of the Young Irelanders.

DUIGENAN, PATRICK 1735–1816

Patrick Duigenan was born in County Leitrim, and though his parents were Catholic, he became a Protestant. He was educated at Trinity College, Dublin, and was called to the Bar in 1767. In 1785 he was appointed King's Advocate-General of the High Court of Admiralty, and in 1790 he was elected as member of parliament for Old Leighlin. He advocated the Union in speeches and pamphlets. For the last sixteen years of his life Duigenan represented Armagh in the Westminster parliament.

DUKE, P. J. 1925–1950

P. J. Duke was a G.A.A. football mid-fielder and right half-back for County Cavan. He played for Stradone and University College, Dublin. He won three Sigerson Cup medals, in 1945, 1949 and 1947, when he was captain. He was a member of the Cavan senior championship side from 1945 and won two All-Ireland Senior Championship medals with Cavan in 1947 and 1948. He won a Railway Cup medal in 1950 for Ulster.

DUNKIN, WILLIAM c.1709–1765

William Dunkin was educated at Trinity College, Dublin and ordained in 1735. He was a friend of Swift, who wrote of him 'he is a gentleman of much wit, and the best English as well as Latin poet in the Kingdom'. Eventually Lord Chesterfield placed Dunkin as Principal of Portora, the endowed school of Enniskillen. His collected work, *Poems and Epistles*, was published in two volumes in 1774.

DUNLAP, JOHN 1747–1812

John Dunlap was born in Strabane, County Tyrone. As a child he went to Philadelphia to live with his uncle William, who was a printer and publisher. By the age of eighteen he was running his uncle's business and had started the newspaper *Pennsylvania Packet*. This venture was extremely successful, and in 1784 it became the first daily newspaper in the United States; it later became known as the *North American and United States Gazette*. He was appointed printer to Congress, and it was his press which first issued the Declaration of Independence. George Washington appointed him an officer in his bodyguard at Trenton and Princeton. In a letter home on the 12th of May, 1785, he wrote 'There is no place in the world where a man meets so rich a reward for good conduct and industry as in America.' He died in Philadelphia.

DUNLOP, JOHN BOYD 1840–1921

John Dunlop was born in Ayrshire, Scotland, and was educated there and at Irvine Academy, where he qualified as a veterinary surgeon in 1859. He moved to Ireland in his late twenties and set up a successful veterinary practice in Belfast. At this point he became fascinated with the improvement of the bicycle wheel, and though he did not actually invent the pneumatic tyre, he was responsible for inventing the first practical form of it. His fascination stemmed from his ailing son, who was prescribed cycling as a therapy and could not endure solid tyres on cobblestones. His application for patent read 'a hollow tyre or tube made of India rubber and cloth . . . said tube or tyre to contain air under pressure or otherwise and to be attached to the wheel'. This patent was bought by Harvey du Cros and developed into the Dunlop Rubber Company. His first experimental bicycle pneumatic tyre was presented by Dunlop to the Royal Scottish Museum, and it is still an exhibit there. The first new tyres were manufactured by Edlin & Sinclair of Belfast and later by a Dublin firm, Bowden & Gillies, of which Dunlop became a director. He died in Dublin.

DUNVILLE, JOHN 1866–1929

John Dunville was born in Holywood, County Down and was educated at Cambridge University. He became chairman of Dunville & Company, Belfast, and twice won the Northcliffe Cup for the greatest distance travelled in a balloon. In 1908 he held the record for the longest time in the air and flew from Holyhead to Dublin in one hour and fifty minutes. He served in the Royal Air Force during the First World War and was promoted to lieutenant-colonel. He was awarded the CBE.

DUNVILLE, ROBERT GRIMSHAW 1838–1910

Robert Dunville was a member of the Dunville whiskey-distilling family and lived at Redburn, near Holywood, County Down. He wrote poetry, and among his volumes are *The Voyage* and *North Sea Bubbles*, which was a collection for young people, illustrated by the author.

E

EATON, TIMOTHY 1834–1907
Timothy Eaton was born near Ballymena, County Antrim. He emigrated to Canada and opened a general shop in St Mary's, Ontario, with his two brothers. He moved to Toronto in 1868 and established a store that sold items for a fixed price in cash, and subsequently created one of the largest department stores in America. He believed in early closing and was the first employer to initiate this. The welfare of his employees was of concern to him. He died in Toronto. [Biography by N. A. Smith, 1923]

EDGAR, JOHN 1798–1866
John Edgar was born in Ballynahinch, County Down, and was educated in Belfast and Glasgow. He was ordained a Presbyterian minister in Belfast in 1820 and became Professor of Theology in 1826. He received a doctorate of Divinity from Hamilton College, New York, in 1836 and in 1842 became Moderator of the General Assembly. The body of his work dealt with his commitment to Temperance though he did not approve of the teetotal movement. He organised relief committees for famine victims in 1847 and later founded a refuge for women. In 1860 he became Doctor of Laws. He edited many periodicals, and his *Select Works* was published in Belfast in 1868. [Memoir by W. D. Killen, 1867]

EDMUNDSON, WILLIAM 1627–1712
William Edmundson was born in Westmorland, and was apprenticed as a carpenter and joiner in the city of York. He served in the army of Cromwell in the campaigns in England and Scotland. In 1652 he came to Ireland and opened a shop in Antrim. On hearing the preaching of the Quaker James Naylor, he was convinced of the worthiness of his doctrine. In 1654 he and other members of his family held at Lurgan, County Armagh, the first regular meeting of the Quakers in Ireland. Subsequently meetings were established at Dublin, Derry, Cork, Waterford and other commercial centres. Because of the unorthodox doctrines which the Quakers practised, they were persecuted, and William Edmundson was imprisoned seven times without charge. He visited the West Indies and America on three occasions, on the first of which he was accompanied by George Fox. During the war of 1689–91 the Friends in Ireland were victimised. William Edmundson appealed to James II to relieve the suffering in Ireland. He died at Rosenallis, near Mountmellick, and his *Journal* was published in 1715.

EDWARDS, R. W. early 20th century
R. W. Edwards was a rugby international forward who played for the Malone Club in Belfast. He played for Ireland when they won against Wales in 1904. He became the only Irish international selected on the 1904 Lions tour of Australia and New Zealand.

EDWARDS, WILLIAM VICTOR 1887–1917
William Edwards was born in Strandtown, Belfast and was a rugby international, a swimmer and water polo player. In rugby he won two international caps for Ireland in 1912. In swimming he was the Irish 200 yard champion and also a water polo champion. He is said to have been the first man to swim Belfast Lough. He was killed in action at Jerusalem.

ELLIOTT, CHARLES 1792–1869
Charles Elliott was born in Killybegs, County Donegal, and was educated in Dublin. When he was twenty-two he went to America and became a superintendent of Methodist missions and Residing Elder of Ohio District. He was appointed Professor of Languages at Madison College and President of Iowa Wesleyan Union. He edited many religious periodicals and wrote several

books, particularly connected with the history of Weslyanism. He died in Iowa.

ELLISON-MACARTNEY, WILLIAM GREY
see MACARTNEY, WILLIAM GREY
ELLISON

EMERSON, NORMAN DAVID 1900–1966
Norman Emerson was born in Lurgan, County Armagh, and educated at Trinity College, Dublin. He was ordained in 1924 and became Canon of Christ Church Cathedral, Dublin, from 1954 to 1961, when he became Dean. He was a member of the Royal Irish Academy and President of the Irish Historical Society from 1960 to 1962. Among his publications are *An Account of Archbishop Ussher* and a *History of the Church of Ireland* in three volumes.

ENSOR, GEORGE 1769–1843
George Ensor was born in Dublin and was educated at Trinity College. He was called to the Bar in 1792 and was a grand juror of County Armagh, where he died at Ardress. He wrote many pamphlets, among which are *Principles of Morality; The Independent Man; National Education; Refutation of Malthus; Defence of the Irish* and *Anti-Union*, 1831.

EOGHAN, ST d.618
Eoghan was born in County Tyrone, and was related to the chieftains of Leinster and Ulster. He was carried off by pirates to Britain as a boy, educated by Ninian and taken to Armorica. When he returned to Ireland, he founded a monastery at Uí Cualann in Wicklow, and is said to have converted the chief of Ardstraw, County Tyrone, to Christianity. He assisted Tigernach to found monasteries in Ulster.

ERARD, ST d.754
Erard was born, it is thought, at Ardboe on the shores of Lough Neagh. He was a missionary in Europe and is especially known in connection with Ratisbon in Germany. He was canonised in 1052, and his feast-day is on the 8th of January. [Biography by O'Hanlon]

ERVINE, ST JOHN GREER 1883–1971
St John Ervine was born in Ballymacarret,

Belfast. After working for three years in an insurance office he emigrated to London at the age of eighteen. For a short period in 1915 he was manager of the Abbey Theatre, where his plays *Mixed Marriage, June Clegg* and *John Ferguson* had already been succesful. He was wounded as a lieutenant in the Dublin Fusiliers, and had a leg amputated. He settled in the south west of England. He wrote biographies of Craigavon and Carson, of William Booth, Oscar Wilde and George Bernard Shaw, as well as publishing seven novels including *The First Mrs Fraser* and some plays, such as *Boyd's Shop* and *Friends and Relations.* Until 1939 he was drama critic for the *Observer.* He became a member of the Irish Academy of Letters and from 1933 to 1936 was Professor of Dramatic Literature for the Royal Society of Literature. His work reflects the change in his political stance away from nationalism and socialism towards unionism.

ESLER, ERMINDA (née RENTOUL) b. *c.*1860
Erminda Rentoul was born in Manor Cunningham, County Donegal. She published many short stories in magazines and her novels, such as *The Way of Transgressors,* were very popular. Among her other works are *The Way They Loved at Grimpat* (1893) and *Maid of the Manse* (1895).

EVANS, EMYR ESTYN 1905–1989
Estyn Evans was brought up on the Welsh border, was educated at Aberystwyth University, and became a lecturer in Geography at Queen's University, Belfast, in 1928. In 1966 the Institute of Irish Studies at Queen's University was founded, and he became Honorary Director. He was particularly interested in the Irish Neolithic. He established scientific archaeology in Belfast and instituted the systematic survey of historic monuments, becoming chairman of the Ancient Monuments Council and helping to found the Ulster Folk and Transport Museum. His research encompassed folklore, myth, legend and the oral tradition, especially in north Antrim and Donegal. His books include *Irish Heritage,* 1942; *Mourne Country,* 1951; *Irish Folk Ways,*

1957; *Prehistoric and Early Christian Ireland*, 1956; *The Personality of Ireland*, 1973, and an essay collection *The Irishness of the Irish*, 1985. He was President of the Institute of British Geographers, and of both the Archaeology and Geography sections of the British Association for the Advancement of Science. He was the recipient of a number of honorary doctorates, and of two awards, the Victorian Medal of the Royal Geographical Society and the Merit Award of the Association of American Geographers.

EVATT, GEORGE 1841–1921

George Evatt was born in County Monaghan. He was educated at Queen's College, Belfast and joined the British army as a medic. He wrote many works, was keenly interested in the health of his soldiers, and became Surgeon General of the army.

EVERETT, JOSEPH DAVID 1831–1904

Joseph Everett was born in England and was educated in England and Glasgow, where he studied classics, moral philosophy and physical science. For a brief period he was Secretary of the Meteorological Society of Edinburgh. For five years, from 1859, he was Professor of Mathematics in Nova Scotia, Canada. His first published paper was on observations of underground temperature. He also investigated atmospheric electricity. He returned to Britain and experimented on the elastic properties of glass, researching under Professor William Thomson in Glasgow. In 1867 he was appointed Professor of Natural Philosophy at Queen's College, Belfast, where he remained for nearly thirty years. He published many theoretical physics and mathematical papers, mainly in the *Philosophical Magazine* and *Nature*. He also wrote several textbooks, including *Units and Physical Constants* and invented the term 'erg' for a unit of energy.

EWALD, PAUL PETER 1888–1985

Paul Ewald was born in Berlin and studied at Cambridge, Göttingen and Munich. He was an X-ray technician in the German army during the First World War. He taught in Munich and in 1921 was appointed Professor of Theoretical Physics at the University of Stuttgart. In 1937 he and his family fled from Nazi Germany, and after two years at Cambridge University he became first lecturer and then professor at Queen's University, Belfast, with a period spent as Professor of Physics in America. For over sixty years he was a key figure in the modern science of X-ray crystallography, which has facilitated the understanding of organic molecules such as proteins and DNA. In 1923 he published *Kristalle und Roentgenstrallen*, and in 1962 *Fifty Years of X-Ray Diffraction*. He founded, with others, the *Strukkurbericht*, a repository for results on crystal structure, edited *Zeitschrift für Kristallographie* and founded and edited the international journal *Acta Crystallographica*. He was Secretary-General and then Vice-President of the International Union of Physics, which he had revived. In 1979 he was awarded the first Gregori Aminoff Medal of the Royal Swedish Academy. The International Union of Crystallography, of which he was a co-founder and President, established the Ewald Prize in his honour. He was a Fellow of the Royal Society and a member of the American Academy of Arts and Sciences. He had five honorary degrees, including those from Stuttgart and the Sorbonne, and in 1978 was awarded the Max Planck Medal, the highest honour of the German Physical Society.

EWART, LAVENS MATHEWSON 1845–1898

Lavens Ewart was born in Belfast and became a linen merchant in the family business. He helped to found the second series of the *Ulster Journal of Archaeology*, which ran from 1895 to 1911, and the first volume of which contained an article by him on the subject of Belfast maps. He wrote *The Diocesan Handbook of Down and Connor and Dromore*. He was interested in the history of printing in Belfast, and his fine collection of books is now in the Linen Hall Library.

F

FABBRINI, GAETANO fl.1816–1845
Gaetano Fabbrini came from Florence. He was appointed drawing master and teacher of Italian at Belfast Academical Institution in about 1816. He quarrelled with the other staff of the school and was eventually dismissed in 1820. During this period, he practised as a portrait painter in Belfast. In 1834 he exhibited at the Royal Hibernian Academy, Dublin, and in 1836 was an honorary member of the Belfast Association of Artists. He had a school, the Belfast Italian Drawing Academy, but in the 1843–44 *Belfast Directory*, he is described as a teacher of dancing.

FAGAN, JAMES BERNARD 1873–1933
James Fagan was born in Belfast and was educated at Clongowes Wood College and Trinity College, Oxford. Abandoning a career in law, he joined the theatre company of Sir Frank Benson and acted with Beerbohm Tree. For fourteen years he wrote plays and then resumed his career as actor and producer. In 1923 he founded the Oxford Playhouse, and the company had among its number Flora Robson, John Gielgud and Tyrone Guthrie. In 1929 he was appointed Director of the Festival Theatre, Cambridge. His plays include *And So To Bed* and *The Improper Duchess*. He died in California.

FAIR, JAMES GRAHAM 1831–1894
James Fair was born in Clogher, County Tyrone, and went to America when he was twelve years old. The gold rush of 1849 drew him to California, and the silver mining of Nevada lured him in 1860. With his friends and fellow-countrymen Mackay, Flood and O'Brien, he became known as one of the 'bonanza kings' who owned large silver mines and founded the Bank of Nevada. He was elected a United States Senator in 1881 and served until 1887. He retired from business in 1886, a millionaire. He died in San Francisco.

FALLS, CYRIL BENTHAM 1888–1971
Cyril Falls was born in Dublin and was educated at Portora Royal School, Enniskillen, at Bradford College and London University. In the First World War he served with the British army, and for sixteen years from 1923 he worked with a team writing the official history of the war. From 1939 to 1953 he was military correspondent of *The Times*. He published many books, including *The History of the 36th (Ulster) Division*; *Elizabeth's Irish Wars* and *Mountjoy: Elizabethan General*. He was a regular contributor to the *Illustrated London News*. He died in England.

FARQUHAR, GEORGE 1678–1707
George Farquhar was born in County Londonderry and was educated at Wall's School in Derry and at Trinity College, Dublin, from which he was expelled. He was befriended by Wilkes the actor and went to work at Smock Alley Theatre in Dublin. His theatrical career lasted only two years and was terminated when he accidentally wounded a fellow-actor. He went to London, where he continued to write comedy and received a commission in the regiment of the Earl of Orrery. Despite having published with great success many plays such as *Love and a Bottle*, *The Constant Couple* and *The Recruiting Officer*, he left the army in 1700 after selling his commission to pay off his debts. In 1707, the year of his death, he published *The Beaux Stratagem*, one of his most widely known plays. He is buried at St Martin-in-the-Fields, London. He ranks, in terms of his contribution to English literature, with Congreve and Etherege.

FARLEY (or FARRELLY), JOHN MURPHY 1842–1918
John Farley was born in Newtownhamilton, County Armagh, and was educated at the local National School. By the time he was

twelve he was an orphan but his maternal uncle, Patrick Murphy, who lived in New York, funded his education at St Macartan's Seminary in County Monaghan. He then went to New York and studied in St Joseph's Seminary. In 1866 he went to Rome to study at the North American College and was ordained in 1870. When he returned to New York he was appointed curate in St Peter's parish, Staten Island, and subsequently became secretary to Archbishop McCloskey. In 1884 he was given his own parish, St Gabriel's, and became Monsignor. Eleven years later he was consecrated Titular Bishop of Zeugma, the first auxiliary Bishop to be appointed to New York. In 1902 he was appointed Archbishop of New York. In 1911 he was elevated to cardinal. He organised the production of the *Catholic Encyclopaedia* and was committed to educational reform. He returned to Newtownhamilton on three occasions. He dedicated two stained glass windows to the memory of his parents, one in St Patrick's Cathedral, Armagh and the other in St Patrick's Church, Cullyhanna, County Armagh.

FAULKNER, ARTHUR BRIAN DEANE 1921–1977

Brian Faulkner was born in Helen's Bay, County Down. He was educated at St Columba's College, Rathfarnham, County Dublin and entered the family shirt-making business. When he was elected for East Down in 1949 he was the youngest ever member of the Northern Ireland parliament. In 1956 he became Government Chief Whip, in 1959 Minister of Home Affairs, and in 1963 Minister of Commerce. Having served as Deputy Prime Minister, he became Prime Minister in 1971. During his term of office he put internment into effect, and direct rule from Westminster was introduced on the 25th of March, 1972. He was Chief of the Executive established by the Sunningdale Agreement, which was set up to implement power-sharing and a Council of Ireland, but this Executive lasted only five months and was terminated by an Ulster Workers' Council strike. He resigned from politics in 1976 and was made Baron Faulkner of Downpatrick in 1977, the year

in which he was killed in a hunting accident.

FAUSSET, ANDREW ROBERT 1821–1910

Andrew Fausset was born at Silverhill, County Fermanagh, and was educated at Dungannon, County Tyrone, and Trinity College, Dublin. He eventually graduated as a Doctor of Divinity in 1843. In 1885 he became a prebendary at York. He edited Terence, Homer, Livy and Euripides, and published many religious and critical works.

FERDOMNACH c. 807

Ferdomnach is known as the scribe of the Book of Armagh, which was compiled from older manuscripts in about 807 at the request of Torbach, Abbot of Armagh. Written in Latin, many of the annotations are in Gaelic, and there is the *Confessio* of St Patrick, as well as a copy of the New Testament. The manuscript is in the library of Trinity College, Dublin.

FERGUS MAC ERC d. c.501

Fergus was the second son of Erc, King of Dalriada, and is one of the chiefs who, with his brothers, led the migration of the Irish to Scotland. Fergus is said to have taken possession of Kintyre in 501.

FERGUS MAC RÓIGH 1st century

Fergus mac Róigh was King of Ulster and a hero of popular romance. He was usurped by his step-son, Conor Mac Nessa. He was killed by a javelin thrown while he was swimming in Loch nÉn. It was by his grave that Murgen the seer is said to have written the story of the great *Táin Bó Cúailnge.*

FERGUSON, HENRY GEORGE 1884–1960

Harry Ferguson was born at Growell, Hillsborough, County Down. He worked on his father's farm before serving an apprenticeship in a car and cycle repair shop in Belfast. In 1903 he and his brother had their own garage in Belfast and were successful in motor-cycle and car racing. In 1909 he had designed, built and flown a monoplane, the first person in Ireland to do so and only four years after the pioneering flight of the Wright brothers. By the next year he was able to fly a distance of twenty miles. He opened his own business in 1911. In 1917, having been approached by the Irish Board of Agriculture, he designed a plough which would increase efficiency in food production. He felt that only a tractor of his own design would do justice to his plough, and the Brown-Ferguson tractor was introduced to the public in 1936. His partnership with Henry Ford, who sold the tractors he had designed, led to the Ford-Ferguson tractor later known as the Fordson tractor. In 1947 Ford's family reneged on the contract, but Ferguson won a legal action against them. He died in England.

FERGUSON, MARY CATHERINE (née GUINNESS) 1823–1905
Mary Guinness was born in Stillorgan, Dublin, and on her marriage to Samuel Ferguson, shared many of his social and literary aspirations. She wrote *Ireland before the Conquest* in 1868 and *Sir Samuel Ferguson in the Ireland of His Day* in two volumes in 1896.

FERGUSON, SAMUEL 1810–1886
Samuel Ferguson was born in Belfast and was educated at Belfast Academy, the Belfast Academical Institution and Trinity College, Dublin, where he was called to the Bar in 1838. Between 1845 and 1846 he went to Europe where he made many sketches, especially of cathedrals and churches dedicated to Irish saints and he studied painting and sculpture in Italy. Some of his sketches are in the Linen Hall Library, Belfast. He became Queen's Counsel in 1859 and Doctor of Laws in 1864. He was published in *Blackwood's Magazine* and in the *Dublin University Magazine*. In collaboration with the Young Ireland movement he founded the Protestant Repeal Association . He kept an open house for the literati of Dublin. In 1867 he became Deputy Keeper of Public Records in Ireland and published many volumes of verse, some of the poems based on Gaelic legends. His collected poems, *Lays of the Western Gael,* appeared in 1865, and *Comgal,* an epic poem in five books, in 1872. He was President of the Royal Irish Academy

and wrote many essays on Irish antiquities. He is renowned for his work *Ogham Inscriptions in Ireland, Wales and Scotland.* He was knighted in 1878. *Poems of Sir Samuel Ferguson* was published in Dublin in 1963 with an introduction by Pádraic Colum. He died at Howth and was interred at Donegore, County Antrim.

FERRIS, SAMUEL 1900–1980
Sam Ferris was born in Magherabeg, near Dromore, County Down. He moved to Glasgow, but returned to Dromore as a young man. At the age of seventeen, he joined the Shelteston Carriers, a running club. A year later he joined the Royal Air Force and was posted to India. After the war he returned to Dromore and took up running. In 1923 he rejoined the Royal Air Force and was stationed at Uxbridge, where he began to take long distance running seriously. He competed in the Olympic Games of 1924, 1928 and 1932 and in the latter he won a Silver Medal. In 1930 he was runner-up in the first Empire Games. He won the London Polytechnic Marathon eight times. He also won the Windsor to London marathon many times. As a warrant officer in the Royal Air Force he served in stations throughout the world, and in Dieppe in 1940 was the officer in charge of evacuation. He is remembered in Dromore by a race held each year.

FINDLATER, WILLIAM HUFFINGTON 1824–1906
William Findlater was born into a Derry family. In 1846 he became a solicitor and was twice President of the Incorporated Law Society. For forty-four years he was a member of the council of the society and served as Chairman of the Solicitors' Benevolent Society for twenty-three years. He was chairman of Findlater's Mountjoy Brewery until it was sold in 1891. He presented to the National Library an autographed letter from Robert Burns which had been sent to a member of his family.

FINDLEY (or FINDLAY), WILLIAM d.1821
William Findley was born in the north of Ireland and when he was young went to America, where he fought in the War of

Independence. He was an able orator and soon became a noted politician and a member of Congress. He supported Thomas Jefferson and opposed the implementation of the United States constitution. His publications include a *Review of the Funding System*, 1794; *Observations* and a *History of the Insurrection in Western Pennsylvania*, an account of the revolutionary war in the area where he lived and eventually died.

FINEGAN, PATRICK 1858–1937

Patrick Finegan was educated at St Patrick's College, Cavan, ordained in 1881, and became Bishop of Kilmore in 1910. He raised money for the new Cathedral of St Patrick and St Phelim, which was eventually dedicated in 1942.

FINLAY, FRANCIS DALZIEL 1793–1857

Francis Finlay was born in County Down and enjoyed the patronage of William Drennan, whose *Fugitive Pieces*, 1815, was the first book he printed. In 1812 he joined the *Belfast Monthly Magazine*, and when it ceased in 1814, he set up a printing office off Joy Street. He later moved to Cornmarket, where he founded the *Northern Whig* in 1824. He was in favour of Catholic Emancipation and supported the tenant right movement. During the course of his career he was imprisoned twice for libel and fined heavily.

FINLAY, PETER 1851–1929

Peter Finlay was born in County Cavan and was educated at St Patrick's College, Cavan, in France and in Germany. From 1874 to 1878 he was a language teacher at Clongowes Wood College. In 1881 he joined the Jesuits and was ordained. He was Professor of Philosophy at Milltown Park, Dublin, from 1881 to 1885, when he was appointed Professor of Theology at St Beuno's in England and the following year at Woodstock, America. From 1912 to 1923 he was the first Professor of Catholic Theology at the National University of Ireland. Among his publications are *Catholics in Civil Life*, *The Catholic Church and the Civil State*, *The Church and Secular Education* and *Socialism and Catholic Teaching*. He was fluent in at least five languages.

FINLAY, THOMAS A. 1848–1940

Thomas Finlay was born in County Cavan and was educated at St Patrick's College, Cavan, St Acheul, Amiens, and the Gregorian University, Rome. He became a Jesuit in 1866, was ordained in 1881, and was appointed Rector of Belvedere College in 1882. He was Professor of Political Economy, University College, Dublin, and President of University Hall, Dublin. He was a member of the Royal Irish Academy and Vice-President of the Royal Irish Agricultural Organisation Society. He founded and edited *Lyceum*, which later merged with *New Ireland Review* which he edited from 1894 to 1910.

FINLEY, SAMUEL 1715–1766

Samuel Finley was born in Armagh and at the age of nineteen went to Philadelphia. In 1742 he was ordained a Presbyterian minister. He travelled the country preaching, despite the laws against this practice. For the next seventeen years, from 1744 to 1761, he directed an academy in Pennsylvania and was for some time Principal of Princeton College. He edited the sermons of President Davies, his predecessor at Princeton, and published some of his own sermons and dissertations. He died in Philadelphia.

FINNCHÚ, ST d.608

Finnchú was Abbot of Bangor, County Down and repelled British pirates who were attacking the King of Meath. He also gave aid in the wars of the Kings of Leinster and Munster.

FINNIAN, ST (FINNBARR or FINDIA) d.576

Finnian was born near what is now Newtownards in County Down, was educated by St Colman at Dromore, County Down and went from there to the school of Ninian in northern Britain. At Newtownards in 540 he established a famous school. He died and was buried there. His feast-day is on the 11th of February. [Biography in William Reeves, *Antiquities of Down and Connor and Dromore*]

FITZPATRICK, MARY (m. SULLIVAN)
early 20th century
Mary Fitzpatrick was born in Farney, County Monaghan and was educated in Dublin and Paris. She published in periodicals in Ireland and America. In 1914 she published *The One Outside*, a collection of short stories.

FITZPATRICK, THOMAS fl. 1857–1868
Thomas Fitzpatrick was probably born in Belfast, and was a student at Belfast School of Design, founded in 1850. Later he and his brothers gave financial support to this establishment. In 1857 he executed the carving on the pediment of the Custom House, and he is also credited with the carved stone work at the Ulster Bank, Waring Street, Belfast.

FITZPATRICK, THOMAS 1832–1900
Thomas Fitzpatrick was born in Virginia, County Cavan, and was educated at Trinity College, Dublin. He took a degree in medicine in 1856. He became a member of the Royal College of Physicians twelve years later. *Tours and Excursions* was published posthumously in 1901, and in the same year his widow founded the Fitzpatrick Lectureship at the Royal College of Physicians in London.

FITZPATRICK, T. 1845–1912
T. Fitzpatrick was born in County Down and was a school-teacher and historian. His novels include *The King of Claddagh* and *Jabez Murdock*, the latter published under the pseudonym 'Banna Borka'. His history books include *The Bloody Bridge and Other Papers Relating to the Insurrection of 1641* and *Waterford During the Civil War*.

FITZPATRICK, WILLIAM. J. 1902–1982
W. J. Fitzpatrick was born in County Down and was educated in Kilkeel, County Down. He was a journalist and a broadcaster and his books *An Old-Timer Talking* and *Margaret O'Mourne* are a record of local folk-tales and superstitions. He also published *Sailing Ships of Mourne* and *A Mourne Man's Memoirs*.

FITZRALPH, RICHARD d.1360
Richard FitzRalph was born in Dundalk, County Louth, and was educated at Oxford, where he became a Doctor of Divinity. In 1333 he was appointed Chancellor of the University of Oxford. Having been promoted from Chancellor of Lincoln to Archdeacon of Chester and then Dean of Lichfield, he was advanced to the see of Armagh in 1346 by Pope Clement VI. In a controversy involving the secular and regular clergy, he sided with the former and appeared at Avignon, where the cardinals ruled against him. He died at Avignon, and in 1370, it is said, his bones were removed to Dundalk. He is believed to have translated, among many other things, the Bible into Irish.

FLACKES, WILLIAM D. 1921–1993
W. D. Flackes was born in Burt, County Donegal. He worked for a number of local newspapers, including the *Fermanagh News* and the *Derry Standard*, before he joined the staff of the *Belfast News-Letter*. From 1947 to 1957 he moved to Westminster as a parliamentary reporter for the press association. Later he worked as chief leader writer and news editor for the *Belfast Telegraph*. He was the BBC's Northern Ireland political correspondent from 1964 to 1982, when he retired. He was awarded the OBE in 1981. He published science fiction and biographies and a political directory of Northern Ireland. He was buried in Lisburn, County Antrim.

FLEMMING, JAMES 1830–1908
James Flemming was born in Strabane, County Tyrone, and was educated at Shrewsbury and Cambridge. He was ordained in 1853 and became chaplain to the royal family in 1876. He was a popular preacher and was made Canon of York in 1879. He published *Art of Reading Sermons* and the *Life of Queen Alexandra*. [Biography by A. R. Finlayson]

FLOOD, WILLIAM HENRY GRATTAN
1859–1928
William Grattan Flood was born in Lismore, County Waterford, and was educated at Mount Melleray and the Catholic Univer-

sity, where he graduated in music. He was organist at Thurles Cathedral, at Belfast Pro-Cathedral in 1879, and at Enniscorthy Cathedral in 1895. He was also Professor of Music at Clongowes Wood College, at Cotton College, Staffordshire, and at St Kieran's College, Kilkenny. He was created a Knight of St Gregory and in 1922, a Chevalier. He wrote prolifically and among his works are *Stories of the Harp, Bagpipes, History of Enniscorthy and Ferns* and a *History of Irish Music* which is a university textbook. He also edited Moore's *Irish Melodies* and *Selected Airs of O'Carolan*.

FORBES, GEORGE 1768–1837

George Forbes was 6th Earl of Granard. He was educated at Armagh and commanded the Longford Militia at Castlebar in 1798. He was an ardent supporter of the Irish Liberal party and was against the Union. In 1806 he was created a peer of Great Britain. He was in favour of Catholic Emancipation and reform. He died in Paris in 1837, having spent many years in France. He is buried at Newtownforbes.

FORDE, FRANCIS 18th century

Francis Forde was born in Seaforde, County Down. He served with the East India Company, second in command to Clive in Bengal in 1758. Having helped drive the French from the Deccan in 1759 and the Dutch from Chinsurah, he returned to England.

FOSTER, ALEXANDER ROULSTON 1890–1972

Alex Foster was born in Derry. He was a schoolteacher and was an international rugby player. Between 1910 and 1921 he was capped seventeen times for Ireland. He played for the British and Irish Lions side which toured South Africa in 1910 and won two test places, scoring a try on his test debut. He captained Ireland three times.

FOSTER, VERE HENRY LEWIS 1819–1900

Vere Foster was born in Copenhagen, where his Irish father was British minister.

He was educated at Eton and Oxford. Having served in the British Diplomatic Corps in South America, he visited Ireland during the Great Famine. The appalling conditions which he witnessed confirmed him in his desire to work for the alleviation of misery. It is said that he gave many emigrants their passage money and that he himself travelled on emigrant ships to America, and the evidence he gathered helped to secure reforming legislation. Several hundred new parish school houses were built with grants which he procured. He assisted in the establishment of the teachers' union which was to become the Irish National Teachers' Organisation. He published a series of drawing and copy books for schools. He wrote *The Two Duchesses* and died in Belfast, where he had been working for the relief of the sick and poor. Virtually his entire fortune had been spent on these causes, yet when he died in Belfast, few newspapers gave him an obituary notice.

FOWKE, FRANCIS 1823–1865

Francis Fowke was born in Ballysillan, Belfast, and studied at Dungannon, County Tyrone, and the military college in Woolwich. He obtained a commission in the Royal Engineers and served with distinction in Bermuda and Paris. When he returned he was appointed architect and engineer in charge of the building of several government structures, among them the Industrial Museum in Edinburgh, the National Gallery, Dublin, and the London Exhibition buildings. He died of a burst blood-vessel before he had time to complete the South Kensington Museum, and his suggested designs became the basis for the plan of the Albert Hall, London.

FOX, CHARLOTTE MILLIGAN 1864–1916

Charlotte Fox was born in Omagh, County Tyrone, and was the sister of Alice Milligan. She founded the Irish Folksong Society in 1904. She was a musician in her own right and collected folk songs and airs throughout Ireland on gramophone. She published *Annals of the Irish Harpers* from Edward Bunting's papers. She died in London.

FOY, WILLIAM 1791–*c.*1861
William Foy was born in County London-derry and was a pupil of the Reverend James Knox, headmaster of the New Free School (later Foyle College). He trained as an artist in the Dublin Society School. He appears to have had a thriving business painting portraits, and his work was in-cluded in principal exhibitions in London from 1828 to 1861. He returned to Dublin and exhibited regularly at the Royal Hibernian Academy from 1836 until 1859. In 1861 he had an exhibition in the British Institution in London. A head and shoul-ders portrait of Knox by Foy is in the Foyle and Londonderry College.

FRASER, DONALD 1912–1993
Donald Fraser was born in Glasgow, and worked for a railway company. He stud-ied for the ministry of the United Free Presbyterian Church at Edinburgh, and was ordained in 1938. In 1949 he came to the Presbyterian Church in Ireland as Sabbath School Society organiser. He edited the *Presbyterian Herald* from 1966 to 1976, and was awarded a Doctorate of Divinity. He was a member of the North-ern Ireland YMCA executive, the Northern Ireland Youth Employment Service Board and the Northern Ireland Orthopaedic Development Committee. In 1971 he was Moderator of East Belfast Presbytery, and in 1974, Moderator of the Synod of Belfast.

FRAZER (or FRASER), HUGH fl.1813–1861
Hugh Frazer was born in Dromore, County Down. He was a pupil in the Drawing School of the Dublin Society in 1812. He published *Essay on Painting*, and from 1826 to 1861 was a regular exhibitor at the Royal Hibernian Academy. His 'River Lagan from Stranmillis' is in the Belfast Harbour Of-fice and he also painted 'Ruins of Old Priory Church, Holywood'. In 1837 he became a member of the Royal Hibernian Academy. He was President of the Association of Art-ists which was founded in Belfast in 1836. Some of his works are in the Ulster Mu-seum, Belfast.

FRENCH, PERCY 1854–1920
Percy French was born in Clooneyquin, County Roscommon, and was educated at Trinity College, Dublin, where he studied civil engineering. In 1881 he became In-spector of Drains for County Cavan. Later he toured the country playing a banjo and singing his own songs. He was an artist and painted water-colours. Among his popular songs are 'Are you Right There, Michael'; 'The Mountains of Mourne'; 'Phil the Fluther's Ball' and 'Slattery's Mounted Fut'. He died in Formby, Lancashire.

FULLER, GEORGE 1829–1907
George Fuller was born in Newbury, Berk-shire and was educated at King's College, London. He was appointed principal asso-ciate in the engineering business of Professor James Thomson in Belfast, and from 1854 to 1888 was employed on rail-way works by Liddell and Gordon, Civil Engineers of Westminster. He then became resident engineer at Madras to the Great Southern of India Railway, and in 1868 took up the position of Professor of Engi-neering at University College, London. Five years later he came to Belfast as Professor of Engineering at Queen's College. After eleven years he resigned to take up private work in London. In 1878 he invented a cylindrical spiral slide-rule which had the accuracy of a straight slide rule of over twenty-five metres long.

FULLERTON, ANDREW d.1934
Andrew Fullerton was born in Dalkey and studied medicine at Queen's College, Bel-fast. He became a surgeon and was President of the Royal College of Surgeons in Ireland and an Honorary Fellow of the American College of Surgeons. Among his publications are *Colles's Fracture*, *Surgical Anatomy of the Knee Joint* and *Operations on the Gall Bladder and Bile Duct*.

G

GAGE, ADELAIDE 1832–1920

Adelaide Gage was born in Ballycastle, County Antrim. She was the daughter of the Reverend Robert Gage, who was both rector and owner of Rathlin island. She travelled in Europe and stayed with her sister, Countess von Roden, in Heidelberg. She was a keen botanist, and the Belfast Natural History and Philosophical Society refers to her illustrated book of flora and fauna of Rathlin, the whereabouts of which is now unknown. Her grave is in Ramoan Churchyard, Ballycastle.

GAGE, CATHERINE (née BOYD) 1791–1852

Catherine Boyd was born in Belfast and lived in Ballycastle, County Antrim. In 1812 she married the Reverend Robert Gage of Rathlin Island, where she lived for the rest of her life. She wrote a two-volume *History of Rathlin Island*, with illustrations and maps, which begins in the prehistoric era and ends in 1851. The manuscript was unpublished.

GAGE, CATHERINE 1815–1892

Catherine Gage was born in County Down. She lived all her life in the Manor House on Rathlin Island. She was an artist, and during her lifetime she painted over five hundred water-colour pictures of birds of Rathlin.

GAGE, DOROTHEA (COUNTESS VON RODEN) 1835–1883

Dorothea Gage was born in County Antrim. In 1864 she went on a visit to Baden Baden, where she met His Serene Highness Albrecht, Prince of Warbeck and Pyrmonte (part of Prussia). He followed her back to Rathlin, and in 1864 they were married in the Chapel Royal, Dublin Castle. In 1867, Queen Victoria created her Countess von Roden. She died in Heidelberg.

GAGE, ROBERT 1813–1891

Robert Gage was born in Ballycastle, County Antrim, and was educated at the Derry Diocesan School and Trinity College, Dublin, from where he received a Master of Arts degree in 1843. He returned to Rathlin and remained there for the rest of his life. On his death, his *Birds of Rathlin Island* was donated to the Belfast Museum.

GALL, ST c.550–c.645

Gall was born in Ireland and educated at Bangor, County Down, by St Columbanus. In 585 he went with Columbanus to Luxeuil in France. He remained in Switzerland when Columbanus departed for Italy, and preached to the people in their own language. Gall established the celebrated monastery of Arbon with its striking architecture and its rich library, and gave his name to the surrounding region. His sermon preached at an ordination ceremony is still extant, and a record of his life written in 771 surviving in fragmentary form is said to be the earliest of its kind. His feast-day is on the 16th of October and he is known as 'the Apostle of Switzerland'.

GALLAGHER, CHARLES fl. 1964–1968

Charlie Gallagher was a dentist and played gaelic football for County Cavan. In 1964, 1967 and 1969 he won Ulster Senior Football Championship medals. He won four Railway Cup medals with Ulster in 1964, 1965, 1966 when he captained the team, and 1968. He is the only Cavan man to score the 'ton up' in one season in 1964. In 1965 and 1967 he was also the country's leading football marksman. He was selected for the the 'Team of the Century' side for football players who had never won an All-Ireland medal. He died in a drowning accident.

GALLAGHER, PATRICK 1873–1966

Patrick Gallagher was born in Cleendra, near Dungloe, County Donegal. For a short period he attended Roshine school. From the age of nine he was hired out as a ploughboy in the Laggan district for very little pay. At the age of seventeen he left to work in Scotland and saved enough money to return home and buy a farm. He was responsible for establishing the Templecrone Co-operative Society, known locally as 'the Cope', and became known as 'Paddy the Cope'. He had a pier built at Dungloe and installed a generator which supplied free power to the local churches and lit the main street. He exported flagstones and knitted garments and improved the prosperity of the town. George Russell (AE) persuaded him to write his autobiography, *My Story*, 1939.

GALLAGHER, PATRICK (PATSY or 'THE MIGHTY ATOM') 1894–1954

Patrick Gallagher was born in Milford, County Donegal. He was a soccer international and joined Glasgow Celtic at the age of seventeen. He won four Scottish Cup medals and six Scottish League Championship medals with Glasgow Celtic. Between 1911 and 1926 he scored one hundred and eighty-four goals in four hundred and thirty-six matches. He later played for Falkirk from 1926 to 1932. He won eleven caps for Northern Ireland between 1920 and 1927 and also a cap for the Irish Free State.

GALLAHER, DAVID 1873–1917

Dave Gallaher was born in Ramelton, County Donegal and emigrated to Auckland, New Zealand. He was an international rugby player and was the first captain of the All-Blacks when they played Australia in 1903. From 1905 to 1906 he was captain of the first All-Blacks side to tour the British Isles. He was killed at Passchendale in the First World War.

GALLAHER, THOMAS 1840–1927

Thomas Gallaher was born at Templemoyle, near Derry. He began to process tobacco in Derry in 1857, but ten years later transferred his business to Belfast and in 1896 opened a large factory in York Street, which produced many types of tobacco, cigarettes and snuff.

GALWAY, MARY *c.* 1871–*c.* 1936

Mary Galway lived in the Springfield Road area of Belfast. She was appointed General Secretary of the Irish Textile Operatives' Union in 1897. She spoke out forcefully on behalf of women textile workers, who suffered atrocious working conditions, and she contributed articles on the linen industry to the *Voice of Ireland*. She addressed rallys and collected funds during the Belfast dockers' and carters' strike. An active member of the executive of the Belfast Trades Council, she was elected Vice-President of the Irish Trade Union Congress in 1910. In the same year she had a rift with James Connolly. In 1915 she set up a Trade Board for outworkers, the most exploited of the textile workers, and she was largely instrumental in getting the first woman factory inspector appointed in Ireland, having approached in person the President of the Board of Trade in London. She was fundamental in banning the system of the half-timers, whereby children divided their week between the factory and the school, and in reducing the working week by seven hours to forty-eight hours.

GALWEY, HONORIA 1830–1924

Honoria Galwey was born in the Waterside, Derry. From an early age she was sung to by her father. She travelled on the continent and when she returned, her enthusiasm for collecting music became central to her life. She once wrote: 'Fiddles, pipes, concertinas, Jews' harps (or trumps), lasses lilting, lads whistling, to each and all I am indebted'. In 1910 she published *Old Irish Croonauns and other tunes*, said to be one of the best collections of Irish melodies extant. The words to many of the tunes were composed by Moira O'Neill of the Glens of Antrim. Honoria Galwey claimed that the Londonderry Air belonged as much to County Donegal as to County Londonderry.

GAMBLE, JOHN 1770–1831

John Gamble was born in Strabane, County Tyrone, and was educated in Edinburgh, where he became a doctor. He served as a surgeon in the army, and after a trip to Holland returned home. He travelled the country and wrote novels and prose sketches which reflect life in Ulster in the early nineteenth century. His titles include *Sarsfield, or Wanderings of Youth; Howard* and *Northern Irish Tales.*

GAMBLE, JOSIAS b.1776

Josias Gamble was born in Enniskillen, County Fermanagh and studied chemistry at Glasgow. He returned to Belfast as a minister, but became interested in the manufacture of bleach for the linen industry. He established himself as a chemical manufacturer producing sulphuric acid and soda for soap. Having settled in St Helens, Lancashire, he played a leading role in the establishment of the British chemical industry.

GANDON, JAMES 1743–1823

James Gandon was born in England and began to practise as an architect in 1764. In 1781 he came to Dublin to supervise the construction of the docks and Custom House and at the same time was working on the design of the Four Courts. Among other things, he designed Bishop's Gate in Derry. He was a member of the Royal Irish Academy. He is buried in Drumcondra churchyard.

GARRETT, JAMES RAMSEY 1817–1855

James Garrett was a solicitor in Belfast who was interested in science and natural history and was also a keen ornithologist. He assisted William Thompson in the publication of *The Natural History of Ireland*, which is still a standard authority on the subject.

GARVEY, JOHN 1527–1595

John Garvey was born in County Kilkenny and was educated at Oxford. He was appointed Dean of Ferns in 1558 and of Christ Church in 1565. After serving as Bishop of Kilmore from 1585 to 1589, he was appointed Archbishop of Armagh and remained there until his death.

GEDDES, WILHEMINA 1887–1955

Wilhemina Geddes was born in Drumreilly, County Leitrim, and was educated at Methodist College, Belfast, the Belfast School of Art and the Metropolitan School of Art,

Dublin. Her work was included in the 1914 Exposition des Arts Decoratifs in the Louvres. Rosamund Praeger recognised her talent and took some of her water-colours to an exhibition in Dublin, where they were brought to the attention of Sarah Purser. She became a member of Sarah Purser's Studio of Ecclesiastical Art, An Túr Gloine. As well as being one of the first of the Dublin stained glass artists, she designed book-jackets, book plates, stamps and posters, as well as illustrating books. She was also a needle worker and produced lino prints. She exhibited at the Society of Scottish Arts, the Ulster Academy, and at the British Empire exhibition at Wembley. The Royal Hibernian Academy held exhibitions of her work in 1913, 1914, 1916 and 1930. She designed a window at St Anne's Church, Dawson Street, Dublin, one at Monea Church, Enniskillen, three at All Saints' Church, Dún Laoghaire, one at St John's Church, Malone Road, Belfast, and two windows at Inver Church, Larne. Her windows in Wellington, New Zealand and Bartholomew's Church in Ottawa, Canada, established her international reputation. In 1929 she completed an eight panelled window on the theme of the Children of Lir for the Ulster Museum and in 1938 she installed the Great Rose Window in the Cathedral of Ypres in memory of King Albert of the Belgians. Her work is represented in many places, including the Victoria and Albert Museum, London, and more than thirty of her designs for stained glass windows are in the National Gallery of Ireland, Dublin.

GETTY, EDMUND 1799–1857

Edmund Getty was born in Belfast and was educated at Belfast Academy and at the Belfast Academical Institution. He rose to be Ballast Master of the Belfast Ballast Board and was later Secretary of the Belfast Harbour Board. He was responsible for the reclamation of the slob-lands on the County Down coast and the construction of a park and 'Crystal Palace' on the site which Harland & Wolff now occupies. He earned a reputation as an antiquary and a linguist, and among his publications are *Chinese Seals in Ireland; The History of the Harbour Board;*

Last King of Ulster and articles on many subject such as Tory Island, round towers and the old ford of Belfast. He promoted Ulster institutions such as the Literary Society, the Natural History and Philosophical Society and the Botanic Gardens. He died in London.

GIBSON, JOHN GEORGE 1846–1924
John Gibson was born in Dublin and educated at Portora Royal School, Enniskillen and Trinity College, Dublin. He achieved a double first and was called to the Bar in 1870. By 1880 he was Queen's Counsel and having served consecutively as Solicitor-General and Attorney-General, he became member of parliament for Walton from 1885 to 1888 and in the latter year was appointed a judge. He died at Colwyn Bay.

GIBSON, JOHN GEORGE 1920–1974
John George Gibson was born in Belfast and was educated at the Royal Belfast Academical Institution and Queen's University, Belfast. After serving in the Royal Air Force in Africa, he became a doctor of medicine in 1946. He trained as a psychiatrist at the Institute of Psychiatry and at Harvard, where he worked at the Massachusetts General Hospital. On his return he became senior lecturer in the Institute of Psychiatry and consultant to the Bethlem-Maudsley Joint Hospital. He published *The Versatile Spud*, which was the result of his research on the possible relationship between the incidence of congenital nervous system anomalies and the consumption of potatoes. His work covered the scientific study of psychosomatic interrelationships, thyroid disorders and muscle-tension pain in anxiety. In 1957 he became Foundation Professor of Mental Health. He was an examiner for, and a Fellow of both the Royal College of Physicians in London and the Royal College of Psychiatrists. In 1973 he was appointed Chairman of the Northern Ireland Association for Mental Health.

GIBSON, WILLIAM 1808–1867
William Gibson was born in Ballymena, County Antrim. He was educated in Belfast and Edinburgh and was ordained in the Presbyterian Church in Ballybay, County Monaghan, in 1834 . After settling in Belfast in 1842 he founded the *Banner of Ulster*, a newspaper which was published three times a week. In 1847 he was appointed Professor of Christian Ethics at the Presbyterian Assembly's College in Belfast. He published in 1860 *The Year of Grace.*

GILBERT, CLAUDIUS 1670–1743
Claudius Gilbert was born in Belfast and was educated at Trinity College, Dublin, where he became a fellow in 1693 and Vice-Provost in 1716. In 1735 he was appointed Rector of Ardstraw, County Tyrone. He bequeathed many of his books to Trinity College Library.

GILBERT, LADY see MULHOLLAND, ROSA

GILLESPIE, ROBERT ROLLO 1766–1814
Robert Gillespie was born in Comber, County Down. He joined the army in 1783 and served in the West Indies. He fought a duel in which William Barrington was killed, though Gillespie was acquitted of murder. He next went to India, where he is said to have suppressed a mutiny at Vellore and was in command of cavalry which fought Runjeet-Singh in 1809. He was appointed Military Governor of the island of Java and in 1812 was part of the force which conquered Sumatra. He was promoted to the rank of major-general, but was killed in action in Nepal in 1814. He was knighted posthumously. His monument is in the square, Comber, County Down.

GILLESPIE, WILLIAM 1891–1981
Billy Gillespie was born in Derry and was an international soccer player. He played for Derry City, Leeds United and Sheffield. Between 1913 and 1931 he scored twelve goals in twenty-five international games for Northern Ireland. He was manager of Derry City Football Club for nine years. He is still the most capped Sheffield United player, and won twenty-five caps while he was at the club.

GILMORE, GEORGE 1898–1985
George Gilmore was born in Belfast and was reared in Howth and Foxrock, Dublin.

He was arrested many times and imprisoned for one year as an active member of the Irish Republican Army. In 1926 he was the leader of a raid made on Mountjoy Prison, which released nineteen prisoners. In 1934 he was instrumental, with others, in establishing the Republican Congress to set up a Workers' Republic. In order to achieve this he had left the Irish Republican Army. The Republican Congress had the support of the Communist Party of Ireland and some trade unions, but dissolved in 1935. During the Spanish Civil War he recruited volunteers to fight on the Republican side. He died in Howth.

GIVEN, THOMAS 1850–1917
Thomas Given lived in Cullybackey, County Antrim. He left school in third class to work on the farm. After a short stay in America, he returned to Cullybackey, where he remained for the rest of his life. He was a justice of the peace and an active Freemason, secretary of his lodge for twenty-five years. His Ulster Scots dialect poems are published, along with those of his brothers, Patrick Given (1837–1864) and Samuel Fee Given (1845–1867) in *Poems from College and Country by Three Brothers* (1900). [Biography by George R. Buick]

GLASGOW, JAMES 1805–1840
James Glasgow was born in Clough, County Antrim. He became a missionary in India with the Irish Presbyterian Church and was a professor of oriental languages.

GLASS, JAMES 1847–1931
James Glass established a business as a portrait and landscape photographer in Derry city in 1870. His speciality was portraits finished in crayon, oil or watercolour and some were executed on porcelain. He is remembered for an album of twenty-four photographs which he took in the Gweedore district, County Donegal, a unique record of the life of the people.

GLENDY, JOHN 1778–1832
John Glendy was born in Maghera, County Londonderry and ordained as a Presbyterian clergyman. Having become involved in the United Irishmen he emigrated to America in 1798. He became a commodore in the United States Navy and was chosen as chaplain of the House of Representatives.

GLOVER, JULIA (née BETTERTON or BUTTERTON) *c.*1779–1850
Julia Betterton was born in Newry, County Down. She began her stage career when she was six years old, as an infant prodigy, reputedly exploited by her father, who was also an actor. She played at York and Bath, and after her unhappy marriage in 1800 she appeared with Edmund Kean at Drury Lane. She is said to have been an accomplished and able actress, the first comic actress of her time. Her last performance, four days before her death, was as Mrs Malaprop in Sheridan's *The Rivals*.

GOBÁN SÁER, (alias GOBBAN, ST) early 7th century
Gobán Sáer was a legendary figure, reputedly born in Turvey, Dublin. He is said to have constructed many ecclesiastical buildings, mainly in the north of the country, and ascribed to him are the towers of Kilmacduagh and Antrim. It is said by some of the annalists that he became blind in old age as a punishment for the exorbitant charges he had made for his services. Near Ballycastle, County Antrim, there are ruins which are said to be Gobán Sáer's church. No fewer than eight saints named Gobán appear in the martyrology of Donegal.

GODKIN, EDWIN LAWRENCE 1831–1902
Edwin Godkin was born at Moine, County Wicklow, and was educated at Queen's College, Belfast, and Lincoln's Inn. He was correspondent of the *Daily News* in the Crimea and emigrated to America in 1856. He was called to the Bar in 1858 and in 1865 founded the influential newspaper, the *Nation*, in New York. He was a renowned journalist and published, among other works, *History of Hungary*. He was made an honorary Doctor of Civil Law at Oxford in 1897 and returned to England in 1900. In Harvard the 'Godkin Lectures' were established in his memory. [Biography by R. Ogden]

GODKIN, JAMES 1806–1879
James Godkin was born in Gorey, County Wexford, and was ordained in the Congregational Church in Armagh. He moved to Belfast, where he founded the *Christian Patriot*, a weekly newspaper. Later he was to become editor of the *Derry Standard* and the *Dublin Express*. In 1868 he started the *National Review* which was published in Dublin. He was author of many works on history and economics and won a prize for his essay on Repeal. He was the father of Edwin Lawrence Godkin.

GODLEY, ALFRED DENIS 1856–1925
Alfred Godley was born in Ashfield, County Cavan. He was educated at Harrow and Balliol College, Oxford. He was a tutor and fellow of Magdalen College from 1883 until 1912. He edited and translated the works of Herodotus, Tacitus and Horace and edited the poems of Thomas Moore and W. M. Praed. From 1910 to 1920 he was joint editor of the *Classical Review*. Among his publications are *Verses of Order*, *Lyra Frivola* and *The Casual Ward*. He died in Oxford.

GOOD, JAMES WINDER 1877–1930
James Good was educated at the Royal Belfast Academical Institution and Queen's College, Belfast. He was a reporter on the *Northern Whig* and then moved to Dublin where he became leader-writer for the *Freeman's Journal*. He was assistant editor of the *Irish Statesman* and joined the staff of the *Irish Independent*. During this period he was correspondent for English and American newspapers and highly regarded in the field of journalism. He was the author of *Ulster and Ireland* and *Irish Unionism*. He died in Dublin.

GORDON, ELLEN late 19th century
Ellen Gordon was a doffing mistress in Owen O'Cork's Mill in Belfast. She was employed, along with Winifred Carney and Marie Johnson, by James Connolly, to help organise the Irish Textile Workers' Union. She was a fine orator and was popular among the mill girls. She campaigned for the Dublin workers during the 1913 lockout and collected money to be sent to the workers' families. Winifred Carney, James Grimley, Cathal O'Shannon and Ellen Gordon became known as the 'Don't Give A Damn' League. In 1915 she married James Grimley. She was an active member of Cumann na mBan and supported the Labour Party. She had a second-hand furniture shop off the Newtownards Road, but left to live in Dublin after sectarian troubles in 1935.

GORDON, JAMES BENTLEY 1749–1819
James Gordon was born at Neeve Hall, County Londonderry. He was educated at Trinity College, Dublin, and ordained in 1773. After a period of ministry in County Cork he became Rector of Killegney. He wrote a *History of the Rebellion of 1798*; a *History of Ireland*, 1806 and *Terraquea*.

GORDON, THOMAS GISBORNE 1852–1935
Thomas Gordon was educated at Rugby and was capped for Ireland three times in international rugby. He played international rugby as a three-quarter without his right hand which he had lost in a shooting accident.

GORMFLAITH *c*.870–925
Gormflaith was the daughter of Flann Sionna, who was High King of Ireland from 879 to 916. She was betrothed to Cormac mac Cuilennáin, the King-Bishop of Cashel, who was killed by King Cerball of Leinster. Cerball then married Gormflaith. Gormflaith's third husband, Niall Glúndubh, who became High King of Ireland in 916 was killed by the Danes in 919. She reputedly wrote poetry about her husbands and her son, some of which is quoted in the Irish annals. Gormflaith became a beggar and died in poverty. Some lyrics attributed to her survive in the Scottish manuscript, the Book of the Dean of Lismore.

GOUDY, ALEXANDER PORTER 1809–1858
Alexander Goudy was born in County Down. He was a Presbyterian minister in Strabane, County Tyrone, from 1833 to 1858 and became Doctor of Divinity in 1851. In 1857 he was appointed Moderator

of the General Assembly. He contributed to *Plea of Presbytery* and *Presbyterianism Defended*. He was the grandson of the Reverend James Porter of Greyabbey, who was hanged in 1798. [Biography T. Croskery]

GOUDY, HENRY 1848–1921
Henry Goudy was born in Strabane, County Tyrone, and was educated in Glasgow, Edinburgh and Königsberg. He was called to the Scottish Bar and became Professor of Civil Law in Edinburgh in 1889 and later at Oxford in 1893. He was made a Fellow of All Souls' College, Oxford. As well as having published many legal works, he was editor of the *Juridical Review*. He died in Oxford.

GRAHAM, JOHN 1776–1844
John Graham was born in County Longford and was educated at Trinity College, Dublin. He was ordained in 1798 and became Rector of Magilligan, County Londonderry, until 1824. He was an Orangeman and was imprisoned for riotous behaviour in the early nineteenth century. Many of his publications appeared in periodicals, and he also published *Annals of Ireland*; *Derriana* and volumes of poetry. He died at Magilligan.

GRAHAM, JOHN 1813–1896
John Graham was born in Downpatrick, County Down and was educated at Belfast and Trinity College, Dublin, where he won the Vice-Chancellor's Prize for both poetry and prose. In 1844 he was ordained in the Church of England and became curate at Margate and later incumbent of St Chad's, Lichfield and Prebendary of Lichfield Cathedral. [Biography by his daughter]

GRAHAM, JOHN 1822–1879
John Graham was born near Omagh, County Tyrone, and was a Methodist minister in Kinsale, Cork, Belfast and Dublin. He went to London to preach in 1855 and to Australia in 1864, where he stayed for twelve years. While attempting to rescue his niece at Cape May in America, he was drowned. Among his publications are poems, memoirs and sermons. [Biography by his brother]

GRAHAM, WALTER *c.*1763–1798
Walter Graham was born near Maghera, County Londonderry. He was a farmer and elder of the Presbyterian Church. He was a colonel in the National Guard, recruited United Irishmen, and was arrested in 1796. In the following year he was released. Having been arrested again for participating in the 1798 rebellion, he was hanged and beheaded.

GRAHAM, WILLIAM 1810–1883
William Graham was born in Clough, County Antrim, and was educated at the Belfast Academical Institution. He was ordained in 1836 and became minister of Dundonald, County Down. He went as a missionary to Hamburg and Bonn and to the Jews at Damascus. He worked in Bonn for thirty years and built a church there. He wrote many works, one of which, *An Appeal to Israel*, was written in four languages. He retired to Belfast, where he died.

GRAHAM, WILLIAM 1839–1911
William Graham was born in Saintfield, County Down, and was educated at Trinity College, Dublin, where he remained as a tutor for some years. He moved to Queen's College, Belfast, where he was Professor of Jurisprudence from 1882 to 1909. He published many works on philosophy and political economy and was thought well of by Gladstone and Carlyle. He died in Dublin.

GRAINGER, JOHN 1830–1891
John Grainger was born in Belfast and was educated at the Belfast Academy and Trinity College, Dublin. After a period in his father's shipping business in Belfast, he was ordained in the Church of Ireland in 1863 and as a curate he worked in Belfast and in the Dublin area for six years. He was a member of the Royal Irish Academy. He gained a Doctorate of Divinity and was an active member of the Belfast Natural History and Philosophical Society and the Belfast Naturalists' Field Club, of which he

was President for some years. He was Rector of Broughshane, County Antrim, and Rural Dean of Antrim and wrote many articles on Irish geology and archaeology. He presented his very fine geological, numismatical and archaeological collections to the city of Belfast, and they are now housed in the Ulster Museum.

GRANARD, EARL OF see FORBES, GEORGE

GRAND, SARAH (CLARKE, FRANCES ELIZABETH) 1854–1943
Sarah Grand was born in Donaghadee, County Down. She was educated at home and when she was fourteen years old was sent to boarding school in England. At the age of sixteen she eloped with a thirty-nine-year-old naval surgeon. After she published her first novel she left her husband and son and went to London in order to write. As well as novels she wrote essays on the plight of women, for example 'Is it ever justifiable to break off an engagement?'. She served as Mayor of Bath for six years in the 1920s and was an active suffragette. Mark Twain and George Bernard Shaw both held her in high regard. Among her titles are *The Heavenly Twins* (1893) and *The Beth Book* (1898).

GRANT, THOMAS 1816–1870
Thomas Grant was born in Newry, County Down. He was educated at the English College at Rome, of which he became rector. He worked for the re-establishment of the Catholic hierarchy in England, was appointed Bishop of Southwark in 1851 and was present at the famous Vatican Council in 1870. He died in Rome later in the same year. [Biography by K. O'Meara]

GRATTAN FLOOD see FLOOD, WILLIAM HENRY GRATTAN

GRAVES, ROBERT JAMES 1796–1853
Robert Graves was born in Dublin and was educated at the Diocesan School of Downpatrick, County Down and Trinity College, Dublin where he took an arts degree in 1815 and a medical degree in 1818. He went on the grand tour of Europe and met Turner the artist. In 1820 he took the licence of the College of Physicians and in 1821 was appointed Physician to Meath Hospital, which became a renowned teaching hospital. With others he helped to found the School of Medicine in Park Street. He introduced to the students the stethoscope and practical diagnosis on real patients. In 1827 he was appointed King's Professor of the Institutes of Medicine in Dublin University. He practised during the famine of 1822 and wrote 'Report on the Fever lately prevalent in Galway'. With Sir Robert Kane he edited the *Dublin Journal of Medical and Chemical Science* and was the author of several papers. Among these was 'Newly Observed Affection of the Thyroid Gland in Females'; the disease, exophthalmic goitre, became known as 'Graves's disease'. He was the first person to describe peripheral neuritis in a seminal paper which is regarded as a historic contribution to neurology. In 1843 he was elected as President of the College of Physicians, and he was also Fellow of the Royal Society and a member of the Royal Irish Academy. His *Studies in Physiology and Medicine* was published posthumously.

GRAVES, THOMAS c.1747–1814
Thomas Graves was born at Castledawson, County Londonderry, and joined the navy when very young. In January 1783 he was in command of a ship which fought the French and in 1801 he was appointed Rear-Admiral. This meant that he was second in command to Nelson when he bombarded Copenhagen. The Order of the Bath was conferred upon him personally by Nelson, and both the House of Lords and the House of Commons gave him a vote of thanks. He was made admiral in 1812 and died at his country seat in Devon.

GRAY, BETSY see GREY, ELIZABETH

GRAY, EDMUND DWYER 1845–1888
Edmund Gray was born in Dublin. He inherited the *Freeman's Journal* from his father. In 1875 he became a member of Dublin City Council and was appointed chairman of the Public Health Committee. In 1880 he was elected Lord Mayor of Dublin and

organised a fund which raised £180,000 for the relief of famine-stricken districts. He was also proprietor of the *Belfast Morning News*. Between 1877 and 1888 he was elected to parliament for Tipperary, Carlow and Stephen's Green, Dublin.

GRAY, ROBERT DISNEY 1896–1980

Disney Gray was born in Ballybay, County Monaghan and was an international rugby player. He played for Old Wesley and the Barbarians and won four international caps for Ireland, two in 1923, and one in 1925 and 1926. He also rowed with the Dolphin club.

GRAY, WILLIAM 1830–1917

William Gray was born in County Cork, where he was educated. He worked as an engineer in England and developed an interest in geology and archaeology, especially the study of fossils. On returning to Ireland he became District Officer for the Board of Works in Belfast. He was a member of the Belfast Naturalists' Field Club and helped discover several important Stone Age sites, among them the early Mesolithic site at Mount Sandel, near Coleraine, County Londonderry, in the 1880s. He correctly dated the raised beach sites at Larne as post Ice Age. He was a member of the Royal Irish Academy and also of the British Association and was involved in the setting up of a Public Library system for Belfast. Among his publications is *Irish Worked Flints, Ancient and Modern*. His collection of Irish antiquities, including flint implements, was given to the Belfast Municipal Museum.

GREEN, EDWARD RODNEY RICHEY 1921–1981

Rodney Green was born in Belfast and was educated at the Royal Belfast Academical Institution and Trinity College, Dublin, where he graduated in Modern History in 1942. After a year working for the Ministry of Agriculture, he took up a lectureship. In 1945 he was appointed staff tutor in the Department of Extra-Mural Studies at Queen's University, Belfast, though he left this post after two years to continue his research in America. In 1950 he went to St

Antony's College, Oxford and subsequently to the University of Manchester, where he was lecturer and then senior lecturer in History from 1954 to 1970. In 1970 he returned to Belfast as Honorary Professor and Director of the Institute of Irish Studies, Queen's University. His interests included archaeology, contemporary economics and Donegal Irish. He published a study of the industrial and commercial history of the Lagan Valley in 1949, and in 1963 a regional study of County Down for the Ministry of Finance. He was a member of the Royal Irish Academy, the Historic Monuments and Historic Buildings Councils, the Cultural Relations Committee of the Department of Foreign Affairs in Ireland, and the Radio Telefís Éireann Authority.

GREEN, EDWARD THOMAS d.1965

E. T. Green was born in Hillsborough, County Down. He owned a mill that manufactured animal feed stuffs. He pioneered the distribution of farmers' informative literature, and had a keen awareness of their problems. He was active in the Young Farmers Clubs of Ulster, the Rural Industries Development Committee and the Royal Ulster Agricultural Society. He also gave his support for the establishment of the Ulster Folk Museum. He was awarded the CBE.

GREEN, WILLIAM ALFRED 1870–1958

William Alfred Green was born in Newry, County Down and was educated at Friends' School, Lisburn, County Antrim. After a decline in his health, which resulted in his having to leave the family business, Forster Green, he became apprenticed to R. J. Welch, a professional photographer, before starting his own photographic business first in Belfast and later in Antrim. His work ranged from lantern slides for educational purposes to photographs for postcards, advertisements and book illustrations but his special interest was to record agricultural practices and folk customs. He carried out much work of this type in the area around Toomebridge, County Antrim. The majority of his pictures were taken between 1910 and 1930, and his collection is now in the Ulster Folk and Transport Museum, Cultra, County Down.

GREER, SAMUEL McCURDY 1810–1880
Samuel Greer was born in Springvale, Castlerock, County Londonderry and was educated at Belfast Academy and in Glasgow. He was called to the Bar in 1835 and was a co-founder of the Tenant League with Gavan Duffy in 1850. He was member of parliament for Derry city and County Londonderry from 1857 to 1859 and was Recorder of Derry from 1870 to 1878, when he became a county court judge in Cavan and Leitrim.

GREER, THOMAS d. *c.*1895
Tom Greer was born in Anahilt, County Down, studied medicine at Queen's College, Belfast and had a medical practice in Cambridge. In 1892 he unsuccessfully contested, as a Liberal Home Ruler, the seat for North Derry. He published *A Modern Daedalus*, which is based on the old Derry folk-tale of Hudy McGuiggen, a boy who had learnt how to fly by watching the sea-birds.

GREEVES, THOMAS JACKSON 1886–1974
Thomas Greeves was an international rugby player who played for the North of Ireland Football Club. Between 1907 and 1909 he won five international rugby caps for Ireland. From 1929 until 1930 he was President of the Irish Rugby Football Union.

GREGG, JOHN ROBERT 1867–1948
John Gregg was born in Rockcorry, County Monaghan, and was educated in Glasgow. For many years he studied stenography, and the natural motion of the hand dictated the construction of his own system of shorthand, which was first published as a twenty-eight-page pamphlet. In 1893 he went to America and published the *Gregg Shorthand Manual* as well as several books on commercial education. In 1895 he settled in Chicago and established a publishing company. From 1920 he edited *American Shorthand Teacher* and in 1938 was given an award by the New York Academy of Public Education. His shorthand system is widely used and has been adapted to other languages. He died in New York.

GREGORY, PÁDRAIC 1886–1962
Pádraic Gregory was born in Belfast and was educated in Ireland and America. He became an architect and designed the Catholic cathedral in Johannesburg and many ecclesiastical buildings in Ireland. Among his publications are *Old World Ballads; Love Sonnets; Ulster Songs and Ballads* and *The Anglo-Irish Folk Songs of Pádraic Gregory* in two volumes.

GREW, GERTRUDE M. early 20th century
Gertrude M. Grew was born in Portadown, County Armagh, and studied at the School of Art in Belfast and at the Royal College of Art in London. In the early 1920s she worked at embroidery before going to Dublin to open the Cluna Studios, where she was later joined by Margaret O'Keefe who specialised in enamelling. The studios produced hand-made jewellery, enamelled metal-work, stencilled fabrics and coloured embroidery. It also produced hand-coloured prints, calendars and cards, and hand-painted woodwork. Gertrude Grew decorated ceramics and won a bronze medal at the Tailteann Exhibition in 1924. By 1925 she had become a member of the Guild of Irish Art Workers.

GREY, ELIZABETH (BETSY) d.1798
Betsy Grey was born near Bangor, County Down and is remembered for having taken part in the Battle of Ballynahinch on the 13th of June 1798. She, with her brother and her lover, Willie Boal, died in the battle. A monument was erected over her grave at Ballycreen in 1898.

GRIFFITH, JOHN PURSER 1848–1938
John Griffith was born in Holyhead, Anglesley, North Wales and was educated at Trinity College, Dublin. After he had qualified as a civil engineer he worked as Assistant Surveyor for County Antrim. From 1898 to 1913 he was Chief Engineer for the Dublin Port and Docks Board and became Commissioner of Irish Lights. He was President of the Institute of Civil Engineers, a Free State Senator from 1922 to 1936 and was given the honorary freedom of Dublin.

GRIFFITHS, AMYAS 1746–1801

Amyas Griffiths was born in Roscrea, County Tipperary. He was Surveyor of Excise at Belfast, but lost his job when he supported Waddell Cunningham, the rich Belfast merchant against the government candidate at Carrickfergus in 1785. In elections he used a portable printing press. Among his writings are *Miscellaneous Tracts*; a play, *The Swaddler*, and a volume of poetry which he published when he was sixteen.

GRIMSHAW, BEATRICE 1870–1953

Beatrice Grimshaw was born at Cloonagh, near Dunmurry, County Antrim. She was educated at Margaret Byers's Ladies' Collegiate College, Belfast, in Caen and in London. She was a keen cyclist, and broke the women's world 24 hour record by five hours. As a journalist in Dublin from 1891 to 1899 she became sub-editor of *Irish Cyclist* and from 1895 edited the *Social Review* for four years. Until 1903 she was a freelance journalist, a tour organiser and an emigration promoter. In that year she went to the Pacific, and from 1907 to 1934 lived in Papua New Guinea, where she ran a coffee plantation for several years. Sixteen of her novels are set in Papua, and nine on other Pacific islands. She published several travel books, including *In the Strange South Seas*, (illustrated by her own photographs) 1907; *From Fiji to the Cannibal Islands*, 1907 and *The New New Guinea*, 1910. Among her novels are *When the Red Gods Call*; *Guinea Gold*; *The Mystery of Tumbling Reef* and *South Sea Sarah*. She also published ten volumes of short stories and contributed articles to the *National Geographic*. There is a misleading claim, possibly based on the 1928 British *Who's Who* entries, 'that she was the first white woman to ascend the notorious Sepic and the Fly River'. She prided herself in writing for 'the-man-who-could-not-go' and said of herself: 'I have no new range of rivers to my credit, though I have mapped a few odd corners here and there, and often met natives who had never seen a white person – that is easy in Papua.' She died in Bathurst, New South Wales.

GRIMSHAW, JAMES 1798–1857

James Grimshaw was probably born in Whitehouse, County Antrim, and went to work in the family linen business. He was interested in natural history and was a member of the Belfast Natural History and Philosophical Society, to which he contributed various papers, such as *Flora of the Cave Hill*. He was one of the founders of Belfast Botanic Gardens.

GRIMSHAW, WILLIAM 1782–1852

William Grimshaw was born at Greencastle, County Antrim, and emigrated to Philadelphia. He was the author of many books, including an etymological dictionary and numerous text books. He also wrote the *Life of Napoleon*. He died in Philadelphia.

GRUBB, THOMAS 1800–1878

Thomas Grubb was born in Kilkenny. While working in Dublin he designed a machine which engraved, printed and numbered Bank of Ireland notes. He became interested in optics, and in 1835 he erected one of the first refractors at the Armagh Observatory. He also provided the refractors for Markree and Dunsink Observatories and for Melbourne, Australia. He was a member of the Royal Irish Academy and Fellow of the Royal Society of London.

GUTHRIE, TYRONE 1900–1971

Tyrone Guthrie was born in Tunbridge Wells, Kent, but came to live in his parental home at Annaghmakerrig, Newbliss, County Monaghan when he was six months old. He was educated at Wellington College and St John's College, Oxford. In 1923 he was invited to join the Oxford Playhouse, but after a short time left to join the BBC in Belfast. He became Director of the Scottish National Theatre Society in Glasgow for two years. He worked with the BBC in London and with the Canadian Broadcasting Corporation, as well as with the Festival Theatre, Cambridge, and the Westminster Theatre, London. In 1931 he directed plays for Sadler's Wells and the Old Vic. He became Director of the latter in 1951. Many of his productions were staged in Australia, England, America, Finland and Israel, and he became first Director of the Old Minnesota Classical Theatre in Minneapolis. He was given honorary degrees by, among others, Queen's University, Belfast, and Trinity College, Dublin, and from 1963 to 1970 served as Chancellor of Queen's University. He was also Chairman of the Ulster Theatre Council and in 1961 was knighted for his service to the theatre. In 1962 he established a jam factory in Newbliss, in an attempt to alleviate high unemployment. Among his publications are *Theatre Prospect*, *Top of the Ladder*, *In Several Directions* and *A Life in the Theatre*. He died in Annaghmakerrig House, Newbliss, County Monaghan, and in his will left his house to the Irish government as a retreat for artists and writers.

GWYNN, JOHN 1827–1917
John Gwynn was born in Larne, County Antrim, and was educated at Portora Royal School, Enniskillen, and Trinity College, Dublin, where he became a fellow in 1853. He qualified as Doctor of Divinity and Doctor of Civil Law, the latter at Oxford. For eight years from 1856 he was warden of St Columba's College, Rathfarnham. He was Dean of Raphoe and Derry and in 1888 was appointed Regius Professor of Divinity at Trinity College, Dublin, a position which he held until 1907. Among his publications are translations from the Syriac and he also edited The Book of Armagh in 1913.

GWYNN, LUCIUS HENRY 1874–1902
Lucius Gwynn was born in Ramelton, County Donegal. He played rugby for Dublin University and won seven caps for Ireland between 1893 and 1898. He and his brothers played rugby for Leinster. He was also an Irish cricket international and played for Lancashire and the Gentlemen of England. His playing record for Ireland in eleven international cricket matches gives him the best average runs-per-innings of any pre-Second World War cricketer.

GWYNN, ROBERT MALCOLM 1877–1962
Robert Gwynn was born in Ramelton, County Donegal. He was educated at St Columba's College, Rathfarnham, and Trinity College, Dublin. Between 1916 and 1952 he held appointments at Trinity, including Professor of Biblical Greek, Professor of Hebrew and Vice-Provost.

GWYNN, STEPHEN LUCIUS 1864–1950
Stephen Gwynn was born in Dublin, but spent his formative years in County Donegal. He was educated in Dublin and Oxford. He became a teacher, then journalist and author and from 1906 to 1918 he was a Nationalist member of parliament for Galway and later a member of the Irish Convention. In 1899 he published *Highways and Byways in Donegal and Antrim*, and his collected poems were published in 1923. *The Old Knowledge*, *John Maxwell's Marriage*, *The Glade in the Forest*, and *Robert Emmet* are among his novels and short-story collections. His autobiography, *Experiences of a Literary Man*, was published in London in 1926. Regarded as an expert on 18th-century Ireland, he wrote *Henry Grattan and his Times*, as well as several biographies, including *Dean Swift* and *Goldsmith*. He was awarded membership of the Legion of Honour for his service in France during the First World War. Before his death he was honoured by the Irish Academy of Letters and had an honorary doctorate conferred upon him by the National University of Ireland. In the Municipal Gallery of Modern Art, Dublin, there is a portrait of Gwynn by Sir William Rothenstein.

H

HACKETT, FELIX 1882–1975
Felix Hackett was born in Omagh, County Tyrone, and was educated at Trinity College, Dublin, and in America. From 1905 to 1909 he was a junior fellow of the Royal University of Ireland. For twelve years after that he was a physics lecturer at the Royal College of Science, Dublin. He served as Professor of Physics until the College of Science amalgamated with University College, Dublin. From 1930 to 1962 he was Treasurer of the Royal Irish Academy, and for twenty years he was Honorary Secretary of the Royal Dublin Society and served as its President from 1953 to 1956. From 1951 he was chairman of the governing board of the School of Theoretical Physics, Dublin Institute for Advanced Studies.

HACKETT, FLORENCE 1884–1963
Florence Hackett was born in Omagh, County Tyrone. She was a writer. Her plays were broadcast by Radio Éireann, and some of her stories were published in the *Dublin Magazine*. She wrote a novel, *With Benefit of Clergy*, which was published in New York in 1922.

HALIDAY, ALEXANDER HENRY 1728–1802
Alexander Haliday was born in Belfast and was educated in Glasgow. He practised as a doctor in Belfast, was prominent in the Volunteer movement and active in the Hearts of Steel secret society. He was a friend of Lord Charlemont, with whom he founded the Belfast Whig Club in 1790.

HALIDAY, SAMUEL 1685–1739
It is likely that Samuel Haliday was born in Omagh, County Tyrone. He was educated in Glasgow and Leiden and ordained a Presbyterian minister at Geneva in 1708. He became an army chaplain and was subsequently posted to Belfast in 1719. He refused to subscribe to the Westminster Confession of Faith, an issue which caused a split in the Presbyterian Church. He was the author of many pamphlets on this subject.

HALL, JOHN 1829–1898
John Hall was born in Ballygorman, County Armagh, and was educated in Belfast. He was ordained and became a Presbyterian minister in Armagh and later in Dublin. As well as contributing prose and poetry to local papers, he edited the *Evangelical Witness*. He went as minister to Fifth Avenue Presbyterian Church, New York, in 1867, and had a doctorate conferred on him by Trinity College, Dublin in 1891. He returned to Ireland and died in Bangor, County Down. [Biography by his son]

HALL, JOHN CAREY 1844–1921
John Hall was born in Coleraine, County Londonderry, and educated at Coleraine Academical Institution and Queen's College, Belfast. He became British Consul General at Yokohama, Japan.

HALL-THOMPSON, ROBERT LLOYD 1920–1992
Lloyd Hall-Thompson was born in Belfast and was educated at Campbell College, Belfast, and worked for a time in the family business before joining the Royal Regiment of Artillery, in which he served in the Second World War. He was a major in the Territorial Army from 1946 to 1956 and was awarded the Emergency Reserve Decoration and the Territorial Decoration. He was a member of the Not Forgotten Association and was elected its Vice-President. He stood as Unionist candidate for North Belfast in 1969 and held this seat until 1975. He was Chief Whip of the Northern Ireland Executive in 1974. He was a member of the Samaritan Hospital Management Committee from 1957 to 1973, member of the Belfast Newsboys' Club, member of the

Northern Ireland Nurses' Housing Association, and President of the North Belfast Working Men's Club. He founded, with his wife Alison, the Half-Bred Horse Breeders' Society; they were both involved in the Down Royal Corporation of horse breeders, and he was Chairman of the Irish Horse Draft Society. He was also appointed Deputy Governor of the Maze racecourse.

HAMILL, MICHAEL b. 1889

Mickey Hamill was born off the Falls Road in Belfast and was an international soccer player. He played for St Paul's Swifts, Belfast Rangers, Belfast Celtic, Manchester United, Manchester City, Glasgow Celtic and the Forth River team in Boston. He was capped seven times for Northern Ireland between 1912 and 1921 and scored an international goal. He was captain of the Home International Championship side of 1913–1914 . He later managed Distillery

HAMILTON, ANDREW c. 1639–1691

Andrew Hamilton was probably born in County Tyrone. He was ordained in 1661, went to Kilskerry, County Tyrone, as rector in 1689, and organised his parishioners so that they could defend themselves. He was agent to William and Mary for the Enniskilleners. The parliament of James II accused him of treason. He published *True Relations of the Actions of Inniskilling Men* in 1690.

HAMILTON, ANTHONY 1645–1720

Anthony Hamilton may have been born in County Tyrone. He served in France. He was the brother of Elizabeth Hamilton, Countess of Grammont. Under James II he was Governor of Limerick and he led the retreat of the Irish cavalry from the Battle of the Boyne. He retired to France, where he wrote *Memoirs of Count Grammont* as well as a volume of fairy tales and other works. He died in Saint-Germains. [Biography by Ruth Clarke, 1921]

HAMILTON, CHARLES 1753–1792

Charles Hamilton was born in Belfast and was a captain in the service of the East India Company. He studied oriental languages and was one of the founding members of the Asiatic Society of Calcutta. He was chosen by the Governor-General to translate Muslim law, which he did in four volumes in 1791. He was regarded extremely highly by Sir William Jones. He was buried in London. He was a brother of Elizabeth Hamilton.

HAMILTON, ELIZABETH 1641–1708

Elizabeth Hamilton was probably born in County Tyrone and was known as 'La Belle Hamilton', one of the most brilliant and beautiful women at the court of Charles II. Her portrait was painted by Lely, and she married Philibert, Comte de Grammont, in 1663 and went with him to France.

HAMILTON, ELIZABETH (pseud. ALMERIA) 1758–1816

Elizabeth Hamilton was born in Belfast and, when her parents died, went to live with an aunt in Scotland. There is no doubt that her brother, Charles Hamilton, influenced her book *Letters of a Hindu Rajah*. She wrote many essays under the pseudonym 'Almeria', in one of which she warned women that they could expect 'an inexhaustable source of delight' in learning, but that they would not thereby attract men. Her second novel, *Memoirs of Modern Philosophers*, was a parody of the Godwin circle. She was very radical in what she wrote about education and she spent much of her life in philanthropic work. *The Cottagers of Glenburnie* was her most popular novel. When she died in Harrogate her writings received praise in the *Edinburgh Review*, and she was mentioned by Jane Austen and Maria Edgeworth.

HAMILTON, GEORGE 1783–1830

George Hamilton was born in Armagh and was educated at Trinity College, Dublin. In 1809 he became a Church of Ireland rector. He was a biblical scholar and wrote, along with many other works, *Introduction to Hebrew Scriptures* and *Codex Criticus of the Hebrew Bible*.

HAMILTON, GEORGE 1797–1883

George Hamilton, 3rd Marquis of Donegall,

was educated at Eton and Oxford and joined the 18th Light Dragoons in 1818, moving to the 7th Hussars the next year. He was promoted to the rank of lieutenant, and eight years later, he retired as captain of the same regiment. He served as captain of the Yeomen of the Guard and was Colonel of the 4th Battalion of the Irish Rifle Volunteers. He was member of parliament for Carrickfergus, and for Belfast from 1820 to 1830. He served as member of parliament for County Antrim from 1830 to 1837, and for Belfast in 1837–38. He was Vice-Chamberlain of the Household and was appointed to the Privy Council in 1830. He was Lord Lieutenant of County Antrim and militia aide-de-camp to the Queen. In 1841 he was created Baron Ennishowen and Carrickfergus. He died in Brighton.

HAMILTON, GEORGE ALEXANDER 1802–1871

George Hamilton was born in Tyrella, County Down and was educated at Rugby and Oxford. He stood for election to parliament on five occasions, on the last of which he was successful. From 1843 to 1859 he was member of parliament for Dublin University and a prominent Conservative leader. He was made a privy councillor in 1869 and died in Kingstown.

HAMILTON, GUSTAVUS 1639–1723

Gustavus Hamilton is thought to have been born in County Fermanagh. He entered the army and was appointed to defend the town of Coleraine in the war of 1689–1691. He was forced to retreat towards Enniskillen and was later appointed Governor there. He organised regiments known as 'the Enniskilleners', the predecessors of the Inniskilling regiments, which had a reputation for being extremely fierce in battle. Gustavus Hamilton commanded a regiment at the Battle of the Boyne, and was afterwards made Governor of Athlone. He served as member of parliament for Donegal and was created Baron Hamilton in 1715. After the war he was made privy councillor and brigadier general. He was presented with a gift by Queen Anne, and George I bestowed on him a peerage as Viscount Boyne.

HAMILTON, HENRY 1851–1932

Henry Hamilton was born in Coolaghey, County Donegal, and was educated at Raphoe and Queen's College, Belfast. He became a Doctor of Medicine in 1875 and entered the Indian military service a year later. In 1878 he took part in the march to Kandahar and was appointed Senior Medical Officer on the Chitral expedition. He served as Principal Medical Officer on the Chinese expedition of 1900–1901. He was knighted and died in Mentone.

HAMILTON, HUGH d.1679

Hugh Hamilton was born in County Fermanagh and entered the Swedish army, where he became a general. By 1648 he had become a naturalised Swedish noble and was created a baron. Charles II gave him an Irish peerage, as Baron of Glenawley. He settled at Ballygawley, County Tyrone, and eventually died there. He was the uncle of Hugh Hamilton.

HAMILTON, HUGH d.1724

Hugh Hamilton was born in Ballygawley, County Tyrone. He served in the Swedish army from 1680, was given a title and became a general after distinguishing himself in the wars of Charles XII.

HAMILTON, JAMES ARCHIBALD 1747–1815

James Hamilton was born in Athlone, County Dublin, and was educated in Armagh and at Trinity College, Dublin. He was a rector and had an observatory in Cookstown, County Tyrone, where he made detailed observations of the planet Mercury, and in 1791 he was appointed the first Astronomer of Armagh Observatory. In 1804 he was appointed Dean of Cloyne. He published several papers in *Transactions of the Royal Irish Academy*.

HAMILTON, JAMES 1811–1885

James Hamilton succeeded his grandfather as 2nd Marquis of Abercorn in 1818, thereby inheriting the estates in Counties Tyrone and Donegal. He was Groom of the Stole to Prince Albert from 1846 to 1859. From 1866 to 1868 and from 1874 to 1876, he was Lord Lieutenant of Ireland. In 1868 he was created a duke by Disraeli.

HAMILTON, JOHN 1755–1835
John Hamilton was born in Woodbrook, Strabane, County Tyrone. He joined the army and was enlisted in the Bengal Infantry. After eighteen years he was transferred to the regular army and was active at the Cape and in the Peninsular War. He was appointed a general and in 1814 became Governor of Duncannon fort. He had a baronetcy bestowed on him in 1815 and was subsequently knighted.

HAMILTON, M. see CHURCHILL-LUCK, MRS.

HAMILTON, MALCOLM 1635–1699
Malcolm Hamilton was born in Ballygawley, County Tyrone. He went to Sweden to join his uncle Hugh and became a naturalised Swedish noble in 1664. He rose to the rank of general and by 1698 was Governor of Wester-Howland. He died in Stockholm.

HAMILTON, ROBERT 1749–1830
Robert Hamilton was born in Coleraine, County Londonderry, and was educated in Edinburgh where he became a doctor. After he had joined the army he wrote *Duties of a Regimental Surgeon* and also a paper on *Influenza*. He practised in Ipswich for ten years and died there.

HAMILTON, THOMAS 1842–1926
Thomas Hamilton was born in Belfast and educated at the Royal Belfast Academical Institution and Queen's College, Belfast. He was ordained as a Presbyterian minister and served from 1865 to 1889, when he was appointed President of Queen's College, Belfast. He gained Doctorates of Divinity and Laws and established a newspaper, the *Witness*. He was Vice-Chancellor of Queen's University, Belfast, from 1908 to 1923, and in 1921 was appointed a Privy Councillor. He published among other works a *History of the Presbyterian Church* and *Irish Worthies*.

HAMILTON, WILLIAM d.1729
William Hamilton was probably born in County Antrim and was educated at Trinity College, Dublin. He took Holy Orders and was appointed Archdeacon of Armagh in 1700. Among his many published works is *The Exemplary Life of James Bonnell*, which appeared in numerous editions. He died in Carnteel, County Tyrone.

HAMILTON, WILLIAM c.1755–1797
William Hamilton was born in County Londonderry. He was educated at Trinity College, Dublin, and became a fellow there in 1779. He was Rector of Clondevaddock on the Fanad peninsula in County Donegal, and he did much to improve the area, though it is said by some that he abused his power. He was appointed magistrate and murdered on the shores of Lough Swilly. He was renowned for his *Letters on the Coast of the County of Antrim*, a geological treatise which was translated into German, and *Letters on the Principles of the French Democracy and their Influence on Britain and Ireland*. He often contributed to the *Transactions of the Royal Irish Academy*.

HAMMERSCHLAG, ALICE BERGER 1917–1969
Alice Berger Hammerschlag was born in Vienna and educated by Professor Cizek, The Kunstgewerbeschule, and Vienna Academy of Arts. In 1938 she came to Belfast and worked as a publisher's designer and on stage sets, both in Belfast and Dublin. She held many exhibitions in Belfast, London, Manchester, New York, Rome, Derry, Florida and Paris. Her work is in the collections of Queen's University, Belfast, the Ulster Museum, the Arts Council for Northern Ireland and An Chomhairle Ealáion as well as many others.

HANCOCK, THOMAS 1783–1849
Thomas Hancock was born in Lisburn, County Antrim and was educated at Edinburgh, where he studied medicine. He practised in Liverpool and London and returned to Lisburn in 1838. He published many works including *The Principles of Peace* in 1825 which contained eye-witness accounts of the rebellion of 1798.

HANCOCK, WILLIAM NEILSON 1820–1888
William Hancock was born in Lisburn, County Antrim. He was educated at

Dungannon, County Tyrone, and at Trinity College, Dublin. He attained a Doctorate in Laws, was called to the Bar in 1844, and became Queen's Counsel in 1880. He was Professor of Political Economy at Queen's College, Belfast, from 1849 to 1851, and he served as secretary on many Royal Commissions. He was President of the Statistical Society and published several pamphlets and reports.

HANGER, GEORGE 1751–1824
George Hanger was born in County Londonderry and was educated at Reading and Eton. In 1771 he joined the army as an ensign in the Foot Guards and fought as a colonel in the American war with the German Hessian Corps. He was wounded at the siege of Charlestown and retired on half pay. He was a friend of the Prince of Wales, one of those described as 'creatures with whom a man of morality or even common decency could not associate'. George Hanger tried to live as lavishly as his royal friend, and he had a weakness for gambling and a preference for bright pink, turquoise blue and orange clothing. He was caricatured by Gilray and was sent to a debtor's prison where he wrote his autobiography, *The Life and Adventures and Opinions of Colonel Hanger*. On his release he was given money by a friend and set up as a coal merchant. He inherited his father's Irish estates and the title of Lord Coleraine, but refused the latter. He died of convulsions, and his obituary in the *Gentleman's Magazine* referred to him as 'one of the most prominent features of his time'.

HANNA, HENRY 1871–1946
Henry Hanna was educated at Belfast Royal Academy, Queen's College, Belfast, and London University. He was called to the Bar and became King's Counsel in 1911. He served as a member of the Executive Committee of the International Academy of Comparative Law at the Hague. He was a High Court judge from 1925 to 1943.

HANNA, HUGH 1824–1892
Hugh Hanna was born in Dromara, County Down. He was educated in Belfast and ordained there and in 1885 became Doctor of Divinity. A former schoolteacher and prominent educationalist, he was made Commissioner of National Education in 1880. In 1872 he built St Enoch's, the largest Presbyterian church in Belfast. He gained a reputation as a street preacher, and his meetings gave rise to sectarian disturbances in the streets of the city. He was known as 'Roaring Hanna', and he published many pamphlets.

HANNA, SAMUEL 1771–1852
Samuel Hanna was born in Kellswater, County Antrim, and was educated in Glasgow. He was ordained a Presbyterian minister in the parish of Drumbo and moved to Belfast in 1799. He was leader of an evangelical revival in Ulster. He was appointed Professor of Divinity in 1817 and Doctor of Divinity the following year. He was Moderator of the first General Assembly of the Presbyterian Church in 1840. His publications include sermons and pamphlets.

HANNA, WILLIAM 1808–1882
William Hanna was born in Belfast, and was educated in Glasgow and Edinburgh and ordained in Scotland in 1835. He edited the *North British Review* and published, among other works, a *Life of Dr Chalmers* (in 4 volumes). In 1852 he became Doctor of Laws and later Doctor of Divinity. He settled in Edinburgh and died in London.

HANNAY, JAMES OWEN (pseud. BIRMINGHAM, GEORGE A.) 1865–1950
James Hannay was born in Belfast and educated at Haileybury and Trinity College, Dublin. He was rector of Delgany, Westport, County Mayo from 1892 to 1913. From 1892 he was a member of the General Synod of the Church of Ireland. His works, which he produced almost annually, include *Spanish Gold; The Seething Pot* and *The Bad Times*. His play, *General John Regan*, upset the local people when produced in Westport, especially when they discovered the identity of the pseudonym under which he wrote. Consequently he left to serve first as chaplain to the British Embassy in Budapest and then in France as army chaplain during the First World War. By 1924

he was a clergyman in Somerset and later in London. As well as fiction he published other writings, which appeared under his own name, such as *A Padre in France, A Wayfarer in Hungary*, and biographies of *Isaiah* and *Jeremiah*. His autobiography, *Pleasant Places*, was published in 1934.

HANSARD, RICHARD fl.1600–1619
Richard Hansard came from England and was a military engineer and builder. He was granted the town of Lifford, County Donegal, in 1610, and he designed and built a new fort there. In his will he made provision for the building of a church and a free school at Lifford, County Donegal.

HARDEBECK, CARL GILBERT 1869–1945
Carl Hardebeck was born in London. His father was German and his mother Welsh. Despite being blind from birth, in 1892 he gained a diploma as an organist, pianist and music teacher. A year later he left London for Belfast and began his collection of Irish music. He was awarded eleven first prizes for compositions he had submitted to the Feis Ceoil in Dublin between 1897 and 1908. He went to Donegal to take down the songs of the native speakers, and devised a Braille alphabet for this purpose which was later adopted by the National Institute for the Blind. He became the best-known musical adjudicator of his day and his choral works were often performed. He lived in Cork from 1919 to 1923 and returned to Belfast until 1932. He published *Gems of Irish Melody.*

HARDING, MORRIS 1874–1964
Morris Harding was born in Stevenage, Hertfordshire, England. He trained as an artist in the studio of his uncle, and worked under J. M. Swan. He taught sculpture and life drawing at the London County Council Technical Institute. He was a member of the Royal Society of British Sculptors and the Society of Animal Painters. He exhibited at the Royal Academy and the Glasgow Institute. In 1925 he came to Belfast, to work on his major achievement, St Anne's Cathedral. He settled in Holywood, County Down, and for the next twelve years

worked on the nave columns and corbels of St Anne's. He also provided the portraits of dignitaries in corbels above the pillars. He carved the font in St Peter's Church, Antrim Road and the coats of arms of the old government house, Hillsborough. In 1932 he became a member of the Royal Hibernian Academy in Dublin, and was President of the Royal Ulster Academy for several years. In 1953, his work was represented at an exhibition of sculpture held at the Belfast Museum. He was awarded the OBE in 1950.

HARDY, EDWARD JOHN 1849–1920
Edward Hardy was born in County Armagh and was educated at Portora Royal School, Enniskillen, and at Trinity College, Dublin. He was awarded a gold medal for his studies and was ordained in 1874. As an army chaplain from 1878 to 1908 he served in many countries. His first book was translated into various languages and though he wrote many works, *How To Be Happy Though Married* is the only one for which he is remembered. He died in Blackrock, County Dublin.

HARKIN, HUGH 1791–1854
Hugh Harkin was born at Magilligan, County Londonderry. He practised as a doctor in Coleraine and was a prolific poet and writer. He composed *Sacred Songs of the People*, which were adapted to popular airs. His book *The Quarter Clift, or The Life and Adventures of Hudy M'Guigan* was serialised in 1840, but had a court injunction placed upon it because it was said to refer to persons in the Randalstown and Draperstown districts.

HARLAND, EDWARD JAMES 1831–1895
Edward Harland was born in Scarborough, Yorkshire, was educated there, and was apprenticed to the firm of Robert Stephenson & Company, Newcastle-upon-Tyne. He became a draughtsman in Glasgow, and in 1853 he was appointed manager of a shipyard on the Tyne. In 1854 he came to Belfast as manager of a Belfast shipyard. He and his associates bought the business in 1859 and developed it so that it became one of the most important shipyards in the

world. In 1862 G. W. Wolff became his business partner. From 1875 to 1886 he was Chairman of Belfast Harbour Commission. A baronetcy was conferred upon him and he served as Mayor of Belfast. In 1887 he was High Sheriff of County Down, and from 1889 to 1895 he was member of parliament for the North Belfast constituency.

HARREL, DAVID 1841–1939
David Harrel was born in Mountpleasant, County Down. From 1859 to 1879 he served in the Royal Irish Constabulary and after some years as a resident magistrate was appointed Chief Commissioner of the Dublin Metropolitan Police. He was Under-Secretary for Ireland from 1893 to 1902. He was knighted in 1893.

HARRIS, JAMES THOMAS (or FRANK) *c.*1855–1931
Frank Harris was born in Galway and was educated at the Royal School, Armagh and at an English grammar school. He ran away to America when he was fifteen years old, where he attended the State University of Kansas after having worked as a bootblack, a hotel clerk and a cowpuncher. When he returned to Europe he studied at Heidelberg and at the age of twenty-seven came to London, where he became editor of the *Evening News* and the *Fortnightly Review* and proprietor of the *Saturday Review*, a leading literary and political paper, between 1894 and 1899. He founded *Candid Friend* and, as well as short stories and novels, wrote several plays of which *Mr and Mrs Daventry* was the most successful. He went to jail for contempt of court, and on his release in 1914 he emigrated to America, where he bought *Pearson's Magazine*. At this time he began a series of books published between 1915 and 1920 as *Contemporary Portraits*, and he also wrote biographies of Oscar Wilde and George Bernard Shaw. His autobiography in five volumes, *The Life and Loves of Frank Harris*, was written between 1923 and 1927 and was banned in England. He died in Nice. It is said that Bernard Shaw remarked of Frank Harris: 'He is neither first-rate nor second-rate nor tenth-rate. He is just his horrible unique self'. [Biography by H. Kingsmill, 1932]

HARRIS, WALTER 1686–1761
Walter Harris was born in Queen's County (Laois) and was educated at Trinity College, Dublin. He was called to the Bar in 1713, and in the same year received an honorary doctorate. Through marriage he inherited Sir James Ware's manuscripts. The manuscripts, many of which he translated and expanded, were edited and published by him. They were eventually divided between the National Library and Armagh Library. Among his publications were *Life and Reign of William III*; *History of Dublin*, and, in 1744, *The Ancient and Present State of the County of Down*.

HARRISON, HENRY 1867–1954
Henry Harrison was born in Holywood, County Down, and was educated at Westminster School and Balliol College, Oxford, and he became secretary of the Oxford Union Home Rule Group. He was elected Nationalist member of parliament for Mid-Tipperary in 1890, but in his support of Parnell, lost his seat in 1892. In 1915 he joined the Royal Irish Regiment and won the Military Cross. He became known as Captain Harrison and later became Irish correspondent of *The Economist*. He defended Parnell at all times and in 1931 published *Parnell Vindicated: The Lifting of the Veil*. A second book *Parnell, Joseph Chamberlain and Mr Garvin* and a further book, *Parnell, Joseph Chamberlain and 'The Times'* followed. Trinity College, Dublin gave him an honorary doctorate in 1953.

HARRISON, SARAH CECILIA 1863–1941
Celia Harrison was born in Holywood, County Down. She spent her early life in London and from 1878 until 1885 she attended the Slade School of Art where she won many awards. Despite living in London, she maintained her links with Belfast by exhibiting with the Ladies' Sketching Club of Belfast in 1879. In 1880 she moved to Dublin and during the 1890s, spent time painting in Brittany. She was a regular exhibitor at the Royal Hibernian Academy and was a member of the Ulster Academy of Arts and the Royal Ulster Academy. During 1912 she became involved with the quest for a location for Hugh Lane's

pictures, and was the first woman to serve on Dublin City Council. She was devoted to the task of getting poor relief extended to include the able-bodied unemployed. She ran an advice centre from a room in her home, worked tirelessly for women's rights and was an ardent nationalist. She was 6ft. 2" tall, was well known in Dáil Éireann, and was a great grand niece of Henry Joy McCracken. Examples of her work are in the National Gallery of Ireland, the Hugh Lane Municipal Gallery, Dublin, and the Ulster Museum, Belfast.

HART, ALICE mid 19th century
Alice Hart and her husband Ernest, who was a surgeon and editor of the *British Medical Journal,* visited Donegal in 1883. The county had suffered severely from bad harvests, and a Donegal Famine Fund was set up by the Harts. Alice Hart felt that a possible short-term solution to the economic distress was the revival of cottage industries and in 1883, the Donegal Industrial Fund was started. After a successful showing of woven tweeds from Donegal at the Health Exhibition in London, Alice Hart opened a small shop in London to sell Donegal products. She personally experimented with the dying properties of the wild plants of Donegal: the heathers, mosses, roots and leaves, as well as soot and bog-ore. The hosiery made in Donegal and dyed with these dyes won the medal of the Sanitary Institute of Great Britain for 'inocuous vegetable dying'. She instigated a scheme whereby Irish women were encouraged to teach embroidery, later known as 'Kells Embroidery'. The designs were taken from early Irish manuscripts, and worked on linen with dyed and polished threads of flax. In 1885 'Kells Embroidery' won the gold medal at the Inventions Exhibition in London. In 1886 the Donegal Industrial Fund moved to a larger shop which became known as Donegal House. In addition, Alice Hart brought specialist teachers specifically to Donegal and woodcarving and carpentry were revived. The work was exhibited at Edinburgh, Liverpool, Paris, Dublin, Chicago and Olympia, where a model Donegal Industrial Village was built. The venture, though a resounding success, lacked the motivation to survive after the Harts retired in 1896.

HART, GEORGE VAUGHAN 1752–1832
George Hart was born in County Donegal. He joined the army and served with the 46th Regiment during the War of American Independence. He saw action in Long Island, Brandywine and Monmouth. He moved to India, where he took part in the battles of Seringa, Patan and Bangalore. In 1811 he became a lieutenant-general. From 1812 to 1831 he served as member of parliament for County Donegal.

HART, ROBERT 1835–1911
Robert Hart was born in Milltown, County Armagh, and was educated at Queen's College, Belfast. He joined the British consular service and became a commissioner of customs in Shanghai. He met General Gordon and it is said that he reconciled him to Li Hung Chang. By 1863 he had been promoted to Inspector General of Chinese Maritime Customs, a Chinese government appointment, not a British Foreign Office one. The post, which he held for the next forty-three years, led to the conferral of the rank of mandarin. He was instrumental in restoring the Manchu dynasty and had both a knighthood and a baronetcy bestowed upon him. [Biography by Julia Bredon 1909]

HARTY, HAMILTON (or HERBERT) 1880–1941
Hamilton Harty was born in Hillsborough, County Down, and was educated by his father. He became an organist, first in Belfast and then in Dublin. In 1900 he left for London and was soon known as an accompanist and composer, as well as being able to play the violin, cello and piano. He performed on many occasions with the soprano, Agnes Nicholls who was his wife. He was conductor with the London Symphony Orchestra, and from 1920 to 1933 was conductor of the Hallé Orchestra, Manchester, with which he toured. He was knighted in 1925. Among his compositions are *With the Wild Geese, An Irish Symphony; The Mystic Trumpeter* and *Violin Concerto in D minor.* He also wrote songs and orchestral arrangements. He died at Hove, Sussex.

HARTY, WILLIAM 1859–1941
William Harty was, from 1878 to 1918, organist at St Malachy's Church Belfast. He was a composer and conductor and he was the father of Hamilton Harty.

HARVEY, CHARLES W. 1895–1970
Charles Harvey was born in London. His father was a map-maker with the Ordnance Survey, and his family moved to Belfast in 1906, and lived on the Antrim Road. Charles studied at the Belfast School of Art and won a gold medal in the National Competition for Design. For a short time in 1914 he attended the Metropolitan School of Art, Dublin. He trained as a damask designer and was also knowledgeable about antique furniture. From 1932 to 1960 he taught in St Mary's Training College, Belfast, and retired as head of the art department. He often exhibited in the Ulster Arts Club. His landscape painting was generally of Ireland: Connemara, Donegal and County Down. In the 1930s he went to paint in Brittany. In 1976, a retrospective exhibition was held at the Arts Council Gallery.

HASTINGS, FRANCIS RAWDON- 1754–1826
Francis Rawdon-Hastings was educated at Harrow and University College, Oxford. In 1775 he distinguished himself at Bunker's Hill and a year later fought in the Battles of Brooklyn and White Plains. In 1778 he was Adjutant-General to the forces in America and two years later fought at Camden. In 1781 he defeated Greene at Hobkirk's Hill, and was captured by the French on his voyage home. In 1783 he was created Baron Rawdon, and in 1790 assumed the additional name of Hastings. Three years later he succeeded as Irish Earl of Moira. The same year he commanded an expedition to Brittany, and a year later brought reinforcements for the Duke of York in Flanders. In 1799 he spoke against Irish Union. In 1803 he became a general and Commander-in-Chief in Scotland. From 1806 to 1807 he was Master of the Ordnance, and from 1813 to 1822 served as Governor-General of Bengal. In 1817 he was created Marquis of Hastings and estab-

lished British supremacy in central India. He died at sea in Baia Bay. A summary of his Indian administration was published in 1824. His statue is at the Dalhousie Institute, Calcutta.

HAWKSETT, SAMUEL 1776–1851
Samuel Hawksett was the principal portrait painter of his time in Belfast. He painted portraits of, among others, Robert Langtry, Thomas Mulholland and the Marchioness of Donegall. He exhibited portraits in the Royal Hibernian Academy, Dublin, from 1826 to 1834. He was commissioned by the Royal Belfast Academical Institution to paint a portrait of King William IV. He was first Treasurer of the Belfast Association of Artists.

HAYES, EDMUND 1804–1867
Edmund Hayes was born in County Down, and was educated at Trinity College, Dublin. He was called to the Bar in 1827 and attained a Doctorate in Laws by 1832. Twenty years later he was made Queen's Counsel and became law adviser to Dublin Castle. He was raised to the Bench in 1859. He is the author of several legal works.

HAYWARD, RICHARD 1898–1964
Richard Hayward was born in Belfast and began his career as a dramatist there. He specialised in works in dialect and became an expert on Ulster dialect. He published a travel series on Ireland in four volumes *This is Ireland: Leinster* (1949); *Ulster* (1950); *Connacht* (1952) and *Mayo, Sligo, Leitrim and Roscommon* (1955). He also wrote *The Story of the Irish Harp*.

HEAD, RICHARD c.1637–c.1686
Richard Head is thought to have been born in Carrickfergus, County Antrim, and educated at Oxford University. He is author of *The English Rogue, The Canting Academy, Life of Mother Shipton* and *The Humours of Dublin*. He was for a time a bookseller in London. He died in a drowning accident.

HEALY, CAHIR 1877–1970
Cahir Healy was born in Mountcharles, County Donegal, but at an early age moved to Enniskillen, County Fermanagh. He

worked as a journalist with the *Fermanagh News*. He joined Sinn Féin in 1905 and in May 1922 was arrested and interned in Belfast Lough on board the prison ship *Argenta*. He was later moved to Larne workhouse and published articles about the appalling conditions there in the *Sunday Express*. The Westminster constituency of Fermanagh and Tyrone elected him Sinn Féin member of parliament in 1922, but he was not released to take up his office until 1924. In 1925 he was elected Nationalist member of parliament at Stormont for Fermanagh, and he held the seat for forty years. From 1950 to 1955 he again became a member of the Westminster parliament. Cahir Healy was a prolific writer and had many of his articles and letters published in newspapers. He produced a volume of poems, *The Lane of the Thrushes*, with Cathal O'Byrne, and also a novel and a children's story.

HEARN, WILLIAM EDWARD 1826–1888
William Hearn was born in Belturbet, County Cavan, and educated at Trinity College, Dublin. He was Professor of Greek at Queen's College, Galway from 1849 to 1854, and Professor of History and Literature at Melbourne University from 1854 to 1872. He became Dean of that university and a member of the Legislative Council of Victoria. He published many works and died in Melbourne in 1888.

HEFFERNAN, JAMES 1785–1845
James Heffernan was born in Derry. He went to Cork, and became a sculptor. The monument of Bishop Florence MacCarthy in the South Chapel, Cork and the monument to Bishop Bennet in the Protestant cathedral, Cloyne, are examples of his work.

HEMPHILL, CHARLES HARE 1822–1908
Charles Hemphill was born in Cashel, County Tipperary, and was educated at Trinity College, Dublin. Having been called to the Bar and made a Queen's Counsel he served as a county court judge from 1863 to 1877. In 1895 he was elected member of parliament for North Tyrone after having served as Solicitor-General for the three previous years. He was created a peer in 1906, and he died in Dublin.

HEMPSON, DENIS see O'HEMPSEY, DENIS

HENDERSON, HENRY 1820–1879
Henry Henderson was born in Belfast and installed as a Presbyterian minister in Holywood in 1844. From 1869 to 1878 he was a contributor on current affairs to the *Belfast Weekly News*, where he used the pseudonym 'Ulster Scot'. He also published sermons. Among his works are *The True Heir of Ballymore* (1859) and *The Dark Monk of Feola* (1859).

HENDERSON, JAMES 1848–1914
James Henderson was born in Belfast and was educated at Trinity College, Dublin. He was called to the Bar in 1872 and was editor of the *Newry Telegraph* for ten years from 1873. From 1883 to 1914 he was managing proprietor of the *Belfast Weekly News* and the *Belfast News-Letter*. In 1898 he was appointed the first Lord Mayor of Greater Belfast, and in 1900 was the first High Sheriff of Belfast.

HENRY, AUGUSTINE 1857–1930
Augustine Henry was probably born in Cookstown, County Tyrone and was educated at Cookstown Academy and in Galway and Belfast, graduating in medicine in 1879. Having acquired a working knowledge of the Chinese language while employed in the imperial Chinese customs service, he travelled into the interior of the country to collect plants and seeds unknown in Europe. A thousand plants, regarded as constituting one of the most important collections to come out of inland China, were sent to Kew Gardens. In the journal of the Chinese Royal Asiatic Society he published a list of Chinese plants, and in 1888 was elected a Fellow of the Linnean Society of London. He was the first to publish an account of the flora of Formosa (Taiwan), and while he was there he studied law and became a member of the Middle Temple. He compiled a dictionary of the Lolos language, the language of a minority people in south-west China whose existence had been unknown to Europeans. He returned to Europe in 1900 and studied at the National School of For-

estry in France and began his collaboration with H. G. Elwes on *The Trees of Great Britain and Ireland* in seven volumes. He was appointed Reader in Forestry at Cambridge in 1908, and developed the university's School of Forestry. He was later appointed Professor of Forestry at the College of Science in Dublin. He was a member of the forestry institutions of many countries, and of the Royal Horticultural Society. In 1908 Cambridge University awarded him an honorary Master of Arts degree. He published *Forests, Woods and Trees in Relation to Hygene* in 1919. His collection of trees and plants were bequeathed to the National Botanical Gardens and a catalogue, *The Augustine Henry Forestry Herbarium at the National Botanic Gardens Glasnevin, a Catalogue of the Specimens*, was published in Dublin in 1957. He died in Dublin.

HENRY, DENIS STANISLAUS 1864–1925
Denis Henry was born in Draperstown, County Londonderry, and was educated at Dundalk, Chesterfield and Queen's College, Belfast. He was called to the Bar in 1885 and became a Queen's Counsel in 1896. He became Unionist member of parliament for South Londonderry in 1916. In 1918 he was appointed Solicitor-General, and in 1919 Attorney-General and a Privy Councillor. In 1921 he became first Lord Chief Justice of Northern Ireland and was created a baronet in 1922.

HENRY, PAUL 1877–1958
Paul Henry was born in Belfast, and was educated at the Royal Belfast Academical Institution, where he met Robert Lynd. He was an apprentice designer with the Broadway Damask Company in Belfast before entering the Belfast School of Art. He studied at the Académie Julian in Paris and in Whistler's studio. When he moved to London, he shared rooms with Robert Lynd for eleven years until 1912. He contributed illustrations to magazines such as *The Graphic, The Lady* and *Black and White*. He visited Achill, County Mayo, for a holiday and stayed for seven years. Instead of using charcoal, he began to use oils for his West of Ireland pictures, those for which he is best known. He held many exhibitions

when he moved to Dublin in 1920 and was elected to the Royal Hibernian Academy in 1929. He was a founder member of the Dublin Painters. He designed posters for the Irish Tourist Board and the London, Midland & Scottish Railway. His biography, *An Irish Portrait*, was published in 1951. He exhibited in London, Paris, Belfast, Brussels, Boston, New York and Toronto. From 1920 onwards, he had red/green colour blindness, and he lost his sight in 1945. He died in Enniskerry, County Wicklow. He is represented in all the principal Irish collections, and in the Victoria and Albert Museum, London.

HENRY, ROBERT MITCHEL 1873–1950
Robert Henry was born in Belfast. He was educated at the Royal University, Dublin, and London University in 1895. For thirty years he was Professor of Latin at Queen's University, Belfast, and in 1938 became Pro-Vice-Chancellor. In 1939 St Andrew's University appointed him Professor of Humanities. He was a member of the Royal Irish Academy, and in 1920 he was appointed President of the Classical Association of Ireland. Among his publications are *The Evolution of Sinn Féin* and editions of Livy, Cicero, Virgil and a study of the Roman epic.

HENRY, SAMUEL d. 1952
Sam Henry was a customs man, a pension officer, a traditional fiddle player, and a popular lecturer. He wrote extensively for the local papers, and went into the countryside to collect the songs he printed in his series of ballads and songs which, from 1923 until 1939, appeared in the *Northern Constitution*, Coleraine. These songs were collected into *Songs of the People*. He presented a manuscript to the Belfast Free Library, to the National Library of Ireland in Dublin, and to the Library of Congress in Washington. It remained unpublished. Sam Hanna Bell, when he was producer with the BBC in Belfast, commissioned Sean O'Boyle to examine the Sam Henry collection, and to prepare an index to be used by the BBC. John Moulden published in 1979, *Songs of the People: selections from the Sam Henry Collection*, Volume I, but it was not until 1990 that

the collection was finally published in entirety by the University of Georgia Press. It is the largest single collection of songs from Ulster between the world wars.

HENTY, GEORGE ALFRED 1832–1902
G. A. Henty was born in Cambridgeshire. As Purveyor to the Forces he spent some time in Belfast. He published more than eighty-six books for boys, which cover almost all countries and every period in history. Among his works are *Friends Though Divided* (1883); *In the Irish Brigade* (1901) and *Orange and Green* (1907).

HERBISON, DAVID 1800–1880
David Herbison was born in Ballymena, County Antrim. He went blind when he was three years old, but four years later regained the sight of his left eye. After helping on his father's farm, at the age of fourteen, he was apprenticed to hand-loom weaving. In 1827 he emigrated to Canada but on being shipwrecked in St Laurence, returned home and after a few months became a weaver. Later he was a local agent for a Belfast linen firm. He published many poems in newspapers in Belfast, Dublin and London, written in Ulster Scots, using some dialect words. He published three volumes of poems, *Midnight Musings; or Thoughts from the Loom* (1848); *Children of the Year* (1876) and *The Snow Wreath* (1869). He wrote poetry up until the time of his death, but had to adopt standard English in order to get published. A monument was erected to him in 1883.

HERON, ARCHIBALD 1894–1971
Archie Heron was born in Portadown, County Armagh, and was educated locally. In 1912 he went to Dublin as an organiser with the Irish Republican Brotherhood. He was one of the first organisers of the Irish Transport and General Workers' Union, and was in close association with James Connolly. He was briefly Labour member of the Dáil for Dublin North-West from 1937 to 1938. He served as General Secretary of the Local Government Officers' Union. He worked as Labour Relations Officer in various departments of local government. He died in Dublin.

HERON, HILARY 1923–1977
Hilary Heron was born in Dublin and spent her childhood in New Ross, County Wexford, and Coleraine, County Londonderry. She was educated at a single-teacher school and the National College of Art, Dublin, where she won three Taylor Prizes. For sculpture in wood, limestone and marble she was awarded the first Mainie Jellett Memorial Travelling Scholarship in 1947. In the same year, she went to Italy and France to study Romanesque carving. She was instrumental in founding the Irish Exhibition of Living Art, and first exhibited there in 1943. With Louis Le Brocquy, she represented Ireland at the Venice Biennale in 1956. In 1950 and 1953 she held one-woman shows in Dublin. In the 1950s she began to work in metal. She travelled in Asia, America and Europe, and her works are in many countries in both private and public collections.

HERON, MATILDA 1830–1877
Matilda Heron was born in County Londonderry and was an actress.

HERRON, THOMAS 1949–1979
Tommy Herron was born in Newcastle, County Down. He was a motor cycle racer and when he was twenty-one years old he won the North-West 200. He raced in Europe at most of the Grand Prix and international events in the 1970s. He won the 1976 Senior and 250cc races and the 1978 Senior T.T. race in the Isle of Man. In 1978 he set the then fastest ever lap of a road race circuit with 127.63 miles per hour. He joined the Suzuki team in 1979 but was killed in an accident in the North-West 200 the same year.

HERVEY, FREDERICK AUGUSTUS 1730–1803
Frederick Hervey was born in Surrey and his christening took place in the distinguished presence of the Duchess of Marlborough, the Duke of Richmond and the Prince of Wales. He was educated at Winchester, Westminster School and Corpus Christi College, Cambridge, and became a chaplain to the Lord Lieutenant of Ireland, who was his brother. In 1767

he was appointed Bishop of Cloyne and in the following year was translated to Derry. He built houses at Downhill and Ballyscullion, County Londonderry, in which he stored his vast art collection. He was in favour of Catholic Emancipation and was renowned for his support of the Volunteer movement, which was uncommon for an English aristocrat (in 1779 he succeeded as 4th Earl of Bristol). He provided the money which built the spire of Derry Cathedral and was made a freeman of Derry and Dublin. He is remembered as a colourful and unorthodox cleric. The end of his life was spent in Italy, and he is buried at Bury St Edmunds, Suffolk, where the inhabitants of Derry erected an obelisk to his memory.

HEWITT, JOHN HAROLD 1907–1987
John Hewitt was born in Belfast and was educated at Methodist College and Queen's University, Belfast. He was Keeper of Art at the Ulster Museum, Belfast, from 1930 to 1957, and was Director of the Herbert Art Gallery and Museum, Coventry, from 1957 to 1972. He returned to Belfast on his retirement. He was a director of the Lyric Theatre and poetry editor of *Threshold*. For a period he was writer-in-residence at Queen's University, Belfast, and he was a member of the Irish Academy of Letters. He published many volumes of poetry, including *No Rebel Word*; *Collected Poems 1932–1967*; *Out of My Time* and *Time Enough*, which won a Poetry Book Society award. He also published *The Rain Dance*, *The Selected John Hewitt* and *Mosaic*. His books of art criticism include *Art in Ulster 1* and a monograph on Colin Middleton. He edited the *Rhyming Weavers and other Country Poets of Antrim and Down* as well as the poems of William Allingham. Seamus Heaney said of him that he was 'the discoverer of the nugget of harmony in the language and ourselves', and Michael Longley's tribute maintains that 'John Hewitt the poet made himself heard in a land of bellowers without raising his voice. He held out the creative hand rather than the clenched fist'. *The Collected Poems of John Hewitt*, edited by Frank Ormsby and published by the Blackstaff Press in Belfast in November 1991, were given special commendation by the Poetry Book Society.

HEZLET, CHARLES OWEN 1891–1965
Charles Hezlet was a major in the army and an amateur international golfer. He played for the Royal Portrush Golf Club. In 1920 he won the Irish Close title and in 1926 and 1929 he won the Irish Open Amateur title. He played thirteen international matches for Ireland between 1923 and 1931 and was Ireland's first player to win Walker Cup honours. In 1927 he also played for Ireland against South Africa and in 1952 captained a British team to Africa. He was Irish team captain ten times before 1932 and six times after 1948. From 1947 to 1953 he was a selector for Ireland. He is the brother of Mary, Florence and Violet.

HEZLET, MARY LINZEE (MAY) 1882–1969
May Hezlet was born in Gibraltar, and played golf for the Royal Portrush Golf Club. She was an amateur international golfer and won three British Ladies' Open Amateur Championships in 1899, 1902 and 1907. She won the Irish Championship five times. In the 1905 British Ladies' team she played with her two sisters, Florence and Violet.

HIGGINS, FRANCIS 1746–1802
Francis Higgins was born in Downpatrick, County Down, and became an attorney's clerk in Dublin. He married, leading his wife to believe that he was a country gentleman, for which offence he was imprisoned and became known as 'the Sham Squire'. He was the owner of gaming houses. He bought the *Freeman's Journal* and in its pages frequently denounced opponents of the government, in particular the United Irishmen. He was rewarded £1,000 for revealing the hiding place of Lord Edward FitzGerald in 1798. He died in Dublin. [Biography, *The Sham Squire* by W. J. Fitzpatrick]

HIGGINS, HENRY BOURNES 1851–1929
Henry Higgins was born in Newtownards, County Down, and was educated at Newry and Dublin. Before he went to Australia he was in business in Belfast. From 1871 to

1875 he studied at Melbourne University and was called to the Bar in 1876 and the Inner Temple in 1886. He served as member of parliament for North Melbourne from 1901 to 1906 and during that period was appointed Attorney-General for the Commonwealth. From 1907 to 1921 he was President of the Court of Conciliation and Arbitration. He died in Melbourne and bequeathed a legacy of £25,000 to the Royal Irish Academy. [Memoir by N. Palmer, 1931]

HIGGINS, JOHN PATRICK BASIL (EOIN) 1927–1993

Eoin Higgins was born in Magherafelt, County Londonderry. He was educted at St Columb's College, the Christian Brothers' School, Derry and at Queen's University, Belfast. In 1948 he was called to the Bar and in 1967 became Queen's Counsel, having served in the county courts of Armagh, Fermanagh and Antrim. In 1982 he became Recorder of Belfast. He became a judge of the High Court of Northern Ireland in 1984, and was in charge of the Family Division. He was the target of several assassination attempts, and his home was attacked in 1987. As a Puisne Judge, he had heard a number of controversial appeals, such as those of the UDR Four, and the Supergrasses Case. He first came into prominence at the Bar with the Scarman Tribunal, which inquired into the causes of the riots in 1969. He was President of the Welfare Society of St Vincent de Paul, and was governor of St Joseph's College, Belfast and the Dominican Convent in Portstewart. He was knighted in 1988 and he served from 1989 to 1993 as Deputy Chairman of the Boundary Commission for Northern Ireland.

HILL, GEORGE 1810–1900

George Hill was born in Moyarget, near Ballycastle, County Antrim. He was educated in Belfast and ordained in Ballymoney and in 1837 was minister of a parish in Crumlin. From 1850 to 1880 he was Librarian of Queen's College, Belfast. His verse appeared in various periodicals, including the *Nation*. He published *The Stewarts of Ballintoy*, 1865; *The Montgomery Manuscripts*; *The Mac Donnells of Antrim*, 1873 and *The Plantation in Ulster*, 1877. He retired to Ramoan, County Antrim.

HILL, GEORGE FITZGERALD 1763–1839

George Hill was born in Derry and was educated at Trinity College, Dublin. He became member of parliament for Derry and later Lord of the Treasury and a Privy Councillor. In 1798, he betrayed Wolfe Tone, whom he recognised from their time at Trinity College. He was Governor of St Vincent's and Trinidad, where he died.

HILL, ROWLEY 1836–1887

Rowley Hill was born in Derry and was educated in London and at Cambridge University. He was ordained in 1860 and worked in London and in Sheffield. In 1877 he was appointed Bishop of Sodor and Man. He died in London.

HILL, WILLS 1718–1793

Wills Hill succeeded his father as Lord-Lieutenant of County Down and was appointed to the Irish Privy Council in 1746. During the early years of George III's reign, he held many ministerial posts. From 1763 to 1765 and in 1768 he was President of the Board of Trade, and in 1768 he became the first Secretary of State for the Colonies, though he was forced to resign after four years, for mishandling the American colonists. In 1751 he was created Earl of Hillsborough in the Irish peerage and five years later entered the House of Lords at Westminster as Baron Harwich. In 1772 he was recognised as Earl of Hillsborough and Viscount Kilwarlin in the British peerage, and finally became Marquis of Downshire in 1789. He was responsible for rebuilding the mansion in Hillsborough, County Down, (now Government House) the parish church, and many houses in the village.

HILLHOUSE, JAMES A. 1789–1841

James Hillhouse's family had emigrated to America from Ballykelly, County Londonderry, in 1720. James was considered an American poet of eminence.

HINCKS, EDWARD 1792–1866

Edward Hincks was born in Cork, and was educated at Trinity College, Dublin, where he became a fellow in 1813. In 1819 he was appointed Rector of Ardtrea, County Armagh, and in 1826 moved to the parish of Killyleagh, County Down where he remained until his death. He was an oriental scholar and published a Hebrew grammar, but it was in the field of Egyptian and Assyrian translation that he excelled. His contribution to the deciphering of cuneiform writing was extremely valuable, and he discovered the Persian cuneiform vowel system at the same time as Rawlinson discovered it in Baghdad. Many of his papers were published in the *Transactions of the Royal Irish Academy*. In 1854 he published a *Report to the Trustees of the British Museum respecting certain Cylinders and Terracotta Tablets with Cuneiform Inscriptions* and a *Letter on the Polyphony of the Assyrio-Babylonian Cuneiform Writing* in 1863. There is a bust of him in the entrance to Cairo Museum as one of the pioneers of Egyptology.

HINCKS, FRANCIS 19th century
Francis Hincks was educated in Belfast and apprenticed to a firm of shipowners. He emigrated to Canada, where he entered politics and eventually became Prime Minister in 1851. He was knighted and was later appointed Governor of Barbados.

HINCKS, THOMAS DIX 1767–1857
Thomas Hincks was born in Dublin, was educated at the Crumlin Academy, Trinity College, Dublin, and London, and was ordained a Presbyterian minister in Cork. He was a member of the Royal Irish Academy and after teaching in the Cork Institution, which he founded, taught in Fermoy, County Cork. In 1821 he was appointed classics master at the Belfast Academical Institution, where in 1822 he was appointed Professor of Oriental Languages. He gained a Doctorate in Laws from Glasgow in 1834 and, as well as writing many educational works, edited the *Munster Agricultural Magazine* in Cork. He was father of Edward and Francis Hincks. He died in Belfast.

HIND (or HINE), GERTRUDE ELIZABETH HERON (pseud. SHANE, ELIZABETH) 1877–1951
Gertrude Hind was born in Glassdrummond, Annalong, County Down. She

was a poet, musician and dramatist, and one of her plays, *The Warming Pan*, a comedy, was performed in Belfast in 1933. She lived in Carrickfergus, County Antrim, for a time and sailed her boat on Belfast Lough. She was first violinist in the Belfast Philharmonic Orchestra, and judged original poems by young people at Larne Music Festival. She published three volumes of poems, *Tales of the Donegal Coast and Islands*; *By Bog and Sea in Donegal* and *Piper's Tunes and Later poems*. Some of her poems were set to music.

HOBART, HENRY 1858–1938
Henry Hobart was born at Lagan Lodge, Dromore, County Down. He was educated at the Royal Belfast Academical Institution and was then articled to William Lynn to train as an architect. In 1890 he began to design buildings, and four years later went into partnership with Samuel Heron. In 1905 the firm moved to Belfast. He designed buildings all over Ulster, such as Gardenmore Presbyterian Church, County Antrim, Mill Street, Tandragee, County Armagh, the Ulster Bank, Irvinestown, County Fermanagh, and the Technical School, Magherafelt, County Londonderry. In Dromore, he designed Holm Terrace on the Lurgan Road, the Gate Lodge at the Cowan Heron Hospital, and the parochial house.

HOBHOUSE, VIOLET (née McNEILL) 1864–1902
Violet Hobhouse was born in County Antrim and was extremely interested in Irish folklore and culture. She was a fluent speaker of Irish, and a keen Unionist, and she toured England, where she spoke publicly against Home Rule. She published poetry and novels, among which were *An Unknown Quantity* (1898) and *Warp and Weft* (1899).

HOBSON, BULMER 1883–1969
Bulmer Hobson was born in Holywood, County Down, and being a Quaker was educated at Friends' School, Lisburn. He was an ardent admirer of Wolfe Tone and was to publish *The Life of Wolfe Tone* in 1919.

He worked in the printing business in Belfast and began a club for boys which evolved into the Protestant National Society and was used to recruit young Protestants into the Nationalist Movement. He was secretary of the first Antrim County Board of the Gaelic Athletic Association but resigned and established Na Fianna Éireann. Constance Markievicz and he in 1909 expanded this club to a national scout organisation. The Ulster Literary Theatre had Hobson as one of its founding members, and he wrote a poetic drama, *Brian of Banba*. He was dissatisfied with Cumann na nGaedheal and began a club for which he wrote *To the Whole People of Ireland: The Manifesto of the Dungannon Club* in 1905. His weekly newspaper, the *Republic*, merged with the *Peasant* after six months. He was invited to America to introduce the Sinn Féin movement, and when he returned to Ireland Hobson amalgamated the Dungannon Clubs and Cumann na nGaedheal. He became Vice-President of Sinn Féin. He collaborated with F. J. Bigger and produced *William Orr*, which was one of a projected series of studies of prominent northern United Irishmen. In 1909 he published *Defence of Warfare: A Handbook for Irish Nationalists*. Because of policy disagreements in 1910, he left Sinn Féin and devoted his time to the Irish Republican Brotherhood, for whom he started a newspaper, *Irish Freedom*. Bulmer Hobson was a founder member of the Irish Volunteers, and he published *A Short History of the Irish Volunteers*. He resigned in 1914 from the Supreme Council of the Irish Republican Brotherhood because of opposition from militant members. In 1916 he opposed the Easter Rising and his own Irish Republican Brotherhood colleagues arrested him and released him only when the rising had started. He withdrew from the revolutionary movement after the Rising and became involved in the Dublin Gate Theatre, in afforestation projects, and in writing of a non-political nature. When the Free State was established in 1922 he was appointed chief of the Revenue Commissioners' Stamp Department in Dublin Castle. Among his later writings are *A National Forests Policy* and *Ireland Yesterday and Tomorrow*.

HOBSON, FLORENCE b.1881
Florence Hobson was born in Monasterevan, County Kildare. She had her mind set on becoming an architect, but at the turn of the century there were no women with architects' professional qualifications in Ireland, Wales or Scotland, though two women had been articled in England. Florence Hobson went to London where her proposal to become an architect met with 'if you were a little less good looking, you'd have a better chance'. She was eventually accepted by James Phillips, the leading Methodist Church architect. By 1893 she had passed two qualifying examinations held under the Royal Institute of British Architects. In 1905 she was appointed to assist the Royal Commission on the City of Belfast's Health and Housing, and spent the next fifteen years making a thorough report. She travelled to Germany and Switzerland to ascertain how these countries dealt with similar problems. She was a member of the Belfast Naturalists' Field Club and delivered a lecture on town planning at the library in Royal Avenue in 1913. She was Bulmer Hobson's sister and Ireland's first woman architect.

HODGES, JOHN FREDERICK 1815–1899
John Hodges was born in Downpatrick, County Down, and was educated in Dublin, Glasgow and finally in Giessen University where he studied chemistry. In Downpatrick he founded the Mechanics' Institute in 1847. He became Professor of Chemistry in the Royal Belfast Academical Institution and Professor of Agricultural Chemistry and Lecturer in Medical Jurisprudence in Queen's College, Belfast. He was Chemical Director of the Chemico-Agricultural Society of Ulster, whose journal he edited. He was one of the founders of the Royal College of Chemistry in London and was employed by the government as an analyst. He had honours conferred on him by Russia, Stockholm, Turin, Germany, France and Amsterdam.

HOGG, DAVID JAMES 1870–1939
James Hogg was born in Tullywest, near Ballynahinch, County Down. He lived in

Belfast and was a joiner by trade. In 1905 he became a member of the Ulster Amateur Photographic Society, and won prizes for his photographs. Subsequently he became a professional photographer. All that has survived of his work is an album of photographs taken in 1909, all of which relate to the temperance issue. He was one of the leading photgraphers in Belfast.

HOGG, JAMES WEIR 1790–1876

James Hogg was born in County Antrim, and was educated at Trinity College, Dublin. He was called to the Bar and practised in Calcutta, and was subsequently Registrar of the Supreme Court and a director of the East India Company. From 1835 to 1857 he was member of parliament for Beverley and Honiton. In 1846 he was created a baron and in 1872 a Privy Councillor.

HOLDEN, JOHN SINCLAIR 1837–1923

John Sinclair Holden studied medicine at Queen's College, Belfast. He had a medical practice at Glenarm, County Antrim. As a founder member of the Belfast Naturalists' Field Club he took many photographs between 1867 and 1870, showing the antiquities, harbours and geology of the east Antrim coast. He went to live in Sudburn in southern England, where he remained for the rest of his life.

HOLMES, HUGH 1840–1919

Hugh Holmes was born in Dungannon, County Tyrone, and was educated there and at Trinity College, Dublin. In 1865 he was called to the Bar and was appointed Queen's Counsel in 1877. He served as Solicitor-General from 1878 to 1880 and Attorney-General from 1885 to 1886. He was member of parliament for Queen's College from 1885 to 1887, in which year he became a judge. In 1897 he was appointed Lord Justice of Appeal. His autobiography is in manuscript.

HOLLAND, MARGARET 1872–1950

Margaret Holland was born in Belfast. Her great wish was to become a doctor, and though her father did not object to education for women – providing they did not take jobs away from men – the era dictated that she 'learned domestic arts and waited for a good husband'. At the age of twenty she accompanied her mother to the Canary Islands, where she kept a journal. She was actively involved in the temperance movement, the Working Men's Sunday School attached to Rosemary Street Presbyterian Church, and charitable work such as food distribution in East Belfast, especially during the depression in the 1920s. She was a member of the Belfast Field Club and of the Presbyterian Women's Missionary Association, and a year after her mother's death in 1921 she embarked for India on a visit to the Presbyterian Zenana Mission. The mission provided medical and educational welfare for Indian women and orphaned children and trained Indian women in the medical profession. Her book *My Winter of Content* follows her journey across northern India and is illustrated by her own photographs and Frank McKelvey's paintings.

HOLLAND, NAN late 19th, early 20th century

Nan Holland was born and educated in Ulster and around 1910 moved to Dublin where she was a student at the Dublin School of Art. Her painted enamel plaque, 'Blue Bird', was exhibited at the Arts and Crafts Society in 1917, though for the rest of her life she concentrated on making fine jewellery.

HOLYWOOD, JOHN d.1250

John Holywood was probably born in Holywood, County Down, at the end of the twelfth century. He was a mathematician and author of *Tractatus de Sphaera*, which was printed in Ferrara in 1472, and *Algorisms*, which was edited by Halliwell-Phillips in 1838. John Holywood was known as Sacro Bosco. He died in Paris.

HOMES, WILLIAM 1663–1746

William Homes was born in the north of Ireland and went to New England, where he was a school teacher for three years. When he returned to Ireland in 1692 he was ordained a Presbyterian minister at Strabane, County Tyrone. In 1714 he once again went to New England and had a parish in Chilmark. He published his sermons, *Sabbath*; *Secret Prayer* and *Church Government*.

HONNER, MARIA (née McCARTHY) 1812–1870

Maria McCarthy was born in Enniskillen, County Fermanagh. She married Robert Honner who was manager of the Surrey Theatre. She was an actress and performed with Edmund Keane.

HOOD, JOHN 1720–1772

John Hood was born in Moyle, County Donegal. He was a surveyor and inventor, and he invented a surveying instrument known as Hood's Compass Theodolite. He published *Treatise on Land Surveying* in 1772.

HOOKE, RICHARD 1822–1887

Richard Hooke was born in County Down, and was a carpenter. He showed a gift for painting, and this was encouraged by Samuel Ferguson, manager of the Sion flax-spinning mills. Ferguson taught him photography, which Richard Hooke used in his portrait painting. He moved to Belfast, and painted the portraits of many people, including those of Samuel McCausland and John Browne. He exhibited at the Royal Hibernian Academy from 1850 to 1856, and from 1873 until his death. He painted a portrait of the Marquis of Downshire, his patron, and this was exhibited at the Royal Academy in 1872.

HOPE, JAMES (JEMMY) 1764–1846

Jemmy Hope was born in Templepatrick, County Antrim. He worked as a labourer, and was taught to read and write by the various farmers who employed him. He was a weaver from the age of ten, then a journeyman, and continued his education at night classes. In 1795 he joined the Society of United Irishmen. In 1796 he went to Dublin to enlist members for the society and during this period he worked as a cotton weaver. He was the friend of McCracken, Russell and Emmet. He led the 'Spartan Band' in the Battle of Antrim in 1798 and after its defeat fled to Dublin. In 1806 he returned to Belfast and resumed work as a linen weaver after the political amnesty. He wrote poetry and his memoirs were published. [Biography by Denis Smyth]

HORNER, JOHN 1858–1919

John Horner was born in Belfast. He became an engineer and an industrialist, but was also a linguist, a scientist and a botanist, accumulating a rich collection of books, art and scientific specimens. He helped initiate the University Extension Lectures, which brought international scientists to Belfast, and in 1895 he was one of the main organisers of the Industrial Exhibition. He was a member of the Belfast Natural History and Philosophical Society and acted as its treasurer and secretary. He is best known as the author of *The Linen Trade of Europe during the Spinning-Wheel Period* (1920). His unique collection of spinning wheels was bequeathed to the Ulster Museum.

HOUSTON, JOHN 1802–1845

John Houston was born in Ulster, and was educated in Dublin and Edinburgh, where he became a doctor in 1826. He was Curator of the Royal College of Surgeons in Ireland, where he compiled a catalogue. He lectured on surgery and was a physician in the City of Dublin Hospital and contributed to many medical journals.

HOUSTON, MARGARET J. (née SINCLAIR) d.1895

Maggie Houston was born at Moneymore, County Londonderry and lived at Portglenone, County Antrim. She wrote novels in which she used Donegal and Palestine as her scenarios. Among her titles is *A Bunch of Shamrocks*, 1888.

HOUSTON, MARY GALWAY b. 1871

Mary Houston came from Coleraine, County Londonderry and in 1890 went to study at the Dublin Metropolitan School of Art. In 1894 and 1895 she exhibited lace and crochet at the Royal Dublin Society and black and white drawings at the Arts and Crafts Society of Ireland. The following year she won prizes for leather-work and repoussé metal-work. In 1896 she moved to London to study at South

Kensington where she became successful. She began to exhibit with the English Arts and Crafts Society, and won a gold medal for a modelled leather book cover. In 1901 she exhibited with the Royal Academy. Her book bindings, including the *Rubiayat* of Omar Kayam were very popular and she embossed and modelled leather panels. She was also a fine metal-worker, working in silver, copper and pure tin and in 1900, her toilet set in beaten silver was sent to the Paris exhibition as an example of work from British Art Schools. She often used designs inspired by Irish myth and legend. She was commissioned by the *Studio* to design two silver trophies. Although an international artist, she continued to exhibit at the Royal Dublin Society and at the Irish Decorative Art Association Exhibitions held in Portrush, County Antrim. She joined the staff of Camberwell School of Art and became interested in costume design, and wrote three books on the subject: *Ancient Egyptian, Assyrian and Persian Costumes* (with Florence Hornblower); *Medieval Costume in England and France* and *Ancient Greek, Roman and Byzantine Costume.*

HOUSTON, THOMAS 1803–1882
Thomas Houston was born in County Antrim but settled in Knockbracken, County Down. He was a Doctor of Divinity, and a Covenanting Presbyterian, and he edited the *Covenanter* and published many theological works. He was a professor at Belfast Theological Hall.

HOUSTON, THOMAS b. 1879
Thomas Houston was born in Coleraine, County Londonderry, and was educated at Coleraine Academical Institution, Queen's College, Belfast, and the Royal University of Ireland, where he graduated with a degree in medicine. He became an authority on clinical pathology and was a pioneer in bacteriological research.

HOUSTON, THOMAS GALWAY b.1843
Thomas Houston was born at Mountpottinger, Belfast, and was educated at Cookstown Academy, Royal Belfast Academical Institution and Queen's College, Belfast. He was Principal of Coleraine Academical Institution from 1870 to 1915. He was a distinguished educationalist.

HOWARD, GEORGE EDMUND 1715–1786
George Howard was born in Coleraine, County Londonderry, and was educated in Dublin. He was a solicitor , a land agent and later an architect. He supported Catholic Emancipation. Among his publications are many legal works and some plays, *Almeyda, or The Rival Kings* and *The Female Gamester. His Miscellaneous Works in Prose and Verse* was published in 1782. He was a Freeman of the City of Dublin, and he died there.

HUDDLESTON, ROBERT c.1817–1868
Robert Huddleston was born in Moneyrea, County Antrim, and became known as the bard of Moneyrea. In 1844 he published *A Collection of Poems and Songs on Rural Subjects,* (2 volumes). He used Ulster Scots dialect in his poems and in 1850 began to write a novel, *The Adventures of Hughey Funny or The Many Tales of Love,* though it was never published. He died lamenting his lack of fame.

HUGHES, FREDERICK DESMOND 1919–1992
Desmond Hughes was born in Belfast and was educated at Campbell College, Belfast, and Pembroke College, Cambridge. In 1939 he joined the Royal Air Force and fought in the Battle of Britain, rising to the rank of wing commander during the Second World War. He received numerous military decorations for his ability as a nightfighter. In 1968 he became Commander of No.18 Group, Coastal Command. From 1970 to 1972 he was appointed Commandant of the Royal Air Force College at Cranwell and from 1972 to 1974 was Deputy Commander of British Forces in Cyprus. He was awarded the CBE. He died near Lincoln.

HUGHES, HERBERT 1882–1937
Herbert Hughes was born in Belfast and became the first organist at St Peter's Church, Antrim Road, when he was still a boy. He made his first of many trips to

Donegal in 1899 to collect traditional songs. He met Pádraic Colum on one of these expeditions and Colum translated from the Irish many of the songs which Hughes collected. He studied at the Royal College of Music in London. 'The Star of the County Down', 'I Know Where I'm Going', 'The Next Market Day' and 'She Moved Through the Fair' were all songs collected and adapted by Colum and set to airs collected and arranged by Hughes. Herbert Hughes lived in England for some years and died in Brighton. His collection of folk-song arrangements is famous.

HUGHES, JOHN 1797–1864
John Hughes was born in Annaloghlan, County Tyrone, and emigrated to America in 1817. He worked as a gardener before being accepted as a student at the Emmitsburg Seminary, Maryland. He was ordained in 1826 and built St Joseph's Church in Philadelphia. He was consecrated Bishop of New York in 1842 and in 1850 became the first Archbishop of the diocese. He lectured before Congress and was thanked by President Lincoln for his support of the Union in the Civil War. He was chosen to represent America on a mission to Napoleon III. He founded a college at Fordham which is now the Jesuit University, and before his death he laid the foundation stone of St Patrick's Cathedral, Fifth Avenue, New York. [Biographies by Hassard and Braun]

HULL, EDWARD 1829–1917
Edward Hull was born in County Antrim, and was educated at Trinity College, Dublin. He joined the Geological Survey, and in his capacity as geologist worked in Ireland, Scotland and Palestine, where he met Lord Kitchener. He was secretary to the Victoria Institute and published many papers in scientific journals. His autobiography, *Reminiscences*, was published in 1910.

HULL, ELEANOR HENRIETTA 1860–1935
Eleanor Hull was born in England of a County Down family and was educated at Alexandra College, Dublin. She was a student of Irish Studies under Kuno Meyer and Standish Hayes O'Grady. She was a journalist and scholar of Old Irish and in 1899 was co-founder of the Irish Texts Society for the publication of early manuscripts, remaining its honorary secretary for nearly thirty years. Her published works include *The Cuchulain Saga in Irish Literature* (1898); *Pagan Ireland; Early Christian Ireland; A Textbook of Irish Literature*, in 2 volumes; *The Poem-Book of the Gael; The Northmen in Britain; Folklore of the British Isles* and *A History of Ireland* in 2 volumes. She was president of the Irish Literary Society. She died in Wimbledon.

HULL, FRED W. 1867–1953
Fred Hull was born in Drogheda, County Louth. He came to Belfast and established a business. When he was thirty years old he took up painting as a hobby, attending evening classes at the Government School of Design. In 1902 he was elected a member of the Belfast Art Society, and exhibited in the Ulster Arts Club of which he was a founder member and later president. From 1904 he exhibited in the Royal Hibernian Academy, Dublin, and in 1924 his work was on view at the British Empire exhibition, London. His favourite painting area was the Lagan Valley, and he painted many scenes of Barnett's Park and Shaw's Bridge. His work is in the Ulster Museum.

HUME, ABRAHAM 1814–1884
Abraham Hume was born near Hillsborough, County Down, and was educated in Belfast and at Trinity College, Dublin. Before he became Vicar of Vauxhall in 1847 he was a teacher in the Liverpool Institution. He explored Chile and Peru, and was a Fellow of both the Royal Society and the Society of Antiquaries. He became a Doctor of Laws and of Civil Law and was Canon of Chester Cathedral. He published over a hundred pamphlets dealing with topics such as Irish dialect and folklore, as well as several volumes dealing with antiquities. He died in Liverpool. [Biography by J. C. Morley]

HUME, ALEXANDER HAMILTON 1797–1843
Alexander Hume was born in Australia,

the son of Andrew Hamilton Hume. He became a famous explorer and is said to have made the first overland journey from Sydney to Port Phillip, discovering five rivers. He accompanied Sturt on the MacQuarie expedition.

HUME, ANDREW HAMILTON 1762–1849
Andrew Hume was born near Hillsborough, County Down. He emigrated to Australia and was known as the 'Father of New South Wales', having lived and prospered there longer than any other settler. He died there.

HUNTER, JOHN F. 1893–1951
John Hunter was born in Manchuria, where his father was an Irish Presbyterian church missionary. He was educated at Trinity College, Dublin, and the Royal College of Art. He became inspector of art for the Ministry of Education in 1923. In 1934 he completed, with W. R. Gordon, the large mural, 'The Bronze Age in Belfast', at the Ulster Museum. He was President of the Ulster Academy of Arts. He served in both world wars, and was promoted to the rank of lieutenant colonel. He was awarded the OBE. His wood engravings and landscape pictures are in the Ulster Museum and the Arts Council of Northern Ireland. He was the brother of Mercy Hunter.

HUNTER, MERCY 1910–1989
Mercy Hunter was born in Belfast. When she was four years old, she travelled on the Trans-Siberian Railway, to China, where she spent her childhood in Manchuria. She was educated in Toronto and the Belfast Royal Academy. From 1927 to 1929 she studied at the Belfast College of Art, and at the Royal College of Art, London from 1930 to 1933. Her special interest was calligraphy, and in London she met other Ulster artists including William Scott and F. E. McWilliams. She returned to Belfast in 1937 and married George McCann, the sculptor. She taught art in Dungannon High School for Girls, County Tyrone, Banbridge Academy, County Down, Armagh High School and Victoria College, Belfast, where she was head of the art department from 1947 until her retirement in 1970. As well as illuminated addresses and other calligraphic commissions, she lectured and broadcast extensively on art. She also designed costumes for the theatre, opera and ballet, and illustrated books. She was a member of the Royal Ulster Academy, and served as its president, and was founder member of the Ulster Society of Women Artists. She was awarded the MBE in 1970. Her work is in the Ulster Museum collection.

HUNTER, ROBERT c.1715–1803
Robert Hunter was born in Ulster, but worked as a portrait painter in Dublin from 1750 to 1780. The principal portrait painter in Ireland, he painted portraits of, among others, John Wesley, Lord Harcourt and Lord Naas. He helped found the Society of Artists in Dublin, and often exhibited there. Many of his portraits were engraved. Five of his paintings are in the National Gallery of Ireland.

HUTCHESON, FRANCIS 1694–1746
Francis Hutcheson was born near Saintfield, County Down, and was educated at James McAlpine's Academy, Killyleagh, County Down, and at Glasgow where he studied theology in order to become a Presbyterian minister. He opened an academy in Dublin. He published *Inquiry into the Original of Our Ideas on Beauty and Virtue*. He later published *The Passions and Affections*, and as a consequence of this became Professor of Moral Philosophy in Glasgow. One of his students was Adam Smith. He became known as 'the father of the Scottish school of philosophy'. It was not until after his death in Glasgow that his *System of Moral Philosophy*, his best-known work, appeared. He coined the phrase 'the greatest happiness of the greatest number', usually attributed to Jeremy Bentham. [Biography by W. R. Scott]

HUTTON, HENRY TOMMASCO 1874–1952
Henry Hutton spent most of his life in Donaghadee, County Down. A series of his photographs from the 1890s depict a number of subjects, including Ballynahinch, County Down, on market day. In addition to his photography, he invented

an early foot pump for pneumatic car tyres. He eventually became a full-time market gardener.

HUTTON, MARY A. (née DRUMMOND)
1862–1953

Mary Hutton was born in Manchester, and was educated at University College, London. When she was forty-nine she became a convert to Roman Catholicism. She was a Celtic scholar and in 1909 was the Margaret Stokes Memorial Lecturer and a member of the Senate of Queen's University, Belfast. Among her publications are an edition of *Táin Bó Cúailnge* (1907), which she spent ten years translating into English. To this she attached appendices which explained place-names, the names of people, tribes and animals and Gaelic terms.

HYNDMAN, GEORGE CRAWFORD
1796–1867

George Hyndman was educated at the Belfast Academy, and when he was fourteen entered his father's auctioneering business; in 1825 he inherited this business. He was a founder member of the Belfast Natural History and Philosophical Society and of the Botanical and Horticultural Association which established the Botanic Gardens. He was a keen conchologist and bequeathed his unique collection of shells to the Belfast Natural History and Philosphical Society.

I

INGLIS, CHARLES 1734–1816
Charles Inglis was born in County Donegal. He went to America, where he worked as a teacher from 1755 until 1758. He was ordained in London and returned to New York, where he became incumbent of Holy Trinity Church. He was later consecrated Bishop of Nova Scotia.

INGRAM, JOHN KELLS 1823–1907
John Ingram was born in Temple Carne, near Pettigo, County Donegal, and was educated in Newry, County Down, and Trinity College, Dublin, where he became a senior fellow. He was Professor of Oratory, Professor of Greek, Librarian and Vice-Provost of Trinity College, Dublin. He helped to found the Dublin Philosophical Society in 1842, and was published in the *Nation* in 1843, although he supported the Union. He was instrumental in founding the Dublin Statistical Society in 1847 and served as its President from 1878 to 1880. He served as President of the Royal Irish Academy from 1892 to 1896. He founded and edited *Hermathena*, a series of papers produced by members of Trinity College. Among his major works are *A History of Political Economy*, which was translated into French and Japanese; *Sonnets*; *A History of Slavery and Serfdom*; *Outlines of the History of Religion*; *Practical Morals* and *The Final Transition*. He was the author of the poem 'Who Fears to Speak of '98?'

INGRAM, THOMAS DUNBAR 1826–1901
Thomas Ingram was born in County Donegal, and was educated at Trinity College, Dublin, and Queen's College, Belfast. In 1853 he graduated in law and in 1856 was called to the Bar. From 1856 to 1867 he was Professor of Hindu Law in Calcutta. Among other works he wrote *History of the Union*.

IRELAND, DENIS 1894–1974
Denis Ireland was born in Belfast, and was educated at the Royal Belfast Academical Institution and at Queen's University, Belfast. He interrupted his degree in medicine in 1914 and joined the Royal Irish Fusiliers, serving in France and Macedonia. He was invalided home with the rank of captain. He represented the family linen business in Canada, Britain and the United States, but retired in 1930. He was a freelance writer and broadcaster for nearly forty years. He was elected to the Senate of the Irish Free State and was the first member of the Oireachtas to be resident in Northern Ireland. Among his works are *Red Brick City*; *Patriot Adventurer*, a life of Wolfe Tone; *The Age of Unreason*; *Six Counties in Search of a Nation* and *From the Irish Shore*, his autobiography. A further volume of autobiography, *Statues Round the City Hall*, was published in 1939.

IRVINE, ALEXANDER 1863–1941
Alexander Irvine was born in Pogue's Entry, Antrim. He was the ninth of twelve children. Before he emigrated to America he worked in various jobs, as a newsboy, a coal-miner and a soldier. He graduated from Yale as an ordained minister and preached for some years in New York's Fifth Avenue Church of the Ascension. It is said that he served as chief morale officer at the front in the First World War, at the personal request of Lloyd George. Among his publications are *My Lady of the Chimney Corner* which is a tribute to his mother Anna née Gilmour; *The Souls of Poor Folk* and *The Man From World's End and other stories*. He is buried in Antrim parish churchyard and the family home has been preserved.

IRVINE, JOHN 1903–1964
John Irvine was born in Belfast and published several collections of poems: *A Voice in the Dark*, (1932); *Willow Leaves: Lyrics in the Manner of the Early Chinese Poets*, (1941) and *Lost Sanctuary and other poems* among

others. He edited *The Flowering Branch: An Anthology of Irish Poetry Past and Present.*

IRVINE, WILLIAM 1741–1804

William Irvine was born in County Fermanagh, and was educated at Trinity College, Dublin. He was a surgeon in the Royal Navy during the Seven Years' War and then emigrated to America, where he had a medical practice in Carlisle, Pennsylvania. He was elected representative for Carlisle and raised and commanded the 6th Pennsylvania Regiment. As a prisoner he was exchanged in 1778. In the autumn of 1781, he was stationed as brigadier-general at Fort Pitt and made responsible for defending the northwest-frontier. He was appointed Examiner of Public Lands and was a member of Congress from 1793 to 1795. He died in Philadelphia.

IRVING, SAMUEL JOHNSTONE 1884–1969

Samuel Irving was born in Belfast and was an international soccer player. He played for Newcastle United, Galashiels United, Bristol Shields, Shildon, Dundee, Cardiff City, Chelsea and Bristol Rovers. Between 1923 and 1931 he was capped eighteen times for Northern Ireland, all in the Home international series.

IRWIN, THOMAS CAULFEILD 1823–1892

Thomas Irwin was born in Warrenpoint, County Down, and was educated privately. As a young man he travelled to Europe and North Africa. His poems, which he had published in Irish magazines such as the *Nation,* and the *Dublin University Review,* have been collected into eight volumes. Richard Dowling called him 'the Irish Keats'. He published a selection of prose sketches, *Winter and Summer Stories*; a biography of Swift; *Irish Poems and Legends* and *Songs and Romances.* He died in Rathmines, Dublin.

ITEN, HANS 1874–1930

John Iten was born in Zurich, and studied at the School of Art in St Gall, Switzerland and in Paris. He arrived in Belfast in 1904 to work as a damask designer with McCrum, Watson & Mercer, and remained for the rest of his life. He painted many pictures of Belvoir Park and of County Down and County Donegal. He was a member of the Belfast Art Society, vice-president of the Ulster Arts Club and exhibited in Paris, Glasgow and Dublin. He died in Switzerland. His portrait, by Pierre Montezin, was presented to the Ulster Museum.

J

JACKSON, RICHARD 1720–1787
Richard Jackson was born in Ballycastle, County Antrim, and was educated at Trinity College, Dublin. He was called to the Bar in 1744 and became member of parliament for Weymouth and later for New Romney. He was appointed Lord of the Treasury and was known as 'Omniscient Jackson'.

JACKSON, THOMAS 1841–1915
Thomas Jackson was born in Crossmaglen, County Armagh, and was educated privately. He was a bank clerk in Belfast and went to the Agra Bank in India in 1864 and in 1866 joined the Hong Kong and Shanghai Bank, where he became chief manager. He was knighted in 1899 and created a baronet in 1902.

JEBB, JOHN 1775–1833
John Jebb was born in Drogheda, County Louth, and was educated at Celbridge, Foyle College, Derry, and Trinity College, Dublin. From being a curate in Swanlinbar in 1799 he eventually became Bishop of Limerick in 1823. He was a pioneer of the Oxford Movement. His works include *Essays on Sacred Literature* and *Practical Theology*, and his correspondence with Alexander Knox was published posthumously. He died in London. [Biography by C. Forster]

JOCELYN, ROBERT 1788–1870
Robert Jocelyn succeeded his father as 3rd Earl of Roden. He was created a peer of the United Kingdom and in 1821 a Knight of St Patrick. He was Grand Master of the Orange Order and on the 12th of July 1849 Orangemen paraded to Roden's estate through a Catholic district, Dolly's Brae, near Castlewellan, County Down. Troops escorted the Orangemen back through the area and there was an encounter that left a number of Catholics dead. After an investigation Roden was dismissed from the magistracy.

JOHNSON, JAMES 1747–1845
James Johnson was born in Ballinderry, County Antrim, and was apprenticed to an apothecary in Portglenone, County Antrim. After a stay of two years in Belfast he went to London and entered the navy as a surgeon. He served from 1800 to 1814 and afterwards started a medical practice in Portsmouth, where he began *The Medico-Chirurgical Review*. He also edited the *British and Foreign Medical Review* from 1836 to 1844. He served as Physician-in-Ordinary to William IV. He died in Brighton. [Biography by his son 1846]

JOHNSON, MARIE b.1874
Marie Johnson married Thomas Johnson, who later became leader of the Irish Labour Party. Marie and her husband made the first attempt to organise the Belfast Mill Workers. She was Secretary of the Textile Workers' Union and worked closely with James Connolly until 1912. She was a suffragist. When Winifred Carney stood for election as a Sinn Féin candidate, Marie Johnson campaigned tirelessly on her behalf.

JOHNSON, WILLIAM 1715–1774
William Johnson was born in Waringstown, County Down, and in 1738 emigrated to America, where he engaged in trade with the Indians. It is said of him that he learned the Mohawk language and accepted their manners and dress, and was consequently adopted as one of their tribe. He was made superintendent of the six nations. In 1755 Johnson, as Commander-in-Chief, defeated the French and received a baronetcy. George II placed him in charge of the Indians in 1756. Three years later he was given supreme command of the army. The expedition of 1760 ended in the surrender of Canada to the British. For this victory he was rewarded with a huge tract of land. After the death of his first wife he married

a Mohawk woman, and they had eight children. He is remembered for his authorship of his paper on 'The Customs, Manners and Language of the Indians', published in the *Philosophical Transactions*, 1772. [Biography by W. L. Stone]

JOHNSTON, ANNA see MacMANUS, ANNA

JOHNSTON, FRANCIS *c.*1760–1829
Francis Johnston was born in Armagh, and from 1786 to 1793 he was involved as an architect in the restoration of Armagh Cathedral. He rebuilt the Irish House of Commons, and among other buildings, designed St George's Church in Dublin, parts of the Bank of Ireland, the General Post Office in O'Connell Street and the Chapel Royal in Dublin Castle. He was founder of the Royal Hibernian Academy, and at his own expense erected its building. He died in Dublin.

JOHNSTON, JOSEPH 1890–1972
Joseph Johnston was born in Castlecaulfield, County Tyrone, and was educated in Dungannon, at Trinity College, Dublin, and Lincoln College, Oxford, where he graduated in Classics and Ancient History. In 1914 he was awarded the Albert Cahn Fellowship and he spent a year studying economics in India, America, Java, China and Japan. He returned to Trinity College, Dublin, where he became a lecturer in Ancient History but later moved to Economics. From 1928 to 1929 he was the Rockefeller Fellow for Economic Research in Europe and in 1939 became Professor of Applied Economics. He served as a Senator of the Irish Free State for twelve years and sat on many government commissions. He published his first book in 1914, entitled *Civil War in Ulster*, and was a prolific writer. In 1970 he gained the degree of Doctor of Literature from Trinity College, Dublin, when he published *Berkeley's Querist in Historical Perspective*. He took on the management of several farms as a practical means of experimenting with agricultural economics.

JOHNSTON, WILLIAM 1818–1894
William Johnston was born in Ballybay,

County Monaghan, and was educated in Belfast and Edinburgh. In 1842 he was ordained a Presbyterian minister in Belfast, where he spent the rest of his life. He founded the Presbyterian Orphan Society and was a popular preacher and educationalist. [Biography by Prenter 1895]

JOHNSTON, WILLIAM 1829–1902
William Johnston was born in Ballykilbeg, County Down, and was educated at Trinity College, Dublin. He was called to the Bar, but never practised. He joined the Orange Order in 1848, and was a prominent member throughout his life. In 1853 he began the publication of tracts, novels, and a newspaper, the *Downshire Protestant*, which ran from 1855 to 1862. In 1867 he was imprisoned under the Party Processions Act for heading an Orange parade on the 12th of July, from Newtownards to Bangor. He was an independent Orange member of parliament for Belfast from 1868 to 1878, when he was appointed Inspector of Fisheries. Because of his verbal attacks on Home Rule supporters and the Land League, he was dismissed. He served as member of parliament for South Belfast from 1885 until his death. [*William Johnston of Ballykilbeg*, Aiken McClelland, 1992]

JOHNSTON, WILLIAM DENIS 1901–1984
William Johnston was born in Dublin and was educated at Dublin, Edinburgh and Christ's College, Cambridge, where he studied law and was President of the Union. He went to Harvard as a Pugsley Scholar, was called to the English Bar in 1925 and the Northern Ireland Bar in 1926. From 1931 to 1936 he was Director of the Gate Theatre. During the Second World War he was a correspondent for the BBC and was subsequently awarded the OBE for his services. Having been a BBC drama producer, he became Director of Programmes in 1946 for two years. From 1952 until 1960 he was a member of the English Department at Mount Holyoke, Massachusetts. In 1955 he was given a Guggenheim Fellowship, and in 1961 was appointed head of the Theatre Department at Smith College, Massachusetts. He was a member of the Irish Academy of Letters and a playwright.

Among his works are *The Old Lady Says No;, The Moon on the Yellow River; A Bride for the Unicorn; The Golden Cuckoo* and *The Scythe and the Sunset*. He also wrote a biography, *In Search of Swift*, and two autobiographies, *Nine Rivers from Jordan* and *The Brazen Horn*. In 1977 the Allied Irish Bank gave him their award for literature, and in 1979 the New University of Ulster bestowed on him an honorary doctorate.

JOHNSTONE, W. E., RALPH and ROBERT late 19th century
The Johnstone brothers were born in Donegal and they were all international rugby players. They represented Dublin University and Wanderers and from 1884 to 1892 won six Irish rugby caps between them. Robert was a member of the British and Irish Lions tour of South Africa in 1896. He was awarded the Victoria Cross for his bravery in the Boer War. Ralph also played cricket for Ireland.

JOHNSTON, WILLIAM JOHN 1869–1940
William Johnston was born in Belfast, and was educated at Methodist College, Belfast, and Queen's College, Belfast. In 1892 he was called to the Bar and eight years later was appointed editor of the *New Irish Jurist*. In 1906 he became editor of the *Irish Law Times*. He became a county court judge and then served as a High Court judge from 1924 to 1939. In the following year he was judge of the Supreme Court before becoming Commissioner of Charitable Donations and Bequests.

JONES, AGNES 1850–1886
Agnes Jones lived at Fahan House, County Londonderry. She was a close friend of Cecil Frances Alexander and took upon herself the task of visiting the sick of the parish. She trained as a nurse and later went to St Thomas's Hospital, London. Florence Nightingale put her in charge of a vast workhouse in Liverpool, but after three years she died of typhus. She is buried in the old churchyard at Fahan.

JONES, HENRY 1605–1682
Henry Jones was educated at Trinity College, Dublin, and was then ordained. He was living in Ballanagh Castle, County Cavan, when the rebellion began in 1641, and he surrendered the castle to the Irish forces. He and his family eventually escaped to Dublin, and in 1645 he was appointed Bishop of Clogher. In 1646 he became Vice-Chancellor of Trinity College, Dublin and gave to the college library the Book of Durrow. In 1642 Jones was asked to collect evidence of crimes committed during the rebellion, and ten years later, he was similarly employed in investigating robberies and murders alleged to have been committed in Munster and Leinster. He was translated from Clogher to Meath in 1661. At the time of the 'Popish plot' he gathered information which implicated the Archbishop of Armagh, Oliver Plunkett.

JONES, LES d. 1992
Les Jones was educated at Queen's University, Belfast. He was an athlete and represented Ulster in the 800 metres and in cross-country runs. On leaving university, he joined the Customs service. He was prominent as an administrator in Northern Ireland athletics. For a period he was Team Manager for men's and women's cross-country teams in New Zealand. He attended Seoul Olympics in 1988 as assistant coach to the British Men's Team. He became chairman of the Northern Ireland Amateur Athletic Association, and Team Manager for the British Olympic Team in Spain.

JONES, THEOPHILUS d.1685
Theophilus Jones was a soldier who fought with the English army when they attempted to crush the rebellion of 1641. Three years later he was appointed commander of the Lisburn garrison and in 1646 was taken prisoner and held for two years. From 1649 to 1659 he was Governor of Dublin. He was elected to the British parliament in 1656, and given a troop of cavalry in the puritan army, with which he fought against the Irish for three years. He was dismissed in 1659, after which point he associated with Sir Charles Coote and Lord Broghill when they took over the government of the country from the Commonwealth commissioners. In 1661 he became a privy

councillor, and from that year until 1685, was Scoutmaster-General in Ireland.

JONES, WILLIAM TODD 1755–1818
William Todd Jones was born in Lisburn, County Antrim, and was educated at Trinity College, Dublin, where he studied law. He was an active Volunteer and sat in the Dungannon Convention in 1782. He was elected member of parliament for Lisburn. He was arrested for high treason in 1803 and was imprisoned for two years. He was the author of poems and pamphlets, and he claimed that he was a descendant of Jeremy Taylor, Bishop of Down and Dromore. He died in Rostrevor, County Down.

JORDAN, JOHN NEWELL 1852–1925
John Jordan was born in Balloo, County Down, and was educated at the Royal Belfast Academical Institution and Queen's College, Belfast, where he graduated as a Master of Arts. In 1876 he went as a student interpreter to China and by 1896 had been appointed Consul-General for Korea. He was knighted in 1904. From 1906 to 1920 he was Envoy Extraordinary and Minister Plenipotentiary in Peking and in 1915 was appointed a privy councillor. For his work as a diplomat he had conferred upon him the honour of Knight Commander of the Order of the Bath. He died in London.

JOY, FRANCIS 1697–1790
Francis Joy was born in Belfast and in 1737, founded the *Belfast News-Letter* which is now the oldest newspaper in Ireland. In 1745 he gave over the newspaper to his sons and started a paper mill at Randalstown, County Antrim. He was the first paper-maker in Ulster.

JOY, HENRY 1754–1835
Henry Joy was born in Belfast and worked for his grandfather's newspaper, the *Belfast News-Letter* from 1782, becoming its editor in 1789. In 1794 he jointly published *Belfast Politics : A Collection of the Debates, Resolutions and Other Proceedings of that Town in the years 1792 and 1793*. When the rebellion of 1798 broke out, Henry Joy served in the yeomanry. He was anonymous author of *Historical Collections relative to the Town of Belfast* in 1817, which retrospectively modified a number of the moderate editorial comments of *Belfast Politics*.

K

KANE, GEORGE MacDOWELL 1890–1954
George Kane was born in Belfast and was educated at Belfast Mercantile Academy. He took up architecture as a profession and worked with the firm Blackwood & Jury. He attended the Belfast School of Art and won a Dunhill Scholarship to the Metropolitan School of Art in Dublin. He taught art for a short time at the Royal Belfast Academical Institution, but left for Edinburgh to work on the Bradstone Memorial, St Andrew Square. In 1917 he returned to Belfast, and devoted his time to portrait drawings; some of these depict actors and actresses preparing for performance. He painted a mural in the kitchen of the family house, at 8 Dunluce Avenue, Belfast. His bronze bust of John Whaley, and his drawing of Hans Iten are in the Ulster Museum.

KANE, RICHARD 1666–1736
Richard Kane was born in Duneane, County Antrim, entered the army in 1689 and was wounded at the Battle of Blenheim in 1704. From 1720 to 1725 he served as Governor of Gibraltar and of Minorca, where he died. He published *Narrative of the Campaigns in the Reigns of William the Third and Anne*, and his letters are in a collection in the British Library. He was knighted, and a monument was erected to him in Westminster Abbey.

KANE, ROBERT ROUTLEDGE 1841–1898
Robert Kane was born in Newtownstewart, County Tyrone, and became the Church of Ireland Rector of Tullylish, County Down, in 1872. He studied at Trinity College, Dublin and gained a Master of Arts degree in 1880 and a doctorate in 1882. He moved to Christ's Church, Belfast in that same year, and was renowned not only for his violent speeches against Home Rule but also for his nationalist stance which he paradoxically adopted when economic aspects of Irish politics were being debated.

KANE, WILLIAM FRANCIS DE VISMES b.1840
William Kane lived at Drumreaske House, Monaghan. He was a member of the Royal Irish Academy. He published a *Handbook of European Butterflies* and *A Catalogue of European Butterflies*.

KAVANAGH, PATRICK 1905–1967
Patrick Kavanagh was born in Mucker, Iniskeen, County Monaghan, where he grew up on a small farm. For a time he worked as a shoemaker. *Ploughman and other poems* was published in 1938, and in 1939 he moved to Dublin, where he contributed to the *Bell, Envoy* and the *Dublin Magazine*. He wrote film criticism for the *Irish Press* under the pseudonym Piers Plowman. With his brother Peter he published *Kavanagh's Weekly*. In 1957 he became a lecturer in Extra-Mural Studies at University College, Dublin. His publications include novels, *The Green Fool* (1938) and *Tarry Flynn* (1948) and several collections of poetry: *The Great Hunger, A Soul for Sale* and *Come Dance with Kitty Stobling*. His collected poems appeared in 1964 and his collected prose in 1967. *By Night Unstarred*, his last novel, was published posthumously in 1977. He is recognised as a major Irish poet.

KAVANAGH, ROSE (pseud. UNCLE REMUS II or RUBY) 1859–1891
Rose Kavanagh was born in Kiladroy, County Tyrone. She was educated at the Loreto Convent, Omagh, and the Metropolitan School of Art, Dublin. She published in the *Shamrock*, as 'Ruby', in the *Irish Monthly* and in *Young Ireland*. In 1887 she produced a literary page for children in *Irish Fireside* under the pseudonym 'Uncle Remus II'. She was the subject of a poem by Katherine Tynan and another by

Charles Kickham, whom she looked after when he became blind and deaf. W. B. Yeats said that she was 'a young inspiration whose great promise was robbed of fulfilment first by ill-health and then by an early death'. She died of tuberculosis.

KEIGHTLEY, SAMUEL ROBERT b.1859
Samuel Keightley was born in Belfast and educated at Queen's College, Belfast, where he studied law. He contested Antrim as Independent Unionist candidate in 1903, and in 1910 he contested South Derry as a Liberal candidate. As well as being a member of the university senate, he was a poet and novelist and, among other works, published *The Pike Men* in 1903.

KEITH, ROBERT M. 1933–1977
Dick Keith was born in Belfast and was an international soccer player. He played for Linfield, Newcastle and Bournemouth. He won three Irish League medals in 1954, 1955 and 1956 and an Irish Cup medal in 1953. He was capped twenty-three times for Northern Ireland between 1958 and 1962 and played in all five games in the 1958 World Cup in Sweden. He was killed in an accident.

KELBURN, SINCLAIR 1754–1802
Sinclair Kelburn was born in Dublin and educated at Trinity College, Dublin and Edinburgh University where he studied theology and medicine. He was ordained in 1780 in Belfast as a Presbyterian minister. As a convinced Volunteer he preached in his uniform, with his musket beside him and in 1797 was imprisoned in Kilmainham on suspicion of links with the United Irishmen. During his imprisonment he developed paralysis. He published several works, including *The Morality of the Sabbath Defended* (1781) and *The Divinity of our Lord Jesus Christ asserted and proved and the connection of this Doctrine with Practical Religion pointed out* (1792). In 1799 his congregation requested that he should resign.

KELLY, EUGENE 1808–1894
Eugene Kelly was born in County Tyrone and in his twenties emigrated to America. It is said that he took with him £100. In America he became a banker and a multi-millionaire. He founded and was benefactor of the Catholic University of Washington.

KELLY, FRANCIS 1813–1889
Francis Kelly was born in Drumragh, County Tyrone, and was educated at Maynooth. He was ordained, became first parish priest of Upper Fahan and then Coadjutor Bishop of Derry in 1849, eventually succeeding as Bishop in 1864.

KELLY, JAMES 1912–1970
Jimmy Kelly was born in Ballybofey, County Donegal and was an international soccer player. He played for Coleraine, Liverpool and Derry City for which he scored three hundred and sixty-three goals over a period of twenty years. He represented the Irish League sixteen times and played for the League of Ireland three times. From 1927 to 1937 he was capped eleven times for Northern Ireland and scored four international goals. He was capped four times for the Irish Free State from 1932 to 1936.

KELLY, JOAN 16th century
Joan Kelly was brought up at Dungannon, County Tyrone, in the house of Art Braddagh O'Hagan. In 1594 she was a camp-follower in the relief column which went to the besieged Enniskillen Castle. The relief column were captured by the confederates. Some days later she was called to the Earl of Tyrone to give him an account of government losses. She overheard O'Neill's conversations, and saw him receive his share of the booty. She knew the names of the O'Neill family who had taken part in the battle, and that while O'Neill was pretending to be a neutral intermediary between the English crown and the confederacy headed by O'Donnell, he was actually in liaison with the confederates. She later gave a sworn confession, which was taken as evidence.

KELLY, JOHN SHERWOOD 1880–1931
John Kelly was a soldier and served in the Boer War, where he was promoted on the field. He was Commander of the Inniskilling Fusiliers during the First World

War. He was awarded the Distinguished Service Order, the George Cross Medal and the Victoria Cross. He was court-martialled for telling the truth, it is said, regarding the unfortunate expedition to northern Russia.

KELLY, SÉAMUS 1912–1979
Séamus Kelly was born in Belfast, and was educated at St Mary's Christian Brothers' School, at Queen's University, Belfast, where he was a boxing champion, and at University College, Cork. In 1940 he joined the army and was a lieutenant on the intelligence staff. By 1945 he was drama and ballet critic of the *Irish Times*. In 1946, having left the army, he became a public relations officer for Aer Lingus and wrote a daily column for the *Irish Times*, a task he performed for the next thirty years. He played the part of Flask in John Huston's film of Moby Dick in 1954. He contributed to many prominent international newspapers and died in Dublin.

KELLY, WILLIAM 1823–1914
William Kelly was born in Millisle, County Down, and was educated at Trinity College, Dublin. He joined the Plymouth Brethren in 1841 and edited the thirty-four volumes of J. N. Darby's works, as well as *Bible Treasury*. He died in Exeter and left his library of fifteen thousand volumes to Middlesborough.

KELVIN, LORD see THOMSON, WILLIAM

KENNEDY, ANDREW 1897–1963
Andy Kennedy was born in Belfast and was an international soccer player. He played for Belfast Celtic, Glentoran, Crystal Palace, Arsenal, Everton and Tranmere. He was capped twice for Northern Ireland in 1923 and 1925.

KENNEDY, ARTHUR EDWARD 1810–1883
Arthur Kennedy was born in Cultra, County Down, and was educated at Trinity College, Dublin. He retired from the army after twenty-one years' service and became a Poor Law inspector during the Famine.

In 1851 he was appointed Governor of Gambia and in 1854 of West Australia. He was knighted in 1868 and served as Governor of Hong Kong in 1872 and of Queensland in 1877. He died at sea when he was returning home.

KENNEDY, EVORY 1806–1886
Evory Kennedy was born in Carndonagh, County Donegal, and was educated in Derry, Dublin, Edinburgh, London and Paris. He settled in Dublin as an obstetrician and established a large medical practice. He was appointed Master of the Rotunda Hospital in 1833 and in 1839 was made a Fellow of the Royal College of Physicians in Ireland. From 1853 to 1854 he was President of the College of Surgeons. When he retired from medicine he became Deputy Lieutenant for County Dublin. He stood unsuccessfully as a parliamentary candidate in support of Home Rule for County Donegal in 1874. He died in London.

KENNEDY, GILBERT 1678–1745
Gilbert Kennedy was born in Dundonald, County Down, and was educated in Glasgow. He was ordained Presbyterian minister of Tullylish, County Down in 1704, and during the next forty years, published many pamphlets.

KENNEDY (later KENNEDY-BAILIE), JAMES b.1793
James Kennedy was educated at Trinity College, Dublin where he became a fellow in 1817. He was Rector of Ardtrea, County Tyrone, from 1830 to 1864, having gained a Doctorate of Divinity in 1828. He was a classical scholar and published Greek verses and a work on *Greek Inscriptions* in three volumes. He also edited Demosthenes, Homer and Aeschylus.

KENNEDY, JAMES 1903–1984
Jimmy Kennedy was born in Omagh, County Tyrone, but was reared in Portstewart, County Londonderry, and was educated at Trinity College, Dublin. He went to England where he taught before taking up song-writing as a full-time profession. Many of his songs were very successful, including 'The Teddy Bears' Picnic'; 'Red

Sails in the Sunset'; 'South of the Border'; 'Love is Like a Violin' and 'The Hokey-Cokey'. He won two Ivor Novello awards, was awarded an honorary degree from the New University of Ulster and an OBE. Bing Crosby, who became a personal friend, recorded nine of his songs. He lived in County Wicklow and died in England.

KENNEDY, JOHN PITT 1796–1879
John Kennedy was born at Carndonagh, County Donegal, and was educated at Foyle College, Derry, and the Royal Military Academy, Woolwich. He served in the Engineering Corps from 1815 until 1831. Having been Sub-Inspector of Militia in the Ionian Islands, Greece, he returned to County Tyrone to be an estate manager. He was appointed Inspector-General in the National Education Department in 1837 and set up a model farm as a training etablishment for teachers at Glasnevin, Dublin. Facing apathy from the government in response to the need for agricultural education, he resigned in 1839. He was secretary to the Devon Commission on Land Law in Ireland from 1843 to 1845, and superintendent of relief work until 1848, when he was given the task of organising the defence of Dublin against Smith O'Brien's rebellion. He rejoined the army in India in 1849 and helped build a road from Simla towards Tibet: the road bears his name. In 1853 he was promoted to the rank of lieutenant-colonel and became managing director of the Bombay, Baroda and Central Indian Railway. He was the author of many pamphlets.

KERNOHAN, JOSEPH WILLIAM 1869–1923
Joseph Kernohan was born in Kilrea, County Londonderry, and was educated at Belfast Academy and Queen's College, Belfast. In 1906 he founded the Presbyterian Historical Society of Ireland and served as its honorary secretary until his death. From 1909 to 1923 he was Librarian of the Presbyterian College, Belfast. His works include *The Parishes of Kilrea and Tamlaght O'Crilly*; *The County of Londonderry in Three Centuries* and an *Historical Account of Boveedy Congregation*.

KERR, ROBERT b.1882
Bobbie Kerr was born in Enniskillen, County Fermanagh. He and his family emigrated to Hamilton, Ontario, Canada, when he was seven years old. He represented Canada in the 1904 Olympic Games in three sprint events. In the 1908 London Games he won a bronze medal in the 100 metres and a gold medal in the 200 metres sprint. He set a new Canadian record in 1908. He represented Ireland for the first time in 1909 and won both the 100 and 200 yards events. He was captain of the Canadian team in the 1928 Olympic Games in Amsterdam and was later manager of the Canadian track and field division.

KETTLE, THOMAS MICHAEL 1880–1916
Thomas Kettle was born in Dublin, and was educated at Clongowes Wood College and University College, Dublin, where he studied law. He was member of parliament for East Tyrone from 1906 to 1910. He practised law and was made the first Professor of Economics at University College, Dublin. In 1913 he joined the Irish Volunteers, but in 1914 joined the Dublin Fusiliers and was employed in a recruitment capacity. His writings include *Miscellaneous Essays*; *The Open Secret of Ireland*; *The Ways of War* and *The Day's Burden*. He died leading a bayonet charge in the Battle of the Somme. One of his own poems served as his epitaph: 'Died not for flag, nor King, nor Emperor,/But for a dream born in a herdsman's shed/And for the secret scripture of the poor'. It is inscribed on his memorial in St Stephen's Green, Dublin. Robert Lynd said of him that he was the most brilliant Irishman of his generation.

KIDD, GEORGE HUGH 1824–1895
George Kidd was born in Armagh, and was educated in Dublin and Edinburgh. He became a Licentiate of the Royal College of Surgeons of Ireland and practised medicine in Edinburgh. He served as Master of Coombe Hospital for seven years from 1876. He was a leading obstetrician and surgeon and was a founder of the Stewart Institute for Imbeciles. In 1876 he was President of the Royal College of Surgeons in

Ireland, and he edited for many years the *Dublin Journal of Medical Science.*

KIDD, JAMES 1761–1834
James Kidd was born in Loughbrickland, County Down, and in 1784 emigrated to America. He taught himself Hebrew and other eastern languages and returned to Edinburgh to study. In 1793 he was appointed Professor of Oriental Languages at Aberdeen University. In 1796 he procured a licence to preach, and his sermons were extremely popular. He published many theological works and died in Aberdeen.

KIDD, WILLIAM LODGE 1784–1851
William Kidd was born at Thornhill, County Armagh. He joined the navy and was on active service during the Napoleonic War. After 1816 he had a medical practice in Armagh and in November 1817 he read before the Royal Physical Society an important paper dealing with typhus which was then raging in Ireland. He is also remembered for his untiring care during the cholera epidemic of 1832. In 1844 he was appointed Fellow of the Royal College of Surgeons in Ireland.

KILLEN, JAMES BRYCE 1845–1916
James Killen was born in Kells, County Antrim, and was educated at Queen's College, Belfast where he studied law. He was called to the Bar in 1869. With Michael Davitt he founded the Land League in 1879 and was later arrested. In Belfast he edited the *Northern Star*, subsequently working as a journalist in Dublin.

KILLEN, THOMAS YOUNG 1826–1886
Thomas Killen was born in Ballymena, County Antrim, and was educated in Belfast. He was ordained a Presbyterian minister in Ramelton, County Donegal, and came to Belfast in 1862, where he built up a large congregation at Duncairn. He edited the *Evangelical Witness* for four years and was Moderator of the General Assembly in 1882, gaining a Doctorate of Divinity in 1883.

KILLEN, WILLIAM DOOL 1806–1902
William Killen was born in Ballymena,

County Antrim, and was educated at the Belfast Academical Institution. In 1829 he was ordained Presbyterian minister of Raphoe, County Donegal, and was appointed Professor of Church History in the Presbyterian College, Belfast, a post which he held for forty-eight years. In 1869 he became President of the college. The University of Glasgow conferred upon him two doctorates. Among other works, he published *Reminiscences of a Long Life; The Ecclesiastical History of Ireland* in two volumes and *History of the Presbyterian Church in Ireland,* in three volumes, a work begun by J. S. Reid, which he completed.

KINAHAN, GEORGE HENRY 1820–1908
George Kinahan was born in County Down, and was educated at Trinity College, Dublin. After having been engaged on the construction of the Boyne Viaduct, he entered the Geological Survey and became a district surveyor in 1869. He published many papers on geology and was a member of the Royal Irish Academy. It is said of him that few had his knowledge of Irish geological structures. He died in Clontarf.

KING, ROBERT 1815–1900
Robert King was born in Cork, was educated at Trinity College, Dublin, and was ordained in 1841. He was curate in Armagh from 1851 to 1858 and headmaster of the Diocesan School, Ballymena, for the next forty-two years. He was a close friend of William Reeves and John O'Donovan, and he published, among other works, *A Primer; A Catechism; A Life of Christ; The History of the Church of Ireland* in three volumes and a *Memoir of the Primacy of Armagh.* He was a devoted scholar of the Irish language, and published an Irish translation of the Book of Common Prayer. He died in Ballymena.

KING, WILLIAM 1650–1729
William King was born in Antrim, and was educated at Dungannon, County Tyrone and Trinity College, Dublin. After his ordination he became rector of St Werburgh's parish in Dublin. He was a pioneer of the Royal Irish Academy, and a founder member of the Dublin Philosophical Society in

1683. In 1688 he was appointed Dean of St Patrick's Cathedral, but was imprisoned when he sided with King William; he was released after the Battle of the Boyne in 1690 and appointed Bishop of Derry. His publication, *The State of the Protestants of Ireland under the late King James's Government* was reprinted three times. In 1703 he was translated to Dublin as archbishop. He supported the penal laws, and his correspondence, which was prolific, is historically illuminating. He was in favour of the teaching of Irish at Trinity College, Dublin. Among his published work is *De Origine Mali* and many sermons. Some of his manuscripts are in Trinity College, Dublin, and in the British Library. [Biography by C. S. King.]

KINGSMILL, ROBERT BRICE 1730–1805
Robert Brice was born in County Donegal, and Kingsmill was added to his name by act of parliament on his marriage to Elizabeth Corry, grand-daughter of Sir William Kingsmill. He entered the navy as lieutenant in 1756, and by 1761 he had gained the rank of commander. In 1784 he was elected member of parliament and in 1799 he was promoted to the rank of admiral. A year later he was created baronet. He died in Sidmouth.

KINNEAR, JOHN 1824–1909
John Kinnear was born in Clonaneese, County Tyrone, and was educated in Belfast. He spent the rest of his life in Letterkenny, County Donegal, where he was ordained a Presbyterian minister in 1848. He received a Doctorate of Divinity in 1874. He was elected Liberal member of parliament for County Donegal from 1880 to 1885; consequently he was the first clergyman in charge of a congregation to sit in parliament. He supported the Tenant Right movement and left his fine collection of books to the Presbyterian College, Belfast.

KINOULTY, JOHN CHARLES 1910–1981
John Charles Kinoulty was born in Belfast and when he was two years old, moved to County Kilkenny. He was educated there, in Cork and at the Bablake School, Coventry. He worked in commercial offices and

qualified as a solicitor in 1942. He entered local government and was assistant solicitor at Batley, and Deputy Town Clerk of Bilston. He was assistant legal adviser to West Midland Gas in 1950, and later was legal adviser. When he retired in 1975, he began to compile *A Dictionary of Irish Biography*, which contains 2468 entries and which covers the period 1500 to 1980. He completed the book three months prior to his death. A copy presented by Mary Kinoulty is in the library of Queen's University, Belfast.

KIRKPATRICK, WILLIAM BAILLIE 1808–1882
William Kirkpatrick was born in Ballynahinch, County Down, and was educated at Glasgow. He became Presbyterian clergyman of Mary's Abbey, Dublin and was instrumental in building a new church in Rutland Square. Among his publications is *Chapters in Irish History*. He died in Bray.

KNOWLES, JAMES 1759–1840
James Knowles was born in Dublin and worked as a schoolteacher in Cork and London. The Belfast Academical Institution appointed him teacher of English in 1815, but dismissed him in 1816. He went to London, where he pursued study in lexicography and produced a *Pronouncing Dictionary* in 1835. He was a cousin of Richard Brindsley Sheridan, the playwright.

KNOWLES, JAMES SHERIDAN 1784–1862
James Sheridan Knowles was born in Cork. For a time he was an ensign in the militia and then studied medicine at Aberdeen. He taught in Belfast and Glasgow, but his principal activity was the writing of plays, among which are *Virginius*; *The Hunchback*; *The Wife*; *The Love Chase* and *William Tell*. In 1844 he became a Baptist preacher and published religious literature. He died in Torquay.

KNOWLES, WILLIAM JAMES 1832–1927
W. J. Knowles was born in Fenagh, near Cullybackey, County Antrim. He was educated privately, and later taught botany and geology. He taught in Cullybackey,

Portglenone and Ballymena, such diverse subjects as heat and light and the principles of agriculture. He was the land agent for the Casement estate, and from 1879 to 1920, secretary of the Antrim County Land, Building and Investment Company. He embarked on his antiquarian career in 1870 and in 1871 discovered sandhill settlement sites in Portstewart, excavated at Whitepark Bay and at Tievebulliagh, where his major achievement was the discovery of a Neolithic Axe Factory. In 1878 he was secretary of the committee set up by the British Association for the Advancement of Science, in order to investigate such sites. He founded the Ballymena Naturalists' Field Club and the Ballymena Archaeological Society. He was a member of the Royal Irish Academy, a fellow of the Royal Society of Antiquaries of Ireland, a member of Belfast Naturalists' Field Club, and a fellow of the Royal Anthropological Institute of Great Britain and Ireland. He published more than seventy papers in journals. His fine collection of antiquities was dispersed in 1924 and he left Ballymena and retired to Ballycastle. He is buried at the Craigs.

KNOX, ALEXANDER c.1757–1831
Alexander Knox was born in Derry and was educated privately. He was Lord Castlereagh's private secretary and he lived the life of a hermit, studying theology and writing. He was a forerunner of the Oxford Movement. He published *Correspondence with Bp. Jebb* and *Remains*. He died in Dublin.

KNOX, J. 1851–1907
J.Knox was born in Armoy, County Antrim, and owned the mills at Armoy. In 1872 he emigrated to America and became editor of *Texas Siftings*. He was a colonel and wrote plays, books and humorous articles.

KNOX, ROBERT 1815–1883
Robert Knox was born in Clady, County Tyrone, and was educated in Glasgow. He was ordained as a Presbyterian clergyman in Strabane, County Tyrone, in 1840 and moved to a congregation in Coleraine, County Londonderry, and then to Belfast in 1843. He published many sermons and was editor of the *Irish Presbyterian*.

KNOX, ROBERT b.1884
Robert Knox was born at Drumaduan, Coleraine, County Londonderry. He was a lieutenant-colonel in the Inniskilling Fusiliers. He was awarded the Distinguished Service Order in the First World War.

KNOX, ROBERT BENT 1808–1893
Robert Knox was born in County Tyrone and was educated at Trinity College, Dublin. He gained a Doctorate of Divinity in 1858, and having served as Bishop of Down and Connor from 1849 to 1886, he then became Archbishop of Armagh. He was author of the important *Ecclesiastical Index* (of Ireland), which was published in 1839.

KNOX, THOMAS FRANCIS 1822–1882
Thomas Knox was born in County Armagh, and was educated at Cambridge University. He converted to Catholicism. He and F. W. Faber founded the London Oratory, and of this institution he became Superior. He became Doctor of Divinity in 1875 and was the author of many religious and historical works. He died in London.

KNOX, THOMAS GEORGE 1824–1887
Thomas Knox was born in Maghera, County Londonderry, and served with the English army from 1840 to 1848. From 1851 to 1857 he served with the Siamese army and became first interpreter, then British consul and finally Consul-General in Siam. He was knighted in 1880 and married a Siamese woman. He died in the Pyrenees.

KNOX-LITTLE, WILLIAM JOHN 1839–1918
William Knox-Little was born in Stewartstown, County Tyrone, and was educated at Cambridge University. He was Rector of St Alban's, Manchester, having been a curate in London. He was mentioned in dispatches during the Boer War, in his capacity as army chaplain. He published fiction and religious work and was made Canon of Worcester Cathedral in 1881. He died in Worcester.

KYLE, GEORGINA MOUTRAY 1865–1950
Georgina Kyle was born in Craigavad, County Down. She was educated privately

and at the Colarossi Studio in Paris. She travelled a great deal and exhibited in Paris, Glasgow, Belfast, Dublin and Liverpool. In 1924 her work was in the Wembley Exhibition. She was a member of the Ulster Academy of Arts and from 1902 she ran the Belfast Art Society's Life Class. Her work is in the collection of the Ulster Museum, Armagh County Museum and Queen's University, Belfast.

L

LAMB, CHARLES 1893–1964

Charles Lamb was born in Portadown, County Armagh and was educated at Portadown Technical School. He was apprenticed to his father, who was a painter and decorator, and in 1913 he attended evening classes at the Belfast School of Art. He won a scholarship to the Metropolitan School of Art in Dublin in 1917. He began to exhibit in the Royal Hibernian Academy and was elected as a member in 1938. He is known for his paintings of Carraroe in the Connemara Gaeltacht, where he settled permanently. He lived for one year in Brittany, and spent another year painting in the Aran Islands. He had an exhibition in New York in 1929 and was represented in the Irish Exhibition in Brussels. He illustrated Máirtín Ó Cadhain's book *Cré na Cille* and exhibited in Los Angeles and Chicago and at the Royal Academy.

LAMBERT, OLIVER d.1618

Oliver Lambert came to Ireland in 1580. He was a soldier in the English army. In 1584 he fought against the Scots in Ulster, and in 1601 he was appointed supreme military commander of Connacht. He was given land in Roscommon and at Clonmahon in County Cavan.

LAMONT (LA MONT), ELISH *c.*1800–1870

Elish Lamont was born in Belfast. As an artist she was self-taught and was a successful miniature painter. She went to England and was acquainted with Charles Dickens whom she had met when he had given readings in Belfast. She exhibited at the Royal Hibernian Academy, Dublin, from 1842 to 1857, and published with her sister Frances, *Christmas Rhymes, Three Nights' Revelry*, which she had illustrated. The book was dedicated to the Right Honorable the Lady Dufferin and Clandeboye. She exhibited at the Royal Academy, London in 1846, and among her miniatures was one of Lady Dufferin. She lived in Dublin for a period, and moved to England where she died.

LANGBRIDGE, ROSAMUND b.1880

Rosamund Langbridge was born in Glenalla, County Donegal and was educated in Limerick. She was a journalist who contributed to the *Manchester Guardian* and other newspapers. She published many novels which included *The Flame and the Flood* (1903); *Land of the Ever Young* and *The Green Banks of Shannon*.

LANGHAM, HERBERT CHARLES ARTHUR early 20th century

Charles Langham, 13th baronet of Tempo, was born in Cottsbrooke, Northamptonshire and was educated at Eton. He became a lieutenant in the Northamptonshire Regiment. He married Ethel Tennent and came to live in Tempo, County Fermanagh. He was Deputy-Lieutenant and a justice of the peace for the county. In 1930 he was appointed High Sheriff. He was a noted amateur photographer and naturalist, and his large collection of butterflies is now housed in the Ulster Museum.

LANYON, CHARLES 1813–1889

Charles Lanyon was born in Sussex but came to Ireland as a young man. He was apprenticed to Jacob Owen of the Board of Public Works in Dublin, was appointed Surveyor of Kildare, and then of County Antrim in 1835. In 1836 he built the Gledun Road viaduct from local stone, and 'The Frosses' road between Ballymena and Ballymoney, where avenues of fir trees were planted so that their roots would support the road and prevent it from sinking into the bog. In addition to being County Surveyor, he undertook private commissions and designed at least fourteen churches. At the age of twenty-six he designed the palm house in the Botanic Gardens,

Belfast, and in 1846 built Crumlin Road Gaol. He became one of Belfast's leading architects. Among other buildings in the city designed by him are Queen's College (now Queen's University) in 1849, the Presbyterian Theological College in College Park, the Custom House, Sinclair Seamen's Church, Corporation Square and the Ulster Club. In 1865, he and W. H. Lynn built the Old Library at Queen's University. In 1866 he was elected member of parliament for Belfast, and in 1867, President of the Royal Institute of Architects of Ireland. He was knighted in 1868.

LANYON, WILLIAM OWEN 1842–1887

William Lanyon was born in County Antrim and joined the army in 1860. He served in Jamaica and South Africa, where he became an administrator. He was involved in the Egyptian campaign of 1882 and the Nile expedition of 1884. He was knighted in 1880 and died in New York.

LARCOM, THOMAS AISKEW 1801–1879

Thomas Larcom was born in Gosport, Hampshire, and attended the Royal Military Academy at Woolwich. In 1821 he was stationed at the Royal Engineers' Depot, Chatham, and for the next three years in Gibraltar. In 1824 he was employed by the Ordnance Survey in England, and two years later transferred to the Ordnance Survey of Ireland. By 1828 he was in charge of the Survey's headquarters office in Dublin and in 1833 the first full maps were published. He invented the limelight for surveying, later used to light the stage in theatres. It was his idea to accompany the maps with a written account of Ireland's physical and human resources, which became known as the *Ordnance Survey Memoirs*. The first was published in 1837 of Templemore, County Londonderry, under Larcom's editorship. Though many memoirs had been compiled in draft, they were not published because of excessive cost. In 1841 Larcom was appointed Commissioner for the census of population in Ireland, and two years later a census report was published. In 1845 he was employed on the commission which chose a site for a university in Ulster and he opted for Belfast. The Ordnance Survey

of Ireland's six inch maps were completed in 1846, and Larcom then joined the Irish Board of Works where he supervised the first collection of agricultural statistics of Ireland. In 1848 he worked on the revision of the boundaries of the Irish Poor Law Unions and the District Electoral Divisions and two years later was appointed Deputy Chairman of the Irish Board of Works. From 1853 to 1868 he served as Under-Secretary of Ireland. He died in Hampshire.

LARKIN, DELIA 20th century

Delia Larkin, the sister of James Larkin, founded a small shirt manufacturing co-operative which employed girls victimised after the 1913–14 lock-out. She was the first Secretary of the Women's Labour Union, which was closely allied to the Suffrage Movement. She instigated improved coverage of Suffrage meetings in Labour journals.

LARKIN, JAMES 1876–1947

James Larkin was born of Irish parents in Liverpool and became a docker. He was a member of the National Union of Dock Labourers, and as an official he went to Scotland where he remained until 1907. He came to Belfast and led a successful dockers' strike which resulted in wage increases and recognition for the union. He became General Secretary of the newly established Irish Transport and General Workers' Union in 1909, was involved with unskilled workers and organised the Dublin workers' strike in 1913, which led to a lock-out by the employers. Larkin was arrested at a protest rally and later imprisoned for a short time. From 1914 to 1923 he was in America, but returned to Ireland and reoccupied his post with the union until his expulsion in 1924 when he formed the Workers' Union of Ireland and became its General Secretary. For two brief periods, 1937–1938 and 1943–1944, he was Dáil deputy for North-East Dublin. Seán O'Casey says of him 'Lectures, Concerts and other activities, he brought into Liberty Hall and the social centre he organised in Croydon Park coloured the life of the Dublin workers.' He was a powerful orator. His statue was erected in O'Connell Street in 1979.

LARKIN, PHILIP ARTHUR 1922–1985

Philip Larkin was born in Coventry, Warwickshire. He was educated in Coventry and at St John's College, Oxford. He became a librarian, and spent from 1950 at Queen's University, Belfast, moving to Hull in 1955. He published two novels, *Jill*, 1946, and *A Girl in Winter*, 1947. He edited the *Oxford Book of Twentieth Century English Verse* in 1973. Among his poetry collections are *The North Ship*, 1945; *The Less Deceived*, 1955; *The Whitsun Weddings*, 1964 and *High Windows* in 1974. The *Collected Poems* were published posthumously in 1988. His articles on jazz were collected in *All What Jazz?* in 1970, and a volume of essays, *Required Writing*, was published in 1983. His *Selected Letters 1940–1985* were published in 1992.

LARMOR, JOSEPH 1857–1942

Joseph Larmor was born at Magheragall, County Antrim, and was educated at the Royal Belfast Academical Institution, Queen's College, Belfast, and St John's College, Cambridge. He was appointed Professor of Natural Philosophy at Queen's College, Galway, in 1880, but returned to St John's five years later as a lecturer in Mathematics. He was appointed Lucasian Professor of Mathematics in Cambridge in 1903, the chair once occupied by Sir Isaac Newton. He published a book, *Aether and Matter* in 1900, and it is for this that he is remembered, as well as for the formula for radiation of energy from an accelerated electron, and for an explanation of the effect of a magnetic field in splitting the lines of the spectrum into multiple lines. He was elected Fellow of the Royal Society in 1892 and became its Secretary, having earlier received the Society's Royal Medal and the Copley Medal. In 1909 he was knighted and became Unionist member of parliament for the University of Cambridge for eleven years from 1911. He was given the freedom of the city of Belfast and many honorary degrees. He died in Holywood, County Down.

LATIMER, WILLIAM THOMAS 1842–1919

William Latimer was born in Ballynahetty, County Tyrone, and was educated at Queen's College, Belfast. He was ordained in Eglish, County Tyrone, and became a Doctor of Divinity in 1915. Among his publications are *History of the Irish Presbyterians*; *Ulster Biographies relating to 1798*; *Life of Dr Cooke* and many articles in Irish periodicals.

LAVERY, CECIL 1894–1967

Cecil Lavery was born in Armagh and educated at St Patrick's College, Armagh, St Vincent's College, Castleknock, and University College, Dublin. In 1915 he was called to the Bar. During the first meeting of the Irish Volunteers he joined the Armagh division, and though he was prepared to command them in Easter Week 1916, he was not called upon to do so. From 1921 to 1922 he was a judge in the Dáil Courts, took silk in 1927 and served on the bench of the King's Inns. He was a member of the Dáil for North County Dublin for three years from 1935 and acted as Attorney-General in the first inter-party government in 1948, subsequently becoming a senator. He helped to draft the Convention of Human Rights for the Council of Europe, and the Republic of Ireland Bill in 1948, and attended a meeting which decided Ireland's relationship with the Commonwealth. In 1950 he was appointed to the Supreme Court, and he was a Steward of the Turf Club.

LAVERY, JOHN 1856–1941

John Lavery was born in Belfast and was left an orphan at the age of three. He was sent to relatives near Moira, County Down, and attended Magheralin National School. At the age of ten, he went to live with relatives in Scotland and was apprenticed at the age of seventeen to a painter-photographer in Glasgow. He studied at the Glasgow School of Art and in London and Paris. In 1886 the Royal Academy showed his 'Tennis Party', which was bought for Munich. In 1888 he was commissioned to paint the state visit of Queen Victoria to the Glasgow Exhibition. He was knighted in 1918, was elected to the Royal Academy in 1921, was a member of the Royal Hibernian Academy and the Academies of Scotland, Rome, Antwerp, Milan, Brussels and Stockholm. He received honorary degrees from Queen's University, Belfast, and Trinity College, Dublin, and was made a freeman of both cities. In 1940 his autobiography, *The Life of a Painter*, was published. His paintings are exhibited in galleries internationally.

LAW, EDWARD FITZGERALD 1846–1908
Edward Law was born in Rostrevor, County Down, and was educated at Woolwich, after which he joined the Royal Artillery in 1868. He resigned after four years and became British Consul at St Petersburg in Russia. In 1885 he served in the Sudan and was later Finance Minister of India. He was knighted in 1898 and died in Paris. He invented a flying machine. [Biography, 1911]

LAW, HUGH 1818–1883
Hugh Law was born in County Down and was educated at Dungannon, County Tyrone, and Trinity College, Dublin. He was called to the Bar in 1840 and was made Queen's Counsel in 1860. He was responsible for drafting the Irish Church Disestablishment Bill (1869) and Gladstone's First Land Bill (1870), and from 1874 served as member of parliament for County Londonderry. In 1880 he was appointed Attorney-General, and in 1881 he became Lord Chancellor. He died at Rathmullen, County Donegal.

LAWLESS, JOHN 1773–1837
John Lawless was born in Dublin and having been refused admission to the Bar, investigated brewing as an occupation. He became a journalist in Newry with the *Ulster Recorder*, in Belfast with the *Ulster Register* from 1817 to 1819, and with the *Irishman*. He was a strong supporter of Catholic Emancipation and his exemplary behaviour which helped to prevent bloodshed at a demonstration at Ballybay is said to have softened Wellington's attitude towards Catholic Emancipation. His most important works are *A Compendium of the History of Ireland* and *An Address to the Catholics of Ireland*. He died in London.

LAWLOR, HUGH JACKSON 1860–1938
Hugh Lawlor was born in Ballymena, County Antrim, and was educated at Trin-

ity College, Dublin, where he later became Professor of Ecclesistical History, a post which he occupied from 1898 to 1933. From 1924 to 1933 he was Dean of St Patrick's Cathedral and from 1919 until 1930 he was Secretary of the Royal Irish Academy. Among his publications are *Chapters on the Book of Mulling; The Manuscripts of the Vita S. Columbani; The Reformation and the Irish Episcopate; Saint Malachy of Armagh* and *The Martyrology of Tallaght.*

LAWRENCE, ALEXANDER 1764–1835
Alexander Lawrence was born in Coleraine, County Londonderry. He served in the 19th and 77th Regiments. He returned after fifteen years service in India, having risen to the rank of colonel. He had four sons, three of whom served with distinction in India: Sir George Alexander Lawrence (1804–1884); Sir Henry Lawrence (1806–1857); Lord John Lawrence (1811–1879).

LAWRENCE, JOHN LAIRD MAIR 1811–1879
John Lawrence was educated at Bristol, Foyle College, Derry, Bath and Haileybury. He joined the East India Company in Calcutta in 1830 and served as administrator and magistrate and finally became Chief Commissioner for the Punjab from 1853 to 1857. In 1857, during the Indian Mutiny, he recaptured Delhi from the mutineers. He was Viceroy of India from 1863 to 1869, when he was created first Baron Lawrence of the Punjab and of Grately. He is buried in Westminster Abbey.

LAWRENCE, WILLIAM 1862–1940
William Lawrence was born in Belfast and was a drama critic for the *Stage* as well as being an historian of the Elizabethan theatre. His books include *Pre-Restoration Stage Studies; The Physical Conditions of the Elizabethan Public Play-House; Shakespeare's Workshop; Those Nut-Cracking Elizabethans; Old Theatre Days and Ways* and *Speeding up Shakespeare* in 1937.

LAWSON, JOHN 1709–1759
John Lawson was born in Omagh, County Tyrone, and was educated at Trinity Col-

lege, Dublin, where he became a Doctor of Divinity in 1745. He was a lecturer in history and oratory and later Professor of Divinity. In 1743 he was appointed the first Librarian of the college. He published many of his sermons and was a distinguished linguist.

LECKY, EMILIA c.1788–c.1844

Emilia Lecky was born in Dublin. She moved to Derry, but later returned to Dublin. From 1826 to 1842 she exhibited at the Royal Hibernian Society. She painted portraits, where generally the sitter was anonymous, as well as religious and historical themes. Her portrait of the Honorable William Porter, Attorney General of the Cape of Good Hope, suggests that her subjects were prominent members of society. There are no known surviving examples of her work.

LECKY, THORNTON STRATFORD 1838–1902

Thornton Lecky was born in Downpatrick, County Down, and was educated at Gracehill, County Antrim. In 1852 he went to sea, conducted many sea surveys and was involved in charting. He was Commodore Captain of the American Line and Marine Superintendent of the Great Western Railway. Much of his writing deals with navigation. He died in Las Palmas.

LECKY, WILLIAM EDWARD HARTPOLE (pseud. HIBERNICUS) 1838–1903

William Lecky was born in County Dublin, and was educated in Armagh, Cheltenham and Trinity College, Dublin. He was a member of parliament for Dublin University from 1895 until a few months before his death, and was in favour of a Catholic university. His manuscripts, both published and unpublished are in Trinity College, Dublin, and under the pseudonym 'Hibernicus' he was author of a volume *Friendship and other poems*. He published anonymously *Leaders of Public Opinion in Ireland* and in 1865, under his own name, the *History of Rationalism*, followed by *History of European Morals*. For nineteen years he worked on his *History of England* and it finally appeared in eight volumes. Other works include *Democracy and Liberty* and *The Map of Life* though he was probably best known for his five volume *History of Ireland in the Eighteenth Century*, published in 1892. He received the Order of Merit in 1902. The Lecky Chair of History at Trinity College, Dublin, was endowed by his widow. [Biography by his wife, 1909]

LEE, ALEXANDER b.1870

Alex Lee was born in Barrow-in-Furness, though his family had just moved from Ballycastle, County Antrim. They then moved to Blackpool, where they lived next door to a photographer. Alex and his elder brother, Robert, had a photographic studio in Cape Town, and when they returned from South Africa, Alex set up studios in Bath Cottage in Portrush. He went from there to the Giant's Causeway once a week, and photographed people in front of the rock formation known as the wishing chair. With the introduction of the amateur camera, Alex bought a Kodak dealership, which meant that he was permitted to sell cameras and films, and to process films. Many of the views of Portrush which he took were sold as postcards. The photographs were embossed in gold lettering with 'Lee's Studios at Cape Town, Portrush and the Giant's Causeway'. His brother Robert and his sister Henrietta also had photographic studios in Portrush.

LEE, SAMUEL 1871–1944

Sammy Lee was educated at the Royal Belfast Academical Institution, played for the North of Ireland Football Club and was an international rugby player. Between 1891 and 1898 he won nineteen international caps for Ireland. He captained Ireland in the 1892–1893 season and again in 1895–1896. In 1894 he was a member of Ireland's first Triple Crown triumph. In 1899 to 1900 he was president of the Irish Rugby Football Union and was also a selector. In 1904 he refereed the Scotland v England match.

LEES, HARCOURT 1776–1852

Harcourt Lees was born in Dublin, and was educated at Trinity College, Dublin, and Cambridge. He was vicar of Killaney, County Down. He published a number of anti-Catholic tracts and was an ardent advocate of the Protestant ascendancy. He died in Blackrock.

LENNON, JOHN 1768–1842
John Lennon was born in Downpatrick, County Down and was a sailor. He is remembered for having brought his ship, the *Hibernia*, through the American fleet in 1812. He died in Devonport.

LENTAIGNE, JOHN FRANCIS O'NEILL 1805–1886
John Lentaigne was born in Dublin and was educated at Trinity College, Dublin, where he graduated in medicine and became a Fellow of the Royal College of Surgeons in Ireland. He was appointed Commissioner of Loan Funds and served as Inspector-General of Prisons, Reformatories and Industrial Schools from 1854 until 1877. He was elected President of the Statistical Society from 1877 to 1888. He was Deputy Lieutenant for County Monaghan and from 1861 to 1886 was a Commissioner of National Education. He was knighted in 1880.

LEPPER, JOHN HERON b.1878
John Lepper was born in Belfast and was educated in Scotland and Trinity College, Dublin. He was a barrister and wrote several novels, including *A Tory in Arms* and *The North-East Corner*. He also published short stories and a book *Famous Secret Societies*. In 1914 he moved to London.

LESLIE, CHARLES 1650–1722
Charles Leslie was born in Dublin and was educated at Enniskillen, County Fermanagh, and Trinity College, Dublin. He is best known for his numerous theological works, though as Chancellor of Connor he refused to take the oath of allegiance to William III and wrote *Answer to the King's State of Protestants* and a *Short and Easy Method with Deists*. He died at Glaslough, County Monaghan. [Biography by Leslie, 1885]

LESLIE, JOHN 1571–1671
John Leslie was born in Scotland and lived in Europe for many years. In 1633, having been Bishop of the Isles, he was translated to Raphoe. He built a fortified palace there, and when the 1641 rebellion broke out he raised a company of foot soldiers who fought for the king. He became known as 'the fighting bishop'. He became Bishop of Clogher in 1661 and was granted money by parliament. He wrote many books and collected European manuscripts, all of which were destroyed. He bought property at Glaslough, County Monaghan, where he died.

LESLIE, JOHN 1882–1916
John Leslie was born in County Monaghan. He was educated at Harrow and Oxford. He served as member of parliament for Monaghan from 1871 to 1880. He was an artist and exhibited for many years in the Royal Academy. His picture, 'Peter denying Christ', was presented to the City of Belfast Public Library. He received a letter of commendation from Prince Albert for his picture 'Children, Christ Died For You'. He won the Grand Military Steeplechase on his own horse.

LESLIE, JOHN RANDOLPH (SHANE) 1885–1971
Shane Leslie was born in Glaslough, County Monaghan, and was educated at Eton, Paris and King's College, Cambridge. On a visit to Russia in 1907 he met Tolstoy. In 1908 he became a Catholic. In two elections he stood for Derry as a Nationalist candidate and in 1911 went on a fund-raising mission to the USA. In 1916 he was appointed editor of the *Dublin Review*. He was a prolific writer of poetry, prose, biography and stories of the supernatural. Among his works are *An Anthology of Catholic Poets; The Skull of Swift; Verses in Peace and War; The Film of Memory; From Cabin Boy to Archbishop; The Irish Tangle for English Readers; Shane Leslie's Ghost Book; The Oxford Movement* and *George the Fourth*. He was an Associate Member of the Irish Academy of Letters and was made a Privy Chamberlain by Pope Pius XI. He succeeded his father as baronet in 1944 and was subsequently knighted. He presented a 9th-century manuscript to the University of Notre Dame, Indiana, of which he was Rosenbach Fellow of Bibliography.

LESLIE, THOMAS EDWARD CLIFFE
1825–1882
Thomas Leslie was born in Wexford and was educated at Trinity College, Dublin. In 1853 he became Professor of Political Economy at Queen's College, Belfast. Among numerous articles and pamphlets he published *Land Systems* in 1870 and *Essays* in 1879. He died in Belfast.

LESTER, SEÁN 1888–1959
Seán Lester was born in Carrickfergus, County Antrim, and was educated at Methodist College, Belfast. He worked as a journalist on the *North Down Herald* and later the *Freeman's Journal.* In 1922 he joined the new Department of External Affairs of the Irish Free State, and in 1929 he was the Irish representative at Geneva. When he was appointed to the High Commission for the League of Nations he protested vehemently against the Nazi persecution of the Jews. In 1940 he became the League's Acting Secretary-General. He stayed in Europe until 1947 to supervise the winding-up of the League, before retiring to Galway where he died. He received the Woodrow Wilson Award and honorary doctorates from the National University of Ireland and Trinity College, Dublin.

LETHLOBAR d.873
Lethlobar was King of Dál nAraide and was reputed to have defeated the Danes in County Down. He overcame the invading forces of Áed Finnliath mac Néill. He eventually died of wounds received in battle.

LETTS, EDMUND ALBERT 1852–1918
Edmund Letts was born in Kent and was educated at Bishop's Stortford, Hertfordshire, King's College, London, and briefly at the Universities of Vienna and Berlin. At the age of twenty he became chief assistant in the Chemistry Department of Edinburgh University. Four years later he was appointed the first Professor of Chemistry at University College, Bristol. In 1879 he became Professor of Chemistry at Queen's College, Belfast, where he remained for thirty-eight years. His main areas of research were: the chemistry of organic compounds of sulphur and phosphorus; the detection of carbon dioxide in air and water (his methods were employed by the first Scott Antarctic expedition); and the pollution of rivers and tidal waters. He published *Some Fundamental Problems of Chemistry, Old and New* and many papers in journals. He was a prominent member of the Belfast Natural History Society and was a Fellow of the Royal Society of Edinburgh and of the Institute of Chemistry. Upon the foundation of Queen's University, Belfast, he was one of the first members of Senate. He returned to England and was killed in a cycling accident.

LEVER, CHARLES 1806–1872
Charles Lever was born in Dublin and educated at Trinity College, Dublin. He went to Göttingen and Louvain to study medicine and then travelled in Canada and America. In 1832, having worked in Dublin throughout the cholera epidemic, he was appointed medical officer at the dispensary at Portstewart, County Londonderry. As a student his *Log Book of a Rambler* had been published in the *Dublin Literary Gazette*, and his novel *Harry Lorrequer* had been serialised in the *Dublin University Magazine*, of which he became editor in 1842. After a stay in Belgium, Germany and Italy he was appointed British consul at La Spezia and in 1867 became the consul at Trieste. His other novels include *Con Cregan; Arthur O'Leary; Charles O'Malley; The Knight of Gwynne* and *The Bramleys of Bishop's Folly.*

LEWIS, ANDREW *c.*1720–*c.*1781
Andrew Lewis was born in County Donegal into a Huguenot family of settlers, who later emigrated to America. They were said to be the first white settlers in Augusta County, Virginia. He volunteered for the expedition in Ohio in 1754, and at the surrender of Fort Necessity served with Washington. He was promoted to the rank of major, commanded the Sandy Creek expedition and the expedition of Major Grant, after which he was taken prisoner in Montreal. He was appointed commissioner with the six nations in 1768 and was brigadier-general in command of the Virginia troops who gained a victory against

an Indian force. During the war of the revolution he was made colonel. He contracted a fever, having driven Lord Dunmore from Gwynne's Island, and died in Bedford County, Virginia. His statue stands on one of the pedestals around the Washington Monument at Richmond.

LEWIS, CLIVE STAPLES 1898–1963
C. S. Lewis was born in Belfast and was educated at Malvern College and University College, Oxford. During the First World War he interrupted his studies to serve with the Somerset Light Infantry. He graduated with a triple first. From 1925 to 1954 he was a fellow and tutor at Magdalen College, Oxford, before being appointed Professor of Medieval and Renaissance Literature at Cambridge. His book *The Allegory of Love* won the Hawthornden Prize, and he published many other works, including *The Discarded Image, The Problem of Pain* and *The Screwtape Letters.* His autobiography, *Surprised by Joy,* was published in 1955, and his 'Narnia' books are a great favourite with children everywhere. He died in Cambridge.

LINDON, PATRICK d.1734
Patrick Lindon was born in Fews, County Armagh. He was a poet and song-writer, and his songs were extremely popular. One of his manuscripts is in the British Library.

LINDSAY, HAROLD A. late 19th century
Harry Lindsay was born in Armagh and was educated at Santry College. Between 1893 and 1898 he was capped thirteen times for Ireland. He was a member of the Triple Crown-winning Irish side of 1894 and the International Championship-winning side of 1896.

LINDSAY, JAMES GAVIN 1835–1903
James Lindsay was born in Downhill, County Londonderry. He entered the Madras army and served through the Indian Mutiny in 1857. He was chief engineer during the construction of many Indian railways and was promoted to the rank of colonel in 1882. He took part in the great march to Kandahar in 1878, and died at sea.

LITTLE, JAMES 1837–1916
James Little was born in Newry, County Down, and was educated in Armagh and Dublin. In 1856 he became Licentiate of the Royal College of Surgeons in Ireland and spent the next three years in India. He became a Doctor of Medicine in Edinburgh in 1861, after which he settled in Dublin, where he became Professor of Medicine at the Royal College of Surgeons. He was a member of the Royal Irish Academy, consulting physician to several hospitals, Regius Professor of Medicine, and Physician to the King. He served as President of the Royal College of Physicians in Ireland and of the Royal Academy of Medicine. He edited the *Journal of Medical Science* and published many medical works. He died in Dublin.

LLOYD, RICHARD AVERIL 1891–1950
Dickie Lloyd was born in Tamnamore, Dungannon, County Tyrone. He played rugby for Dublin University and Liverpool. Between 1910 he was capped nineteen times for Ireland. He captained Ireland on eleven occasions. He was also an international cricketer.

LOFTIE, WILLIAM JOHN 1839–1911
William Loftie was born in Tandragee, County Armagh, and was educated at Trinity College, Dublin. He was ordained in 1865 and for the next thirty years preached in many English churches. He was a prolific writer and wrote much on art, architecture and on the history and antiquities of London, as well as editing the *People's Magazine.* He died in Kensington.

LOFTUS, ADAM 1533–1605
Adam Loftus was born in Yorkshire and was appointed Archbishop of Armagh in 1562. Five years later he became Archbishop of Dublin and was appointed ecclesiastical commissioner to further the Reformation in Ireland. From 1582 to 1584 he was Lord Justice, and he became the first Provost of Trinity College, Dublin, where there are two portraits of him. There is another portrait in the Archbishop's Palace, Armagh.

LOGAN, JAMES 1674–1751

James Logan was born in Lurgan, County Armagh, and was educated by his father, a Quaker schoolmaster. He was apprenticed to a Dublin linen draper, and it would appear that he taught for some years in England and was involved in trade between Dublin and Bristol. He went to America as the secretary of William Penn in 1699. He became Chief Justice of Pennsylvania, Mayor of Philadelphia, and State Governor in 1736. He is remembered for his considerate treatment of the Indians. He became interested in botany and natural science and Linné named the *Loganiacae* for him. He contributed papers on scientific subjects to the Royal Society, and his translation of Cicero's *De Senectute* was published. He bequeathed his extensive library to Philadelphia. He died on his estate at Germantown.

LOGUE, MICHAEL 1840–1924

Michael Logue was born in Carrigart, County Donegal. He was educated at a hedge school, a school in Buncrana, and at Maynooth. In 1866 he was appointed Professor of Dogmatic Theology at the Irish College in Paris, where he had been ordained. He returned to Donegal as a curate in 1874. In 1879 he became Bishop of Raphoe; he was translated to Armagh in 1887 and in 1893 was created a cardinal. His denunciation of Parnell after the O'Shea divorce case had a significantly adverse effect on the politician's career. In 1880 he went to America to raise funds, and further fund-raising efforts by him resulted in the completion of Armagh Cathedral in 1904. He was a native Irish speaker and supported the Gaelic League. He disapproved of Sinn Féin's use of physical force and was opposed to partition.

LOMBARD, PETER 1554–1625

Peter Lombard was born in Waterford. In 1572 he went to Louvain where he later became Professor of Philosophy and then Professor of Theology. He served as Provost of Cambria Cathedral from 1594. Four years later he was sent to Rome where he became O'Neill's agent. He was appointed Archbishop of Armagh by Pope Clement VIII in 1601. Among his works are *Commentaries on the Kingdom of Ireland* which was written in Latin, and published posthumously in 1632. Latterly he abandoned O'Neill and sought agreement with James I. He was involved in debates in the church, and sat on the committee which tried Galileo. He established a Catholic diocesan system. He never came to Ireland as Archbishop of Armagh and died in Rome.

LONDONDERRY, LADY EDITH HELEN VANE-TEMPEST-STEWART (née CHAPLIN) 1878–1949

Edith, Lady Londonderry, was active in many war-time organisations and charities. She hosted functions for the Conservative Party and was also very friendly with the Labour Party leader, Ramsay MacDonald. She was President of the Women's Advisory Committee of the Northern Counties Provisional Area of the National Union of Conservative and Unionist Associations. She was President of the War Service Legion and Chairman of the Queen's Institute of District Nursing. She was in charge of the Red Cross Casualty Station at Mount Stewart. She designed the garden at Mount Stewart.

LONDONDERRY, LADY FRANCES ANNE (née VANE-TEMPEST)

Frances, Marchioness of Londonderry, was the Countess of Antrim in her own right. She corresponded with major political and diplomatic figures of her day, such as Benjamin Disraeli, Prince Gortchekov, Count Brunov and Mary, Duchess of Gloucester. Among her letters are many from Tzar Alexander I. She travelled widely, visiting the continent and Russia, and kept journals of these visits. She also wrote a history of the Vane-Tempest family.

LONDONDERRY, LADY THERESA VANE-TEMPEST-STEWART 1856–1919

Theresa, Lady Londonderry, was known as the foremost Tory political hostess of her day. She entertained royalty both at Wynyard Park, County Durham, and at Mount Stewart, County Down. *The Londonderrys: A Family Portrait*, published in 1979 by H. Montgomery Hyde, refers to her as 'one of the most striking and dominating feminine personalities of our time . . . with unrivalled experience of men, and things social and political'.

LONG, ARTHUR W. b.1874

Arthur Long was born in Coleraine, County Londonderry and was educated at Coleraine Model School. He emigrated to South Africa and worked for a leather merchant. He took up the study of astronomy in 1910 and two years later was one of the founders of the Cape Astronomical Association, serving as its President from 1919 to 1921. This association combined with the Johannesburg Astronomical association to form the Astronomical Society of South Africa. In 1921 he was elected Fellow of the Royal Astronomical Association. He wrote articles for the *Cape Times* and was active as a lecturer and demonstrator. He was the first astronomer to map the southern sky, and in 1922 published a star atlas for the southern hemisphere. His special interest was variable stars.

LOUGHLIN, JOHN 1817–1891

John Loughlin was born in County Down and went to America as a boy. He was educated there and ordained in Albany in 1840. In 1853 he was consecrated first Bishop of Brooklyn, and began building the cathedral there in 1868. He died in Brooklyn.

LOWRY, CHARLES GIBSON 1880–1951

Charles Lowry was born in Limavady, County Londonderry and was educated at Foyle College, Derry, and Queen's College, Belfast, where he obtained a degree in medicine. He was a Fellow of the Royal College of Surgeons in Ireland and became consultant surgeon at the Ulster Hospital for Women. He was consultant gynaecologist at the Royal Victoria Hospital, Belfast and was Pro-Chancellor and Emeritus Professor of Midwifery and Gynaecology at Queen's University, Belfast.

LOWRY, ROBERT WILLIAM 1824–1905

Robert Lowry was born in Drumreagh, County Tyrone, and was educated in Dungannon and Belfast. He joined the 47th Regiment and served in the Crimea and the Ionian islands. In 1863 he was promoted to the rank of colonel and commanded field forces in the defence of Canada in 1866. He eventually became a lieutenant-general and was created a Companion of the Order of the Bath.

LOWRY, STRICKLAND 1737–c.1785

Strickland Lowry was a portrait painter who came from Cumberland, and worked in Ireland. He came to Belfast around 1762. He contributed thirteen engraved views of churches, which appeared in *History and Antiquities of Shrewsbury* (1779). Sir John Rawdon, 1st Earl of Moira was his patron.

LOWRY-CORRY, DOROTHY 1885–1967

Dorothy Lowry-Corry was born at Castlecoole, County Fermanagh. She was interested in history and genealogy and particularly in archaeology of the Early Christian period. She was Vice-President of the Royal Society of Antiquaries. She contributed many papers to the Royal Irish Academy; perhaps the most important was the recording of the Boa Island and Lustymore stone figures. When the Ancient Monuments Advisory Committee was established, she represented County Fermanagh. She conducted a survey of the monuments of County Fermanagh, and discovered the Corracloona megalithic tomb in County Leitrim. She contributed many articles to the *Ulster Journal of Archaeology*.

LOWRY–CORRY, SOMERSET 1835–1913

Somerset Lowry-Corry was born in London and was educated at Eton and Cambridge. He was appointed Under-Secretary for Home Affairs, and in 1867, privy councillor. Having governed New South Wales, and received a knighthood, he became Lord Lieutenant of Tyrone. He published several books on the history and landscape of Tyrone and Fermanagh.

LUKE, JOHN 1906–1975

John Luke was born in Belfast, was educated at Hillman Street National School, and became a riveter's boy in the shipyards. He later worked in the York Street

Flax-spinning Company and attended the School of Art for evening classes. He won the Sorella Scholarship, which enabled him to attend day classes. In 1927 the Dunville award meant he was able to study at the Slade School of Art, London, and during his stay he won the Robert Ross Scholarship. He worked for a short period in London, exhibiting at the Westminster School of Art, but returned to Belfast in 1931. He exhibited at the Royal Hibernian Academy, Dublin, and in 1938 assisted Morris Harding in the work for the Northern Ireland government's pavilion at the Glasgow Empire Exhibition. During the air raids in Belfast in 1941, he went to live in Killylea, County Armagh. A one–man exhibition was held in 1946 in the Ulster Museum. He painted a large mural in the dome of the City Hall, Belfast, which was commissioned to commemorate the Festival of Britain in 1951. Another of his murals is in the Masonic Hall in Rosemary Street, Belfast. He was a member of the Royal Ulster Academy. He carved two coats of arms for Lord Wakehurst and Lord Erskine, both in Hillsborough. The Ulster Museum has 'Natas', his self-portrait, painted in 1928. Other works include 'The Rehearsal'; 'The Dancer' and a portrait of Roberta Hewitt.

LUNDY, ROBERT 17th century
Robert Lundy was sent to Derry in 1688 to command a small garrison which had declared allegiance to William III and opposition to James II. As soon as he was threatened with the approach of the opposing army, he announced his intentions of surrendering, and those who desired to resist removed him from office. He was permitted to escape to Scotland in disguise, where he was captured and was for a short time held in the Tower of London. His fate after his release is not known. His effigy is burnt each year when the siege of Derry is commemorated.

LYLE, THOMAS *c.*1857–1944
Thomas Lyle was born in Coleraine, County Londonderry, and was educated at Trinity College, Dublin, where he was 100 yards sprinting champion and an international

rugby player. He made important contributions to theories of transformers and alternators and was a pioneer in using the operator *j* in alternating current theory. He became Professor of Natural Philosophy at the University of Melbourne and held many public appointments in Australia. He received a knighthood.

LYNAS, J. LANGTRY 1879–1956
Langtry Lynas was born at Greenock, Scotland, but came to Belfast in 1882. During his life he had many jobs, at one time housepainting and signwriting. In 1904 he went on a trip through Europe, and later spent a short time at the Belfast School of Art. In 1928 he published *Psychological Satyr or The Hounds of Hell*, which he had written and illustrated. In 1935 *Why* was published. In 1939 he held an exhibition of sculpture, paintings and drawings at Magee's Gallery, Belfast. A self-portrait is in the Ulster Museum, and County Armagh Museum has his picture, 'Creation of Man'.

LYND, ROBERT WILSON 1879–1949
Robert Lynd was born in Belfast and was educated at the Royal Belfast Academical Institution and Queen's College, Belfast, where he studied classics. Having trained with the Belfast daily, the *Northern Whig*, in 1901 he went to Manchester and then London, working as a free-lance journalist and sharing a studio with Paul Henry, the artist, with whom he had graduated. He joined the staff of the *Daily News* (subsequently called the *News Chronicle*) and from 1912 to 1947 was its literary editor. As well as making contributions to the *Nation*, he wrote a weekly essay under the pseudonym 'Y.Y.' for the *New Statesman* from 1913 to 1945. He was a Republican and a Gaelic Leaguer and taught Irish classes in London. He wrote for the Sinn Féin movement under the name of Riobard Ó Floinn, and edited some of the works of James Connolly. Among his books, which number over thirty, are *Home Life in Ireland*; *Ireland a Nation*; *The Art of Letters* and *Doctor Johnson and Company*. He died in Hampstead.

LYNN, SAMUEL FERRIS 1834–1876
Samuel Lynn was born in County Wexford.

He was educated at Belfast Academy and studied architecture in his brother's Belfast office, at the same time attending classes at the Belfast School of Design. In 1854 he went to London and entered the Royal Academy, where, in 1875 one of his exhibits was a statue of Lord Lurgan's greyhound, Master McGrath, who had won the Waterloo Cup in 1868, 1869 and 1871 and had been beaten only once in thirty-seven races. He was an associate of the Royal Hibernian Academy and a member of the Institute of Sculptors. Other works include the statues of Prince Albert on the Albert Memorial Clock, Belfast, of Dr Henry Cooke in Belfast and of Lord Downshire in Hillsborough. He died in Belfast.

LYONS, FRANCIS STEWART LELAND
1923–1983
F. S. L. Lyons was born in Derry and was educated at Tunbridge Wells, the High School, Dublin and Trinity College, Dublin. He was a lecturer in history at Hull University and at Trinity College, Dublin, before becoming Professor of History at Kent University in 1964. In 1969 he was appointed Master of Eliot College on the Kent University campus. He became Provost of Trinity College, Dublin in 1974, but in 1981 he relinquished the post in order to devote himself to writing. He won the Ewart-Biggs Memorial Prize and the Woolfson Literary Prize for History for his book *Culture and Anarchy in Ireland, 1890–1939*, published in 1979. Five universities awarded him honorary doctorates. He was a Fellow of the Royal Society of Literature and of the British Academy and was Visiting Professor at Princeton University. Among his other publications are *The Fall of Parnell; Charles Stewart Parnell*, which won the Heinemann Prize in 1978; *John Dillon, a Biography* and *Ireland since the Famine*. He died in Dublin.

LYTLE, JAMES HILL and JOHN N. late 19th century
James Lytle and his brother were educated at Methodist College, Belfast and both were international rugby players. In the 1890's they played twelve times and eight times respectively for Ireland. James played in two Triple Crown wins in 1894 and 1899.

LYTTLE, WESLEY GUARD 1844–1896
Wesley Lyttle was born in Newtownards, County Down, and he wrote several poems and sketches in a County Down dialect. He gave popular readings which were published as *Robin's Readings*. He edited a newspaper, the *North Down and Bangor Gazette*, and he was one of the first people to teach shorthand in Belfast. He wrote many novels, among them *Sons of the Sod* and *Betsy Gray: A Tale of Ninety-Eight*.

142

M

MacADAM, JAMES 1801–1861
James MacAdam was born in Belfast and was educated at the Belfast Academical Institution, and at Trinity College, Dublin. He was a Fellow of the Geological Society and used the opportunity to examine excavations made during the construction of the Irish railway systems. He had a private museum of geological specimens which was regarded as the best in Ireland. In 1849 he was appointed the first Librarian of Queen's College, Belfast. He was President of the Belfast Natural History Society and a founder of the Botanic Gardens, Belfast.

MacADAM, ROBERT SHIPBOY 1808–1895
Robert MacAdam was born in Belfast and was educated at the Belfast Academical Institution. It is said that he had the ability to speak and write in thirteen languages. He was fluent in Irish and encouraged its study and the collection of Irish manuscripts. He was the principal founder of the *Ulster Journal of Archaeology* in 1853 and was its editor for nine years. He was a member of the Belfast Literary Society, the Belfast Natural History and Philosophical Society, and the Belfast Harmonic Society. Among his publications is a *Gaelic Grammar*. He and his brother James established the Soho Foundry in Townsend Street in 1832.

McADOO, ANNIE FLORENCE VIOLET *c.*1925–1965
Violet McAdoo was born in Cookstown, County Tyrone, and studied at the Belfast School of Art and at the Royal College of Art. She was a member of the Watercolour Society of Ireland. She worked in Belfast and exhibited at the Royal Hibernian Academy and the Royal Ulster Academy. A collection of her work is in the Ulster Museum.

McADOO, WILLIAM 1853–1930
William McAdoo was born in Ramelton,

County Donegal, and went to America as a boy. He was educated there, was called to the Bar in 1874, and was elected to Congress. In 1904 he was appointed Police Commissioner for New York, and in 1910 became Chief Magistrate.

McAFEE, DANIEL 1790–1873
Daniel McAfee was born in Bushmills, County Antrim, and was a Wesleyan minister, preaching all over Ireland for a period of thirty-eight years. He published many controversial tracts and several poems. He died in London.

MAC AINGIL, AODH, see MacCAGHWELL, HUGH

MAC AIRT, SEÁN 1918–1959
Seán Mac Airt was born in Keady, County Armagh, and was educated at Queen's University, Belfast. He established the Ulster Place-name Society in 1952 and was editor of its bulletin. He prepared two editions of ancient texts for the Dublin Institute of Advanced Studies: *Leabhar Branach* and *The Annals of Innisfallen*.

MacALEESE, DANIEL 1833–1900
Daniel MacAleese was born in Randalstown, County Antrim. He was self-taught and a shoemaker by trade. In his youth he wrote much poetry. He served on the staff of several Belfast newspapers and edited the *Ulster Examiner*. He was fined and imprisoned for four months in 1872 for contempt of court. He was founder of the *Vindicator* and the *Citizen* in Belfast, and of the *People's Advocate* in Monaghan. He served as member of parliament for North Monaghan from 1895 until his death.

McALLISTER, JOHN A. 1896–1925
John McAllister attended the Belfast School of Art and the Metropolitan School of Art, Dublin. Before that point he had worked

as a designer in the linen trade. He opened a studio in College Street, Belfast. His paintings were often of the Glens of Antrim, and he exhibited at the Ulster Arts Club. His portrait of William J. Coombes is in the Ulster Museum, and other work is in the Town Hall, Bangor.

MACAN, TURNER 1792–1836
Turner Macan was a captain in the 16th Hussars. He had a thorough knowledge of Persian language and literature and for many years was Persian interpreter to the Commanders-in-Chief of the British forces in India. He translated and published the work of the Persian poet Firdausi. He is buried in the East, and a memorial plaque has been erected by his widow in St Mark's Church, Armagh.

MAC AN BHAIRD, AODH BUIDHE, see WARD, HUGH

MAC AN BHAIRD, EOGHAN RUADH (WARD, OWEN ROE) c.1570–1630
Eoghan Ruadh Mac an Bhaird was probably born in Donegal. He was of the family of hereditary poets to the O'Donnells, which flourished from the twelfth to the seventeenth centuries. About 1600 he became chief poet to Red Hugh O'Donnell, and when Red Hugh fled to Spain, Eoghan Ruadh stayed in Ireland in the service of Rory O'Donnell. He composed a poem condemning Rory for surrendering to the English, but he also wrote a lament for him on his death. His last datable work was a lament for Niall Garbh O'Donnell, who died in the Tower of London in 1625.

MAC AN BHAIRD, FEARGHAL ÓG (WARD, FERGAL OGE) c.1550–c.1620
Fearghal Óg Mac an Bhaird was probably born in Donegal, a member of the great bardic family. He worked under the patronage of Turlough Luineach O'Neill. He wrote many poems in Ireland and for a period lived in Scotland, where he wrote a great deal of verse expressing his misery. He went from Scotland to Europe and appealed for sanctuary in Louvain.

MAC AN FHIR LÉIGHINN, EOIN, see MacERLEAN, JOHN

McARTHUR, KENNEDY 1882–1960
Kennedy McArthur was born in Dervock, County Antrim, and was a postman. He emigrated to South Africa in 1905, where he joined the Transvaal Mounted Police. In 1907 and 1908, he won the South African five mile and cross country titles. In 1911 he set a South African record for the ten mile distance. He won the South African marathon in 1908, 1909 and 1912. He won the marathon at the Olympic Games in Stockholm in 1912. A marathon is still held annually in Dervock in his memory. He died in South Africa.

McARTHUR, WILLIAM 1809–1887
William McArthur was born in Malin, County Donegal. He was a woollen draper in Derry and exported woollen goods to Australia. In 1857 he moved his business to London and was a member of the Corporations of Londonderry and London. In 1867 he was appointed Sheriff of London, and five years later an alderman. In 1880 he became Lord Mayor of London. From 1868 to 1885 he served as Liberal member of parliament for Lambeth. He was knighted in 1882. [Biography by McCullough, 1891]

MacARTHUR, WILLIAM P. 20th century
William MacArthur was born in Belmont, County Down, and was educated at Bangor Grammar School and Queen's University, Belfast. He was clinical lecturer in Tropical Medicine at the University of Oxford, and Director-General of the British Army Medical Services. He was a fluent Irish speaker and helped found the Queen's University Gaelic Society. He contributed a chapter on 'The Medical History of the Famine' to Edwards and Williams' *The Great Famine* (1956). He was knighted in 1939.

MACARTNEY, A. fl. 1903–1909
A. Macartney was an international soccer player and played for Ulster, Linfield, Everton, Belfast Celtic and Glentoran. He was capped fifteen times between 1903 and 1909.

MACARTNEY, GEORGE 1737–1806

George Macartney was born in Lisanoure, Loughgiel, County Antrim, and was educated locally and at Trinity College, Dublin. In 1760 he went on a European tour and was knighted four years later when he was sent as an envoy to the court of Catherine the Great in Russia. He was honoured by Stanislaus of Poland with the Order of the White Eagle in 1767. In 1768 he was member of parliament for Cockermouth, Cumberland, later taking a seat in the Irish parliament. In 1769 he became Chief Secretary for Ireland and held the position until 1772, in which year he was made a Companion of the Bath. Two years later he again entered the British parliament and was sent as Governor to the Island of Granada where he was captured by the French; he was eventually released and returned to England. In 1776 he received a barony in the Irish peerage and in 1781 went to Madras as Governor and served for four years. He then resided at Lisanoure, tending and expanding his estate and rebuilding Dervock, a nearby village. From 1792 to 1794 he served as Ambassador to Peking. In 1795 he was sent on a mission to Italy, and in 1798 was appointed Governor of the Cape of Good Hope. He was a Trustee of the British Museum, a member of the Literary Club, a Fellow of the Royal Society, and a member of the Privy Council. He was created a viscount in 1792 and an earl in 1794, becoming a British peer in 1796. He died in Chiswick. [Memoir by J.Barrow (includes Macartney's *Journal of the Embassy to China, An Account of an Embassy to Russia* and *A Political Account of Ireland*). Biography by Peter Roebuck, 1983]

MACARTNEY, GEORGE 1660–1730

George Macartney was born in Belfast and joined the army, serving in Flanders and Spain. He was dismissed after the fall of Marlborough. He was accused of causing the death of the Duke of Hamilton, when he served as his second in a fatal duel. He was tried and found guilty as an accessory in 1716, but was later readmitted into the army and promoted to the rank of general. He died in London.

MACARTNEY, JAMES 1770–1843

James Macartney was born in Armagh and was educated there. He joined the United Irishmen, became a member of the Royal College of Surgeons, and was a surgeon in the Radnor Militia from 1803 to 1812. From 1813, when he became a Doctor of Medicine, to 1837, he was Professor of Anatomy at Trinity College, Dublin. He published many works on anatomy and was a Fellow of the Royal Society. He died in Dublin. [Biography by Macalister].

MACARTNEY, JOHN WILLIAM ELLISON- 1818–1904

J. W. Ellison-Macartney was called to the Bar in 1846, and to the Irish Bar in 1848. In 1870 he was High Sheriff of County Armagh, and from 1874 to 1885 was member of parliament for County Tyrone. He was a justice of the peace and Deputy Lieutenant.

MACARTNEY, WILLIAM GREY ELLISON 1852–1924

William Ellison Macartney was born in Dublin and was educated at Eton and Oxford. He was called to the Bar in 1878 and served as member of parliament for South Antrim for eighteen years until 1903, when he became Deputy Master of the Royal Mint. From 1913 to 1917 he was Governor of Tasmania, and for the next three years, Governor of Western Australia. He was a privy councillor, and was knighted in 1913. He died in London.

McATEER, EDWARD 1914–1986

Edward McAteer was born in Coatbridge in Scotland. When he was two the family moved to Derry. In 1949 he was returned to Stormont for Mid-Londonderry, unopposed. In 1953 he became leader of the Nationalist Party, and he accepted the role of Leader of the Opposition at Stormont in 1965. After the Civil Rights marches in 1968 he relinquished this position. In the 1969 general election he was defeated by John Hume in Derry's Foyle constituency, and in 1970 he was defeated for the Londonderry seat in Westminster.

MACAULAY, WILLIAM J.B. 1892–1964
William Macauley was born into a County Antrim family and was educated privately. He entered the diplomatic service, and his first appointment, from 1925 to 1929, was as Secretary at the Irish Legion, Washington. Before being appointed Minister to the Holy See, a post which he occupied until 1941, he spent two years as Consul and four years as Consul-General.

MacAULEY, JOHN HENRY d.1937
John Henry MacAuley was born on a farm in Glenshesk, County Antrim; owing to an accident when he was a child, he was disabled. He was taught to carve wood by the woman for whom his mother worked as cook. He opened his own shop in Ann Street, Ballycastle, County Antrim, selling objects carved out of bog oak, and his window displays of farm animals, circus caravans, and even an Irish funeral, were renowned. He was a well-known fiddle player and wrote a number of songs, though the only one published was the famous 'The Ould Lammas Fair in Ballycastle O'

McBRIDE, DAVID 1726–1778
David McBride was born in Ballymoney, County Antrim, and studied medicine in Edinburgh, and London, where he graduated in 1764. He served in the navy and advocated yeast as a preventive against scurvy. He settled in Dublin and was a popular teacher and physician. He published *Experimental Essays on the Fermentation of Alimentary Mixtures*, a work which made him known in Europe, and his *Methodical Introduction to Medicine* was translated into Latin, German, French and Dutch. He was awarded the Gold Medal of the Society of Arts for inventing a process in tanning. He died in Dublin.

McBRIDE, JOHN 1650–1718
John McBride was born in Ulster and educated in Glasgow. He was ordained in the Presbyterian Church in Clare in 1680 and installed in Belfast in 1694. He declined to take the Oath of Abjuration in 1703 and was forced to escape to Scotland on two occasions. Much of his written work has survived.

McBRIDE, JOHN 1730–1800
John McBride was born in Ballymoney, County Antrim and was a brother of David McBride. He was a merchant seaman but joined the navy in 1724. He was promoted to admiral and became a member of parliament for Plymouth. He died in London.

McBRIDE, JOHN JOSEPH b.1898
John McBride was born in Belfast and was the author of a number of plays, among which are *The Yellow Rose, The Colorado Beetle* and *Down by the Glenside*.

McBURNEY, JOHN 1877–1917
John McBurney was born in Belfast and attended the Government School of Design, where he specialised in designs for damask linen. He was awarded an exhibition to study art in South Kensington for two years, after which period he returned to Belfast. He was deeply involved with the Belfast Art Society, the Ulster Literary Theatre, and was President of the Ulster Arts Club. He also designed embroidery.

McBURNEY, WILLIAM B. (pseud. CARROL MALONE) 1844–1890
William McBurney was born in County Down and contributed articles to the *Nation*. When he emigrated to America, he wrote for the *Boston Pilot* under his pseudomnym. He wrote the ballad 'The Croppy Boy'.

MAC CÁBA, CATHAOIR, see McCABE, CHARLES

McCABE, CHARLES (MAC CABA, CATHAOIR) c.1700–1740
Charles McCabe was born near Mullagh, County Cavan. He was a poet and harpist and among other works is remembered for his elegy on the death of Carolan who was his friend. Most of McCabe's work has been assimilated into the oral tradition, but some manuscripts are in the British Library. He is buried near St Ultan's Well in the barony of Castlerahan, County Cavan.

McCABE, WILLIAM PUTNAM 1775–1821
William Putnam McCabe was born in Belfast and was an ardent United Irishman, his interest stemming from Wolfe Tone's visit to Belfast in 1791. He became an active organiser and was responsible for Leitrim and Roscommon, and it is said that he was a master of disguise. He was arrested as one of a bodyguard to Lord Edward FitzGerald but was freed when he convinced the Scottish soldiers that he was Scottish. He escaped to France, having been specifically named in the Banishment Act. He established a cotton mill near Rouen, which was favoured by Napoleon. He returned to Ireland on three occasions, and on each one was arrested and imprisoned for short periods. He pleaded that he was travelling on behalf of his business, but the Home Secretary's comment was: 'It is very extraordinary that, in whatever part of the king's dominions his own business brought him, some public disturbance was sure to take place'. He died in Paris.

MacCAFFREY, JAMES 1875–1935
James MacCaffrey was born in Fivemiletown, County Tyrone. He was educated at St McCartan's College, Monaghan and Maynooth. In 1899 he was ordained and then carried out research in Paris and at the University of Freiburg. He was a monsignor and President of Maynooth from 1918 until 1935. He was editor of *Archivium Hibernicum*. Among his publications are *History of the Catholic Church in the Nineteenth Century*; *School History of the Catholic Church*; *History of the Catholic Church from the Renaissance to the French Revolution* and an edition of *The Black Book of Limerick*.

MacCAGHWELL, HUGH (MAC CATHMHAOIL, or MAC AINGIL, AODH) 1571–1626
Hugh MacCaghwell was born in Downpatrick, County Down. He became tutor to Hugh O'Neill's sons, having spent some years in the Isle of Man. He went to Spain and entered the Franciscan Order in Salamanca after the Flight of the Earls. He was appointed Guardian of the Irish Franciscan College in Louvain and taught there. In 1626 he was appointed Arch-

bishop of Armagh, though five months later he died in Rome, where he had been involved in the founding of the Irish College, and never reached his see. His writings deal with theology, philosophy and history, such as *Scáthán Shacramuinte na hAithridhe*, *Scoti Commentaria* and *Quaestiones in Metaphysicam* as well as two books on Duns Scotus. He wrote in Irish and Latin and is the foremost composer of Christmas carols in Irish.

McCALMONT, HUGH 1809–1887
Hugh McCalmont was born in Abbeylands, County Antrim. He became a wealthy stockbroker and settled in London, where he bestowed much money on hospitals. He died in London and his estate was valued at over three million pounds.

McCALMONT, HUGH 1845–1924
Hugh McCalmont was born in County Antrim. He joined the army in 1865, serving in Canada, Egypt and South Africa. He was promoted to the rank of major-general in 1896, and was member of parliament for North Antrim for four years until 1899, and for the next four years was army commander in the Cork District. He was knighted in 1900, and his autobiography was published in 1924.

McCALLUM, JOHN D. M. 20th century
Johnnie McCallum was a badminton and cricket player. He was capped eight times for Ireland between 1913 and 1926 in badminton. He introduced the game into Denmark and in Ireland founded the Strollers Club. He was a major in the army in the Second World War and was awarded the Distinguished Service Order and the CBE. From 1961 to 1963 he was President of the International Badminton Federation, and served as Secretary for fifty-two years in the Northern Branch of the Badminton Union of Ireland. He was also capped for Ireland as a cricket wicket-keeper.

McCANDLESS, REX 1915–1992
Rex McCandless was born in Hillsborough, County Down. He began work in a miller's when he was thirteen. In his early twenties he went to London and worked at

servicing lorries, and before the Second World War he returned to Belfast, where Short Brothers & Harland employed him to install brake systems in Bristol Bombay aeroplanes. In 1943 he went into partnership with his brother Cromie to repair vehicles for the Ministry of Supply. During this period he built his own motor-cycle and this became the prototype for the 'Featherbed' adapted by Norton. In the 1950s McCandless refined the design, calling it the 'Kneeler', and it broke many world speed records. In 1953 he designed two aluminium-bodied racing cars for Harry Ferguson. He developed a light cross-country vehicle which he called the 'Mule', but on Ferguson's death McCandless had no means of legally proving that the design was his. After a visit to Germany he devised a method of burning coal at low temperatures, an idea which saved the National Coal Board millions of pounds. In the 1960s he built his own autogiro. Towards the end of his life he perfected the technique of producing blackberry wine.

MacCANN, GEORGE 1909–1967

George MacCann was born in Belfast and was educated at the Royal Belfast Academical Institution and in 1926 entered the Belfast School of Art to study sculpture. In 1929 he was awarded a scholarship to the Royal College of Art, London, and won a prize on the commendation of Henry Moore. When he returned to Ulster, he taught at the Royal School, Armagh, Portadown College, County Armagh, and from 1938 to 1939 he lectured in sculpture at the Belfast College of Art. During the Second World War he served in Burma as a captain in the Royal Inniskilling Fusiliers. In 1942, his collection of short stories, *Sparrows Round My Brow*, was published under the pseudonym of George Galway. When he returned to Belfast, he taught art at Sullivan Upper School, Holywood. During the Festival of Britain in 1951, two sculptures were commissioned, one depicting St Columba for the Guild Hall, Derry. He also painted murals for the Northern Ireland section of the Festival of Britain. In 1955 he becme a free-lance designer and painter, and worked for the Group Thea-

tre and the Lyric Theatre, and painted murals for public houses. He was an associate of the Royal Ulster Academy, and exhibited in Belfast and Dublin. He was the husband of Mercy Hunter, and in 1963, he made the death mask of the poet Louis MacNeice.

McCANN, JACK 1917–1993

Jack McCann lived all his life on the Broughshane Road, Ballymena, County Antrim. He joined the family business and qualified as a lawyer in 1944. He practised as a solicitor in Ballymena. He had an enduring interest in the theatre, especially the Slemish Players and the Open Door Theatre, and he was involved in the North West 200 motorcycle race, on which he commentated. He founded the Glens of Antrim Historical Society in 1965 and the John Hewitt International Summer School in 1988.

McCANN, LOUISA fl. 1890s

Louisa McCann was born in Belfast. She went to Paris in the 1890s and studied at the Académie Julian. In 1890 a watercolour portrait was exhibited at the Paris Salon. All that is known is that it had been sent from the Hotel de Chartres, Rue Brea.

MacCANN, SOMHAIRLE 1901–1975

Somhairle MacCann was born in Belfast and educated at the Christian Brothers' School. He was appointed a textile designer to a damask and linen manufacturers in 1915, and attended Belfast School of Art, studying damask and embroidery design. In 1921 he was sentenced to death by British court martial but the sentence was revoked. He won the Sorella Art Scholarship in 1923 and in 1924 taught in the School of Art. He won the Dunville Scholarship in 1925 and went to study at the Royal College of Art, London. He became an art master at Galway Technical School from 1929 to 1935, and later became art inspector for the Department of Education, Dublin. In 1937 he became Principal of the Crawford Municipal School of Art, Cork, a post which he held until retirement. He exhibited at the Royal Hibernian Academy, Dublin, and he illustrated books. His work is held at the Cork Municipal Art Gallery.

McCARRISON, ROBERT 1878–1960

Robert McCarrison was born in Portadown, County Armagh, and studied medicine at Queen's College, Belfast, and at the Richmond Hospital, Dublin. In 1900 he joined the Indian Medical Service. His study of goitre, cretinism and deficiency diseases had to be put in abeyance because of active service during the First World War. In 1918 he returned to India and continued his research and from 1929 until 1935 held the position of Director of the Nutrition Research Laboratories at Coonoor. He retired from the Indian Medical Service with the rank of major-general. During the Second World War he was official medical adviser and for ten years from 1945 he was the first Director of Post-Graduate Medical Education at Oxford. He was awarded the Kaisar-i-Hind Gold Medal for public service in India, and the Prix Amussat of the Academy of Medicine of Paris for his original research. From 1928 to 1935 he served as Honorary Physician to the King, and in 1933 he was knighted. On a tour of America he lectured extensively in leading universities and medical centres. *The Work of Sir Robert McCarrison*, which was presented to him on his seventy-fifth birthday, included all his important papers. In London a McCarrison Society has been founded.

McCARTAN, PATRICK 1878–1963

Patrick McCartan was born in County Tyrone. He took a degree in medicine and was appointed Resident Medical Officer of the General Hospital in New York. He returned to Ireland and in 1917 was sent as a member of the Irish Republican Brotherhood to the American President with a message that Ireland intended to fight for its independence. In 1918 he was elected unopposed as member of parliament for King's County and in the same year was appointed Irish Envoy to America. Although he was opposed to the Treaty he felt that failure to accept it would lead to war. From 1948 to 1961 he was a member of the Senate.

McCARTHY, JAMES JOSEPH 1845–1895

James McCarthy was a prominent Irish architect. He built, among others, the churches at Ballitore, County Clare; Clogheen, County Tipperary; St Michael's, Ballinasloe and St John's, Tralee. He built the cathedrals at Monaghan and Thurles, the mortuary chapel at Glasnevin and the college chapel and senior infirmary at Maynooth. After 1854 he became the architect of Armagh Cathedral.

McCARTHY, JUSTIN 1830–1912

Justin McCarthy was born in Cork and was a journalist there before going to Liverpool and London, where he edited the *Morning Star* from 1864 to 1868. In 1870 he wrote for the *Daily News*. From 1879 to 1885 he served as member of parliament for Longford, and from 1886 to 1892 for Londonderry. As a writer he was highly regarded and wrote biography, history and fiction Among his titles is *Gladstone's Life*, 1898. He died in Kent.

MAC CATHMHAOIL, AODH see MacCAGHWELL, HUGH

Mac CATHMHAOIL, SEOSAMH see CAMPBELL, JOSEPH

McCAUGHEY, SAMUEL 1835–1919

Samuel McCaughey was born near Ballymena, County Antrim, and emigrated to Australia in 1856. He became manager of a sheep station in Victoria after a two-year apprenticeship. By 1860, with two partners, he had built up a famous marino stud farm in New South Wales. After this he bought other stations and introduced methods to improve the yield and quality of wool. He was the first to adopt irrigation and to improve the breed of sheep. At one point he had one million sheep to shear. He became the wealthiest man in the state and was known as the 'Sheep King'. He served as a member of the Legislative Assembly for twenty years until 1919 and was knighted in 1905. He gave twenty war planes to the government in the First World War, and £2,000,000 for charitable and educational purposes.

McCAULEY, LEO 1895–1979

Leo McCauley was born in Derry and was educated at University College, Dublin, where he became a lecturer in Classics. He then became a civil servant and in 1926 was secretary of the committee chaired by W. B. Yeats which was to advise on the new coinage of the Irish Free State. He later moved to the diplomatic service and was posted to Berlin as First Secretary. He served as Irish Ambassador to Spain, Canada and the Vatican.

MacCAUSLAND, DOMINIC 1806–1873
Dominic MacCausland was born in Daisy Hill, County Londonderry, and studied law at Trinity College, Dublin. He was called to the Bar in 1835 and became Queen's Counsel in 1860. He published many works on religion, the most popular of which, *Sermons in Stones*, has gone through thirteen editions. He died in Dublin. [Memoir by W.D.Ferguson, 1873].

McCLEERY, WILLIAM VICTOR 1887–1957
William McCleery was educated privately. From 1945 to 1958 he served as a Unionist member of the Northern Ireland parliament. From 1949 to 1953 he was Minister of Commerce. He was a prominent Orangeman, and in 1954 was Grand Master of the Grand Orange Lodge of Northern Ireland; in 1955 he became Grand Master of the Imperial Grand Orange Council of the World.

McCLELLAND, JOHN ALEXANDER 1870–1920
John McClelland was born in Coleraine, County Londonderry. He was educated at the Academical Institution, Coleraine, and Queen's College, Galway. In 1895 he became a junior fellow of the Royal University of Ireland, and in 1901 was appointed a Fellow. He was Professor of Physics at University College, Dublin, and he specialised in atmospherical electricity. He was a member of the governing body of University College, Dublin, a member of the Senate of the National University of Ireland, a Fellow of the Royal Society, London, and Secretary of the Royal Irish Academy.

McCLELLAND, JOHN T. 1940–1976
Jack McClelland was born in Lurgan, County Armagh and was an international goalkeeper, playing soccer for Glenavon, Arsenal, Fulham, Lincoln City and Barnet. Between 1961 and 1967 he was capped for Northern Ireland six times.

McCLINTON, ARTHUR NORMAN 20th century
Arthur McClinton was a rugby international who played for the North of Ireland Football Club. In 1908 he won an Ulster Senior Cup medal. He was capped for Ireland on two occasions and was selected for the 1910 Lions tour of South Africa.

McCLOY, SAMUEL 1831–1904
Samuel McCloy was born in Lisburn, County Antrim and was apprenticed to a firm of engravers. From 1850 to 1851 he studied at the School of Design. He worked in Belfast, London and Cork and in 1853 became Master of the Waterford School of Art. He exhibited at the Royal Hibernian Academy Exhibition in Dublin in 1862, and in London. In 1875 he returned to live in Belfast, six years later moving to London. 'At The Pantomime' is one of his best known oil paintings. His work is represented in The Victoria and Albert Museum, and the Ulster Museum.

McCOAN, JAMES CARLILE 1829–1904
James McCoan was born in Dunlow, County Tyrone, and was educated in Dungannon, County Tyrone, and Homerton. He was called to the Bar in 1856 and was war correspondent for the *Daily News* during the Crimean War. The first newspaper in English in Turkey, the *Levant Herald*, was founded by him in 1864. He was member of parliament for County Wicklow from 1880 to 1885. He died in London.

MacCOLGAN, JOHN d.1765
John MacColgan was born in Cregamullen, Inishowen, County Donegal. In 1752 he was appointed Bishop of Derry. He resided at Muff until he fled the authorities and found refuge with Joseph Campbell. From there he fled to Omagh where he died.

McCOMB, WILLIAM 1793–1873
William McComb was born in Coleraine, County Londonderry. Before becoming a

bookseller in Belfast he was a schoolteacher. He published six volumes of poetry, and a collected edition was published in 1864. He was responsible for establishing the *Presbyterian Almanac*, a publication which ran for nearly fifty years.

MAC CONMARA, SEÁMUS 1909–1936
Seámus Mac Conmara was born in Newry, County Down, where his father, a member of the Royal Irish Constabulary, was a native Irish speaker. He was the author of a successful novel, *An Coimhthíoc* (The Stranger).

MAC CON MIDHE, GIOLLA BRIGHDE *c.* 1210–1272
Giolla Brighde Mac Con Midhe was born in County Tyrone and seems to have travelled mostly within Ulster and Connaught. Little is known of his life but it appears from his surviving poems that some of his children died when very young. He came under the patronage of the O'Neills and the O'Donnells, and latterly of the O'Gormleys. His poetry is much quoted in early sixteenth century tracts as an example of bardic style. Until recently his identity was confused with that of the Scottish poet, Giolla Brighde Albanach (fl. *c.* 1220), and some of the latter's poems were erroneously attributed to him.

McCONNELL, ADAMS ANDREW 1884–1972
Andrew McConnell was born in Belfast and was educated at the Royal Belfast Academical Institution and Trinity College, Dublin, where he was later Provost, having been first Senior Moderator of Science. From 1946 to 1961 he was Regius Professor of Surgery, Trinity College, Dublin, and had served as Professor of Surgery in the Royal College of Surgeons in Ireland.

McCONNELL, ALBERT JOSEPH 1903–1993
Albert McConnell was born in Ballymena, County Antrim. He entered Trinity College, Dublin, in 1922, where he studied both mathematics and philosophy. He went to Rome for his doctoral studies and on returning to Dublin in 1930 was elected a

fellow of Trinity. In the same year he was appointed Professor of Natural Philosophy. In 1931 his book, *Applications of the Absolute Differential Calculus*, was published, reflecting his interest in Riemannian geometry and tensor calculus. He had been elected to the Royal Irish Academy in 1929, and collaborated with A. W. Conway in preparing the second volume of the collected mathematical works of William Rowan Hamilton, which was published in 1940. He was elected Provost of Trinity College, Dublin, in 1952, a position which he held for twenty-two years. During that period he instigated many reforms, including introducing a retiring age for all staff. In 1973, was appointed to the Council of State.

MacCORMAC, HENRY 1800–1886
Henry MacCormac was born at Fairlawn, County Armagh, and studied medicine in Dublin, Paris and Edinburgh. Before settling in Belfast in 1828, he travelled in Africa and America. In 1832 he was placed in charge of the fever hospital in Belfast, and during the epidemic of that year he took charge of the cholera hospital. He improved the conditions and diet of the patients in the district lunatic asylum, of which he was visiting physician. In 1836 he was one of the founders of the Belfast Medical Society, and he was among the first physicians to suggest that tuberculosis sufferers ought to be exposed to fresh air. He is said to have had a knowledge of twenty languages and was particularly interested in the study of comparative philology.

MacCORMAC, WILLIAM 1836–1901
William MacCormac was born in Belfast and was educated at Queen's College, Belfast. He was appointed surgeon to the Royal Hospital and in 1870–1871 was in charge of the Anglo-American Ambulance in the Franco-Prussin war. In 1873 he was surgeon to St Thomas's Hospital, London, and was employed as a consultant surgeon during the Boer War. He was knighted in 1881, created a baronet in 1897 and was President of the Royal College of Surgeons. He wrote many books on surgery and on his war experiences. He died in London.

McCORMICK, ARTHUR DAVID 1860–1943

Arthur McCormick was born in Coleraine, County Londonderry and was educated locally. He studied art at the Government School of Design in Belfast and later in London, where he worked for the *English Illustrated Magazine*. In 1889 the Royal Academy exhibited his work. From 1922 to 1933 he accompanied Sir Martin Conway as artist on his expedition to Karakoram in the Himalayas, and later accompanied Clinton T. Dent to Central Caucasus. His illustrations appeared in Conway's *Climbing and Exploring in the Himalayas* in 1894, and in 1895, McCormick produced his own book, *An Artist in the Himalayas*. He worked in many parts of the world, including Africa, the Netherlands, New Zealand, Norway and India, and he was a Fellow of the Royal Geographical Society. In 1927 the tobacco manufacturers, John Player & Son commissioned him to paint the head and shoulders of a sailor on their cigarette packets. He is represented, among other places, in the Victoria and Albert Museum.

M'COSH, JAMES 1811–1894

James M'Cosh was born in Ayrshire, Scotland, was educated at the Universities of Glasgow and Edinburgh, and was ordained in the Presbyterian ministry. In 1850 he was appointed Professor of Logic and Metaphysics in Queen's College, Belfast. This appointment was satirised by Thackeray in *Punch*. He was appointed President of Princeton College, America, in 1868 and remained there for twenty years.

McCOUBREY, MARGARET 1880–1955

Margaret McCoubrey was born in Eldersley, near Glasgow. At the age of twelve she began working for a men's outfitters shop in Glasgow, though she continued her education at night school. In 1896 she qualified as a junior shorthand typist, and three years later became secretary to the managing director of the first private telephone service in Scotland. She taught in the Skerries Business Training College, of which she became deputy headmistress at the age of twenty-four. She married and came to live in Belfast in 1905. She joined the Suffragette movement in 1910, and was an active militant. At the outbreak of the First World War she joined the peace movement, and gave refuge to conscientious objectors. She became General Secretary of the Co-operative Guild, and from 1910 to 1916 was elected onto the board of management. During this period she sat on all the sub-committees in turn, and she taught economics and the history of the Co-operative Society in the educational department. In the 1920s she took a one-year course in economics at Manchester Universtiy. She contributed articles to many periodicals, including the Co-op magazine, the *Wheat Sheaf*, and she had a weekly column in the *Co-op News*. Her history of the Co-op movement was unfinished at the time of her death. She was an active member of the independent Labour party, and in 1920 was elected Labour councillor for Dock ward. In 1933 she went to live in Carnlough, County Antrim, where she ran Drumalla House as a non-profit making base for members of the Belfast Girl's Club Union to come on holiday. Throughout her life she was a powerful orator, and refused to use a microphone. [Reminiscence by Elizabeth Hutchinson]

McCRACKEN, ELIZABETH A. M. (pseud. L. A. M. PRIESTLY) c.1865–1944

Elizabeth McCracken lived during the summer in Bangor, County Down. She was one of Ulster's leading sufragettes and published under her pseudonym. Among her publications is *The Feminine in Fiction*.

McCRACKEN, HENRY JOY 1767–1798

Henry Joy McCracken was born in High Street, Belfast. He was put in charge of a cotton factory at the age of twenty-two, and with Thomas Russell formed the first Society of United Irishmen in Belfast in 1791. In 1796 he was imprisoned for over a year, but was released and was appointed Commander-in-Chief of the forces which were defeated at the Battle of Antrim in 1798. He was prevented from escaping to America and was court-martialled. On refusing to turn informer, he was hanged in Belfast on the evening of the day of his trial.

McCRACKEN, MARY ANN 1770–1866

Mary Ann McCracken was born in Belfast and was educated at David Manson's school in Clugston's Entry, Belfast. She collected Irish harp music and was closely involved with the establishment of the United Irishmen. She was present when her brother, Henry Joy McCracken, was hanged in 1798. In partnership with her sister she started a muslin business which closed in 1815. She was a prolific writer and worked energetically for the poorhouse which had been designed and built by her uncle Robert Joy. A Ladies' Committee was formed in 1827 to supervise the treatment of women and children there, and she was its secretary for twenty-five years. All her life she actively opposed slavery and campaigned against the use of small boys as chimney sweeps. She was President of the Committee of the Ladies' Industrial School for the Relief of Irish Destitution which was established in 1847 to assist famine victims. She believed in the equality of women. In her nineties she assisted Dr R. R. Madden in the writing of the history of the United Irishmen.

McCRACKEN, WILLIAM 1883–1979

Billy McCracken was born in Belfast and was a soccer international full-back. He played for Distillery, Newcastle United and won medals in 1905, 1907, 1908, 1909, 1910 and 1911. He also played for Hull City. He was capped fifteen times for Northern Ireland between 1902 and 1923, and scored an international goal. He later managed Hull City, Millwall and Aldershot.

McCREERY, JOHN 1768–1832

John McCreery was born in Strabane, County Tyrone. He went to Liverpool, where he worked as a printer and became renowned for the high quality of his work. His poem, 'The Press', was printed and used as a specimen of his workmanship. He moved to London, where he continued to work as a printer. He died in Paris.

MAC CUBHTHAIGH (McCOOEY), ART c.1715–1773

Art Mac Cubhthaigh was born in Ballinaghy, Creggan, County Armagh, and was a major poet, although his livelihood depended on labouring and gardening jobs. He wrote an *aisling* or vision poem, *Úir-chill an Chreagáin* which became a popular song in south Ulster. He dedicated some of his poems to the O'Neills of Glassdrummond, a branch of the family who were traditionally patrons of poetry. Much of his work was set to music, and he was known as 'Art na gCeoltaí'.

McCULLAGH, JAMES 1809–1847

James McCullagh was born in Badoney, County Tyrone and educated at Trinity College, Dublin, where in 1832 he became a fellow and, in 1838, Doctor of Laws. He served first as Professor of Mathematics, then as Professor of Natural Philosophy, and he was Secretary of the Royal Irish Academy and Fellow of the Royal Society. He received the Cunningham Medal and won the Copley Medal. He published many papers on geometry and the wave theory of light. His failure to win the Dublin University seat for the Liberals, combined with overwork on his researches, contributed to his death by suicide. He presented the Cross of Cong and other antiquities to the National Museum.

McCULLOUGH, JOHN EDWARD 1837–1885

John McCullough was born in Coleraine, County Londonderry, emigrated to America, and worked in Philadelphia as a chair-maker. He made his first appearance on the stage in 1857. He played Shakespearean parts, the most successful of which was Othello, and appeared at Drury Lane, London in 1881. He suffered a nervous breakdown and died in Philadelphia.

McCURRY, NORMAN ERNEST (NORRY) 1919–1993

Norry McCurry was born in Belfast and moved to Oxfordshire where he spent his youth. He was educated at St Edward's and later St Edmund Hall. He served as a sailor on the Atlantic convoys, first as a seaman and then as an officer, and later he went to Chichester Theological College. He was appointed curate in Staveley and in Leeds, was priest in charge near High Wickham, and was vicar to St Edward's, Holbeck, Leeds. He finally moved to St Bartholomew's, Armley, Leeds, where he stayed for ten years from 1963. From 1973 to 1985 he was rector of St Dunstans, Stepney and from 1980 to 1985, was Prebendary of St Paul's Cathedral. He was appointed to the Advisory Council for the Church's Ministry, and Archbishop Runcie invited him to look after clergy who had particular difficulties. In 1985 he became Prebendary Emeritus and Honorary Priest to St James's, Picadilly.

MacDERMOTT, JOHN CLARKE 1896–1979
John MacDermott was born in Belfast and was educated at Campbell College, Belfast, and Queen's University, Belfast, where from 1931 to 1935 he was a lecturer in Jurisprudence and, from 1951 to 1969, Pro-Chancellor. He was Unionist member of parliament for Queen's University and in 1941 he was appointed Attorney-General. In 1944 he became a High Court judge and in 1947 Lord of Appeal in Ordinary. From 1951 to 1971 he served as Lord Chief Justice for Northern Ireland. He was created a baron.

MacDEVITT, PHILIP 1724–1797
Philip MacDevitt was born in Fahan, County Donegal, and was educated at the Sorbonne. In 1766 he became Bishop of Derry. He founded a bursary at Maynooth for students from Derry and raised money for a seminary at Claudy. He began building the Long Tower Church in 1786, towards which his Church of Ireland counterpart, Bishop Hervey, is said to have contributed two hundred guineas.

MAC DIARMADA, SEÁN 1884–1916
Seán Mac Diarmada was born in Kiltyclogher, County Leitrim, and at sixteen went to work in Glasgow as a gardener and later a tramway conductor. He moved to Belfast in 1902, worked as a tram conductor there and as a barman. He joined the Gaelic League, where he met Bulmer Hobson, who asked him to act as organiser for the Dungannon Clubs set up by the Irish Republican Brotherhood. In 1906 he joined the Irish Republican Brotherhood and was appointed Treasurer of its Supreme Council. He was a full-time organiser for Sinn Féin by 1907, and in 1910 he was appointed manager of *Irish Freedom*, a monthly journal. Despite being crippled by polio, he continued to work and was elected to the Provisional Committee of the Irish Volunteers in 1913. He was a member of the Military Council set up by the Irish Republican Brotherhood to plan a rising, and he fought in the General Post Office in Easter 1916. The Proclamation of the Republic carried his signature. He was court-martialled, sentenced to death and executed.

McDONAGH, W. PATRICK 1902–1961
Patrick McDonagh played hockey for Dublin University, East Antrim and Cliftonville. Between 1923 and 1934 he was capped twenty-nine times for Ireland. He was a cricketer and tennis player as well as an artist and a poet.

MacDONALD, FINULA 16th century
Finula MacDonald was the daughter of James MacDonald of Isla, and Agnes Campbell, and gained the nick-name Inghean Dubh. She was brought up at the court of the Stuarts and in 1569 married Hugh O'Donnell. Together with her mother, she recruited the majority of Scots mercenaries into Ireland at that time. She was given lands by her husband, on the banks of Lough Foyle, and fortified houses at Mongavlin and Carrigans, which allowed her to retain close contact with her homeland. She maintained a body-guard of Scottish auxiliaries. She bore Sir Hugh O'Donnell four male children and was determined to ensure the succession of her eldest son, Hugh Roe O'Donnell, to whom she gave birth in 1572. While Hugh Roe was imprisoned, and his competitor Hugh O'Gallagher was gaining strength, she arranged for O'Gallagher to visit Mongavlin, and had him killed. She offered bribes, sureties and hostages to Perrot in 1588 to

try and obtain Hugh Roe's release and in 1590, seeing Donnell O'Donnell as a threat, she defeated and killed him at Doire Leathan, Tirconnell. In 1593 she was described by Miler Magrath as 'a cruel, bloody woman who has committed sundry murders'. Her military strength and influence is seen as the decisive factor in the ultimate election of Hugh Roe O'Donnell to succeed his father as king of Tirconnell.

MacDONALD, JAMES ALEXANDER 1849–1928

James MacDonald was educated at Methodist College, Belfast and played rugby there and for the Royal University of Ireland. He played in Ireland's first international in 1875 and won thirteen caps in ten seasons. He was a doctor and was Chairman of the British Medical Association.

MacDONLEVY, CORMAC see MAC DUINNSHLÉIBHE, CORMAC

MacDONNELL, ALASDAIR (mac COLLA) d.1647

Alasdair mac Colla was a Scottish chieftain, related to the MacDonnells of Antrim. He was given the rank of major-general and led a company of soldiers to Ulster, where he refused to accept the Covenant and fought in the war of 1641–1652. He won a decisive victory near Ballymoney. Later he was appointed Lieutenant-General of Munster. He was killed in battle and is buried in Clonmeen churchyard, Kanturk.

MacDONNELL, ALEXANDER d. 1696

Alexander MacDonnell was the 3rd Earl of Antrim. In 1689 he led his Redshanks, on behalf of James II, to take Derry City. The Apprentice-Boys closed the gates against him and his lands were confiscated. After the Treaty of Limerick, however, he recovered his estates.

MacDONNELL, ALEXANDER 1794–1875

Alexander MacDonnell was born in Belfast and was educated at Westminster School and Oxford University. He was called to the Bar in 1824 and became Resident Commissioner of National Education, a post which he occupied for thirty-two years. He was appointed a privy councillor in 1846 and was created a baronet in 1872. He died in Drogheda. A statue of him by Farrell stands in Marlborough Street School, Dublin.

MacDONNELL, ALEXANDER 1798–1835

Alexander MacDonnell was born in Belfast and was involved in business in Demerara in the West Indies between 1820 and 1830. He was appointed Secretary to the West Indies Merchant Committee. He was one of the finest chess-players in the world, and a number of his games are in a publication by W. G. Walker.

MacDONNELL, JAMES 1763–1845

James MacDonnell was born in Cushendun, County Antrim, and studied medicine at Edinburgh, where he graduated in 1784. When he settled in Belfast he was one of the founders of the Royal Hospital, eventually becoming renowned as a doctor all over Ulster. He was a member of the Literary Society and a founder of the the Linen Hall Library and was active in many institutions. He was a keen amateur minerologist and geologist and an early member of the Belfast Natural History Society. Among his personal friends were Henry Joy McCracken and Wolfe Tone. He was involved with the Belfast Harp Festival of 1792.

MacDONNELL, RANDAL d.1636

Randal MacDonnell was the son of Sorley Boy and in 1601 inherited his father's lands. He was fostered on the island of Arran, and was known as 'Arranach'. In 1602 he changed allegiance and offered to attack Hugh O'Neill, whom he had formerly supported. He was knighted and in 1603 was granted three hundred and thirty-four thousand acres between Larne and Coleraine. The following year he married O'Neill's daughter, and when O'Neill and O'Donnell fled in 1607, it left him in a perilous position. He turned his attention to improving his estates. He was received well at the court in London, and in 1618 was created Viscount Dunluce, and became a member of the Privy Council and Lieutenant of the County of Antrim. In 1620 he was made Earl of Antrim. He died at Dunluce and was buried at Bonamargy, Ballycastle, County Antrim.

MacDONNELL, RANDAL 1609–1682

Randal MacDonnell was the son of the 1st Earl of Antrim. He travelled on the continent and was well received at the court in England. Charles I appointed him one of his commissioners in the Highlands of Scotland on the outbreak of war. He took a seat in the Irish House of Lords. In 1642 he was imprisoned in Carrickfergus Castle and supposedly escaped by being smuggled out in a bed as a sick person. He fled to York, and on returning to Ireland was again taken prisoner and again escaped. For helping raise troops in Antrim for the king's service, he was rewarded by being created a marquis. Under the Cromwellian settlement his estates were confiscated but restored to him in 1666. He died at Ballymagarry and is buried at Bonamargy, Ballycastle, County Antrim.

M'DONNELL, RANDAL WILLIAM b.1870

Randal M'Donnell was born in Dublin and was educated at Armagh Royal School and Trinity College, Dublin. He worked as assistant librarian in Marshes Library, and then as an inspector. He published three volumes of poetry, and many works of fiction among which are *Kathleen Mavourneen* (1898); *When Cromwell Came to Drogheda* (1906); *My Sword For Patrick Sarsfield* (1907) and *Ardnaree* (1911).

McDONNELL, SCHOMBERG KERR 1861–1915

Schomberg Kerr McDonnell was born in Glenarm, County Antrim, and was educated at Eton and Oxford. He served as Private Secretary to Lord Salisbury when the latter was Prime Minister. He fought in the Boer War and was knighted in 1902. He subsequently became Secretary to the Office of Works and died in Flanders, fighting with the Cameron Highlanders.

MacDONNELL, SORLEY BOY c.1505–1590

Sorley Boy MacDonnell was probably born in Ballycastle, County Antrim. Having been imprisoned for a year in Dublin Castle, he came to prominence in 1552 when he drove the English from Carrickfergus, stating 'playnly that Inglische men had no ryght to Yrland'. In 1559 the MacQuillans tried to retrieve the Route, which had been their territory, and a battle was fought at Bonamargy, with Sorley Boy leading the MacDonnells. He was imprisoned for two years following a defeat by Shane O'Neill. On his release, Sorley Boy, with help from supporters in Scotland, opposed the government's efforts to take his lands. His territory was invaded by the Earl of Essex, and his wife and children who had been sent to Rathlin for sanctuary were murdered, while, as Essex's account puts it, 'Sorley then stood upon the mainland of the Glynnes, and saw the taking of the island and was likely to run mad for sorrow saying that he had lost all he ever had'. For eight years from 1576 Sorley Boy ruled the north coast, which after many skirmishes remained in his command, including the MacDonnells' seat at Dunluce, which he had lost and reclaimed. In 1587 he settled his quarrel with the English. He was buried in Bonamargy, Ballycastle, County Antrim.

McDOWELL, FLORENCE MARY (née DUGAN) 1888–1977

Florence McDowell was born in Doagh, County Antrim. She was a primary schoolteacher and her first book *Other Days Around Me* was written after she retired. *Roses and Rainbows* was published posthumously in 1986. Sam Hanna Bell said of her first book: 'For myself, I recognised with pleasure my own country childhood, in a different county, but filled with much the same sounds and sights and odours'.

MacDOWELL, PATRICK 1799–1870

Patrick McDowell was born in Belfast and was educated at a school run by Hugh Gordon, an engraver. When his mother moved to London, he was apprenticed to a coach-builder there. He was taught how to draw and sculpt by Peter Francis Chenu, a French sculptor with whom he lodged. The work which first brought him to public attention was his statue 'The Girl Reading'. He exhibited at the Royal Academy in

1822 and was commissioned to execute statues of Pitt the Elder and Pitt the Younger, Lord Belfast for the city of Belfast, and Viscount Fitzgibbon for Limerick. He became a member of the Royal Academy in 1846, and his last piece of sculpture was 'Europa', commissioned for the Albert Memorial, London. He died in London.

MAC DUINNSHLÉIBHE, CORMAC c.1420–1480

Cormac Mac Duinnshléibhe was born in County Donegal. He and his family were heriditary physicians to the O'Donnells. He translated into Irish *De Dieties* written by Isaac and *De Dosibus* written by Walter de Burley. It is said that Cormac was trained in the Arabian school of medicine.

McDYER, JAMES 1911–1987

James McDyer was born in Kilraine, Glenties, County Donegal, and was educated at St Eunan's College, Letterkenny, and Maynooth. During the Second World War, after his ordination in 1937, he worked in England with Irish immigrants. From there he was transferred to Tory Island, County Donegal, and remained a curate in Glencolumbkille, County Donegal, from 1951 for twenty years. He was instrumental in having water and electricity brought to the area, and he instigated many co-operative projects to attract visitors and provide employment. He published his autobiography, *Father McDyer of Glencolumbkille* and *The Glencolumbkille Story*. In 1971 he was appointed parish priest of Carrick and Glencolumbkille.

McELDERRY, ROBERT KNOX 1869–1949

Robert McElderry was born in Ballymoney, County Antrim, and was educated at Queen's College, Belfast, and St John's College, Cambridge. From 1902 to 1916 he was Professor of Greek at Queen's College, Galway, and from 1916 until 1926 he was Professor of Ancient Classics there. He was later Emeritus Professor of Greek at Queen's University, Belfast.

McELROY, JOHN 1782–1877

John McElroy was born in Brookeborough, County Fermanagh and emigrated to America in 1802. He entered the Society of Jesus as a laybrother and was ordained in 1817. He built a church, a college, schools and an orphanage in Frederick, Maryland. He served as army chaplain during the Mexican War, and from 1847 to 1862 he was in Boston, where he built a church and a college. He died in Frederick, Maryland.

MacENTEE, SEÁN 1889–1984

Seán MacEntee was born in College Square, Belfast and was educated at St Malachy's College, Belfast, and Belfast Municipal College of Technology, where he qualified as an electrical engineer. For his part in the Easter Rising of 1916 he was sentenced to death. This sentence was commuted to life imprisonment, and he was released after the general amnesty of 1917. In 1918 he was elected Sinn Féin member of parliament for Monaghan. He was imprisoned for a second time by the Free State government for his active oppostion to the Treaty. He was a founder member of Fianna Fáil and held many ministerial posts. In 1918 he published *Poems*. He was given an honorary doctorate by the National University of Ireland and made a Knight Grand Cross of the Pian Order.

MacERLEAN, JOHN (MAC AN FHIR LÉIGHINN, EOIN) 1870–1940

John MacErlean was born in Belfast and educated at St Malachy's College, Belfast. He joined the Society of Jesus as a novice in 1888, and in 1904 was ordained. He collected and edited the poems of Seathrun Ceitinn (Geoffrey Keating). He spent a year in Spain, and on his return collected and edited the poems of Dáibhidh Ó Bruadair for the Irish Texts Society in three volumes.

McFADDEN, JAMES 1842–1917

James McFadden was born in Doochary, County Donegal, and was educated at Maynooth. He came to Gweedore, County Donegal, where he was appointed parish priest in 1875. He campaigned against the drinking of poteen and inhibited traditional gatherings where it might be consumed. He was known as 'An Sagart Mór': 'The Big Priest' and 'The fighting priest of

Gweedore', although he was a small man. He championed the cause of the Land League and in 1888 was imprisoned for encouraging tenants not to pay rent. In 1889, District Inspector Martin attempted to serve a summons on him outside Derrybeg Chapel after mass; a scuffle broke out, and Martin was allegedly murdered by bystanders. Cannon McFadden, along with others, was arrested and tried for murder. He was released, although some of the participants were imprisoned for up to thirty years. He became parish priest of Iniskeel and died in Glenties. He was a prolific pamphleteer.

MacFARLAND, JOHN HENRY 1851–1935
John MacFarland was born in Omagh, County Tyrone and educated at Queen's College, Belfast and at Cambridge. In 1881 he went to Ormond College, Melbourne and in 1886 became a member of the University Council. A Doctorate of Laws was conferred upon him by the Royal University of Ireland in 1892. He was appointed Vice-Chancellor of Melbourne University in 1910 and became Chancellor in 1918. He was knighted the following year.

MAC FHIONNGHAILE (or MAC FHIONNLAOICH), PEADAR (Mac GINLEY, PETER) 1857–1940
Peadar Mac Fhionnghaile was born in County Donegal and though he learned some Irish as a child, he was not an Irish-speaker. In 1878 he joined the civil service in England. When he returned to Ireland in 1893, he joined the Gaelic League, and from 1923 served as its President. As well as *A Handbook of Irish Teaching*, he wrote plays and edited anthologies of Irish verse. Among his works, many of which were written under the pseudonym Cú Uladh, are *Eachtra Aodha Ruaidh Uí Dhomhnaill, Conchubhar Mac Neasa* and *An Cogadh Dearg agus Sgéalta Eile*.

MAC GABHANN, MICÍ 1865–1948
Micí Mac Gabhann was born in County Donegal, the eldest child of a Gaelic-speaking family. When he was nine years old he was hired out as a herder. At the age of fifteen he went as a labourer to Scotland, and when he was twenty went to America

as a gold prospector. In 1902 he returned to Ireland, rich with Klondyke gold and bought a farm. His story, which was transmitted orally to Seán Ó hEochaidh was published as *Rotha Mór an tSaoil*, and it won the Club Leabhar award. Valentin Iremonger translated it into English as *The Hard Road to Klondyke*.

MAC GABHRÁIN, AODH 18th century
Aodh Mac Gabhráin was from County Cavan. His 'Pléaráca na Ruarcach' was translated by Swift as 'O'Rourke's Feast' and set to music by Carolan.

MacGAURAN (or MAGAURAN), EDMUND 1548–1593
Edmund MacGauran was born in County Cavan and was educated abroad. In 1581 he was appointed Bishop of Ardagh, and in 1587 became Archbishop of Armagh. He was opposed to the rule of Elizabeth and sought help from Philip II of Spain. On his return to Ireland, he had to take refuge with Hugh Maguire. He was killed when Maguire, at his instigation, rebelled against the English. His followers are said to have taken away his head.

McGEE, JAMES E. 1830–1880
James McGee was born in Cushendall, County Antrim, and was educated in Wexford where he joined the staff of the *Nation*. He emigrated to New York and practised law. He joined the army during the Civil War, rising to the rank of colonel. He published *The Men of '48; Sketches of Irish Soldiers*; and *Priests and Poets of Ireland*.

McGETTIGAN, DANIEL 1815–1887
Daniel McGettigan was born in Mevagh, County Donegal. He was educated at Navan and Maynooth and was ordained in 1839. He served as parish priest in Ballyshannon until he became Coadjutor to the Bishop of Raphoe in 1856, eventually succeeding to the see in 1861. In 1870 he was appointed Archbishop of Armagh, his original refusal to accept the position having been overruled by the Pope.

MACGILL, PATRICK 1891–1963
Patrick MacGill was born in Glenties,

County Donegal, where he left school when he was ten years old and was hired out at the Strabane hiring fair. He emigrated to Scotland when he was fourteen and worked as a navvy, a platelayer and a labourer. He published *Gleanings from a Navvy's Scrapbook*; *Songs of a Navvy* and *Songs of the Dead End*, all of which were very popular, the former procuring him a job on the editorial staff of the *Daily Express*. The archivist of the Chapter Library of Windsor Castle appointed MacGill, who was twenty-three, to the position of editor of ancient manuscripts. In 1914 he wrote a semi-autobiographical novel, *Children of the Dead End*, which in its first week of publication sold thirty-five thousand copies in England. During the First World War he served with the London Irish Rifles and later published *The Great Push : An Episode of the Great War*, *Soldier Songs* and *The Amateur Army*. His play, *Suspense*, which also deals with the war, was published in 1930. Among his other works are *Maureen*; *The Glen of Carra* and *The Rat Pit*. He went to America in 1930 on a proposed lecture tour, but due to the depression, the tour fell through. Because he had no money, he and his family were stranded in Los Angeles. His wife, Margaret Gibbons MacGill opened a dramatic school in Los Angeles and later in Florida. She published twenty novels, and several collections of short stories. Patrick lived in America for the rest of his life, and died at Fall River, Massachusetts, where he is buried.

McGILLIGAN, PATRICK 1889–1979
Patrick McGilligan was born in Coleraine, County Londonderry, and was educated at St Columb's, Derry, Clongowes Wood College and University College, Dublin. He was called to the Bar in 1921. After an unsuccessful attempt to win a seat for Sinn Féin in 1918, he became a member of the Dáil for the National University of Ireland. From 1924 to 1932 he was Minister of Industry and Commerce, during which time he set up the Electricity Supply Board to harness the waters of the Shannon. In 1927 he had the additional office of Minister of External Affairs. During 1929 and 1930 he was heavily involved in the Imperial Conference and the Committee on the Operation of Dominion Legislation. From 1937 to 1965 he represented Dublin constituencies in the Dáil. During this period he was Minister of Finance, and he also became Professor of Constitutional and International Law at University College, Dublin. In 1946 he was appointed Senior Counsel and served from 1951 to 1954 as Attorney-General.

MacGINLEY, PETER, see MAC FHIONNGHAILE, PEADAR

MAC GIOLLA GHUNNA, CATHAL BUIDHE *c.*1680–1756
Cathal Mac Giolla Ghunna was born in County Cavan or County Fermanagh, and though he had been educated for the priesthood, he wandered the roads as a poet and gained such an infamous reputation that the priests of County Cavan ordered that no Catholic home should shelter him. It is said that on his death, when a priest was being fetched, he wrote a poem of repentance, 'Aithreachas Chathail Bhuidhe', on the wall of a hut and that a halo of light surrounded his dead body. A few poems survive which are attributed to him, the most celebrated of which is 'An Bonnán Buidhe'.

McGONAGLE (Mac CONGHÁIL), DONALD *c.*1520–1598
Donald McGonagle was a native of Killybegs, County Donegal, and in 1562 was appointed Bishop of Raphoe. In the same year he was consecrated in Rome and took part in the Council of Trent. He returned to Ireland and attended a provincial synod in Ulster in 1587 when the decrees of the Council of Trent were promulgated. He lived in the Manor House at Killybegs and, according to a manuscript in the British Library, 'could write well and spoke Latin and English as well as Irish'.

McGONIGAL, AMBROSE JOSEPH 1917–1979
Ambrose McGonigal was educated at Clongowes Wood College and Queen's University, Belfast. He served with distinction in the Royal Air Force during the Second

159

World War and was decorated. In 1948 he was called to the Northern Ireland Bar and later became a High Court judge. In 1975 he became Lord Justice of Appeal. He was subsequently knighted.

McGONIGAL, JOHN 1870–1943
John McGonigal was born in Sydenham, County Down, and educated at St Malachy's College, Belfast, and Blackrock College. In 1892 he was called to the Bar, and from 1910 to 1913 was Professor of the Law of Personal Property, Contracts and Torts at King's Inns. In 1917 he was appointed Senior Crown Prosecutor in Belfast and in 1939 he became county court judge for Tyrone.

McGOUGH, JOHN 1887–1967
John McGough was born in County Monaghan and emigrated to Scotland. He was a middle-distance athlete and won a silver medal for Great Britain in the 1,500 metres race.

McGOWAN, JAMES 1841–1912
James McGowan was born in Comber, County Down. He emigrated to New Zealand in 1865 and began a business which was successful. He was elected Mayor of Thames, New Zealand, and on entering political life became Minister of Justice and Mines. While he was in office he wrote on mines and minerals and introduced prison reforms. He died in New Zealand.

McGOWN, THOMAS MELVILLE WHITSON 1876–1956
Tom McGown played international rugby for the North of Ireland Football Club. He won three international caps for Ireland and played in all four Test matches when he went with the Lions on the 1899 tour of Australia. In 1896 he won a Blue at Cambridge.

McGRATH, MILER see MAGRATH, MILER

McGREDY, SAMUEL 1828–1903
Sam McGredy had been a head gardener but in 1880 leased ten acres of ground outside Portadown, County Armagh and established the firm of Samuel McGredy & Son, Nurserymen. He grew and sold fruit trees, shrubs and pansies and his business flourished. He was appointed a justice of the peace. When he died the business was run by his son.

McGREDY, SAMUEL b. 1861
Samuel McGredy was born in Gilford, County Armagh and educated there. He inherited his father's nursery business at Woodside, Portadown, County Armagh and began to grow his own roses in 1891. Already there was competition from Dicksons in Newtownards, County Down. He began by raising a few hundred seedlings and in 1886 won first prize for roses at Douglas, Isle of Man. This was followed by a first prize and cup in Glasgow the following year and many awards followed. He won a Gold medal for his salmon pink rose 'Countess of Gosford' with the National Rose Society and in 1921 won the Society's Dean Hole Medal. He became a justice of the peace and was known as 'The Irish Wizard'.

MAC GRIANNA, SEOSAMH (GREENE, JOSEPH) 1900–1990
Seosamh Mac Grianna was born in Ranafast, County Donegal. He was educated at St Columbkille's College in Derry and St Patrick's, Drumcondra, where he qualified as a schoolteacher in 1921. During the civil war and its aftermath (1922–4) he was interned as a political prisoner. He is regarded as one of the finest writers in Irish of the 20th century. He translated many books from English into Irish under the auspices of An Gúm working on the belief that only a writer can translate a writer. He visited Wales in the mid–1930s and his experience there is recorded in his autobiography, *Mo Bhealach Féin*. From late 1935, when he felt his creativity had failed him, he suffered a nervous disorder. This was exacerbated by the fact that he was living in penury. Eventually he returned to Donegal and spent a long period in a mental institution in Letterkenny, where he died. Among his publications are *An Druma Mór, An Gradh agus an Ghruaim, Eoghan Rua Ó Néill, Pádraic Ó Conaire agus Aistí Eile,* and *An Bhreatain Bheag.*

McGUINNESS, NORAH 1903–1980

Norah McGuinness was born in Derry and was educated at Victoria High School, Derry. In 1921 she entered the Metropolitan School of Art, Dublin, and later studied at Chelsea Polytechnic, London, and in Paris. She went to India to stay with her sister, and on her return to London, became engaged in book illustration. She exhibited in New York shortly before the Second World War and created window displays for stores. Having returned to Ireland, she was President of the Living Art Exhibition from 1944 to 1972, during which period she was elected to the Royal Hibernian Academy. She illustrated books by W. B. Yeats, designed window displays for shops, and sets for the Abbey and Peacock Theatres. At the Venice Biennale she was one of the Irish representatives and her paintings have been exhibited in London, Dublin, Belfast, New York, Monaco, Derry and Paris. In 1980 she received an honorary degree from Trinity College, Dublin. She died in Dublin and the Douglas Hyde Gallery held a retrospective exhibition in 1968.

MACHA

Macha, a mythological figure, was the queen of Uladh who won her right to the throne by killing one rival and marrying the other. She compelled the sons of the dead man to build the palace of Emain Macha, the site of which is near the city of Armagh.

McHENRY, JAMES 1753–1816

James McHenry was born in Ballymena, County Antrim, and emigrated to America, where he joined the army as a surgeon. He became Private Secretary to George Washington. He was elected to Congress and served as Secretary of War from 1786 to 1800. He died in Baltimore.

McHENRY, JAMES 1785–1845

James McHenry was born in Larne, County Antrim, and published poetry in order to pay for his education at Glasgow. He emigrated to America in 1817, where he traded, edited the *American Monthly Magazine* and practised medicine. He published many novels, including *O'Halloran, the Insurgent Chief, The Hearts of Steel* (1825); *The Wilderness* and *Meredith.* Edgar Allan Poe praised his poem 'The Antedeluvians'. He was American consul in Derry from 1842 to 1845.

McHENRY, JAMES 1816–1891

James McHenry was a leading Irish-American financier and patron of the arts. He is remembered for having introduced Indian corn into Ireland at the time of the Famine. He published the *Life and Works of J. Sheridan Knowles* (5 volumes) and the *Geneological Table of Sheridan, Lefanu and Knowles Families.* He was the son of James McHenry (1785–1845).

McILHAGGER, DAVID SHERWOOD 1911–1993

David McIlhagger was born in Belfast and at the age of sixteen was an apprentice with the Belfast Omnibus Company, during which period he attended evening classes at the Belfast School of Technology. In 1933 he graduated in electrical engineering from Queen's University, Belfast, and in 1935, was appointed lecturer at the Belfast College of Technology. In 1942 he gained his doctorate from Queen's University and became lecturer there in 1955, and senior lecturer in 1960. In 1970 he was given a readership. He was a senior research fellow in Civil Engineering after retirement, and in 1977 joined the wave power research group. He contributed to the rebuilding of St Barnabus Church, Belfast, after the war, and in 1963 was lay representative from Connor diocese at the Anglican Congress in Toronto. He was Chairman of the local branch of the Institute of Electrical Engineers, and was the Northern Ireland Representative on the Council of the Benevolent Fund.

MacILROY, ARCHIBALD 1860–1915

Archibald MacIlroy was born in Ballyclare, County Antrim, and worked in insurance and banking and was a local councillor. He wrote many stories and novels, including *A Banker's Love Story* (1901); *The Humour of Druid's Island* (anecdotes of Islandmagee) and *The Auld Meeting House Green* (1898). He died at sea in the *Lusitania* which was sunk off the coast of Cork in 1915.

MacILWAINE, JOHN ELDER 1874–1930
John MacIlwaine was born in Belfast and was educated at the Royal Belfast Academical Institution, Queen's College, Belfast, and Glasgow University, where he was a student of engineering and naval architecture. In 1894 he took a degree in the latter after serving an apprenticeship in a shipyard. He then studied medicine and graduated as a doctor from the Royal University of Ireland in 1904. He studied at the Universities of Berlin, Cambridge, Paris and Vienna and held the Chair of Materia Medica and Theraputics at Queen's University, Belfast.

MacILWAINE, WILLIAM 1807–1880
William MacIlwaine was rector of St George's Church, Belfast. He was a classical and English scholar and was a member of the board of the Linen Hall Library. His works include *Death Conquered and other poems*; *A Vision of Italy: a poem*; *Heotha and Melech and other poems* and *The Thistle, Rose and Shamrock*, as well as several religious texts. He was editor of the second edition of *Lyra Hibernica Sacra* in 1879.

McINERNEY, MICHAEL 1906–1980
Michael McInerney was born in Limerick and was educated at Limerick Vocational School. While working as a clerk on the railways in London he joined the Communist Party and was co-founder of the London Connolly Club. He contributed to the *Daily Worker* and was editor of the *Irish Front* from 1939 to 1941, when he became a clerk for the Great Northern Railway in Belfast. During this period he was an active trade unionist and editor of the Communist Party of Ireland's newspaper, *Unity*. In 1946 he moved to Dublin as a reporter on the *Irish Times* and was appointed political correspondent in 1951. Among his many writings are biographies of Erskine Childers and Peadar O'Donnell. He was President of the Irish branch of the National Union of Journalists and was elected an honorary life member in 1974.

McIVOR, JOHN b.1894
John McIvor was born in Ballybay, County Monaghan. He was a school teacher and published many books, including *Popular Education in the Irish Presbyterian Church*; *Extracts from a Ballybay Scrapbook* (1974) and *Divining in Ireland* (1980).

MacKAY, WILLIAM b.1846
William MacKay was born in Belfast, and he and both his brothers Wallace and Joseph wrote fiction, plays and poetry. William published several novels among which is *Beside Still Waters*.

McKEE, EVA b.1890
Eva McKee studied at the School of Art in Belfast where she attended evening classes. It is likely that at the same time she was working with the Irish Decorative Art Association. She first exhibited her work in 1921 at the Arts and Crafts Society of Ireland and later took part in most of the major craft exhibitions. She formed a partnership with Eveline McCloy, and together they produced decorated wood-work, ceramics, embroidery, jewellery, leather-work, repoussé metal-work, lace-work, enamelling and calendars and cards, containing the hand-lettered verses of writers such as James Stephens and Joseph Campbell. They used Celtic and Oriental designs. Eva McKee specialised in painted pottery and used the products of Belleek and Wedgewood on which to work. She won a medal in 1922 at the Tailteann Exhibition in Dublin. She also produced ceramic tiles and ceramic brooches. Into the 1940s, the studio in Wellington Place was active and producing innovative work.

McKEE, FREDERICK 20th century
Fred McKee played soccer for Cliftonville and won Irish Cup medals in 1907 and 1909. He played for Belfast Celtic and won three Irish Football Association Cup medals in 1915, 1916 and 1919. He also played for Linfield. He was capped five times for Northern Ireland .

McKEE, WILLIAM DESMOND 1923–1982
Des McKee was both a rugby and cricket international. He played for the North of Ireland Football Club and was capped twelve times for Ireland between 1947 and 1951. He scored two international tries, both against England, one in 1948 and the other in 1949. He played cricket for Ireland on one occasion against Scotland in 1946.

McKELVEY, FRANK 1895–1974
Frank McKelvey was born in Belfast. He worked as a poster designer before entering the Belfast School of Art. In 1911–12 he won the Sir Charles Brett Prize for figure drwaing, the Fitzpatrick Prize for figure drawing in 1913–14 and a bronze medal in 1917. He was commissioned by Thomas McGowan to paint pictures of old Belfast, and this collection is in the Ulster Museum. He was a member of the Royal Hibernian Academy, and exhibited in Belfast, Dublin and Derry. He had a one-man show in 1936 where three of his landscapes were purchased as a wedding present for Queen Juliana by Dutch people residing in Ireland. He painted many portraits, amongst them Sir William Whitla, the Duke of Abercorn, first governor of Northern Ireland and Professor Sir William Thomson. He illustrated Margaret Holland's book *My Winter of Content*, and his work is represented in many collections.

MACKEN, JOHN, (pseud. FITZADAM, ISMAEL) 1784–1823
John Macken was born in Brookeborough, County Fermanagh, and served in the navy. He was one of the founders of the *Erne Packet* in 1808. In 1818 he went to London, where he was involved with the *Literary Gazette*, but he returned to Ireland in 1821. Much of his literary work appeared under the pseudonym Ismael Fitzadam. He published volumes of poetry: *The Harp of the Desert* (1818) and *Lays on Land*. He died in Enniskillen.

McKENNA, ANDREW JOSEPH 1833–1872
Andrew McKenna was born in County Cavan. He moved to Belfast in 1862 as editor of the *Ulster Observer*. After a quarrel with Bishop Dorrian in 1868 he left the *Observer* and founded the second *Northern Star*, which ceased publication on his death in 1872. He wrote poetry. He died in Holywood, County Down.

McKENNA, ELLEN (REV. MOTHER AUGUSTINE) 1819–1883
Ellen McKenna was born at Aghaninimy, near Monaghan. She emigrated to the USA after the Great Famine, and taught in a school in New York, before she entered the Sisters of Mercy in 1855. She was a committed social worker, particularly during the American Civil War. She published many poems and articles anonymously. She died in Balmville.

McKENNA, JAMES EDWARD 1868–1931
James McKenna was born in Truagh, County Monaghan, and was educated at St Macartan's College and Maynooth. He was curate in Enniskillen from 1893 to 1909 and parish priest of Dromore, County Tyrone, from 1909. He was a member of the Royal Society of Antiquaries of Ireland and of the Royal Irish Academy. He contributed to journals, especially the *Ulster Journal of Archaeology*. Among his works are *Parish of Dromore* (1916); *A History of the Diocese of Clogher* (printed in sections by the *Fermanagh Herald* from 1920); *Lough Erne, Lough Derg, Fermanagh and its Princes* and *Devenish* (1899).

MacKENNA, JOHN (or JUAN) 1771–1814
John MacKenna was born either in Clogher, County Tyrone or in Aghaninimy, County Monaghan, and was educated at the Royal Academy of Mathematics in Barcelona. He was appointed a cadet in the Irish Corps of Military Engineers in the Spanish army. In 1796 he sailed to Peru and served as a military engineer in Chile. In 1797 he was appointed Governor of Osorno. He became Commander-in-Chief of Artillery and Engineers in Carrera's revolutionary organisation. After a disagreement he was banished, but was recalled in 1813, at which point he became military commander of Santiago, having been promoted to brigadier-general. He changed allegiance to Carrera's rival, Bernardo O'Higgins and

became second-in-command after O'Higgins's victory. In 1814 Carrera was restored to power and MacKenna was banished. He died the same year in a duel with Carrera's brother in Buenos Aires. [Biography by his grandson, 1859]

MacKENNA, NIAL early 18th century
Nial MacKenna was born in Fews, County Armagh and settled at Mullaghcrew, County Louth. He was a prolific song-writer, and his Gaelic songs were extremely popular. Some of them are preserved in the *Transactions of the Iberno Celtic Society* (1808).

McKENNA, SIOBHÁN 1923–1986
Siobhán McKenna was born in Belfast and moved to Galway when she was five years old. She was educated at the Dominican Convent, Galway, St Louis Convent, Monaghan, and University College, Galway. Her acting career began in An Taibhdhearc (the Irish-language theatre in Galway), after which she joined the Abbey Theatre in 1944. The *Evening Standard* named her actress of the year in 1958, and she was famous for performances in plays such as *St Joan* by Bernard Shaw and Synge's *Playboy of the Western World. Here are Ladies,* her one-woman show, was a tremendous success, especially her delivery of Molly Bloom's soliloquy from Joyce's *Ulysses.* The honours conferred on her include the gold medal of the Éire Society of Boston, an honorary doctorate from Trinity College, Dublin, and in 1983, life membership of the Royal Dublin Society. In 1975 she was appointed President of Ireland's advisory Council of State.

McKENZIE, G. W. 1857–1924
G. W. McKenzie was born in Belfast and trained in the Governmnet School of Design. He won the National Scholarship which allowed him to study at the Royal Academy, London, where he exhibited, and at Julian's, Paris. He was involved with the Belfast Ramblers' Sketching Club and the Belfast Art Society and he became one of the foremost portrait painters in Ulster. He was an associate of the Royal Hibernian Academy, Dublin and he exhibited there. The Ulster Museum holds his portrait of William Gray.

MacKENZIE, JOHN *c.*1648–1696
John MacKenzie was born near Cookstown, County Tyrone, and was ordained as a Presbyterian minister in Cookstown in 1673. Having taken refuge in Derry during the siege of 1688–9, he wrote *A Narrative,* which showed George Walker, who had written his own account, in a very different light. McKenzie's is regarded as the more accurate.

McKEOWN, JAMES 1814–1889
James McKeown, after a brief schooling, went to work in Barbours, the thread-manufacturers, in Hilden, County Antrim. He contributed poems to the *Nation* using the pen-name 'Curlew' and 'Kitty Connor'. He became known as the Bard of Lambeg. For forty years he worked at Richardson's Glenview Bleachworks and received a pension. It was said that he frequently walked from Lambeg to Belfast to attend the theatre. His poems were written in Ulster Scots dialect and appeared in *The Harp of Erin;* a book of ballad poetry and native song, collected, arranged and annotated by Ralph Varian, in 1869.

McKINNEY, WILLIAM FEE 1832–1917
William Fee McKinney was born in Sentry Hill, Carnmoney, County Antrim. He farmed the family land. He was a member of the Belfast Naturalists' Field Club and he collected fossils and stone axes which he displayed at Sentry Hill. He compiled family histories of the people of Carnmoney and collected ballads and books of local poetry. He helped to found the Carnmoney Mutual Improvement Society in 1869. He was a keen photographer and six hundred photographic plates remain in his collection.

MACKLIN, CHARLES, see McLAUGHLIN, CHARLES

MacKNIGHT, JAMES 1801–1876
James MacKnight was born near Rathfriland, County Down, and was educated in Belfast. In 1826, in the absence of the librarian, he was appointed deputy librarian of the Linen Hall Library. He became editor of the *Belfast News-Letter* in 1827 and when he went to Derry he worked

on the *Londonderry Standard* though for a brief period he returned to Belfast to edit *Banner of Ulster*. He was an opponent of Repeal, but a strong supporter of the Tenant Right movement, and in 1852 he joined the Tenant League. Among his work is *The Ulster Tenants' Claim of Right*, published in 1848.

MacKNIGHT, THOMAS 1829–1899
Thomas MacKnight was born in County Durham and educated at Gainsford and King's College, London. From 1865 he was editor of the *Northern Whig*, Belfast. He published *A Literary and Political Biography of the Right Honorable Benjamin Disraeli, MP*, in 1853; *The History of the Life and Times of Edmund Burke* in three volumes, 1856 to 1860, and *Ulster as it is or Thirty Years Experience as an Irish Editor*, 1896.

MacLAINE, ARCHIBALD 1722–1804
Archibald MacLaine was born in Monaghan and was educated in Glasgow. He was Presbyterian minister of the English Church at the Hague and Preceptor of the Prince of Orange. He translated Moscheim's *Ecclesiastical History* in 1765. He died in Bath.

MacLAINE (or McLEAN), JAMES 1724–1750
James MacLaine was born in Monaghan. He went to London as a servant and set up a grocer and chandler's shop in Cavendish Square. In 1748 he took to the road as a highwayman, and among his victims was Horace Walpole. In Ireland his gain from robbery allowed him to live like a squire. In 1750 he was sent for trial to the Old Bailey, and among his possessions were found twenty-three purses. He was found guilty and hanged at Tyburn. He was a brother of Archibald MacLaine.

McLAUGHLIN (or MACKLIN), CHARLES *c.*1697–1797
Charles McLaughlin was born in Culdaff, County Donegal and was educated in Dublin. Before he appeared in London in 1725 he had been a member of a company of strolling players. It is said that he stabbed a fellow actor in a quarrel. By 1740 he had become popular at Drury Lane and was a friend of Garrick's. He wrote many plays, among which are *The True-Born Irishman; The Man of the World* and *Love à la Mode* and he was renowned for his performance of Shylock in Shakespeare's *The Merchant of Venice*. He died in London. [Biographies by Congreve, Cooke and Parry].

McLAVERTY, MICHAEL FRANCIS 1904–1992
Michael McLaverty was born in Carrickmacross, County Monaghan, and moved to Belfast as a child. He was educated at St Malachy's College, Belfast, and Queen's University, Belfast. He was a teacher of mathematics and physics until 1957, when he became headmaster of St Thomas's Secondary School in west Belfast. He was a member of the Irish Academy of Letters, and among his works are several novels, including *Call My Brother Back; Lost Fields; In This Thy Day; The Three Brothers* (1948) and *Truth in the Night* (1951). He also published collections of short stories: *Game Cock and other Stories* and *The Road to the Shore*. He died in Ardglass and is buried in Strangford, County Down.

McLEAN, JOHN ROBINSON 1813–1873
John McLean was born in Belfast, trained as a civil engineer in Glasgow, and in 1844 was working as an engineer in London. He constructed many docks, harbours and railways and was asked to report on the feasibility of the Suez Canal. He was a Fellow of the Royal Society and member of parliament for East Staffordshire. He died in Kent.

MACLEAR, THOMAS 1794–1879
Thomas Maclear was born in Newtownstewart, County Tyrone, and was educated at Guy's Hospital and St Thomas's Hospital in London. In 1815 he became a member of the Royal College of Surgeons and worked in Bedford Infirmary. He began to study astronomy and mathematics. In 1833 he was appointed Royal Astronomer at the Cape of Good Hope. He won the Lalande Prize and a Royal Medal for work which had been published in 1866. He made observations of many of the stars in the southern hemisphere, erected

lighthouses on the African coast, and it is said that he taught David Livingstone the use of a sextant. He was knighted in 1860, and in 1876 became totally blind. He died in Cape Town.

MAC MAGHNUSA MHÉIG UIDHIR, CATHAL see MAGUIRE, CATHAL MacMANUS

MacMAHON, BERNARD d.1747
Bernard MacMahon was born in County Monaghan, and was educated in Rome. In 1718 he was appointed Vicar Apostolic of Clogher, becoming Bishop of the diocese in 1727, and in 1737 Archbishop of Armagh and Primate of All Ireland.

MacMAHON, HEBER 1600–1650
Heber MacMahon was born in Farney, County Monaghan, was educated at the Irish College, Douai, and was ordained at Louvain in 1625. He was Vicar-General of Clogher and later Bishop of Down and Connor. In 1643 he was translated to the see of Clogher. Owen Roe O'Neill chose him as his adviser and on O'Neill's death in 1649 he was asked to lead the Ulster army. He stormed Dungiven, County Londonderry. His troops were defeated near Letterkenny, County Donegal, in an engagement in which he was badly wounded. He fled to Enniskillen, where he was taken prisoner by Cromwellian troops and executed.

MacMAHON, HUGH c.1606–1644
Hugh MacMahon was born in County Monaghan and after serving in the Spanish army returned to Ireland in 1641. He attempted to capture Dublin Castle, was betrayed, arrested and sent to London. He escaped from the Tower of London in 1644, but was recaptured, tried and hanged at Tyburn.

MacMAHON, HUGH d. 1737
Hugh MacMahon was born in County Monaghan, was appointed Bishop of Clogher in 1707, and Archbishop of Armagh in 1715. In 1728 he published *Jus Primatiale Armachamum*, which argued the question of precedence between Armagh and Dublin.

MacMAHON, JAMES 1865–1954
James MacMahon was born in Belfast and was educated at Armagh Christian Brothers' School, St Patrick's College, Armagh, and Blackrock College, Dublin. On leaving school he joined the civil service and in 1913 he was appointed Assistant Secretary to the Post Office. In 1916 he became Secretary. He was Under-Secretary to the Lord Lieutenant from 1918 to 1922.

MacMAHON, ROSS ROE 1698–1748
Ross MacMahon was born in County Monaghan and was educated in Rome. In 1727 he returned to Ireland and in 1738 was appointed Bishop of Clogher. In 1747 he became Archbishop of Armagh.

MacMANUS, ANNA (née JOHNSTON; pseud. CARBERY, ETHNA) 1866–1902
Anna Johnston was born in Ballymena, County Antrim. She wrote many poems which were published in the *Nation* and *United Ireland* and in a collection, *The Four Winds of Eirinn*. In collaboration with Alice Milligan, she founded a monthly paper, the *Northern Patriot* and later the *Shan Van Vocht*, of which she was editor from 1896 to 1899. She was a member of Inghinidhe na hÉireann, which provided free classes in Irish, music, dance, history and drama, and gave Yeats the impetus to launch the Irish National Theatre. Two volumes of her collected short stories appeared posthumously under the titles *The Passionate Hearts* and *In the Celtic Past*. Her collected poems, together with the poems of her husband, Séamus MacManus and of Alice Milligan, were published as *We Sang For Ireland*.

McMANUS, HENRY d.1873
Henry McManus was born in Monaghan and was educated at the Hibernian School in Phoenix Park, Dublin. He worked in Monaghan as an artist and painted many religious works for churches in the area. In 1835 he moved to Dublin and two years later, to London. In 1839 the Royal Academy accepted 'An Irish Market Day at Ballybay' and 'May Day at Finglas'. He became head of the Glasgow School of Design in 1845 and four years later, head of the Dublin School of Design. His

illustrations were included in Hall's *Ireland* and Carleton's *Traits and Stories of the Irish Peasants.*

MacMANUS, SEAMUS 1869–1960
Seamus MacManus was born in Inver, County Donegal. He was educated at Glencoagh National School and in 1888 became its Principal. He began to write for the *Weekly Irish Times* and other journals, and in 1899 went to America, where his stories were popular. He wrote many fairy-tales, poems and novels, among which are *Shuilers; Humours of Donegal; Through the Turf Smoke; The Bewitched Fiddle* and *Land of the O'Friels.* He was also a playwright and published *The Woman of Seven Sorrows; Orange and Green; Dinny O'Dowd* and *Father Peter's Miracle.* Though he continued to be based in America, he returned to Donegal every year, and is remembered for having told stories to the children at the village pump. In 1938 he published his autobiography, *The Rocky Road to Dublin.*

MacMANUS, TERENCE BELLEW c. 1823–1861
Terence Bellew MacManus was born in Tempo, County Fermanagh. He went to Liverpool, where he was engaged in shipping. After returning to Ireland, he joined the Young Ireland movement in 1843, was arrested as a rebel in Cork, tried and sentenced to death. In 1849 he was transported to Tasmania, but he escaped in 1852. He died in San Francisco, and his body was brought back to Ireland and buried in Glasnevin cemetery, attended by masses of sympathisers, the funeral having been organised by the Fenian Brotherhood.

MAC MAOLÁIN, SEÁN 1886–1973
Seán Mac Maoláin was born in County Antrim. In 1912 he won first prize for the Oireachtas Ode. He published many plays, stories and poems, among which are *Éan Corr; Finnscéal agus Fírinne; Lomramh Ghlómair* and an autobiography, *Gleann Airbh go Glas Náion.*

McMASTER, ANEW 1894–1962
Anew McMaster was born in Monaghan and was educated in England. He became an actor. In 1911 he appeared in *The Scarlet Pimpernel* and played opposite Peggy O'Neill in *Paddy the Next Best Thing.* In 1921 he toured Australia and on his return to England formed a company which he managed, as well as directing and acting in performances. He was renowned for his portrayal of Shylock and Coriolanus, and in 1933 appeared at the Shakespeare Memorial Theatre, Stratford-on-Avon, as Hamlet. He toured the Near East, Ireland and Australia, returning to Dublin in 1951.

MacMASTER, GILBERT 1778–1854
Gilbert MacMaster was born in Saintfield, County Down, and was educated in Philadelphia, where he became a medical doctor. He served as pastor of the Reformed Church at Duanesberg, New York, from 1808 until 1840 and of a church at Princetown for the next six years. He became Doctor of Divinity, and among his publications are *Apology for the Book of Psalms* and an *Essay in Defence of Christianity.* He died in Albany.

McMASTER, WILLIAM 1811–1887
William McMaster was born in County Tyrone and became a merchant in Toronto. He was a member of the Legislative Council from 1862 to 1867 and was called to the Senate. He was appointed President of the Bank of Commerce and was founder of a Literary Institute and a Baptist church, as well as McMaster Hall, which is now the University of Toronto. He died in Toronto.

MAC MEANMAIN, SEÁN 1891–1962
Seán Mac Meanmain was born in County Donegal and was a teacher of Irish in the McDevitt Institute in Glenties, County Donegal. Among his works are *Scéalta Goiridhe Geimhridh; Inné agus Inniú; Mám as mo Mhála; Trí Mhion-Dráma; Crathadh an Phocáin* and *Stair na h-Éireann.*

McMILLAN, HECTOR 1923–1993
Hector McMillan was secretary of the Sandy Row and Lower Donegall Road Redevelopment Committee. He was Chairman of the Mid-Donegall Road and Sandy Row Tenants' Association. He was a prominent

member of the Orange and Black Institutions in the Sandy Row District, and Treasurer of the Sandy Row Arch Committee. He was one of the founders of the Shaftsbury Credit Union. He served in the Ulster Special Constabulary and the Royal Ulster Constabulary Reserve and was an elder in Great Victoria Street Presbyterian Church.

McMONAGLE, ALEXANDER 1848–1919

Alexander McMonagle was born near Derry and worked as a journalist in Belfast. He was founder of the *Ulster Echo* and the *Witness*, which he edited until his death.

McMORRAN, EDWARD J. 1923–1984

Eddie McMorran was born in Larne, County Antrim and was educated at Larne School where he won a schoolboy international cap for soccer. He played for Ballyclare, Larne, Belfast Celtic, Leeds United and Crewe Alexander. Between 1947 and 1957 he was capped fifteen times for the Northern Ireland senior side and scored four international goals.

MacMOYER, FLORENCE d.1713

Florence MacMoyer was born in Ballymoyer, County Armagh. He was a school master and his family were hereditary keepers of the Book of Armagh, a manuscript thought to date back to 807. It is said that he pawned the book for £5, a sum which took him to London to give evidence against Archbishop Oliver Plunkett. He returned to Ireland in 1683, his reputation totally discredited. In the nineteenth century, the Book of Armagh eventually came into the care of Bishop William Reeves, who donated it to the library of Trinity College, Dublin.

McMULLEN, JOHN 1833–1883

John McMullen was born in Ballynahinch, County Down, and was educated in Chicago and Rome. He was ordained in 1858 and became President of the University of St Mary, Chicago. In 1870 he was given responsibility for Chicago Cathedral. In 1877 he was appointed Vicar-General, and in 1880 was consecrated Bishop of Davenport.

MacNAGHTEN, EDWARD 1830–1913

Edward MacNaghten was born at Dundarave, near Bushmills, County Antrim, and was educated at Cambridge, where he rowed twice in the boat race. He was called to the Bar and later became Queen's Counsel. He served as member of parliament for County Antrim from 1880 until 1885, and for North Antrim from 1885 to 1887, in which year he became a life peer.

MacNAGHTEN (or MacNAUGHTON), JOHN 1724–1761

John MacNaghten was born in Benvarden, near Ballymoney, County Antrim, and was educated at the Royal School, Raphoe, County Donegal, and Trinity College, Dublin. He gambled away an inheritance and left Trinity College without taking a degree. He was given a post as the Collector of the King's Duty in Coleraine, but he squandered the money he had collected. His first wife having died in childbirth, it is said that he tried to abduct and trick into marriage the fifteen-year old Miss Knox, whose father had befriended him, but who opposed the proposed marriage. A member of the Knox family challenged him to a duel and wounded him, but he returned and attacked the Knox family when they were travelling to Dublin by coach and Miss Knox was accidentally shot dead. He was tried and convicted at Strabane in 1761. The public were not in favour of the hanging, so that the Knox family had to erect the scaffold themselves and an executioner had to be summoned from Cavan. It is said that the rope broke, but MacNaghten refused his liberty.

MacNAGHTEN, WILLIAM HAY *c.*1793–1841

William MacNaghten was born at Dundarave, near Bushmills, County Antrim, and was educated at Charterhouse School. He entered the service of the East India Company in 1809. It is said that he learned many languages and dialects. In 1840 he was created a baronet, in 1841 became Governor of Bombay, and in 1848 Envoy to Kabul. While quelling a rising in Kabul, he angered the Afghans by seeming to negotiate different settlements with both sides, and was shot dead.

McNAMARA, GERALD see MORROW, HAROLD

MacNEICE, LOUIS 1907–1963
Louis MacNeice was born in Belfast and was educated in Dorset and at Merton College, Oxford. He lectured in classics at Birmingham and was a lecturer in Greek at Bedford College, University of London. He was in Spain towards the end of the civil war. From 1941 he worked for the BBC as a scriptwriter and producer. He wrote many radio plays, among which are *Christopher Columbus; The Mad Islands; The Administrator; Out of the Picture; One For the Grave* and *The Dark Tower*. MacNeice was first and foremost a poet and his collections include *Autumn Journal* 1938–1939; *Holes in the Sky*, 1947; *Collected Poems, 1925–48; Autumn Sequel*, 1954; *Visitations*, 1957; *The Burning Perch* and *Solstices*, 1961. His collected poems were edited by E. R. Dodds and reprinted in 1979, and his autobiography, *The Strings are False*, was published posthumously in 1965.

McNEILE, HUGH 1795–1879
Hugh MacNeile was born in Ballycastle, County Antrim. He was educated at Trinity College, Dublin and was ordained as curate of Stranorlar, County Donegal in 1820. He preached in London and Liverpool and published many controversial works. He became canon of Chester in 1860 and Dean of Ripon in 1868. He died in Bournemouth.

MAC NÉILL, EOIN (MacNEILL, JOHN) 1867–1945
Eoin Mac Néill was born in Glenarm, County Antrim, and was educated at St Malachy's College, Belfast, and the Royal University of Ireland. He worked as a civil servant and in 1893 he was a founder member of the Gaelic League, editing its publication, the *Gaelic Journal*. From 1908 to 1945 he was Professor of Early Irish History at University College, Dublin. He became a commander of the Irish Volunteers, which he had helped to organise, and on Easter Sunday 1916 he countermanded orders for the Easter Rising

because he felt that there could be no success. He was imprisoned and released in 1917. In 1918 he was elected member of parliament for the National University of Ireland. From 1922 to 1925 he was Minister of Education and served on the 1925 Boundary Commission, from which he resigned just as its report was about to be published, and he retired thereafter from active politics. In 1927 he was appointed Chairman of the Irish Manuscripts Commission. He published *Phases of Irish History; Celtic Ireland; St Patrick* and *Early Irish Laws and Institutions*.

McNEILL, HENRY 1836–1904
Henry McNeill (Knockems) was born at Deerpark, Glenarm, County Antrim. He was a hotel proprietor and tourist pioneer in the Larne district. Even in winter, seventy horses were needed and in the summer, two hundred vehicles in which to transport the tourists. The average number of tourists dealt with was six thousand per year. Henry McNeill's portrait was painted by M. G. MacKenzie in 1903. He is buried in McGarel Cemetery.

MacNEILL, HUGH HYACINTH 1900–1963
Hugh MacNeill was born in Glenarm, County Antrim, and was a soldier in the Irish army. He was appointed Chief of the Military Mission to the United States from 1924 until 1926. From 1941 to 1946 he served as General Officer Commanding the 2nd (spearhead) Division.

MacNEILL, JAMES 1869–1938
James MacNeill was born in Glenarm, County Antrim, and was educated at Belvedere College, Dublin, and Emmanuel College, Cambridge. After a successful career in the Indian civil service he returned to Ireland in 1914 and joined the Sinn Féin movement. In 1923 he was appointed High Commissioner for the Irish Free State in London and in 1928 was made Governor-General. The post became defunct in 1932. He died in London.

McNEILL, RONALD 1861–1934
Roland McNeill, Lord Cushendun, was

born in County Antrim and educated at Harrow and Oxford. He was called to the Bar in 1887, and from 1900 to 1904 was editor of the *St James Gazette*. From 1906 to 1911 he was assistant editor on the eleventh edition of the *Encyclopaedia Britannica*. He wrote several works defending the Union and was member of parliament for St Augustine's and Canterbury. In 1924 he was appointed a privy councillor, and as acting Foreign Minister signed the Kellogg Pact at Geneva. He was created a peer in 1927 and died at Cushendun.

McNULTY, EDWARD MATTHEW 1856–1943
Edward McNulty was born in Antrim and was educated in Dublin with George Bernard Shaw, who became his close friend. He wrote a memoir of Shaw which remains unpublished. During his lifetime he published two plays, *The Lord Mayor* and *The Courting of Mary Doyle*. Among his novels is *Misther O'Ryan* published in 1894.

McPEAKE, FRANCIS 1885–1971
Francis McPeake was born in Belfast, worked in a factory as a boy, and at the age of nine years played in the O'Connell Flute Band. Six years later he had graduated to second flute. He took the initiative of writing to *Ireland's Own* for information on Irish pipes and harp, as there was a decline in traditional Irish music at that time. He won many awards. When his daughter Mary died at the age of nineteen, followed a year later by his wife, 'he put his pipes away under the table' and did not play again until his son Francis formed the McPeake Trio.

McPEAKE, FRANCIS 1917–1986
Francis McPeake was born in Belfast and began to play the pipes when he was eighteen years old. He formed the first McPeake Trio, which included his father, and they were to win the Llangollen International Music Eisteddfod three times. He afterwards included his children, which meant that the group had six members and was known as the McPeake Family. Among other places, they played in the Royal Festival Hall in London. He also formed the

Clonard Traditional Music School, and many young people learned how to play traditional music there.

McQUAID, JOHN CHARLES 1895–1973
John McQuaid was born in Cootehill, County Cavan, and was educated at St Patrick's College, Cavan, Blackrock College, Clongowes Wood College, and University College, Dublin. In 1924 he was ordained a priest and seven years later became President of Blackrock College. From 1940 until 1972 he was Archbishop of Dublin. In 1941 he established the Catholic Social Welfare Conference, and in 1942 the Catholic Social Welfare Bureau from which he resigned in 1972. He opposed the Mother and Child Scheme of 1950 and the entry of Catholic students to Trinity College, Dublin.

Mac RÓICH, FERGUS see FERGUS MAC RÓIGH

MacRORY, JOSEPH 1861–1945
Joseph MacRory was born in Ballygawley, County Tyrone, and was educated at St Patrick's Seminary, Armagh and at Maynooth. Immediately after his ordination in 1885 he was appointed President of Dungannon Academy. In 1887 he was appointed Professor of Moral Theology and Sacred Scripture in Birmingham. At the age of twenty-seven he returned to Maynooth and was appointed successively Professor of Sacred Scripture and Hebrew and Professor of Hermeneutics and Exegesis; in 1909 he became Vice-President of the college. He with others founded the *Theological Quarterly* and was a regular contributor to theological journals. In 1915 he was appointed Bishop of Down and Connor, and in 1928 became Archbishop of Armagh and Primate of All Ireland. In the following year he was created a cardinal in Rome. In 1933 he served as Papal Legate in Liverpool, being present at the laying of the foundation stone of the cathedral. He attended the National Eucharistic Congress at Melbourne in 1934. Among his publications are works on the Gospel of St John and the Epistles to the Corinthians. He died in Armagh.

MacRORY, PATRICK ARTHUR 1911–1993

Patrick MacRory was born in Limavady, County Londonderry. He was educated in Donegal, Cheltenham and Trinity College, Oxford, and was called to the Bar at Middle Temple in 1937. For four years during the war he was a parliamentary draughtsman, and in 1947, he joined Unilever. He became a director in 1968. He served on the Devlin Commission of Inquiry into industrial representation, and sat on a committee on the preparation of legislation. He was treasurer of the British Association for the Advancement of Science, and was a director of Rothman Carreras and of the Bank of Ireland. He served for eight years on the Northern Ireland Development Council and on the Regional Committee of the CBI. He wrote military histories and thrillers, among which are *Borderline* (1932); *Signal Catastrophe* (1952); *The Siege of Derry* (1980) and *The Ten Rupee Jezail*, in 1992 with George Pottinger. It was his interest in Indian history and his ancestral links with the Indian army that instigated his becoming Chairman of the Merchant Ivory production company from 1976 to 1992. Both he and his wife had walk-on parts in E. M. Forster's *Room With A View*, which was produced by Merchant Ivory.

McSKIMMIN, SAMUEL 1775–1843

Samuel McSkimmin was born in Carrickfergus, County Antrim, and served in the yeomanry in 1798. He wrote for *Fraser's Magazine* and the *Gentleman's Magazine*. His outstanding achievements are his *History of Carrickfergus* and *The Annals of Ulster, or Ireland Fifty Years Ago*, which was published posthumously and based on his manuscripts. These were scattered at his death. Bishop William Reeves said of him: 'He possessed a marvellous taste and faculty for archaeological pursuits'.

McSPARRAN, ARCHIBALD 1786–1848

Archibald McSparran was born in Drumseerin, County Londonderry, and was a schoolmaster at Glenkeen from 1802 to 1816. He then entered Trinity College, Dublin, where he wrote the very successful *MacDonnell and the Norman de Burgos* in 1829. He subsequently emigrated to America, and his later published works include *Tales of the Alleghanies* and *The Hermit of the Rocky Mountains*. He died in Philadelphia.

MacSPARRAN, JAMES d.1757

James MacSparran was born in Dungiven, County Londonderry, and was educated in Glasgow. In 1720 he was ordained in the Church of Ireland and frequently spoke and preached in Irish. He went to America as a missionary on Rhode Island where he entertained Bishop Berkeley. In 1737 he gained a Doctorate of Divinity from Oxford. He published, among other works, *America Dissected* in 1753. He died in Rhode Island.

McSPARRAN, JAMES 1892–1970

James McSparran was born in Glasgow of Irish parents and was educated at Queen's University, Belfast, and the National University of Ireland. In 1916 he was called to the Bar and was later appointed Chairman of the Anti-Partition League. He was a Nationalist member of the the Northern Ireland parliament from 1945 to 1958.

MacSWEENEY, TURLOGH (MAC SUIBHNE, AN PÍOBAIRE MÓR TURLOUGH) 1831–1916

Turlogh MacSweeney was born in Glenfin, County Donegal, and lived near Gweedore, County Donegal. He was known as 'the Donegal Piper' and also (on account of his great physical stature) as 'An Píobaire Mór' (the big piper). In 1893 such was his international reputation that he went to play at the World Exhibition in Chicago where he won the world championship. His pipes and fiddle are on display in the Franciscan Friary Museum, Rossnowlagh, County Donegal.

McTIER, MARTHA *c.* 1743–1837

Martha McTier was a sister of the United Irishman, William Drennan and knew many of her brother's friends. Her husband, Samuel McTier, was President of the First Belfast Society of United Irishmen. She was a prolific writer, and her letters provide historians with a unique commentary on the political situation in Ireland during this period. She was a keen gambler, and wrote 'I play as well as any of them, and when I lose too much, will quit it'.

McWILLIAMS, FREDERICK EDWARD 1909–1992

F. E. McWilliams was born in Banbridge, County Down and was educated at Campbell College, Belfast. In 1926 he attended the Belfast School of Art and in 1928, Slade School, London, where he won a leaving scholarship which took him to Paris for a year. On his return from Paris, he settled in London, and in 1933 started to sculpt. He had a one-man show in a London Gallery, and exhibited with the British Surrealist Group in 1938. During the Second World War, from 1940 to 1945, he served in the Far East as intelligence officer with the Royal Air Force. After the war he taught for a short period in Chelsea, and at the Slade School. In 1951 he was invited to Dublin as a guest artist to the Irish Exhibition of Living Art. He was given a number of important commissions, notably the Festival of Britain and Altnagelvin Hospital, Derry. He exhibited in Dublin and Belfast and in 1960 had a one-man show at Queen's University, Belfast. His work became internationally known, and he exhibited in Japan, London and America. In 1966 he was awarded the CBE and in 1971 was the winner of the Oireachtas Gold Medal, for sculpture. He was the principal exhibitor at the opening of the Hillsborough Arts Centre, County Down.

McWILLIAMS, HUGH c.1783–1831

Hugh McWilliams was born in Glenavy, County Antrim. From 1800 to 1816 he was a school teacher in North Down. He was school teacher in the parish of Loughgiel, County Antrim from 1819 to 1831. He wrote songs in Irish and in Scottish dialect. He published two books, both called *Poems and Songs on Various Subjects*, one in 1816 and the other in 1831. A selection of his songs is published by John Moulden in his Ulstersongs series.

MADDEN, SAMUEL 1686–1765

Samuel Madden was born in Dublin and was educated at Trinity College, Dublin.

He moved to Newtownbutler, County Fermanagh, as a clergyman. In 1729 his tragedy, *Themistocles*, was produced in London and was very successful. With Thomas Prior he founded the Dublin Society in 1731, and he began a scheme to give financial assistance to students at Trinity College, Dublin. For this he became known as 'Premium' Madden. In 1738 he published *Reflections and Resolutions Proper for the Gentlemen of Ireland, as to their Conduct for the Service of their Country.* Among his friends were Swift and Dr Johnson. He died in County Fermanagh.

MÁEL BRIGTE MAC TORNÁIN d.927

Máel Brigte was Archbishop of Armagh from 885 until his death. The city of Armagh was burned three times by the Danes in his lifetime. He was said to have been a pious and learned man and settled disputes between northern chieftains.

MÁEL ÍSU UA BROLCHÁIN c.970–1038

Máel Ísu Ua Brolcháin was probably born in Derry. He is the author of religious poetry, some of which is preserved in the *Liber Hymnorum* and *The Yellow Book of Lecan.*

MÁEL MÁEDÓC UA MORGAIR see MALACHY, ST

MÁEL MUIRE MAC EOCHADA (MARIAN) d.1020

Máel Muire was Archbishop of Armagh from 1001 until his death. He is said to have followed the body of Brian Bórumha from Swords to Armagh, and to have performed the funeral rites. He is called by the Four Masters 'the head of the clergy of the west of Europe'.

MÁEL MURA d.886

Máel Mura was born in County Donegal and joined the monastery in Fahan. He is spoken of in the Annals of the Four Masters as an exceptional poet and an historian. The Book of Leinster and the Book of Lecan contain some of his poems.

MAGEE early 19th century

'Big Magee' was born in Clogher, County Tyrone. He was a neighbour of William

Carleton's in the early 1800s. He was an inventor of clocks and watches, and Carleton described him as 'a most ingenious man'. He was diminutive in size, and for a period of almost thirty years he went around the world exhibiting himself. He retired to Maynooth.

MAGEE, JAMES 1707–1797
James Magee was a printer and bookseller in Belfast. He was the most prolific supplier in Ulster of popular literature, mainly in the form of chapbooks, during the eighteenth century. In 1736 he was in partnership with J. Potts and S. Wilson, but by 1744 was printing on his own account in Bridge Street, Belfast, where he remained in business until he retired in 1790.

MAGEE, JOHN 1750–c.1809
John Magee was born in Belfast and came from a family of printers. He went to Dublin where he published *Magee's Weekly Packet* in 1777, and by 1779 he had acquired the *Dublin Evening Post*. He was imprisoned in Newgate for exposing the Earl of Clonmel and the 'Sham Squire', Francis Higgins.

MAGEE, MARTHA MARIA (née STEWART) d.1846
Martha Magee was born in Lurgan, County Armagh. She was responsible for bequeathing £60,000 to various societies and institutions. One of the buildings which was erected as a result of her benefaction was Magee College, Derry, which became part of the New University of Ulster in 1970.

MAGEE, WILLIAM 1766–1831
William Magee was born in Enniskillen, County Fermanagh and was educated at Trinity College, Dublin, where in 1788 he was appointed a fellow. He was ordained in 1790 and ten years later became Professor of Mathematics. He was appointed Dean of Cork in 1813, Bishop of Raphoe in 1819, and Archbishop of Dublin in 1822. He regarded it as one of his main duties to make converts from Roman Catholicism, and was a fervent promoter of the 'new reformation society', claiming that 'in Ireland the reformation may, strictly speaking, be truly said only now to have begun'. In 1827 he led a deputation which petitioned George IV against the Emancipation Bill. He published *Discourses on the Scriptural Doctrine of Atonement and Sacrifice*. He died in Dublin. [Memoir by Dr Kenny, 1842]

MAGEE, WILLIAM CONNOR 1821–1891
William Magee was born in Cork and was educated at Trinity College, Dublin. He was ordained and became curate of Bath in 1848. In 1861 he was rector of Enniskillen, County Fermanagh. He became Dean of Cork in 1864, and four years later Bishop of Peterborough. In 1891 he was appointed Archbishop of York. He died in London. [Memoir by J. C. MacDonnell, 1896]

MAGENNIS, BERNARD 1833–1911
Bernard Magennis was born at Ballybay, County Monaghan. He was a schoolteacher and wrote and published poems in newspapers. For a number of years he lived in New York and England and was an advocate of temperance, editing the Dublin newspaper *The Social Mirror and Temperance Advocate*. His books include *The Catapult: a satire* and *Antihumbug, or Mansion House Banquets midst Ireland's Poverty*.

MAGENNIS, EDWARD d.1938
Edward Magennis was born in County Down and was educated at Queen's College, Belfast and King's College, London. He was Ophthalmic and Aural Surgeon at St Michael's Hospital, Dún Laoghaire. He was a governor of the Apothecaries' Hall and examiner in Ophthalmology. From 1920 to 1923 he was President of the Irish Medical Association. Among his publications are *Dictionary of Ophthalmic Terms* and *Eye Systems as Aids in Diagnosis*.

MAGENNIS, PETER 1817–1910
Peter Magennis was born in County Fermanagh and became a National School teacher. *The Ribbon Informer*, 1874, was among his most successful novels, and he also wrote poetry. He was known as the Bard of Knockmore.

MAGENNIS, PETER E. 1868–1937
Peter Magennis was born in Tandragee, County Armagh, and was educated at St

Malachy's College, Belfast, and the Royal University of Ireland. He entered the Carmelite novitiate and was ordained in 1894. From 1908 to 1919 he was Assistant General and from 1919 to 1931 General of the Order of Calced Carmelites, the first Irishman to occupy this position.

MAGENNIS, WILLIAM 1869–1946
William Magennis was born in Belfast and was educated at Belvedere College, Dublin, and University College, Dublin. In 1893 he was called to the Bar, and from 1922 to 1927 he represented the National University of Ireland in the Dáil. He held the Chair of Metaphysics at University College, Dublin.

MAGILL, ROBERT 1788–1839
Robert Magill was born in Broughshane, County Antrim, and was educated in Glasgow. He was ordained a Presbyterian minister in Antrim. He wrote poems, among which is 'The Thinking Few', which attacks Arianism.

MAGINESS, WILLIAM BRIAN 1901–1967
William Maginess was born in Lisburn, County Antrim, and was educated at Trinity College, Dublin. In 1922 he was called to the Bar and from 1938 to 1964 he represented the Iveagh constituency as a Unionist in the Northern Ireland parliament, where he held various ministerial appointments. He was appointed county court judge for Down.

MAGINN, EDWARD 1802–1849
Edward Maginn was born in Fintona, County Donegal, and was educated at the Irish College, Paris, where he was ordained in 1825. He supported the Repeal movement, but transferred his allegiance to the Young Irelanders. He was appointed coadjutor to the Bishop of Derry in 1845. He wrote frequently to local newspapers on political matters.

MAGLONE, BARNEY, see WILSON, ROBERT ARTHUR

MAGRATH, GEORGE 1775–1857
George Magrath was born in County Tyrone and joined the navy as a surgeon.

He was medical officer to Lord Nelson. In 1822 he gained his Doctorate of Medicine and became a Fellow of the Royal Society. He was supervisor of various naval hospitals over the course of eleven years and was knighted in 1831. He later received the distinction of Companion of the Bath. After he retired he practised medicine in Plymouth. He was a Fellow of the Linnean Society and Fellow of the Geological Society.

MAGRATH, MILER c.1522–1622
Miler Magrath was born in County Fermanagh. He was a Franciscan friar and spent time in Rome before he was appointed Bishop of Down and Connor in 1567. On entering the Church of Ireland he was then appointed Anglican Bishop of Clogher in 1569 and Archbishop of Cashel and Bishop of Emly in 1571, at the same time continuing to be papal Bishop of Down until 1580, when he was decried for heresy. In 1581 he added to this the bishoprics of Lismore and Waterford, which he later exchanged for Achonry and Killala. It is said that in 1604 he held four bishoprics and seventy parishes and had two wives and many children. He attended parliament in Dublin in 1613. He is buried in Cashel Cathedral under a monument erected by himself.

MAGUIRE, ANNE 1964–1992
Anne Maguire was born in Enniskillen, County Fermanagh, and was educated at Mount Lourdes Grammar School, Enniskillen, and Queen's University, Belfast, where she studied Social Anthropology. She was active in the Students' Union as women's rights and welfare representative. From 1986 to 1987 she was President of the Students' Union of Queen's University. In 1988 she began working free-lance on the *Belfast News Letter*, and later joined the staff as a reporter. She became education correspondent. In 1991 she joined the *Irish Times*. She wrote on behalf of the sisters of Brian Keenan, *For Brian's Sake*, 1992. She had a reputation for ensuring that the rights of the people about whom she was writing, were respected. She died in a car crash.

MAGUIRE, CATHAL MacMANUS 1439–1498

Cathal Maguire was born in Ballymacinis, Lough Erne. He was rector of Inniskeen, County Monaghan,Canon of Armagh and Archdeacon of Clogher. He was a collector of manuscripts and compiled a portion of the Annals of Ulster covering the period from prehistory to the fifteenth century.

MAGUIRE, CONOR 1616–1645

Conor Maguire was born in County Fermanagh and was the 2nd Baron of Enniskillen. He participated in the attempt to take Dublin Castle in 1641, was arrested and sent to the Tower of London. He was tried, convicted and hanged, drawn and quartered. [Memoir by F. J. Bigger]

MAGUIRE, CUCONNACHT d.1608

Cuconnacht Maguire succeeded his brother Hugh as Lord of Fermanagh in 1600. He is said to have procured the ship for the 'Flight of the Earls', whom he accompanied into exile. He died in Genoa and his lands were confiscated and settled.

MAGUIRE, FRANCIS c.1930–1981

Frank Maguire was a publican in Lisnaskea, and was member of parliament for County Fermanagh-South Tyrone for seven years from 1974. During this period he thwarted the Conservative attempt to bring down the Labour government in 1976. However, by witholding his vote three years later he helped to bring down James Callaghan's government. He supported the H Block campaign and defended the interests of Irish Republican Army prisoners in Britain.

MAGUIRE, HUGH d.1600

Hugh Maguire became Lord of Fermanagh after his father's death. He had various confrontations after he defied the English government, and he is said to have slain Sir Warham St Leger with his own hand a mile outside Cork, dying of wounds in the same conflict. An ode was written to him by his bard, O'Hussey, and translated into English by James Clarence Mangan.

MAGUIRE, WILLIAM HENRY fl. c.1830–1840

William Maguire was an artist who painted 'View of Belfast' in 1838. He worked in Belfast during the period 1830 to 1840. He was one of two associate members of the Association of Artists founded in Belfast in 1836.

MAGUIRE, WILLIAM JOSEPH d.1934

William Maguire was educated at Queen's College, Belfast where he became a Doctor of Medicine. He was a visiting physician to the Mater Hospital, Belfast, and a clinical lecturer and examiner in Queen's University, Belfast. He was also an examiner for the National University of Ireland and Medical Commisssioner for the National Insurance Commission.

MAHAFFY, JOHN PENTLAND 1839–1919

John Mahaffy was born in Switzerland of Irish parents. From the age of nine he was educated at home in Monaghan. In 1855 he entered Trinity College, Dublin, and became Professor of Ancient History from 1869 to 1899. Flinders Petrie asked him to decipher Egyptian papyri, and he subsequently published *The Empire of the Ptolemies* (1895). His publications until then had been mainly on the civilisation of the Ancient Greeks, except for *Principles of the Art of Conversation,* which appeared in 1887. From 1911 to 1916 he served as President of the Royal Irish Academy, and in 1918 he was knighted. He was appointed Provost of Trinity College in 1914.

MAKEMIE, FRANCIS 1658–1708

Francis Makemie was born in Ramelton, County Donegal. He was ordained as a Presbyterian minister in 1682 and went to America as a missionary. In 1706 he formed the first Presbytery there. He published many sermons and is honoured as the 'Father of American Presbyterianism'.

MALACHY, ST (MÁEL MÁEDÓC UA MORGAIR) d.1148

Malachy was born in Armagh and was ordained in the priesthood in 1119. He was Vicar to the Archbishop and substituted the Roman for the Celtic liturgy. He rebuilt the church which had been destroyed by the Danes, and became head of the school in Bangor, County Down. In 1124 he was appointed Bishop of Down and Connor and in 1132 was consecrated Archbishop of Armagh. He resigned the sees of Armagh and Connor in 1136, retaining Down until his death. He founded a priory of Augustinian canons at Downpatrick and a monastery at Saul. He led the party intent on reforming the Irish church by proposing the diocesan system and the jurisdiction of bishops as opposed to the great monastic abbots. He met his biographer, St Bernard of Clairvaux, when he was appointed Apostolic Legate for Ireland. In 1142 he established the first Cistercian abbey in Ireland at Mellifont, County Louth, and introduced a branch of the monks of St Bernard. He made a second journey to Rome in 1148 and having been taken ill, died in St Bernard's arms at Clairvaux, where he is buried. He was canonised by Pope Clement III in 1190 (the first papal canonisation of an Irishman). His feast-day is on the 3rd of November. [Biographies by Canon O'Hanlon and Monsignor O'Laverty]

MALBY, NICHOLAS *c.* 1530–1584
Nicholas Malby served in Ireland in the army of Sir Henry Sidney, from 1567. Four years later he received a grant of land in County Down, on condition that, within the next eight years, he planted it with loyal subjects. He failed, but in 1576 was knighted and became Governor of Connaught, where he antagonised the population. He managed to establish his family in lands in Roscommon.

MALCOM, ANDREW GEORGE 1782–1823
Andrew Malcom was born at Hillhall, County Down, and was educated in Glasgow. He was ordained a Presbyterian minister in Dunmurry in 1807 and two years later moved to Newry, County Down. He was a hymn-writer and published *A Collection of Four Hundred and Five Psalms and Hymns* in Newry in 1811. He contributed to the *Newry Magazine* and was one of its founders.

MALCOLM, ANDREW 1818–1857
Andrew Malcolm was born in Newry, County Down, was educated at the Royal Belfast Academical Institution, and in Dublin, Glasgow and Edinburgh. He was a doctor of medicine and worked in the Belfast General Hospital, which is now the Royal Victoria Hospital. He wrote a history of that establishment. He lived in York Street, Belfast, all his life, and was devoted to the care of the poor, and to the encouragement of education. He died in Dublin, but later was brought to Belfast for burial. [Life by H. G. Calwell, 1977]

MANBY, PETER *c.*1638–1697
Peter Manby was probably born in Dublin and was educated at Trinity College, Dublin. In 1670 he became Canon of Kildare, and two years later Dean of Derry. It is said that he was disappointed at not being offered a bishopric, so he joined the Catholic Church. He wrote *The Considerations which Obliged Peter Manby, Dean of Derry, to Embrace the Catholic Religion* which evoked a retort by William King and a counter-reply by Manby. He was appointed an alderman of Derry and retired to France after the Battle of the Boyne. He died in London.

MANNING, OLIVIA 1908–1980
Olivia Manning was born in Portsmouth, but spent much of her youth in Bangor, County Down. Her first novel *The Wind Changes* contains references to Bangor. Her best known work is the Balkan trilogy and the Levant trilogy. It was televised as 'Fortunes of War'.

MANSON, DAVID 1726–1792
David Manson was born in Cairncastle, County Antrim. As a child he was very ill and had no formal schooling, learning from his mother 'by amusement'. He became a teacher and started an evening school in Belfast in 1755 at his house in Clugston's Entry. He was extremely innovative in the way in which he viewed education. The school moved to Donegall Street in 1768. He taught 'without the discipline of the rod' and was very successful in his methods. His income from the school was supplemented by brewing beer. He published several school books, including a spelling book, an English dictionary, a new primer and a pronouncing dictionary.

MANT, RICHARD 1776–1848

Richard Mant was born in Southampton and was educated at Oxford. He was appointed Bishop of Killaloe in 1820 and Bishop of Down and Connor in 1823. He published many works including a *History of the Church of Ireland* (2 volumes), in 1840. He oppposed Catholic Emancipation.

MARRINAN, PÁDRAIG 1906–1973

Pádraig Marrinan was born in Belfast. He was educated privately after he had contracted infantile paralysis at the age of five. He was a self-taught artist. He painted landscapes in Antrim, Kerry, Connemara and Donegal, and was interested in Celtic mythology and in religious art. He painted the Stations of the Cross for St Colman's Church, Lambeg, County Antrim, and 'Our Lady of Belfast' is in Holy Cross Church, Ardoyne, Belfast. 'The Madonna and Child of Loreto' is in the Convent School, Omagh, County Tyrone. He was a member of the Royal Ulster Academy, and exhibited there. The National Gallery of Dublin has one of his charcoal drawings. He died in Omagh.

MARSH, NARCISSUS d.1713

Narcissus Marsh was born in Wiltshire and was educated at Oxford, where he became Doctor of Divinity in 1638. He was appointed Provost of Trinity College, Dublin. He became Bishop of Ferns in 1683, and then successively Archbishop of Cashel 1691, of Dublin 1694 and of Armagh 1703. He bestowed many gifts, the most magnanimous being a free public library next to St Patrick's Cathedral, Dublin, the first of its kind in Ireland. Archbishop Marsh is buried in the churchyard of St Patrick's Cathedral, where a monument was erected to his memory.

MARSHALL, ANN 1792–1860

Ann Marshall was admitted as a patient to the hospital in West Street, Belfast in 1810. After her treatment she was employed as a domestic. By 1812 she had become an assistant nurse and had been promoted to nurse by 1819. In 1832 she was Head Nurse. She remained working in the hospital until her death. In 1849, when the hospital was facing a financial crisis, she donated her entire life savings. A plaque was erected in her honour and a copy is in the entrance hall of Bostock House, the Royal Hospital.

MARSHALL, W. F. 1888–1959

W. F. Marshall was born in Omagh, County Tyrone, and was educated at his father's primary school in Sixmilecross, County Tyrone, the Royal School, Dungannon, County Tyrone, University College, Galway, and the Presbyterian College, Belfast. In 1916 he became Presbyterian minister in Sixmilecross, moving to Castlerock, County Londonderry, in 1928. He published a novel, *Planted by a River*, a book of sermons for children, *His Charger White*, a history of 18th-century Ulster emigration to America; a play, *The Corduroy Bag*, and four books of poetry and became known as the 'Bard of Tyrone'. He was a member of the Royal Irish Academy, lectured on elocution in Magee College, Derry, and wrote an Ulster dialect version of Shakespeares's *A Midsummer Night's Dream*. In 1936 his research on Ulster dialect was broadcast by the BBC. He is said to have compiled a dictionary of Ulster dialect which was destroyed in manuscript form by a puppy before it reached the publisher.

MARTIN, GEORGE 1822–1900

George Martin was born in Kilrea, County Londonderry and went to Canada when he was ten years old. He was educated at the Black River Literary Institute in New York and when he was thirty, settled in Montreal where he was a photographer and later a merchant. He was a frequent contributor to the Canadian press and published a volume of poetry, *Marguerita and other poems*, three years before his death.

MARTIN, JAMES 1893–1981

James Martin was born in Crossgar, County Down. He was an engineer by the time he was twenty years old, and shortly afterwards, designed a three-wheeled enclosed car. He went to London in 1924 and invented various types of machines. In 1929 he moved to Middlesex, to what is now known as the Martin Aircraft Works. The company built a plane, the MB1. James Val Baker joined the company as a partner and they began to design fighter planes for the Royal Air Force, the MB2 and the MB3. Captain Baker was killed trying to land the MB3, and this may have been a reason why Martin focussed his energy on methods of saving pilots' lives. The MB4 and the MB5 aircraft were developed. Martin's inventions, such as gun mountings and barrage-balloon cable cutters were manufactured. Many pilots were unable to escape from their cock-pits during the Battle of Britain because the canopies would not open when damaged, and Martin devised a way of blowing the canopy off the aircraft. He invented the ejector seat and it was so successful that by 1947, MB ejector seats were being fitted in all British military jet aircraft. He was awarded two honoray doctorates and an OBE and he was knighted. He won the Wakefield Gold Medal of the Royal Aeronautical Society, the Laura Taber Barbour Air Safety Award, the Cumberbatch Air Safety Trophy (1959) and the Royal Aero Club Gold Medal in 1964.

MARTIN, JOHN 1812–1875
John Martin was born in Loughorne, near Newry, County Down, and was educated at Trinity College, Dublin, where he studied medicine. He travelled in Europe and America, and on his return to Ireland he became a Young Irelander. He was the schoolfellow and brother-in-law of John Mitchel. He produced the *Irish Felon*, a militantly nationalist journal, and was tried and sentenced to transportation for ten years. He was pardoned and returned to County Down in 1856, where he established the National League in 1864. He was elected member of parliament for Meath in 1871 and held the seat until his death. He was known as 'Honest John' Martin. He died in Newry. [Biography by P. A. Stillard]

MARTIN, NOEL b. 1891
Noel Martin was born in Portrush, County Antrim and was a brigadier general. He was also an amateur international golfer and played for the Royal Portrush Club. In 1920 and 1923 he won the Irish Open Amateur title and in 1928, he won the British Army Championship. He won the North Indian Championship twice while serving in India. He played international golf for Ireland on seven occasions and captained the side in 1930. In 1928 he was a member of the Walker Cup team. He was awarded the Victoria Cross.

MARTIN, ROBERT MONTGOMERY 1803–1868
Robert Martin was born in County Tyrone and travelled from the age of seventeen. He published as many as twenty-six books, among which is *History of the British Colonies*. The *Colonial Magazine* was founded and edited by him. In 1844 he became Treasurer of Hong Kong. He died in Surrey.

MARTIN, SAMUEL 1801–1883
Samuel Martin was born in Culmore, County Londonderry, and was educated at Trinity College, Dublin, where he became a Doctor of Laws in 1857. He was called to the Bar in 1830 and became a Queen's Counsel in 1843. In 1847 he served as member of parliament for Pontefract. In 1850 he was appointed Chief Baron of the Exchequer and was knighted. He retired after twenty-five years on the bench and died in London. He was known affectionately as 'the good Sam Martin'.

MASSEY, WILLIAM FERGUSSON 1856–1925
William Fergusson Massey was born in Limavady, County Londonderry, and was educated in Derry. In 1870 he emigrated to New Zealand, where he hoped to become a farmer. By 1894 he had entered the New Zealand parliament, and seven years later had become leader of the opposition. By 1912 he had been elected Premier. He had the unique experience of retaining office before, during and after the First World War – the only Prime Minister in the world to do so. In 1914 he was appointed a privy councillor, and his was one of the signatures on the Versailles Treaty. Ten cities made him a freeman, including Derry and Belfast. He died in Wellington, New Zealand. [Biography by H. J. Constable]

MAXWELL, ARTHUR 1875–1935

Arthur Maxwell was born in County Down and was educated in Dublin. He joined the civil service in 1893, but retired in 1905 to become secretary to the banking company Glynn Mills, and rose to be a managing partner. He served in the First World War and was severely wounded in 1916. He was awarded the Distinguished Service Order, made a Companion of the Order of St Michael and St George, and was promoted to the rank of brigadier-general.

MAXWELL, HUGH 1733–1799

Hugh Maxwell was born in Ulster and went to America as a child. He joined the revolutionary army and served at Bunker's Hill, Saratoga and Valley Forge. He was appointed Brigadier-General and died at sea.

MAXWELL, JOHN 1824–1895

John Maxwell was born in Ulster. He was a publisher and founder of the *Temple Bar* in 1860; *St James's Magazine*, *Belgravia* and other popular monthly magazines. He died in Lyndhurst.

MAXWELL, WILLIAM 1732–1818

William Maxwell was born in Donagh, County Monaghan, and was educated at Trinity College, Dublin. In 1777 he became Doctor of Divinity and was appointed rector of Mount Temple, Westmeath. He was a close friend of Dr Samuel Johnson. He erected a school in Glaslough, County Monaghan. He died in Bath.

MAXWELL, WILLIAM HAMILTON 1792–1850

William Maxwell was born in Newry, County Down, and was educated at Trinity College, Dublin. He was ordained in Carlow in 1813 and the same year became curate of Clonallon. He fought in the Peninsular War and at the Battle of Waterloo. In 1820 he was appointed rector of Balla, County Mayo. He made contributions to many periodicals, but he was primarily a novelist and his titles include *Wild Sports of the West* and *Stories of Waterloo*. He also published a *History of the Irish Rebellion of 1798* and the *Life of Wellington*. He died in Musselburgh, near Edinburgh.

MAY, ANDREW McLEAN 1880–1971

Andrew May was born in Helensborough in Argyll and was Keeper of the Tropical House of the Royal Botanic Gardens in Edinburgh. He came to Coleraine in 1914 as Horticultural Instructor for County Londonderry and his job necessitated travelling in the country-side, which facilitated his love of archaeology. He recorded carefully all sites and artefacts that came to his notice. He was a keen angler and played competitive tennis and badminton. He was a member of the Route Naturalists' Field Club, Coleraine Angling Club, the Coleraine Art Society, and was a fellow of the Royal Horticultural Society. In 1969 he was the first Honorary Member of the Ulster Archaeological Society. He was responsible for horticulture and rural science being added to the syllabus in Ulster schools. He excavated Portbraddan cave in 1931; sites near Portstewart; Gortcorbies, and Cornaclaery, near Garvagh and worked on the Beaghmore stone circles, County Tyrone. He contributed the County Londonderry section to the *Preliminary Survey of the Ancient Monuments of Northern Ireland* and was a member of the Northern Ireland Ancient Monuments Advisory Council from 1937. He published many articles in archaeological journals and collected five thousand artefacts.

MAY, GEORGE AUGUSTUS CHICHESTER 1815–1892

George May was born in Belfast and was educated at Cambridge University. He was called to the Bar in 1844 and was appointed Queen's Counsel in 1865. In 1875 he became Attorney-General, having in the previous year unsuccessfully contested Carrickfergus in the general election. In 1877 he was appointed Lord Chief Justice. He was to have tried Parnell and others, but was accused of partiality and declined. He resigned in 1887.

MAYNE, ROBERT BLAIR 1915–1955

Blair Mayne was born in Newtownards, County Down. He played rugby for Queen's University, Belfast and Malone. He won six caps for Ireland between 1937 and 1939 and toured with the British and Irish Lions on their tour of South Africa in 1938. He was also an Irish Universities Boxing Champion. He served in North Africa in the Second World War, was given three bars on his Distinguished Service Order and was awarded the Legion d'Honneur. He was killed in a car accident.

MAYNE, RUTHERFORD, see WADDELL, SAMUEL

MAYNE, THOMAS EKENHEAD 1867–1899
Thomas Mayne was born in Belfast. He wrote short stories and poetry and published *Blackthorn Blossoms*; *Belfast* and *The Heart of the Peat.*

MAYNE REID, META 1905–1990
Meta Mayne Reid was born and reared in Yorkshire, though she lived much of her life in Crawfordsburn, County Down. She wrote over twenty children's novels, a collection of poetry and two novels for adults.

MEARS, JOHN *c.*1695–1767
John Mears was born in Loughbrickland, County Down, and was educated at Glasgow University. He was ordained as a Presbyterian minister in Newtownards in 1720 and later moved to Clonmel. In 1732 he published *A Catechism* which was in use for almost a hundred years. He died in Dublin.

MEASE, JOHN 1740–1826
John Mease was born in Strabane, County Tyrone and emigrated to America. He became a merchant in Philadelphia. He joined the revolutionary army and crossed the Delaware with Washington. It is said that he subscribed a large sum of money towards army supplies in 1780 and suffered much personal loss. He was made Admiralty-Surveyor of Philadelphia where he died.

MEENAN, JAMES NAHOR 1879–1950
James Meenan was born in Fintona, County Tyrone and educated at the Catholic University Medical School, Dublin. He was

Professor and Examiner in Medicine at University College, Dublin, Physician to St Vincent's College, Dublin, and Consulting Physician to the National Maternity Hospital and Maynooth.

MEGAW, ERIC CHRISTOPHER STANLEY 1908–1956
Eric Megaw was born in Belfast and was educated at Campbell College, Belfast, and Queen's University. He had a natural talent with radios and in 1923 picked up a radio message from New Zealand. In 1924 he transmitted the first radio signal by an amateur from Ireland and in the next two years established the first radio contact between Ireland and Australia and the west coast of America. He worked for sixteen years with the General Electric Company in Wembley on the development of the cavity magnetron which proved critical to the success of the radar. In 1943 he was awarded the MBE. In 1951, he became Director of Physical Research with the Admiralty.

MICHELBURNE, JOHN 1647–1721
John Michelburne was born in Sussex. Between 1680 and 1683 he served in Tangiers and in 1689 took part in the attack on Carrickfergus. During the siege of Derry he commanded a regiment of foot. In 1689 he became Governor of Derry, and refused to accept a bribe from King James. He wrote a play based on his observations: *Ireland Preserved, or the Siege of Londonderry.* He commanded an army at the Boyne and at the siege of Sligo, of which he became Governor in 1691. He spent much time extracting the money which he felt to be rightfully his, from the English Treasury. He died in Derry.

MIDDLETON, CHARLES COLLINS 1878–1935
Charles Middleton was born in Manchester. He studied at Manchester College of Art and became a cotton damask designer. He holidayed in Ulster and decided to stay, finding a job with William Moyes as a damask designer. He was a founder member of the Ulster Arts Club, and in 1902 was elected a member of the Belfast Art Soci-

ety. He formed a damask designing partnership with Hugh Page. He visited Belgium in 1931 and painted Bruges. One of his paintings is in the Ulster Museum. He was the father of Colin Middleton.

MIDDLETON, COLIN 1910–1983

Colin Middleton was born in Belfast and attended Belfast Royal Academy. He was apprenticed in his father's firm as a damask designer and studied part-time in the Belfast School of Art. He was a member of the Royal Ulster Academy and exhibited at the Royal Hibernian Academy of which he became a member in 1970. In 1943 he had a one-man show at the Belfast Museum and Art Gallery, and the following year, a one-man show in Dublin and he exhibited in Ireland, and abroad. He spent a year with his family at the Middleton Murray Community in England and returned in 1948 to Ardglass, County Down, moving to Bangor in 1954. From 1954 to 1955 he taught at the Belfast College of Art, and from 1955 to 1961 at Coleraine Technical School. From 1961 to 1970 he lived in Lisburn and was head of the art department of Friends' School. During his period of teaching, he exhibited widely and received many commissions. In 1970 he was the recipient of an Arts Council award which enabled him to devote himself to his painting. He moved back to Belfast and then to Bangor. His work was bought by the Ulster Museum, the Municipal Gallery, Dublin and is in many other collections. He received an honorary degree from Queen's University, Belfast. He was awarded the OBE.

MIDDLETON, JOHN b. 1945

John Middleton was born in Ulster and studied at the Belfast College of Art from 1963 to 1966, and the Royal College of Art, London, from 1966 until 1969. From 1969 to 1971 he was a lecturer in printmaking in London, and he returned to Belfast to teach art in Kelvin Secondary School. He received three commissions from the Arts Council of Northern Ireland, and from 1974 worked as a graphic designer. He exhibited widely and had many one-man shows. The Arts Council of Northern Ireland and the

Belfast Education and Library Board hold examples of his work. He was the son of Colin Middleton.

MIDGLEY, HAROLD 1892–1957

Harry Midgley was born in North Belfast. He served in the First World War and published a collection of poems, *Thoughts from Flanders*. When he returned from the war, he joined the Belfast Labour Party. In 1921 he unsuccessfully contested the East Belfast parliamentary seat and in 1923 and 1924, he fought the West Belfast seat. He polled over twenty-one thousand votes and appealed to the working-class constituents on both the Falls and the Shankill. He was first secretary of the Northern Ireland Labour Party, and in 1925 was elected a city councillor for Dock ward. He gained a seat in the Northern Ireland parliament in 1933. He lost his seat in Dock ward in 1938, because of the unpopularity of his support for Republican Spain. During the Second World War he formed the commonwealth labour party and held the post of Minister of Public Security in the Stormont war-time government. He joined the Unionist party in 1947, was appointed Minister of Labour in 1949 and Minister of Education in 1950. He joined the Orange and Black Orders and became chairman of Linfield Football Club.

MILLER, PHILIP HOMAN d. 1928

Philip Miller was born in Derry and was educated at Queen's College, Belfast. He studied architecture and painting, and in 1879 began to exhibit at the Royal Academy, London. In 1890 he was elected to the Royal Hibernian Academy.

MILLER, WILLIAM fl. 1762–1778

William Miller was born near Lurgan, County Armagh. He was a portrait painter and sometimes painted on glass. He painted likenesses of the Lurgan people of his time. He invented a speaking clock which was modelled as the figure of an old man standing in a case, though when he could not find a buyer, he dismantled it.

MILLIGAN, ALICE c. 1865–1953

Alice Milligan was born in Omagh, County Tyrone, and was educated at Methodist

College, Belfast, Magee College, Derry, and King's College, London. She went to Dublin to learn Irish, and as organising secretary of the 1798 centenary celebrations in Ulster, she invited John O'Leary to Belfast. She was a friend of James Connolly, a member of Inghinidhe na hÉireann and of Sinn Féin, supporting Winifred Carney when she stood for parliamentary election in Belfast in 1918. For some years she was organiser for the Gaelic League and gave history lectures throughout Ireland. She published poetry in the *United Irishman* among other journals, and with Ethna Carbery founded and edited the *Northern Patriot*; she also edited the *Shan Van Vocht* from 1896 to 1899. In 1900 she wrote a play, *The Last Feast of the Fianna,* for the Irish Literary Theatre, and *The Daughter of Donagh* for the Abbey Theatre. She also published a *Life of Wolfe Tone* and a novel, *A Royal Democrat* as well as a book of poetry *Hero Lays* (1908). She published two other books, one of them, *Glimpses of Erinn*, in collaboration with her father, and the other, *Sons of the Sea Kings*, with her brother. She was a founder member of the Ulster Anti-Partition Council. In 1941 she received an honorary degree from the National University of Ireland. She died in Omagh.

MILLIGAN, SEATON FORREST 1836–1916

Seaton Milligan was born in Cloncur, County Tyrone, and was educated locally. Through his business travels he became familiar with Ulster and Connaught. He was interested in Irish antiquities and in 1884 became a member of the Royal Society of Antiquaries and a Fellow in 1888. He contributed many papers to the journal of that society. With his daughter Alice, he published *Glimpses of Erinn* and also a guide to Tyrone and Fermanagh.

MITCHEL, JANE (JENNY) (née VERNER) 1820–1900

Jane Verner is thought to have been born in County Armagh and educated at Miss Bryden's School for Young Ladies in Newry. At the age of fourteen she married John Mitchel. Under the pseudonym Mary, which she shared with other contributors, she published controversial articles in the *Nation*. Following John Mitchel's arrest in 1848, she organised his defence campaign. With her five children she emigrated to Australia, where her husband had been exiled, and later, on his escape, she joined him in New York. During the American Civil War, she supported the Confederates, and two of her sons were killed fighting. As a mark of public respect, a large sum of money was raised in America to support her at the time of her husband's death. Her house in New York became a focus for political and cultural activity.

MITCHEL, JOHN 1815–1875

John Mitchel was born in Dungiven, County Londonderry, and was educated in Newry, County Down and at Trinity College, Dublin. In 1840 he became a lawyer and settled in Banbridge, County Down, where he met Thomas Davis, whose place he took on the journal the *Nation*. In 1848 he founded the *United Irishman*. He felt that a complete break with England was necessary for the survival of Ireland. He was tried for treason and felony and sentenced to transportation for fourteen years, but he eventually escaped to America in 1853, where he published *Jail Journal, or Five Years in British Prisons*. He attempted to found newspapers which supported the cause of the South in the American Civil War. When he returned to Ireland in 1874 he was elected member of parliament for Tipperary, but he was declared ineligible as an undischarged felon, even when subsequently re-elected in 1875. He died in Newry, County Down. He edited the poems of Mangan and the poems of Davis as well as publishing a *History of Ireland from the Treaty of Limerick* and the *Life of Hugh O'Neill, Prince of Ulster*. [Biography by William Dillon]

MITCHELL, ALEXANDER 1780–1868

Alexander Mitchell was born in Dublin and became blind when he was twenty-two years old. He moved to Belfast, where he became a brick-maker, and he invented machines used in that trade. He is best known for his invention the 'screw pile', which allowed lighthouses to be erected on mud banks and shifting sands. It is used with great success internationally, from the Portland Breakwater to the bridges of Bombay. In 1837 he became an associate and in 1848 a member of the Institute of Civil Engineers, who awarded him the Telford Medal for his invention. He died in Belfast. [Memoir by F. J. Bigger].

MITCHELL, CRAWFORD 1908–1976
Crawford Mitchell was born on the Grosvenor Road, Belfast, and was educated at the Belfast Model School, Falls Road. He studied at the Belfast School of Art and won a scholarship to the Royal College of Art, London. He returned to Ulster in 1935 and taught at the Rainey Endowed School, Magherafelt, at Lurgan College and Portadown College, County Armagh. He was head of the art department of Grosvenor High School in 1950 and remained there for the next twenty years, after which he taught part-time at the Rupert Stanley College of Further Education, Belfast. He was a lino-cut artist and wood engraver, and his work is in the Victoria and Albert Museum. He won the Silver Medal of the Royal Ulster Academy in 1975.

MITCHELL, WILLIAM 1910–1978
Billy Mitchell was born in Lurgan, County Armagh. He was an international soccer player and played for Cliftonville, Distillery, Chelsea and Bath City. Between 1932 and 1938 he was capped fifteen times for Northern Ireland.

MOCHÁEMÓG, ST d.655
Mocháemóg was born in Connemara, but studied under St Comgall at Bangor, County Down. He founded churches in Kilkenny and Tipperary and is said to have cured many people of blindness.

MOCHOÍ, ST d.497
Mochoí was born in County Antrim, and it is said that as a young man in Saul, near Downpatrick, he met St Patrick who baptised and ordained him. He founded and became Bishop of churches on Nendrum, now known as Island Mahee. St Finian of Moville and St Colman of Dromore were educated at his schools.

MOCHUA, ST c.580–637
Mochua was born in Ulster and was educated by St Comgall at Bangor, County Down. He travelled to Westmeath, where he was the guest of St Feichín of Fore. It is thought that he had considerable skill as an engineer. He worked in Connemara, for thirty-one years.

MODWENNA, ST d.518
Modwenna was the daughter of the King of Iveagh. It is said that she was blessed by St Patrick. She founded churches at Louth, Wexford, Kileevy, Armagh, Swords and the Aran Islands. As well as travelling around Ireland, she crossed to England and Scotland and had churches built from Warwickshire to Dundee, where she died.

MOIRA, EARL OF, see HASTINGS, FRANCIS RAWDON

MOLAISSE (or LASRÉN), ST 533–564
Molaisse founded a monastic settlement on Devenish Island, County Fermanagh. He made a pilgrimage to Rome. An ancient Gaelic life of Molaisse is preserved in the British Library and has been edited and published by S. H. O'Grady. A prayer to Molaisse has been preserved: 'Molaisse the superior/may he protect me from annihilation/from blood-flux, from small pox/from violent death and from oppression ... I entreat Molaisse/both sleeping and waking/I pray to him at all times/the Fair One from the Lakes of the Erne.'

MOLINES (or MULLEN), ALLAN 1654–1690
Allan Molines was born in Ballycoulter, County Down, was educated at Trinity College, Dublin, and became a doctor of medicine. In 1681 he dissected the body of an elephant accidentally burnt in Dublin, and published his account of it. He contributed much original research to comparative anatomy, was a Fellow of the Royal Society and was elected as a Fellow of the Royal College of Physicians in Ireland in 1683. He went to the West Indies, where he died in Barbados.

MOLLOY, FRANCES 1947–1991
Frances Molloy was born in County Londonderry. Her short stories have appeared in various magazines. In 1985 her first novel, *No Mate for the Magpie*, was published by Virago Press.

MOLLOY, JOSEPH 1798–1877
Joseph Molloy was appointed art master of the Belfast Academy in 1828 and master of the Belfast Academical Institution in 1830. He retired from this position in 1870. He was a member of the Association of Artists, founded in Belfast in 1836. He illustrated *Belfast Scenery*, which was published in 1832 by E. K. Proctor. The Ulster Museum have two of his sea-scapes and a portrait.

MOLUA (or LUGIDUS), ST 6th century
Molua became a disciple of Comgall at Bangor, County Down in about 559. He founded a monastery at Clonfert, and Killaloe (Church of Lua) may be named after him. His feast-day is on the 4th of August.

MOLYNEUX, SAMUEL fl. 1594–1625
Samuel Molyneux was Clerk of the Royal Works in Ireland. He was actively involved in the Tyrone war, and in 1601 he was paid for work and fortifications carried out at Carrickfergus, County Antrim.

MONAGHAN, JOHN JOSEPH (RINTY) 1920–1984
Rinty Monaghan was born in Belfast and became a professional boxer. He began his boxing career in Ma Copley's boxing booth, Belfast. On the 23rd of March, 1948 he knocked out Jackie Patterson in the King's Hall, Belfast, and won the world championship. He defended his title the following year and in 1949 drew with Terry Allen. Six months later he retired undefeated. He lost only eight, drew three and won forty-three out of fifty-four professional fights. As well as holding the World Championship, he held the British European and Commonwealth Championships. He died in Belfast.

MONCK, GEORGE 1608–1670
George Monck came to Ireland in 1641 as commander of an English regiment sent to crush the rebellion. After he returned to England he was taken prisoner by the parliamentary forces, but on changing sides, he was released and appointed general of the English parliamentary army in Ireland. He was Governor of Ulster and in 1648 was responsible for the capture of Robert Monro. In 1649, as Governor of Carrickfergus, he made peace with Owen Roe O'Neill and surrendered Dundalk. He then left Ireland.

MONRO, ROBERT d.1680
Robert Monro, when the rebellion of 1641 began in Ireland, came as a major-general in the Scottish army. That year he sacked Newry, County Down and three years later defended the Scots in east Ulster against the confederates and royalists. Owen Roe O'Neill defeated him at the Battle of Benburb in 1646. He was sent to England and was detained there until 1654 when he returned to Ireland.

MONSELL, DIANA 1813–1851
Diana Monsell was probably born in Derry. She produced flower and foliage water-colour drawings. Her work deals with more common flowers of the fields and hedge-rows, and is meticulously accurate and realistic. An album of her drawings is in the National Gallery of Ireland.

MONTGOMERY, HENRY 1788–1865
Henry Montgomery was born in Killead, County Antrim, and was educated at Crumlin Academy and the University of Glasgow. In 1800 he was ordained in Dunmurry, County Antrim, and in 1817 became English master of Belfast Academical Institution. Glasgow University conferred upon him a Doctorate of Laws. He was elected Moderator of the General Synod of Ulster. An opponent of Henry Cooke, he led the Arian section of the Synod, and on being defeated, formed the Remonstrant Synod of Ulster in 1829, which later led to the establishment of the Non-Subscribing Presbyterian Church of Ireland. He published pamphlets and edited the *Bible Christian*, was in favour of Catholic Emancipation, but strongly opposed Repeal.

MONTGOMERY, HENRY RIDDELL 1818–1904

Henry Montgomery was born in Belfast and went to Alabama, where he started a newspaper. When he returned to Belfast he established the *Belfast Illustrated Monthly Magazine*, wrote the lives of Steele and Moore and published an anthology, *Early Native Poetry of Ireland*. He published *Essay on Irish Literature* in 1840 when he was President of the Rhetorical Society.

MONTGOMERY, HUGH *c.*1623–1663

Hugh Montgomery was born in County Down and was taken prisoner at the Battle of Benburb in 1646 and later banished to Holland. He was appointed Master of Ordnance and was created an earl at the Restoration. Hervey, the celebrated doctor, described how Hugh Montgomery had a gap in his side through which the action of his heart was visible. He succeeded his father as Viscount and died in Dromore, County Down.

MONTGOMERY, HUGH 1871–1954

Hugh Montgomery was born in Blessingbourne, County Tyrone and was educated at Eton and The Royal Miltary Academy, Sandhurst. He served with the Royal Artillery in the Boer War and in the First World War. He held many honours, including the Order of St Anne (3rd class), conferred by the Tzar of Russia; the Legion of Honour and the Croix de Guerre. He retired from the army in 1925, having attained the rank of major-general. He was a Unionist member of Tyrone County Council for several years and served as chairman for the Regional Education Committee for five years, although this office was removed from him when he antagonised other Unionist councillors by supporting the appointment of James Hackett, a Catholic Nationalist, as Deputy Vice-Chairman of the local Board of Guardians. He was a patron of the Marie Stopes Clinic in Belfast and in 1938 he was co-founder of the Irish Association, which sought to 'make reason and goodwill take the place of passion and prejudice in Ireland, north and south'. He was Companion of the Order of the Bath, Companion of the Order of St Michael and St George and Deputy Lieutenant.

MONTGOMERY, JEMIMA (TAUTPHOEUS, BARONESS von) 1807–1893

Jemima Montgomery was born in Seaview, County Donegal. When she married Baron von Tautphoeus in 1838 she went to Germany, where she spent the rest of her life. Her husband was Chamberlain to the King of Bavaria, and many of her novels, for example, *The Initials*; *Cyrilla*; *Quits* and *At Odds*, are set in that country.

MONTGOMERY, JOHN WILSON 1835–1911

John Wilson Montgomery was born in Virginia, County Cavan. He was master of the workhouse in Bailieborough for some years and became known as the 'Bard of Bailieborough'. He spent much of his life in Downpatrick, County Down, where he was clerk to the Poor Law Board of Guardians. He was an antiquarian and contributed articles on this subject to local newspapers. He published volumes of poetry, including *Rhymes Ulidian* and *Fireside Lyrics*, and a collection of prose sketches, *Round Mourne*.

MONTGOMERY, LESLIE ALEXANDER (pseud. LYNN C. DOYLE) 1873–1961

Leslie Montgomery was born in Downpatrick, County Down, and educated in Dundalk, County Louth. At the age of sixteen he joined the Northern Banking Company in Belfast and worked in Cushendall, County Antrim, and Keady, County Armagh. When he was thirty-three he was transferred to Skerries, County Dublin, where until 1934 he was Branch manager. He wrote more than twenty books under his pseudonym, 'Lynn C. Doyle'. The popular 'Ballygullion' stories ran into several volumes and later editions were illustrated by William Connor. His comedy, *Love and Land* was produced in London at the Little Theatre. Other plays among which are *The Lilac Ribbon* and *The Turncoats* were staged by the Ulster Literary Theatre. Among his novels is *Mr Wildridge at the Bank*, and he also wrote an autobiography, *An Ulster Childhood*. He broadcast regularly for the BBC in Belfast and for a short period served as a member of the Censorship of Publications Board. He was President of the Consultative Council of Irish PEN in 1954. He died in Dublin.

MONTGOMERY, MARY 19th century
Mary Montgomery was the wife of a local landowner in Fivemiletown, County Tyrone. She ran embroidery and sewing classes for girls in Fivemiletown, but in 1891 went to London to learn repoussé metalwork. She returned home and started a metal-work class, and in 1893 their work was shown at the Home Arts and Industries Association Exhibition at the Albert Hall in London. The class produced furnishings in copper and brass, such as candle-sticks, tankards and mirror frames and won frequent awards at exhibitions: a silver cross and sixty-nine awards of merit at the Home Arts and Industries Association; five first, seven second, and four third prizes at the Royal Dublin Society and first prizes at Cheltenham and Bristol. Queen Victoria is said to have purchased Fivemiletown work. The classes received more orders than they were able to fulfil, and silver and pewter were added to the materials used. Mary Montgomery set up her own annual exhibition in Fivemiletown, but both this and the Art Metal-work Class ended at the beginning of the First World War.

MONTGOMERY, ROBERT 1809–1887
Robert Montgomery was born in Moville, County Donegal, and was educated in Derry. In 1827 he joined the Bengal civil service and in 1849 was appointed Commisssioner at Lahore. In 1859 he was appointed Governor of the Punjab and was knighted. He died in London.

MONTGOMERY, WILLIAM 1633–1706
William Montgomery was born in Aughaintain, County Tyrone, and was educated in County Down, Glasgow and Leyden. Having returned to Ireland in 1652 and repossessed the family estate of Rosemount House, Greyabbey, in 1661 he became a member of parliament for Newtownards. He was High Sheriff of County Down from 1670. He wrote *A De-scription of the Ards*, and his family history *The Montgomery Manuscript*, which was first published in the *Belfast News-Letter* from 1785 onwards, and then in book form in 1830. He is buried at Greyabbey.

MONYPENNY, WILLIAM FLAVEL 1866–1913
William Monypenny was born in Ballyworkan, County Armagh, and was educated at Trinity College, Dublin, and Oxford. He was assistant editor of *The Times* from 1894 to 1899, and when he returned from South Africa, having been editor of the *Star*, he became Director of *The Times*. He published posthumously *Two Irish Nations* and was chosen as biographer of Disraeli.

MOODY, THEODORE WILLIAM 1907–1984
Theodore William Moody was born in Belfast and was educated at the Royal Belfast Academical Institution and Queen's University, Belfast. From 1940 until 1977 he was Professor of Modern History in Trinity College, Dublin, where he became an Emeritus Fellow in 1977. He was the joint editor, with R. Dudley Edwards, of *Irish Historical Studies* from 1938 until 1977, and he collaborated with Professor J. C. Beckett on *Thomas Davis, 1814–1845* and *Queen's, Belfast, 1845–1849: the History of a University* in two volumes. He planned and established the major *New History of Ireland*, of which he was joint editor of Vols. III: *1534–1691* (1976); IV: *1691–1800* (1986); VIII: *Chronology of Irish History to 1976* (1982) and IX: *Maps, Genealogies, Lists* (1984). He edited and contributed to *Nationality and the Pursuit of National Independence*, which was published in Belfast in 1978, and in 1982 he published *Davitt and Irish Revolution, 1846–1882*. He died in Dublin.

MOORE, ALFRED S. early 20th century
Alfred S. Moore was educated at the Royal Belfast Academical Institution and Queen's University, Belfast. He was the editor of *Nomad's Weekly*, a magazine which ran from 1895 until 1914. It satirised politicians, churchmen, trade union officials, councillors and businessmen. It pressed for social

reform, for example shorter hours for shop assistants, and at the height of its popularity it claimed a readership of 40,000. From 1901 to 1914 he also edited the *Investor*. During the First World War he served abroad. Other publications include *Straggler from Saturn* (1908); *Belfast Today* (1912) and *Linen* (1922).

MOORE, ARTHUR *c.*1666–1730

Arthur Moore was born in Monaghan and went to England where he made a fortune trading. In 1695 he was member of parliament for Grimsby, and subsequently became a director of the South Sea Company. In 1712 he was instrumental in bringing about the Commercial treaty with France and Spain. By the time of his death he owned large estates in Surrey.

MOORE, FRANCIS FRANKFORT 1850–1931

Francis Moore was born in Limerick, but grew up in Belfast, where he attended the Royal Belfast Academical Institution. From 1876 to 1892 he worked as a reporter for the *Belfast News-Letter* before moving to England. Among his novels are *The Jessamy Bride*, *Castle Omeragh*, *The Ulsterman* and *The Truth about Ulster*. Some of his novels were serialised in magazines such as the *Graphic* and the *Queen*. He wrote many successful plays, including *The Queen's Rooms* and *I Forbid the Banns*, which was a hit in London in 1893. He published a book of poetry, *Flying from Shadows*, as well as journalistic pieces.

MOORE, GARRETT 1560–1627

Garrett Moore was visited by Hugh O'Neill at Mellifont before the Flight of the Earls in 1607. As a consequence, he was implicated in the charge of disloyalty, but was able to clear his name. He was granted a thousand acres in County Armagh as part of the plantation settlement. In 1615 he was created a baron, and in 1621 a viscount.

MOORE, WILLIAM 1864–1944

William Moore was born in Ballymoney, County Antrim, was educated at Trinity College, Dublin, and was called to the Bar in 1887. He was a Unionist member of parliament for eighteen years from 1899 to 1917, before being appointed a High Court judge. When a Court of Appeal was established in Northern Ireland he was appointed its judge until 1925 and eventually became Lord Chief Justice of Northern Ireland.

MOORE, WILLIAM ARTHUR 1880–1962

Arthur Moore was born in Glenavy, County Antrim and was educated at Campbell College, Belfast and St John's College, Oxford. In 1904 he was elected President of the Oxford Union. He was secretary of the Balkan Committee from 1904 to 1908 and penetrated central Albania in 1908. He became correspondent for various newspapers, and reported on the constitutionalist rebellion in Persia. He was besieged for one hundred days at Tabriz, joined the anti-Shah forces, and in 1909 took part in the final sortie. He worked for a number of years for *The Times* in Teheran and St. Petersburg. From 1922 to 1923 he was editor of the *New Age*, and in 1924 became assistant editor of the *Statesman* in Calcutta, rising to the post of Managing Editor. Between 1927 and 1933 he was a member of the Indian Legislative Assembly in Delhi but was dismissed for persistent criticism of the Viceroy, Lord Linlithgow, and the British Government for their indifference to the role of India in the Second World War. He spent the remainder of the war as a public relations officer for the Supreme Allied Command in South East Asia. He founded the journal *Thought* and retired to England in the 1950s. He died in London.

MOORHEAD (MOOREHEAD), THOMAS GILLMAN 1878–1960

Gillman Moorhead was born in Benburb, County Tyrone, but grew up in Bray, County Wicklow. He was educated at the Aravon School in Bray and Trinity College, Dublin, where he took a degree in medicine in 1901 before continuing his research in Vienna. In 1905 he became a member of the Royal College of Physicians in Ireland, in 1906 was elected a fellow, and by 1910 had become its President. His clinics at the

Royal City of Dublin Hospital and Sir Patrick Dun's Hospital were very popular. He served in Cairo with the Royal Army Medical Corps during the First World War. On his return to Dublin he was appointed consulting physician to a number of hospitals, Professor of Medicine in the Royal College of Surgeons in Ireland, and Regius Professor of Physic at Trinity College, Dublin, where he had been King's Professor of Materia Medica. In 1933 he was elected President of the British and Irish Medical Associations. Among his works are *A Short History of Sir Patrick Dun's Hospital* and *Surface Anatomy*. He fell from a train on a journey to England in 1926, and the blow to his head detached his retina and left him permanently blind. Though clinical work was of necessity curtailed, he continued to teach and write. He was Director of the National Cancer Campaign.

MORANT, GEORGE DIGBY 1837–1921
George Morant was born in Carrickmacross, County Monaghan. In 1850 he joined the navy and served in Burma, the Baltic, Crimea and China. He was promoted to the rank of admiral. At Pembroke and Chatham he supervised the dockyards. Before his retirement he was the Inspector of Irish Lights. He was knighted and died in London.

MORGAN, JAMES 1799–1873
James Morgan was born in Cookstown, County Tyrone, was educated in Glasgow and was ordained as a Presbyterian minister in Carlow in 1820. He became a minister in Lisburn in 1824, and in Belfast in 1827. In 1846 he was appointed Moderator of the General Assembly. He published theological works and was active in founding the Presbyterian College. He was a noted philanthropist. [Recollections of Life and Times, edited by his son, 1874]

MORRIS, HENRY 1874–1945
Henry Morris was born near Lisdoonan, County Monaghan. He was educated at Lisdoonan School and taught there from 1888 to 1901. He founded the Gaelic League in Lisdoonan and promoted it throughout County Monaghan. From 1901

to 1907, he taught in Dundalk and was co-founder of the Louth Archaeological Society in 1903. In 1907 he moved to Strabane, County Tyrone, and was organiser of Irish in schools. In 1912 he moved to Derry and later became a school inspector in Skerries, and in 1923 became a divisional inspector in Sligo. By 1932 he was Deputy Chief Inspector. He published widely in many journals and newspapers, and his books include *Greann na Gaedhilge* (1901); *Seanfhocla Uladh* (1907); *Ceithearnach Uí Dhomhnaill* (1912); *Céad de Cheoltaibh Uladh* (1915) and *Amhráin na Midhe* (1933). He was an educationalist, an Irish scholar, a folk-lorist, an archaeologist, a historian and a prolific writer.

MORROW, GEORGE 1870–1955
George Morrow was born in Belfast and studied art at the Government School of Design. Later he exhibited at the Royal Academy and the Royal Society of British Artists. He began to contribute to *Punch* in 1906, joined the staff in 1924 and became art editor from 1932 until 1937. He illustrated many books and collaborated with E. V. Lucas in *George Morrow: His Book* (1920); *More Morrow* (1921) and *Some More* (1928). His work is in the Ulster Museum, the Linen Hall Library, Belfast, and the British Museum. His four brothers, Albert, Edwin, Jack and Norman were connected with painting and drawing.

MORROW, HAROLD (pseud. McNAMARA, GERALD) 1866–1938
Harry Morrow was a founder member of the Ulster Literary Theatre. He was an actor as well as a playwright. Among his plays is *Thompson in Tír-na-n-Óg*, which was first performed in 1912 in the Grand Opera House in Belfast. Other plays which were never published are *Suzanne and the Sovereigns; The Throwbacks; No Surrender* and *Who Fears to Speak*. The *Dublin Magazine* published many of his sketches and short plays.

MORTON, MARY (MAY) ELIZABETH 1876–1957
May Morton was born in County Limerick and when she was twenty-four came to live in Belfast. She was secretary of the Belfast

PEN and became its chairperson. She was also a founder member of the Young Ulster Society and was vice-principal of a girls' model school until 1934. She published poetry in many magazines including *Rann, Poetry Ireland* and the *Cornhill Magazine* and broadcast on the BBC and Radio Éireann. Among her publications are *Dawn and Afterglow, Masque in Maytime* and *Sung to the Spinning Wheel.*

MORYSON, FYNES 1566–1630

Fynes Moryson was educated at Peterhouse College, Cambridge, and in 1589 obtained a licence to travel. He visited, among other places, Germany, Denmark, Poland, Italy, France, the Holy Land, and Constantinople. In 1600 he came to Ireland as Chief Secretary to Sir Charles Blount. He helped to suppress Tyrone's Rebellion, and published an account of his travels and a history of Tyrone's rebellion in 1617.

MORYSON, RICHARD 1571–1628

Richard Moryson came to Ireland in 1599 as a soldier in the English army and was knighted. He was Governor of Dundalk and then of Lecale, County Down. He fought in the campaign against Hugh O'Neill, Earl of Tyrone. In 1604 he was appointed Governor of Waterford and Wexford, and in 1609 Vice-President of Munster. He proposed the transportation to Virginia of Irish pirates. In 1613 he was elected member of parliament for Bandon, but returned to England when he was not appointed President of Munster. He became Lieutenant-General of the Ordnance in England from 1616 to 1628. In 1621 he was member of parliament for Leicester.

MOYES, JAMES 1851–1927

James Moyes was born in Draperstown, County Londonderry and educated at Coleraine Model School. He was private secretary to Archbishop Bourne and contributed to theological journals. He was Monsignor in the Roman Catholic Cathedral, Westminster, London.

MUIRCHERTACH MAC ERCAE d. c.534

Muirchertach, an Ulsterman, is first mentioned in the Irish annals in 482. He was appointed king in 507, and he defeated the Leinstermen at the Hill of Allen in 526. It is said that a jealous concubine set fire to his house on the banks of the Boyne and that he was burnt to death.

MUIRCHÚ, ST 7th century

Muirchú is known as the author of the Life of St Patrick in the Book of Armagh. His feast-day is on the 8th of June.

MULCAGHY, MATT (GUY, WILSON) 1875–1959

Matt Mulcaghy was born in County Tyrone and spent most of his youth in America, but as a young man returned to Ireland. He became a dialect story-teller, and eventually had his own weekly radio programme, which was extremely popular.

MULDOON, JOHN 1865–1938

John Muldoon was born in Dromore, County Tyrone, and was educated at Queen's College, Galway. In 1894 he was called to the Bar and in 1913 was appointed King's Counsel. From 1921 to 1926 he was Registrar of Lunacy, and from then until 1938 Registrar to the Chief Justice.

MULHOLLAND, ANDREW 1791–1866

Andrew Mulholland was born in Belfast and went into the cotton trade. On the destruction of his mill by fire, he decided to establish a mechanised flax-spinning factory, which was in operation by 1830. In 1845 he was appointed Lord Mayor of Belfast. The Ulster Hall recieved his gift of an organ.

MULHOLLAND, CLARA d.1934

Clara Mulholland was born in Belfast and was educated at home and in England and Belguim. She produced her first novel in the 1880s and was a prolific novelist throughout her life. She also wrote books for young people. Among her titles are *Percy's Revenge* (1888); *In A Roundabout Way* (1908) and *Sweet Doreen* (1915). She died at Littlehampton.

MULHOLLAND, JOHN 1819–1895

John Mulholland was the son of Andrew Mulholland and entered the family flax-spinning company. He became a justice of the peace for County Antrim and County Down and served as Deputy Lieutenant, then High Sheriff for County Down in 1868 and for County Tyrone in 1873. He was member of parliament for Downpatrick from 1874 to 1885. In 1892 he was created Baron Dunleath.

MULHOLLAND, ROSA (pseud. RUTH MURRAY) 1841–1921
Rosa Mulholland was born in Belfast and was educated privately. Charles Dickens encouraged her to write and printed her early stories in *Household Words*. Her first novel, *Dunmara*, was published in 1864, under her pseudonym. She produced many novels over a period of fifty years, among which are *A Fair Emigrant* (1889); *Marcella Grace* (1886) and *The Wild Birds of Killeevy* (1883). She died in Dublin.

MULLAN, DAVID
David Mullan was a clergyman who wrote several books on religious and ecclesiastical topics. These include *The Nature of the Pentecostal Baptism*. He propagated the unity ideal long before the Edinburgh world mission conference of 1910 which brought it to public notice. He wrote many lectures and pamphlets.

MULLIGAN, SYLVESTER 1875–1950
Sylvester Mulligan was born in Tassan, Clontibret, County Monaghan, and was educated at the Capuchin College, Rochestown, County Cork, and at Louvain. In 1892 he entered the Capuchin Order and was ordained in 1901. He taught moral theology at Louvain and in 1925 was elected Minister Provincial of his order, a year later becoming Definitor General. In 1937 he was the last non-Indian to be appointed to Delhi-Simla as Archbishop. For a period he was editor of the *Father Mathew Record*. He is buried in the Capuchin plot in Glasnevin Cemetery, Dublin.

MULLIN, JAMES 1846–1920
James Mullin was born in Cookstown, County Tyrone. He left school at the age of eleven and worked on a farm, after which he spent nine years as a carpenter. He was one of the first recruits of the Fenian Brotherhood which he joined in 1865, and he and other members were denounced by their church. When he was twenty-two years old he went to Cookstown Academy and supported himself by working part-time. He took a Bachelor of Arts degree at Queen's College, Galway. He tutored students to fund himself for the degree of Doctor of Medicine and he subsequently practised in London and Cardiff. At one period of his life he served as a ship's surgeon, and at another as a journalist. He wrote a great deal, including his autobiography, *The Story of a Toiler's Life*. Although he was a Catholic, he went to a Protestant school, and of this he said: 'The intermingling of the sects was attended by the happiest results, inasmuch as it allowed the young people to understand one another and contract friendships which no subsequent surroundings or whispers of bigotry could ever wholly efface'.

MULVANY, JOHN SKIPTON
John Mulvany was an architect and he designed the Georgian Terrace in the Mall, Armagh, the Railway Station in Athlone and the renowned Broadstone Station, Dublin.

MUNRO, HENRY 1758–1798
Henry Munro was born in Lisburn, County Antrim, where he worked as a linen draper in Market Square, Lisburn, and attended the Linen Halls of Lurgan, Banbridge and Tandragee, where he bought webs for the bleachers. He was an adjutant in the Volunteers, whom he joined at the age of twenty, and in 1795 he joined the United Irishmen. He was a Freemason and was head of the Lodge in Lisburn. In 1798 he led the men of Down when they seized Ballynahinch, which was occupied by English forces. The signal for the garrison's retreat was mistaken as a signal for its advance and Munro's men scattered. He was arrested, tried by court-martial and hanged in Lisburn opposite his own door. His body was decapitated and displayed.

MURA, ST d.645
Mura was born in County Tyrone. He founded the abbey of Fahan on Lough

Swilly and a church at Banagher in Derry. His feast-day is on the 12th of March. He was regarded by the O'Neills as their patron saint.

MURNAGHAN, SHEELAGH MARY 1924–1993
Sheelagh Murnaghan was born in Dublin and was a barrister and politician. From 1961 to 1969, she served as a Liberal member of the Northern Ireland parliament for Queen's University, Belfast, the only Liberal to have been elected to that body. She spoke on a wide range of issues: electoral equity, proportional representation, fair employment, fair allocation of houses and the introduction of an ombudsman. From 1969 to 1972 she served on the first Northern Ireland Community Relations Commission and when Direct Rule was introduced, on Whitelaw's Advisory Commission. Later she chaired National Insurance and Industrial Relations Tribunals.

MURPHY, EDWARD SULLIVAN 1880–1945
Edward Murphy was educated at Trinity College, Dublin, where he studied classics. In 1903 he was called to the Bar, and from 1929 to 1939 represented Derry city in the Northern Ireland parliament. From 1937 to 1939 he was Attorney-General, before becoming Lord Justice of Appeal in the Northern Ireland Supreme Court.

MURPHY, GERARD 1900–1959
Gerard Murphy was born in Clones, County Monaghan. He was educated at University College, Dublin. He was Assistant Librarian of the National Library before becoming Professor of the History of Celtic Literature at University College, Dublin, from 1938 to 1959. From 1939 to 1957 he edited *Éigse* and collected, edited and translated into English, an anthology of Gaelic verse, published as *Early Irish Lyrics*, 1946. Among his other publications are *Tales from Ireland* (1947); *Ossianic Lore and Romantic Tales of Medieval Ireland*, (1955); *Saga and Myth in Ancient Ireland* and *Early Irish Metrics*, both 1961.

MURPHY, JAMES GRACY 1808–1896
James Murphy was born in Comber, County

Down, and was educated at Trinity College, Dublin. He became a Presbyterian minister in Ballyshannon in 1836, and was Professor of Hebrew in Belfast in 1847. He translated the Book of Daniel and wrote Latin and Hebrew grammars, as well as publishing *The Human Mind*.

MURPHY, JOSEPH JOHN 1827–1894
Joseph Murphy was born in Belfast and was educated at the Royal Belfast Academical Institution. He was a linen mill-owner. He was President of the Belfast Literary Society, President of the Natural History and Philosophical Society and President of the Linen Hall Library. Among his publications are *Habit and Intelligence, The Scientific Basis of Faith; Sonnets and other poems* and *Natural Selection and Spiritual Freedom*.

MURPHY, PATRICK 1834–1862
Patrick Murphy was born in Killowen, County Down, and at the height of eight foot one and a half inches, claimed to be the tallest man alive. He exhibited himself on the continent and died in Marseilles. His embalmed body was brought back for burial in Killbrony, County Down.

MURRAY, JAMES 1788–1871
James Murray was born in Culnady, County Londonderry, and was educated in Dublin and Edinburgh, where he took the degree of Doctor of Medicine. He was a member of the College of Surgeons in Dublin. When he settled in Belfast he published a paper on the value of fluid magnesia, and eventually patented his process and started manufacturing it, utilising the waste product as fertiliser. He produced a booklet, *Advice to Farmers*, and devoted attention to development of fertilisers on a large scale. In 1843 he published *Trials and Effects of Chemical Fertilisers with Various Experiments in Agriculture*, and subsequently, *Heat and Humidity* and *Medical Effects of Atmospheric Pressure*. He was innovative in his exploration of electricity as a cause of illness and in 1849 published *Electricity as a Cause of Cholera and Other Epidemics, and the Relation of Galvanism to the Action of Remedies*, which was translated into Italian. He became Inspector of Anatomy in Dublin. He was

Resident Physician to three Lords Lieutenant and was knighted in 1831. He died in Dublin.

MURRAY, JAMES 1831–1863
James Murray was born in Armagh and trained as an architect in Liverpool. He designed public buildings and churches in many cities, and he published *Gothic Buildings* and *Modern Architecture*. He died in Coventry.

MURRAY, JOHN 1742–1793
John Murray was born in Antrim and was educated in Edinburgh. He emigrated to America in 1763 and supported the revolution, involving himself in enlisting young men for the army. As well as other religious works, in 1780 he published *Sermons on Justification* and *Original Sin*. He died in Newburyport, Massachusetts.

MURRAY, JOHN FISHER 1811–1865
John Murray was born in Belfast and was educated there and at Trinity College, Dublin, where he qualified in medicine. He contributed to many journals, including *Blackwood's Magazine*, and wrote *The Irish Oyster-Eater*, *The Viceroy*, in three volumes, published in 1841; *The Environs of London* and *The World of London*. He joined the Young Ireland movement.

MURRAY, LAURENCE PATRICK (LORCAN O MUIREADHAIGH) 1883–1941
Laurence Murray was born in Carlingford, County Louth. He was educated locally and at St Patrick's College, Armagh, before going to Maynooth in 1901. He won many prizes for academic achievement, and wrote articles for the *Louth Archaeological Journal* and *Irisleabhar Maighe Nuadhat*. In 1908 he was asked to leave the college. He went as a student to St Paul in the United States, was ordained a priest there in 1910, and became mathematics teacher in the College of St Thomas. After the foundation of the Omeath Irish College in 1912, he spent every summer teaching in the Omeath Gaeltacht, and began collecting songs, stories and prayers. In 1917 he lost his post at St Paul for refusing to take the oath of allegiance, and he returned to Ireland as stoker on a ship because the British Embassy refused him a visa. In 1918 he was appointed curate in the parish of Clonfeacle, where he taught Irish and Irish dancing. In 1921 he became Religious Inspector for schools, and he remained in that position for the next sixteen years. In 1924 he established the Gaelic monthly, *An tUltach*. In 1925 he built St Brigid's College, Ranafast, County Donegal, and in 1926 set up a Gaelic League Provisional Council for the nine counties of Ulster and County Louth. He was an active Gaelic Athletic Association supporter and team coach. He wrote prolifically all his life, and his publications include a collection of songs, *Ceolta Óméith* (1920) and *Pota Cnuasaigh* (1924).

MURRAY, PATRICK ANTHONY 1811–1882
Patrick Murray was born in Clones, County Monaghan, and educated locally and at Maynooth, where he was ordained. In 1838 he was appointed Professor of French and English to Maynooth and in 1841, transferred to Theology. He contributed frequently to the *Dublin Review* and other journals, and after 1850 produced an *Annual Miscellany*. Among his publications are *De Ecclesia Christi*; *Essays, Chiefly Theological* and *De Gratia*.

MUSGRAVE, JAMES 1826–1904
James Musgrave was born in Lisburn, County Antrim and established a firm of patent stove-makers and iron mongers in Belfast. During his term of office as Chairman of the Harbour Commissioners, he greatly improved the harbour and the docks. He gave his name to a new channel, was created baronet in 1897, and founded the Musgrave Chair of Pathology in Queen's College, Belfast.

MUSHETT, WILLIAM 1712–1792
William Mushett was born in County Londonderry, and was educated at Trinity College, Dublin, Leyden and Cambridge, where he became a Doctor of Medicine in 1746. He was elected Fellow of the Royal College of Physicians and was physician to the armed forces. He declined a baronetcy and died in York.

N

NAPIER, JOSEPH 1804–1882
Joseph Napier was born in Belfast and was educated there and at Trinity College, Dublin. He was called to the Bar in 1831. He became Queen's Counsel in 1844 and was member of parliament for Dublin University from 1848 to 1858. In 1852 he was appointed Attorney-General and received a Doctorate of Civil Law in 1853, becoming Lord Chancellor five years later. In 1867 he was created a baronet. His publications include educational and legal works. [Biography by A. C. Ewald, 1887]

NASH, JOHN 1752–1835
John Nash came to work in Ireland as an architect after 1793. He designed Caledon House, County Tyrone; Killymoon Castle, near Cookstown, County Tyrone, and Kilwater Castle, Larne, County Antrim.

NEILL, HAROLD ECHLIN b.1888
Harry Neill was born in Belfast and was educated at Willowfield National School, Woodstock Road. He studied at the Belfast School of Art and became a lithographic artist. In 1912 he became a member of the Belfast Art Society. He exhibited at the Royal Hibernian Academy, Dublin and in Belfast.

NEILL, HAROLD JAMES 1861–1949
Harry Neill played rugby for the North of Ireland Football Club. He was capped eight times for Ireland between 1885 and 1888. He captained the team in its first shared win in the International Championship, when Ireland defeated Wales.

NEILSON, SAMUEL 1761–1803
Samuel Neilson was born at Ballyroney, County Down, and was educated locally. At the age of sixteen he was apprenticed to a woollen draper and at twenty-four established his own business. He abandoned business for politics, joined the Volunteers and in 1791 suggested to Henry McCracken the idea of a political society of Irishmen of every religious persuasion. He and Wolfe Tone established the United Irishmen in Belfast. The *Northern Star* was founded by Neilson in 1792, and he became its editor. In 1796 he was arrested and imprisoned in Dublin, being released in 1798. He was captured trying to devise a release plan for Lord Edward FitzGerald at Newgate Jail. He was detained in Scotland until 1802, when he was deported to the Netherlands. He made his way to America and died there.

NEILSON, WILLIAM 1774–1821
William Neilson was born in Rademon, County Down, and was educated in his father's school, Patrick Lynch's Irish school at Loughinisland, and Glasgow University. He became a schoolmaster and later a Presbyterian minister in Dundalk, where he opened his school, the Classical and Mercantile Academy, which admitted children of every religion and class. He often preached in Irish and in 1805 was awarded a Doctorate of Divinity by the University of Glasgow. While a student he had written an English grammar, *Elements of English Grammar Expressed in Easy Language,* which became a textbook in English schools and his *Greek Exercises in Syntax, Ellipsis, Dialects, Prosody and Metaphrasis* passed through eight editions in forty-two years. Among his other works are an abridgement of Begley's and McCurtin's *English-Irish Dictionary; An Introduction to the Irish Language* (specifically County Down Irish); *Greek Idioms*; and *Elementa Linguae Graecae.* In 1810 he published, *Céad Leabhar na Gaoidheilge.* He was Moderator of the General Synod of Ulster at the age of thirty-one and a member of the Royal Irish Academy. In 1818 he moved to the Belfast Academical Institution, where he was appointed headmaster of the Classical School and Professor of Latin, Hebrew, Greek, Irish and Oriental

Languages. He was a member of Belfast Literary Society, served as its President from 1809 to 1820, and as a dedicated musician he revived the Harp Society. He was a leading member of the Belfast Society for Promoting Knowledge. In 1821 he learned that he had been appointed Professor of Greek at Glasgow University, but died before he could take up the post.

NELSON, GARIBALDI 1840–1910
Garibaldi Nelson was born in Crossgar, County Down and was educated in Downpatrick, at the Royal Belfast Academical Institution and at Queen's College, Belfast. He was given a commission in the Regimento Inglese, in Italy, and fought for Garibaldi, who presented him with a sword of honour. He received two medals. Three years after his return he qualified as a medical doctor, and became a Licentiate of the Royal College of Surgeons of Ireland. He then went to India for fourteen years, where he worked on a tea plantation. In 1877 he returned to Ireland and worked in Dublin. He learned German and proceeded to Vienna, where he took classes in eye, ear and throat diseases. He returned to Belfast in 1880, and three years later was appointed the first Ophthalmic Surgeon in the Royal Hospital, and subsequently in the Hospital for Sick Children. In 1898 he was President of the Ulster Medical Society. He died in Downpatrick, County Down.

NELSON, ISAAC 1812–1888
Isaac Nelson was born in Belfast, was educated there, and ordained in Comber, County Down. He moved to Belfast where he wrote *The Year of Delusion*, an account of the Revival movement in Ulster in 1859. He served as Home Rule member of parliament for Mayo from 1880 to 1885, and died in Belfast.

NESBITT, JAMES 1913–1992
James Nesbitt was an international discus-thrower. He won twelve Northern Ireland titles between 1935 and 1950. He represented Great Britain six times from 1937 to 1949, and at the Olympic Games in London in 1948.

NETTERVILLE, LUKE d.1227
Luke Netterville was appointed Archdeacon of Armagh in 1207 and in 1217 became Archbishop of Armagh. In 1224 he erected the Dominican monastery in Drogheda.

NEVILL, FRANCIS c.1648–1727
Francis Nevill is noted in 1688 as one of the committee members who were to regulate the concerns of the City of Derry. He acted as an engineer to the Corporation of Derry. When he returned to Derry after the siege he published a map and tract entitled *A Description of Londonderry as it was closely besieged by ye army in 1689. A description of the Towne and Workes about it. A description of the Enemy's Camp.* In 1689 he was sworn a burgess of the City of Derry, and he built a town house and repaired Charlemont Fort. In 1703 he surveyed the Glan Bog between County Down and County Armagh, with the intention of creating a canal between Lough Neagh and Newry. He published *Some Observation of Lough Neagh,* in 1713. By 1726 he was residing at Belturbet, County Cavan.

NEWELL, EDWARD JOHN 1771–1798
Edward Newell was born in Downpatrick, County Down. He was a sailor and later a painter and glazier, and eventually worked as a miniature portrait painter. In 1796 he joined the United Irishmen and became an informer. He published *The Life and Confessions of Newell, the Informer,* which proved to be very popular. He was about to leave Ireland for America when he was assassinated at Roughfort, Antrim.

NEWMAN, ALEC 1905–1972
Alec Newman was born in Waterford but his family moved to Belfast when he was seven, and he was educated at the Royal Belfast Academical Institution and Trinity College, Dublin. He worked for a time as a teacher in Dublin High School, but joined the *Irish Times* in 1930. He became assistant editor in 1934 and editor from 1954 to 1961, at which point he joined the *Irish Press* as leader-writer and journalist on current affairs.

NIALL CAILLE MAC ÁEDO 791–846
Niall Caille was King of Ireland and de-

feated the Danes at Derry in 833 and at Lough Swilly in 843. He drowned in the River Callan, near Armagh.

NIALL GLÚNDUB 870–919

Niall Glúndub, King of Ireland, won a military victory at Glaryford, County Antrim, and at Ballymena, County Antrim, when he led his army into Dalriada. He was killed by the Danes at Kilmashoge.

NIALL MAC ÁEDA d.1139

Niall, the grandson of Máel Ísu, Archbishop of Armagh, claimed the primacy and is known as the 'False Primate'. He seized and held the pastoral staff and book for seven years before he was driven out, and it is said that he performed severe penance before his death.

NIALL MAC EOCHADA d.1063

Niall, King of Ulidia, defeated a Danish fleet in 1022 and gained a great victory when he invaded Armagh. It is said that during his reign in 1047 there was a great famine followed by a great snow.

NIALL MAC MÁEL SECHNAILL d.1061

Niall became King of Ailech when he killed his brother Lochlain in battle near Dungiven, County Londonderry. He ravaged Down and Monaghan and extended his territory into County Louth.

NICHOLL, ANDREW 1804–1886

Andrew Nicholl was born in Church Lane, Belfast, and was apprenticed as a compositor with the *Northern Whig* when it started in 1824. He was a watercolourist and painted a series of views of the Antrim coast, and in 1830 he moved to London. Two years later he had moved to Dublin, and was exhibiting in the Royal Hibernian Academy, of which he became a member in 1860. He also exhibited in the Royal Academy, London. His drawings appeared in the *Dublin Penny Journal* from its first issue in 1832, and he was one of the artists selected to illustrate *Hall's Ireland, its scenery, character* (1841–43). He published *Fourteen Views of the County of Wicklow* with F. W. Wakeman. He was associated in 1835, with *Picturesque Sketches of Some of the Finest*

Landscape and Coast Scenery of Ireland. In 1840 he published twelve lithographs, *The Northern Coast of Ireland*. He moved to London in 1840 and in 1846 travelled to Ceylon, where Sir James Emerson Tennent, a friend of his from Belfast, was the Colonial Secretary. In 1848 he accompanied Tennent on an official tour of the island, and sketched for five weeks. His account appeared in the *Dublin University Magazine*, 1852. He returned to London, then moved to Dublin, then to Belfast, where he taught landscape drawing. He died in London. His work is represented at the British Museum and the Victoria and Albert Museum, as well as in major galleries and museums in Ireland.

NICHOLL, WILLIAM 1794–1840

William Nicholl was born in Church Lane, Belfast. He was in business as a ship's chandler and flax merchant in Belfast. He exhibited with his brother Andrew, at the Royal Hibernian Academy, Dublin, in 1832. He painted many water-colours around the Knock area in Belfast, where he lived and died, and is buried in Knock graveyard. The Ulster Museum has some of his paintings.

NICHOLSON, JOHN 1821–1857

John Nicholson was born in Dublin. His father died when he was nine years old, and his mother moved to Lisburn, County Antrim. He was educated at Dungannon School and in 1837 became an ensign in the Indian army. When serving in the Afghan war in 1842 he met his brother Alexander, and three days later discovered his murdered body. In 1847 he became assistant to Sir Henry Lawrence, Resident at Lahore, and he distinguished himself in the Sikh war of 1848. When he was only twenty-eight years old he was appointed Deputy Commissioner of the Lahore Board. He was Governor of the Punjab for several years, and by 1857, the year of the mutiny, he had been promoted to the rank of colonel and was stationed at Peshawar. He fought ferociously and was said to have been in the saddle for twenty hours during one battle. A Hindu guru deified Nicholson as an incarnation of Brahma. As a result, a sect of 'Nikalsainis' grew up, and though

Nichloson in his embarrassment had them whipped and imprisoned, they persisted in worshipping him. Having won various victories against the mutineers, he was soon appointed Brigadier-General. He was killed in action at the age of thirty-five. There is a memorial tablet dedicated to him in Lisburn Cathedral, and though it portrays the storming of Delhi, it was deemed politic by Nicholson's family to omit any depiction of Nicholson himself because of the 'Nikalsaini' episode. [Biography by Trotter]

NÍ DHOMHNAILL, NEILÍ 1907–1984

Neilí Ní Dhomhnaill was born in Ranafast, County Donegal, and she traced her ancestry to the O'Donnell poets of Donegal. As a child she had poor eye-sight, and spent much time with the adults and this is how she acquired her vast wealth of traditional song and story. She was a singer and story teller, and for her the story which preceded the song was important. Eventually, she became completely blind. She remained active and took up knitting, working as a home knitter and producing two aran sweaters each week. She composed songs and for two consecutive years she won first prize in the Radio na Gaeltachta competition for setting new words to old airs.

NIETSCHE, PAUL 1855–1950

Paul Nietsche was born in Kiev and educated in Odessa. He studied art in Berlin, Munich, London and Paris, and it was not until the 1920s that he arrived in England. In 1926 he travelled to Ulster and lived there for the next four years, after which point he travelled to France, Switzerland, Cornwall, the United States and Canada. He was interned on the Isle of Man during the war because of his German parentage. During this period he made crayon studies of other internees. He died in Belfast. Among his works at the Ulster Museum, is a self portrait.

NIXON, JOHN 1750–1818

John Nixon's place of birth remains uncertain. He lived in London and exhibited at the Royal Academy from 1784 to 1815.

Between 1780 and 1790 he visited Ireland on several occasions, and he drew locations such as Dunluce Castle, Carrickfergus Castle, Shane's Castle and the Cave Hill. His work is held at the British Museum, the Victoria and Albert Museum, the National Library of Ireland and the National Museum of Wales.

NOBLE, MARGARET (SISTER NIVEDITA) 1867–1911

Margaret Noble was born in Dungannon, County Tyrone, and was educated at Halifax College. She taught in Keswick, north Wales and in Chester. She studied the teaching methods of Fröebel and Pestalozzi and was co-founder of a school in Wimbledon which put these principles into action. In 1893, as a member of the London Sesame Club, she spoke in favour of the Home Rule Bill. She met Swami Vivikananda in London in 1895 and joined his Ramakrishna Mission. In 1897 she went as a missionary nun to India, where she founded a school in Calcutta, the Sister Nivedita Girls' School. Among her publications are *Kali the Mother, The Master as I Saw Him* and *The Web Of Indian Life* which is regarded in India as one of the few fair accounts of Hindu society written in English. She was in favour of Indian nationalism and lobbied British members of parliament to this end. When she died her body was cremated in Darjeeling, and a memorial to her is inscribed: 'Here reposes Sister Nivedita, who gave her all to India'. A commemorative Indian stamp was issued in her honour, and her school has published an official biography, *Sister Nivedita of Ramakrishna-Vivikananda.* Among those who paid her tribute was Rabindranath Tagore who said: 'She was, in fact, a mother of the people'.

NOBLE, WILLIAM HENRY 1834–1892

William Noble was born in Lisnaskea, County Fermanagh, and was educated at Trinity College, Dublin, after which he joined the Royal Artillery. Having attained the rank of general, he commanded a field train in a march to Kandahar. He became superintendant of Waltham Abbey Powder Factory, and his researches led to the manufacture of cordite. He was elected Fellow of the Royal Society and died in Waltham.

NOLAN, JOHN J. 1888–1952
John Nolan was born in County Tyrone and was educated at the Christian Brothers' School, Omagh, and University College, Dublin. In 1920 he became Professor of Experimental Physics, and in 1940 was Registrar of the College. He was President of the Royal Irish Academy and Chairman of the School of Cosmic Physics in the Dublin Institute of Advanced Studies. He published several papers on atmospheric electricity and ionisation.

NORMAN, CONOLLY 1853–1908
Conolly Norman was born in Fahan, County Donegal, and was educated in Dublin. In 1876 he became a Fellow of the Royal College of Surgeons in Ireland; his specialist subject was the study of insanity. From 1886 to 1908 he was superintendent of Richmond Asylum, where he instigated improved methods of treatment.

NORRIS, JOHN *c.*1547–1597
Sir John Norris came to Ireland as a soldier in the English army. He captured the castle on Rathlin Island and all the inhabitants were massacred. His brief was to colonise and when this was not achieved Norris was recalled to England and served in the Low Countries. In 1584 he was appointed President of Munster but left his brother as deputy and returned to Europe. In 1595 he was the general chosen to try to quell the rebellion of Hugh O'Neill. He was instructed to negotiate peace, but retired to Munster in 1597 without having succeeded in this. He died a month later.

NORTON, CAROLINE (née SHERIDAN) 1807–1877
Caroline Norton was the sister of Lady Dufferin and a granddaughter of Richard Brinsley Sheridan. In 1829 she published *The Sorrows of Rosalie: a Tale with other poems*, and a year later, *The Undying One*. These were met with popular acclaim. In 1827 she had married the Honorable George Chapel Norton and they established a circle of social and political friends, including Lord Melbourne. The marriage quickly deteriorated, with Norton physically mistreating his wife, at the same time as asking her to use her political influence with her friends. Lord Melbourne, who was then Home Secretary had Norton appointed to a Metropolitan Police Magistracy in 1831. It was alleged that Caroline was Melbourne's mistress. In 1840 she published *The Queen and other poems*, and in 1845, *The Child of the Islands*. George Norton claimed the proceeds of her literary works, and the matter came to court, which declared its support for her husband. Caroline privately published a pamphlet, *English Laws for Women in the 19th century*, together with pamphlets on the Divorce Bill and on the rights of mothers to custody of their children. Her work culminated in the Married Woman's Property Act (1883).

NORTON, KATHARINE (née MacLAUGHLIN) 17th century
Katharine Norton was born near Coleraine, County Londonderry and educated in Derry. She was an Irish speaker and at the age of sixteen took a ship for Barbados. She was a Quaker minister. In 1678 she returned to Ireland where she often preached in Irish.

NUGENT, WILLIAM d.1625
William Nugent is said to have abducted the titular Baroness of Skryne in 1573. The O'Neills gave him refuge. He made various forays into the Pale and escaped to Scotland with the help of the O'Neills, and then to Rome in 1582. He later returned to Ulster disguised as a friar and subsequently received a pardon.

O

O' BEIRNE, BRIAN OSWALD (pseud. BYRNE, DONN) 1889–1928
Brian O'Beirne was born in New York and came to Forkill, County Armagh, as an infant. He was educated locally and at the National University. In 1911 he went to America, but returned eight years later. As well as factual works, he wrote novels, which include *Brother Saul; Blind Raftery; Hangman's House* and *Destiny Bay*. He accidentally drowned at Courtmacsherry, County Cork. [Biography by T. Macauley]

O'BRIEN, BARNABAS d.1657
Barnabas O'Brien was member of parliament for Coleraine in 1613. In 1639 he became 6th Earl of Thomond and in 1640, Lord Lieutenant of Clare, a position which he held for one year. In the rebellion he relinquished Bunratty Castle and fled to England. He was made Marquis of Billing and was compensated for his losses by King Charles.

O'BRIEN, CATHERINE d.1963
Catherine O'Brien was an artist in stained glass with An Túr Gloine (the Tower of Glass). She has windows in Killoughter Church, Ballyhaise, County Cavan, in St Nicholas's Church, Carrickfergus, County Antrim, in Downpatrick Church, County Down, in St John the Baptist's Church, Clontarf, Dublin, and in many other locations throughout Ireland.

O'BRIEN, DONOUGH d.1624
Donough O'Brien was brought up at the court of Queen Elizabeth I. In 1581 he became Earl of Thomond. He assisted in quelling Tyrone's rebellion and defended Newry, County Down, on behalf of the English. In 1601 he took part in the Battle of Kinsale and in 1605 became President of Munster. In 1615 he was appointed Governor of Clare.

O'BRIEN, EILEEN 1925–1986
Eileen O'Brien was born in Galway and was educated at University College, Galway. She was a journalist and worked on various newspapers in England and Ireland, eventually becoming Belfast editor for the *Irish Press*. She became Irish language editor and columnist for the *Irish Times* in 1965.

O'BRIEN, FLANN, see Ó NUALLÁIN, BRIAN

O'BRIEN, NORA CONNOLLY d.1981
Nora Connolly O'Brien formed around she and her sister, Ina, a young republican party in Belfast. She was principal organiser of the Belfast section of Inghinidhe, a branch of Cumann na mBan. In her book *We Shall Rise Again* she discusses the Easter Rising of 1916 and her father, James Connolly's role in it. She went to America as a propagandist and in 1923 was Acting Paymaster General in Ireland. She also published *Memoirs of a Rebel Father* and she was a Senator in the Dáil.

Ó BROLCHÁIN, FLAITHBHERTACH d.1175
Flaithbhertach Ó Brolcháin, as Abbot of Derry, was responsible for raising funds to rebuild the city when it had been burnt. In 1158 he was given jurisdiction over all Columban churches, and he completed the rebuilding of Derry Cathedral in 1164.

O'CAHAN, DONNELL BALLAGH d.1617
Donnell O'Cahan inherited property and land around Dungiven, County Londonderry, but lost a third of this to County Tyrone, the boundaries of which were delineated in 1591. In 1607, after the Flight of the Earls, he was knighted. Suspicion rested on him when his brother joined Sir Cahir O'Doherty's rebellion, and though he was never brought to trial, he was imprisoned in the Tower until his death.

O'CAHAN, RORY DALL *c.*17th century
Rory Dall O'Cahan was a harper and composer descended from the Dunseverick branch of the O'Cahans. He composed 'Tabhair Dom Do Lámh' (Give me your hand), and also, it is said, the 'Londonderry Air', which in 1851 was noted down at Limavady by Jane Ross from a traditional fiddler named MacCormick. George Petrie included the air in *The Traditional Music of Ireland*, 1855.

Ó CARÁIN, GILLA AN CHOIMDED d.1180
Gilla an Choimded Ó Caráin witnessed the charter granted to the Abbey of Newry, County Down, and was appointed Archbishop of Armagh in 1175. It is said that he was present at the battle near Downpatrick when John de Courcy defeated the Ulstermen in 1177.

Ó CASAIDE, TOMÁS 18th century
Tomás Ó Casaide was born in either Roscommon or Ulster and entered the Augustinian novitiate. However, he was expelled and went to Europe, where he joined the French army, from which he soon deserted. He travelled to Germany where he was captured by bandits, but eventually made his way back to Ireland as a travelling story-teller. *Eachtra an Bhráthair Ultaigh* is an account of his adventure; a copy of the manuscript is in the Royal Irish Academy and another in the British Library.

Ó CIANÁIN, TADHG *c.*1575–1625
Tadhg Ó Cianáin was born in County Fermanagh and was a chronicler for the Maguires of Fermanagh. He left for Europe with Hugh O'Neill during the the Flight of the Earls and kept a journal of the departure and the journey to Rome which is a valuable and detailed account. An edition has since been translated into English.

Ó CLÉIRIGH, CÚ CHOIGRÍCHE *c.*1590–1664
Cú Choigríche Ó Cléirigh was born in Kilbarron, County Donegal. He was asked by his cousin Mícheál to help with what became the Annals of the Four Masters.

During the period when he was living and working in Donegal from 1625 to 1636 he forfeited his land. He settled in Ballycroy, County Mayo. His poems in Irish still exist in manuscript form.

Ó CLÉIRIGH, LUGHAIDH *c.*1570–*c.*1620
Lughaidh Ó Cléirigh was probably born in Donegal. He contrbuted to the Contention of the Bards of 1617 to 1620. Among other works, he wrote a life of Red Hugh O'Donnell in Irish.

Ó CLÉIRIGH, MÍCHEÁL 1575–1643
Mícheál Ó Cléirigh was born in Kilbarron, County Donegal. He was baptised Tadhg, and was the son of a chieftain, but he took the name Mícheál when he entered Louvain as a member of the Franciscan Order. Hugh Ward, the Franciscan Guardian at Louvain, sent him to Ireland to collect manuscripts on the lives of the Irish saints. He collected material avidly and in 1630 compiled *An Réim Ríoghraidhe*, a list of kings, and lives and genealogies of the saints. He later prepared a definitive redaction of the *Leabhar Gabhála*, which dealt with the invasions of Ireland, and *Annála Ríoghachta Éireann*, covering the history of Ireland to 1616. This book was written by Ó Cléirigh and three assistants between 1632 and 1636 in a cottage on the banks of the River Drowes, which flows from Lough Melvin to Donegal Bay. The work is known as the Annals of the Four Masters. In 1634 a Martyrologium of Irish saints and a glossary of Irish words was printed at Louvain. He died there.

O'CLERY, CUCHOIGCRICHE, see Ó CLÉIRIGH, CÚ CHOIGRÍCHE

O'CLERY, MICHAEL see Ó CLÉIRIGH, MÍCHEÁL

Ó COLGÁIN, SEÁN see COLGAN, JOHN

Ó CONCHÚIR, TOMÁS early 19th century
Tomás Ó Conchúir lived at Greaghnaroog, County Monaghan. He flourished in the Carrickmacross, County Monaghan area in the early part of the 19th century. He was a

scribe and story-teller, and he translated *Topography of Ireland*, by Gerald Cambrensis, into Irish. The manuscript is in the Royal Irish Academy.

O'CONNOR, DANIEL 1843–1919
Daniel O'Connor was born in Cornenty, County Monaghan, and was ordained priest for the diocese of Clogher in 1868. He became Dean of the diocese in 1914. In 1916 he transferred to Carrickmacross, County Monaghan. He wrote a *History of St Patrick's Purgatory* in 1879, and this became the standard work on the subject.

O'CONNOR, JOHN 1830–1889
John O'Connor was born in County Londonderry, and was orphaned at the age of twelve. He was educated in Dublin at the Church of Ireland Education Society, and when he came to Belfast he was a call-boy in the theatre and assisted in scene-painting. He worked in the Dublin theatre for a short time and in 1845 joined a travelling company as scene-painter, but the tour failed and he was reduced to making silhouettes with the pantograph. He went to work in the Drury Lane and Haymarket theatres in London and became principal scene-painter. He took up landscape painting and architectural drawing and visited Italy, France and Spain. He taught drawing in London and exhibited at the Royal Academy and the Royal Hibernian Academy. In 1864 he painted the scenery for the Shakespeare Tercentenary performances at Stratford-on-Avon. His work is represented at the National Gallery of Ireland, the British Museum, the Ulster Museum and others.

Ó CREAG, SÉAMUS 1861–1934
Séamus Ó Creag was born in County Donegal and collected Irish songs which were published as *An Craoibhín Úr* and *An Craoibhín Ceoil*. He also arranged the music for many of the songs. In 1900 he wrote a *Modern Irish Grammar*.

O'DEVANY, CONOR (CORNELIUS) 1533–1612
Conor O'Devany was born in Ulster and educated at the Franciscan convent in Don-

egal. He was consecrated in Rome in 1582. He was imprisoned twice and compiled *Index Martyralis*, which was a list of his fellow-prisoners. He was tried for high treason in Dublin, and was hanged there.

O'DOHERTY, CAHIR 1587–1608
Cahir O'Doherty was Lord of Inishowen and knighted for his bravery in the Battle of Augher. He was received in London by Queen Elizabeth I and had his territorial rights confirmed. When he returned to Ireland he was made justice of the peace and alderman of the new city of Derry. He was foreman of the jury that found those participating in the Flight of the Earls in 1607 guilty of treason. The Governor of Derry, Sir George Paulet, charged O'Doherty with treason and in 1608 struck him during an argument. O'Doherty killed Paulet, slaughtered the garrison and sacked and burnt Derry. A force which was dispatched from Dublin shot him at the Rock of Doon near Kilmacrenan, County Donegal.

Ó DOIRNÍN, PEADAR d.1768
Peadar Ó Doirnín was born in Tipperary and moved to Drumcree, County Armagh. He was tutor to Arthur Brownlow's children in Lurgan, after which he was a schoolmaster at Forkill, County Armagh. He wrote nature poems, political verses and humorous verse. Some of his manuscripts are in the Cambridge University Library.

Ó DOMHNAILL, MAGHNUS, see O'DONNELL, MANUS

O'DONNELL, FRANK HUGH 1848–1916
Frank Hugh O'Donnell was born in County Donegal and educated at St Ignatius' College, Galway and Queen's College, Galway. He worked as foreign editor on the *Morning Post*. He was elected Home Rule member of parliament for Galway in 1874 and served as member of parliament for Dungarvan from 1877 to 1885. He stirred up the Parnell controversy because of Parnell's refusal to allow him to be nominated in the general election of 1885. For many years he lived in Europe and he died in London. Among his

publications are *A History of the Irish Parliamentary Party* (2 volumes, 1910); *The Stage Irishman and pseudo-Celtic Drama* and *The Message of the Masters*.

O'DONNELL, HUGH 1739–1814

Hugh O'Donnell was born in Glenarm, County Antrim, and was educated at Salamanca in Spain. He was sent to Belfast as curate and in 1784 opened St Mary's Church. In 1808 he was appointed parish priest of Belfast, where he opened St Patrick's Church, Donegall Street, in 1811.

O'DONNELL, HUGH BALLDEARG d.1704

Hugh Balldearg O'Donnell was born in County Donegal and he joined the Spanish army. After the Battle of the Boyne he raised ten thousand men in Ulster. Following a quarrel with Tyrconnell, he joined the Williamite forces and helped to attack Sligo. Before returning to Spain, where he died, he fought for the Austrians in Italy.

O'DONNELL, (RED) HUGH c.1571–1602

Red Hugh O'Donnell was the son of Sir Hugh O'Donnell. He undertook his first military action at twelve years of age. At the age of sixteen he was taken hostage and after four years as a prisoner in Dublin Castle, managed to escape to his father's castle in Ballyshannon, County Donegal. The frostbite suffered during the winter journey necessitated the amputation of his two big toes. He married Finula, daughter of Hugh O'Neill, which consolidated his power. He was inaugurated as chief of the O'Donnells in 1592 and took Sligo and Connaught. Together with Hugh O'Neill he achieved a crushing victory over the English army at the Yellow Ford in 1598. In 1600 the Spaniards sent help, but nonetheless the Irish lost to Mountjoy at the Battle of Kinsale. O'Donnell went to the court of the Spanish king, Philip III, to ask for further assistance, but he fell ill and died there, possibly as a result of poisoning by an ally of Mountjoy. He was buried at the Franciscan monastery at Valladolid. [Biography by Lughaidh Ó Cléirigh, published 1948–57]

O'DONNELL, MANUS c.1500–1563

Manus O'Donnell was born in Donegal, and in 1537 was inaugurated Lord of Tyrconnell at Kilmacrenan. He invaded the Pale in 1539, but two years later submitted to the Lord Deputy. His son Calvagh deposed him in 1555. He wrote love poetry and satiric verse and undertook to supervise the writing of a life of St Colmcille at Lifford Castle, where he was captive. The manuscript is now in the Bodleian Library, Oxford.

O'DONNELL, MARY STUART fl.1632

Mary Stuart O'Donnell was born in England and reared in Ireland until she was twelve years old, when she returned to England to the care of her grandmother, Lady Kildare. She was the daughter of Brigid Fitzgerald and Rory O'Donnell, who fled with the Earls in 1607. In 1626, because she objected to her grandmother's choice of suitor, she dressed in men's clothes and with friends, made her way to Bristol where she boarded a vessel to Brussels. It was in Europe that she met her brother Hugh for the first time, but is said to have antagonised him by continuing to dress and behave as a man. She was betrothed to O'Neill, but married Dudley O'Gallagher who was killed in 1635. She remarried four years later, a 'poor Irish captain', and returned to Rome. Nothing further is known of her.

O'DONNELL, NIALL GARBH 1569–1626

Niall Garbh O'Donnell was born in County Donegal and opposed the election of Red Hugh O'Donnell as chief. He took Lifford and Donegal from him and was himself inaugurated at Kilmacrenan. In 1608 he was accused of conspiring with Cahir O'Doherty in a rebellion, and in 1609 he was committed to the Tower of London where he remained until his death.

O DONNELL, NUALA fl. 1608–1617

Nuala O Donnell was a daughter of Hugh O'Donnell, and probably of Finula O'Donnell. She was a sister of Red Hugh, and the subject of a poem, 'Truagh liom Máire agas Mairghrég', by Fearghal Óg Mac an Bhaird. She was exiled in Rome, returning to Louvain some time after the death of the last of her four brothers, in 1608. She is believed to have brought the son of the Earl of Tyrconnell, who was seven years of age, to be educated by the Irish Franciscans in Flanders, and she herself also tutored him. A letter addressed to James I prior to 1613, mentions her request that the boy be pardoned, be permitted to return to Ireland, and have his father's lands restored to him. She died some time after 1617 and is buried in the chapel of the Franciscans at Louvain near the high altar. It is probable that she was the owner of the *Book of O'Donnell's Daughter*, which contains sections by Eoghan Ruadh Mac an Bhaird, Ferghal Óg Mac an Bhaird and Eochaidh Ó hEoghusa.

O'DONNELL, PATRICK 1856–1927

Patrick O'Donnell was born in Kilraine near Glenties, County Donegal, and was educated locally and at Letterkenny. In 1880 he was ordained at Maynooth and was appointed Professor of Theology. In 1888 he became Bishop of Raphoe. He instigated the building of many churches, including Letterkenny Cathedral, a school at Killybegs, County Donegal, and a seminary at Letterkenny. In 1896 he was chairman of the Irish Race Convention, and in 1900 chaired the National Convention. In 1908 he was instrumental in founding the National University of Ireland. In 1924 he became Archbishop of Armagh and in the following year was created a Cardinal. In 1927 he introduced reforms at a Synod at Maynooth. He was a native Irish speaker and an active member of the Irish Convention in 1917. He died in Carlingford, County Louth.

O'DONNELL, PEADAR 1893–1986

Peadar O'Donnell was born in Meenmore, near Dungloe, County Donegal, and educated at St Patrick's Training College, Dublin. He went to Arranmore and Inisfree islands as a teacher, but having witnessed the hardships of Irish migrant labourers in Scotland, in 1918 he became a full-time organiser for the Irish Transport and General Workers' Union. He opposed conscription, and in 1920 he became a member of the Irish Republican Army and was imprisoned for his opposition to the Anglo-Irish Treaty of 1921. He escaped in 1924, but was imprisoned again in 1927. *The Way It Was With Them* was written on his release, when he went to the south of France. In 1930 he was President of the European Peasant Congress in Berlin. For a period he was editor of *An Phoblacht*, but left the Irish Republican Army to work for the Republican Congress, which was intended to establish a workers' republic. He recruited volunteers to fight in the Spanish Civil War on the republican side. Among his publications are *Storm* (begun in prison); *Islanders; The Knife; On the Edge of the Stream; The Big Windows* and *Proud Island. The Gates Flew Open; Salud!: An Irishman in Spain* and *There Will Be Another Day* are autobiographical works. From 1946 until 1954 he was editor of the literary monthly journal the *Bell.* He was a member of the Irish Academy of Letters and served as its President. His play, *Wrack* was performed in the Abbey Theatre in 1932. He was a campaigner all his life, and in his later years was in favour of nuclear disarmament. He died in Dublin.

O'DONNELL, RORY 1575–1608

Rory (Ruaidhrí) O'Donnell was born in County Donegal and became chief of Tyrconnell when Red Hugh went to Spain after the defeat at the Battle of Kinsale. In 1602 he submitted to Mountjoy and went with him in 1603 to London to visit King James I and was created first Earl of Tyrconnell. Later that year he was knighted in Dublin. Discontented with the lands granted to him, it is said that he planned to seize Dublin Castle, but on discovery he and Tyrone fled in what became known as the 'Flight of the Earls' in 1607. He died in Rome.

O'DONOVAN, GERALD 1871–1942

Gerald O'Donovan was born in County Down and was educated in Cork, Galway and Sligo. After having attended Maynooth, he was ordained for the diocese of Clonfert. He was involved with the Gaelic League and the co-operative movement. He left the priesthood and went to London where he became a businessman and a novelist. His publications include *Father Ralph; How They Did It* and *Vocations*. His work was admired by Frank O'Connor. He died in Surrey.

O'DUFFY, EOIN 1892–1944
Eoin O'Duffy was born in Cargaghdoo near Castleblayney, County Monaghan. He worked as an engineer and architect in County Monaghan and then became an auctioneer. He was a prominent volunteer in the 1916 uprising. In 1917 he joined the Irish Republican Army and was imprisoned on several occasions. In 1921 he became Director of Organisation of the Irish Republican Army and in the following year was appointed its Chief of Staff. He supported the Treaty and became first chief commissioner of the Garda Síochána, but in 1933 de Valera dismissed him. He became leader of the National Guard (known as the Blueshirts) and was appointed President of the Fine Gael party upon its formation in 1933, resigning in 1934. In 1935 he founded the National Corporate Party and in 1936 organised an Irish brigade to fight in the Spanish Civil War. He described his campaign in *Crusade in Spain*. He was given a state funeral.

Ó DUILEARGA, SÉAMAS see DELARGY, JAMES

O'FARRELLY, AGNES MARY WINIFRIDE d.1951
Agnes O'Farrelly was born at Raffenny House, County Cavan, and was educated at University College, Dublin. She was a member of the senate of the National University of Ireland and of the governing body of University College, Dublin. She pioneered the Irish language revival, was a member of the Executive Committee of the Gaelic League and President of the International Celtic Congress. She wrote many works both in English and Irish.

O'FARRELLY, FEARDORCHA 18th century
Feardorcha O'Farrelly was born in Mullagh, County Cavan. He was a farmer and a friend of the harper O'Carolan for whom he wrote

poems in Irish. Among his poems are 'Beir Beannacht uaim síos go Baile na Croabh' and 'Siubhal mé Cúig Cóige na Fódhla'.

O'FEE, THOMAS, see Ó FIAICH, TOMÁS

Ó FHLOINN, RIOBARD, see LYND, ROBERT

Ó FIAICH, TOMÁS 1923–1992
Tomás Ó Fiaich was born in County Armagh and was educated at Maynooth and University College, Dublin. He was ordained in 1948 and went to Louvain to further his studies. He was Professor of History at Maynooth and became deeply involved in the language revival. In 1977 he was consecrated Archbishop of Armagh and Primate of All Ireland, and in 1979 he was created cardinal. In 1980 he received the Irish American Cultural Institute Award for translating the Bible into Irish. Among his publications are *Gaelscrínte i gCéin; Má Nuad; Oliver Plunkett: Ireland's New Saint; Art Mac Cumhaigh: Dánta* and *Saint Oliver of Armagh*.

Ó GALLCHOBHAIR, SÉAMUS (GALL-AGHER, JAMES) 1681–1751
Séamus Ó Gallchobhair was born in County Donegal and from 1725 to 1737 was Bishop of Raphoe and then Bishop of Kildare until his death. There were periods of his life as Bishop of Raphoe when he sought refuge at Lough Erne from the authorities. He preached in Irish, and his sermons, which were popular, were printed as *Sermons in Irish Gaelic*.

O'GALLAGHER, REDMOND 1521–1601
Redmond O'Gallagher was born in Raphoe, County Donegal. In 1545 he was consecrated Bishop of Killala. He was translated to Derry in 1569 and was appointed Vice-Primate in 1570. It is said that he helped survivors of the Spanish Armada in 1588, but that he was killed by English soldiers at Killea, County Londonderry. [Biography by Bishop O'Doherty]

O'GARA, FERGAL 17th century
Fergal O'Gara was born in County Sligo and was the patron of the Four Masters

while they were compiling the famous Annals in Donegal from 1632 to 1636.

OGILBY, DAVID 1755–1834
David Ogilby was born in Limavady, County Londonderry, and went to India to serve with the East India Company. After twenty-two years he was knighted and returned to Ireland. He wrote and published poems, which included translations of Indian poets, in *Walker's Hibernian Magazine* in 1804.

O'GLACAN, NIAL *c.*1590–1655
Nial O'Glacan was born in County Donegal, though few details of his early life remain. He was a physician, and it is possible he left Ireland when he was young because of his support for Hugh O'Donnell who died in 1602 in Spain. He spent many years practising in Salamanca and Valencia, using the latinised version of his name, Mellanus Galacanus, for professional purposes. By the 1620s he was treating cases of the plague in Claremont and Toulouse. In 1629 he published his famous *Tractatus de Peste*, which was printed by the university printers; it includes personal observations such as the fact that the plague doctors wore long leather gowns, gauntlets, leather masks with glass protection for the eyes and a long beak filled with fumigants for the nose. The University of Toulouse appointed him to its Chair of Medicine, and he was physician to the King of France. In 1646 he moved to Bologne and visited Rome. He edited a collection of poems with the Bishop of Ferns and Sir Nicholas Plunkett: *Regni Hiberniae ad Sanctissimus Innocenti Pont. Max Pyramides Encomiasticae.* In 1655 he published *Cursus Medicus* (2 volumes), based on the writings of Galen.

Ó GNÍMH, FEARFLATHA *c.*1540–1640
Fearflatha Ó Gnímh was the bard of the O'Neills of Clandedoye and went with Shane O'Neill to London to meet Queen Elizabeth I. His two best-known poems are 'Mo Thruaigh Mar Táid Gaoidhil' and 'Beannacht ar Anmain Éireann'.

Ó GORMÁIN, (MAC GORMAIN), MUIRIS *c.*1700–1794
Muiris Ó Gormáin was born in Ulster and was a schoolmaster, scribe and poet. The manuscripts upon which he worked are in the British Library and other Irish collections. He assisted Charlotte Brooke in her publication *Reliques of Irish Poetry*.

O'GOWAN, ERIC EDWARD DORMAN 1895–1969
Eric O'Gowan was born in County Cavan and was educated in England. He joined the British army and was commissioned. He fought in both world wars. In 1942 he was dismissed as Deputy Chief of the General Staff, British Middle East Command, though a footnote on a report by Sir Winston Churchill states that O'Gowan 'only became Deputy Chief of Staff on 16th June, 1942' and could not have been responsible for the fall of Tobruk. The Chief Herald, in 1949, authorised him as being the representative of the ancient sept of the O'Gowans of Ballygowan, County Down.

Ó GRIANNA, SÉAMUS (pseud. MÁIRE) 1891–1969
Séamus Ó Grianna was born in Ranafast in the Donegal Gaeltacht. He taught in Tyrone, Dublin and Donegal, and in 1919 was employed as an organiser for Dáil Éireann's Ministry of Education. In 1921 he was imprisoned for two years because of his opposition to the Anglo-Irish Treaty. When the first Fianna Fáil government had taken office in 1932 he once more became a civil servant and was employed in making translations from English and French into Irish. Among his publications are two novels, *Mo Dhá Róisín* and *Caisleáin Óir* and many collections of short stories, including *Cioth is Dealáin*. In 1945 *Saoghal Corrach*, his autobiography, was published.

O'HAGAN, JOHN 1822–1890
John O'Hagan was born in Newry, County Down, and was educated at Trinity College, Dublin. He was called to the Bar in 1842 and defended Gavan Duffy in 1848. He was made Queen's Counsel in 1865 and became a judge of the Land Court in 1881. Many of his poems were published in the *Nation* and he translated the *Song of Roland* in 1883.

O'HAGAN, JOHN TULLYHOGUE d.1979
John O'Hagan was born in Coalisland, County Tyrone. In 1939 he went to England to pursue a business career, and became known as a woodcarver. In St Michael's Church, West Bromwich hangs his carving 'Madonna and Child'. Another of his carvings was presented to Queen Elizabeth II by Sandwell Metropolitan Borough Council. The artist's family own his carved chairs and chests which carry the armorial bearings of the O'Neills.

O'HAGAN, MARY 1823–1876
Mary O'Hagan was born in Belfast and entered the Sisters of Poor Clares in Newry in 1844, where she became Abbess in 1853. She founded the Convent of Poor Clares, Kenmare in 1861 and was Abbess there until her death. [Biography by M. F. Cusack]

O'HAGAN, THOMAS 1812–1885
Thomas O'Hagan was born in Belfast and was educated at the Belfast Academical Institution. He was called to the Bar in 1836 and defended Gavan Duffy both in a libel action and when he was tried by the state in 1844. In 1860 he became Solicitor-General and in 1861 Attorney-General, and from 1863 to 1865 he served as member of parliament for Tralee. Within the next seven years he was appointed judge, and Lord Chancellor in 1868. He became a peer in 1870 as Lord O'Hagan of Tullyhogue. He published *Speeches and Papers* and died in London.

O'HANLON, JOHN J. 1874–1960
John O'Hanlon was born in Portadown, County Armagh. He won nine Irish Chess Championship titles, from 1912 to 1940. He also won many minor chess tournaments in England and in Europe.

O'HANLON, REDMOND 1640–1681
Redmond O'Hanlon was born in Aghantaraghan, near Poyntzpass, County Armagh, and took up service in the French army. His family were dispossessed of property in Tandragee, their ancestral home, after the Cromwellian wars. When Redmond returned he led a band of outlaws or rapparees and exacted tribute in Armagh,

Down and Louth. In 1676 a reward of £100 was offered for his body, dead or alive. He was regarded by many people as a folk hero, and gave money he had robbed from the rich to the poor. It is said that he frequently evaded capture and once swam the width of Carlingford Lough to escape. He was shot in his sleep while hiding at Eightmilebridge, County Down, by his foster-brother. His head was placed on a spike over Downpatrick jail, and he is buried in the graveyard of Relicarn, adjacent to Balinabeck, outside Tandragee, County Armagh. He is the subject of many songs and stories.

O'HARA, HELEN 1881–1919
Helen O'Hara was probably born in Portstewart, County Londonderry. She exhibited at the Royal Hibernian Academy, the Royal Institute of Painters in Watercolours, and the Society of Women Artists. She was elected Vice-President of the Belfast Art Society in 1904. She lived in Belfast and Waterford, and her work is represented in the Ulster Museum, Belfast.

O'HARA, WILLIAM 1816–1899
William O'Hara was born in Derry and was taken to Philadelphia when he was four. After studying in Rome he was ordained in 1843 and became Vicar-General of Philadelphia in 1860, and eight years later was consecrated first Bishop of Scranton.

O'HARTAGAN (UA hARTACÁIN), CINÁED d.975
Cinaed O'Hartagan was born in Ulster and was a Gaelic poet. Several of the poems ascribed to him appear in the Book of Leinster and the Book of Ballymote.

O'HEMPSY (HEMPSON), DENIS 1695–1807
Denis O'Hempsy was born in Craigmore, near Garvagh, County Londonderry. Owing to smallpox he became blind at the age of three years, but was taught to play the harp by Bridget O'Cahan when he was twelve. He travelled throughout Ireland for ten years playing his harp, and when he visited Scotland in 1745 he played before Prince Charles Edward at Holyrood. He lived in a house at Magilligan, County

Londonderry, which had been given to him by Bishop Hervey, and in 1792 he attended the famous Harp Festival in Belfast. He is mentioned by Edward Bunting for his expertise as a musician. It is said that he lived on a diet of milk, water and potatoes, that he married when he was eighty-six and had a daughter, and that he lived until he was one hundred and twelve years old. Many of Ireland's very old harp tunes are attributed to him. His harp was made out of white willow with a back of fir which had been dug out of a bog.

Ó hEODHASA, EOCHAIDH, see O'HUSSEY, EOCHAIDH

Ó hEODHASA, GIOLLA-BHRIGHDE or MÁELBHRIGHID, see O'HUSSEY, BONAVENTURE

Ó hUALLACHÁIN, COLMÁN 1922–1979
Colmán Ó hUallacháin was born in Dublin and was educated at Coláiste Mhuire, University College, Galway, and at Louvain. He was ordained a Franciscan priest. He studied linguistics at Georgetown University and proceeded to apply his knowledge to the Irish language. He initiated a television programme, 'Buntús Cainte' to promote Irish. He was lecturer in philosophy through Irish in University College, Galway, and held the Chair of Ethics and Logic at Maynooth. He was Director of the Institiúid Teangeolaíochta Éireann and a senior lecturer in Irish at the New University of Ulster. Among his publications is *Ridire Mhuire gan Smál.*

Ó hUIGINN, TADHG DALL 1550–1617
Tadhg Ó hUiginn is thought to have been born in County Sligo, but fostered in County Donegal. He was a bard, and about forty of his poems survive, some of which are addressed to the O'Neills, the O'Rourkes and the Maguires. He was murdered by the O'Haras because he had satirised them in one of his poems.

O'HUSSEY, BONAVENTURE (Ó hEODHASA, GIOLLA-BHRIGHDE or MÁELBHRIGHID) 1574–1614
Bonaventure O'Hussey was born in Enniskillen, County Fermanagh, and was educated at Douay and Louvain, where he became a Franciscan in 1607. He was one of the original members of the community of St Anthony's at Louvain and was Guardian there at the time of his death. In 1608 he published *An Teagasc Críostaidhe*, a book on Christian doctrine, later publishing a long poem with the same title. His works were written in Irish, and his manuscripts are in the British Library, the Royal Irish Academy and the Vatican.

O'HUSSEY (Ó hEODHASA), EOCHAIDH *c.*1570–*c.*1630
Eochaidh O'Hussey was an ollamh, and the last of the bards of the Maguires of Fermanagh. The winter campaign of 1599 to 1600 is the subject of his most famous poem. His poetry celebrates the escape of Hugh O'Donnell from Dublin Castle and praises the Earls of Tyrone and Tyrconnell. His manuscripts are preserved in the Royal Irish Academy.

OISÍN or OSSIAN
Oisín was the son of Fionn mac Cumhaill and is the legendary warrior poet of the Fianna. The *Transactions of the Ossianic Society* have printed the poems which are ascribed to him. Local tradition in the Glens of Antrim associates his name with the Neolithic court cairn at Lubitavish, Glenaan, close to which a memorial has been erected to John Hewitt.

O'LAVERTY, JAMES 1828–1906
James O'Laverty was born in Lecale, County Down, and was educated at St Malachy's College, Belfast, and Maynooth, where he was ordained in 1851. He was curate in Ahoghill and Portglenone, County Antrim, and in 1857 he became dean of the diocesan seminary in Belfast and chaplain to the Belfast Workhouse. He was parish priest of Holywood, County Down, for over thirty years until the time of his death. He established a National School in 1869 and erected a church dedicated to St Colmcille. He wrote many articles for the *Ulster Journal of Archaeology.* From 1878 until 1887 he produced the *Historical Account of Down and Connor*

(4 volumes), which he acknowledged as owing a debt to the work of Bishop William Reeves. A fifth volume dealt with the bishops of the diocese. In 1904 he became Monsignor. He is buried in the churchyard in Holywood.

Ó LOCHLAINN, DOMHNALL 1048–1121
Domhnall Ó Lochlainn was King of Ailech. In 1083 he invaded Connaught, crossing into Ulidia, where he won the battle of Creeve in County Antrim in 1100. It is said that he cut down the great tree under which the kings were crowned. By 1091 he had become ruler of Ireland and in 1103 he defeated the Danes and Leinstermen. He died in Derry.

O'MALLEY, ERNEST 1898–1957
Ernie O'Malley was born in County Mayo and as a medical student joined the Irish Volunteers in 1917. With the rank of captain he was sent as an organiser to north-west Ulster. He fought in both the Anglo-Irish War and the civil war, was wounded on several occasions and was told by a doctor that he would never be able to walk again. He recovered in Spain and travelled in Europe and America, where he collected funds for the establishment of the *Irish Press*. He was elected a member of the Irish Academy of Letters and published *On Another Man's Wound* which was republished as *Army Without Banners*. He also published *The Singing Flame* and *Raids and Rallies*. He died in Howth.

O'MALLEY, GRACE *c.*1530–*c.*1600
Grace O'Malley was born in County Mayo; the name Granuaile, by which she is sometimes known, is a corruption of the Gaelic form of her name, Gráinne Ni Mháille. The O'Malleys were seafarers, and Grace spent her childhood on the islands off the west coast of Ireland, becoming a proficient sea-captain. She was accused of robbing from the Aran Islands, and a gallows was built for her execution. She fled to Ulster and stayed with the O'Neills until her eventual pardon by Queen Elizabeth I. It is believed that she is buried on Clare Island off County Mayo.

Ó MAOIL CHONAIRE, FEARFEASA 17th century
Fearfeasa Ó Maoil Chonaire (O'Mulconry) was a native of County Roscommon and one of the Four Masters who worked in Donegal transcribing the manuscripts which comprised the Annals of the Four Masters. He also recorded the lives of forty Connaught bards, c. 1636.

Ó MEALLÁIN, FEARDORCHA 17th century
Feardorcha Ó Mealláin is thought to have been born in County Down. Little is known of his life, but he may have been a priest. He has left only one known work; this deals with the act of parliament of 1652 which banished all opponents of the British parliament east of the Shannon to Connaught and Clare on pain of death.

O'MULCONRY, see Ó MAOIL CHONAIRE, FEARFEASA

O'NEILL, ARTHUR 1737–1816
Arthur O'Neill was born in County Tyrone and was a traditional harper who collected many ancient tunes. He was blind, played the harp with extraordinary skill, and was considered one of the last of the itinerant bards. He was one of the performers at the great Harp Festival in Belfast in 1792. He died in County Armagh.

O'NEILL, BRIAN MacPHELIM d.1574
Brian O'Neill was chief of the O'Neills of Clandeboye, County Down, and was knighted in 1567. He had fought for the English against his cousin Shane O'Neill, but later joined with Turlough Luineach in attacking the Ards peninsula and resisting plantation. Essex compelled him to submit, but he disobeyed in 1573 and, although he was pardoned, Essex insisted on his execution.

O'NEILL, CONN BACACH *c.*1484–*c.*1559
Conn O'Neill was inagurated chief of the Tyrone O'Neills in 1519. He attacked the Pale, and his lands were ravaged three times in reprisal. In 1537 he attacked Ardglass, but when he went to London he was given the title of Earl of Tyrone by Henry VIII, which made him unpopular in Ulster. He died in the Pale.

O'NEILL, DANIEL c.1612–1664

Daniel O'Neill served at the court of Charles I, and as a royalist soldier fought abroad. After attempting to regain his own estates, he commanded the foot soldiers at Marston Moor (1644) and Naseby (1645), and for a period was in command of the Ulster Confederate army. He was committed to the Tower, but escaped wearing women's clothes. After the Restoration he was rewarded with an estate in England and was appointed Postmaster-General. He built Belsize House in London and died in Kent.

O'NEILL, DANIEL 1920–1974

Daniel O'Neill was born in Belfast and worked as an electrician. He attended Belfast Technical School for art classes, and held his first exhibition in Belfast in 1940. He undertook night work so that he could use the day for painting. He had a very successful one-man exhibition in Dublin, and Victor Waddington subsidised him so that he could become a full-time artist. After a period abroad he returned to Kerry in the 1960s. He had occasional exhibitions at the Royal Hibernian Academy and in London and Boston.

O'NEILL, FELIM, see O'NEILL, PHELIM

O'NEILL, FLAITHBERTACH d.1036

Flaithbertach O'Neill was King of Ailech. He ravaged Lecale, County Down, and killed its king in 1004. In 1014 he attacked Kilmacrenan, County Donegal, and the Ards peninsula, County Down, and carried off plunder. In 1031 he went on a pilgrimage to Rome.

O'NEILL, GEORGE 1863–1947

George O'Neill was born in Dungannon, County Tyrone, and was educated at St Stanislaus' College, Tullamore, and at the Universities of Prague and Paris. In 1900 he became a Fellow of the Royal University of Ireland. He was Emeritus Professor of English at University College, Dublin, and Professor of Modern Languages at Corpus Christi College, Melbourne. Among his publications are *Could Bacon have Written the Plays?*; *Five Centuries of English Poetry*; *Golden Years on the Paraguay*; *The Psalms* and *The Book of Job*, the last two being translations with commentary.

O'NEILL, GORDON d.1704

Gordon O'Neill was the son of Sir Phelim O'Neill and was Lieutenant and member of parliament for Tyrone in 1689. He fought in the Battle of the Boyne and at Aughrim and was left for dead on the battlefield. He later went to France and served with the Irish Brigade.

O'NEILL, HENRY d.1489

Henry O'Neill was King of Tyrone and was captured by the O'Donnells in 1431 but defeated them four years later. He fought on the side of the McQuillans against the O'Neills of Clandeboye, County Down. In 1470 he took Sketrick Castle and six years later demolished Belfast Castle. He received a gift of scarlet cloth and a gold chain from the king of England in 1463.

O'NEILL, HUGH d.1230

Hugh O'Neill was King of Tyrone from 1196 and opposed the Anglo-Normans, whom he defeated at Larne in 1198. He defeated the English at Narrow-water near Warrenpoint, County Down, in 1211 and destroyed the castle of Clones, County Monaghan. Within the next few years he had razed Carrickfergus, County Antrim, Carlingford, County Louth, and Coleraine, County Londonderry.

O'NEILL, HUGH c.1550–1616

Hugh O'Neill was born in Dungannon, County Tyrone, and as an infant was fostered in Tyrone by the O'Hagans and the O'Quinns. After the death of his father, he became a ward of the crown and lived with an English settler family in the Pale. When war broke out between the crown and Shane O'Neill in 1566, he fought on Queen Elizabeth's behalf. Between 1573 and 1575 he soldiered for the Earl of Essex in Ulster, but in 1579, he reached an agreement with the Crown which lasted until 1587. The English government became increasingly dependent upon him to defend the Pale, and he had the title Earl of Tyrone conferred on him. He was proclaimed a traitor when he declared himself The O'Neill, chief of Tyrone in 1595. He captured the Blackwater fort and fought in Munster during the Nine Years' War against the English. After many military successes he was eventually defeated at the Battle of Kinsale in 1601 and returned to Ulster to find that the majority of his lands had been confiscated; though he accepted the terms of Queen Elizabeth I in order to retrieve them. Possibly learning that in response to an alleged conspiracy, the English government was planning to arrest him, he fled to France and then to Rome, where he spent the rest of his life. In his later years he became blind. There is a memorial stone to him in the Church of San Pietro in Montorio. [Biography by John Mitchel]

O'NEILL, HUGH DUBH d.1660
Hugh O'Neill served in Spain with Owen Roe O'Neill, and when he returned to Ireland in 1642 he was taken prisoner in Monaghan, but in 1646 was released in an exchange of prisoners. He was appointed general of the Irish forces in Ulster and Governor of Limerick, where he fought Cromwell's army. In 1651, as Governor of Limerick, he capitulated and was sent as a prisoner to London. On his release he returned to Spain, where he died.

O'NEILL, JOHN 1740–1798
John O'Neill was born in Shane's Castle, County Antrim, and served as member of parliament for Randalstown from 1761 to 1793. He supported Catholic Emancipation and was raised to the peerage of Antrim in 1793 and created a viscount in 1795. In 1798 he was, as the Governor of Antrim, involved in the battle which took place there during the rebellion, and was killed by his own park-keeper.

O'NEILL, JOHN 1834–1878
John O'Neill was born in Drumgallon, County Monaghan. In 1857 he emigrated to America. He served throughout the Civil War with the Federal army. He joined the Fenians. With fifteen hundred men he crossed the Niagara into Canada and captured Fort Erie. He was imprisoned, and on his release he returned to the United States. He died in Omaha.

O'NEILL, JOHN BRUCE RICHARD 1780–1855
John O'Neill joined the British army and reached the rank of general. In 1841 he became 3rd Viscount O'Neill. He was Constable of Dublin Castle and Vice-Admiral of the coast of Ulster.

O'NEILL, MOIRA, see SKRINE, AGNES NESTA SHAKESPEARE (née HIGGINSON)

O'NEILL, NIAL 1658–1690
Nial O'Neill was born in Shane's Castle, County Antrim, and in 1687 recruited regiments of dragoons for King James I. He was present at the siege of Derry and was wounded at the Battle of the Boyne. He died in Waterford. A famous portrait of him in Gaelic dress by John Michael Wright hangs in the Tate Gallery.

O'NEILL, NIALL MORE d.1398
Niall More O'Neill was King of Tyrone and fought many battles in the fourteenth century. It is said that in 1387 he built a house at Emain Macha, now Navan Fort, near Armagh, and entertained there the learned men and the bards of Ireland. In 1397 he abdicated in favour of his son.

O'NEILL, OWEN c.1380–1456
Owen O'Neill was King of Tyrone. He defended east Ulster in 1417, and in 1422 with English assistance attacked Connaught. During 1435 he fought the Maguires of Fermanagh, and it is said that the people fled before him carrying their possessions across the frozen surface of Lough Erne. He was captured by the English at Trim, when he turned against them. He had been inaugurated O'Neill in 1432, but in 1455 was deposed by his son.

O'NEILL, OWEN ROE c.1590–1649
Owen Roe O'Neill accompanied his uncle, Hugh O'Neill, Earl of Tyrone, when he fled to Europe in 1607. He was educated at Louvain, served in the army in Spain around 1610, and fought with distinction in the Netherlands and against the French. He returned to Ulster in 1642, and arriving in

Sheephaven Bay, County Donegal, was chosen by the Ulstermen as their general. He swore allegiance to King Charles I and won the Battle of Benburb, County Tyrone, in 1646. Shortly after Cromwell's arrival in Ireland in 1649, O'Neill died in County Cavan, on his way to join the royalist army.

O'NEILL, PHELIM 1604–1652
Phelim O'Neill was born in Kinard, County Tyrone, studied at Lincoln's Inn, and served as member for Dungannon in the Irish parliament. He was expelled in 1641 for his part in the rebellion. After seizing Charlemont castle, he was chosen leader of the Ulster forces at Monaghan. He was defeated at Lisburn, County Antrim, but captured Lurgan, County Armagh, and burnt Armagh. In 1650 he was forced to capitulate and was tried and executed in Dublin.

O'NEILL, PHELIM d.1709
Phelim O'Neill was a Jacobite who took part in the siege of Derry. He also fought at the Battle of the Boyne, at Aughrim, and at Limerick. When Limerick capitulated, he went into exile in France with his regiment and was killed at the Battle of Malplaquet, fighting for the Irish Brigade.

O'NEILL, ROSA (O'DONNELL, née O'DOGHERTY) c.1582–1660
Rosa O'Neill was a sister of Cahir O'Dogherty. She married Cathbar O'Donnell, brother of the Earl of Tyrconnell, and bore him a son, Hugh. In 1607 they accompanied the Earl of Tyrone to the continent, and then to Rome, having left Hugh in Louvain. A year later, when her husband died of fever, she returned to Louvain, and in 1613–14 married Owen Roe O'Neill. They had one son, Henry. Rosa was politically active on Owen Roe's behalf, often representing him and acting as his intermediary and purchasing agent. In 1643, she and Henry Roe returned to Ireland, where her husband was campaigning, but six years later, Owen Roe died of a fever. In 1651 she gained permission to resettle in Flanders, from where she petitioned the Spanish authorities for Owen's military pensions. Towards the end of her life she lived in Brussels. She was buried at the Franciscan College of St Anthony of Padua in Louvain. Her crypt and Latin inscription survive.

Ó NÉILL, SÉAMUS 1910–1981
Séamus Ó Néill was born in Clarkhill, near Castlewellan, County Down and was educated at Queen's University, Belfast, and Innsbruck. He gave lecture tours in America and Canada and was, for forty years, Professor of History at Carysfort College of Education. He wrote short stories, *An Sean Saighdiúir agus Scéalta Eile*, poetry, essays and plays including *Faill ar an bhFeart*. His novel *Tonn Tuile* was a bestseller. He died in Dublin.

O'NEILL, SHANE c.1530–1567
Shane O'Neill, born in Ulster, was known as 'Shane the Proud' and was elected The O'Neill in 1559. In 1562 he submitted to Queen Elizabeth I, but she later withdrew her support in favour of Shane's stepbrother. Despite being a supporter of Mary, Queen of Scots, he destroyed the Scottish settlements of the MacDonnells in County Antrim, burnt Armagh, and invaded the Pale. He defeated the MacDonnells and took Sorley Boy prisoner at Ballycastle in 1565, but they killed him at Cushendun, having invited him to a banquet as a guest.

O'NEILL, SHANE MacBRIAN d.1616
Shane O'Neill was one of the last chiefs of Clandeboye and took part in the rebellion of Hugh O'Neill. He captured Edenduffcarrick and Belfast from the English in 1597, but later surrendered and was pardoned. The O'Neills of Clandeboye were dispossessed of six hundred thousand acres under the Ulster plantation of James I. Shane was allowed to keep one hundred and twenty thousand acres, his castle in Edencarrickduff at Randalstown, County Antrim, and the baronies of Antrim and Toome. The castle, of which only a ruined tower now stands, is known as Shane's Castle.

O'NEILL, TERENCE 1914–1990
Terence O'Neill was born in London, the son of a member of parliament for

Mid-Antrim at Westminster. When he was only three months old, his father was killed in the First World War. He was educated at Eton and became an army officer. In 1946 he was elected representative for Bannside, and from 1953 to 1956 was Deputy Speaker. For the next seven years he worked for the Ministry of Finance, and from 1963 to 1969 Captain Terence O'Neill was Prime Minister of Northern Ireland. He resigned in 1969 and returned to England. He became Lord O'Neill of Maine and died in Hampshire.

O'NEILL, TURLOUGH LUINEACH c.1530–1595

Turlough O'Neill came from a subordinate branch of the O'Neills and was fostered amongst the Muintir Luinigh. He was inaugurated chief of the O'Neills after the death of Shane O'Neill. He resisted the colonisation of Antrim and maintained his power base, west of the River Blackwater. He built the castle of Strabane, which developed into a small town. In 1583 he fought against the Scots. Although he had defeated the rival claimant, Hugh O'Neill in 1588, five years later he resigned in Hugh's favour. He died in Strabane, County Tyrone, and is remembered for his support for the bards and brehons.

O'NOLAN, BRIAN see Ó NUALLÁIN, BRIAN

Ó NUALLÁIN (O'NOLAN), BRIAN (pseud. FLANN O'BRIEN and MYLES NA GOPALEEN) 1912–1966

Brian Ó Nualláin was born in Strabane, County Tyrone, graduated in Celtic languages at University College, Dublin, and for many years was a civil servant. He wrote a column for the *Irish Times* under the pseudonym Myles na Gopaleen. His first novel, *At Swim-Two-Birds*, which was published in 1939, is regarded as a masterpiece. He wrote two plays, *Thirst* and *Faustus Kelly* which was produced in 1943 in the Abbey Theatre. Other books include *The Hard Life*, 1961; *The Dalkey Archive*, 1965 (dramatised by Hugh Leonard as *When the Saints Go Cycling In*) and *The Third Policeman*, 1967. *The Poor Mouth (An Béal Bocht)*; *The Best of*

Myles and *Myles Away from Dublin* were published posthumously.

Ó NUALLÁIN, CIARÁN 1910–1983

Ciarán Ó Nualláin was born in Strabane, County Tyrone, and was educated at Synge Street Christian Brothers' School, Dublin, Blackrock College and University College, Dublin. For some years he worked as subeditor on the *Irish Independent* and was co-founder of the newspaper *Inniu*. He was the brother of Brian Ó Nualláin and published a memoir *Óige an Dearthair* in 1973. He also published a collection of essays *Amaidí* and a novel, *Oíche i nGleann na nGealt*. He died in Dublin.

Ó NUALLÁIN, GEARÓID 1874–1942

Gearóid Ó Nualláin was born in Omagh, County Tyrone, and was educated in Dublin and Germany. From 1909 to 1940 he was Professor of Irish at Maynooth. He wrote textbooks and short stories and among his publications are *The New Era Grammar of Modern Irish*; *Dia Diabhail agus Daoine* and *Sean agus Nua*. He was President of the Society for the Preservation of the Irish language.

O'QUINN, JEREMIAH d.1657

Jeremiah O'Quinn was born in Templepatrick, County Antrim. He was a native Irish speaker and a Catholic, but he converted to Protestantism and was educated in Glasgow, where he qualified as a Presbyterian minister. He was appointed to the parish of Billy, County Antrim, in 1645 and was suspended for his stand on the execution of Charles I, though he was later reinstated. He died at Billy.

Ó RAIFEARTAIGH, TARLACH 1905–1984

Tarlach Ó Raifeartaigh was born in Carrickmore, County Tyrone, and was educated at St Patrick's College, Armagh, and University College, Dublin. He was Professor of History at St Patrick's Training College, Drumcondra, Dublin before joining the Department of Education as a secondary schools inspector. Before becoming Chairman of the Higher Education Authority, he served as Secretary to the Department of Education. He was a member of the Royal Irish Academy and had bestowed upon him the Legion of Honour. Dublin University and the National University of Ireland gave him honorary doctorates and he received a papal knighthood.

O'REILLY, EDMUND 1606–1669
Edmund O'Reilly was born in Dublin and was educated abroad. In 1642 he became Vicar-General of the diocese of Dublin. After being imprisoned and banished, he returned and was appointed Archbishop of Armagh in 1657, though as a Catholic Archbishop he was only able to visit Armagh surreptitiously on a few occassions. Nine years later he was again imprisoned and deported to Europe. He died in France.

O'REILLY, EDWARD 1770–1829
Edward O'Reilly was born in County Cavan and moved to Dublin at the age of twenty. He compiled a dictionary of Irish, with the help of William Haliday, which was printed in Dublin in 1817 as *Irish-English Dictionary*, prefixed by an introduction to Irish grammar. The Iberno-Celtic Society, whose aim it was to preserve Irish literature, appointed him its assistant secretary. In 1820 it published his *Dictionary of Irish Writers*. The Royal Irish Academy awarded him two medals, one for his essay on the brehon laws, and the other for his discussion of the authenticity of the poems of Ossian. He catalogued Irish language manuscripts in Dublin libraries and provided Irish nomenclature for the maps of the Ordnance Survey of Ireland.

O'REILLY, HUGH d.1653
Hugh O'Reilly was appointed Bishop of Kilmore in 1625 and became Archbishop of Armagh in 1628. He died on Trinity Island, Lough Erne and is buried in County Cavan.

O'REILLY, MICHAEL d.1758
Michael O'Reilly was the parish priest of Drogheda, County Louth, and was appointed Bishop of Derry in 1739, during which period he lived in Maghera, County Londonderry. He became Archbishop of Armagh in 1749. For many years his two catechisms, one in Irish and the other in English were used throughout Ulster.

O'REILLY, PHILIP MacHUGH d.1657
Philip O'Reilly lived in County Cavan and was a soldier. In 1639 he became a member of parliament. In 1641 he and his nephew, who was Sheriff of Cavan, captured Belturbet. He was one of those who signed the petition regarding the grievances of the Catholics in Cavan. In the following year he failed to capture Drogheda, though he took some castles in the vicinity. He was appointed a colonel in the army of Owen Roe O'Neill and fought at Benburb in 1646. In 1653 he laid down arms. He later went to Spain to command a regiment and died in Louvain.

ORR, ANDREW 1822–1895
Andrew Orr was born in Macosquin, near Coleraine, County Londonderry, and was educated at Kilure. He worked at Mulamore bleachgreen, Aghadowey and wrote poetry, some of which was published in magazines. In the 1830s he went to Australia where he worked as a journalist and became editor of the *Ballarat Chronicle*. The poem for which he is remembered, 'In Exile', was often anthologised. He died in Ballarat.

ORR, JAMES 1770–1816
James Orr was born near Ballycarry, County Antrim. He was educated at home and was a weaver and small farmer. He wrote political pieces for the *Northern Star* and poetry in Ulster Scots dialect. In 1798 he went towards Antrim with the Ballycarry contingent of United Irishmen, but arrived too late to take part in the battle. Nevertheless, he had to flee to America where he worked as a journalist and published poetry until a government amnesty was declared and he was able to return home. His *Poems* were published in 1804 and in 1817, *The Posthumous Works of James Orr: with a Sketch of His Life*, was published. He founded the Masonic Lodge in Ballycarry, which he headed for many years. In 1816 they erected a monument over his grave.

ORR, WILLIAM 1766–1797
William Orr was born at Farranshane, County Antrim. He was arrested for administering the oath of the United Irishmen to two soldiers, and despite widely signed

petitions and the jury's appeal, he was hanged in Carrickfergus, County Antrim, in 1797. William Drennan's 'The Wake of William Orr' was extremely popular. [Biography by F. J. Bigger]

Ó SEARCAIGH, SÉAMAS 1887–1965

Séamas Ó Searcaigh was born in County Donegal and was educated at Queen's University, Belfast. He was a lecturer in the Department of Celtic Studies, University College, Dublin, and at Maynooth. He was President of the Irish College of Cloghaneely (Falcarragh), County Donegal. His publications include, *Faire Phaidi Mhóir; Ceol Na nÉan agus sgéalta eile; Foghraidheacht Ghaeilge an Tuaiscirt; Padraig Mac Piarais* and *Beatha Cholm Cille.*

O'SHANNON, CATHAL 1889–1969

Cathal O'Shannon was born in Randalstown, County Antrim, and was educated at St Columb's College, Derry. He worked as a clerk in the Belfast office of the Heysham Steamship Company. He was a member of the Irish Republican Brotherhood and of the Gaelic League. At James Connolly's request, he joined the staff of the Irish Transport and General Worker's Union in Belfast. He wrote for the Gaelic League's newspaper and other periodicals. In Coalisland, County Tyrone, on Easter Saturday 1916 he mobilised a hundred Volunteers, but without orders they dispersed.

He was imprisoned in Wales and England, and after the general amnesty in 1917 he returned to Ireland and edited the *Voice of Labour.* He addressed meetings all over London in 1920, advocating Irish independence, and was arrested and imprisoned in Mountjoy Jail. He campaigned both as a trade union official and as a Volunteer, and in 1922 was elected to the Dáil for Louth-Meath. In 1941 he became Secretary of the Irish Trade Union Congress, and afterwards of the Congress of Irish Unions. He served for twenty-three years as one of the workers' representatives when the Labour Court was established in 1946. He died in Dublin.

O'SULLIVAN, MORTIMER *c.*1791–1859

Mortimer O'Sullivan was born in Clonmel, County Tipperary. He converted to Protestantism and was ordained. He became the first headmaster of the Royal School, Dungannon, County Tyrone, and was known for his opposition to landlordism. Among his publications are *Digest of Evidence of the State of Ireland.*

Ó TIGHEARNÁIN, POALL early 19th century

Poall Ó Tighearnáin was an Irish scribe who flourished in Clones, County Monaghan. A composite volume of his tracts, prose and poetry is preserved in the National Library.

P

PALLES, CHRISTOPHER 1831–1920
Christopher Palles was born at Mount Palles, County Cavan, and was educated at Clongowes Wood College and Trinity College, Dublin. In 1853 he was called to the Bar, becoming Doctor of Laws and Queen's Counsel in 1865. He served as Solicitor-General in 1872 and from then until 1874 was Attorney-General. He unsuccessfully contested the parliamentary constituency of Londonderry. In 1874 he was raised to the bench, gaining the title Lord Chief Baron of the Exchequer.

PALMER, ARTHUR HUNTER 1819–1898
Arthur Palmer was born in Armagh and was educated in Youghal before emigrating to Australia in 1838. He represented Brisbane in the Legislative Assembly, and from 1870 to 1874 was Premier of Queensland. He was knighted in 1881 and became Lieutenant-Governor of Australia in 1893.

PAPS, NICHOLAS fl. 1614
Nicholas Paps was a mason who was commissioned by Sir Arthur Chichester to rebuild the ruined church of St Nicholas in Carrickfergus, County Antrim. The alterations were to include the construction of the Donegall Aisle which was to house a large monument to the Chichester family.

PARKE, JAMES CECIL 1881–1946
James Parke was born in Clones, County Monaghan. He played rugby with both Monkstown and Dublin University and between 1901 and 1908 played ten times for Leinster. Between 1903 and 1907, he won twenty international caps. As a tennis player he won the Wimbledon Mixed Doubles title in 1914. He won the Australian Men's singles and doubles tennis titles in 1912. He was Singles Champion of Europe in 1907 and played for Britain in the Davis Cup. In 1908 he won an Olympic silver medal in the Men's Doubles. He won eight Irish Lawn Tennis Singles titles, four doubles and two mixed titles. In 1914 he was ranked No.6 and in 1920 he was ranked No.4. He played golf for Ireland in 1906. He was also a top-class track and field sprinter and a cricketer. He played chess for the Clones team when he was nine years old.

PARKE, THOMAS HEAZLE 1857–1893
Thomas Parke was born in Drumsna, County Roscommon, and was reared in Carrick-on-Shannon, County Roscommon. He graduated from the College of Surgeons in Dublin and was appointed to a post in Ballybay, County Monaghan. In 1881 he joined the British army and served in Egypt. He offered to accompany Stanley in his African explorations and reputedly became the first Irishman to cross the African continent. During the expedition Parke bought a pygmy girl. For more than a year they travelled together and she nursed him through malaria. He was forced to leave her behind eventually because her eyes could not adapt to sunlight after the darkness of the forest. When Parke returned home he received an Honorary Fellowship of the Royal College of Surgeons in Ireland. Among his published works are *My Personal Experiences in Equatorial Africa* and *A Guide to Health in Africa*. When he died in Scotland his coffin was brought back to Ireland and drawn on a gun carriage from the Dublin docks to Broadstone station. A statue of him stands outside the Natural History Museum in Merrion Street, Dublin, and he is commemorated by a bust in the Royal College of Surgeons in Ireland.

PARKER, STEWART 1941–1988
Stewart Parker was born in Belfast and was educated at Queen's University, Belfast. He was a member of the Philip Hobsbaum Belfast Writing Group and published two

volumes of poetry: *The Casualty's Medita-tion*, which appeared as part of the Queen's University Festival Series in 1965, and *Maw* in 1968. He taught for five years at Hamilton College, New York, and then returned to Belfast to write in 1969. His play, *Spokesong* was refused in Belfast and Edinburgh, but was staged at the Dublin Theatre Festival in 1975. In the following year he won the *London Evening Standard* award as the most promising playwright. In 1978 he moved to Edinburgh and later settled in London. Among his many plays written for theatre, radio and television are *Catchpenny Twist* ; *I'm A Dreamer Mon-treal*, *Iris in the Traffic*, *Ruby in the Rain*; *Northern Star*, *Heavenly Bodies*; *Pentecost*; *The Traveller* and *Lost Belongings* (a six-part television series based on the Dierdre myth). He died in England.

PARNELL, JOHN HOWARD 1843–1923

John Howard Parnell was born in Avondale, County Wicklow and was a soldier in the Armagh Militia. He spent many years in America as a fruit-grower and when he returned to Ireland served as member of parliament for South Meath from 1895 to 1900. He was a brother of Charles Stewart Parnell, and published his memoir in 1916. He served as City Marshal of Dublin.

PARROTT (PARRAT), WILLIAM fl.1627

William Parrott was a builder and his name first occurs in 1627 in a letter to the Secretary of State from the Earl of Antrim requesting that Parrott be relieved from military service in England. In the same year Parrott won the contract to build St Columb's Cathedral in Derry at the cost of £3,400. It is likely that he undertook the restoration of the chapel at Dunluce Castle, County Antrim. In 1642 a William Parrott was Mayor of Coleraine.

PARRY, EDWARD 1600–1650

Edward Parry was born in Newry, County Down, and was educated at Trinity College, Dublin. In 1638 he became Dean of Waterford, and in 1647 Bishop of Killaloe. He died of the plague.

PARSONS, WILLIAM c.1570–1650

William Parsons came from England and in 1602 was appointed Surveyor-General. Between 1610 and 1620 he acted as Commissioner of Plantations and was largely responsible for implementing the scheme for the plantation of Ulster. He obtained for himself a thousand acres of land in County Tyrone, as well as vast tracts in County Wexford and County Leitrim. In 1640 he became Lord Justice. In 1643 he was relieved of his office because he opposed conciliation and in 1648 he returned to England.

PATERSON, THOMAS GEORGE FARQUHAR 1888–1971

George Paterson was born in Canada, but the family returned to Cornascreeb, near Tandragee, County Armagh, when he was an infant. He was educated at the National School, Aghory, County Armagh and was then apprenticed to a grocer in Portadown, County Armagh. In 1911 he became manager of Couser's Provision Store, Armagh. He was an amateur historian who collected traditional tales and dialect phrases and proverbs, and made detailed sketches of local architecture and furniture in South Armagh. In 1931 he became honorary curator, and in 1935, full-time curator of Armagh County Museum, retiring in 1963. When the Ulster Folk Museum was established in 1958, he was a Foundation Trustee. He wrote prolifically, and compiled 25 volumes of *Armagh Miscellanea*, including many articles of his own. He contributed to the *Ulster Journal of Archaeology*, and wrote for local newspapers under the pseudonym 'Cornascreeb'. His accounts of archaeological sites were published in the official *Preliminary Survey of Ancient Monuments of Northern Ireland, 1940*, and he subsequently published *Country Cracks*. He served on the South Armagh Hospital Committee and the Northern Ireland Committee of the National Trust. He was an active member of the Armagh Field Club and of the Naturalists' Society, and in 1941 became a member of the Royal Irish Academy. In 1954 he was awarded an OBE. He was a genealogical researcher, and an honorary member of the Disciples of

Christ Historical Society in Nashville, Tennessee for his research on the Campbellites. The society established a fund in his memory.

PATERSON, WILLIAM 1745–1806

William Paterson was born in the town of Antrim. Two years later his family emigrated to America and settled in Princeton, New Jersey. He was educated at Princeton University and chose to follow a legal career. In 1775 he was elected to the New Jersey Provincial Congress and became its Secretary. He was later appointed first Attorney General of the State of New Jersey, a position which he held until 1783. In 1787 he represented New Jersey at the Philadelphia Convention. In 1788 he was elected to serve in the Senate of the United States and in 1791 he was elected second Governor of the State of New Jersey. In 1793 he was appointed Justice of the United States Supreme Court and in 1795 he declined to become Secretary of State. He was given an honorary degree by Harvard University and became a Trustee of the College of New Jersey.

PATRICK, ST c.385/400–c.461/490

Patrick was born somewhere in Roman Britain and was carried off as a slave to Ireland, where he herded sheep on Slemish Mountain, County Antrim. It is said that he escaped, and according to tradition he studied at Auxerre and Tours and was ordained as a bishop. He returned to Ireland, landing at Strangford Lough, and supposedly first preached the Christian faith in Saul, County Down. He founded a settlement in Armagh and wrote a letter to a hostile chieftain named Coroticus, and his *Confession*, which are the main sources of information concerning his life and are generally accepted as authentic. He is believed to be buried in Downpatrick, and his feast-day as patron saint of Ireland is on the 17th of March.

PATTERSON, ANNIE d.1934

Annie Patterson was born in Lurgan, County Armagh, and was educated at Alexandra College, Dublin, and the Royal Irish Academy of Music, where she won a gold medal for playing the organ. She was examiner in Music for the Royal University of Ireland from 1892 to 1895 and gained a Doctorate of Music. She was conductor of the Dublin Choral Union and instigated the Feis Ceoil movement. She lectured on Irish music at University College, Cork from 1924 and published many works, including *The Story of Oratorio, Great Minds in Music* and *Native Music of Ireland.* She composed music and Gaelic songs.

PATTERSON, ROBERT 1743–1824

Robert Patterson was born in Ulster and in 1768 went to Philadelphia, where he became Principal of Wilmington Academy in Delaware. He joined the revolutionary army and was promoted to the rank of brigadier-general. From 1779 to 1814 he was Professor of Mathematics at the University of Pennsylvania, later becoming Vice-Provost, and in 1805 he was appointed Director of the United States Mint. He was a Doctor of Laws and President of the American Philosophical Society, and he published several works, including the *Newtonian System* and *Treatise on Arithmetic.* He died in Philadelphia.

PATTERSON, ROBERT 1802–1872

Robert Patterson was born in Belfast, was educated at the Belfast Academical Institution and entered the family business. He became interested in the study of natural history and was one of the eight founders of the Belfast Natural History Society, serving as its president for many years. He discovered, during dredging excursions, several forms of marine life. He was a Fellow of the Royal Society and a member of the Royal Irish Academy, and he published numerous works, including *Zoology for Schools* and *First Steps to Zoology.* He also published *Letters on the Insects Mentioned in Shakespere.* He was one of the earliest members of the British Association.

PATTERSON, ROBERT LLOYD 1836–1906

Robert Patterson was born in Belfast and was educated at the Royal Belfast Academical Instution and at Stuttgart before becoming an apprentice in the linen business. He was President of the Chamber of Commerce on three occasions and served as President of the Natural History and Philosophical Society. In 1902 he was knighted. He published *The Birds, Fishes and Cetacea of Belfast Lough*. He was an art collector and bequeathed his collection to the city of Belfast.

PATTERSON, SAIDIE 1906–1985

Saidie Patterson was born on the Falls Road, Belfast, and lived there all her life. When she was twelve years of age she began working in the Belfast Linen Mills. She was active in her union, the Amalgamated Transport and General Workers' Union. She helped to organise many strikes to try and improve the conditions of the mainly female workforce. She became involved with the Moral Re-armament Movement after the Second World War, and she was a founder member of Women Together, an organisation which preceded the Peace People. She won the Methodist Peace Award in 1978 as well as five international peace awards. The prize money she donated to charities for children and arthritis sufferers. In the elections of 1945 she worked for the Northern Ireland Labour Party.

PATTERSON, WILLIAM HUGH 1835–1918

William Patterson was born in Belfast and was educated at the Royal Belfast Academical Instution and Queen's College, Belfast. When he was sixteen he entered his father's linen business. He was one of the original members of Belfast Naturalists' Field Club and of Belfast Natural History and Philosophical Society and served as President of both societies. He was a member of the Royal Irish Academy and of the Royal Historical and Archaeological Association of Ireland. He served as Honorary Secretary of the Ulster Society for the Prevention of Cruelty to Animals, of which he was a founder member. Some of his paintings were accepted for exhibition by the Belfast Arts Society. He had a fine collection of shell cameos, part of which he bequeathed to the city of Belfast. As a member of the English Dialect Society he published *A Bibliography of Anglo-Irish Dialects* and *A Glossary of Words and Phrases used in Antrim and Down*.

PAUL, JOHN 1777–1848

John Paul was born in Tobernaveen, County Antrim, and was educated in Glasgow. From 1805 until 1848 he was Presbyterian minister of Loughmorne near Carrickfergus. He wrote many works, some of which were controversial, such as *Refutation of Arianism*.

PEERS, RICHARD 1645–1690

Richard Peers was born in Lisburn, County Antrim, and was educated at Oxford. He translated Anthony à Wood's *History and Antiquities* of Oxford University and compiled a *Catalogue of Graduates* in 1689. He also published volumes of poetry.

PELAN, MARGARET McLEAN 1908–1978

Margaret Pelan completed a doctoral thesis in 1937 and was appointed lecturer in Mediaeval French at Queen's University, Belfast, in the following year. She became Professor of the department in 1966. Her publications include several editions of *Floire et Blancheflor* and, with Professor Arnold, *La Partie Arthurienne du Roman de Brut* (1962).

PENDER, MARGARET T. (née O'DOHERTY) b.1865

Margaret O'Doherty was born in County Antrim and was educated locally and in Belfast. Her poetry and short stories were published in newspapers, and she wrote several historical novels, among which are *The Green Cockade: A Tale of Ulster in '98*; *The Last of the Irish Chiefs*; *The Outlaw* and *Spearmen of the North*.

PENPRASE, NEWTON b.1888

Newton Penprase was born in Redruth, Cornwall, and studied art at the Redruth School of Art. As a student he had nine sheets of drawings and studies purchased by the Victoria and Albert Museum, London. In 1911 he came to Belfast as a teacher in the College of Technology, College Square and retired forty-two years later. He exhibited at the Royal Ulster Academy and at the Ulster Arts Club of which he was President. In 1936 he began to build Bendhu House at Ballintoy, County Antrim. He held an exhibition at the Arts Council of Northern Ireland in 1977.

PENTLAND, JOSEPH BARCLAY 1797–1873

Joseph Pentland was probably born in Armagh. He studied in Paris, and between 1826 and 1827 surveyed the Andes in Bolivia. He travelled in Peru in 1838 and was the author of several of Murray's *Handbooks*.

PEPPERGRASS, PAUL see BOYCE, JOHN

PERCY, THOMAS 1729–1811

Thomas Percy was born in England and was educated at Christ Church, Oxford. He became vicar of Easton Maudit, Northamptonshire in 1753, and rector of Wilby three years later. In 1770 he became Doctor of Divinity at Emmanuel College, Cambridge. He was appointed chaplain to the Duke of Northumberland and George III, and from 1778 was Dean of Carlisle. In 1762 he published *Miscellaneous Pieces*, translated from the Chinese. He edited and published a manuscript containing medieval poems, *Reliques of Ancient English Poetry*, 1765, and in 1770 published *Northern Antiquities*. In 1771 he wrote a ballad, 'The Hermit of Warkworth'. He was Bishop of Dromore from 1782 to 1811 and lived in the Bishop's Palace, Dromore, County Down.

PERRIN, LOUIS 1782–1864

Louis Perrin was born in Waterford and was educated in Armagh and at Trinity College, Dublin, where he was acquainted with Robert Emmet. He was called to the Bar in 1806 and served as member of parliament for Dublin City, Monaghan and Cashel. He became a judge in 1835.

PERRY, ANTHONY d.1798

Anthony Perry was born in County Down. He joined the United Irishmen, having resigned from the Coolgreany Cavalry in County Wicklow. When he was arrested in 1798 he was tortured and revealed information about his comrades. On his release he took part in the rebellion in County Wex-

ford and was one of the principal military leaders at the battles of Arklow and Vinegar Hill. He was arrested after the rebellion had been crushed, and was executed.

PERRY, JOHN 1850–1921

John Perry was born in Garvagh, County Londonderry and was educated at Queen's College, Belfast. He taught at the University of Glasgow and from 1875 to 1879 was Professor of Engineering at the University of Tokyo, Japan. He also taught in South Kensington where he was Professor of Mathematics, and was Treasurer of the British Association. He was known as an inventor and a researcher into the properties of electricity.

PHELAN, WILLIAM 1789–1830

William Phelan was born in Clonmel, was educated at Trinity College, Dublin, and was ordained in 1814. He was a schoolteacher in Derry. He was rector of Killyman from 1824, and was co-author, with Mortimer O'Sullivan, of *Digest of Evidence*, a publication about the state of Ireland compiled from evidence given to a committee of parliament in 1825.

PHILIPS, GEORGE 1599–1696

George Philips was probably born in Limavady, County Londonderry. He was a soldier and was appointed Governor of Culmore during the siege, and later, in 1688, Governor of Derry, but resigned in favour of Robert Lundy.

PHILIPS, WILLIAM c.1675–1734

William Philips was the son of George Philips, the Governor of Derry, and was born there. He was a soldier and a dramatist and his tragedy *The Revengeful Queen* was produced at Drury Lane in 1698. Another of his plays, *St Stephen's Green*, was produced in Dublin in 1700. In 1722 *Hibernia Freed* was staged and printed in London and *Belisarius*, a tragedy in blank verse, was published in 1724.

PIM, HERBERT MOORE (pseud. A. NEWMAN) b.1883

Herbert Pim was born in Belfast and was educated at Friends' School, Lisburn. He was prominent in the Belfast YMCA, and later converted to Roman Catholicism and became a Nationalist. He joined the Irish Volunteers and was imprisoned in Belfast. He published works of poetry which included *Selected Poems; Songs from an Ulster Valley* and *New Poems*. Among his novels are *A Vampire of Souls* and *The Man with Thirty Lives*. His other works include *The Pessimist: A Study of the Problem of Pain*, which is partly autobiographical and *Unknown Immortals in the Northern City of Success*, published under the psuedonym A. Newman. After 1918 he reverted to Unionism, in 1919 publishing, *Unconquerable Ulster* followed in 1920 by *A Short History of Celtic Philosophy*. He went to England, where he edited *Plain English* and its successor, *Plain Speech*. He was involved with the Fascist movement in Italy in the 1930s. He died in England.

PINKERTON, JOHN 19th century
John Pinkerton was born in Seacon More, County Antrim. He rose to prominence as a member of Ballymoney Debating and Agricultural Societies, and as a radical member of Coleraine Board of Guardians. In 1885 he contested the election for North Antrim as an Independent candidate. Though defeated, he impressed the Parnellites and was adopted as party candidate for Galway in 1886. He won the election, and held the seat until 1900.

PINKERTON, WILLIAM 1809–1871
William Pinkerton was born in Belfast and became a sailor. His life was devoted to collecting printed material which related to the history of Belfast, and he owned a large collection of books which had been printed there. He was a Fellow of the Society of Antiquaries and was responsible for the reprinting of *Hounslow Heath*, which he funded.

PIRRIE, MARGARET MONTGOMERY (née CARLILE) 1857–1935
Margaret Carlile married Viscount Pirrie in 1879 and became the first woman justice of the peace in Belfast and also the first to receive the freedom of the city. She was involved in charity work and was President of the Royal Victoria Hospital. She was elected to the Senate of Queen's University, Belfast and was President of Harland & Wolff, the Belfast shipbuilding firm. She died in London.

PIRRIE, WILLIAM JAMES 1847–1924
William Pirrie was born in Quebec into a County Down family and was educated at the Royal Belfast Academical Institution. In 1862 he was apprenticed to Harland & Wolff's shipbuilding firm and in 1874 became a partner and later the Chairman. He insigated the innovation in design which led to the building of large liners. In 1896 he became Lord Mayor of Belfast, and in 1897 he was made a privy councillor. He was Controller of Shipping during the First World War and was raised to the peerage and knighted. On his yacht at the Kiel Regatta he hosted the Kaiser. He was Pro-Chancellor of Queen's University, Belfast, and sat in the Northern Ireland Senate. He died on board ship near Panama.

PLUNKET, WILLIAM CONYNGHAM 1764–1854
William Plunket was born in Enniskillen, County Fermanagh, and was educated at Trinity College, Dublin. He was called to the Bar in 1787 and became King's Counsel in 1797. He was member of parliament for Charlemont and voted against the Union. In 1803 he became Solicitor-General, in 1805 Attorney-General, and two years later was elected member of parliament for Midhurst. He was a strong supporter of Catholic Emancipation. In 1812 he became member of parliament for Dublin University, and from 1822 to 1827 served a second term as Attorney-General. In 1827 he was appointed Chief Justice with a peerage and three years later became Lord Chancellor, remaining in office (with one short break in 1835) until 1841. There is a bust of Lord Plunket in the library of Trinity College, Dublin. [Biography by Hon. D. Plunket].

PLUNKETT, OLIVER 1625–1681
Oliver Plunkett was born at Loughcrew near Oldcastle, County Meath, was educated at the Irish College in Rome, and was ordained in 1654. He taught theology in Rome and was the representative of the

Irish Bishops. He composed a poem, 'O Tara of the Kings'. In 1669 he became Archbishop of Armagh and began to reorganise his neglected diocese. He established the Jesuits at Drogheda, County Louth. In 1673 he was forced to go into hiding, and he was arrested in 1679. All Catholic Bishops and regular priests were to be expelled, and in 1680 Oliver Plunkett was brought to Dundalk and charged with activating an uprising. He was tried in London and sentenced to be hanged, drawn and quartered at Tyburn. His death is looked upon as martyrdom, subsequent events proving him innocent of all the charges brought against him. His relics are enshrined in Downside Abbey and his head is preserved in St Peter's Church, Drogheda. In 1920 he was beatified, and in 1975 canonised.

POCKRICH (POCKERIDGE or PUCKERIDGE), RICHARD 1690–1759

Richard Pockrich was born in County Monaghan. His nickname was 'projecting Pock'. At the age of twenty-five he inherited his father's estate which he spent on impractical ventures such as planting vineyards on reclaimed bogs, rearing huge numbers of geese for the European market, or fitting wings to enable every Irish person to fly. However, some of his ideas were genuinely innovative, such as his lifeboat made from unsinkable tin, a projected system of canals for linking the Liffey to the Shannon, and his design for an observatory to be built on a mountain peak. He invented a new form of dulcimer consisting of pins hammered into a pub table and two pieces of brass wire, and developed musical glasses, which he demonstrated at many concerts in England. Dubbed 'the angelic organ', the glasses caught the imagination of Walpole, Gray, Gluck and Benjamin Franklin. He published *Miscellaneous Works* in 1750 and a volume of poetry. He died in a fire at Hamlin's Coffee House in London.

POË, WILLIAM HUTCHESON 1848–1934

William Poë was born in Donaghadee, County Down, and was educated at Gosport. He joined the Royal Marines in 1867 and served in the Sudan, where he was wounded in 1884. The following year he had a leg amputated at Metemneh. He became Companion of the Order of the Bath and was promoted to the rank of lieutenant-colonel. In 1891 he became High Sheriff for Queen's County, and in 1893 for County Tyrone. He was a member of the Land Conference in 1902, in 1904 was appointed a governor of the National Gallery, and eight years later was created a baronet. In 1915 to 1916 he served in Egypt in the First World War, and from 1916 to 1919 with the Red Cross in France. From 1922 to 1925 he served as a Senator of the Irish Free State. He died at Littlehampton.

POLSON, THOMAS R.J. c.1820–1908

Thomas Polson was born in Enniskillen, County Fermanagh. He wrote a novel, *The Fortune Teller's Intrigue*, set in Ireland of the late eighteenth century, and published in three volumes.

PORTER, ALEXANDER 1786–1844

Alexander Porter was born in County Down, son of Reverend James Porter. He is reputed to have fought in the Battle of Ballynahinch in 1798. In 1801 he went to America, and in 1807 was called to the Bar. By 1821 he was a judge in Louisiana and served as a member of Senate from 1834 to 1837, during which time he strongly upheld the institution of slavery, and was himself a slave-owner. He died in Attakapas, Louisiana.

PORTER, ANDREW MARSHALL 1837–1919

Andrew Porter was born in Belfast and was educated at the Royal Belfast Academical Institution, and Queen's College, Belfast. In 1860 he was called to the Bar and by 1872 had become Queen's Counsel. From 1881 to 1884 he was a member of parliament for County Londonderry. He became Solicitor-General in 1881 and Attorney-General in 1883, at which time he was appointed Master of the Rolls. In 1902 he was created a baronet.

PORTER, CLASSON EMMET 1814–1885

Classon Porter was born in Artikelly, County

Londonderry, and was educated at York. In 1834 he was ordained a Presbyterian minister in Larne where he spent the rest of his life. He wrote and published a great deal of local history and biography, some of which was reprinted in a collection in 1883. He died at Ballygally, County Antrim.

PORTER, JAMES 1753–1798
James Porter was born near Ballindrait, County Donegal. In 1773 he taught in Dromore, County Down and later, having studied divinity in Glasgow, became a Presbyterian minister in Greyabbey, County Down. He supported Catholic Emancipation and joined the Volunteers. His contributions to the *Northern Star* were published as a satire of Lord Londonderry in 1796, entitled *Billy Bluff and Squire Firebrand* which was regarded as treasonable. He also published *Sermon, Wind and Weather* in 1797. He was captured at the outbreak of the 1798 rebellion, tried, testified against by an informer, found guilty and, despite the pleas of his wife and seven children, hanged in front of his own meeting-house.

PORTER, JOHN SCOTT 1801–1880
John Porter was born in Limavady, County Londonderry, and was educated locally and at the Belfast Academical Institution. For a time he was a schoolteacher and edited *The Christian Observer* in London. In 1826 he became a Presbyterian minister, and from 1831 he had a congregation at Rosemary Street, Belfast. In 1838 he was appointed Professor of Theology and in 1851 Professor of Hebrew to the Association of Irish Non-Suscribing Presbyterians. He edited the *Christian Moderator* and the *Bible Christian* and was a prolific theological writer. Among his works was *Principles of Textual Criticism*, published in 1848. He was devoted to the preservation of the Irish language.

PORTER, JOSIAS LESLIE 1823–1880
Josias Porter was born in Burt, County Donegal, was educated in Glasgow and Edinburgh, and was ordained in 1846. He spent ten years as a missionary in Damascus and recorded his experiences. In 1860 he became a professor in the Presbyterian

College, Belfast and in 1875, Moderator of the Presbyterian Church. In 1879 he was appointed President of Queen's College, Belfast. He wrote the *Life of Dr Henry Cooke*, his father-in-law and predecessor as chaplain of Queen's College.

PORTER, WILLIAM 1805–1880
William Porter was born in Artikelly, County Londonderry. He was called to the Bar in 1831, and in 1839 was appointed Attorney-General at the Cape. He was offered a knighthood and Premiership of the Cape, both of which he declined. He endowed a university there and was its first Chancellor. In 1873 he returned to Ireland. He died in Belfast.

POTTER, ARCHIBALD JAMES 1918–1980
James Potter was born in Belfast, but moved to England with his family when he was still a child. He sang in the choir of All Saints' Church, Margaret Street, London and then became an organ scholar at Clifton College. He was later a composition student at the Royal College of Music. After serving in the Second World War he returned to St Patrick's Cathedral, Dublin, as vicar. He was appointed Professor of Composition at the Royal Irish Academy of Music in 1955. He was a composer, and his works include a television opera, *Patrick*, and four ballets, among which are *Careless Love* and *Caitlín Bocht*. He arranged traditional music for Radio Éireann Light Orchestra and wrote an opera, *The Emigrants*.

POTTINGER, ELDRED 1811–1843
Eldred Pottinger was born in Mountpottinger, County Down, and entered the Bengal Artillery as a soldier. In 1837 he travelled through Afghanistan disguised as a horse dealer and took part in the siege of Herat a year later. He was made a Companion of the Bath and succeeded William MacNaghten in Kabul. Though he was held a prisoner there in 1842, he was released and went to Hong Kong on leave. He died there of fever.

POTTINGER, HENRY 1789–1856
Henry Pottinger was born in Mountpottinger, County Down, and was educated

221

at Belfast Academy. In 1804 he went to India to serve in the army and explored the lands between the Indus and Persia, travelling in disguise as a Mohammedan merchant and studying native languages. In 1816 he published his *Travels in Beloochistan and Sinde*. He served in the Mahratta War and rose to the rank of colonel. He undertook a mission to Sind which is said to have opened up the traffic of the Indus. He was created a baronet when he returned to England. He was sent as a plenipotentiary to China in 1842 and eventually made peace by which Hong Kong was ceded. He became Governor of Hong Kong and later Governor of the Cape and Governor of Madras. The Grand Cross of the Bath was conferred upon him, and he was made a privy councillor. He died in Malta on his way home.

POYNTZ, CHARLES d.1605

Charles Poyntz fought against Hugh O'Neill, Earl of Tyrone, as an officer in the Elizabethan army. During the battle Poyntz defended a pass five miles south of Tandragee. The village on this site is known as Poyntzpass.

PRAEGER, ROBERT LLOYD 1865–1953

Robert Lloyd Praeger was born in Holywood, County Down, and was educated at the Royal Belfast Academical Institution and Queen's College, Belfast, where he qualified as an engineer. He was a member of the Belfast Naturalists' Field Club, of which he was twice President, and he received their gold medal. He wrote many papers on post-glacial geography, especially on the raised beaches of the north-east of Ireland, which gave information on the climate in Neolithic times. In 1893 he joined the staff of the National Library of Ireland in Dublin as assistant librarian. He organised the Lambay Survey in 1905, which studied the natural resources of Ireland, and this led to the famous Clare Island Survey of 1909 to 1922. He was a prolific writer and was co-founder and editor of the journal, the *Irish Naturalist*. He published *Flora of the County Armagh*; *Irish Topographical Botany*; *A Tourist's Flora of the West of Ireland* and *The Botanist in Ireland*.

Other publications include *The Way That I Went*; *Some Irish Naturalists*; *The Natural History of Ireland* and *The Irish Landscape*. He was given the gold medal of the Royal Horticultural Society on two occasions and later became its President. He was elected President of the Royal Irish Academy, the British Ecological Society, the Royal Zoological Society of Ireland, the Geographical Society of Ireland and the Bibliographical Society of Ireland, and he was first President of the Library Association of Ireland. An honorary doctorate was conferred on him by Queen's University, Belfast, Trinity College, Dublin, and the National University of Ireland. He was elected an associate of the Linnean Society of London, was an honorary life member of the Botanical Society of the British Isles and in 1948 was first President of the National Trust for Ireland.

PRAEGER, SOPHIA ROSAMUND 1867–1954

Rosamund Praeger was born in Holywood, County Down, and was educated at Sullivan School, Holywood, the School of Art, Belfast, and the Slade School, London. Before returning to Ireland to open a studio in Belfast and then in Holywood, she studied art in Paris. She wrote and illustrated children's books, but achieved fame with her sculpture 'The Philosopher' which was exhibited in the Royal Academy, bought by an American collector, and is now on display in the Colorado Springs Museum and Art Gallery. She mostly worked in plaster, but also used stone, marble, terracotta and bronze, and her work included relief panels, memorial plaques and stones. She exhibited in London and Paris, at the Royal Hibernian Academy, as well as at the Irish Decorative Art Association Exhibitions. She was a member of the Guild of Irish Art Workers. Among her other works are 'The Waif'; 'Johnny the Jig'; 'These Little Ones'; 'St Brigid of Kildare' and 'The Fairy Fountain'. For the Causeway School near Bushmills, County Antrim, she carved 'Fionnula the Daughter of Lir' in stone. She modelled a heraldic figure for the Northern Bank in Donegall Square West, Belfast, and bronze plaques for the front door of the Carnegie Library, Falls Road, Belfast, as well as the angels on Andrews Memorial Hall in Comber, County Down, and some work in St Anne's Cathedral, Belfast. She illustrated three books for her brother, Robert Praeger. She was President of the Royal Ulster Academy, and she received an honorary doctorate from Queen's University, Belfast. In 1939 she was awarded the MBE.

PRENDERGAST, THOMAS *c.*1660–1709
Thomas Prendergast was implicated in plans to assassinate William III in 1696 at Turnham Green. He informed the king of the conspiracy and was created a baronet in 1699. In 1703 he was member of parliament for Monaghan. He was a brigadier and was killed leading his forces at the Battle of Malplaquet.

PRESTON, THOMAS 1860–1900
Thomas Preston was born in Kilmore, County Armagh, and was educated at the Royal School, Armagh, the Royal University of Ireland and Trinity College, Dublin. From 1891 to 1900 he was Professor of Natural Philosophy at University College, Dublin. He was a Fellow of the Royal University of Ireland and of the Royal Society, London and was a distinguished spectroscopist. Among his works are *The Theory of Light* and *The Theory of Heat*.

PRIOR, JAMES 1790–1869
James Prior was born in Lisburn, County Antrim. He became a naval surgeon and was present at Napoleon's surrender in 1815. He was a member of the Royal Irish Academy and a Fellow of the Society of Antiquaries, and in 1843 became Deputy Inspector of Hospitals. He was knighted in 1858. He wrote many biographies, including those of Burke and Goldsmith, and several volumes recording his travels such as *Voyage to the Indian Seas*. He died in Brighton.

PULLEN, SAMUEL b.1713
Samuel Pullen was born in Dromore, County Down, and was educated in Newry and Trinity College, Dublin. He won the Madden Prize given by the Royal Dublin Society for a poem, 'The Silk Worm', which he translated from Latin and which was judged the written work of the year in 1750. He was also the author of other works.

PURSER, JOHN 1835–1903
John Purser was born in Dublin and was educated in Wiltshire and Trinity College, Dublin, where he distinguished himself in mathematics. He was tutor to the children of Lord Ross at Parsonstown. In 1863 he became Professor of Mathematics at Queen's College, Belfast, where he remained until 1901. In 1878 he was made Registrar of the college. He was a member of the British Association, and his seminal paper *The Source from which the Kinetic Energy is Drawn that Passes into Heat in the Movement of the Tides* was presented at the meeting of the British Association in Belfast in 1874.

PURSER, LOUIS CLAUDE 1854–1932
Louis Purser was born in Dungarvan, County Waterford and was educated at Middleton, Portora Royal School, Enniskillen and Trinity College, Dublin, where he became a fellow in 1881. He was appointed Professor of Latin from 1898 to 1904 and received honorary degrees from Glasgow, Durham and Oxford. He was Vice-President of the Royal Irish Academy and a Fellow of the British Academy. He translated many works and collaborated with R. Y. Tyrrell in publishing *Cicero's Correspondence* in seven volumes.

Q

QUIGG, ROBERT fl. 1914–1918
Robert Quigg lived in Bushmills, County Antrim, and was a private in the 12th Battalion, Royal Irish Rifles, Ulster Division. He was awarded the Victoria Cross for acts of bravery near Hamal in France in 1916. It is said that he made seven attempts to find his wounded officer, and that he continued to rescue the wounded on the frontline. He is buried in Billy churchyard, County Antrim.

QUIGLEY, EDWARD J. 1872–1942
Edward Quigley was born in Killeevan, County Monaghan and ordained in 1897 as priest of Clogher. He contributed to theological and religious journals and wrote a number of religious works, including *The Divine Office, A Book for Altar Servers; Ceremonies and Rights of Confirmation* and the *Visitation of Parishes.*

QUINN, WILLIAM PATRICK 1901–1978
William Quinn was born in Iniskeen, County Monaghan. On the dissolution of the Royal Irish Constabulary in 1922, he was among the first to join the Garda Síochána. He became Deputy Commissioner, and in 1965 Commissioner, the first member of the force to occupy this post.

QUINTON, JAMES WALLACE 1834–1891
James Quinton was born in Quinton, County Fermanagh, and was educated at Trinity College, Dublin. He served in India in the Bengal civil service from 1856 and was made a Companion of the Order of the Star of India. In 1889 he was appointed Chief Commissioner of Assam and in 1891 he was murdered while attempting to quell a rebellion.

R

RADCLIFFE, THOMAS *c.*1526–1583
Thomas Radcliffe, 3rd Earl of Sussex, was an English nobleman who came to Ireland in 1556 as Lord Deputy and after 1560 as Lord Lieutenant. In an attempt to subdue Shane O'Neill he burnt Armagh, and three years later he again made the attempt as part of a venture undertaken jointly with the O'Donnells and the Maguires, but failed. He reneged on his promise not to implement the Act of Supremacy, and three years later used the act to dissolve parliament.

RAMSEY, JOHN late 19th century
John Ramsey was born at Carnkirk near Bushmills, County Antrim. He became minister of the Ballymoney Reformed Presbyterian Church. At Niagara Falls he saved the life of a woman by climbing down the girders of the suspension bridge 160 feet above the water and bringing her to safety.

REA, JOHN *c.*1822–1881
John Rea was born in West Street, Belfast, and in 1847 became a solicitor. He played an active role in the Young Ireland movement and was imprisoned in Kilmainham Jail for nine months after conducting the defence of John Mitchel. He acted for the Catholics in the Dolly's Brae inquiry and defended Michael Davitt in 1879. He won an appeal in the House of Lords for an action he had taken against Belfast City Council in regard to misappropriation of funds. In the 1874 general election he contested Belfast unsuccessfully. He committed suicide.

READ, CHARLES ANDERSON 1841–1878
Charles Read was born in Sligo. He had a business in Rathfriland, County Down, but went to London as a journalist when it failed. He wrote two much-acclaimed novels *Savourneen Dheelish* and *Aileen Aroon*.

Only three of the four projected volumes of *The Cabinet of Irish Literature* were completed before his death. The final volume was edited by T. P. O'Connor. He died in Surrey.

REDFERN, PETER 1820–1912
Peter Redfern was born in Derbyshire and educated at the Universities of Edinburgh and London, where he studied medicine. He was Professor of Anatomy and Physiology in Queen's College, Belfast, from 1860 to 1893. He was responsible for the building of dissecting and lecture rooms and a medical museum.

REDMOND, WILLIAM HOEY KEARNEY
c. 1861–1917
William Redmond was born in Wexford and was educated at Clongowes Wood College. He was a member of parliament for Wexford, Fermanagh and Clare. He joined the army during the First World War and became a major. He contributed articles to the London *Chronicle* and published two travel journals about Australia. He was killed in action in France. A collection of his articles from the front was published posthumously.

REEVES, WILLIAM 1815–1892
William Reeves was born in Charleville, County Cork, and was educated at Trinity College, Dublin. He was ordained in 1838 and two years later became a master of the Diocesan School in Ballymena, County Antrim. In 1847 he published *Ecclesiastical Antiquities of Down and Connor and Dromore*, and ten years later *The Life of St Columba*, which is regarded as the best collection of materials on the early Irish Church. He was the rector of Tynan and the Librarian at Armagh from 1861 to 1886, during which period he purchased the Book of Armagh for the library. From 1886 he was Bishop of Down, Connor and Dromore and lived in

Conway House, Dunmurry, County Antrim. In 1891 he became President of the Royal Irish Academy, to whose journal he contributed many papers. He died in Dublin. [Biography by Lady Ferguson].

REICHEL, HAROLD RUDOLF 1856–1931
Harold Reichel was born in Belfast and was educated at Christ's Hospital and Balliol College, Oxford. In 1884 he took charge of the new University College at Bangor, Wales, which became the University of Wales and of which he became Vice-Chancellor. He learned the Welsh language and promoted Welsh culture. He was knighted in 1907. He died in France.

REID, FORREST 1875–1947
Forrest Reid was born in Belfast and was educated at the Royal Belfast Academical Institution and Christ's College, Cambridge, where he read medieval and modern languages. He returned to Belfast and lived there for the rest of his life. He was a friend of E. M. Forster. His novels include *The Kingdom of Twilight; Following Darkness; Uncle Stephen; The Retreat; Peter Waring* and *Young Tom* which won the James Tait Black Memorial Prize. He also published criticism of W. B. Yeats and Walter de la Mare, as well as *Illustrators of the Sixties*, a study of Victorian woodcut artists. He published articles in many magazines, including the *Westminster Review* and the *Ulster Review*, and he reviewed books for the *Manchester Guardian*. *Apostate*, an autobiography, was published in 1926, and its sequel, *Private Road*, was published in 1940. He was a founder member of the Irish Academy of Letters.

REID, JAMES SEATON 1798–1851
James Reid was born in Lurgan, County Armagh, and was educated at Glasgow University, where he gained a Doctorate of Divinity in 1833. He was ordained at Donegore, County Antrim. In 1827 he was elected Moderator of the Synod of Ulster and co-founded a journal *Orthodox Presbyterian* to which he contributed. From 1837 he was Professor of Ecclesiastical History in the Belfast Institute, and from 1841 Professor of Ecclesiastical and Civil History in the University of Glasgow. As well as

other works he wrote a *History of the Presbyterian Church in Ireland* in three volumes (1867), which was unfinished at the time of his death and was completed by W. D. Killen.

REID, META MAYNE see MAYNE REID, META

REID, THOMAS 1791–1825
Thomas Reid was born in Eglish, County Tyrone. In 1815 he became a member of the Royal College of Surgeons. On two occasions he sailed to Australia in charge of convicts and denounced their treatment in a work which he dedicated to Elizabeth Fry. He published *Travels in Ireland* after having travelled on horseback observing social conditions. He died in Pentonville, England.

REID, THOMAS MAYNE 1818–1883
Thomas Reid was born in Ballyroney, County Down, and was educated for the Presbyterian ministry. He ran away to sea and settled in America in 1840. He worked as a storekeeper, actor, schoolteacher, slave overseer, hunter, and as a soldier in the Indian wars. In 1842 he began work with the *Pittsburgh Morning Chronicle*. He then moved to Philadelphia where he met Edgar Alan Poe, began publishing poems and had a play produced in the Walnut Street Theatre. He volunteered for the Mexican war (1846–8), where he distinguished himself, having been left for dead on the battle field. He produced his first novel while recovering from this ordeal and when he returned to England he wrote adventure novels for the next thirty years, among which are *Scalp Hunters; Rifle Rangers* (1850); *Boy Hunter; Headless Horseman* and *The Castaways*. Altogether he published seventy novels, and was translated into ten languages. He returned to America and founded and edited the *Onward Magazine*. He died in London. [Memoir by Mrs Thomas Mayne Reid]

REILY, HUGH c.1630–1695
Hugh Reily was born in County Cavan and in the reign of James II became a Master in Chancery and Clerk of the Council in Ireland. After the Battle of the Boyne he went

into exile with James II. Among his publications are *Ireland's Case Briefly Stated*, which has been reprinted as *Impartial History* and *Genuine History*, one of the few peices of contemporary writing which attempted to articulate the cause of Irish Catholics. James disliked the tone which Reily had adopted and dismissed him from service.

REILLY, THOMAS DEVIN 1824–1854
Thomas Reilly was born in Monaghan and was educated there and at Trinity College, Dublin. He joined the Young Ireland movement and was a journalist with the *Nation* in 1845 but in 1847 he followed John Mitchel's example in leaving that paper and began contributing to the *United Irishman*, Mitchel's new paper. In this he published 'The French Fashion', a revolutionary article which provided ammunition for Mitchel's prosecutors. In 1848, after the arrest of Mitchel, he went to New York, where he edited the *Democratic Review* and later the *Washington Union*. He died in Washington.

REILLY, WILLIAM EDWARD MOYSES 1827–1886
William Reilly was born in Scarva, County Down, and was educated at Woolwich. He entered the Royal Artillery and served in the Crimean War. In 1868 he was promoted to the rank of colonel and was made Companion of the Bath. He saw action in the Franco-Prussian War and was taken prisoner by the Prussians, and later served in the Zulu War. In 1885 he became major-general. He died at sea.

REYNOLDS, DORIS 1899–1985
Doris Reynolds was an international authority on granites and specialised on the local igneous rocks of Counties Down and Armagh. She published on the igneous complexes of Newry and Slieve Gullion and revised *Principles of Physical Geology*, which is a textbook written by her husband, Arthur Holmes. She is renowned for the thoroughness of her scientific data and her accurate field mapping.

REYNOLDS, OSBORNE 1842–1912
Osborne Reynolds was born in Belfast and was educated at Cambridge University. In 1867 he was made a Fellow of Queen's College, Belfast, and from 1868 to 1905 he was Professor of Engineering at Owen's College, Manchester. He published much original research under the title *Papers on Mechanical and Physical Subjects* in three volumes and died in Somerset.

RHIND, ETHEL early 20th century
Ethel Rhind was born in Bengal, India and educated at Londonderry High School and the School of Art, Belfast. In 1902 she attended the Dublin Metropolitan School of Art where she was awarded a scholarship in mosaic. Her window in the Old Court Chapel, Strangford, County Down won first prize at the Royal Dublin Society in 1908. She worked at An Túr Gloine and specialised in 'opus sectile', a technique involving a mosaic of glass set into the plaster of a wall. She designed the stations of the cross for St. Enda's Church at Spiddal, County Galway, using this process. Further examples of her work can be seen in Grangegorman Church in Dublin, and in Magheralin Church, County Down. Her work was shown at the Arts and Crafts Society of Ireland in 1910, 1917 and 1921 and she was a member of the Guild of Irish Art-Workers.

RICE, PETER 1935–1992
Peter Rice was born in Ulster. He studied engineering at Queen's University, Belfast, and at Imperial College, London. His first job, when he went to work for Ove Arup, was to raise the roofs of Sydney Opera House, designed by Jorn Utzon. From that point he was commissioned to work on the Centre Pompidou in Paris; the Menil Art Collection Museum in Houston and the Kansai International Airport in Japan. He worked on the Lloyd's Building in London, the new pavilion at Stanstead Airport and the Pavilion of the Future at the Seville Expo. He collaborated on these projects with Sir Richard Rogers and Renzo Piano. He had his own practice in Paris, and was director of Arup's, London. He was awarded the Royal Gold Medal for architecture. He was fond of poetry, philosophy, mathematics, football, racing, wildflowers, wine and whiskey.

RICHARDSON, JAMES NICHOLSON 1846–1921

James Richardson was born in Belfast and was educated in Tottenham. He joined the family linen business in Bessbrook, County Armagh, the model village set up by his father, John Grubb Richardson. He was interested in the welfare of his workers and did much to improve their quality of life. He was a member of parliament for County Armagh from 1880 to 1885 and frequently travelled abroad. He published a Quaker biography and several volumes of poetry, and died at Malvern. [Memoir by C. F. Smith]

RICHARDSON, JOHN 1664–1747

John Richardson was born in County Armagh and was educated at Trinity College, Dublin. In 1693 he was ordained and became rector of Armagh, where he preached in Irish. He published a volume of sermons in Irish and a *Church Catechism*. He became Dean of Kilmore and was involved in a project for the printing and distribution of an Irish translation of the bible. He died in Clogher.

RICHARDSON, WILLIAM 1740–1820

William Richardson was a geologist who lived in Portrush, County Antrim, for much of the year, so he knew the Giant's Causeway intimately. It is therefore surprising that, along with Richard Kirwan, he reverted to the erroneous Neptunian theory of the Causeway's formation and disregarded William Hamilton's suggestions. The volcanic theory of Hamilton and Desmarest was suspected of being subversive of the existing order.

RIDDELL, CHARLOTTE ELIZA LAWSON (née COWAN) 1832–1906

Charlotte Cowan was born in Carrickfergus, County Antrim. She began to write when she was a girl, and during her lifetime produced over thirty novels and collections of short stories among which are *The Race for Wealth*; *Above Suspicion* and *The Banshee's Warning*. She encouraged young writers. Her book *Struggle for Fame* is interpreted as being autobiographical. She died in Ashford, Middlesex.

RIDDELL, HENRY 1851–1923

Henry Riddell was born in Belfast and was educated at Belfast Model School and Belfast Academy. Before entering Queen's College, Belfast, to study engineering in 1876, he was apprenticed at Milford Mill, Belfast. He turned down a professorship in Newfoundland to go into business as an engineer and eventually became managing director of his father's business. He was a member of Belfast Corporation and of the Senate at Queen's University, Belfast. He served as Honorary Treasurer of the Belfast Natural History and Philosophical Society and also as its President from 1921 to 1923.

RITCHIE, WILLIAM 1756–1834

William Ritchie was born in Ayrshire, Scotland. He was a shipbuilder and visited Belfast in 1791 with the aim of transferring his shipyard from Scotland to Belfast. In 1791 he founded a shipyard on the site of the Old Lime Kiln Dock. As well as building ships, he was also employed by the Ballast Board to construct their first dock, which was completed in 1800. He was involved in charitable work for the Poor House, and the House of Industry.

ROBINSON, BRYAN 1808–1887

Bryan Robinson was born in County Cavan and was educated at Trinity College, Dublin. In 1828 he went to Newfoundland, where in 1831 he was called to the Bar and three years later became Master in Chancery. In 1842 he was elected member of the Newfoundland parliament for Fortune Bay. In 1858 he was appointed a judge, and in 1877 he was knighted. He died in Ealing.

ROBINSON, HUGH 1845–1890

Hugh Robinson was born in Belfast and was educated at the Royal Belfast Academical Institution, after which he served his apprenticeship with a firm of wholesale drapers. He was a founder member of Belfast Naturalists' Field Club, acted as Honorary Secretary for eleven years and was President from 1887 to 1889. His presidential address on the progress of science in Belfast was republished after his death. He was Secretary of the Belfast School of

Art and Registrar of the Academical Institution.

ROBINSON, MARJORIE 1858–1924
Marjorie Robinson was born in Belfast. She became a skilled illuminator and attended the Government School of Design. In 1907 she went to London to take up portraiture, where she worked under Alyn Williams of the Royal Society of Miniature Painters. While she was in London she also studied modelling, and remained there until the outbreak of the First World War when she returned to Belfast. She exhibited in London and Belfast, and a collection of twenty-two miniatures was presented by her brother to the Belfast Museum and Art Gallery, where she is also represented by sculpture, watercolours and a self-portrait in oil.

ROBINSON, MINA late 19th century
Mina Robinson held art classes in Belfast in the early 1890s which evolved into the Irish Decorative Art Association. The group, established along with Eta Lowry, was first known as the Belfast School of Poker-work. In 1894 at the Irish Decorative Art Association Exhibition in Portrush, County Antrim, she exhibited poker-work and at the Belfast Art and Industrial Exhibition of 1895, she showed an oak settle decorated in poker-work and 'hot air paints' which was a method invented by her. She also exhibited art needle-work. By 1896 the Belfast School of Poker-Work was involved in large scale decorations for house interiors, railway carriages and steamers. Often Celtic ornamentation was used in the designs. In 1904 the water-colour paintings of Percy French were framed in poker-work frames at the Portrush Exhibition and the decoration of harps and harp chairs were added to the School's output, as well as hand-painted china and leather book-binding, such as that used on the books of Moira O'Neill and AE. The work was widely exhibited, from Cork to St Louis.

ROBINSON, RICHARD c.1709–1794
Richard Robinson was born in Yorkshire and came to Ireland as chaplain to the Duke of Dorset. In 1765 he was made Arch-bishop of Armagh and Primate of All Ireland, and in 1777 was created Baron Rokeby. He built himself a palace in Armagh, was responsible for the construction of the public library, and in 1789, built the observatory at his own expense.

ROBINSON, ROBERT SPENCER 1809–1889
Robert Spencer Robinson was born in County Armagh. In 1821 he joined the navy and took part in operations on the coast of Syria, and in 1854 he commanded a ship in the Baltic fleet. He became a vice-admiral in 1860 and was Lord of the Admiralty from 1868 to 1871. He was created a Knight Commander of the Bath.

ROBINSON, SANDY 1909–1989
Sandy Robinson lived near Ballyclare, County Antrim, and was known as the Bard of Ballyalbanagh. He recited poems, told stories and played the fiddle, and in his will he left all his writings to his great niece, Joanne Robinson, who has published them with her own illustrations.

ROBINSON, THOMAS fl. 1790–1810
Thomas Robinson was born in Westmoreland. He studied under the famous portraitist, George Romney, and then went to Dublin. He moved to Laurencetown, near Dromore, County Down in order to be close to the Bishop of Dromore, Dr Thomas Percy. He then went to Lisburn, where he painted 'The Battle of Ballynahinch', which is now in the National Gallery of Ireland, Dublin. In 1801 he moved to Belfast, and painted 'A Military Procession in Honour of Lord Nelson', which portrays many of the prominent citizens of Belfast. He left Belfast in 1808 and settled in Dublin, where he died. His work is held by collectors in America, Belfast and Dublin.

ROBINSON, THOMAS ROMNEY 1792–1882
Thomas Romney Robinson was born in Dublin and was taken to Dromore, County Down, when he was two years old. His family settled for a period in Lisburn, County Antrim, before moving to Belfast. He was

educated at Belfast Academy and published *Juvenile Poems* in 1806, the same year as he entered Trinity College, Dublin. He became a fellow of the college in 1814 and served as Deputy Professor of Natural Philosophy. During this period he became a member of the Royal Irish Academy. He was curate in Enniskillen before being appointed rector of Carrickmacross, County Monaghan, and he also worked as an astronomer in Armagh from 1823. There he gained international fame for his observations, some of which he published in 1854 in *Places of 5,345 Stars Observed at Armagh from 1818 to 1854*. In 1851 he became President of the Royal Irish Academy, a position which he filled for five years, contributing many papers to its *Transactions*. He was a Fellow of the Royal Society, which presented him with a gold medal in 1862 for his valuable work in astronomy, and a member of the British Association. He invented the cup anemometer and researched in physics. He died at Armagh Observatory.

ROBINSON, WILLIAM 1838–1935
William Robinson was probably born in Ulster. He was an Irish gardener and writer and began work on the estate of the Marquess of Waterford at Curraghmore. He went to the Irish National Botanic Garden at Glasnevin, where he was a student. From 1860 to 1861 he worked at Ballykilcavan and then moved to London where he joined the staff of the Royal Botanic Garden in Regent's Park and became the foreman in charge of the herbaceous plants. He contributed articles to the *Gardeners' Chronicle* and in 1866 was elected to the Linnean Society on the sponsorship of, among others, Charles Darwin. He spent 1867 in France, visiting gardens and produced two books: *Gleaning from French Gardens* (1868) and *Parks and Gardens of Paris* (1869). In 1870 he published *Alpine Flowers for Gardens* and *The Wild Garden* and a year later established a weekly journal *Garden* which he edited until 1899. It was then edited by Gertrude Jekyll and in 1927 became part of *Homes and Gardens*. In 1883 he published *The English Flower Garden* which ran to fifteen editions during his life. Other periodicals were established:

Gardening Illustrated; Gardener's Chronicle; Cottage Gardening and *Flora and Sylva*. He edited W. Miller's translation of the Vilmorin book, *The Vegetable Garden* (1885 and reprinted in 1976) and published *The Virgin's Bower*, a book on clematis. He influenced the taste for informality in gardens.

RODEN, 3rd EARL OF see JOCELYN, ROBERT

RODGERS, JAMES GUINNESS 1822–1911
James Rodgers was born in Enniskillen, County Fermanagh, and was educated at Trinity College, Dublin. He was a popular preacher and President of the Union of Churches. From 1865 to 1900 he resided in Clapham and was a good friend of Gladstone. He edited the *Congregationalist* and the *Congregational Review* and had a Doctorate of Divinity conferred upon him by the University of Edinburgh. He published many works, including his autobiography.

RODGERS, WILLIAM ROBERT 1909–1969
W. R. Rodgers was born in Belfast and was educated at Queen's University, Belfast. He served in Loughgall, County Armagh, as Presbyterian minister from 1934 to 1946. *Awake and Other Poems* appeared in 1941. He joined the BBC in 1946 as a scriptwriter and producer for the Third Programme. He collaborated with Louis MacNeice in the unpublished *The Character of Ireland*. In 1951 he was elected to the Irish Academy of Letters, and in 1952 produced his second collection of poetry, *Europa and the Bull*. From 1967 to 1969 he was Poet–in–Residence at Pitzer College, Clairmont, California, where he died.

ROE, SAMUEL BLACK 1830–1913
Samuel Roe was born in Ballyconnell, County Cavan, and was educated at Trinity College, Dublin. In 1855 he joined the Gordon Highlanders and served in the Crimea, the Indian Mutiny, the Afghan War and the Boer War and participated in the march to Kandahar. In 1881 he was made a Companion of the Bath. He was appointed Deputy Surgeon General, and served as High Sheriff of Cavan in 1892–1893.

ROGERS, JOHN *c.*1740–1814
John Rogers was ordained in Cahans, County Monaghan, in 1767. In 1782 he attended the Volunteer Convention in Dungannon. He was appointed clerk of the Burgher Synod and Professor of Divinity. He published many sermons and addresses and died at prayer.

ROS, AMANDA MALVINA FITZALAN ANN MARGARET McLELLAND (née McKITTRICK) 1860–1939
Amanda McKittrick Ros was born in Drumaness, near Ballynahinch, County Down. She was educated at Drumaness School, where her father was Principal, and Marlborough Teacher Training College in Dublin. She was appointed monitor at Millbrook National School, Larne, before completing her training in Dublin. She married Andy Ros, who was station master in Larne. She wrote many novels in her own idiosyncratic fashion, among which are *Irene Iddesleigh*, *Delina Delaney* and *Helen Huddleson*, the latter completed by her biographer, Jack Loudan, after her death. She referred to her critics as the 'maggoty throng', 'claycrabs of corruption' and 'hogwashing hooligans'. She was greatly admired by Mark Twain and Aldous Huxley, and there was an Amanda Ros fan club at St John's College, Cambridge. She also published collections of verse entitled *Poems of Puncture* and *Fumes of Fomentation*. At the age of sixty-two, after her first husband had died, she re-married a farmer. She also wrote music, songs, and, during the First World War, she wrote ballads under the pseudonym Monica Moyland, which were printed in broadsheets. She saw her own death as joining 'the boundless battalion of the breathless'. [*O Rare Amanda: The Life of Amanda McKittrick Ros*, Jack Loudan, 1954]

ROSS, EDWARD CHARLES 1836–1913
Edward Ross was born in Rostrevor, County Down, and educated in Edinburgh. He entered the service of the East India Company in 1855 and was highly proficient in Arabic and Persian. He served as colonel during the Indian Mutiny. In 1863 he joined the political service and served as consul-gen-

eral in South Persia from 1872 to 1891. In 1892 he was knighted and he died in Clifton.

ROSS, JOHN 1854–1935
John Ross was born in Derry and was educated at Foyle College, Derry, and Trinity College, Dublin. He gained a Doctorate in Law, was called to the Bar in 1879, and became Queen's Counsel two years later. From 1892 to 1895 he was a member of parliament for Londonderry and from 1896 to 1921 was judge in Chancery. In 1919 he became a privy councillor and was created a baronet. He served as Lord Chancellor in 1921–1922. Among his publications are *The Years of My Pilgrimage*, *Pilgrim Scrip*, and a collection of presidential addresses to college societies.

ROWAN, ARCHIBALD HAMILTON 1751–1834
Archibald Hamilton Rowan was born in London and was educated at Westminster School and Queen's College, Cambridge. He went to live in Rathcoffey, County Kildare, in 1784 and joined the Volunteers. In 1790 he was a founder member of the Northern Whig Club, Belfast, and joined the United Irishmen in 1791. In 1794 he was tried for sedition and sentenced to two years' imprisonment, but fled to France, where he witnessed the atrocities of the Terror. While he was there he met Mary Wollstonecroft. In 1795 he went to America and was joined by Wolfe Tone and Napper Tandy. He was pardoned in 1803 and settled on his estate at Killyleagh Castle, County Down. He was a supporter of Catholic Emancipation.

ROWAN, CHARLES 1780–1852
Charles Rowan was born in Mullans, County Antrim, and joined the 52nd Foot Regiment. He served throughout the Peninsular campaign and was wounded at the Battle of Waterloo. When the London police were formed he was appointed Chief Commissioner. He was knighted in 1848 and died in London.

ROWAN, WILLIAM 1789–1879
William Rowan was born in Mullans, County

Antrim, and in 1803 joined the 52nd Foot Regiment. He, like his brother Charles, served during the Peninsular War and took part in the famous charge against the Imperial Guards at Waterloo. In 1856 he was awarded the Grand Cross of the Bath. He became a major-general in 1877, and was made a field-marshal. He died in Bath.

RUSHE, DENIS CAROLAN 1852–1928
Denis Rushe was born in Monaghan town, and educated at St Louis Convent, McCartan's Seminary, and Trinity College, Dublin. In 1878 he became a solicitor and in 1880, President of the Monaghan Conference of the St Vincent de Paul Society. He was involved in the Home Industries Association, and the Monaghan Show. He was secretary of the Fermanagh Board of Education from 1891 until his death, and also secretary of Monaghan County Council from 1899 until 1924. He was a keen student of the Irish language and an advocate of the Gaelic League. He wrote three books on the history of Monaghan, *Historical Sketches of Monaghan* (1894); *Monaghan in the Eighteenth Century* (1916) and the *History of Monghan for Two Hundred Years* (1921).

RUSK, WALTER 1910–1940
Walter Rusk was born in Belfast and was a motor-cycle road racer. In 1934 he finished second in the European 350cc Championship. He won two third places and won second place in the Isle of Man TT Race. In 1939 he was the first rider to lap the Ulster Grand Prix Circuit. He took part in the German and Swiss Grand Prix in 1935. At the start of the Second World War he became a pilot. He died of pneumonia.

RUSSELL, CHARLES 1832–1900
Charles Russell was born in Ballybot, near Newry, County Down, and was educated at a private school in Newry, the Belfast Diocesan Seminary and the Vincentian College, Castleknock, Dublin. He practised as a solicitor for two years in Belfast and was called to the English Bar in 1859. In 1872 he became Queen's Counsel and served as a member of parliament for Dundalk from 1880 until 1885, when he was elected for South Hackney. In the following year he was appointed English Attorney-General. He published *New Views of Ireland or Irish Land; Grievances; Remedies*. In 1893 he was advocate for Britain in the Bering Sea arbitration and was awarded the Grand Order of St Michael and St George. In 1894 he was made Lord of Appeal and was knighted, became Lord Chief Justice and was made a life peer, Baron Russell of Killowen. He died in Kensington. [Biography by Barry O'Brien]

RUSSELL, CHARLES WILLIAM 1812–1880
Charles Russell was born in Killough, County Down, and by 1835 was appointed Professor of Humanities at Maynooth. In 1837 he was made President of the college, and he is said to have been instrumental in the conversion of Cardinal Newman. He was co-editor of the *Dublin Review* and collaborated with J. P. Prendergast on the eight-volume *Report on the Carte Manuscripts* and the four-volume *Calendar of State Papers of James I*. He also wrote the *Life of Cardinal Mezzofanti*. He died after falling from his horse.

RUSSELL, GEORGE WILLIAM (pseud. AE) 1867–1935
George Russell was born in Lurgan, County Armagh, and after his family moved to Dublin he was educated at Rathmines School and the Metropolitan School of Art, where he and W. B. Yeats became friends. He worked as a clerk and then became editor of the *Irish Homestead*, the journal of the Irish Argicultural Organisation Society. He published *Homeward: Songs by the Way*, his first book of poems, and his play *Deirdre* was one of the first to be staged by the Irish Literary Society. He was a painter and writer and was interested in mysticism, economics and politics: he was also a founder of the Irish Theosophical Society. Among his publications are *New Visions; The Divine Vision; The Mask of Apollo; Enchantment; The Renewal of Youth* and *The Interpreters*. In 1913 he published his *Collected Poems* and he was editor for seven years of the *Irish Statesman*. He was also an artist and kept open house in Dublin for the intellectuals of his day.

He painted in Donegal, often near Dunfanaghy. His work is represented in the Ulster Museum and the Armagh County Museum. His portrait of W. B. Yeats is in the National Gallery of Ireland, Dublin. He died in Bournemouth.

RUSSELL, JAMES 1842–1893

James Russell was born in Broughshane, County Antrim, and was educated at Queen's College, Belfast. He was a cadet in Hong Kong in 1865 and was called to the Bar in 1874. In 1879 he became Attorney-General and a member of the Legislative Council. He was appointed a puisne judge in 1883.

RUSSELL, KATHERINE (name in religion, MARY BAPTIST) 1829–1898

Katherine Russell was born in Ballybot, near Newry, County Down, and was educated in Belfast and Kinsale. She was a pioneer Sister of Mercy in California, and in 1854 became Mother Superior in San Francisco, where she was instrumental in founding hospitals and convents. She died there. [Biography by Reverend Matthew Russell]

RUSSELL, MATTHEW 1834–1912

Matthew Russell was born at Ballybot, near Newry, County Down, and was educated at Castleknock and Maynooth. He became a Jesuit priest and established the *Irish Monthly* in 1873 and edited it for nearly forty years. He also wrote many volumes of poetry, and a biography of his sister Katherine.

RUSSELL, NELSON 1897–1971

Nelson Russell was born in Lisburn, County Antrim and was educated at Campbell College, Belfast. In 1915 he joined the Royal Irish Fusiliers and won the Military Cross in 1916 for having led the first day-light raid of the First World War. In 1923 he played hockey for Ireland and the following year represented the Gentlemen of Ireland at cricket. He was given command of the 38th Irish Brigade who fought in Sicily in 1942 and was awarded the Distinguished Service Order the following year. He commanded a Territorial Army brigade after the Second World War and from 1951 to 1968 was Sergeant-at-Arms in the Northern Ireland Parliament. He died in Newcastle, County Down.

RUSSELL, THOMAS 1767–1803

Thomas Russell was born in Betsborough, Kilshanick, County Cork. He served in the Army and was posted to Belfast. From 1794 to 1796 he was Librarian of the Linen Hall Library and contributed to the *Northern Star*. He took an active part in the organisation of the United Irish Society, and in 1796 he was arrested and deported, but was liberated in 1802. He met Robert Emmet in Paris and went to Ulster hoping to provoke a rising, but failed. He was arrested in Dublin and hanged in Downpatrick. He was known as 'the man from God knows where', the title of a ballad written about him by Florence Wilson of Bangor, County Down in 1918.

RUTHVEN, EDWARD SOUTHWELL 1772–1836

Edward Ruthven was born in County Down and was educated at Trinity College, Dublin, and Oxford University. He assumed the surname Ruthven rather than his family name, Trotter. He was member of parliament for Downpatrick in 1806 and again from 1830 to 1832 and for Dublin city (together with O'Connell) in 1832, and was returned again in 1835 but was later unseated. He was an advanced radical reformer. He fought a duel with Louis Perrin. He died in Westminster.

S

ST JOHN, OLIVER 1559–1630
Oliver St John, Viscount Grandison and Baron Tregoz, came to Ireland in 1601. Having taken part in the Battle of Kinsale, he then became a member of the Ulster Plantation Commission, gaining land for himself in County Armagh. In 1616 he was appointed Lord Deputy and banished all friars and monks who had been educated abroad. After Ulster, he went on to plant County Leitrim and County Longford. He was recalled to England in 1622.

SAMPSON, GEORGE VAUGHAN 1763–1827
George Sampson was born in County Antrim, and was educated at Trinity College, Dublin. He was headmaster of Foyle College, Derry for four years before becoming rector of Aghaboe. He published *Statistical Survey of Derry* and *Memoir of Chart and Survey of Derry.*

SAMPSON, WILLIAM 1764–1836
William Sampson was born in County Londonderry, and was educated at Trinity College, Dublin, and Lincoln's Inn, London. He was a United Irishman and held a commission in the Volunteers. He wrote for the the *Press* and the *Northern Star,* was arrested and deported to France and from there he went to America, where he rose to prominence as a lawyer. He published his *Memoirs* in New York and *Discourse showing the Origin, Progress, Antiquities, Curiosities and Natures of the Common Law,* which was recognised as an important contribution to legal studies.

SANDS, ROBERT 1954–1981
Bobby Sands was born in Belfast and was apprenticed to a coachbuilder. He joined the Irish Republican Army in 1972 and in 1973 was charged with having in his possession four guns. He was sentenced to five years' imprisonment. In 1977, after his release, he was again arrested when a furniture factory was bombed in Belfast. He was sentenced to fourteen years' imprisonment in the H-Block of the Maze Prison, Long Kesh. He began a hunger-strike on the 1st of March, 1981 as part of a campaign to demand, among other things, political status. In April 1981 he was elected member of parliament for Fermanagh and Tyrone. He died on the 5th of May 1981, the sixty-sixth day of his hunger-strike. His prison diary and poems were published by Sinn Féin in 1981, and in 1982 an anthology of his writings, *Skylark, Sing Your Lonely Song,* was published.

SAUNDERSON, EDWARD JAMES 1837–1906
Edward Saunderson was born in Castle Saunderson, Belturbet, County Cavan, though he spent his boyhood in Nice. In 1858 he returned to Ireland, becoming Sheriff of Armagh in 1859, and was elected Liberal member of parliament for Cavan, serving for nine years from 1865. He joined the Orange Order, which was organizing opposition to Home Rule, and within a short period was selected as Deputy Grand Master for Ireland. As colonel he led a militia battalion of the Royal Irish Fusiliers, and from 1885 to 1906 was Unionist member of parliament for North Armagh. In 1900 he was appointed Lord Lieutenant of Cavan, and he led the Unionist Parliamentary Party in Westminster against Home Rule. [Biography by Reginald Lucas, 1908]

SAURIN, WILLIAM 1757–1839
William Saurin was born in Belfast and was educated at Dubourdieu's school in Lisburn, County Antrim, Trinity College, Dublin, and Lincoln's Inn, London. He was called to the Irish Bar in 1780, was member of parliament for Blessington, and opposed the Union. In 1807 he was appointed Attorney-General for Ireland,

remaining in that post for fifteen years, during which he became noted for his bitter opposition to Catholic Emancipation. When he was replaced in 1822, he refused both a peerage and judgeship and returned to practice at the Bar.

SAVAGE, ROLAND 15th–16th century
Roland Savage was born in Ardkeen and was Seneschal of Ulster in 1482. He was knighted and was Lord of Lecale, County Down. He was known for his allegiance to the English, but by 1515 he reversed his position and fought on the side of the Irish and as a consequence had his lands confiscated by Gerald Fitzgerald, 9th Earl of Kildare.

SAVAGE-ARMSTRONG, GEORGE FRANCIS see ARMSTRONG

SAVORY, DOUGLAS LLOYD 1878–1969
Douglas Savory was born in Suffolk and from 1909 to 1941 was Professor of French and Roman Philology at Queen's University, Belfast, and then became Professor Emeritus. He sat as Unionist member of the Westminster parliament, representing Queen's University from 1940 to 1950, and from 1950 to 1955 representing South Antrim. He was knighted.

SCHOMBERG, FRIEDRICH HERMAN 1615–1690
Friedrich Schomberg was born in Heidelberg of a German father and an English mother. By 1687 he was second-in-command of William III's army and was appointed commander of the Williamite forces in Ireland in 1688. He landed at Bangor, County Down, and occupied Belfast, Carrickfergus, Dundalk and Charlemont. When William III came to Ireland in 1690, he and Schomberg marched southwards. He was killed during the Battle of the Boyne and buried in St Patrick's Cathedral, Dublin.

SCOTT, CHARLES STEWART b.1838
Charles Scott was born at Willsborough, near Derry. He was educated at Cheltenham College and Trinity College, Dublin, and entered the Diplomatic Service. In 1859

he was appointed Attaché to the Embassy in Paris and in 1862 was appointed to Copenhagen as Third Secretary, and this appointment coincided with the war between Denmark, Austria and Prussia. In 1866 he was appointed Second Secretary to Her Majesty's Legation in Mexico during the final stages of the civil war, the seige of Mexico City and the downfall of Emperor Maximilian. He also served in Lisbon, Stuttgart, Munich and Vienna and in 1874 was appointed Second Secretary and Head of the Chancery in St. Petersburg and witnessed the outbreak of the Russian-Turkish war. He later served in Darmstadt and Coburg and in 1883 was transferred to Berlin as Her Majesty's Secretary of the Embassy. He served as Envoy to Switzerland and Copenhagen and in 1898 was promoted to the post of Ambassador to Russia. He was knighted in 1896 and in 1898 became a privy councillor. He was awarded the Grand Cross of the Order of the Bath as well as that of St Michael and St George. He received an honorary degree from Trinity College, Dublin. He died in Scotland.

SCOTT, ELISHA (LEE or LI) c. 1894–1959
Elisha Scott was born in Belfast and was an international goal-keeper. He played for Broadway United, Liverpool, and Belfast Celtic, where he was manager from 1946 to 1949. During that period the team won thirty-one major trophies, including eight gold cups and five County Antrim Shields. He won thirty-one caps for Northern Ireland between 1920 and 1936.

SCOTT, JAMES HENDERSON 1913–1970
James Scott was born in Dundalk and was educated in Dundalk and at the Methodist College, Belfast. From 1964 until 1970 he was Professor of Dental Anatomy at Queen's University, Belfast. Among his publications are *Introduction to Dental Anatomy, Essentials of Oral Anatomy* and *The Christian Vision* (with N. B. B. Symonds).

SCOTT, WILLIAM (alias TANTRA BARBUS) 1778–1837
William Scott was born near Ballynahinch, County Down. He was a chapman, an

itinerant pedlar who sold such items as cloth, combs and books. He became well known throughout the countryside for his eccentric behaviour: he stole pewter from his customers and the brass knockers from their doors to finance his drinking habits. He died in a fit of inebriation at the age of fifty-nine. His *Life* was published in 1833.

SCOTT, WILLIAM b.1913

William Scott was born in Greenock, Scotland, though his family moved to Enniskillen, County Fermanagh when he was eleven. He was educated at the Model School and attended night classes in art at the Technical School, under Kathleen Bridle. He studied at the Belfast College of Art in Belfast in 1928. He won a scholarship to the Royal Academy School, London, won a silver medal and became a Landseer scholar in painting. He was awarded a Leverhulme scholarship in 1935. During the early years of the Second World War he helped to run an art school in France and from there went to live in Dublin and then London. From 1942 to 1946 he served with the Royal Engineers, and learned lithography in the map-making section. From 1946 to 1956 he taught art at Bath Academy of Art and from there went to Canada and America as a guest instructor. He exhibited in London, America, Italy, Switzerland, West Germany, France, Canada and Australia, as well as Belfast and Dublin. In 1961, he executed a mural for the Altnagelvin Hospital, Londonderry. He is represented in many collections at home and abroad and was awarded many honours.

SCRIVEN, JOSEPH 1819–1886

Joseph Scriven was born near Banbridge, County Down, and was educated at Trinity College, Dublin. In 1847 he emigrated to Canada where he settled at Port Hope, Ontario, and became a teacher and a preacher with the Plymouth Brethren. He wrote the hymn 'What a Friend We Have In Jesus'.

SEMPLE, PATRICK 1875–1954

Patrick Semple was born in Derry and was educated at the Royal University of Ireland, where he became a fellow. He was appointed Professor of Classics at University College, Dublin, and then Professor of Latin in 1909. He was a Senator of the National University of Ireland.

SEXTON, THOMAS 1848–1932

Thomas Sexton was born in Waterford and was educated locally. When he was thirteen he went to work for the railway service, and six years later he joined the staff of the *Nation*. In 1880 he was elected member of parliament for Sligo, and Gladstone is said to have remarked that his speech on the Land Bill in 1881, was the finest he had ever heard in the house. From 1886 to 1892 he was member of parliament for West Belfast, and from 1892 to 1896, for North Kerry. He was High Sheriff of Dublin in 1887, and Lord Mayor from 1888 to 1889. He served as chairman of the *Freeman's Journal* from 1892 to 1912. [Biography by T. Sherlock]

SHANE, ELIZABETH see HIND GERTRUDE ELIZABETH HERON

SHARMAN CRAWFORD, WILLIAM, see CRAWFORD, WILLIAM SHARMAN

SHAW or SHAW-GRAETZ, ELIZABETH 1920–1992

Elizabeth Shaw was born in Belfast and studied art at Chelsea Art School, with Henry Moore and Graham Sutherland among her teachers. She established herself as an illustrator and cartoonist during the Second World War and was regarded on a par with Ronald Searle, publishing in *Our Time* and *Lilliput*. She moved to Germany in 1946 and married Rene Graetz from Switzerland. They were committed to the establishment of a new Communist society in Berlin and both learned the German language. They attended the founding meetings of UNESCO in Paris. Elizabeth Shaw made her reputation with her caricatures of the East Berlin intellectual world. She produced, with Bertha Waterstradt, *Das Magazin*, which published the contributions of women artists and writers for twenty years. She wrote and illustrated children's books which sold in East Germany. She illustrated Brecht's poems for children and these brought her international acclaim. During the McCarthy era, Rene and Elizabeth Graetz had a wide coterie of dissident friends from both America and Britain. She began to publish books on places she had visited and loved, particularly Ireland, and there were Arts Council Exhibitions of her work in Coventry and Belfast. In 1981 she was awarded the Kathe Kollwitz Prize. She published her autobiography, *Irish Berlin*, in German in 1990.

SHAW, EYRE MASSEY 1830–1908
Eyre Massey Shaw was born in Ballymore, County Cork, and was educated at Trinity College, Dublin. In 1859 he was Chief Constable in Belfast, and he reorganised the city's fire brigade. He was appointed head of the London fire brigade in 1861 and was severely injured while directing operations. He was knighted in 1891, and in 1892 was given the freedom of the city of London. He wrote many works on fire protection and served on the boards of companies.

SHAW, JAMES JOHNSTON 1845–1910
James Shaw was born in County Down and educated at Queen's College, Belfast. From 1869 to 1878 he was Professor of Metaphysics at Magee College, Derry, and in 1878 was called to the Bar. He served as Whately Professor in Trinity College, Dublin, from 1876 to 1891, and in 1891 became Commissioner of Education and a county court judge in County Kerry, transferring to County Antrim in 1909. He was Chairman of the Commissioners who framed the statutes of Queen's University, Belfast, and he became Pro-Chancellor. In 1909 he was Recorder of Belfast.

SHAW, ROSE early 20th century
Rose Shaw lived in the Clogher Valley, County Tyrone. She was a governess to the Gledstanes who lived at Fardross, near Clogher. She was an amateur photographer. Only about thirty of her photographs have survived and these are in the Ulster Folk and Transport Museum, Cultra, County Down. She published *Carleton's Country* 1930, which had an introduction by Sir Shane Leslie and included many of her own photographs.

SHAW, WILLIAM 1823–1895
William Shaw was born in The Moy, County Tyrone. He was a Congregational minister of a church in Cork for four years, but resigned in 1840. He went into business and became a director of the Munster Bank. In 1868 he was elected to parliament. He was an advocate of Home Rule and by 1873 was Chairman of the Home Rule Convention in Dublin. He was elected Home Rule member of parliament for County Cork and succeeded Butt as leader of the party in 1879. In the general election of 1880 he was re-elected for Cork but was replaced as party leader by Parnell. He withdrew from the Home Rule Party because of his differences of opinion with the Land League. He retired from politics in 1885, and with the insolvency of the Munster bank of which he was now Chairman, he became bankrupt.

SHEA, PATRICK 1908–1986
Patrick Shea was born in County Westmeath and since his father was a policeman, he spent his childhood in Athlone, Clones, County Monaghan, Rathfriland and Newry, County Down. He was educated at the Christian Brothers' School, Newry, among other places. He joined the Northern Ireland civil service and attained the rank of permanent secretary in the Department of Education. He wrote *Voices and the Sound of Drums*.

SHEPPARD, OLIVER 1865–1941
Oliver Sheppard was born in Cookstown, County Tyrone. After his birth the family moved to Dublin, and he studied at the Metropolitan School of Art. He won a scholarship to the South Kensington Art School, where he studied from 1889 to 1891 before spending a year in Paris. He taught in Leicester and Nottingham. When he returned to Dublin in 1902 he was appointed instructor in modelling at the Metropolitan School of Art. He was Professor of Sculpture to the Royal Hibernian Academy and exhibited there and at the Royal Academy. He represented Ireland in exhibitions in Europe, and in 1905 founded the Royal Society of British Sculptors. His work 'The Death of Cuchulain' was chosen

as a memorial to the 1916 Rising and is in the General Post Office in Dublin.

SHEIL, CHARLES LEO 1897–1968
Charles Sheil was born in Portadown, County Armagh, and was educated at Clongowes Wood College, and Queen's University, Belfast. In 1921 he was called to the Bar and was Crown Counsel for County Antrim from 1926 to 1943. He served as county court judge and Senior Crown Counsel and was then appointed a judge of the Northern Ireland High Court.

SHEIL, EDWARD 1834–1869
Edward Sheil was born in Coleraine, County Londonderry, and was educated at the Cork School of Art. In 1857 he became second master and from 1859 to 1860 he was headmaster. In 1861 he was elected an associate of the Royal Hibernian Academy where he had exhibited for the previous five years and he became an Academician in 1864. Among his pictures are 'Excelsior'; 'The Angel of Intercession'; 'Spring'; 'Jacob's Dream' and 'Gethsemane', a work exhibited at the Royal Academy, London in 1866.

SHERIDAN, PHILIP HENRY 1831–1888
Philip Sheridan was born in Killinkere, County Cavan, and as a young boy was taken to America. From 1848 to 1853 he was educated at Westpoint. He served in the American Civil War and rose to the rank of major-general in the Union army by 1862. He is remembered for his success at the Potomac, the Shenandoah and for his campaign against the Confederates which ended the war in north Virginia. In 1865 he won the Battle at Five Forks. In 1883 he was promoted to the rank of commander-in-chief, and among his publications are his memoirs.

SHERIDAN, THOMAS 1687–1738
Thomas Sheridan was born in County Cavan and was educated at Trinity College, Dublin. In 1726 he attained a Doctorate of Divinity. He taught in the school which he had opened in Capel Street, Dublin. He was a friend of Swift and in 1738 sold his school and went to live in the Deanery of St Patrick's with him. He wrote prolifically,

yet published little, except for his translations from the classics.

SHERIDAN, THOMAS 1719–1788
Thomas Sheridan was born in Quilca, County Cavan, and was educated at Westminster School and Trinity College, Dublin. He was an actor and appeared in Covent Garden, Drury Lane and Smock Alley, where he became manager. He went to England, where he enjoyed great success as a teacher of elocution. He befriended Samuel Johnston, but lost his friendship when he proposed to publish a dictionary of pronounciation. Among his publications are *A General Dictionary of the English Language*, and he edited *The Works of Swift* in eighteen volumes. Swift was his godfather, and he himself was the father of Richard Brinsley Sheridan.

SHERIDAN, WILLIAM 1636–1711
William Sheridan was born in Togher, County Cavan, and was educated at Trinity College, Dublin, where he became Doctor of Divinity in 1682. He was chaplain to the Duke of Ormond, and in 1667 became rector of Athenry. Two years later he was appointed Dean of Down, and in 1682 became Bishop of Kilmore and Ardagh. When William III came to the throne, Sheridan left Kilmore and went to London to avoid taking the oath of allegiance, as a result of which he was deprived of his bishopric in 1691. His letters are preserved in the Sloane Manuscripts in the British Library. He died in London.

SHIELDS, JAMES 1806–1879
James Shields was born in Altmore, Dungannon, County Tyrone. In 1826 he went to America, settled in Illinois and studied law, becoming a judge of the Supreme Court in 1843. He once challenged Abraham Lincoln to a duel which was compromised. In 1846 he was appointed Brigadier-General in the Mexican War, where he was severely wounded, and in 1849 was elected Senator for Illinois. From 1858–1859 he was Senator for Minnesota. He served in the American Civil War as Brigadier-General from 1861 to 1863 and fought against Stonewall Jackson. He

settled in Missouri and in 1879 was again elected to the Senate. He died in Iowa.

SHIELS, GEORGE (pseud. MORSHIEL, GEORGE) *c.*1881–1949

George Shiels was born in Ballymoney, County Antrim, and was educated locally. He emigrated to the USA and Canada and after an accident sustained while working on the Canadian Pacific Railway was left disabled for life. He returned to Ireland, where he began to write plays; the first of these, *Bedmates and Insurance Money*, was performed at the Abbey in 1921. Other works, some of which were also performed at the Abbey theatre, Dublin, include *Paul Twyning*, *Passing Day*, *Professor Tim*, *The Fort Field*; *The Summit* and *The Rugged Path*.

SIGERSON, GEORGE (pseud. ERIONNACH) 1836–1925

George Sigerson was born in Holy Hill, Strabane, County Tyrone, and was educated in Letterkenny, France, Galway, Cork and Dublin, graduating as a Doctor of Medicine in 1859. Ten of his poems were published in the *Harp of Erin* in 1869. He taught himself Irish, for which he won a prize. He specialised in neurology and was appointed Professor of Botany and Biology in the Catholic University and later in the National University of Ireland. He published, often under the pseudonym Erionnach, articles in newspapers such as the *Freeman's Journal*, the *North British Review* and the *Irishman*. His first book, *The Poets and Poetry of Munster*, was followed by *History of the Land Tenures and Land Classes of Ireland*; *The Last Independent Parliament of Ireland* and medical works, which included *Diseases of the Nervous System*. He published poems and translations from the Irish, such as the popular *Bards of the Gael and Gall*. His last book, *The Easter Song of Sedulius* was published when he was eighty-six years old. He was a Senator of the Irish Free State and President of the National Literary Society and was a founder member of Feis Ceoil.

SIMMS, JOHN GERALD 1904–1979

Gerald Simms was born in Lifford, County Donegal, and was educated at Winchester and Oxford. Before entering Trinity College, Dublin, in 1950 as a lecturer in Modern History, he had been a civil servant in the Indian administration. In 1966 he was elected a fellow of Trinity, and in 1974 became Keeper of Marsh's Library, Dublin. He was a member of the Royal Irish Academy. Among his publications are *The Williamite Confiscation in Ireland, 1690–1703*; *Jacobite Ireland, 1685–91* and *William Molyneux of Dublin*.

SIMMS, JOHN MORROW 1854–1934

John Simms was born in Newtownards, County Down, and was educated at Queen's College, Belfast, and in Edinburgh, where he studied theology, afterwards becoming a Presbyterian minister. In 1887 he was appointed an army chaplain and served in the Sudan and in South Africa. In the First World War he was Principal Chaplain to the British forces in France, with the rank of major-general. He was made a Companion of the Order of St Michael and St George and a Companion of the Order of the Bath. In 1919 he became Moderator of the General Assembly, and in 1922 member of the Westminster parliament for North Down, retaining his parliamentary seat until 1931. He was the King's Honorary Chaplain. He died in Newtownards. In his obituary *The Times* said of him: 'He was no mere arm-chair minister, but shared the risks and hardships of military life'.

SIMPSON, ALAN 1920–1980

Alan Simpson was born in Dublin and was educated at Campbell College, Belfast, and Trinity College, Dublin, where he graduated in engineering in 1946. During the Second World War he served with the Irish army. He was commissioned as captain with the Corps of Engineers in 1950. He was interested in the theatre, and he and his wife, Carolyn Swift, founded the Pike Theatre in Dublin, where the first Irish productions of Samuel Beckett's *Waiting for Godot* and Brendan Behan's *The Quare Fellow* were staged. His book *Beckett and Behan and a Theatre in Dublin* recalls those years. He went to London and Edinburgh to work in theatre, and from 1968 to 1969 was artistic adviser to the Abbey Theatre. While in Dublin he directed musicals. He lectured in the State University of New York in 1978 and directed productions in America. He died in Dublin.

SIMPSON, JONATHAN 1817–1900
Jonathan Simpson was born at Inchadoghill, Aghadowey, County Antrim and educated at Belfast College and the University of Edinburgh. He became a minister in Portrush, County Antrim in 1842 and resigned in 1890. He was a keen exponent of Temperance and Social Reform. He swam all year round and saved many lives from drowning. He travelled in Europe, Palestine and the United States of America and published *The Annals of My Life*.

SIMPSON, MAXWELL 1815–1902
Maxwell Simpson was born in County Armagh and was educated at Trinity College, Dublin, and later studied chemistry in London and Germany. He was a Fellow of the Royal Society and Professor of Chemistry in Queen's College, Cork, from 1872 to 1891. His research placed him as one of the most prominent chemists of his time.

SIMS, JAMES 1741–1820
James Sims was born in County Down and graduated from Leyden, afterwards settling in London. For twenty-two years he was President of the Medical Society and wrote many medical works which were translated into French, German and Italian. In 1802 he presented his library to the Medical Society. He died in Bath.

SINCLAIR, ELIZABETH 20th century
Betty Sinclair was a trade unionist and political campaigner. She was one of the organisers of the 1932 outdoor relief workers' strike. She was a former chairperson of the Civil Rights Association, and until her retirement in 1975, full-time secretary of the Belfast Trades Council. She was a founder member of the Communist Party of Ireland.

SINCLAIR, EVERINA 1870–1966
Everina Sinclair was born in Holyhill, County Tyrone and when she went to live in Bonnyglen, Inver, County Donegal, she

taught three classes of wood carvers, all of which exhibited at the Royal Dublin Society. She was herself a skilled carver and in 1890 won a prize at the Royal Dublin Society for a folding chair. She exhibited a carved head at the Royal Dublin Society in the same year. As well as Celtic designs she used Moorish designs from Spain.

SKEFFINGTON, CLOTWORTHY 1742–1805
Clotworthy Skeffington, 2nd Earl of Massereene, was probably born in County Antrim and was educated at Cambridge University. As a youth he fell from his horse and this seems to have had a permanent effect on his posture, since he insisted on crossing his arms across his chest and holding both shoulders. He was considered a dandy and when his business ventures failed and Antrim Castle would no longer pay his debts, he went to a debtor's prison in France for eighteen years. He married (against the wishes of his family) Marie-Ann Barcier, who tried for twelve years to win his release, and when she eventually succeeded in doing so he deserted her. He returned to Ireland, and a neighbour is reputed to have remarked that she 'had previously heard a report that he was a lunatic, but she then thought that if he was a lunatic he was the pleasantest one she had ever met'. It is said that when his second wife's dog died, he decreed that fifty local dogs in white scarves should attend the funeral.

SKEFFINGTON, FRANCIS SHEEHY 1878–1916
Francis Skeffington was born in Bailieborough, County Cavan, and was educated at home and at University College, Dublin where, in 1902, he became Registrar and began a campaign for the admission of women to the college. When asked to drop the campaign or resign, he resigned and became a journalist and social reformer. In 1908 he helped to form the Independent Labour Party and with Hanna Sheehy, the leading Irish suffragist to whom he was married, helped found the Irish Women's Franchise League. He co-edited the *Nationalist* and later became editor of the *Irish*

Citizen, writing prolifically for various newspapers. He joined the Young Ireland branch of the United Ireland League and was a member of the Peace Committee in the 1913 lock-out. He was a pacifist, a vegetarian and an anti-vivisectionist. In 1913 he was elected Vice-Chairman of the Irish Citizen Army. When the First World War broke out, he campaigned against recruitment and was arrested. When, after six days on hunger-strike, he was released, he went to campaign in America. Although he advocated non-violent action, he was arrested during the insurrection in Dublin at Easter 1916, and having witnessed the shooting of an unarmed boy, was himself arbitrarliy executed. His executioner was declared of unsound mind. Among his publications are *A Life of Michael Davitt* and *In Dark and Evil Days*, which was published posthumously.

SKEFFINGTON, JOHN FOSTER 1812–1863

John Skeffington was born in Dublin and was educated at Eton and Oxford University. He wrote a *Metrical Version of the Psalms; Church Melodies* and, along with other volumes of poetry, *O'Sullivan*. He was the 10th Viscount Massareene, and he died in Antrim Castle.

SKEFFINGTON, WILLIAM d.1535

William Skeffington came to Ireland in 1530 as Lord Deputy, but he was recalled in 1532 because of accusations of abuse of power. He returned again as Deputy in 1534 and was knighted. He besieged the castle at Maynooth a year later, and after nine days the garrison surrendered and its surviving defenders were executed. This led to the submission of the rebellious lords Conn O'Neill and Silken Thomas Fitzgerald.

SKELTON, PHILIP 1707–1787

Philip Skelton was born in Derriaghy, near Lisburn, County Antrim, and was educated at Trinity College, Dublin. He was curate at Drummully, near Newtownbutler, County Fermanagh, to Dr Samuel Madden and was tutor to his children. He had parishes in Pettigo, Devenish, Enniskillen, and Fintona, County Tyrone, and his advice to his congregation was: 'If you have not food, beg it; if you can't get for begging, steal; if you can't get for stealing, rob and don't starve'. It is said that on two occasions he sold his library to feed his parishioners. He sometimes locked the church doors so that they could not escape his hell-fire sermons, and he frequently called upon them to witness his death. He was a man of 'gigantic size', a keen boxer and brandisher of the cudgel, a 'bullet'-thrower in his youth, and he loved flowers. He published a *Description of Lough Derg, Deism Revealed* and *Proposals for the Revival of Christianity*. He died of pneumonia in Dublin, leaving instructions that his throat should be cut before he was placed in his coffin. [Life by Samuel Burdy, 1792]

SKRINE, AGNES NESTA SHAKESPEARE (née HIGGINSON; pseud. O'NEILL, MOIRA) 1865–1955

Moira O'Neill was born in Cushendun in the Glens of Antrim. Her *Songs of the Glens of Antrim* and *More Songs of the Glens of Antrim* were very popular and ran to many editions. She also published *An Easter Vacation* and *The Elf Errant*, and her collected poems were published in 1933. After a period living in Canada, she returned to Ireland to live in County Wicklow, where she died. She was the mother of Molly Keane, the novelist.

SLEATOR, JAMES 1889–1950

James Sleator was born in County Armagh and was educated at the Belfast School of Art. He won a scholarship in 1910 which enabled him to attend the Metropolitan School of Art in Dublin. He studied for a time in Paris and at the Slade School of Art in London, but returned to Dublin and the Metropolitan to take up a teaching post in 1915, exhibiting at the Royal Hibernian Academy, to which he was elected in 1917. He spent five years in Florence from 1922 and returned to London, where he opened a studio, taught Sir Winston Churchill, and received commissions for portraits. He exhibited at the Royal Academy and at the Royal Society of Portrait Painters. In 1945 he became President of the Royal Hibernian Academy.

SLOANE, HANS 1660–1753

Hans Sloane was born in Killyleagh, County Down, and studied medicine at London, Paris and Montpelier and graduated from the Huguenot University of Orange near Avignon in 1683. From 1687 to 1689 he was physician to the Governor of Jamaica, and surgeon to the West Indies fleet. In 1696 he published a catalogue in Latin of eight hundred new specimens of plants he had collected. He practised medicine in London, where he set aside his early mornings to treat the poor without payment. It is said that he attended Samuel Pepys, and in 1712 he was appointed physician to Queen Anne and set up his Physic Gardens in Chelsea. He was made a baronet in 1716, and three years later became President of the Royal College of Physicians. He was appointed physician to King George II. He was a friend of Robert Boyle and Isaac Newton, whom he succeeded as President of the Royal Society in 1727. He published *A Voyage to the Islands of Madeira, The Natural History of Jamaica* (2 volumes, 1707 and 1725) and the fourth *London Pharmacopoeia*, a catalogue of medicinal herbs. He was honoured by many foreign academies of science. As a physician he introduced drinking-chocolate, which he considered a health-giving beverage. His library was said to contain 50,000 books, 3,500 manuscripts, 32,000 medals and coins, 3,000 cameos, seals and precious stones, and over 25,000 natural history specimens. This collection, which he bequeathed to the nation, and which was purchased by a special act of parliament, became the nucleus of the British Museum, which was opened to the public in 1759. Sloane Square in London is named after him.

SMITH, ALFRED JOHN 1865–1925

Alfred Smith was born at Kevit Castle in Crossdoney, County Cavan, and was educated at St Patrick's College, Cavan. He studied medicine in Dublin, Leipzig and Vienna, became Professor of Midwifery and Gynaecology at the National University of Ireland and Consultant Gynaecologist at St Vincent's Hospital, Dublin.

SMITH, CHARLES 1715–1762

Charles Smith was born in Waterford and became an apothecary. He published a history of County Down in conjunction with Walter Harris in 1744. He was one of the founders of the Physico-Historical Society in Dublin which published histories of Waterford, Cork and Kerry. He was a pioneer of topography.

SMITH, THOMAS d.1573

Thomas Smith was the son of Queen Elizabeth's secretary and was given land on the Ards peninsula. Sir Brian O'Neill, chief of the O'Neills, declared that he would not relinquish any of his land, and with the force which Smith was leading dwindling in numbers. Smith was killed at Comber by Irish servants he had employed.

SMITH, SYDNEY 1912–1982

Sydney Smith was born in Belfast and educated at the Royal Belfast Academical Institution. He attended evening classes at the Belfast College of Art, and also had private tuition in drawing. He painted landscapes and portraits and made a drawing of the poet W. R. Rodgers. He painted Belfast scenes during the Second World War, and made portraits of American army officers. In 1948 he went to London, and concentrated on painting murals. He also painted murals in ships. He exhibited frequently in Belfast and in Dublin.

SMITH, WILLIAM CUSACK see CUSACK

SMYTH, RICHARD 1826–1878

Richard Smyth was born in Dervock, County Antrim, and was educated at Bonn and Glasgow, where he gained Doctorates of Divinity and of Laws. He was a Presbyterian minister in Derry from 1857 to 1865, and from 1865 to 1868 was Professor of Oriental Languages and Theology at Magee College, Derry. From 1874 to 1878 he served as member of parliament for County Londonderry.

SMYTH, THOMAS 1884–1928

Tom Smyth was born in County Antrim, was educated at Ballymena Academy and eventually gained a doctorate. He was a rugby international and played for Malone and Newport, Wales. Between 1908 and

1912 he was capped for Ireland fourteen times, and was captain of the team only once in 1910. He was appointed Captain of the British and Irish Touring Side who went to South Africa. Both his brothers, William and Patrick, played for Ireland, and were capped several times.

SMYTHE, WILLIAM JAMES 1816–1887
William James Smythe was born in Carnmoney, County Antrim, and was educated at Woolwich. He joined the Royal Artillery in 1833 and served in Africa, St Helena, Nova Scotia and the Fiji Islands. He went to India in 1865 and was promoted to the rank of major-general in 1868. When he returned home he built a church with a round tower at Jordanstown, County Antrim, and took an active interest in local antiquities. He was a Fellow of the Royal Society and bequeathed money to the Royal Irish Academy to encourage the study of Irish. He died at Carnmoney.

SOUTHWELL, EDWARD 1671–1730
Edward Southwell succeeded his father, Sir Robert Southwell, as Secretary of State, in 1702, occupying the position until his death. He also served two terms of office as Chief Secretary to the Lord Lieutenant (1703–7 and 1710–13). He was a member of parliament for Kinsale, County Cork, and acquired, by marriage to Elizabeth Cromwell, daughter of the Earl of Ardglass, Downpatrick, the Manor of Down. He was founder of the Southwell Charities in Downpatrick.

SPENCER, BRENT 1760–1828
Brent Spencer was born in Trumery, County Antrim, and in 1778 joined the 15th Regiment of Foot. For twenty years he served in the West Indies and later at Aboukir and Alexandria. He became a major-general in 1805 and commanded a division in the Peninsular War. Wellington is supposed to have said of him: 'There never was a braver man'. In 1809 he was knighted, in 1811 he became lieutenant-general and in 1825 general. He was appointed member of the consolidated board of general officers, and Governor of Cork.

STACPOOLE-KENNY, LOUISE d.1933
Louise Stacpoole-Kenny was born in Dublin and was educated at the Loreto Convent, Omagh, and in Paris. She was a prolific writer, and the subjects of her biographies included St Martin of Tours, St Francis of Sales and Pius X. She also wrote more than twelve novels.

STANFORD, WILLIAM BEDELL 1910–1984
William Stanford was born in Belfast and educated at the Bishop Foy School, Waterford, and Trinity College, Dublin where he studied classics. In 1934 he was elected a fellow and was appointed Regius Professor of Greek in 1940. From 1948 to 1969 he was a Senator representing Dublin University in Seanad Éireann. He undertook an extensive lecture tour of America and was visiting Professor at Berkeley, at Wayne Park University, and at McGill University, Toronto. From 1972 to 1980 he was the Chairman of the Dublin Institute of Advanced Studies, and he was Pro-Chancellor of Dublin University from 1974 to 1982 and Chancellor from 1982 to 1984. He was a member of the Royal Irish Academy and of the General Synod of the Church of Ireland. He is recognised for his edition of Homer's *Odyssey* and his many papers on Greek literature. Among his other works are *Greek Metaphor, Aeschylus in his Style, The Sound of Greek, Ireland and the Classical Tradition, Enemies of Poetry, Greek Tragedy and Emotions* and an edition of Sophocles' *Ajax*. He was co-author of a biography of Provost Mahaffy of Trinity College.

STANNUS, ANTHONY CAREY 1830–1919
Anthony Stannus was born in Carrickfergus, County Antrim, and was educated at the Royal Belfast Academical Institution, before studying art at the Belfast School of design from 1850 to 1854. He moved to London to study in the Training School for Masters, and Dowlais School in Wales. He went to Mexico from 1864 to 1868, and was employed as an artist in the army of Maximilian, and later as a correspondent for the *Illustrated London News*. He returned to London, and then moved to Belfast in 1882. He exhibited in both Belfast and

London. He was a member of the Belfast Ramblers' Sketching Club, and was its President for five years. He was elected an honorary member of the Belfast Art Society in 1891. He died in London. His work is represented in the Ulster Museum, the Belfast Harbour Office and the Victoria and Albert Museum.

STANNUS, EPHRAIM GERRISH 1784–1850

Ephraim Stannus was born in Camus, County Tyrone. He joined the Bombay army in 1800 and distinguished himself in the Pindari war. From 1823 to 1826 he resided in the Persian Gulf. From 1834 he was the Governor of Addiscombe College. He was knighted in 1837 and became a general in 1838. He died in Addiscombe.

STAPLES, ROBERT PONSONBY 1853–1943

Robert Ponsonby Staples was born at Lissan House, Cookstown, County Tyrone and was educated at home by his father and at the Academy of Fine Arts, Louvain, studying in Dresden, Paris and Brussels. In 1875 he held his first exhibition with the Royal Academy, London and four years later he visited Australia. He taught art in London from 1897. He was a member of the Union International des Beaux-Arts and of the United Irish League. His paintings include 'Cardinal Manning's Last Reception' which was presented to Cardinal Vaughan and two triptychs illustrating ship-building, for the City Hall, Belfast. He also drew political cartoons. He was a baronet.

STEARNE, JOHN 1660–1745

John Stearne was born in Dublin and educated at Trinity College, Dublin, where he gained a Doctorate of Divinity. He was appointed vicar of Trim and Dean of St Patrick's, in 1713 became Bishop of Dromore, and in 1717 Bishop of Clogher. He rebuilt the episcopal residences at Dromore and Clogher and the deanery house in Dublin. He bequeathed his manuscripts to Trinity College, Dublin, and erected the university printing house.

STEENSON, BRIAN 1947–1970

Brian Steenson was born in Crossgar, County Down. He was a motor-cycle road racer. He competed in many moter-cycle races in both Ireland and England. In the World Championship Grand Prix events from 1967 until 1970, he finished five times in the top five places. He was killed in a crash at the Senior T.T in the Isle of Man.

STEPHENSON, GEORGE VAUGHAN 1901–1970

George Stephenson was educated at the Royal Belfast Academical Institution, and later became a Doctor of Medicine. He played rugby for Queen's University, Belfast, and London Hospitals. Between 1920 and 1930 he won forty-two rugby international caps with Ireland. Until very recently he had scored more international tries than any other Irishman. During his last three seasons in the side he captained the Irish team.

STEPHENSON, HENRY WILLIAM VAUGHAN 1900–1958

Harry Stephenson was born in Dromore, County Down. He was an international rugby player who played for United Services, and between 1922 and 1928, he won fourteen caps for Ireland. In the international championship season in 1925 he scored three tries.

STEPHENSON, SAMUEL MARTIN 1742–1833

Samuel Stephenson was born in County Antrim and was educated at Glasgow. In 1773 he was ordained a Presbyterian minister at Greyabbey, County Down. He graduated as a Doctor of Medicine in 1776 and settled in Belfast where he helped to found the Dispensary (1792) and the Fever Hospital (1797). He wrote a *History of Greyabbey* and a *History of Templepatrick* among other works. He was Vice-President of the Linen Hall Library from 1814 to 1817 and President from 1817 to 1828.

STEVENSON, PATRIC 1909–1983

Patric Stevenson was born in Wadhurst, Sussex. He was educated at Methodist College, Belfast, and from 1926 to 1928 studied at the Belfast School of Art, and later at the Slade School, London. He served in the Royal Air Force as a radar mechanic from

1940 to 1945, and was a lecturer in art and music in Tring, Hertfordshire, from 1946 to 1950. One of his pictures was bought by the Duke of Edinburgh. He returned to Ulster in 1950. He exhibited in Belfast, Dublin and England, and he pioneered open-air exhibitions during the summer at Rostrevor from 1951 to 1954, and at the Shambles, Hillsborough, from 1955 to 1968. He was President of the Royal Ulster Academy, and examples of his work are in the Ulster Museum, the Ulster Folk and Transport Museum, Cultra, County Down, and the Waterford Municipal Art Gallery.

STEVENSON, ROBERT 1866-1960
Robert Stevenson was educated at the Royal School, Dungannon, County Tyrone. He was a linen manufacturer and became an international rugby player, who played for Dungannon and Lisburn. During the period between 1887 and 1893, he was capped for Ireland fourteen times. In 1912–13 he was President of the Irish Rugby Football Union. His brother also won two international caps for Ireland, in 1888 against the Maoris, and in 1889 against Scotland.

STEVENSON, SAMUEL MARTIN 1742–1833
Samuel Stevenson studied for the ministry in Glasgow, and was licensed by Templepatrick Presbytery in 1767. He served as master in the Church of Ireland Diocesan School in Monaghan, where he lodged with an apothecary and developed an interest in medicine. From 1773 to 1776 he studied medicine in Dublin and Edinburgh, and was also minister for Greyabbey, County Down. He settled in Belfast, and resigned from the ministry in 1785. He set up a medical practice and specialised in the treatment of fever. He was physician to the Belfast Dispensary from 1796 to 1799, attending physician to the hospital from 1800 to 1810, and consulting physician from 1830 to 1833. He was President of the Belfast Library Society from 1803 to 1804 and was involved with the Belfast Academical Institution.

STEVENSON, WILLIAM 1719–1783
William Stevenson was probably born in County Tyrone, studied medicine at Edin-

burgh and practised in Coleraine, County Londonderry. He later moved to Bath and Wells and wrote many medical works. He is remembered as a venomous lampooner.

STEVENSON, WILLIAM FLEMING 1832–1886
William Stevenson was born in Strabane, County Tyrone, and was educated at Belfast and Glasgow. In 1860 he was ordained as Presbyterian minister for Rathgar, where a new church was built for him. He travelled extensively as Convenor of Foreign Missions, and in 1882 was appointed Professor of Theology at Edinburgh University. He gained a Doctorate of Divinity and became Senator of the Royal University in 1879. Many of his works on the missions are published. [Biography by Ms Stevenson].

STEWART, ALEXANDER TURNLEY 1803–1875
Alexander Stewart was born in Lisburn, County Antrim, and emigrated to America, where he opened a drapery shop in New York. During the Great Famine he sent a shipload of food over to his fellow-countrymen, and in 1863 sent a further shipload to Lisburn during the cotton srike. He left a fortune of £15,000,000 when he died in New York.

STEWART, ANDREW *c.*1620–1671
Andrew Stewart was born in Donegore, County Antrim, and became Presbyterian minister of Donaghadee in 1645. He was imprisoned at Carlingford, County Louth, and wrote an account of the early settlement of the Presbyterians in Ireland.

STEWART, CHARLES 1764–1837
Charles Stewart was born in Lisburn, County Antrim, and joined the Bengal army in 1781. By 1800 he was Professor of Persian at Calcutta, and in 1827 Professor of Arabic and Hindustani at Haileybury. He wrote a great deal on oriental languages and eastern biography.

STEWART, CHARLES JOHN 1851–1932
Charles Stewart was born in Rock Hill, County Donegal, and was educated at Harrow. He was called to the Bar and to

the Inner Temple in 1883. From 1890 to 1897 he was a senior official receiver in bankruptcy cases. In 1897 he was appointed Clerk to the London County Council. He was the First Public Trustee from 1907 until 1919, and he was knighted.

STEWART, CHARLES WILLIAM 1778–1854

Charles Stewart was born in Dublin and joined the army, serving in the Netherlands and in the Peninsular War. He was promoted to the rank of general and in 1814 was appointed Ambassador to Vienna. He was a member of parliament for County Londonderry from 1801 to 1814, and Joint Governor of County Down. In 1852 he was knighted, and he succeeded as 3rd Marquis of Londonderry. He wrote narratives of military campaigns. A monument to him was erected at Scrabo, County Down. [Biography by Sir A. Alison]

STEWART, ELLIE c.1867–c. 1948

Ellie Stewart grew up in Derry, and was educated at Victoria High School, Derry. She taught French in Scotland. When she retired, she lived in Ann Street, Ballycastle, County Antrim, and attended the Presbyterian College in Belfast. Women could not be ordained, but she did preach widely from the pulpit, and wore a cap and gown. She published a volume of poetry and prose, *From a Ballycastle Garden*. She was a Suffragist and published monthly articles in the *People's Friend*. During the period when she was studying for her degree, rheumatic fever confined her to a wheel-chair.

STEWART, GEORGE VESEY 1832–1920

George Vesey Stewart was born in Martray, County Tyrone. He was educated at Trinity College, Dublin, and eventually emigrated to New Zealand after a period of farming. He planned a settlement of Ulster gentry and tenant farmers, of which he would become the patriarchal head. Twenty-eight families arrived by sailing ship in 1875, and in 1878 were joined by another three hundred and seventy-eight people. Stewart bought land from the New Zealand Government and sold it in farm lots to the immigrants who settled at Katikati on the shores of Tauranga Harbour. After an initial period of disillusionment the community thrived, especially after the discovery of the Martha gold mine in Waihi, just twenty miles away. Dairy farming was developed. In 1880 to 1881 Stewart founded another settlement, Te Puke. After a short stay in England he returned to Katikati where he died. It is estimated that he was responsible for settling four thousand people from Ulster in New Zealand.

STEWART, ROBERT d.1670

Robert Stewart came from Scotland and in 1617 was granted lands in Cavan, Fermanagh and Leitrim. He was appointed Governor of Culmore Castle on Lough Foyle in 1638, and became Governor of Derry in 1643. He had defeated Owen Roe O'Neill near Clones, County Monaghan. In 1648 he was arrested by the Parliamentarians and taken to London, but he managed to escape and join the Royalist army. He then returned to Scotland until the Restoration, after which he served a term as Governor of Derry.

STEWART, ROBERT 1739–1821

Robert Stewart was a member of parliament for County Down and in 1789 was created Baron Londonderry. In 1795 he became Viscount Castlereagh; in 1797 he was created an earl, and in 1816 1st Marquis of Londonderry. He was a prominent member of the Volunteer movement. He was opposed to Catholic Emancipation. He died at Mountstewart, County Down, and was succeeded by his son Robert, Lord Castlereagh.

STEWART, ROBERT TEMPLE 1769–1822

Robert Stewart, Viscount Castlereagh and 2nd Marquis of Londonderry, was born in Dublin and was educated at the Royal School, Armagh, and St John's College, Cambridge. In 1790 he was elected to the Irish parliament, where he advocated the suppression of the Volunteers, and in 1798 he became Chief Secretary. He believed the Act of Union in 1800 was essential to preserve the Empire. When Catholic Emancipation did not follow as had been promised, he resigned . In 1805 he was appointed Secretary for War and until his death he played a prominent role in British politics. In 1812 he was appointed Foreign Secretary and master-minded the coalition against Napoleon, and he was instrumental in negotiating terms for peace at the Congress of Vienna in 1815. After this point his popularity waned, and in 1822 he committed suicide. His *Correspondence and Despatches* (12 volumes) was published between 1847 and 1853.

STEWART, SAMUEL ALEXANDER *c.*1826–1910
Samuel Stewart was born in America, and at the age of eleven accompanied his family when they returned to Ireland. From that age he was an errand boy and later worked in factories and shops. In 1880 he became assistant curator of the Belfast Museum and in 1891 was appointed curator. He was the foremost authority on botany, zoology and geology in the north of Ireland. He published, among other papers, *The Latest Fluctuations of the Sea Level on our Own Coasts* and *A List of the Fossils of the Estuarine Clays of the Counties of Down and Antrim.* In 1874 he produced a list of the mosses of the north-east of Ireland. He contributed to the botanical publications of the Royal Irish Academy and the British Academy. He edited the *Flora of the North East of Ireland* and made a botanical study of the Mourne Mountains. He died as a result of a street accident.

STEWART, WILLIAM 1653–1692
William Stewart, 1st Viscount Mountjoy, was a soldier in the English army. He became Commissioner for Managing Claims, and in 1684 was made Master-General of the Ordnance for life. He was appointed Governor of Derry for a short time. He went to Paris, where he was arrested and dismissed from the Master-Generalship. He was held in custody until 1692, and on his release joined William's army and was killed at the Battle of Steenkirk.

STEWART, WILLIAM JOSEPH 1900–1958
William Stewart played rugby at Queen's University, Belfast. Between 1924 and 1928

he was capped for Ireland ten times.

STOCK, JOSEPH 1740–1813
Joseph Stock was born in Dublin and was educated at Trinity College, Dublin. He became rector of Conwall, Letterkenny, County Donegal, and headmaster of Portora Royal School, Enniskillen, in 1795. In 1798 he became Bishop of Killala and was taken prisoner by the French. He was a scholar and linguist and wrote *What Passed at Killala*, an account of the French occupation of the town. In 1810 he was appointed Bishop of Waterford.

STOKES, GABRIEL 1849–1920
Gabriel Stokes was born in County Kilkenny and was educated at Kilkenny, Armagh and Trinity College, Dublin. In 1871 he entered the Indian civil service, became a member of Council and Governor of Madras. He was knighted in 1909.

STONE, GEORGE *c.*1708–1764
George Stone was born in London and was educated at Westminster School and Christ Church, Oxford. After he had taken holy orders he came to Dublin as chaplain to the Lord Lieutenant, the Duke of Dorset. In 1733 he became Dean of Ferns, and in 1734 Dean of Derry. In 1740 he became Bishop of Ferns and Leighlin, and in 1743 Bishop of Kildare and Dean of Christ Church. He was appointed Bishop of Derry in 1745, and Archbishop of Armagh, Lord Justice and a member of the Irish Privy Council in 1747. In 1758 he was again appointed Lord Justice and, with the Earl of Shannon and John Ponsonby, was responsible for the government of Ireland until 1764.

STORY, GEORGE WALKER d.1721
George Story came to Ireland as an English clergyman in 1689 and was an army chaplain at the Battle of the Boyne. From 1694 to 1705 he was Dean of Connor and then became Dean of Limerick. Among his publications are *An Impartial History of the War in Ireland*, published in two parts.

STOTHERD, RICHARD HUGH 1828–1895
Richard Stotherd was born in Augher, County Tyrone, and was educated at

Woolwich. He joined the Royal Engineers in 1847 and served in Canada. While working as an instructor at Chatham he organised the first field telegraph. From 1876 to 1881 he served with the Royal Engineers in Belfast, was placed in charge of Ordnance Survey in Ireland, and two years later of the United Kingdom Ordnance Survey. In 1886 he retired with the rank of major-general and nine years later died in Surrey.

STOTT, THOMAS 1755–1829

Thomas Stott was born in Hillsborough, County Down. His family were involved in linen bleaching. He contributed poetry to the *Northern Star* in Belfast and the *Morning Post* in London and was satirised by Lord Byron in *English Bards and Scotch Reviewers*. He published *Songs of Deardra*, and when Bishop Percy died he erected a memorial to him at Dromore, County Down. He wrote under the pen-name 'Hafiz', or 'Banks of Banna'.

STOUPE, SEAMUS 1872–1949

Seamus Stoupe was born in Belfast and educated at the Belfast Model School. In 1904 he was Modelling Master at the Belfast School of Art, and remained until 1938. He was a sculptor and a painter. He was President of the Ulster Arts Club and a member of the Belfast Art Society. He exhibited in Belfast and Dublin, and his self-portrait is in the Ulster Museum.

STRATHDEE, ERNEST d.1971

Ernie Strathdee was educated at Belfast High School. He was a Presbyterian minister and a T.V. sports journalist. He played rugby for Queen's University, Belfast and won nine caps for Ireland. He was a member of the Grand Slam side of 1948 and the Triple Crown sides of 1949. In 1947 he captained Ireland against Australia, and in 1948 against France. He died in a hotel fire in Belfast.

STUART, JAMES 1764–1840

James Stuart was born in Armagh and was educated at Armagh Royal School and Trinity College, Dublin. In 1811 he published *Poems on Various Subjects* and was called to the Bar. He was the first editor of the *Newry Telegraph* in 1812, and editor of the *Newry Magazine* from 1815 to 1819. In 1819 he published *Historical Memoirs of the City of Armagh*, which is reckoned to be one of the most valuable works of its kind, and in 1825 *The Protestant Layman*. From 1821 to 1826 he edited the *Belfast News-Letter* and was co-founder of the *Guardian* and *Constitutional Advocate*.

SULLIVAN, ROBERT JOSEPH 1803–1868

Robert Sullivan was born in Holywood, County Down, and was educated at the Belfast Academical Institution and Trinity College, Dublin. In 1850 he gained a Doctorate of Laws and was appointed Inspector of National Schools and Professor of English at Marlborough Street College, Dublin. He wrote many textbooks and books on education.

SWANZY, HENRY BIDALL 1873–1932

Henry Swanzy was born in Newry, County Down, and was educated locally and at Trinity College, Dublin. He was ordained in 1899, and in 1926 became a canon of St Patrick's Cathedral, Dublin, and five years later Dean of Dromore. He was an ardent genealogist and was the author of many family histories and of the *History of the Diocese of Dromore*. He was a member of the Royal Irish Academy and of the Royal Society of Antiquaries of Ireland. He died in a street accident in London.

T

TALBOT, RICHARD 1630–1691

Richard Talbot was appointed Commander-in-Chief of the army in Ireland under King James II, who created him Earl of Tyrconnell. He restructured his force, recruiting many Catholics, and in 1687 became Viceroy. Talbot's troops, numbering over fifty-thousand, were defeated at Enniskillen and in Derry. When King James arrived from France in 1689 Talbot was created a duke. He fought at the Battle of the Boyne and died during the second siege of Limerick.

TANDY, JAMES NAPPER 1740–1803

James Napper Tandy was born in Dublin. He was a prominent Volunteer and radical politician who supported the French Revolution. He was Secretary of the United Irish Society in 1791 and was imprisoned in 1792. He had organised two of the National Guard battalions, and when these were vetoed by the authorities he escaped to America in 1795. In 1798 he returned to France. He then sailed for Donegal and landed on Rutland Island where he hoisted the Irish flag, but after eight hours left for Bergen. Subsequently he was arrested in Hamburg and condemned to death at Lifford. He was released as a special concession to Napoleon and died in Bordeaux.

TATE, FAITHFULL see TEATE, FAITHFULL

TATE, NAHUM 1652–1715

Nahum Tate was born in Dublin into a family with County Cavan origins. He was educated at Trinity College, Dublin. As well as his own drama, such as *A Duke and No Duke* and *Injured Innocence*, he adapted many plays, one of which was *King Lear*, and in 1692 became Poet Laureate in England. He wrote the hymn 'While shepherds watched their flocks by night' and collaborated in the metrical version of the Psalms.

TAUTPHOEUS, BARONESS von, see MONTGOMERY, JEMIMA

TAYLOR, JEREMY 1613–1667

Jeremy Taylor was born in Cambridgeshire, was educated at Cambridge and took holy orders in 1633. He preached in London and became a Fellow of All Souls' College, Oxford. He was, for a period, attached to the royal household and he later spent much time in Wales at the estate of the Earl of Carbey. During that period he wrote *A Discourse on the Liberty of Prophesying*, 1647. After the Restoration he lived in London and in 1660 he became Bishop of Down and Connor, and the following year Administrator of Dromore. He was not in favour of the use of the Irish language. Among his publications are *Dissuasive from Popery; Rule and Exercises of Holy Living*, 1650; *Rule and Exercises of Holy Dying*, 1651 and *Discourse on Friendship*.

TAYLOR, JOHN WILGAR 1859–1924

John Taylor was an international rugby player who played for Queen's University, Belfast, and the North of Ireland Football Club. Between 1879 and 1883, he played eight rugby international matches for Ireland.

TEATE (or TATE), FAITHFULL *c.*1600–*c.*1672

Faithfull Teate was born in Ballyhaise, County Cavan, and was educated at Trinity College, Dublin. In 1625 he was appointed rector of Castleterrogh. In 1641, because he informed against the rebels, his house was burnt and his children injured, and he escaped to England for a period. He was a writer. He died in Dublin.

TEDFORD, ALFRED 1877–1942

Alfred Tedford was educated at Methodist College and played rugby for the Malone Club. Between 1902 and 1908 he won twenty-three international caps for Ireland, and scored six international tries in all. In 1903 he was selected for the British and Irish tour of South Africa, and was voted the outstanding forward on the tour. In 1923 and 1924 he was an Irish selector and from 1919 to 1920, President of the Irish Rugby Football Union.

TEELING, BARTHOLOMEW 1774–1798

Bartholomew Teeling was born in Lisburn, County Antrim. He was educated in Dublin at the Dubordieu School. He joined the United Irishmen and went to France in 1796 to enlist support for a French invasion of Ireland. He returned to Ireland, landing at Killala. He fought at Ballinamuck and surrendered at Collooney. He was court-martialled and hanged in Dublin.

TEELING, CHARLES HAMILTON 1778–1850

Charles Teeling was born in Lisburn, County Antrim, the brother of Bartholomew Teeling. In 1802 he was a linen bleacher but became a journalist and established the *Northern Herald* and the *Ulster Magazine* in Belfast, and the *Newry Examiner* in Newry. He wrote a *Personal Narrative of '98* and *A Sequel*, as well as *The History and Consequences of the Battle of the Diamond*. He died in Dublin.

TELFAIR, CHARLES c.1777–1833

Charles Telfair was born in Belfast and qualified as a surgeon. He settled in Mauritius and established a botanical garden, and sent many plant specimens to Kew Gardens. A botanical genus was named after him. He died in Port Louis.

TEMPLETON, JOHN 1766–1825

John Templeton was born in Bridge Street, Belfast, and was educated privately. He was one of the first people to make accurate observations of the plants, animals, rocks and minerals found in the north of Ireland, and he was a founder member of the Belfast Academical Institution. He was a supporter of the United Irishmen, but became disillusioned by what he saw as a rise in sectarian nationalism. He devoted a great deal of time to the study of botany and the improvement of various species of plants. He laid out an experimental garden at the family estate at Cranmore, near Belfast, and grew many foreign trees, shrubs and flowers from seeds sent by other botanists. He studied, noted and illustrated not only flowering plants, but also algae, fungae, lichens and mosses. He was interested in geology, meteorology and many aspects of zoology, especially birds, fish and molluscs. His book on the natural history of Ireland was not completed but the illustrated manuscripts of his *Catalogue of Native Plants*; *Hibernian Flora* and *Hibernian Zoology* have constituted invaluable source material. Many contemporary English botanists have included his work in their publications and a genus of Australian legumes is named *Templetonia*. He published in the *Transactions of the Royal Irish Academy*, and his observations on weed control and his description of a new rose (*Rosa hibernica*) were published by the Dublin Society. Much of Templeton's collection, which was donated to the Belfast Natural History Society Museum, still survives in the Ulster Museum, Belfast. The British Library possesses his manuscript of fungus and lichen drawings. He was an associate of the Linnean Society of London; Vice-President of Belfast Literary Society; and first honorary member of Belfast Natural History Society. He left an unpublished journal covering the years 1806 to 1825.

TEMPLETON, ROBERT 1802–1892

Robert Templeton was born in Belfast and was educated at the Belfast Academical Institution, which his father, John Templeton, had helped to found. From 1821 to 1831 he studied medicine at Edinburgh University and was an active entymologist, accumulating his own collection of insects and contributing significantly to entymological, meteorological and botanical research being carried out by the Belfast Natural History Society. His 'Figures and Descriptions of Irish Archnida and Acari' was incorporated into Blackwall's *History of the Spiders of Great Britain and Ireland* and the *Transactions of the Entomological Society of London* (1836) included his paper on

Thysanurae hibernicae. As a tribute to his fascination with the latter species, a thysanuran genus was named *Templetonia.* From 1829 he began meticulously to prepare his father's manuscripts for publication. In 1833 he was appointed assistant surgeon in the Ordnance Medical Department of the Royal Artillery, which took him to Mauritius and Ceylon, where he again conducted original and comprehensive research into the flora and fauna. He was recalled to Europe in 1852 and served in the Crimean War, where he was promoted to surgeon-major in 1855. His collection from Ceylon was received by the Belfast Museum, though the main collection of his work is in the British Museum, London. He retired with the honorary rank of Deputy Inspector-General of Hospitals in 1860. He died in Edinburgh.

TENISON, RICHARD *c.*1640–1705

Richard Tenison was born in Carrickfergus, County Antrim, and was educated at Trinity College, Dublin, where he achieved a Doctorate of Divinity in 1682. He was a schoolteacher in Trim and rector of Laracor. In 1675 he became Dean of Clogher, in 1682 Bishop of Killala, and nine years later Bishop of Clogher. In 1697 he was appointed Bishop of Meath.

TENNENT, GILBERT 1703–1764

Gilbert Tennent was born in Armagh and emigrated to America. He was educated at Yale University and ordained a Presbyterian minister at New Brunswick in 1726. He preached in New England and founded a church in Philadelphia in 1743. He visited England and Ireland, where it is said he collected £500 to establish a college. He was a prolific writer and his works include *The Lawfulness of Defensive War*, 1747, and *Sermons on Important Subjects*, 1758. He died in Philadelphia.

TENNENT, JAMES EMERSON 1804–1869

James Emerson was born in Belfast and was educated at Belfast Academy and Trinity College, Dublin. He was called to the Bar in 1831, and in 1832 he assumed his wife's surname, Tennent. He served as member of parliament for Belfast from 1832 to 1845, and for Lisburn in 1852. In Greece, where he had gone to fight, he met Lord Byron and subsequently published *Travels in the Egean.* His *Spanish Grammar*, now in the Linen Hall Library, is a tribute to his abilities as a linguist. In 1841 Sir Robert Peel appointed him Secretary to the India Board, and he wrote an account of Ceylon when he served as Civil Secretary there from 1845 to 1850. He was knighted and had honorary doctorates conferred upon him by Trinity College, Dublin, and Cambridge University. He was Secretary to the Poor Law Board and Permanent Secretary to the Board of Trade in Belfast. Charles Dickens dedicated *Our Mutual Friend* to him and attended his funeral.

TENNENT, JOHN *c.*1772–1813

John Tennent was born in County Antrim, and was educated at home by his father, where he was trained for a career in the family wine and spirit business. He joined the United Irishmen and left Ireland for London and later went to Hamburg and The Hague in 1797 on a secret mission on behalf of the society. Two years later he fought for Napoleon against the British, and in 1803 was appointed captain. He joined the newly-established Irish Battalion and he represented his unit at Napoleon's coronation in 1804. The Emperor presented him with an eagle standard. Tennent fought in the Napoleonic campaigns in Spain, Holland and Germany, and was appointed Chef de Bataillon of the 4th Battalion of the Irish Regiment in 1809. He took command of the 1st Battalion at Landau in 1810. In 1813 Napoleon named him a knight of the Legion of Honour. He died at Lowenberg, Germany, in a conflict with Russian troops in 1813.

TENNENT, ROBERT 1765–1837

Robert Tennent was born in County Antrim. He studied medicine, went to the West Indies and worked as an agent for several properties in Jamaica. He joined the Royal Navy as a surgeon in 1793, and served on the *Europe.* He left the navy in 1799 and settled in Belfast where he became Treasurer of the Belfast Hospital and was involved with the Hibernian Bible Society and the Belfast Harp Society.

TENNENT, WILLIAM 1705–1777

William Tennent was born in County Antrim, the brother of Gilbert Tennent. It is said that as a young man he fell into a trance which lasted for three days during which he was 'cold and stiff as a stake'. He recovered, but could not remember anything, and had to begin the learning process again. In 1733 he was ordained and served as a pastor until his death in New Jersey. [Memoir 1847]

TENNENT, WILLIAM 1760–1832

William Tennent was born in County Antrim and served as an apprentice with John Campbell, a Belfast merchant and banker. He joined the Belfast Chamber of Commerce in 1783, and was junior manager in the New Sugar House in Waring Street. He eventually became a partner in this business, and he held partnerships in the distilling firm of John Porter & Company and the Belfast Insurance Company. He was co-founder, in 1809, of the Commercial Bank, and he worked in the bank until it became the Belfast Banking Company in 1827. He was on the Board of the Spring Water Commissioners and the Belfast Banking Company, was manager of the Belfast Academical Institution and Vice-President of the Chamber of Commerce. After the rebellion of 1798, he was arrested on suspicion of belonging to the United Irishmen, and imprisoned in Scotland for two years. He returned to Belfast and in 1814, purchased the village and demesne of Tempo, County Fermanagh. He bequeathed property to the Presbyterian Church, and died in the cholera epidemic.

THOM, JOHN HAMILTON 1809–1894

John Thom was born in Newry, County Down, and was educated in Belfast. He was ordained as a Unitarian minister and moved to Liverpool, where he edited the *Christian Teacher*. He founded the Domestic Mission and wrote and edited many works, among which is the *Life of Blanco White*. [Memoir and sermons, 1901]

THOMPSON, BONAR 1888–1963

Bonar Thompson was born in Carnearney, near Antrim, where he was brought up by an elderly aunt. He was educated in Ladyhill National School. When he was fourteen he went to England and did a variety of jobs. He listened to open-air orators, and at the age of seventeen, made his first speech in Salford. He became involved with the unemployment movement, was arrested for smashing shop windows during a protest, and was sentenced to a year in Rochester Borstal. In 1910 he went to London, where for the next four years he survived by collectiong money after his speeches, and by selling pamphlets which dealt with issues such as his theory on birth control. He opposed the First World War and refused to serve, which stance, when the war was over, made him very unpopular. He addressed large crowds at Speakers' Corner in Hyde Park and was known as 'The Prime Minister of Hyde Park'. He wrote poetry and articles for the *Worker* and published three autobiographies: *An Agitator of the Underworld*; *An Evangel of Unrest* and *Hyde Park Orator*, though the biographical details often contradict each other. He took part in several radio shows, including *Gossip Hour*, *In Town Tonight* and *Variety in a Taxi Cab*, and in 1948 performed in a production of *Coriolanus* broadcast on the radio. Throughout the 1940s, he put on satirical one-man shows, with titles such as *Macbeth with Pat Geary*. In 1945 he toured abroad with Basil Langton's Travelling Repertory Theatre Company. Michael Foot acknowledged him as a powerful influence.

THOMPSON, CHARLES fl. 1907–1910

Charles Thompson was an international rugby player and played for Belfast Collegians. Between 1907 and 1910 he won thirteen international caps for Ireland. In 1909 he became the first Irish player to score against France.

THOMPSON, HAROLD NEVILLE 1861–1925

Harold Thompson was born in Clonmany, County Donegal, and was educated at Trinity College, Dublin. In 1884 he joined the army and took part in the Nile expedition and served in South Africa. He received the Distinguished Service Order and in 1904 was promoted to the rank of lieutenant-colonel. During the First World War he was Director of Medical Supplies, was taken prisoner and then released. In 1917 he rose to the rank of major-general and was honoured by the French, American and Portuguese governments. In 1919 he was knighted. He died on the Isle of Wight and is buried in Omagh, County Tyrone.

THOMPSON, SAMUEL 1916–1965

Sam Thompson was born in Belfast and was educated locally. He worked as a painter in the shipyards and wrote documentary scripts on the shipyards for the BBC. His first play *Over the Bridge*, though accepted for performance in 1957, was not staged until 1960 in Belfast and Dublin because of fear of a hostile response. In 1963 *The Evangelist* was staged in the Opera House, Belfast, with Ray McNally in the leading role, and *Cemented with Love* was performed on television a year after his death.

THOMPSON, SYDNEY MARY (MADAM CHRISTEN) 1847–1923

Sydney Mary Thompson was born in Whitehouse, County Antrim. She studied art from 1870 at the Belfast Government School of Art and won many prizes. She was a member of the Belfast Ramblers' Sketching Club and the Belfast Art Society. She married Randolph Christen, an art instructor from Switzerland, in 1900 and they left to live in Scotland. In 1921 she became a patron of the Belfast Art Society. She wrote a tribute to her husband, *Randolph Christen: The Story of an Artist's Life*, which was published in 1910. As well as art, her other consuming interest was geology, and she visited the volcanoes at Auvergne at the age of seventy-five.

THOMPSON, THOMAS CLEMENT 1780–1857

Thomas Thompson was born in Belfast. He studied art at the Dublin Society Schools and began his career as a miniature painter. He later abandoned this for large-scale portraiture, and after 1817 established a successful studio in London. Among his

sitters were George IV and the 2nd Marquis of Ormond. He was a founder member of the Royal Hibernian Academy, and exhibited there between 1826 and 1852. He also painted landscapes, such as 'Belfast from the banks of the Lagan'. He died in Cheltenham.

THOMPSON, WILLIAM 1805–1852

William Thompson was born in Belfast and was expected to manage the family linen business, but became instead a full-time naturalist. He had joined the Belfast Natural History Society when he was twenty-one and his first paper was 'On the Birds of the Copeland Islands'. He published many of his observations between 1827 and 1852, and eighty of his scientific papers on Irish Natural History appeared in journals such as the *Magazine of Zoology and Botany* and *Proceedings of the Zoological Society of London*. Between 1840 and 1843 he produced reports for the British Association for the Advancement of Science. His papers were collected in three volumes entitled *The Natural History of Ireland* (the fourth volume was published posthumously), and these books remain an indispensable reference work on Irish zoology of the early nineteenth century. He added about a thousand species to Irish fauna lists and discovered a number of species new to science. He was the first to describe the breeding places of rare birds on the Donegal coast. He was President of the Natural History Section when the British Association met in Cork in 1843, and was President of the Belfast Natural History and Philosophical Society from 1843 to 1852.

THOMPSON, WILLIAM MARCUS 1857–1907

William Thompson was born in Derry, was educated privately, and worked on local newspapers such as the *Belfast Morning News*. He then went to London to join the staff of the *Standard*. He edited *Reynolds' News*, stood as a Progressive candidate for London County Council and was elected. In 1880 he was called to the Bar and defended trade unionists, among them John Burns.

THOMSON, CHARLES 1729–1824

Charles Thomson was born in Maghera, County Londonderry. He emigrated to America in 1740 and was educated by Quakers. He was an acquaintance of Franklin and Secretary to the American Continental Congress in 1789. He was an ardent campaigner for the preservation of Indian tribes and he was chosen by the Indians to record on their behalf the proceedings of the Treaty of Easton in 1757. In 1758 he was adopted into the Delaware tribe, with the Indian name equivalent to 'the man who tells the truth'. He translated the Gospels and died in Pennsylvania.

THOMSON, CHARLES WYVILLE 1830–1882

Charles Thomson was born in Linlithgowshire, Scotland, and educated at Merchiston Castle School, Edinburgh, and the University of Edinburgh. He was appointed a lecturer in Botany at the University of Aberdeen in 1851, and two years later Professor of Natural History in Queen's College, Cork. In 1854 he became Professor of Geology in Queen's College, Belfast, where, in 1860, he also became Professor of Botany and Zoology. He published work on fossils and as a consequence became interested in oceanography. He returned to Edinburgh in 1870 to become Professor of Natural History at the university and undertook several scientific deep-sea explorations which he recounted in *The Depths of the Sea*. He was director of the scientific staff on the *Challenger* expedition, which, between 1872 and 1876, explored sixtynine thousand miles of the Atlantic and Pacific Oceans. Fifty volumes of reports were published as a result. He was elected a Fellow of the Royal Society, and in 1876 was knighted.

THOMSON, GORDON AUGUSTUS 1799–1886

Gordon Thomson was born in Belfast and lived for a time in the West Indies and also visited South Africa, China and India. In 1834 he reached Australia and subsequently explored that country. He went to South America via New Zealand and the Sandwich Islands, and travelled on horseback from Rio de Janeiro to Valparaiso with naval dispatches. From Valparaiso he travelled through Chile, Peru and Mexico to the United States of America. He returned to England by way of Canada and the Prince Edward Islands in 1842. During his journeys he made a collection of ethnological objects, some of which he donated to the Belfast Museum. He built his house 'Bedeque' on the site of the present Mater Hospital in Belfast, and was a regular vistor at the Royal Hospital before leaving in 1866 to explore Egypt, Palestine and part of Arabia. He returned to Australia in 1873 to live in Melbourne, which had been an Aboriginal village when he had seen it forty years earlier. On his death a monument was erected to his memory in Melbourne.

THOMSON, HUGH 1860–1920

Hugh Thomson was born in Coleraine, County Londonderry, and was educated at the Model School in Coleraine, later training as a draughtsman in Belfast. In the 1880s he went to London, where he worked for the *English Illustrated Magazine*. He gained a reputation for his work in black and white. He illustrated the novels of Jane Austen, George Eliot, Thackeray and Dickens, and made many drawings for the *Graphic*. He received a civil list pension and died in London.

THOMSON, JAMES 1786–1849

James Thomson was born near Ballynahinch, County Down, and when he was twelve years old witnessed the battle there. He was educated in Glasgow, and became a mathematics teacher in the Academical Institution, Belfast. In 1832 he was appointed Professor of Mathematics at Glasgow University and he wrote a great deal on mathematics and geography. He was the father of Lord Kelvin (William Thomson) and James Thomson.

THOMSON, JAMES 1822–1892

James Thomson was born in Belfast and was educated from 1832 at Glasgow University, where his father was Professor of Mathematics. He graduated in 1839 and served his engineering apprenticeship in England. In 1851 he became a civil engineer in Belfast and patented his invention of an inward-flow vortex turbine. He worked for Belfast Waterworks and was Professor of Engineering at Queen's College, Belfast, from 1857 to 1873, when he was appointed professor at Glasgow University. He was an inventor and contributed to the knowledge of centrifugal and jet pumps, paddle-boats and water-wheels. He published in scientific journals on such subjects as plasticity of ice, crystallisation, liquefaction and air and water currents. He was interested in the social life of Belfast and recommended the purchase of land for Ormeau Park for the people of the city. In 1877 he was elected a Fellow of the Royal Society and received honorary doctorates from Glasgow, Belfast and Dublin. He was the brother of Lord Kelvin.

THOMSON, SAMUEL 1766–1816

Samuel Thomson was born near Templepatrick, County Antrim. He became a school-master and lived in the townland of Carngranny. In 1793 he published his first volume, *Poems on Different Subjects, Partly in the Scottish Dialects*, and it was dedicated to Mr Robert Burns. In 1779 he published a second volume, *New Poems*, and in 1806 a third volume, *Simple Poems*.

THOMSON, WILLIAM 1726–1796

William Thomson was born in Maghera, County Londonderry, and went to Pennsylvania in 1740. He was placed as general in command of the South Carolina Rangers in the War of Independence. He was the brother of Charles Thomson, and he died in Virginia.

THOMSON, WILLIAM (LORD KELVIN), 1824–1907

William Thomson was born in College Square East, Belfast. He was educated at Glasgow University from the age of eleven and at Peterhouse, Cambridge. In 1846 he became Professor of Natural Philosophy at Glasgow, a post which he held for fifty-three years. He discovered the second law of thermo-dynamics, but also carried out considerable research on electric currents which was to prove invaluable in submarine telegraphy and accounted for the

success of the Atlantic cables. He also devised a more accurate way of determining the size of the earth. He invented depth-sounding apparatus, tide gauges, a new type of ship's compass, and instruments for measuring electricity. In 1866 he was given a knighthood. In 1892 he was created Baron Kelvin of Largs, and in 1902 received the Order of Merit. An exhibition of his inventions in 1896 attended by prominent international scientists was held as part of his fifty years' service as professor. He wrote prolifically and his works are collected as *Mathematical and Physical Papers*. He died in Scotland and is buried in Westminster Abbey. His statue stands at the entrance of Botanic Gardens, Belfast, and the Kelvin temperature scale is a memorial to his name. [Biographies by Professor Thomson and Ms King]

THORNTON, MATTHEW 1714–1803

Matthew Thornton was born in County Londonderry, and his family emigrated to America when he was four years old. He was educated at Worcester, Massachusetts and graduated as a Doctor of Medicine. He practised at Londonderry, New Hampshire, and presided over the Provincial Convention in 1775. In 1776 he was a delegate to the Congress and was one of the signatories of the Declaration of Independence. In 1782 he became a judge and later a senator. He died at Newburyport.

THORNTON, WILLIAM 1779–1840

William Thornton was born in Muff, County Londonderry, and joined the army in 1796. He served in Malta, Canada and in the Peninsular War, and in 1814 in America. He was wounded at Bladensburg and in New Orleans. He was knighted in 1836 and became a general in 1838. He committed suicide in England.

TICHBORNE, HENRY 1581–1667

Henry Tichborne came to Ireland in 1620 as a soldier in the English army. In 1623 he was appointed a commissioner of plantations in County Londonderry. By 1641 he owned land in Tyrone, Donegal and Leitrim and was appointed Governor of Drogheda, where he withstood a siege by

Sir Phelim O'Neill. He captured Dundalk and Ardee and was made Lord Justice in 1643. Though he had shifted his allegiance from the king to the parliament, at the Restoration he was made a marshal of the army and was granted the estate of Beaulieu, County Louth.

TISDALL, WILLIAM 1669–1735
William Tisdall was born in Dublin and was educated at Trinity College, Dublin, where he became a fellow. It is said that he and Jonathan Swift quarrelled because of Stella. He was vicar of Skerry and Racavan and of Antrim. In 1712 he became vicar of Belfast. He witnessed Swift's will.

TOD, ISABELLA 1836–1896
Isabella Tod was born in Edinburgh and was educated privately. She came to live in Belfast and contributed to the *Dublin University Magazine*, the *Banner of Ulster* and other journals, with a view to raising the status of women. During the period when she was working with the temperance movement, she, along with Caroline Norton and others, formed a society which agitated for changes in the law which culminated in the Married Women's Property Bill. She was a campaigner for votes for women and was secretary of the Northern Ireland Branch of the National Society for Women's Suffrage, established in 1871. She published many articles on social issues and campaigned against the Contagious Diseases Act which allowed magistrates in garrison towns to force women suspected of being prostitutes to undergo medical examinations for venereal disease. The act was repealed in 1886. In 1867 she was Secretary of the Ladies Institute in Belfast, which played a prominent role in achieving the rights of girls to take recognised academic tests. Throughout her life she was a supporter of higher education for girls and petitioned the Queen's University of Ireland to allow girls to take university examinations. The university agreed to admit girls to tests, though they were awarded certificates, not degrees. She was vehemently opposed to Home Rule and was involved in the Women's Liberal Unionist Association.

TOLAND, JOHN 1670–1722
John Toland was born in Clonmany, County Donegal. He was educated in Prague, Scotland, Leyden and Oxford and although raised a Catholic, became a Protestant when he was sixteen years old. He believed that the Church and the Christian hierarchy had perverted true Christian religion, and he advocated reading the bible with a cognisance of who wrote it, in what cultural context, and for what purpose. His books were extremely controversial. He paid a brief visit to Ireland in 1697 but the hostility occasioned by his book, *Christianity not Mysterious*, forced him to flee, and he never returned to Ireland. His other works include *Amyntor; Nazarenus; Life of Milton; Tetradymus; Pantheisticon; Account of Prussia and Hanover* and *History of the Druids*. He was a native Irish speaker and knew at least fifteen other languages. He became increasingly involved in politics and latterly turned to Pantheism. He died in poverty, in Putney, near London.

TONE, THEOBALD WOLFE 1763–1798
Wolfe Tone was born in Dublin and was educated at Trinity College, Dublin. In 1787 he was called to the Bar and wrote a pamphlet, *An Argument on Behalf of the Catholics of Ireland* in 1791. In the same year he was invited to Belfast by Thomas Russell, where he helped to found the Society of United Irishmen. When he returned to Dublin he established a branch there. A year later he became the assistant secretary of the Catholic Committee and the principal organiser of the Catholic Convention, though he was a Protestant. In 1795 he went to Philadelphia and then to Paris in 1796, where he galvanised support for Ireland. The ship on which Tone sailed in 1798 was captured by the British off Lough Swilly and he was taken prisoner and sentenced to death by hanging. He committed suicide in prison in Dublin.

TOOGOOD, ROMEO 1902–1966
Romeo Toogood was born in Belfast and was educated at Hillman Street Public Elementary School. He became a painter and decorator. He attended the Belfast School of Art and taught part-time, before leaving

for the Royal College of Art in London. When he returned to Ulster he began his teaching career at Larne Technical School, Dungannon Technical School, Down High School and Friends' School, Lisburn. He became painting and drawing master of Belfast College of Art in 1949. He chose the Lagan Valley and the Cushendun area as subjects for his paintings.

TORNA ÉIGEAS (the Learned) *c.*400
Torna Éigeas was the chief poet of Niall of the Nine Hostages. He was also Niall's foster-father. He has three extant poems attributed to him by tradition, and one of these appears in *Lebor na hUidre*.

TORRENS, HENRY 1779–1822
Henry Torrens was born in County Londonderry and joined the army. He served in the West Indies, Nova Scotia and Egypt. In Portugal he was Military Secretary to Sir Arthur Wellesley, and in 1815 he was knighted. He rose to the rank of adjutant-general. He died in England.

TORRENS, ROBERT 1776–1856
Robert Torrens was born in County Londonderry and was educated at Trinity College, Dublin. In 1798 he was called to the Bar and became a serjeant-at-law, and in 1823 a judge of common pleas. He sat on the Bench for thirty-three years. He died in Derrynoid, County Londonderry.

TORRENS, ROBERT b.1780
Robert Torrens was born in Herveyhill, County Londonderry. He served in the Royal Marines in the Dutch campaign and as a colonel of a Spanish legion in the Peninsular War. He was member of parliament for Ashburton and Bolton and a Fellow of the Royal Society. He owned and edited the *Globe* and the *Traveller* and wrote many works on economics, among which are *An Essay on the External Corn Trade* and *An Essay on the Production of Wealth*. He was also the author of two novels, *Celebia Choosing a Husband* and *The Victim of Intolerance, or the Hermit of Killarney: A Catholic Tale*. He was appointed Chairman of the Crown Commissioners to establish the colonisation of South Australia, and Lake Torrens and the River Torrens on which Adelaide stands are named after him. He died in London,

TRAILL, ANTHONY 1838–1914
Anthony Traill was born in Ballylough, County Antrim, and was educated at Trinity College, Dublin, where he studied engineering and became a fellow, later taking the degrees of Doctor of Medicine and Doctor of Laws. He was active in church affairs, represented the landlords' interest on royal commissions and wrote on questions of education. He was also a keen and accomplished sportsman and alpine climber. In 1884 he was appointed High Sheriff of Antrim and became Chairman of Portrush electric railway, which ran from Portrush to the Giant's Causeway from 1883 to 1947. In 1904 he was appointed Provost of Trinity College, Dublin. He received honorary degrees from many universities.

TRAILL, ROBERT 1793–1847
Robert Traill was born in Lisburn, County Antrim. He was rector of Schull, County Cork from 1832 to 1847. He was a Doctor of Divinity and translated the works of the Jewish historian, Josephus, into English. He was a Calvinist and antagonised many of the inhabitants of the county with his fervour. He is credited with having discovered copper at Dhurode, and one of the mine shafts was named after him. He became a principal share-holder in the company. In 1846, when the potato crop began to rot, he felt that if the potatoes were stored in pits, they could be saved, but had to concede that this was not the case. He became Chairman on the Schull Relief Committee and his eloquent letters induced people to subscribe. James Mahoney, an artist working with the *Illustrated London News*, visited Dr Traill and sketched him visiting a family whose father was dying. He wrote 'my house is more like a beleaguered fortress. Ere the day has dawned the crowds are already gathering. My family one and all are perfect slaves worn out with attending them; for I would not wish, were it possible, that one starving creature would leave my door without something to allay the cravings of hunger'. He

set up a soup kitchen, but in 1847, died of famine fever. He was the maternal grandfather of John Millington Synge.

TRAILL, WILLIAM ACHESON 1844–1934
William Traill was born in Ballylough, County Antrim, and was educated at Trinity College, Dublin where he took a degree in engineering. From 1868 to 1881 he served on the Geological Survey of Ireland and built an electrical railway from Portrush to the Giant's Causeway in 1883, the first ever constructed in the world. He was a brother of Anthony Traill.

TRENCH, RICHARD LE POER 1767–1837
Richard Trench was called to the Bar, served as member of parliament for Limavady in 1796 and for Galway in 1798. He voted against the Union in 1799 but in 1800 supported it. He was Master of the Mint and Postmaster-General. In 1813 he was appointed Ambassador at The Hague and two years later was Plenipotentary at the Congress of Vienna. From 1816 to 1822 he served once more in The Hague. He was created a British peer with the title Earl of Clancarty.

TRENCH, WILLIAM STEUART 1808–1872
William Steuart Trench was born near Portarlington, Queen's County (now County Laois) and was educated at the Armagh Royal School and Trinity College, Dublin. He won a gold medal for his essay on land reclamation. He was a land agent for the Shirley estate, County Monaghan, and later for Lord Landsdowne, Lord Bath and Lord Digby. He wrote a contemporary account of the famine, *Realities of Irish Life* which was published in 1868 and reprinted five times during that year. (An abridged edition was produced in 1966 with an introduction by Patrick Kavanagh). Other works include *Ierne, a tale* and *Sketches of Life and Character in Ireland,* which appeared each month from 1871 to 1872 in *Evening Hours.* He died in Carrickmacross, County Monaghan.

TREVOR, HELEN MABEL 1831–1900
Helen Mabel Trevor was born in Loughbrickland, County Down. Having drawn and painted at home, she decided to attend the Royal Academy in London in the late 1870s, and she went from there to Paris. She travelled in France, and in 1883 sent two pictures to the Royal Hibernian Academy. She visited Italy and stayed for six years until 1889 when she returned to Paris. She made sketches of St Germaine, Les Invalides and the Eiffel Tower. She was interested in the lives and traditions of the Bretons and other Celtic peoples and this is reflected in her painting. She was a regular exhibitor in London, Dublin and Paris, and examples of her work are in the National Gallery of Ireland and the Ulster Museum.

TREVOR, MARCUS 1616–1670
Marcus Trevor, was born in Rostrevor, County Down, and served at Marston Moor as a Royalist, in Louth as a Parliamentarian (1647), and then in Drogheda as a Royalist (1649). At this point he submitted to the Parliamentarians, but became a Royalist again before the Restoration. In 1662 he was created Baron Trevor of Rostrevor and Viscount Dungannon of Tyrone. In 1664 he was made Lord-Lieutenant of County Down.

TROBRIDGE, GEORGE 1851–1909
George Trobridge was born in Exeter, and in 1880 was appointed headmaster of the Government School of Design in Belfast, where he remained for the next twenty-one years. He exhibited in England, at the Belfast Ramblers' Sketching Club and in Dublin. He published *The Principles of Perspective as Applied to Model Drawing and Sketching from Nature* (1884); *Swedenborg, His Life, Teachings and Influence,* and *The Foundations of Philosophy* (1904). He wrote a novel and contributed to journals and newspapers and in 1908 he returned to England.

TROTTER, JOHN BERNARD 1774–1818
John Trotter was born in County Down, and was educated at Downpatrick and Trinity College, Dublin. He wrote an account of Charles James Fox, to whom he was private secretary, but is remembered for his *Walks through Ireland.* His 'A Letter to

258

Lord Southwell on the Catholic Question' was published in the *Herald* newspaper and a periodical, the *Political Register*. He died in penury in Cork.

TULLY, CHARLES PATRICK 1924–1973
Charlie Tully was born in the Falls Road, Belfast and played soccer for Whiterock, Forth River, Ballyclare Commrades, Cliftonville, Belfast Celtic and Glasgow Celtic, where he won Scottish League and Cup medals in 1954. He also played for Cork Hibernians. Between 1949 and 1959 he was capped ten times for Northern Ireland, and scored three international goals. He was later manager of Bangor, County Down and Portadown, County Armagh.

TURNER, SAMUEL 1765–1810
Samuel Turner was born in Turner's Glen in County Armagh, and was educated at Trinity College, Dublin. In 1788 he was called to the Bar. He joined the United Irishmen became a member of the Executive Committee and in 1797 went to Hamburg where he informed on his comrades, through Lord Downshire, to the government. It is said that he had a secret service pension. It is thought that he was killed in a duel in the Isle of Man.

TURNERELLI, PETER 1774–1839
Peter Turnerelli was born in Belfast and was the grandson of an Italian refugee. He was educated in Dublin and moved to London, where he became a pupil of the sculptor Chenu and a student at the Royal Academy. He was appointed instructor in modelling to the royal princesses and lived at court from 1797 to 1800. George III, Wellington, Pitt and Grattan were among those whose busts he sculpted. His bust of Daniel O'Connell was extremely popular in Ireland. At Dumfries he designed the memorial over the grave of Robert Burns. He held regular exhibitions at the Royal Academy and died in London.

TYRRELL, RICHARD d.1603
Richard Tyrrell was a member of an old English family. He was a soldier in the service of Hugh O'Neill, Earl of Tyrone. In 1597 he was in command of a force of four hundred men which intercepted an English force advancing from Mullingar. All the English except for the commander and one soldier were killed, and the scene of the battle is known as Tyrrell's Pass. In 1598 he went to Munster in an attempt to oust the planters and joined the garrison at Dunboy. He was thwarted both in Munster and in Kerry and was not heard of again after he took refuge in O'Carroll's country.

TYRRELL, WILLIAM fl. 1910–1951
William Tyrrell became an air vice-marshal with the Royal Air Force in the First World War. He won a Distinguished Service Order with a Bar, a Belgian Croix de Guerre and was knighted in 1947. He played rugby for Queen's University, Belfast and between 1910 and 1914 was capped many times for Ireland, scoring two international tries. In the season 1950–51 he was President of the Irish Rugby Football Union.

U

UPTON, ARTHUR 1623–1706
Arthur Upton was born at Castle Upton, County Antrim. At the Restoration he was elected member of parliament for Carrickfergus and later for County Antrim. He supported William III and raised a regiment to fight for him. He later forfeited his civil liberties on being condemned for treason.

USSHER, HENRY 1550–1613
Henry Ussher was born in Dublin, and was educated at Oxford and Cambridge Universities. He was appointed Archdeacon of Dublin and was the first Fellow of Trinity College, Dublin, to be named in the college's charter. He served as Vice-Provost of the college in 1594 and was appointed Archbishop of Armagh in the following year.

USSHER, JAMES c.1580–1656
James Ussher was born in Dublin. At the age of thirteen he was one of the first students to be admitted to Trinity College, Dublin. In 1600 he became a Master of Arts, was elected to a fellowship, and was ordained in 1601. He was Chancellor of St Patrick's and incumbent of Finglas, and in 1607 he was appointed Professor of Divinity in Trinity College, Dublin. In 1612 he took the degree of Doctor of Divinity and in 1613 published *Gravissimae Quaestiones de Christianorum Ecclesiarum Continua Successione et Statu*. In 1614 and again in 1617 he was chosen Vice-Chancellor of Trinity College, Dublin. During two years in London he met James I, was appointed to the bishopric of Meath and preached before the House of Commons at Westminster. In March 1625 he became Archbishop of Armagh. He was averse to the use of Irish in the Church of Ireland. He drew up the strongly Calvinistic Articles of Religion for the Church in 1634, though they were never brought into use. During a visit to England in 1640 he witnessed the execution of King Charles I and never returned to Ireland, in 1642 holding the bishopric of Carlisle for a short period. In 1645 he took refuge in Wales. He died in Surrey and was buried in Westminster Abbey. Among his works are *Biblical Chronology* or *Annales Vetris et Novi Testamenti* in two volumes, which sets the creation of the world at 4004 B.C. He was a prolific writer on theological and historical topics and his *Works* were published in Dublin between 1847 and 1864. After his death his library of ten thousand volumes, containing many Irish and oriental manuscripts of great value, was purchased by the government and eventually placed in Trinity College, Dublin. [Biographies by Carr and Elrington]

USSHER, ROBERT 1592–1642
Robert Ussher was born in Dublin and was educated at Trinity College, Dublin, where he became a fellow in 1611. He was elected Vice-Provost of the college in 1615 and Provost in 1630. In 1629 he was rector of Lurgan, County Armagh and in 1635 was consecrated Bishop of Kildare.

V

VARIAN, ELIZABETH WILLOUGHBY (née TREACY) 1821–1896

Elizabeth Varian lived in County Antrim. She published her first volume, *Poems by Finola* in 1851. She was often published in the *Nation*, and she married Ralph Varian of Cork, who gave generous representation to northern poets in his anthology. She also published work in the *Belfast Vindictor*.

VERNER, WILLIAM 1782–1871

William Verner was born in Churchill, County Armagh. He joined the army as a young man and survived the Peninsular campaign. At Waterloo he was severely wounded, but was promoted on the battlefield for his gallantry. He served as member of parliament for County Armagh from 1832 to 1868, having been returned nine times uncontested. He was a member of the Orange Order, and although he was dismissed as a magistrate in 1837 for proposing the toast of the 'Battle of the Diamond', he was created a baronet in 1846.

VESEY, JOHN *c.*1637–1716

John Vesey was born in Coleraine, County Londonderry, and educated at Westminster and Trinity College, Dublin. He was appointed Archdeacon of Armagh, Dean of Cork, Bishop of Limerick in 1672, and Archbishop of Tuam in 1678. He went to England in 1689 but later returned. He was Vice-Chancellor of Dublin University and many of his sermons were published.

VINYCOMB, JOHN 1833–1928

John Vinycomb was born in Newcastle-on-Tyne. He studied art at the School of Design there, and in 1855 entered the art department of Marcus Ward & Company as an engraver. He lived as head of the department until the break-up of the firm in 1899, when he became an artist, designer and illuminator. He lived in Holywood, County Down until 1909. He was a member of the Royal Irish Academy; Vice-President of the Royal Society of Antiquaries of Ireland; Vice-President of the Ex-libra Society of London and founder and President of the Belfast Art Society and the Ulster Arts Club. He also served as President of Belfast Naturalists' Field Club. He was a recognised authority on heraldry and illuminating, and he published books, notably on the illustration of book plates. He died in London. The City Hall has his scroll, and the Belfast Harbour Office and the Victoria and Albert Museum also have examples of his work.

W

WADDELL, HELEN JANE 1889–1965
Helen Waddell was born in Tokyo, where she learned to speak both Japanese and Chinese. She was educated at Victoria College, Belfast, Queen's College, Belfast, and Somerville College, Oxford, where she was Susette Taylor Fellow. Her first book was *Lyrics from the Chinese*, but her best-known works are *The Wandering Scholars, The Desert Fathers* and *Mediaeval Latin Lyrics* and she translated from Latin *Beasts and Saints*. Her first play, *The Spoilt Buddha*, was performed at the Opera House, Belfast by the Ulster Literary Society and in 1935 *The Abbé Prevost* was staged. In 1949 she published *Stories from Holy Writ*. Her novel *Peter Abelard*, 1933, has been translated into many languages and has run to over thirty editions. She contributed many articles to the *Standard*, the *Manchester Guardian* and the *Nation* and was engaged in lecturing and broadcasting. She was assistant editor of the magazine the *Nineteenth Century*. Among her friends in London, where she was Vice-President of the Irish Literary Society, were W. B. Yeats, Virginia Woolf, Rose Macaulay, Siegfried Sassoon, Max Beerbohm and George Russell. She received honorary degrees from the universities of Columbia, Belfast, Durham and St Andrew's and is the only woman to have won the A. C. Benson Medal of the Royal Society of Literature. She died in London and was buried in Magherally churchyard, County Down.

WADDELL, SAMUEL JOHN (pseud. MAYNE, RUTHERFORD) 1878–1967
Samuel Waddell was born in Japan, where his father was a Presbyterian minister and a lecturer at the Imperial University of Tokyo. He was the brother of Helen Waddell and was educated at the Royal Belfast Academical Institution, Queen's College, Belfast, and the Royal University of Ireland, where he graduated in engineering. In 1904 he helped to found the Ulster Literary Theatre and began to act and write. His first play *The Turn of the Road* was produced in 1906. *The Drone* was produced in the Abbey Theatre in 1908 and his other plays include *Red Turf, Peter,* and *Bridgehead.* He starred in the title role of Eugene O'Neill's *The Emperor Jones.* He was Chief Inspector for the Irish Land Commission and died in Dalkey, County Dublin.

WALKER, DAVID 19th century
David Walker was born in Belfast and was surgeon and naturalist aboard the yacht *Fox* which went in search of Sir John Franklin who disappeared on the North-West Passage expedition. In 1859 he read a paper entitled 'Notes on the Arctic Regions' to the Belfast Natural History and Philosophical Society.

WALKER, GEORGE *c.*1646–1690
George Walker was born in England and was educated at Trinity College, Dublin. In 1674 he was appointed rector of Donoughmore, County Tyrone, where he formed the Charlemont Regiment which he brought to Derry in 1688. In 1689 he was chosen Governor of Derry during the seige. He was received in England by William III and was promised the bishopric of Derry. He wrote a *True Account of the Siege*, 1689, and was killed at the Battle of the Boyne.

WALKER, SAMUEL 1832–1911
Samuel Walker was educated at Trinity College, Dublin, was called to the Bar, and became Queen's Counsel in 1872. He defended Parnell in 1881 and three years later was elected Liberal member of parliament for County Londonderry. He was knighted and served as Solicitor-General from 1883 to 1885 and Attorney-General in 1886. From 1892 to 1895 and from 1905 to 1911 he was Lord Chancellor. In 1906 he was created a baronet.

WALKER, SAMUEL 1912–1972

Sam Walker was born in Belfast and educated at the Royal Belfast Academical Institution. He played rugby for Instonians, and won fifteen caps for Ireland between 1934 and 1938. He toured South Africa with the British and Irish Lions and played twenty matches on that tour. He was later a BBC commentator.

WALKER, WILLIAM 1871–1918

William Walker was self-educated and at an early age became a founder and leader of the Independent Labour Party in Belfast. He often addressed crowds at the Custom House steps in the 1890s. His particular blend of Labour/Unionism became known as Walkerism. He organised the Carpenters' and Joiners' Union, worked on behalf of unskilled unions and women textile workers, and gained prominence in the Trades Council. In 1898 he was elected Poor Law Guardian and became a city councillor in 1904, when he was also elected President of the Irish Trade Union Congress. In 1905 he stood for the North Belfast parliamentary bi-election, but was defeated following his endorsement of an anti-Catholic questionnaire, by which he lost Catholic votes. He stood in the general election of 1906, 1907 and 1910, but remained unsuccessful. He was in favour of the British Labour Party organising in Ireland, which brought him into conflict with Nationalists in the Labour movement, especially Larkin and Connolly. He became involved in a controversy with Connolly regarding socialism and nationalism, conducted through the letter page of the Glasgow newspaper, *Forward*. In 1912 he was appointed Inspector of the National Insurance Scheme for the north-east.

WALSH, EDWARD 1805–1850

Edward Walsh was born in Derry, was educated at a hedge school and became a hedge schoolmaster. He was imprisoned for his part in the tithe war. He taught in a National School near Mallow, but was dismissed from his post because of his articles published in the *Nation*. He became a National School teacher in County Waterford and published poems and translations in the *Dublin Penny Journal*. He was sub-editor of the *Dublin Monitor* for a short time, and was once more dismissed as a schoolteacher at Spike Island, the convict island in Cork Harbour, reputedly because he said farewell to John Mitchel before his transportation. He was a poet who wrote *Reliques of Irish Jacobite Poetry with Metrical Translations* and *Irish Popular Songs, translated with notes*. He taught in Cork Union Workhouse, where he died.

WALSH, LOUIS JOSEPH 1880–1942

Louis Walsh was born in Maghera, County Londonderry. He was a solicitor in Ballycastle, County Antrim, and in County Londonderry and later a district justice in County Donegal. In 1967 extracts from his unpublished autobiography appeared in the *Irish Times*. Among his other works are *Yarns of a Country Attorney; The Next Time; Memoirs of Men, Places etc.; The Life of John Mitchel* and a number of plays, including *Twilight Reveries* and *The Pope at Killybuck*, which was first performed in Ballycastle, County Antrim by the Dalriada Players in 1915.

WARD, EDWARD 1906–1993

Edward Ward spent his childhood and youth at the family seat of Castle Ward. He was educated at the Royal Military Academy, Woolwich. He left the army and became a journalist, a BBC broadcaster and a war correspondent. In 1952 he succeeded to the title of Viscount Bangor, though Castle Ward was transferred to the care of the National Trust.

WARD, FERGAL OGE see MAC AN BHAIRD, FEARGHAL ÓG

WARD, HUGH (MAC AN BHAIRD, AODH BUIDHE), 1580–1635

Hugh Ward was born in Lettermacaward, County Donegal, a member of the principal bardic family of Ulster. He was educated in Donegal where he joined the Franciscans, and at Salamanca. In 1616 he was appointed the first Professor of Theology at Louvain. He was highly knowledgeable about Irish literature and was himself the author of poetry in the bardic tradition.

He collaborated in the compilation of John Colgan's *Acta Sanctorum Hibernae*. He died in Louvain and is buried there.

WARD, JAMES 1851–1924

James Ward was born and educated in Belfast and studied at the Royal College of Art, London. He exhibited at the Royal Academy and was appointed Principal of the Metropolitan School of Art, Dublin in 1907. Among his publications are *Studies for Decorative Design* and *Fresco Painting: Its Art and Technique*.

WARD, JOHN 1832–1912

John Ward was born in Belfast and was educated at the Royal Belfast Academical Institution. In 1847 he entered the family firm of printers and publishers and studied at the Belfast School of Art and Design. From 1876 he travelled in Europe and Egypt, and devoted his time to collecting Greek coins and Egyptian scarabs. He wrote many works concerning Egypt including *Pyramids and Progress*, *Sketches from Egypt* and *The Sacred Beetle*. He painted many water-colours and exhibited under the name of Bonnington Smith. He was a member of the Belfast Ramblers' Sketching Club, and changed its name to the Belfast Art Society. He contributed to 'Notes and Queries' and 'The Irish Book Lover'. He died in Kent.

WARD, MARY (née KING) 1827–1869

Mary King was born in Ferbane, County Offaly, and was educated privately. She married Henry Ward of Castle Ward, near Strangford, County Down, who later became the 5th Viscount Bangor. She published many scientific papers and books under the name of the Hon. Mrs Ward, such as *Sketches with the Microscope*, reprinted eight times between 1858 and 1888 as *The World of Wonders as Revealed by the Microscope*. This book was revised and reissued as *Microscope Teachings*. *Telescope Teachings*, which appeared in 1859, was based on her observations using the world's largest telescope in the grounds of Birr Castle. She was a gifted artist, naturalist, astronomer and microscopist, and she illustrated her own work as well as that of other people,

for example Sir David Brewster's *Life of Newton*. Two of her books were selected to be displayed at the International Exhibition at the Crystal Palace in 1862. She died tragically in an accident on a steam carriage.

WARD, OWEN ROE, see MAC AN BHAIRD, EOGHAN RUADH

WARREN, WILL 1906–1980

Will Warren was born in England and worked in a printing firm. During the First World War a bomb had demolished his bedroom while he was sleeping. In 1971 he decided to come to Ulster and joined a Fellowship of Reconciliation work camp in Derry. He moved into a house in the Bogside, and was particularly concerned regarding the children in the vicinty. He often approached the paramilitaries in order to urge against retaliation. He was a Quaker and hated violence. In 1977 he had to leave Derry since his health was deteriorating. In 1982 Will Warren House was opened as a base for community groups and as a memorial to his courage and commitment.

WARRINGTON, ROBERT fl. 1831–1839

Robert Warrington's birth and death dates are not known, but it is known that he lived and worked in Belfast for many years. He exhibited at the Royal Hibernian Academy, Dublin, and in 1836, was a member of the Association of Artists when it was established. He painted 'Launch of the Aurora, the first passenger steamer built in Belfast, 1839'. He also painted a portrait of William Tennent of Belfast.

WARWICK, ARCHIBALD d.1798

Archibald Warwick was licensed as a Presbyterian minister but while awaiting a parish taught in Kircubbin, County Down. He was arrested as a United Irishman. In 1798 he was court-martialled and hanged in Kircubbin beside the Presbyterian Meeting House. He was buried in Movilla, Newtownards, County Down.

WATERS, GEORGE 1863–1947

George Waters was born in Holywood, County Down. He studied at the Government School of Design in Belfast and spent much of his life as a lithographic artist. He was a founder member of the Belfast Art Society. He painted many of his water-colours in County Donegal and County Antrim. He was one of a group known as the Ulster Society of Painters, and he was a member of the Ulster Arts Club. His work is represented in the Ulster Museum.

WATTS, ROBERT 1820–1895
Robert Watts was born near Castlewellan, County Down, and graduated at Lexington after having studied at Princeton in the United States of America. In 1863 he returned to Ireland and was appointed Professor of Theology in Belfast. He replied to Tyndall's *Address* and this brought him to public notice.

WAVENEY, LORD see ADAIR, ROBERT ALEXANDER SHAFTO

WEBB, THOMAS EBENEZER 1821–1903
Thomas Webb was born in England and in 1845 won a classical scholarship at Trinity College, Dublin. In 1857 he became Doctor of Laws and was appointed Professor of Moral Philosophy. In 1861 he was called to the Bar, and from 1879 to 1887 was Regius Professor of Law at Trinity College, Dublin. He was then appointed county court judge for Donegal. In 1868 he unsuccessfully stood as a Liberal parliamentary candidate for Trinity College, Dublin. In 1880 he published a pamphlet on the land question.

WEIR, IKE O'NEILL (THE BELFAST SPIDER) 1867–1908
Ike Weir was born in Lurgan, County Armagh and emigrated to the United States in 1886. Up until 1881 he had lost only one of his twenty-eight professional fights as a feather-weight boxer. He claimed the World Featherweight Title, the fight having been stopped in the eightieth round, and the claim is not universally accepted. He was knocked out in 1890 and lost the title to Billy Murphy of New Zealand. For the next four years he remained unbeaten, until in 1894 he lost to the ex-world champion, Young Griffo, and retired. His professional record includes twenty-nine wins, eight draws, three losses and one no-decision, in forty-one contests.

WELCH, ROBERT JOHN 1859–1936
Robert Welch was born in Strabane, County Tyrone and lived for a time in Enniskillen, County Fermanagh. In 1875 he went to Belfast to train as a professional photographer under E. T. Church. He established his own business in 1883 and for the next fifty-three years practised his craft. He was appointed official photographer to the firm of Harland & Wolff, and the Belfast Ropeworks Company but much of his time was spent taking pictures which reflected the life of the people and the contemporary landscape. The Ulster Museum, Belfast, houses the majority of these. He was a member of the Royal Irish Academy, President of the Belfast Naturalists' Field Club, and President of the Conchological Society of Great Britain and Ireland. In 1923 he had an honorary doctorate conferred upon him by Queen's University, Belfast.

WENTWORTH, D'ARCY 1762–1827
D'Arcy Wentworth was born in Portadown, County Armagh and in 1782 held a commission in the Volunteers. He went to New South Wales in 1790 and was appointed Principal Surgeon and later Superintendent of Police in Sydney. He also held the appointment of Colonial Treasurer. The building of the general hospital was financed by the proceeds of a spirit monopoly which he initiated.

WEST, ROBERT d.1770
Robert West was born in Waterford and became a builder and stucco worker. He ran an academy for teaching drawing in George's Lane, Dublin in 1747. It was taken over by the Royal Dublin Society, which then employed him. The rococo plasterwork at Florence Court, Enniskillen, County Fermanagh, is his, and it is thought that he built Newman House, St Stephen's Green. A house built by him in 20 Lower Dominic Street, Dublin, has a magnificent staircase.

WHELAN, CLAUDE BLAKE 20th century
Claude Whelan was a lawyer who became

one of the foremost amateur archaeologists in Ulster. In 1930 he discovered Later Mesolithic material in the peat bogs of Toome Bay, County Londonderry.

WHITE, GEORGE STUART 1835–1912

George White was born at Whitehall, County Antrim, and was educated at Sandhurst. He served in the Indian Mutiny and took part in the Afghan War of 1870 to 1880. In 1879 he was awarded the Victoria Cross and became secretary to the Viceroy of India. He took part in the Nile expedition and commanded a brigade in Burma. From 1893 to 1898 he was Commander-in-Chief of the Indian army. In the Boer War, from 1899 to 1900 he defended Ladysmith for one hundred and eighteen days. From 1900 to 1904 he served as Governor of Gibraltar and from 1904 to 1912 he was Governor of the Chelsea Hospital. He received the Order of Merit in 1905 and became a field-marshal.

WHITE, IDA late 19th century

Ida White lived in Ballymena, County Antrim. She was a Republican, supported women's rights and, later, was exiled in Paris. She was imprisoned in Holloway and made a public attack on the Tzar of Russia. She produced two volumes of poetry, one in 1874 and the other in 1890, though much of the material was written before 1870.

WHITESIDE, JAMES 1804–1876

James Whiteside was born in Delgany, County Wicklow, and was educated at Trinity College, Dublin, and the Inner Temple. In 1830 he was called to the Bar and in 1842 rose to Queen's Counsel. He defended Daniel O'Connell and later Smith O'Brien, and in 1851 was elected Conservative member of parliament for Enniskillen, County Fermanagh, and for Dublin University in 1859. In the same year he became a judge. He served as Solicitor-General from 1852 to 1853 and Attorney-General from 1858 to 1859, and in 1866 became Lord Chief Justice. Among his publications are *Early Sketches of Eminent Persons* and *Italy in the Nineteenth Century*. He died in Brighton.

WHITLA, WILLIAM 1851–1933

William Whitla was born in Monaghan and was educated at the Model School, Monaghan, and Queen's College, Belfast, where he studied medicine, having already completed an apprenticeship in pharmacy. He joined the staff of the Royal Hospital, the Belfast Ophthalmic Hospital and the Belfast Hospital for Women and Children before setting up a private practice. In 1890 he was appointed Professor of Materia Medica at Queen's College, Belfast. He received honorary degrees from many universities and was knighted in 1902. His medical works, in particular his *Dictionary of Medical Treatment* (first edition 1891)were widely sought and translated into many languages, including Chinese. *Elements of Pharmacy, Materia Medica and Theraputics,* published in 1882, went into twelve editions. He was also author of the two-volume *Manual of Practice and Theory of Medicine.* In 1909 he was elected President of the British Medical Association, and from 1917 to 1918 served as a member of the Irish Convention. He was Pro-Chancellor of Queen's University, Belfast, represented the university in parliament from 1918 to 1922 and was appointed physician to the king. He left endowments to Methodist College, Belfast, Queen's University, Belfast, and the Ulster Medical Society.

WILDE, OSCAR FINGAL O'FLAHERTIE WILLS 1854–1900

Oscar Wilde was born in Dublin and was educated at Portora Royal School, Enniskillen, Trinity College, Dublin, and Magdalen College, Oxford. A year after his first volume, *Poems*, was published in 1881 he completed a lecture tour in America and Canada. From 1882 until 1888 he worked in London as a book-reviewer. During the period 1887 to 1889 he edited *Woman's World* and published his collection of fairy stories, *The Happy Prince and other tales.* In 1891 he published *The Picture of Dorian Gray*, his only novel, and another collection of fairy stories, *A House of Pomegranates.* Among his plays are *Vera; The Duchess of Padua; Lady Windermere's Fan; A Woman of No Importance; An Ideal Husband; The Importance of Being Earnest* and *Salome.*

In 1895 Oscar Wilde was charged with homosexual offences and was imprisoned in Reading jail for two years. On his release he left England to live in Italy and France. In 1898 he published *The Ballad of Reading Jail*, and in 1905 *De Profundus*. He died at the Hotel Alsace and is buried in the Père La Chaise cemetery, Paris.

WILES, FRANCIS 1889–1956
Frank Wiles was born in Larne, County Antrim and was educated at Larne Grammar School. He studied sculpture at Belfast School of Art, in Paris, and at the Metropolitan School of Art, Dublin. In the national competition of Schools of Art, he won a gold medal in 1914. He lived in Dublin until 1921, and exhibited with the Belfast Art Society and the Royal Hibernian Academy, Dublin. The war memorial in Newcastle, County Down, was sculpted by him and a bronze plaque to John Moore Killen in the Royal Hospital, Larne, is his work. He died in Larne.

WILKINS, MAURICE b.1885
Maurice Wilkins was born in Dublin and was educated at Trinity College, Dublin. He was headmaster of Bangor Grammar School, County Down, from 1923 to 1947. He published *Sonnets of Love and Friendship* and *The Seeker*.

WILKINSON, HIRAM 1844–1926
Hiram Wilkinson was born in Money-shanere, Tobermore, County Londonderry. He was a civil servant in the Far East, became Chief Justice of the Supreme Court for China and Korea, and was knighted.

WILKS, MAURICE 1910–1984
Maurice Wilks was born in Belfast and was educated at Malone Public Elementary School. He attended night classes at the Belfast School of Art and won a scholarship to the day school. He had several one-man shows, and exhibited regularly in Belfast and Dublin. He also exhibited in Toronto and Montreal, and the United States of America. His work is represented at the Ulster Museum and the Armagh County Museum, as well as other locations.

WILLIAM III (WILLIAM OF ORANGE) 1650–1702
William was the son of William II, Prince of Orange, and Mary, daughter of Charles I. He married Mary, daughter of James II who eventually succeeded to the English throne. Protestants invited William to England to defend their religion when James, a Catholic, had a son thereby ensuring Catholic succession. William arrived in England with an army in 1688, and when James fled, William was declared king. He was supported by the Protestant inhabitants of Ireland. He sent reinforcements to Derry and Enniskillen and a large army under Schomberg, and he himself landed at Carrickfergus in 1690. James was already in the country and their respective armies eventually faced each other across the River Boyne, where James was defeated. William marched south, and after setting up headquarters in Finglas, captured Waterford and tried to take Limerick. He then returned to England, leaving his army to fight on his behalf. It achieved a number of successes, most notably at Aughrim on the 12th July, 1691. Limerick was finally taken, and a settlement was arranged by treaty. When parliament met in Dublin in 1692, William was recognised as the lawful sovereign of Ireland.

WILLIAMS, ALEXANDER d.1930
Alexander Williams was born in County Monaghan and was educated at Drogheda Grammar School. He became a painter in oils and water-colours, having studied drawing at the Art School of the Royal Hibernian Academy. In 1883 he was elected an associate of the Royal Hibernian Academy and a member eight years later. Many of his paintings were of Irish landscapes, and he exhibited in Australia, Canada and England. He was also a soloist in many Dublin choirs.

WILLIAMS, CHARLES 1838–1904
Charles Williams was born in Coleraine, County Londonderry, and was educated at Belfast Academy and in Greenwich. He spent some time in America, and on his return to London became a journalist on the *Evening Standard*. During the Franco-

Prussian war of 1870 he was a war correspondent. He reported on Armenia in 1877, and on the Afghan War of 1879–1880. In 1884 he accompanied the Nile expedition for the relief of General Gordon. From 1881 to 1884 he was editor of the *Evening News* and later worked in Egypt as a correspondent for the *Daily Chronicle*. He reported the Bulgar-Serbian war of 1885, the Greco-Turkish war of 1887, and in 1898 Kitchener's Sudanese campaign. He was founder of the Press Club in London and became its President. He published one novel, *John Thaddeus Mackay*.

WILLIAMS, JOHN 1761–1818
John Williams was born in London and came to Ireland in about 1780. In 1783 he painted a large picture of the Adelphi Club in Belfast. He edited the *Volunteers' Journal* in Dublin and returned to England after he had attacked the government in an article. He published *An Authentic History of the Professors of Painting, Sculpture, and Architecture, who have practised in Ireland* (1796). He died of typhus fever in Brooklyn, New York.

WILSON, DANIEL MARTIN 1862–1932
Daniel Wilson was born in Limerick and was educated at the Royal Belfast Acdemical Institution and Trinity College, Dublin. He was called to the Bar and sat on the bench of the King's Inns. He was Unionist member of parliament for West Down from 1918 to 1921, and during the same period was Solicitor-General. He was then appointed a judge of the newly established Supreme Court of Northern Ireland.

WILSON, DAVID 1873–1935
David Wilson was born at Minterburn, County Tyrone, and when he was ten, the family moved to Belfast. He was educated at the Royal Belfast Academical Institution, and went to work in the Northern Bank in Belfast, attending evening classes in drawing at the Government School of Design. He moved to London, and eventually became recognised as one of the leading artists on Fleet Street. He worked as cartoonist on the *Daily Chronicle*, but he also painted landscapes and flowers. His caricatures were exhibited at the Burlington Gallery, London, in 1921. He was a member of the Royal Society of British Artists and the Royal Institute of Painters in Watercolour. The Ulster Museum and the Victoria and Albert Museum hold examples of his work.

WILSON, FLORENCE MARY *c.*1870–1946
Florence Mary Wilson was born in Lisburn, County Antrim, but lived for most of her life in Bangor, County Down. She published a collection of poems *The Coming of the Earls* which was popular in America. Her work was influenced by Irish archaeology and legend and she is best known for her ballad 'The Man from God Knows Where' (1918) which was written about Thomas Russell who was hanged in 1803.

WILSON, GUY LIVINGSTONE 1886–1962
Guy Wilson went to work in the woollen mill at Broughshane, near Ballymena, County Antrim, after he left school, though even at that early age his major interest was the growing of daffodils. His first crop of seedlings were flowering in 1912, and his last in 1967. He is known in horticultural circles as being associated with white daffodils, but he also created reverse bicolours and small cupped rimmed varieties. In 1913 his first success, the daffodil 'White Dame', received a first-class certificate. Following this, seventy-eight cultivars were registered. He produced an important pink daffodil, 'Irish Rose', which received awards of merit. He achieved international renown as the man who improved garden daffodils, and was awarded the Victoria Medal of Honour in Horticulture, the highest honour given by the Royal Horticultural Society. In 1956 he was guest of honour of the first convention of the American Daffodil Society. A daffodil garden has been planted in his memory at the University of Ulster, Coleraine.

WILSON, HENRY 1864–1922
Henry Wilson was born in Currygrane, Edgeworthstown, County Longford, and joined the British army in 1884. Early in 1914, during the 'Curragh mutiny', he was promoted to the rank of major-general.

He was appointed Chief of the Imperial General Staff in 1918 and was firmly in support of conscription. In 1920 he advocated martial law throughout southern Ireland. In 1922 he was elected Unionist member of parliament for North Down and retired from the army. His speeches regarding Ireland were provocative, and in his capacity as military adviser to the government of Northern Ireland he advised a strengthening of the armed forces. In 1922 he was shot dead in London and two members of the Irish Republican Army were hanged for his murder.

WILSON, HENRY MOIR 1910–1992
Henry Wilson was born in Belfast and was educated at the Royal Belfast Academical Institution and Queen's University, Belfast, where he studied electrical engineering. He began an apprenticeship as a mechanical engineer with Combe Barbour in Belfast and later with Metropolitan–Vicars in Manchester. He joined the Royal Air Force in 1935, and in 1939 was commissioned. He was senior tutor of the Royal Air Force advanced armament force during the Second World War and later became education officer at the Empire Air Armament School. In 1947 he was Superintendent of the Servo Division at the Ministry of Supplies Guided Projectile Establishment and later moved to the Guided Weapons Department at the Royal Aircraft Establishment, Farnborough, where he became Head of Armament in 1959. He was appointed Director-General of Aircraft Equipment, Research and Development at the Ministry of Aviation in 1956. He went to Washington in 1962 to lead the Defence Research and Development staff at the British Embassy as an expert on guided missiles. In 1965 he became the army's Deputy Chief Scientist and in 1967 was promoted to Chief Scientist. He was appointed Director of the Technical Centre at Supreme Headquarters Allied Powers Europe. In 1946 he was created Member of the British Empire, in 1965 Companion of the Order of St Michael and St George, and four years later Companion of the Order of the Bath. In 1961 he was elected a Fellow of the Royal Aeronautical Society. He was involved with Fireflash, an air-to-air guided missile; the Royal Navy's Sea Slug; Bloodhound, a surface-to-air missile and the missile Thunderbird.

WILSON, JAMES B. 1862–1936
James Wilson was educated at the Royal Belfast Academical Institution and Queen's College, Belfast. He served in the army in Africa and India in the First World War and became a major-general. He was made a Companion of the Order of the Bath and Companion of the Order of St Michael and St George.

WILSON, JOHN 1635–1695
John Wilson was probably born in County Londonderry. He became Recorder of Londonderry in 1680. He was a playwright, and his comedy *The Cheats*, 1671, went into numerous editions.

WILSON (or WILLSON), JOSEPH fl. 1770–1793
Joseph Wilson lived near Kircubbin, County Down, but also worked as a portrait painter in Dublin. He painted a portrait of David Manson, the famous Belfast schoolmaster, and a portrait of John Magee. The Ulster Museum and the Armagh County Museum hold some of his portraits.

WILSON, ROBERT ARTHUR (pseud. MAGLONE, BARNEY) 1820–1875
Robert Wilson was born in Falcarragh, County Donegal, but as a young man spent some years in America. After returning to Ulster, he wrote for the *Nation* and Enniskillen newspapers. He made a reputation as a humorous writer under his pseudonym in the *Morning News*, and he published a volume of verse in 1894.

WILSON, SAMUEL 1832–1895
Samuel Wilson was born in Ballycloughan, County Antrim and emigrated to Australia where he became a sheep farmer. He made a great fortune and endowed Melbourne University. When he returned to Ireland, he unsuccessfully contested a parliamentary seat for County Londonderry in 1881, but later served as member of parliament for Portsmouth from 1886 to 1892.

WILSON, WALTER HENRY 1839–1904

Walter Wilson was born in Belfast and was educated at Gracehill School, near Ballymena, and Chester College. He was apprenticed in 1857 to a shipbuilding company where he became a draughtsman. In 1874 he became a partner in the firm of Messrs Harland & Wolff, where he was responsible for many inventions in ship design such as the single-plate rudder and the prevention of electro-chemical corrosion of propellor blades by a method still in use today. He promoted technical education, was a member of the Midland Railways Northern Counties Committee and President of the Chamber of Commerce. He died suddenly on a train travelling between Portstewart and Portrush.

WILSON, WILLIAM EDWARD 1851–1908

William Wilson was born in Belfast and was educated privately. In 1871 he established a private observatory at Daramona, Streete, County Westmeath, and in 1881, built a second one. He also built a laboratory and a mechanical workshop. In 1894 he became High Sheriff of Westmeath; in 1896 was made a Fellow of the Royal Society, and in 1901 gained a Doctorate of Science. He pioneered research on the temperature of the sun and radiation from sun-spots the results of which he published privately in 1900. He died in Daramona.

WITHEROW, THOMAS 1824–1890

Thomas Witherow was born in Limavady, County Londonderry, and was educated in Belfast and Glasgow. He was ordained a Presbyterian minister in Maghera, County Londonderry, when he was twenty-one years old, and in 1865 was appointed Professor of Church History in Londonderry. He wrote many theological works and published in journals. Among his publications are *Derry and Enniskillen*; *The Boyne and Aughrim* and *Historical and Literary Memorials of Presbyterianism* in two volumes, 1879–1880. He gained a Doctorate in Divinity and a Doctorate of Laws.

WOLFE, ARTHUR 1739–1803

Arthur Wolfe was born in County Kildare and was educated at Trinity College, Dublin. In 1766 he was called to the Bar, in 1783 he was elected member of parliament for Coleraine, and in 1798 for Dublin, the year in which he was appointed Chief Justice. He was created Baron Kilwarden and Vice-Chancellor of Trinity College, Dublin. He supported the Union and was killed in Emmet's insurrection.

WOLFE, CHARLES 1791–1823

Charles Wolfe was born in Blackhall, County Kildare, and was educated at Trinity College, Dublin. He was ordained in 1817 and held the curacy of Ballyclog, County Tyrone, and later Donoughmore, County Down. He was a poet and on the 19th of April, 1817, published his lyric 'The Burial of Sir John Moore at Corunna' in the *Newry Telegraph*. He died in Queenstown. [Memoir by J. A. Russell]

WOLFF, GUSTAV WILHELM 1834–1913

Gustav Wilhelm Wolff was born in Hamburg, but served his apprenticeship as an engineer in Liverpool. He then came to Belfast as a draughtsman with Messrs. Hickson & Company, the owners of the Queen's Island shipyard. When the firm was taken over by Edward Harland, Wolff was appointed manager. In 1861 he was made a partner. He was also chairman of Belfast Ropeworks and represented East Belfast at Westminster for eighteen years. He died in London.

WOOD, CHARLES 1866–1926

Charles Wood was born in Armagh and was educated at Armagh Cathedral School. He won a scholarship to the Royal College of Music in London in 1883 and studied under Stanford. In 1890 he graduated in music at Cambridge University. He became organist at Gonville and Caius College, Cambridge, and taught at the Royal College of Music. He succeeded Stanford as Professor of Music at Cambridge in 1924. He composed songs, string quartets and organ preludes, and the latter are still performed regularly. He died in Cambridge.

WOODS, STANLEY 1904–1993

Stanley Woods was born in Dublin, but moved to Downpatrick, County Down.

Between 1923 and 1939 he won ten TT victories in the Isle of Man motorcycle races. He also won the Ulster Grand Prix seven times on the Clady course. He donated most of his trophies to the Ulster Folk and Transport Museum at Cultra.

WORKMAN, THOMAS 1843–1900
Thomas Workman was born in Belfast and went into the family linen business. He was interested in natural history and collected and studied spiders, and his name was given to at least two new tropical spiders: *Damchus workmanii thor* and *Theridium workmanii thor*. He served as Vice-President and President of the Belfast Naturalists' Field Club and was Librarian of the Belfast Museum. His business travels took him to many countries including Egypt, India, the Far East and South America; he studied the natural history of the areas and published and illustrated the accounts of his journeys in various journals. He had a valuable collection of spiders which he bequeathed to the National Museum in Dublin. He was a magistrate for County Down and a founder and vice-chairman of a firm of shipbuilders, Workman Clark (1880). In 1896 he published the first volume of *Malaysian Spiders*, illustrated with plates drawn by himself. The second volume was completed but unpublished at the time of his death, which occurred during a trip to the Rocky Mountains.

WRIGHT, FRANK AMYAS 1948–1993
Frank Wright was born in Oxford and was educated at Trinity College, Oxford. In 1969 he won the Gibbs Prize for politics, and in 1973 he became lecturer in Comparative Politics at Queen's University, Belfast, first having begun research in the Institute of Irish Studies. He wrote *Northern Ireland in Comparative Perspective* and *Developments in Ulster Politics, 1843–1886*. He was active in working for peace in Yugoslavia, though his special area of research continued to be Northern Ireland. In 1992 he was given the Chair of Peace Studies in the University of Limerick. He was deeply involved with the Corrymeela Community, an interdenominational Christian group working for reconciliation, based in Ballycastle, County Antrim, and with the Understanding Conflict Project. He was also an artist.

WRIGHT, JOSEPH 1834–1923
Joseph Wright was born in Cork, was educated at Friends' School, Newtown, County Waterford, and was apprenticed to a grocer in Clonmel. During 1859–1860 he assisted the Professor of Geology in Trinity College, Dublin. He had made a collection of carboniferous fossils which he presented to the British Museum. In 1866 he was elected a member of the Geological Society of London, and two years later he came to live in Belfast, where he concentrated his geological studies on foraminifera, becoming an acknowledged authority on this subject. He was a member of the Cork Cuvierian Society, the Belfast Naturalists' Field Club, the Palaeontographical Society, and an honorary member of various other societies. His unique collection of 'forams' and a collection of his scientific papers are in the National Museum of Dublin.

WRIGHT, WILLIAM 1837–1899
William Wright was born in Finnard, County Down, and was educated at the Royal Belfast Academical Institution and Queen's College, Belfast. From 1865 to 1875 he travelled to Damascus as a missionary and became proficient in Eastern languages. He wrote about his travels and on theological subjects, and was editorial superintendent for the Bible Society. *The Brontës in Ireland*, written with first-hand knowledge, caused considerable controversy. He died in London.

WYATT, JAMES 1746–1813
James Wyatt was an architect who, when he came to Ireland, designed Castlecoole, County Fermanagh. He also modified Westport House, County Mayo, and extended Slane Castle, County Meath. His drawings for the work on Slane Castle are in the Murray Collection in the National Gallery.

WYLIE, JAMES OWENS 1875–1955
James Wylie was born in Rushvale, County Antrim and was educated at the Royal Belfast Academical Institution and Trinity

College, Dublin. He was called to the Bar and eventually became a judge of the Supreme Court and Judicial Commissioner of the Land Commission. During the First World War he served in the British army and was prosecutor at the trial of some of the participants in the 1916 rising. He competed at equestrian events at the Dublin Horse Show and was Chairman of the Racing Board in 1945. He was Vice-Chairman of the Irish Red Cross Society during the Second World War.

WYLIE, WILLIAM EVELYN 1881–1964
William Wylie was born in Dublin and educated in Coleraine, County Londonderry. He became the youngest judge in the United Kingdom and was Crown prosecutor at the trials of the 1916 rebels.

He was Law Adviser to Dublin Castle. [Biography by Leon Ó Broín]

WYSE, ANDREW NICHOLAS BONAPARTE 1870–1940
Andrew Wyse was born in Limerick and was descended from Lucien Bonaparte, brother of Napoleon I. He was educated in Downside in England, and at the University of London. In 1895 he became inspector of National schools, first in County Cork, and then in the Ballymena, County Antrim area. In 1915 he was made Secretary to the Commission of National Education. After partition, he opted for service in the North and in 1927 was appointed Permanent Secretary in the Department of Education. Due to ill health, he retired to Dublin in 1939.

Y

YEATS, JOHN BUTLER 1839–1922
John Yeats was born in Tullylish, County Down. He was educated at Athol Academy, Isle of Man, and Trinity College, Dublin. He was called to the Bar in 1866, but did not practise. He studied at Heatherley's Art School in London, exhibited at the Royal Academy and returned to Ireland in the 1880s to exhibit in the Royal Hibernian Academy, to which he was elected in 1892. His studio was a venue for literary people. In 1901 he had a joint exhibition with Nathaniel Hone. Several of his portraits of leading Irish figures are exhibited in the National Gallery of Ireland, including 'The Artist's Wife' and portraits of John O'Leary and William Butler Yeats. In 1908 he went to America and wrote essays for *Harper's Weekly*, collected in *Essays Irish and American*. His autobiography *Early Memories: A Chapter of Autobiography* was published posthumously. He died in New York. His *Letters to his Son, W. B. Yeats, and others* was published in 1944, and further editions were edited by Ezra Pound and Lennox Robinson.

YELVERTON, BARRY 1736–1805
Barry Yelverton was born in County Cork and was educated at Trinity College, Dublin. He was called to the Bar in 1764, and ten years later was returned as member of parliament for Donegal. In 1776 he became member of parliament for Carrickfergus, County Antrim. In 1783 he was appointed Baron Avonmore, and in 1795 he became a peer of the realm. He supported the Union.

YOUNG, ELLA 1865–1951
Ella Young was born in Fenagh, County Antrim, and took a degree in Political Science and Law at University College, Dublin. She was encouraged in folklore research by George Russell and belonged to his Hermetical Society and later to the Irish Theosophical Society. She had a firm belief in reincarnation. She lived in Connaught for many months and learned to speak Irish. In 1912 she was involved in gun-running for the Irish Volunteers. She lived for a period on Achill Island, but eventually went to Connemara and returned to Dublin in 1919. She went to America to lecture in 1925, studied Mexican and Indian folklore, and lived in Calfornia, until she died. She wrote children's fiction, such as *The Unicorn with Silver Shoes*, and poetry which she published in periodicals. Her autobiography is entitled *Flowering Dusk*.

YOUNG, JAMES d.1974
James Young lived at Ballywalter, County Down and worked in an estate agent's office in Ballymoney, County Antrim. His artistic talents were discovered by Sir Tyrone Guthrie. He became a comedian and actor and Mr Harold Goldblatt, Director of the Group Theatre, offered him work. He played George in Steinbeck's *Of Mice and Men* and was enrolled in the Festival of Britain Company. He played the part of Derek, the window-cleaner, in Joseph Tomelty's radio series, *The McCooeys*, which ran from 1949 to 1955. Many of the shows in which he appeared at the Belfast Empire Theatre were broadcast, and eventually he had his own television programme. From 1960 to 1972 he was manager of the Group Theatre. He toured in the United States and Canada, and after the Group Theatre closed, he gave many performances throughout Ulster.

YOUNG, MARY ALICE (née Mac NAGHTEN) 1868–1946
Mary Young was born at Dundarave, Bushmills, County Antrim. When she married she went to live at Galgorm, Ballymena, County Antrim. She was an enthusiastic and accomplished photographer. She took

over a thousand photographs between 1890 and 1915, and she often experimented with chiaroscuro. Most of the photographs are of her family, and life on the Galgorm Estate. During the Second World War she was actively involved in voluntary work for the armed forces.

YOUNG, ROBERT 1822–1917

Robert Young was born in Belfast and was educated at Belfast Academy and Glasgow University, where he studied mathematics. He assisted Sir Charles Lanyon, County Surveyor of Antrim, on the construction of the Ballymena Railway. He designed the three-arched viaduct in Glendun Valley, County Antrim. In 1849 he moved to Athlone to work on the Midland Great Western Railway, where he designed the bridge that spans the River Shannon. He returned to Belfast to practise as an architect and civil engineer in the 1850s, and his firm was responsible for the design of the Presbyterian Assembly block. In 1907 he was created an Irish privy councillor, and in 1909 became a senator of Queen's University, Belfast. He was interested in archaeology and was convinced that there was evidence for Palaeolithic habitation in Ireland. He was a talented water-colour arist and had a wide knowledge of traditional Irish music and frequented Feis Ceoil meetings.

YOUNG, ROSE MAUD 1865–1947

Rose Young was born in Galgorm House, Ballymena, County Antrim. She was educated at home by a governess and then trained as a teacher in Cambridge. She was committed to learning the Irish language, and kept diaries charting her progress. While in England she visited the Bodleian Library to see their collection of Gaelic manuscripts. She attended Irish classes run by the Gaelic League in London, and on her return to Ireland in the early 1900s, went regularly to Seán Ó Catháin's Irish College in Belfast. She was a close friend of Margaret Dobbs, and supported the Glens of Antrim Feis. She published three collections of Irish songs, and observed the keening tradition which was on the decline.

YOUNG, ROBERT MAGILL 1851–1925

Robert Young was born in Athlone and was educated at Queen's College, Belfast. He trained as an architect under his father, Robert Young. He was a member of the Royal Irish Academy and a Fellow of the Royal Society of Antiquaries of Ireland. In 1895 he became co-editor for the *Ulster Journal of Archaeology*, second series. He compiled *Fighters of Derry*, and edited the *Town Book of Belfast* and *Belfast and Ulster in the Twentieth Century*. He wrote *Ulster in '98* and *Historical Notices of Old Belfast*. He was a justice of the peace.

BIBLIOGRAPHY

Adams, J.R.R.; *The Printed Word and the Common Man*; Institute of Irish Studies, Queen's University, Belfast, 1987.

Akenson, D. H. and Crawford, W. H.; *James Orr – Bard of Ballycarry*; Public Record Office of Northern Ireland, 1977.

Andrews, J.H.; 'Thomas Askew Larcom 1801–1879'.

Atlas of Ireland; Royal Irish Academy, Dublin, 1979.

Banbridge and District Historical Society Journal

Bardon, Jonathon; *A History of Ulster*; The Blackstaff Press, Belfast 1992.

Bardon, Jonathon and Conlin, Stephen; *Belfast 1000 Years*; Belfast 1985

Barrington, Margaret; *David's Daughter Tamar*; Wolfhound Press, Dublin, 1982.

Beckett, J.C.; *A Short History of Ireland*; Hutchinson, 1975.

Belfast Telegraph

Bew, Paul; Darwin, Kenneth and Gillespie, Gordon (eds); *Passion and Prejudice; Nationalist/Unionist Conflict in Ulster in the 1930s and the Founding of the Irish Association*; Institute of Irish Studies, Queen's University, Belfast, 1993.

Black, Eileen; *Irish Oil Paintings 1572–c.1830: a catalogue of the permanent collection III*; Ulster Museum, Belfast, 1991.

Blackburne, E. Owens; *Illustrious Irishwomen*, 1877.

Boswell, James; *The Life of Samuel Johnson*, vols. 1 and 2; Everyman's Library, London, 1946.

Boylan, Henry; *A Dictionary of Irish Biography*, Second Edition; Gill and Macmillan, Dublin,1988.

Brady, A.; *Women in Ireland: an annotated Bibliography*; Westport, Connecticut, Greenwood Press, 1988.

Brady, A. and Cleeve, B.; *A Biographical Dictionary of Irish Writers*; Lilliput Press, 1985.

Browne, Stephen SJ; *Ireland in Fiction*; Maunsel, 1916.

Browning, D. C.; *Dictionary of Literary Biography*; Everyman Series; J. M. Dent and Sons, London, 1969.

Byrne, Art and McMahon, Sean; *Lives: 113 Great Irishwomen and Irishmen*; Poolbeg, 1990.

Byrne, Art and McMahon, Sean; *Great Northerners*; Poolbeg, 1991.

Captain William Coppin; The Foyle Civic Trust, 1992.

Casway, Jerrold; *Owen Roe O'Neill and the Struggle for Catholic Ireland*; University of Pennsylvania Press, Philadelphia, 1984.

Causeway, 1st issue, edited by Damian Smyth; Belfast 1993.

Chambers Biographical Dictionary, edited by Magnus Magnusson, 1990.

Chatto, Mike; *Art In Ulster*; Ulster Museum, Belfast, 1977.

Crone; *Concise Dictionary of Irish Biography*.

Crawford, W.H. and Trainor, B. (eds); *Aspects of Irish Social History 1750–1800*; H.M.S.O., 1969.

Day, Angelique; *Letters From Georgian Ireland: the Correspondence of Mary Delany 1731–68*; Friars Bush Press, 1992.

Day, Angelique and McWilliams, Patrick, (eds); *Ordnance Survey Memoirs of Ireland*; The Institute of Irish Studies, Queen's University, Belfast.

Deane, Arthur, ed.; *The Belfast Natural History and Philosophical Society, Centenary Volume 1821–1921*; published by Society 1924.

Dictionary of National Biography

Did your granny have a hammer??? ; A History of the Irish Suffrage Movement 1876–1922; Attic Press.

Donegal Annual

Dunlop, Eull and Foy, Bob, (eds); *John Carey 1800 – 1891*; Mid-Antrim Historical Group, Antrim and District Historical Society; 1991.

Familia; Ulster Historical Foundation, Belfast.

Fortnight

Fortnight Educational Trust Supplements

Foy, R. H.; *Bonar Thompson: The Old Days at Carnearney*; Antrim and District Historical Society, 1991.

Fyfes Dictionary of Irish Sporting Greats; compiled by John Gleeson; Dublin, 1993.

Gantz, Jeffrey, transl. and intro.; *Early Irish Myths and Sagas*; Penguin Books, London, 1981.

Gardner, Susan Jane; *For Love and Money: Beatrice Grimshaw's Passage to Papua*; PhD, Rhodes University, 1985.

Garvin, Wilburt and O'Rawe, Des; *Northern Ireland Scientists and Inventors*; Blackstaff Press, 1993.

Guide to Sources of Women's History; Public Record Office of Northern Ireland.

Harrison, A.T., ed.; *Graham Indian Mutiny Papers*; Public Record Office of Northern Ireland, 1980.

Henry, Sam; 'Our Hall of Fame : Northern Notabilities. An Ulster Roll of Genius'; *Northern Constitution* c.1928.

Hewitt, John, ed.; *The Poems of William Allingham*; 1967.

Hewitt, John; *Rhyming Weavers*; Blackstaff Press, 1974.

Hewitt, John; *Art In Ulster*, vol.1; Ulster Museum, Belfast, 1977.

Hidden, A. E. and Latimer, C. J.; *Science & Technology: Belfast and its Region*; Institute of Irish Studies, Queen's University, Belfast, 1987.

Hollander, John and Kermode, Frank (eds); *The Literature of Renaissance England*; The Oxford Anthology of English Literature; Oxford University Press, 1973.

Hooley, Ruth; *The Female Line: Northern Irish Women Writers*; Northern Ireland Women's Rights Movement, Belfast, 1985.

Hutchinson, Elizabeth; *Reminiscence*.

Independent.

Ireland: Weekly Bulletin of the Department of External Affairs, No.295; 1955.

Irish News.

Irish Times.

Irish Women Artists from the Eighteenth Century to the Present Day; The National Gallery of Ireland and the Douglas Hyde Gallery, 1987.

Jacobs, Arthur, compiler; *A New Dictionary of Music*, third edition; Penguin Books, London, 1973.

Jordan, Alison; *Margaret Byers*; Institute of Irish Studies, Queen's University of Belfast, 1990.

Journal of the Irish Folksong Society.
Kavanagh, Peter, ed.; *Patrick Kavanagh: The Complete Poems*; The Goldsmith Press, Newbridge, County Kildare, 1972.
Kelly, A.A.; *Pillars of the House*; Wolfhound Press, Dublin, 1987.
Kennedy, S. B.; *Irish Art and Modernism 1880–1950*; Institute of Irish Studies, Queen's University of Belfast, 1991.
Kinoulty, John Charles; *A Dictionary of Irish Biography*, (unpublished).
Labour History News.
Larkin, Philip; *Selected Letters 1940–1985*; Thwaite, Anthony, ed.; Faber, London 1992.
Larmour, Paul; *The Arts & Crafts Movement in Ireland*; Friars Bush Press, Belfast, 1992.
Latimer, W.T.; *Ulster Biographies Relating Chiefly to the Rebellion of 1798*; Belfast – James Cleland. William Mullan and Son; 1897.
Linenhall Review.
Livingstone, Peadar; *The Monaghan Story*; Clogher Historical Society, Enniskillen 1980.
Loeber, Rolf; *A Biographical Dictionary of Architects in Ireland 1600–1720*; John Murray, London 1981.
Lyons, J.B.; *Brief Lives of Irish Doctors 1600–1965*; Blackwater Press, Dublin, 1978.
Mac Cuarta, Brian SJ; *Ulster 1641: Aspects of the Rising*; Institute of Irish Studies, Queen's University, Belfast, 1993.
McDowell, Florence Mary; *Other Days Around Me*; Blackstaff Press, Belfast, 1972.
McKenna, Jill, ed.; *Belfast Women*; Norhthern Ireland Community Education Association, 1991.
McNeill, Mary; *The Life and Times of Mary Ann McCracken 1770–1866: A Belfast Panorama*; Blackstaff Press, Belfast, 1988.
Magee, John; *A Journey Through Lecale*; Friar's Bush Press, Belfast, 1991.
Mallory, J.P. and McNeill, T.; *The Archaeology of Ulster*; Institute of Irish Studies, Queen's University of Belfast, 1991.
Malone, Dumas; *Dictionary of American Biography*; American Council of Learned Societies (in Association with the Oxford University Press), 1936.
Martin, Bill; *Harry Ferguson*; Ulster Folk and Transport Museum, Cultra, 1984.
Mollan, Charles; Davis, William and Finucane, Brendan (eds); *Some People and Places in Irish Science and Technology*; Royal Irish Academy, Dublin, 1985.
Moody, T. W., Martin, F. X. and Byrne, F. J. (eds); *A New History of Ireland* IX; Oxford 1984.
More Missing Pieces; Attic Press, Dublin, 1985.
Morgan, Hiram; *Tyrone's Rebellion*; Gill and Macmillan, Dublin 1993.
Mourne Review; Mourne Local Studies Group.
Mullan, J.E. and Mullin, T.H.; *The Ulster Clans*; Belfast, 1966.
Neilson, William; *An Introduction to the Irish Language*; Original publication 1808, Reprint: Ultach Trust, Belfast 1990.
Nivedita, Sister and Coomaraswamy, Ananda K.; *Hindus and Buddhists: Myths and Legends*; The Mystic Press, London, 1987.
O'Briean, G. and Roebuck, P.; *Nine Ulster Lives*; Ulster Historical Foundation, 1992.

O'Connor, Rebecca; *Jenny Mitchel – Young Irelander : A Biography*; O'Connor Trust Publishers, Dublin and USA, 1988.

O Lochlainn, Colm, ed.; *Irishmen of Learning: Studies by Paul Walsh.*

Ordnance Survey in Ireland: an Illustrated Record; Dublin, 1991.

Ormsby, Frank, ed.; *Northern Windows*; Blackstaff Press, Belfast, 1987.

Ormsby, Frank, ed.; *Thine in Storm and Calm ; An Amanda McKittrick Ros Reader*; Blackstaff Press, Belfast, 1988.

O Tuama, Sean and Kinsella, Thomas, eds and translators; *An Duanaire 1600–1900 : Poems of the Dispossessed*; Dolmen Press, Dublin, 1981.

Oxford Companion to Gardens; Oxford University Press, 1991.

Rankin, Helen and Nelson, Charles, (eds); *Curious in Everything: the career of Arthur Dobbs of Carrickfergus 1689–1765*; Carrickfergus and District Historical Society, 1990.

Reid, Forrest; *The Garden God*; Brilliance Books, London, 1986.

Reid, Forrest; *Peter Waring*; Blackstaff Press, Belfast, 1976.

Roebuck, Peter, ed.; *Public Service and Private Fortune: The Life of Lord Macartney 1737–1806*; Ulster Historical Foundation, Belfast, 1983.

Saunders, Norah and Kelly, A.A.; *Joseph Campbell: Poet and Nationalist 1879–1944*; Wolfhound Press, Dublin, 1988.

Schlueter, Paul and June, (eds); *An Encyclopaedia of British Women Writers*;

Smyth, Denis; *Thomas Carnduff 1886–1956: Poet of the People*; Belfast, 1992.

Somerville-Large, Peter; *Irish Eccentrics: a selection*; London, Hamilton, 1973.

Strabane Historical Society Journal

Templemore. Journal of the North West Archaeological and Historical Society.

Thom's Irish Who's Who 1923; Dublin, 1923.

Ulster Local Studies

Ulster Museum Publication no. 234; *Dr Robert Templeton (1802–1892)*; Belfast 1980.

Walker, Brian Mercer; *Shadows on Glass: a Portfolio of Early Ulster Photography*; The Appletree Press, Belfast, 1977.

Walker, Brian M., O Broin, Art and McMahon, Sean; *Faces of Ireland*; The Appletree Press, Belfast, 1980.

Ward, Margaret; *Unmanageable Revolutionaries: Women and Irish Nationalism*; Pluto Press, 1983.

Warner, Alan; *William Allingham, an Introduction*; 1971.

Webb; *Compendium of Irish Biography.*

Wigham, Maurice J.; *The Irish Quakers: a Short History of the Religious Society of Friends in Ireland*; Historical Committee of the Religious Society of Friends in Ireland; Dublin 1992.

Williams, Nicholas; 'The poems of Giolla Brighde Mac Con Midhe'; Irish Texts Society vol. 51.